Du Fu Transforms

HARVARD-YENCHING INSTITUTE MONOGRAPH SERIES 126

Du Fu Transforms

*Tradition and Ethics
amid Societal Collapse*

Lucas Rambo Bender

Published by the Harvard University Asia Center
Distributed by Harvard University Press
Cambridge (Massachusetts) and London 2021

The Harvard University Asia Center publishes a monograph series and, in coordination with the Fairbank Center for Chinese Studies, the Korea Institute, the Reischauer Institute of Japanese Studies, and other faculties and institutes, administers research projects designed to further scholarly understanding of China, Japan, Vietnam, Korea, and other Asian countries. The Center also sponsors projects addressing multidisciplinary and regional issues in Asia.

The Harvard-Yenching Institute, founded in 1928, is an independent foundation dedicated to the advancement of higher education in the humanities and social sciences in Asia. Headquartered on the campus of Harvard University, the Institute provides fellowships for advanced research, training, and graduate studies at Harvard by competitively selected faculty and graduate students from Asia. The Institute also supports a range of academic activities at its fifty partner universities and research institutes across Asia. At Harvard, the Institute promotes East Asian studies through annual contributions to the Harvard-Yenching Library and publication of the *Harvard Journal of Asiatic Studies* and the Harvard-Yenching Institute Monograph Series.

This book was published with the assistance of the Frederick W. Hilles Publication Fund of Yale University and the Association for Asian Studies First Book Subvention Program.

Library of Congress Cataloging-in-Publication Data
Names: Bender, Lucas Rambo, author.
Title: Du Fu transforms : tradition and ethics amid societal collapse / Lucas Rambo Bender.
Description: Cambridge : Harvard University Asia Center, 2021. | Series: Harvard-Yenching Institute monograph series ; 126 | Includes bibliographical references and index. |
Identifiers: LCCN 2021013698 | ISBN 9780674260177 (hardcover ; acid-free paper)
Subjects: LCSH: Du, Fu, 712-770—Criticism and interpretation. | Manners and customs in literature. | Ethics in literature. | Chinese poetry—Tang dynasty, 618-907—History and criticism | Literature and society—China—History—To 1500. | LCGFT: Literary criticism.
Classification: LCC PL2675 .B45 2021 | DDC 895.11/3—dc23
LC record available at https://lccn.loc.gov/2021013698

Index by Mary Mortensen
∞ Printed on acid-free paper
Last figure below indicates year of this printing
30 29 28 27 26 25 24 23 22 21

For Ronan

Contents

Acknowledgments

In writing this book, I have incurred debts I can never fully repay. My thanks especially to Stephen Owen, Xiaofei Tian, and Lee H. Yearley; to Mo Lifeng, Peter K. Bol, Michael Puett, Wai-yee Li, and Robert Ashmore; to Paul W. Kroll, Anna M. Shields, and Kang-i Sun Chang; to Tina Lu, Jing Tsu, Ed Kamens, Aaron Gerow, and Pauline Lin; to Valerie Hansen, Bryan Garsten, Howard Bloch, Martin Hägglund, and Shawkat Toorawa; to Kristen Wanner, Bob Graham, Susan Stone, Joyce Seltzer, Mary Child, and Mary Mortensen; to Ayesha Ramachandran and Marta Figlerowicz; to Mick Hunter, Eric Greene, and James Reich; and, finally, to my parents, to Nick, and most of all to Claire, who sustained me patiently throughout. The errors that remain are entirely my own.

Note to the Reader

I have designed this book to be accessible to readers with different backgrounds. This effort has involved a few compromises, which I hope readers of all stripes will forgive. The most immediately obvious will be the use of both footnotes and endnotes. Footnotes are provided only for Du Fu's poems. They should be understood as an integral part of the translation and read thoroughly—otherwise, much of what I go on to say about the poems will be incomprehensible. The endnotes, by contrast, are intended primarily for specialists.

Another compromise has involved omitting some of the Chinese that specialists might like to have. In particular, I do not provide the text for quotations before the first year of the Common Era or after 1900, since the former are oft-translated classical materials, and the latter are generally Standard Written Chinese (*baihua* 白話), which does not pose the same problems of translation. I also do not provide the text of Japanese. To avoid breaking up paragraphs with Chinese or Japanese characters that will not be comprehensible to all readers, I do not provide the text for in-line quotations. In block quotations, the punctuation is my own and may not follow the published text.

I do provide the full Chinese text of Du Fu's poetry, of course. In preparing this text, I have replicated to the best of Unicode's ability the so-called *Songben Du Gongbu ji* 宋本杜工部集, which by general consensus represents the earliest surviving editions of his collection.[1] In the few cases in which this edition is missing a character or contains an orthography that cannot be represented in Unicode, I have followed the readings of the recent critical edition compiled under the general editorship of Xiao Difei 蕭滌非. My translations often began as modifications of Stephen

Owen's from *The Poetry of Du Fu*, and I gratefully acknowledge my debt to this enormous undertaking, without which this book would not have been possible.

The apparatus that accompanies this poetry is also more slight than it could be. The references I provide to Du Fu's poems, for instance, give only the *juan* number in the *Songben*, the starting page number in Xiao's edition, and the poem number in Owen's translation; readers are requested to consult Xiao and Owen for references to other editions. Because of the availability of Xiao and Owen, moreover, my footnotes to Du Fu's poems provide only the basic information that I believe a nonspecialist will need in order to understand their core arguments.[2] I do not include variants, and I only provide the Chinese text of passages Du Fu alludes to when their phrasing is of particular importance to the point being made.[3] (References for allusions given in the footnotes can be found in the endnote at the end of the paragraph preceding the poem, where they are ordered by line number.) I also omit discussing alternate grammatical construals of Du Fu's language, do not defend my choices when it comes to interpretive cruxes, and do not cite the studies that I have consulted for my interpretations of Du Fu's language. Note, however, that I have for every poem here reviewed the interpretive glosses, where available, of the following scholars at least: Zhao Cigong 趙次公, Wang Sishi 王嗣奭, Qian Qianyi 錢謙益, Zhu Heling 朱鶴齡, Qiu Zhao'ao 仇兆鰲, Pu Qilong 浦起龍, Yang Lun 楊倫, Shi Hongbao 施鴻保, Guo Zengxin 郭曾炘, Cheng Shankai 成善楷, Fu Gengsheng 傅庚生, Han Chengwu 韓成武 and Zhang Zhimin 張志民, Li Shousong 李壽松 and Li Yiyun 李翼雲, Suzuki Torao 鈴木虎雄, Xiao Difei, Xie Siwei 謝思煒, Xin Yingju 信應舉, Xu Renfu 徐仁甫, Yoshikawa Kōjirō 吉川幸次郎, Zhang Zhilie 張志烈, and Zheng Wen 鄭文.[4] It might have been useful to consult other sources as well (there are many more worth consulting), but eventually one gets one's own feel for Du Fu's language and for the structures that he habitually embeds into his poetry. As a result, many of my interpretations are idiosyncratic. An example of the sort of extensive apparatus it would take to defend them adequately can be found in the appendix of my dissertation.[5]

In other ways as well, I have likewise found it impossible to document thoroughly my debt to the vast edifice of Chinese Du Fu scholarship. For biographical details and chronology, to give just one example, I have regularly consulted the scholarship of Chen Yixin 陳貽焮, Xiao Difei, and

Cai Zhichao 蔡志超, among others, though I have not always cited their work when I follow it.[6] And if my arguments are thus dependent on a magnificent tradition of scholarship I credit only selectively, I am also acutely aware of how much work there is on Du Fu's poetry, on his age, and on his reception that I have not been able to consult or have consulted only summarily. I hope, therefore, that scholars who know more than I do about various aspects of the wide-ranging material I touch on here will offer corrections and amendments to my arguments.

Introduction

Tradition and Transformation

Among the many lures of literature, perhaps the most addictive is its promise to make sense. Though the point is almost too obvious to merit comment, this promise goes down to its simplest linguistic elements, whose basic function is to mean. As readers and writers, we arrange these promising elements into significant patterns, weave those patterns into intelligible ideas and satisfying stories, and translate those ideas and those stories into visions of our lives and of what matters in them. And we do not do so alone: we are always reading what others have written, reading in community, responding in our own writings. As a shared practice by which we involve each other in these projects, literature thus gives voice to a communal hope, against much evidence, that at least some sense can be made in and of this world.

Literature's entanglement with our passion for sense does not, however, guarantee that the "best" literature will most satisfy it. Quite the contrary, readers often demand of those works that would stand the test of time that they retain a certain reticence when it comes to the sense we can make of them. A number of explanations might be offered for this somewhat unintuitive phenomenon. Optimistically, for instance, dissatisfaction with what comes easy might represent a recognition that easy sorts of sense are flimsy things, that what will survive the sequent phases of our interests and capacities will necessarily refuse to be comprehended entire on a first pass. Or, more pessimistically, we might intuit that any sense we can grasp will shortly sour, that culture has an inherent tendency to reduce its achievements to ruins. Whatever explanation we give, however, it seems clear enough that it is not always the particular sense we will ultimately make of a text that defines our attachment to it, but sometimes more the hint, the pursuit, even the frustration that precedes any final articulation, as if it were the promise rather than the promised that we cared most about.

This dynamic generates revealing paradoxes, nowhere more obvious than in literary canons. Though classic works must always remain partly elusive if they are to repay rereading throughout readers' lives and across generations, they come, over time, to constitute the shared reference points by which sense is made elsewhere. As the literary cultures they initially addressed pass away and new cultures form themselves around them, moreover, they become obscure not only in themselves but also through time, forcing readers invested in the stability they supposedly offer to invent new ways of interpreting them. For these reasons, canonical texts always exist at a point of crisis. They prove a culture's most cherished visions of sense while also undermining them, and offer to preserve civilization while simultaneously driving it inexorably to what partisans of any one stage in its progress would recognize as collapse. They are evidence of our need for shared sense and also that we will, collectively, never find it—at least if finding it would mean ceasing to seek further.[1]

These paradoxes are particularly clear in the case of Chinese poetry, where critics of subsequent ages largely remade the art in the image of one medieval poet whose work, written at a moment of quite literal societal collapse, presented an enduring crisis of understanding. This poet is Du Fu 杜甫 (712–70), generally recognized throughout the last millennium as the greatest poet in the tradition, but also as one whose poetry was unusually difficult for his latter-born readers. To reveal what they took to be its secrets, devotees of Du Fu's poetry over a thousand years have engaged in unprecedented feats of historical and biographical research, supplementing his collection with new genres of criticism and inventing new sorts of scholarly apparatus to transform it into the art's most powerful demonstration that sense was always there to be made. In time, these new genres and new apparatus have come to define what it means to make sense of Chinese poetry and have been applied to nearly every important poet in Chinese history, including many who were previously read quite comfortably without them. In this way, the obscurity that has so troubled readers of Du Fu's verse has stimulated the development of new regimes of sense-making for the tradition as a whole.

The obscurity of Du Fu's verse was not merely adventitious, however; nor has it been simply resolved by the work of so many generations of commentators. Instead, his was a poetry originally difficult to make sense of, a fact attested by the limited enthusiasm with which it was received in his lifetime and for the first 250 years after his death. Though this opacity has often been heightened by the passage of time, it derives ultimately from the work's consistent focus on difficult questions about sense-making itself, both in literature and in our lives. For Du Fu, these questions were urgent, sharpened by the sudden violence of the An Lushan Rebellion in 755, which fractured one of the greatest empires the world had ever known. In the wake of this cataclysmic conflict, Du Fu found himself unable to live out the models of the good life provided by "This Culture of Ours" (*siwen* 斯文), the great literary, philosophical, historiographical, and ritual tradition that he and his contemporaries had believed contained the wisdom necessary to guarantee social and personal flourishing.[2] During the fifteen years that remained to him after An Lushan's initial assault on the Tang capitals, therefore, he searched for new ways to make sense of his experience, unmoored from the certainties that had guided him in his youth.[3]

What he found, I will suggest, was less an answer to his questions than a new perspective on them. In the collapse of his civilization's models of sense-making, Du Fu came to recognize that cultural traditions are ineluctably insufficient to changing circumstances; that the understandings of any given cultural moment are, as such, inherently fragile; and that cultural change is thus inevitable. Yet rather than discarding his age's deep investment in the idea of tradition, he came to see value in its inability to offer irrefragable meanings. After the trauma of the Rebellion, he began to discern a richness in his experience's divergence from established paradigms and, in his last years, even began to hope that his apparently failed life might bear a different significance for future readers who derived their models of sense-making from different moral cultures. With increasing self-consciousness, therefore, he came to write a poetry designed to speak to a future he could not predict, as part of a tradition more commensurate with the inevitability of, and more capable of surviving, collapses like that he witnessed in his lifetime.

Over the last thousand years, Du Fu's success in this project has been nothing short of remarkable. Not only has he survived successive waves of cultural change, retaining his position at the apex of the canon in literary cultures organized around values as disparate as loyalty to the emperor and revolutionary solidarity with the masses. Through those changes, moreover, he has also been recognized as a crucial exemplar of virtues he could not have imagined, transfiguring him from a failure in his own age to an epitome of the ethical life. Yet by virtue of this very success, Du Fu's critics have also been blinded to his own evolving interest in the problems of sense-making itself, the interest that rendered his poetry so open to interpretation in the first place. That interest is the focus of this book.

Modes of Sense-Making

This book thus offers two central arguments. The first concerns Du Fu's poetry and how it changed as he thought through the consequences of his society's collapse; the second, a shift in the modes of sense-making that have prevailed in China in the thousand years since he was elevated to the pinnacle of its poetic pantheon. Though different in scope, these two arguments are interrelated. On the one hand, the millennial shift in sense-making described here is written into the very text of Du Fu's collection, which in all its existing forms has been molded by his commentators. On the other hand, Du Fu's collection, thus constituted, has served as a principal justification for the shift these critics have wrought, retrojecting its origin into the deeper past and thus disguising their innovations. When we unearth, therefore, the contemporary assumptions against which Du Fu was writing, we begin to recognize how different he was from either his inheritance or his inheritors. And when we identify the eccentricity of his mature verse to the literary culture of his time, we start to appreciate how radical were the changes wrought upon literary sense-making by the later critics who placed him at its center.

It is this historical intertwining of poetic and critical innovation that makes the concept of "sense-making" useful to me here, highlighting as it does the connections between what we do when we write literature, read literature, and integrate literature into larger visions of significance.[4] The concept is also helpful in explaining why the transformations in literary understanding I will describe have not previously been recognized as such. The sense that we make in and of any given poem, that is, we make beyond the text itself, in the connections we draw between the fragmentary markings on the page and the various conceptual and affective domains that underwrite our sense of poeticity. In this way, both reading and writing poetry involve intuitions about the kind of thing poetry is and should be, intuitions that depend upon larger, generally implicit understandings of human psychology, the nature of reality, and the role of art in a good life— to name just a few of the issues at play. And not only do the intellectual networks that underwrite our intuitions thus guarantee that there is at least a rough alignment between our instincts as to what makes sense as a poem, how a successful poem should make sense of the realities and imaginaries it concerns, and how it is that reading and writing poetry make sense as activities people might want to pursue. Just as important, the inchoate extent of these intellectual networks all but guarantees that we only rarely articulate our sense of the poetic in explicit forms. Readers operating on different models of sense-making can therefore appreciate the same literature in vastly different ways, without recognizing that they are doing so.[5]

The salience of these points is particularly marked when it comes to premodern Chinese verse. This poetry is, for the most part, written in an idiom far removed from everyday speech, omitting the particles and grammatical markers even of literary prose. In its language, then, no less than in its imagery, classical Chinese poetry often provides readers only the barest building blocks of scenes, sentences, and thoughts, as if it were a fragment from a lost fullness inviting their active reconstruction.[6] This participatory quality, not incidentally, is one of the main reasons that the tradition of philological and explanatory commentary on Du Fu is so robust that, by the year 1250, publishers of critical editions of his work could claim to have collected exegesis from "a thousand scholars."[7] When we read classical Chinese poetry, that is, we are quite obviously "making" sense, producing it out of some combination of the fragmentary markings on the page and the assumptions we bring with us about what it would make sense for the poet to be saying. And when these assumptions change, everything down to the basic grammatical construal of a poem can change with them.

We do not, unfortunately, have records of the construals, grammatical or otherwise, of Du Fu's poetry from his own time (or, for that matter, from the three centuries that followed his death). What we do have are statements about poetry and its entailments within other domains of significance, statements that can be usefully compared with the ideas that are articulated in later criticism of Du Fu's work. Among the many contrasts that could be drawn from these materials, I will focus throughout this book on the ways in which Du Fu's contemporaries and his critics discussed the relationship between poetry and what can roughly be termed "ethics"—that is, attitudes towards what is good or praiseworthy in a life.[8] Ethics was central to the literary discourse of Du Fu's time, when poetry was more commonly integrated into visions of the good life than it has been since. Indeed, given that poetry figured almost omnipresently in social rituals among the elite, was discussed in mainstream intellectual circles as central to civilization's flourishing, and served as one of the most prestigious paths of access to real political power, Tang China might represent the world-historical apogee of poetry's assumed ethical significance. After the Tang, the art would never again attain the same general approbation as a moral medium—though Du Fu proved that it still could be one in exceptional cases. He has been, for the critics of the last thousand years, the tradition's "Poet Sage," the most moral of all its post-Classical writers. The entanglement of poetry and ethics was thus salient to Du Fu's context and has been important to his reception, albeit in revealingly different ways.[9]

The question of poetry's ethical significance is also central to the narrative of poetic change that I want to trace in Du Fu's own work. The early eighth century was a golden age of culture and the arts, a flourishing believed to have been matched only in the legendary epochs of early Chinese history. According to contemporary ideology, this cultural flourishing both reflected and contributed to the surging economic and political might of an empire that by the 750s was closing in on a century and a half of almost continuous political stability, military strength, and economic growth. When the empire suddenly crumbled before An Lushan's armies at the apparent height of its cultural achievements, therefore, Du Fu's confidence in poetry's ethical significance crumbled with it—not to mention his hopes that poetry would earn him entry into the halls of power, where he could accomplish the moral goals he cherished most. Unlike most of his contemporaries—who generally wrote in the period immediately following the war in styles that signaled a retrenchment of the visions of poetry's significance that had underwritten the art for Du Fu in his youth[10]—Du Fu's acute sense of being cut off from the promised political and moral ends of his early immersion in literature led him to a thoroughgoing reconsideration of the nature and purpose of the art.

This reconsideration, I suggest, has allowed Du Fu to serve as a pivot between the optimistic assumptions of his time and those of the later ages for which he served as proof, against an ambient doubt, that poetry could at least sometimes be ethically significant. This is partly because his mature work pioneered new ways of understanding poetry's relationship to ethics that would become influential among his critics. His role in catalyzing this shift, however, is even more dependent on the ways in which he did not foreshadow their critical innovations: the ways his reconsideration of the poetic art often presented readers with verse that did not make immediate sense to them. In response to these obscurities, critics from the eleventh century onward have worked diligently to figure out how everything that Du Fu says might, in fact, be what a paradigmatically ethical poet should say, and they have written their conclusions into the text of his collection in the ways they have ordered it, in the paratexts they have provided for it, and in the annotations they have written to accompany it. In these respects, Du Fu's poetry as it exists today is indelibly marked by his postmedieval critics' vision of poetry's ethical significance. What I hope to suggest in this book, however, is that it is possible to read these interventions against the grain as well, as evidence of critical difficulty occasioned by his struggles with the failing ethical paradigms of a cultural world that, by his critics' time, had long since passed.

Before and After Du Fu

When intellectuals theorized the moral character of poetry in the sixth through eighth centuries—what I will call the "late medieval period"—they often depicted it as making effective within exoteric forms values that derived ultimately from esoteric sources.[11] Poetry, that is, was understood to be capable, in its immediate affective power, of both subtly and deeply shifting the dispositions of its readers; in this way, it could inculcate normative moral and political values within individuals who did not themselves have the resources necessary to arrive at those values themselves. Good poetry was thus the product of exceptional moral savants and of individuals who had learned from them, and it was written to mediate their supranormal insights to the limited moral faculties of most people. In this sense, it was understood ideally as offering a medium for the preservation of the great cultural tradition that linked the present to China's ancient sages, as propagating the values initially taught by those sages throughout a society that would otherwise be prone to chaos, and thus as playing an important role in the furtherance of civilization as a whole.

This model contrasts with the most important impulse of Du Fu criticism over the last millennium, towards what I will call "recordizing reading."[12] This impulse—which is often pulled into complex braids with other strands of postmedieval literary thought—is to treat poetry as "recording" (most often *ji* 記) extratextual realities present to the writer at the time of the poem's composition. In recordizing criticism, therefore, accuracy and truth become key values: a poem is thought to be ethically exemplary when it records a clear observation, correct interpretation, and apt emotional response to the salient historical realities of the moment at which the poet wrote. These realities are not esoteric, in contrast to the ethical sources of the late medieval period; to the contrary, recordizing reading by its very nature tends to emphasize the shared access we all have to the moral significance of our experience. For critics persuaded that poems should be records, the art is thus valuable largely insofar as it preserves the moral truth of history and models the process by which individuals should go about understanding the ethical contours of their lives.

From the "late medieval model" to the "recordizing paradigm," then, a shift occurs in the directions in which intellectuals reached when they wanted to justify poetry as a moral practice. In Du Fu's time, poetry's ethical value tended to be thought of as lying in the art's capacity to preserve and develop the animating values of the sagely tradition; in the work of his recordizing critics, it lies in its ability to manifest the inherent moral significance of historical experience as such. Underlying this shift are epochal changes in China's social order, its government, its economy, and even its geography, not to mention fundamental changes in intellectual culture and in the technologies that underwrote literary production and dissemination.[13] All of these changes rippled through the conceptual networks that underlay poetic sense-making, and some of them will be taken up seriatim in the chapters of this book.[14] For now, the core transformation can be neatly illustrated by contrasting two exemplary statements about poetry's ideal function, one from a few decades before Du Fu was born and another from one of his most influential postmedieval commentators.

In the preface to his massive commentary on Du Fu's literary collection, the Qing dynasty critic Qiu Zhao'ao 仇兆鰲 (1638–1717) articulates clearly what he thinks poetry is supposed to be and why it is that Du Fu has been recognized, above all other poets, as realizing this ideal. Conveniently for my argument about the shifts that had occurred between Du Fu's time and Qiu's, he begins his introduction by critiquing two of the earliest readers to have left behind statements appreciating Du Fu's poetry, Han Yu 韓愈 (768–824) and Yuan Zhen 元稹 (779–831), both of whom had praised Du Fu in terms that would have made sense to late medieval readers.[15]

These two masters . . . have not displayed much understanding of Du Fu. When discussing the poems of other writers, one can judge them by the skillfulness of their diction and phrasing; but when you get to Du Fu, and Du Fu alone, you should not be seeking his essence in diction and phrasing. The reason for this is that his poems have in them the true substance of poetry, the true root of poetry. When Mencius discussed the [*Classic of*] *Poetry*, he said, "It is not permissible, when reciting someone's poems or reading his documents, not to know what kind of person he was. This is why we discuss the age in which he lived." Poetry being bound up with the fate of the polity—is this not the true substance of poetry? When Confucius discussed the *Poetry*, he said, "The teaching that occurs through poetry is mild and gentle, sincere and generous." He also said, "Poems can inspire, they can allow for observation, they can bring people together, and they can express resentment. Near at hand one can through them serve one's father, and at a further distance one can through them serve one's lord." Poetry is bound up with natural human emotions and with the principles of inter-personal ethics: is this not the true root of poetry?

Therefore, the men of the Song dynasty who discussed poetry called Du Fu the "Poet Historian." What they meant is that his poems can be used to discuss his historical era and to know what kind of person he was. And the men of the Ming dynasty who discussed poetry called Du Fu the "Poet Sage." What they meant is that, in establishing words, he showed loyalty and generosity, and that his poems can be used to teach these virtues to ten thousand generations. If one gives up on these things and discusses Du Fu as did Yuan Zhen and Han Yu, then he is indeed no different from a mere phrasemaker. . . .

Therefore, one who would annotate Du Fu's verse needs to think deeply and repeatedly, seeking the ultimate referent of each line, phrase, and word.

Only then can such a one hope to grasp the writer's pained mind of so many centuries past, almost as if living through his time with him and meeting him face to face. Then one will feel his lingering sadness and know his lingering yearning. I, a humble servant of the throne, have therefore worked untiringly at this collection to the end of my days.

二子…猶未爲深知杜者。論他人詩，可較諸詞句之工拙，獨至杜詩，不當以詞句求之。蓋其爲詩也，有詩之實焉，有詩之本焉。孟子之論詩曰：頌其詩，讀其書，不知其人，可乎？是以論其世也。詩有關于世運，非作詩之實乎？孔子之論詩曰：溫柔敦厚，詩之教也。又曰：可以興觀群怨，邇事父而遠事君。詩有關于性情倫紀，非作詩之本乎？故宋人之論詩者，稱杜爲詩史，謂得其詩可以論世知人也。明人之論詩者。推杜爲詩聖，謂其立言忠厚，可以垂教萬世也。使舍是二者而談杜，如稹、愈所云，究亦無異於詞人矣。…是故注杜者必反覆沉潛，求其歸宿所在，又從而句櫛字比之，庶幾得作者苦心於千百年之上，恍然如身歷其世，面接其人，而慨乎有餘悲，悄乎有餘思也。臣於是集，矻矻窮年。[16]

In denigrating the Tang dynasty readings of Han Yu and Yuan Zhen in contrast to the more insightful comments of Song and Ming critics, Qiu flags the shift in the appreciation of poetry that I will be arguing for in this book. He does not, however, see recordizing reading as novel, as I do. Rather, it represents for him a return to origins: an attention once again to the normative sources of the literary and cultural tradition, and to the true substance and true root of verse.

For Qiu, this true substance and true root of poetry is a moral orientation towards concrete contemporary circumstances. Great poetry, he avers, will be a record of appropriate moral reactions to historical situations accurately conceived, and it is therefore the critic's job to seek out the "ultimate referent" of those moral feelings and to assess their adequacy to the historical facts. What matters in poetry, then, is finally outside of poetry and needs to be inferred through language that is less an end in itself than a tool for recording what the poet thought about the situation of his time.[17] Here, the two common appellations through which Qiu praises Du Fu, "Poet Historian" and "Poet Sage," reveal much the same desire to get past language to its referents in the real world that is evident in his criticism of Han Yu and Yuan Zhen, who supposedly reduce Du Fu to a "mere phrasemaker." "Poet" by itself is not a title worth attaining:

poetry must be justified through its connection to arenas of human interest whose significance is more unquestionable, such as history or morality. We can perhaps hear in the background here the distrust of poetry, left to its own devices and unanchored in the world of moral commitment, that was endemic to postmedieval China, as well as the solution many critics found to the problems that distrust posed for poetry lovers: Du Fu, who proved that the art could be serious after all.[18]

Poetry aficionados in the late medieval period felt less need to justify themselves, and less need to justify their art in terms of other areas of human concern. Poetry's relative confidence in the Tang makes it more difficult to find cogent articulations of what verse is ideally supposed to do, especially in a vocabulary that (like Qiu's) will be relatively transparent to readers unfamiliar with the tradition being defended. I beg the reader's indulgence, therefore, in citing a longer and more difficult text to compare with Qiu Zhao'ao's statement on Du Fu. The text is Lu Zhaolin's 盧照鄰 (ca. 634–ca. 684) preface to the literary collection of his deceased friend and patron Lai Ji 來濟, former Marquis of Nanyang and prime minister, who had incurred the wrath of Empress Wu and died in exile fighting the Tibetans in 662. Its extreme allusiveness (aggressively paraphrased here) makes in rhetorical form its central point, that literature is a tradition and a crucial part of the inheritance of civilization, and that the responsibility of writers like Lai Ji and Lu Zhaolin is to sustain it.[19]

> Of old, a dragon crouched in Lu in the east [Confucius (551–479 BCE)] and laid out normative *Ritual* and *Music* in order to save the myriad folk, but a tiger grasped Qin in the west [the first emperor of Qin] and burned the *Poetry* and the *Documents* in order to make the common people ignorant. "Numinous" we call that [i.e., the cultural tradition] which can continue through such transformations, acting as a third with heaven and a second with earth; "Sagely" we call that which matches with incipiency, treating as one *yin* and *yang*. . . .
>
> From the time Confucius stopped his brush at the capture of the unicorn, it has been thirteen or fourteen hundred years. The project of study he imparted to [his students] Ziyou and Zixia has since then had [the Confucian masters] Xunzi and Mengzi [third and fourth c. BCE, respectively]; and, after the great writers Qu Yuan and Song Yu [fourth and third c. BCE], there were Jia Yi and Sima Xiangru [both second c. BCE]. Ban Biao and Ban Gu [both first c. CE] recounted the affairs of the Han, getting the wind

and bone of [Confucius's friend the historian] Zuo Qiuming; Lu Ji and Lu Yun [third c. CE] wrote poetry comprising the strange marvelousness of [the earlier poet] Liu Zhen's [second c.] verse.... [Because of these later writers,] the means by which states can be improved and the cultural tradition that has come down from the ancient sages hang like the sun and the moon within our breasts, placing wind and clouds at the tips of our brushes. Holding within the regulations of past and present, this legacy allows us to strike the appropriate notes on the scale. At its most subtle it enters and exits where there is no gap; at its most broad, it regulates the cosmos.... [And yet] people who truly understand it are few, which makes me constantly worry that the forest of letters will come to ruin....

From the time that Lai Ji as a censor castigated flatterers and from the time that in the Secretariat he elevated the worthy, within he was in charge of state secrets, and without he edited the state history.... At royal hunts on Mt. Huang [as described in Zhang Heng's (78–139) "Western Capital Rhapsody"], he several times presented writings of agate; on storied boats on the Fen River [as when Emperor Wu of Han (141–87 BCE) visited], he was able to hear the emperor's jeweled thoughts. At southern fords he mourned for Qu Yuan [as did Jia Yi when he was exiled to the south], going off to follow the clouds at Cangwu [as had Qu Yuan in his own exile]; on western roads he grieved for Gao Ang [501–38, general of the Western Wei dynasty who lost a crucial battle against the Xianbei], gathering snow on the cliffs of Congling.... In his life he wrote over a thousand pieces; here, they are organized into thirty scrolls.

Early in my life I roamed to Hao in the west [the capital of the ancient Zhou dynasty], to the place where the Zhou court scribes left lacunae; late I lie on an eastern mountain, thinking of the forgotten affairs of the Han court.... It is not only Zhuangzi [fourth c. BCE] who grieves to have given up the axe [lost a person who could appreciate his art] and not only Xiang Xiu [ca. 221–ca. 300] who is saddened on hearing a flute [because it reminds him of dead friends]. In vain I have worked to observe the sea yet do not know the beginning of the waves; I have always loved to discuss the workings of heaven but have not penetrated the secrets of cosmic creation. I have therefore taken up my balding brush in order to make this preface for Lai Ji.

昔者龍蹲東魯，陳禮樂而救蒼生；虎據西秦，焚詩書以愚黔首。通其變，參天二地謂之神；合其機，一陰一陽謂之聖。⋯ 自獲麟絕筆，一千三四百年。游夏之門，時有荀卿孟子；屈宋之後，直至賈誼相如。兩班敍事，得邱明之風骨；二陸裁詩，含公幹之奇

偉。…齊魯一變之道，唐虞百代之文，懸日月於胸懷，挫風雲於
毫翰。含今古之制，扣宮徵之聲。細則出入無間，麤則彌綸區
宇。…後生莫曉，更恨文律煩苛；知音者稀，常恐詞林交喪…自
矜冠指佞，難樹登賢，內掌機密，外脩國史。…黃山羽獵，幾奏
瓊篇；汾水樓船，參聞寶思。南津弔屈，去逐蒼梧之雲；西路悲
昂，來挽葱巖之雪。…凡所著述，千有餘篇；今之刊寫，成三十
卷。余早遊西鎬，及周史之闕文；晚臥東山，憶漢庭之遺事。…輟
斤之慟，何獨莊周；聞笛而悲，寧惟向秀。徒勤觀海，未知渤澥之
倪；永好談天，莫究氤氳之數。遂抽短翰，爲之序云。

In its original unexpurgated and unparaphrased form, this is a masterpiece
of late medieval parallel prose, compressing into its allusions traditional
resonances that this translation gestures towards in only the most cursory
way. Lu's readers are expected to know all these references and to be moved
by Lai's resemblance to these figures in cherished texts. Contrary to Qiu
Zhao'ao's impulse to justify Du Fu's poetry through reference to extra-
literary concerns, Lu's allusive rhetoric makes a point of providing no justification of Lai Ji's literary works that will be intelligible to readers who
are not already fully steeped in the tradition it claims they inherit.

The cultural and literary tradition's role in the construction of meaning is crucial here for reasons Lu Zhaolin suggests in the final lines of
this preface. Although he claims to have spent much time discussing and
observing the mysteries of the universe, from which human life derives
and to which Lai Ji's has now returned, Lu disclaims understanding: he
cannot make sense of Lai's life and death through insight into the workings of the cosmos. All he can do is offer Lai the same species of immortality Ziyou had offered to Confucius, and Jia Yi to Qu Yuan: the continuance of his literary projects and the moral interpretation of his life via
the terms and tropes of the tradition. The tradition offers mere guide
ropes through the darkness, and is always in danger of being lost. But so
long as writers like Lu Zhaolin continue it, its wondrous ability to survive
the transformations of history offers a possibility of preservation and
return that we cannot discern in the obscure workings of heaven or the
heavings of the sea.

Though neither the late medieval model exemplified by Lu Zhaolin nor
the recordizing model of Qiu Zhao'ao should be taken as univocal in itself
or unchallenged in its time, these two prefaces provide a useful illustration

of the contrasting directions in which Du Fu's rough contemporaries and his later critics often sought to justify poetry. For Qiu Zhao'ao, the literary tradition is heterogeneous and discontinuous: it contains only isolated positive examples fit for careful study. For Lu Zhaolin, by contrast, the literary tradition is essentially coherent: although different writers and different ages have attained different degrees of success in developing its core concerns, all are engaged in a common civilizing project. This difference is bound up, moreover, with a fundamental epistemological shift whereby the textual tradition goes from being the primary tool of sense-making to being itself in need of discriminating moral interpretation. For Qiu Zhao'ao, critics have to work diligently to understand how obscure texts relate to referents in the external world, since it is in that relationship that their ethical character lies. For Lu Zhaolin, it is the world outside of traditional texts that is obscure, and texts help us make meaning within it. Since the world's deeper processes lie beyond our ken, the textual tradition provides the key epistemological ground for moral understanding.

Du Fu as Pivot

Du Fu's capacity to serve as a pivot between these two models of poetic sense-making can be illustrated by a late poem that explicitly contrasts his own mature verse with that of a contemporary. Old, sick, and stranded in the remote cultural backwater of Kuizhou, he came into possession of a copy of two recently composed poems by Yuan Jie 元結 (719–72), prefect of Daozhou, in which Yuan lamented the suffering of the people under his jurisdiction and argued for a reduction of the taxes levied on them. Yuan was a remarkable man: a successful military strategist who would soon resign his office in high-minded protest of the state's misgovernance, he was also one of the greatest poets of the eighth century and an intellectual whose innovations would inspire some of the revolutions of the ninth.[20] These two poems of Yuan Jie's are, moreover, justifiably famous for their compassionate depiction of the wretched state of the people following the An Lushan Rebellion.[21] Moved by Yuan's poems, Du Fu wrote a companion piece praising both their content and their author. And yet he cannot help but dwell on the differences between Yuan Jie and himself.[22]

同元使君春陵行幷序　　*A Companion Piece for Prefect Yuan's*
"Ballad of Chongling" (with a preface)

覽道州元使君結春陵行兼賊退後示官吏作二首，志之曰：當天
子分憂之地，效漢官良吏之目，今盜賊未息，知民疾苦，得結
輩十數公，落落然參錯天下爲邦伯，萬物吐氣，天下少安可得
矣。不意復見比興體制，微婉頓挫之詞，感而有詩，增詩卷
軸，簡知我者，不必寄元。

I have looked over Prefect Yuan Jie of Daozhou's two poems, "Ballad of
Chongling" and "Shown to the Officials and Clerks after the Marauders
Withdrew." I comment upon them thus: Yuan is worthy of a position
that shares the emperor's worries and enacts the category of the "fine
officer" from the ranks of Han dynasty officialdom.[a] These days, when
rebels and marauders have not ceased, he understands the suffering of
the common people. If we could get people like Yuan Jie to fill the ten
official ranks, and distribute such people throughout the world as elders
of the provinces, the myriad things would give forth [more vital] *qi*,[b] and
it would be possible to pacify the empire somewhat. I did not expect to
see again the normative form of the *Classic of Poetry*[23] or words of such
subtleness or rhythmic sharpness. Stirred by them, I found I had a
poem, which I wrote on the scroll of [Yuan's own] verses. I send it to
those who truly understand me; there is no need to send it to Yuan.

遭亂髮盡白	Meeting disorder, my hair turned full white;
轉衰病相嬰	getting old, sicknesses enwrapped me.
沉緜盜賊際	Sunken so long among rebels and marauders,
4　狼狽江漢行	in desperation, I traveled down to Yangzi and Han.[c]
歎時藥力薄	I sigh for my time as medicine's strength grows thin;
爲客羸瘵成	ever a sojourner, infirmities coalesce.
吾人詩家秀	Yet I am one who, among the finest poets,
8　博采世上名	gathers broadly from the famous of the age.
粲粲元道州	And glorious indeed is Yuan of Daozhou,

a. These are conventional ways of referring to the office of prefect.
b. *Qi* 氣 (breath, vapor) is a crucial concept in this poem. It refers to the matter-and-energy that makes up all things, including human bodies, emotions, and natural phenomena. Moral character can be a kind of *qi*; sickness can be too. Similarly, there are types of *qi* characteristic of war, and types of *qi* characteristic of peace. Note that it is also possible to read "give forth *qi*" as "sigh with relief."
c. That is, to the south, near the confluence of the Yangzi and Han Rivers.

	前聖畏後生	a latter-born former sages would hold in awe.[d]
	觀乎舂陵作	Reading his poem on Chongling
12	欻見俊哲情	in a flash I saw the passions of a hero.
	復覽賊退篇	Then perusing his piece on the marauders' retreat—
	結也實國貞	Jie it is, a true pillar of the state.[e]
	賈誼昔流慟	Jia Yi once shed tears of grief;
16	匡衡常引經	Kuang Heng constantly cited the *Classics*.[f]
	道州憂黎庶	The Prefect of Daozhou worries for the people,
	詞氣浩縱橫	and the *qi* of his words surges without restraint.
	兩章對秋月	His two poems match the autumn moon;
20	一字偕華星	each word the equal of a brilliant star.
	致君唐虞際	He would place his lord between Yao and Shun;
	純樸憶大庭	his purity recalls Dating.[g]
	何時降璽書	When will an imperial summons come down,
24	用爾為丹青	to use you as one of the highest ministers?
	獄訟永衰息	Lawsuits would then permanently cease;
	豈唯偃甲兵	how could it only be war you'd lay to rest?[h]
	悽惻念誅求	Compassionate, you'd think on exactions;
28	薄斂近休明	with lighter taxes, we'd approach enlightened rule.
	乃知正人意	And yet I know the thoughts of this upright man:
	不苟飛長纓	he would not carelessly trail long ribbons.[i]
	涼飇振南嶽	Chilly winds stir the southern marchmount;

d. This line alludes to a saying of Confucius: "The latter-born should be held in awe. How can one know that those to come will not be as good as those of nowadays? If, however, a person reaches forty or fifty and has no fame, this is someone unworthy of being held in awe." The phrase translated as "glorious" in the previous line may echo "Dadong" 大東 from the *Shijing*, where it describes the brilliant robes of court officials. In both lines, a contrast may be intended with Du Fu.

e. The phrasing here echoes Confucius's praise of his disciple Yan Hui 顏回 in the *Analects*: "Hui it is, one who has almost gotten there!" 回也其庶乎.

f. Jia Yi 賈誼 (200–168 BCE) and Kuang Heng 匡衡 (fl. ca. 36 BCE) were exemplary officials of the Western Han. Du Fu's language here echoes their writings and their official biographies.

g. Yao and Shun were legendary sage rulers of high antiquity. Dating was the ruler of an earlier, simpler age.

h. Confucius said of himself that, "when it comes to hearing lawsuits, I am no better than others. What one has to do is make it so there are no lawsuits."

i. These are the long capstrings characteristic of the ceremonial garb of a high minister.

32	之子寵若驚	this personage takes imperial favor with alarm.[j]
	色阻金印大	His face would grow gloomy with a grand golden seal,
	興含滄溟清	his inspiration lies in the purity of distant seas.[k]
	我多長卿病	As for me, I suffer the illness of Sima Xiangru,
36	日夕思朝廷	though day and night I yearn for the court.[l]
	肺枯渴太甚	My lungs are withered, my thirst is extreme;
	漂泊公孫城	I moor here by Gongsun's walls.[m]
	呼兒具紙筆	I call to my boy to prepare paper and ink;
40	隱几臨軒楹	leaning on my armrest, I look out from the railing.
	作詩呻吟內	I compose this poem within my moaning;
	墨淡字欹傾	the ink is light, the characters slant.[n]
	感彼危苦詞	Stirred by that man's words of hardship,
44	庶幾知者聽	I hope people of understanding will heed.[o]

j. This line echoes the *Daodejing* 道德經: "Favor and disgrace should be [equally] alarming" to a wise person. The southern marchmount, Mt. Heng 衡山, was nearby Yuan's post at Daozhou. The chilliness of his aura probably refers to the strict dignity of his comportment. It also contrasts with the heat of the climate in Daozhou, on the empire's less civilized southern frontier.

k. These lines refer to Yuan's sentiments in the final lines of "Shown to the Officials and Clerks after the Marauders Withdrew": "How I long to cast down my symbols of office, / to take a fishing pole and punt my boat away! / I'd take my family where there's plenty fish and grain, / and live out my old age on rivers and lakes."

l. Sima Xiangru 司馬相如 (179–117 BCE) was a great writer of the Western Han whose talent won him high office at court, but whose diabetes gave him a pretext for retiring from it, since he was independently wealthy and had never much aspired to hold a position there.

m. Gongsun is Gongsun Shu 公孫述 (d. 36 CE), who during the Han interregnum set up a rebel regime in Kuizhou.

n. "Moaning" is ambiguous. It might refer to moaning from sickness or to reciting Yuan Jie's poem—"moaning" being a common description of poetic chanting in the Tang. The ink of Du Fu's composition is light, presumably, because he lacks the strength or funds to grind more. "Slanting characters" was a category of negative calligraphic judgment in the Tang. In a treatise on the interpretation of calligraphy, the eminent early Tang literatus Yu Shinan 虞世南 (558–638) wrote: "If one's mind and spirit are not rectified, one's characters will slant; if one's intent and temper are not harmonious, one's characters will topple" 心神不正書則敧斜，志氣不和書則顚仆.

o. There may be a pun in this line. The phrase translated as "I hope," *shuji* 庶幾, also has another canonical meaning, deriving from a passage in the *Yijing* 易經: "Confucius said, 'Yan Hui has gotten close to incipiency (*dai shu ji* 殆庶幾).'" According to the official

Although it occupies a marginal position among the many greater works of Du Fu's collection, this poem forces readers to reckon with the central problematic of his mature verse. As he suggests, the ethical significance of Yuan Jie's poems would have been immediately clear to their contemporaries. Persuasive imitations of the "normative form of the *Classic of Poetry*," Yuan's poems request redress on behalf of the population of Daozhou, remind the court of its proper functions as established by the ancient sage dynasties, preserve the form of poetic remonstrance that those dynasties had instituted, and model for later readers emotional dispositions conducive to good government.[24] The poem in which Du Fu praises Yuan for successfully replicating this model, however, appears to do none of these things and, throughout its course, presents Du Fu as Yuan's near opposite. Whereas Yuan is of the type of the precedent-citing Han ministers Jia Yi and Kuang Heng, Du Fu is a disappointment of inherited tropes, a Sima Xiangru who, unlike the original, is unhappy in retirement. Too old and too sick to hold office, he yearns for the kind of powerful position that Yuan, following the traditional guideline that one should not serve a corrupt state, is about to abandon. And where Yuan is a paradigmatic "fine officer" whose moral aura has tempered even the miasmal southlands, Du Fu's slanting calligraphy reveals that their climate has bred in him infirmities of body and of mind. Yet despite these marked and systematic contrasts, the ambiguity of the poem's final line is clearly intentional. Du Fu hopes that readers will heed both Yuan Jie's poems and also his companion piece for them, affording both writers the sympathetic approbation that was built into the concept of "understanding" (*zhi* 知) in Chinese literary culture.[25]

Recordizing reading offers one possible solution to the challenge the poem thus sets its readers. According to critics of this stripe, Du Fu's verse

---

Tang subcommentary on this text, this passage indicates that "Worthies only come close to incipiency. . . . Sages know incipiency, and Yan Hui was second to the sage. He thus could not know incipiency, but he could get close to it and aspire towards it." To "know incipiency" was to be able to recognize the subtle springs of change before they declared themselves and thus to be able to act with perfect appropriateness to changing circumstances, as only sages could. "Coming close to incipiency," therefore, was sometimes an epithet for "worthies." The line could thus be retranslated, "May his 'coming close to incipiency' be heeded by those who understand."

is just as valuable as Yuan's, since both poets are recording emotions deeply felt and morally appropriate to the historical situations in which these poems were written. This interpretation is already visible in the earliest surviving evaluative comment on the poem, by Liu Chenweng 劉辰翁 (1232–97), who remarks that it is precisely Du Fu's complaints about his own situation that make the poem compelling: "The beginning and the end of the poem being like they are," he writes, shows that "the affairs it describes are true and Du Fu's feelings about them authentic."[26] Similar approbation is offered by Wang Sishi 王嗣奭 (1566–1648), who writes that the poem "comes from Du Fu's guts, and each character is a tear."[27] Pu Qilong 浦起龍 (1697–1762), more elaborately, suggests that Du Fu's description of his own suffering "subtly reveals," as a condensed example, "the way that the populace's desperation has grown worse by the day," thus making the poem a record not merely of Du Fu's sincere feelings, but also of the imperial history about which Yuan Jie was writing more explicitly.[28] Taking this interpretation a step further, the modern scholar Chen Yixin 陳貽焮 (1924–2000) argues that Du Fu in this poem reaffirms his decision not to participate in government but rather to devote his energy to poetry in hopes of adding momentum to the poetic "movement" instigated in Yuan's poems.[29] Mo Lifeng 莫礪鋒 (1949–), similarly, takes the poem as a statement of Du Fu's poetics, a manifesto for "poetry that reflects and criticizes reality, and especially those social phenomena that cause suffering to the people." "This sort of spirit," he writes, "is very similar to what we nowadays call [socialist] realism."[30]

These comments reveal some of the motivations behind recordizing reading. Not only does the paradigm solve particular problems in Du Fu's verse, but it also guarantees in a more global sense that he was not the moral failure he worried that he was. Even though Du Fu's initial ambitions to contribute to the good governance of the state ended in futility, that is, recordizing critics understand poetry to have provided him an alternate arena for significant moral action. Insofar as poetry's ideal sense is, for them, merely a perspicacious perception of historical experience and historical reality as they are—because a successful "poet historian" will be a "poet sage"—they argue that the art offered him the possibility of moral transcendence even in the aftermath of a cataclysm as devastating as the An Lushan Rebellion. This is clearly a compelling and usefully flexible paradigm, having perdured for nearly a thousand years and through the sorts of ideological changes announced by Mo Lifeng's comparison of the poem to the ethical and aesthetic ideal of socialist realism. Yet this recordizing paradigm is also premised on a forgetting of the late medieval ideals against which Du Fu was writing. In this case, these critics solve this poem's challenge by effectively denying it altogether, erasing the pointed contrast between Du Fu and Yuan Jie that the verse itself highlights so consistently.

It is, I will suggest, precisely this challenge that places the poem within the linked series of intellectual problems and possibilities that Du Fu's poetry takes up from the outbreak of the Rebellion in 755 until his death in 770. Du Fu's early poetry, before the traumas of the war years, often expresses a faith similar to Lu Zhaolin's that the types and tropes of the cultural tradition should allow him to cast his experience in its meaningful and lasting patterns. With the outbreak of the Rebellion and his flight to the frontiers, however, he began to find that traditional tropologies distorted his experience, rather than making sense of it. By the time he wrote this poem, therefore, he had come to see moral sense-making as inherently problematic, dependent on categories and concepts that make sense within certain delimited situations but may not translate to others. Where for Lu Zhaolin the sacred cultural tradition had proven its "sageliness" and "numinosity" by surviving history's catastrophes and applying equally well to all its vicissitudes, and where recordizing readers would see the essence of Chinese culture in fidelity to an always available moral reality, Du Fu at this point had come to see ethical judgment as ineluctably ambiguous and contingency as close to absolute. At the same time, however, he had also begun to observe the ways his contingent and ambiguous experience proved richer than traditional precedents could predict, integrating him into communities he had not expected to reach and raising the possibility that his life and work would have greater and different significance for others than he could foresee within the limited horizons of his own understanding. If his sense of his life's failure to conform to the moral scripts available to him threatened the stability of his moral sense-making, then, it also offered the hope that his failed and frustrated life might someday be redeemed. And his poetry had become a discipline by which he sought to make himself equal to this hope.

In the poem at hand, this broader project manifests itself in the systemic ambiguities Du Fu has programmed into the verse. One of these ambiguities I have already noted in the final line. A precise parallel appears as well in the fourth couplet, where it is undecidable whether Du Fu is referring to Yuan Jie as "among the finest poets" or is referring to himself as such. This fourth couplet also begins the poem's reflections on Du Fu's equivocal relationship to Confucius, for even if Yuan Jie is the subject of "among the finest poets"—one way of reading the grammar—the activity of gathering such poets' work is unmistakably reminiscent of Confucius's compilation of the *Classic of Poetry*. And if Du Fu is the Confucius here, then his praise of Yuan Jie throughout the poem may be the equivalent of Confucius's praise of his student Yan Hui, echoed in line 14, as one who had "almost [but not entirely] gotten" what Confucius was teaching (*shu* 庶).[31] Where Confucius was a "sage" (*shengren* 聖人), Yan Hui and most of the poets collected in the *Poetry* were, for medieval thinkers, merely "worthies" (*xianzhe* 賢者), a level of moral achievement categorically inferior to that of the sages. The difference between sages and worthies was understood to lie in their adaptability to circumstance: whereas sages respond perfectly to any contingency without being locked into a predetermined pattern, worthies can only continue the traditions begun by sages responding to situations that have now already passed. This idea was summed up for late medieval Classicists in Confucius's description of Yan Hui as the best of worthies, "almost getting to the incipiencies of change [that sages understand]" (*shuji* 庶幾).[32] When this compound, *shuji*, appears in the final couplet of the poem, therefore, it is ambiguous whether it bears its other common meaning—"I hope," the translation given above—or whether Du Fu is casting Yuan Jie in the role of an excellent, but merely "worthy," student.[33]

In these ambiguities, the poem takes on a shadow of the adaptability that characterizes the infinite responsiveness of the sages. Depending on what makes moral sense to us, we can understand it either as a poem Du Fu wrote "while intoning" Yuan's or as one he wrote "while moaning" about his own helpless frustration—or, perhaps, as both. By allowing these alternatives to proceed despite the tensions between them, Du Fu opens the poem to various possibilities of reconciliation, including the one outlined by his recordizing readers and the rather different one I will offer in this book. This openness seems particularly significant given his statement in the preface that he intends the poem to be sent not to Yuan Jie himself, but rather to "those who truly understand" him. At the time he wrote this verse—in the autumn of 767, most likely, just a few years before his death—Du Fu was living as an exile in Kuizhou, a semibarbarous backwater in the far south of the empire. Most of his close friends were dead, and though he served as something like the court poet for the regional satrap Bai Maolin 柏茂林, fêting officials with gracious verse as they passed through the Three Gorges, he complained of the indignity of these social obligations and chose in his free time to compose some of the strangest poems in the language, addressed to dead luminaries and the marginally literate audiences of his children and his non-Chinese domestic servants.[34] If Du Fu did not expect Yuan Jie to be someone capable of "understanding" him, it is far from clear who he imagined would be able to make sense of this deeply ambiguous poem. He may have had a few surviving friends in mind, and it is possible that he hoped this poem would prompt them to material demonstrations of their sympathy. It is also possible, though, that his readers were speculative and the poem a missive to an unknown future.

This poem's ambiguities are thus one example of the methods Du Fu experiments with for transforming his literary inheritance into something less rigidly normative and more endlessly transformable than the great sagely tradition had seemed when he was young. Having become disillusioned of his early dedication to the tradition's moral scripts, and having witnessed the collapse of a great culture, he had by this point in his career begun to ponder the possibility that ethical values and the communities that hold them may change radically over time. Such change, he imagined, might allow for the future reinterpretation of his life, which, by contemporary standards, seemed an abject failure. The question to which he turns in his last years, therefore, is this: how can one write for a different sort of tradition, one defined by the continual emergence of new moral perspectives?[35]

Transforming Tradition

This transformed idea of tradition represents not merely a solution to the intellectual and moral problems Du Fu faced in the collapse of the Tang dynasty, but also a potentially useful perspective on a signal challenge of the humanities in our time: that is, of integrating our unprecedentedly heterogeneous, global past with the increasing certainty that the moral categories of even the near future will look very different from our own. This is not to step into complicated debates about what the relationship is or should be between our modern age and "traditional" societies, let alone to defend a Burkean concept of tradition as a repository of inherited wisdom.[36] Instead, if his late medieval contemporaries generally saw tradition as roughly such a "handing over" (*trado*) of values from one generation to the next, Du Fu comes over the course of his life to think about tradition as equally involving that other sense of "handing over," betrayal (also *trado*). It will be my contention here that the sharp (but often underappreciated) disagreements between the late medieval model and recordizing reading identify the tradition of Chinese moral poetics as a tradition in this latter, larger, more heterogeneous sense, rather than the former, smaller, more stable one. And yet it is precisely the internal heterogeneity of the values that have serially reanimated the apparently continuous forms, images, themes, and aesthetic intuitions of this tradition that has allowed it to fulfill Du Fu's hopes. What he offers us, then, is a model of the virtues that may render our lives ethically commensurate to the rich transformations of human understanding exemplified in longstanding, complex traditions like that of Chinese moral poetics.

In considering the model Du Fu provides, it is worth noting the millennium of success he has had to date in providing spaces where past and future can meet amidst change. It is, indeed, in hopes of doing some justice to his achievement in this regard that this book considers his poetry in relation to his contemporaries and his critics.[37] Methodologically, I aim in this way both to build on the excellent reception histories that have already been written about Du Fu and also to resist the tendency of reception history in general since the "death of the author" to focus only on the continual construction of figures like him, as if readers were not reading anything in particular and authors had no agency in how they have been received. It is true and well documented that Du Fu's critics have been highly creative, and my account of the shift from the late medieval model to recordizing reading will further undermine their common claim to have tapped the timeless essence of Chinese poetry.[38] At the same time, however, I also hope to demonstrate that even the blindness of Du Fu's recordizing critics derives ultimately from their insight into his poetry.[39] If they have often created new values in their reading of his work, they were impelled to such feats of interpretation precisely by their recognition of the difficult questions his verse raised. Their betrayals are intimate, and, in this sense, even their overreaching in pursuit of what Du Fu could mean for them often points towards the rather different significance he can hold for us now.[40]

Convinced in the aftermath of the An Lushan Rebellion that only a tradition open to transformation in this way might survive the repeated cataclysms of history, Du Fu developed a poetics that pointedly frustrates final interpretations. Exploiting to the fullest the awesome resources, in this respect, of both the classical Chinese language and the allusive tradition, he coded into his poetry puzzles that have allowed the significance of his experience to develop in directions he could not predict and could not, perhaps, even imagine. His transformability, therefore, has been the result neither of "having no one inside him," like Borges's Shakespeare, nor of later writers' willfully misreading their great predecessor.[41] Instead, this transformability has always been his own: the result of using poetry to live more fully the luminous obscurity of his life.

ONE

Time and Authority

Early Poems (before 755)

W e know a great deal about Du Fu's life and times: more, probably, than most of his contemporary readers would have, and certainly more than those contemporaries would have known about even the most famous poets from earlier eras. As will become clear in subsequent chapters, this biographical context allows us to read his corpus in great depth, recognizing in it narrative threads that would be invisible in the work of poets about whom we know less. The project of this first chapter, however, is to suggest that even as it represents the indispensable starting place for researching his poetry, our extensive knowledge of Du Fu's circumstances tends to distort our understanding of the sort of art poetry was in his time.

The forms in which information about Du Fu's biography is now generally transmitted between scholars and to readers were not part of the apparatus of poetry in the Tang. As far as we can tell, Du Fu was the first poet whose work occasioned the composition of a "year chart" (*nianpu* 年譜) tracking his movements and his poetic productivity against the history of his era; his was the first individual collection scholars endeavored to rearrange into roughly chronological (*biannian* 編年) order; and he was among the first poets whose corpus was provided an extensive, historically informative commentary to accompany the text.[1] One or more of these Song dynasty innovations has characterized the vast majority of surviving editions of Du Fu's poetry since the thirteenth century,[2] and all three are now standard in the presentation of his work.[3] The forms in which readers from the Song onward have generally encountered Du Fu are thus different from the forms in which eighth-century readers would have encountered any poetry.

Late medieval readers could not rely on the extensive contextualizing information conveyed by these critical genres when they read verse, and late medieval poets could not have expected that their readers would have access to such paratextual guides. This was not a problem for them, however, since their visions of literary reading emphasized forms of understanding that did not depend on scholarly research, and they mostly wrote poems that could be read well without the benefit of detailed historical knowledge. Du Fu himself wrote poetry that would have fit this description: such poetry makes up a large percentage of what seem to be the earliest poems that survive in his collection. In this chapter, therefore, I want to resist the retrospective application of the reading procedures and literary ideals of the commentary tradition to a poetry that does not call for them, in order in subsequent chapters to highlight the innovative character of his later poetry, which does.

Chronological Interpretation and Authority in Recordizing Criticism

All of Du Fu's works have been dated, whether roughly or precisely, in the hundreds of chronological collections and dozens of year charts that have been produced over the past thousand years. As a result of this work, most of the great poems of his oeuvre have accumulated robust interpretive traditions, and consensus has mostly emerged about the likely historical and biographical contexts in which they might have been written. For a large number of his less famous poems, however, the same cannot be said; and if the forms of the chronological collection and year chart have forced critics working in these genres to shoehorn these pieces into particular periods of his lifetime, their dates are often tentative or contested. Such chronologically uncertain poems are, in this respect, unpropitious to a project like mine that seeks to trace a narrative of Du Fu's poetic development, and I will mostly avoid them here. It is, however, useful to begin with one such poem: a poem that probably is early but has often been thought not to be, whose ambiguous dating thus offers a glimpse back at the situation in which readers of medieval poetry operated before the development of the contextualizing genres in which we now encounter Du Fu's work.[4]

重題鄭氏東亭　*Another Written on Mr. Zheng's Eastern Pavilion*[a]

華亭入翠微	The splendid pavilion recedes into azure
秋日亂清輝	as the autumn sun scatters its clear glow.
崩石敧山樹	Fallen rocks lean the mountain trees;
4　清漣曳水衣	clear ripples tug the water's robes.[b]
紫鱗衝岸躍	Purple scales vault, dashing against the shore;
蒼隼護巢歸	a gray hawk returns to guard its nest.
向晚尋征路	In twilight we'll seek our traveling roads,
8　殘雲傍馬飛	the last clouds accompanying our horses in flight.

Were this poem ascribed to any eighth-century poet but Du Fu, it is unlikely it ever would have invited historicizing comment at all. Poetry in the eighth century was often composed on social occasions so common and repeatable as to be effectively timeless. Excursions, banquets, and partings from friends all came around with such regularity that a poem written on one such occasion could sometimes be reused at others, as seems to have been the common practice with Wang Wei's 王維 (ca. 701–61) famous verse on parting, "Tune of a City on the Wei" 渭城曲.[5] Reading "Another Written on Mr. Zheng's Eastern Pavilion" along these lines, we might imagine it serving as a pleasant accoutrement to one such social outing, the poet's companions recognizing in Du Fu's words much of what they had seen that day and appreciating his skill in representing their experience in the graceful language and strict form of contemporary "regulated verse." They would have thought back to the leaning trees they had remarked along their walk, and they would perhaps still see the fish jumping in the sunset waters. And when the last couplet imagined the party breaking up, the outing would have been gilded for them with the prospect of nostalgia.

This nostalgia for the present pulls the poem out of the normal flow of time, simultaneously hurrying the day to its conclusion and also resisting its loss, a temporal dynamic that echoes throughout the poem's images. Like many of the days Tang poets found most beautiful, this one lingers

a. Early, likely authorial, note: "Within the borders of Xin'an County" 在新安界. Xin'an County was a few kilometers east of Luoyang.

b. Sheets of algae.

on the edge of oblivion. It is autumn, and, as the poem moves on, evening; the proverbially stable mountain is collapsing, the water does not flow. Yet as all things withdraw back into uncreation, Du Fu also focuses on forces that defy this devolution: trees that support the falling rocks and provide nests for fledgling hawks, and fish that with the ripples of their twilight leaping prevent algae from overspreading the pond. This tension, finally, is recapitulated in the equivocal grammar of the final line, which on one construal shows Du Fu and his companions, forced to leave the pavilion by the close of evening and the darkening of winter, nonetheless transcending their mortal limitations, accompanying the clouds in flight.

As a whole, then, the poem would have complexified its initial audience's relationship with the temporally situated experience they were sharing when Du Fu wrote it. Though it forced them to recognize that shortly, the only remnants of their revels would be the fading brushstrokes that likely inscribed this poem on the pavilion wall, it also encouraged them to imagine that that inscription would remain to preserve the outing's ghost on the landscape. That ghost could then be reembodied in other autumns and by other visitors, who could see their own excursions in its images as well.

Fading time transfigured into timelessness: this is one way of reading this poem. Its plausibility is supported by the many critics who have dated the poem to Du Fu's youth, sometime in the flush of the Kaiyuan (713–42) or early Tianbao (742–56) reign period, when he might well have sought to entertain friends and impress patrons through such social verse. Other commentators, however, have assigned the poem to 758 or 759, several years into the An Lushan Rebellion and just before the Xin'an region would fall back into rebel hands.[6] These critics have seen the pavilion as abandoned, the poet as alone (Chinese poetry generally lacks pronouns, and so the "we" in the last couplet could just as easily be "I"). Their attention, commensurately, is drawn to images evoking the chaos of the late 750s: the overgrowth of the vegetation, the "disorder" of the sunlight, the "collapsing" of the mountain, the wariness of the hawk, and the "raggedness" of the evening clouds. Depending upon the vagaries of its dating, therefore, the poem might enact time's transcendence, or it might meditate on a particular historical moment. Such are the uncertainties that accompany the attempt to chronologically contextualize eighth-century verse.

There happen in this case to be convincing biographical reasons to doubt the later dating. Critics who have offered this interpretation have cited as evidence the note attached to the poem's title that the pavilion was located "within the borders of Xin'an County." This note, preserved without comment in our earliest surviving editions of Du Fu's collection, derives from an unknown source. Given that few besides Du Fu himself could have known where this unnamed pavilion was, however, the note is often thought to derive from his own hand, either at the time of composition or, perhaps more likely, at some later point when he was rereading, editing, or preparing his collection for circulation. And if it is indeed Du Fu's own, it can fairly definitively rule out the possibility that the verse derives from any period after 755. Based on the evidence provided by other poems in his collection, we know that Du Fu did pass through Xin'an in both 758 and 759, but only in the late winter and early spring, respectively, of those years. There does not seem to have been any occasion after the outbreak of the war in 755 when he might have had the chance to visit in autumn, the season described in the verse.[7] Considering that he would never again return to the heartland after 759, we can thus say with good confidence that the poem must have been written before the Rebellion, when Du Fu frequently traveled between his hometown of Luoyang and the capital, Chang'an.

There is a serious point that could be made here about the ideological interpretation of Du Fu's collection, which only rarely allows that he might have written poems that do not centrally concern the state. For my present purposes, however, it is more important to note that the uncertainty introduced by chronological contextualization is only cleared up, in this case, by better contextualization. Given the dramatic historical changes that were to condition Du Fu's verse, that is, the authority of any successful argument about this poem must rest not so much on any insight a critic might have into the poem's imagery or tone, but instead on that critic's mastery of the historical circumstances of the period—a mastery that must base itself on the vast body of scholarship that has interpreted the fragmentary historical hints of his collection into a biography that can place him confidently almost every month from 755 to 770. Authority of this sort has been central to the tradition of Du Fu commentary since the eleventh century, when scholars in a newly burgeoning print culture began the cumulative project of empirical research into and evidence-based reasoning about his life and times that continues to inform all readings of his poetry today.[8] We in the modern world are quite comfortable with this sort of scholarly work, of course. But it is not a vision of authority that would have had much resonance in the literary culture of Du Fu's time.

Authoritative Reading in the Late Medieval Period

As would have been the case with many Tang poems, the original audience of "Another Written on Mr. Zheng's Eastern Pavilion" was there at its composition. Although they probably did not feel compelled to consider its biographical and historical contexts beyond the narrow circumscription of the occasion, they knew them well enough, or at least as well as they knew the poet. Readers who read the verse off the wall of Mr. Zheng's pavilion in years to come, however, might not have known exactly when the poem had been written or what was going on in the life of the poet at the time. It might have been one poem among many inscribed there, deriving from many gatherings over many years. In a context like this, readers would have been even further discouraged from seeking the poem's precise biographical situation. They would, instead, likely have read the poem against others written there (and present to them in the vast *déjà lu* of the excursion genre), appreciating the novelty of craft and talent Du Fu applied to the common experience of banqueting in the pavilion's beautiful surroundings.[9]

Most of the other contexts in which late medieval readers encountered poetry would have similarly discouraged historical and biographical speculation. Print had not yet arrived on the scene to render books cheap and widely available, and as a result, when poetry circulated outside of the social situations in which so much of it was composed, it would have been encountered aurally, as recited by a friend or a performer; handwritten on an isolated sheet of paper with little attribution and no commentary; in anthologies that selected a few poems (or even a few lines) from a great many poets; or as part of small, often fragmentarily copied, usually disorganized, individual collections—complete, carefully collated volumes of collected works being vanishingly rare, since they would have taken many hours if not many days of work to copy manually.[10] Beyond the material presentation of any given poem, moreover, Tang readers would often have lacked historical resources to contextualize it. Although a few great aristocrats were able to maintain sizable libraries, most readers had to copy out by hand whatever books they wanted to possess, either borrowing from friends or from local monastery scriptoria, a situation that probably guaranteed that most people most of the time had few sources at hand for figuring out the historical situation in which a given poem might have been composed.[11] Had their enjoyment of verse depended, therefore, on the sort of responsible, research-based scholarly authority recordizing critics have used in reading "Another Written on Mr. Zheng's Eastern Pavilion," Tang literati would rarely have read any poetry at all.[12]

These material circumstances had far-reaching consequences for the late medieval period's understanding of poetry. In keeping with the informationally straitened circumstances in which poetry was generally encountered in this period, for example, contemporary models of readerly authority relied less on the vast availability of empirical evidence characteristic of later print cultures and more on the possibility of immediate, often emphatically miraculous, comprehension—comprehension that went beyond what the fragmentary material or oral text could convey to audiences less capable of transcending its limitations.[13] The standard metaphor in the period for sensitive reading was "knowing the tone" (*zhiyin* 知音), a concept that derived from early anecdotes about extraordinary musical savants who could discern from a performance what the musician was thinking about or what the situation was in his state.[14] According to the official Tang subcommentary on the *Classic of Poetry*, for instance, it was this ability that originally grounded the poetic tradition, allowing the "numinous blind musicians" (*shengu* 神瞽) of the legendary Zhou court to establish the normative moral interpretations of the *Poetry* that were later transmitted by Confucius and his disciples.

> Sound can inscribe emotion and emotions can thus all be seen. Listening to a tone it is possible to know whether it expresses order or disorder, and observing music it is possible to understand whether it purports flourishing or decline. Therefore, the numinous court musicians had the means necessary to recognize the import of the poems. If a poem's words misrepresented what was really on a poet's mind (their *zhi*), this would be called "faked emotion," and the truth would be manifest in the sound, its falseness recognizable. It is like if you took a piece of silk and wove it into brocade, its color might be beautiful even if its material was poor, or its pattern might be ugly though its quality was good; only a good merchant could tell. So too when

they took songs and chants and put them to court music: sometimes the words seemed right but the intention was wrong, and sometimes the words seemed perverse though the *zhi* was normative. Only people who understood music could tell.

聲能寫情，情皆可見。聽音而知治亂，觀樂而曉盛衰，故神瞽有以知其趣也。設有言而非志，謂之矯情，情見於聲，矯亦可識。若夫取彼素絲，織爲綺縠，或色美而材薄，或文惡而質良，唯善賈者別之。取彼歌謠，播爲音樂，或辭是而意非，或言邪而志正，唯達樂者曉之。[15]

The Tang subcommentary draws a clear distinction here between those who "understand" music and those who do not. This distinction is crucial because the texts of the *Poetry* are often obscure, and sometimes seem to say something like the opposite of what the commentary tradition assures readers they mean. In order to forestall dissention, therefore, these interpretations have to be grounded in an authority most interpreters do not have.[16] And it is characteristic of late medieval ideas about reading that this authority should lie not in these musicians' possession of contextualizing information, but rather in their "numinous" insight into the texts themselves.

This capacity to immediately perceive an author's meaning from a text that might be obscure to most people was also claimed by late medieval readers themselves. In his *Statutes of Poetry* 詩式, for example, Jiaoran 皎然 (ca. 720–ca. 798) writes that, when he encounters the poems of a master poet like Xie Lingyun 謝靈運 (385–433), he "sees emotions, not words," thus suggesting that good writing and adept reading transcend the necessity of uncertain inference, speculation, or research.[17] The same point is made by Liu Xie 劉勰 (ca. 460s–520s), author of the late medieval period's only surviving explicit theoretical discussion of reading, who writes that emotions (*qing* 情) need to be understood as the basic materials of the writer, as colors are to a painter, and sounds, to a musician.[18] To read well, for Liu, is to be capable of recognizing the identity of text and emotion, for the words of a well-written text are in fact consubstantial with the mind that created them, as downstream waters are with their source. "Although the temporal distance separating writer and reader may be great," Liu writes, "and the reader will never see the writer's face, nonetheless, by looking at his writing the reader can immediately see his mind."[19]

Characteristically, neither Jiaoran nor Liu Xie—nor, indeed, anyone else from the late medieval period—explains the mechanics of how this perception of a writer's mind is supposed to work. Unlike their postmedieval counterparts, medieval intellectuals did not leave behind tracts on "how to read books" (*dushu fa* 讀書法).[20] This is not merely because, had they wanted to write out methodologies for interpreting poetry, they would have limited themselves neither to "reading" 讀 nor to "books" 書. More important, when they did discuss interpretation, they generally disclaimed the possibility that it might have a "method" 法, or even that it could be satisfyingly explained. In his preface to the *Wuchen* 五臣 commentary on the *Wenxuan* 文選, for example, Lü Yanzuo 呂延祚 (fl. ca. 718) insists that, "if one does not have deep and mysterious insight (*you shi* 幽識), one cannot penetrate" the poetry contained in that anthology to the meanings he and his collaborators have finally revealed.[21] Zhang Huaiguan 張懷瓘 (fl. 713–42), similarly, writes that, though "everyone wants to explore the miraculous and wonderful [in the arts], not everyone can understand it."

> If one does not have a mysterious mind that is inscrutably illuminating, such that one can close one's eyes and see deeply, then the complete recognition [necessary for artistic appreciation] will never be possible. [For such a task,] one's mind can complete the tally, but one cannot speak about it publicly.
>
> 自非冥心元照，閉目深視，則識不盡矣。可以心契，非可言宣。[22]

Zhang here explicitly denies the possibility that others will be able to understand why he makes the judgments he does unless they too have the capacity for mysterious appreciation. This sort of appeal to an incommunicable hermeneutical authority is a common move in late medieval texts, including Jiaoran's *Statutes of Poetry*, which suggests that good reading no less than good writing depends on the unaccountable "incipiencies of heaven" within a person (*tianji* 天機).[23]

Good readers in the late medieval period, then, were not thought of as operating according to some specifiable method, but rather as embodying something others did not, some quality of mind that provided them with the authority to adjudicate insightful readings from dull ones. As

Zhang Huaiguan's metaphor of "completing the tally with one's mind" implies, Tang literati often imagined that texts might appear radically different to different readers, seeming to a nonauthoritative reader, for example, as merely fragmentary, broken things, like half of the sort of wooden "tallies" that were conventionally split between the parties to an agreement, covenant, or debt.[24] An authoritative reader, by contrast, would see the same texts as whole and unambiguously meaningful, for such readers possessed within themselves the "other half of the tally." Crucially, we never find in any surviving material from the late medieval period the claim that the "other half of a poem's tally" might be provided by the sort of specific historical research boasted by Du Fu's recordizing commentators.[25] Instead, the most usual use of the metaphor is in the phrase "mysteriously matching tallies" (*ming qi* 冥契) with the poet or the poem, an expression that assumes the impossibility of justifying good readings on publicly assessable grounds.

In practice, of course, it was probably acquaintance with the literary tradition that provided authoritative readers most of the "other half of the tally" they relied on in confronting new poems. In general, the task of not-yet-authoritative readers in the late medieval period seems to have been the assimilation of canonical texts and the authoritative interpretations that had accrued to them over the centuries. Tang biographies, for instance, routinely describe the textual curricula their subjects had studied when young, commenting on the precocious age at which they "could read" different Classics and histories.[26] This emphasis on basic competence—in contrast, for example, to the deep, lifelong relationships with the Classics that would define the ideal of Neo-Confucian reading in the postmedieval period—suggests that the meanings of these texts were generally understood to be established in their commentaries, which thus effectively served as the gateway into a literate community constituted by the mastery of a shared authoritative corpus. And a similar process might have described initiation into the reading of contemporary poetry as well. Both Zhang Huaiguan and Jiaoran, for instance, articulate their above-mentioned skepticism of method in works that claim to educate aspiring aficionados through the presentation of exemplary judgments—the most common literary- and art-critical form of the period. By providing concatenating examples rather than fixed rules, such pedagogical manuals would have encouraged students to intuitively assimilate the conventions of medieval verse that would, ultimately, allow them to reconstruct the laconic language of poetry into full, moving poetic statements. After working through such manuals, students might not have been able to articulate the methods they had learned to apply, and their newly acquired hermeneutical capacities might have seemed obscure even to them. This obscurity, however, would have bound them even more intimately to other authoritative readers, since their unspoken affinities would have been inexplicable to outsiders.

The attraction of this sort of authoritative community can be discerned in another of Du Fu's early social poems, written in response to others recited at a banquet.[27]

夜宴左氏莊　*A Night Banquet at the Zuo Estate*

風林纖月落	Into windy forests sinks the slender moon
衣露淨琴張	and dew wets our clothes as the clear zither's strung.
暗水流花徑	Dark waters flow on flowered paths;
4　春星帶草堂	springtime stars circle the thatched hall.
檢書燒燭短	Examining manuscripts—the candles burn short;
看劍引盃長	viewing swords—the cups are passed long.
詩罷聞吳詠	Poems finished, we listen to Wu chants:
8　扁舟意不忘	thoughts of a small boat I can't forget.[a]

Like "Another Written on Mr. Zheng's Eastern Pavilion," this poem is a regulated verse. Defined in part by their adherence to tonal prosody, regulated verses are written in couplets, usually four but sometimes more or fewer. By convention, the middle two couplets of a four-couplet poem, or all but the first and last of a longer poem, are structured by parallelism,[28] whereby each word or phrase in one line of the couplet must be matched with a similar word or phrase in the other line, and (in the best instances) in such a way as to enrich the significance of both. "Dark waters"—to give

a. Wu was the regional name of part of southeast China, so called because of an ancient state centered there; the dialect of the Wu region was markedly different from that of the northern region where Du Fu was raised. The phrase "small boat" may recall the story of Fan Li 范蠡 (6th c. BCE). Fan Li was a successful minister of the state of Yue in the Spring and Autumn period; after he helped the king of Yue destroy its longtime rival state of Wu, he retired to live in a "small boat" on the rivers and lakes of the southeast.

an example from lines 3 and 4 of this poem—is parallel to "spring stars," for not only are both compounds structurally the same (adjective-noun), but there were conventional connections between water and the Milky Way, in which China's east-flowing rivers legendarily returned through the sky to the west. The water down on the paths, moreover, probably derives from recent "springtime" rains, and may be known in the "darkness" because it glisteningly reflects the stars above.[29] On a larger scale, such formal interconnections were supposed to obtain between couplets as well. The middle couplets, for example, alternate around the opposition between the natural and the human that is raised in the first two lines of the poem and then resolved in a new way in the final couplet, where Du Fu imagines following the precedent of reclusion set by Fan Li—a legendary exemplar of civilized achievements and also, later on in his life, of intimacy with nature.[30]

Du Fu's companions, no doubt reasonably adept in applying the conventions of contemporary poetry, would thus have intuited in his laconic notation of scenes from the party a meditation on the rich interconnections of the Chinese cultural cosmos. And as they filled in the poem's fragments, they would have recognized in the final couplet Du Fu himself similarly "completing the tally" of another verse from the banquet. Here, Du Fu hears a poem apparently recited in the dialect of Wu, the southeast, and imagines being there, drifting off to a life of reclusion amidst the storied splendors of its riverine and lacustrine landscape. Within the context of the party, this ending might have been pointedly polite, since Mr. Zuo, by virtue of his lack of an official title, is likely himself to have been a "recluse"—a trope often used in the eighth century to flatter those who, for whatever reason, had failed to obtain or maintain that primary aspiration of most educated men, a position in government.[31] Reclusion was a noble alternative to government service, and it had a long tradition, going back to Fan Li and beyond. Within this context, the conventionality of the association between the southeast and reclusion, and the readiness with which even the sound of Wu dialect could evoke it for Du Fu, strengthen the suggestion he makes in intimating his own desire to follow Fan Li's boat: that Mr. Zuo's lack of an official post had not debarred him from a life all civilized men could admire. That such things do not have to be said outright, that they are instead understood implicitly by men of understanding, is here very much the point.

Transpersonal and Transtemporal Orientations

Recordizing critics have, unsurprisingly, often read this final couplet differently. Eager to apply biographical knowledge gleaned from careful study of Du Fu's collection as a whole, many have interpreted the final line not as representing an allusion to a trope well known by all Tang literati, but rather as invoking a memory of Du Fu's travels in Wu in his youth.[32] Though it is perfectly plausible that Du Fu's "thoughts of a small boat" would have been influenced by his time on the rivers and lakes of the southlands, it is worth pointing out how radically this interpretation shifts the poem's momentum. For if Du Fu withdraws here from the shared space of the banquet into a private memory, then he is not flattering Mr. Zuo, and he is not resolving the poem's themes by drawing together civilization and the natural in a traditional reference to someone who embodied the best of both. Equally important, he is not enacting a propensity that I will suggest is common throughout his early work: to end his poems with statements that pointedly blur the boundaries between individuals. Though this propensity will become clearer below, it can already be discerned in the two pieces above, both of which can be seen as ending on the projection of a shared imagination. Both poems, that is, conclude with a vision of the revelers going their separate ways, seeking out their traveling roads amidst the dusky clouds or going off alone to a reclusive life in the southlands. Yet insofar as these visions of each banquet's aftermath gather the about-to-be-isolated revelers in a vision shared by all, they structurally enact a continuance of community against time's encroach. In the social context of a party, it is not difficult to see how this gesture would have recommended itself: part of the point of writing such poetry was to craft shared memories that would continue to link friends across time and distance. By drawing reader and writer together in the prospect of their oncoming separation, these poems promise to become the perduring form of a moment when friends' minds were at one.

Although it is unlikely that social occasions such as these regularly recalled to writers' minds the serious normative prescriptions of the *Classic of Poetry*, it is perhaps not an accident that this aspect of these poems recalls Tang dynasty interpretations of the moral import of that most canonical of all statements about Chinese verse, that "poetry speaks *zhi*"

詩言志.[33] According to the government-sanctioned subcommentary on that Classic, this phrase meant that poetry was the losslessly externalized form of a poet's moral and emotional orientations and obsessions (*zhi*)—the form by which those orientations could come to be publicly shared, as others who read, heard, recited, and acted out the poem came to embody them as well. The ancient sage kings, therefore, had directed their subjects to recite praiseworthy poems regularly so that they gradually came to adopt as their own the normative dispositions of the original poet.

> When a poet first speaks his *zhi*, he just speaks it normally. If he speaks it normally, this will not satisfy, and he will feel that his words have not expressed his *zhi*; therefore he will sigh those words in order to harmoniously continue them. When he sighs them, he will still find it insufficient, and therefore will sing them in long form. Upon singing them in long form, he will still find it insufficient, and so without knowing it, his hands will be dancing and his feet stomping. The poet's body, that is, is put in service by his mind, and without knowing it, he will raise his hands and dance with his body, moving his feet and stomping the earth, and only in this way will his emotions inside find release. . . . The sage kings knew that human emotions worked like this, so they set poems [embodying normative ethical dispositions] to music, making their people sing them with their voices in order to image the poets' singing of their words and dance them with their forms in order to image the poets' dancing with their bodies. When one completely images the form of the poets' emotions, then one gets completely the way they used their minds.

> 初言之時，直平言之耳。平言之而意不足，嫌其言未申志，故咨嗟歎息以和續之。咨嗟之猶嫌不足，故長引聲而歌之。長歌之猶嫌不足，忽然不知手之舞之、足之蹈之。言身爲心使，不自覺知舉手而舞身、動足而蹈地，如是而後得舒心腹之憤。⋯聖王以人情之如是，故用詩於樂，使人歌詠其聲，象其吟詠之辭也；舞動其容，象其舞蹈之形也。具象哀樂之形，然後得盡其心術焉。[34]

This account of poetry's capacity to transmit moral and emotional orientations between individuals articulates in compressed fashion poetry's fundamental claim to ethical significance in the late medieval period. As chapter 3 will discuss in more detail, this mythology of the art's derivation from the ancient sage courts encouraged Tang intellectuals to think of verse as capable of molding diverse individuals into a harmonious society characterized by shared moral commitments. In this sense, although banquet poetry along the lines of Du Fu's two poems above has sometimes been scorned as a frivolous pastime by moralist critics of the postmedieval period, the community such social verse formed by uniting friends' minds in linguistic crystallizations of experience and imagination could seem to Tang intellectuals a microcosm of the ideal society Confucius envisioned when he edited the *Classic of Poetry*.[35]

This Tang idea that poetry paradigmatically allowed for the interpersonal sharing of moral and emotional dispositions also imputes to the art a temporal structure inherently at odds with the contextualizing imperatives of recordizing reading. For Tang dynasty Classicists, that is, the harmonious society that the *Classic of Poetry* was intended to create was not just horizontal, as it were, but also vertical.[36] The ancient sages were understood both to have promulgated praiseworthy poems throughout their lifetimes and to have established poetry as a perduring ritual institution for their dynasties. The poems produced by the original poets of the *Shijing* were thus supposed to shape not merely the dispositions of their contemporaries, who would necessarily apply them within the different individual circumstances of their own lives. Equally important, those poems were supposed to shape the minds of readers over time, working to ensure that future generations would not deviate from the moral commitments of their ancestors. In this sense, the meaning of poetry was not delimited to the particular historical moment of its composition but was rather imagined as transcending it.

The ancient institution of poetry had, of course, eventually collapsed, as had all the sages' institutions. Yet the legacy of these institutions was nonetheless preserved in the Classics and in many of the cultural mores and literary products of succeeding eras, all of which went into making up the cumulative tradition Tang intellectuals had inherited from the past: what they referred to as This Culture of Ours (*siwen* 斯文). This Culture was, by virtue of its origins, accounted normative, and, in many contexts, the question of whether a given literary work displayed its author's assimilation of the styles and concerns of exemplars from the precedent tradition was central in determining its moral value.[37] As a result, late medieval poets often sought explicitly to transcend their limited historical situations so as to merge themselves with what was timeless in the tradition.[38]

This aspiration animates a number of Du Fu's early verses. In the following poem, for instance, he dedicates his art to the overcoming of time.[39]

登克州城樓   *Climbing the Wall Tower at Yanzhou*

東郡趨庭日	In this eastern province, in days of "rushing through the yard,"
南樓縱目初	from this south tower I first let my eyes roam free.[a]
浮雲連海岱	Drifting clouds reach Mount Tai and the sea;
4　平野入青徐	the level moors go off into Qing and Xu.[b]
孤嶂秦碑在	The Qin stele is still there on the lonely cliff;
荒城魯殿餘	an overgrown wall remains from the Lu palace.[c]
從來多古意	Always many ancient thoughts:
8　臨眺獨躊躇	looking out, alone, I pace back and forth.

If in the case of the first poem discussed above we were able to solve, fairly confidently, the problems recordizing reading raises, here we are not so lucky. "Rushing through the yard" was what Confucius's son had done to avoid disturbing his father; from this allusion, many commentators have understood that Du Fu wrote this poem while visiting his own father at Yanzhou, perhaps while the latter was serving in a government position there.[40] Others, however, have worried that the poet's known travels in the vicinity of Yanzhou occurred in around his thirtieth year, when, they think, his father might have already been dead, rendering the first line a reminiscence of an earlier trip to the region.[41] Unfortunately, there simply is not enough evidence in the poem or beyond it to decide which is the case. Yet whereas for recordizing reading this contextual ambiguity must present a momentous uncertainty—suspending the poem between apparently irreconcilable alternatives: youthful prospect or mournful reminiscence— a late medieval reader might have seen Du Fu dedicating himself here to

a. "Rushing through the yard" alludes to a story from the *Analects*, cited below.

b. These are all ancient toponyms found together in the *Classic of Documents*: "Mount Tai and the sea were the boundaries of Qingzhou. . . . Mount Tai, the sea, and the Huai were the boundaries of Xuzhou."

c. The Qin stele is an inscription by the First Emperor of Qin 秦始皇, written in 219 BCE to commemorate his completion of the *feng* and *shan* sacrifices, which marked his consolidation of the empire. It is preserved in Sima Qian's (ca. 145–ca. 86 BCE) *Shiji*. The Lu Palace in question was the subject of a famous rhapsody (*fu* 賦) by Wang Yanshou 王延壽 (2nd c. CE), preserved in the *Wenxuan* 文選.

the mission of This Culture of Ours in a way that obviated the question of its precise moment in his life.

Whether or not Du Fu's father had already passed away when he wrote this poem, the relationship between individual patrimony and the larger claims of tradition is at its center. This theme is invoked in the first line, which alludes to a story of Confucius's son Boyu.

> Chen Kang once asked Boyu whether his father had passed on any special teaching within the family. Boyu answered, "No. But once he was standing alone, and I rushed through the courtyard. He said to me, 'Have you studied the *Poetry*?' I answered, 'Not yet.' [He said,] 'If you do not study the *Poetry*, you will not be able to articulate.' I then withdrew and studied the *Poetry*." . . . Chen Kang was pleased at this response and said, "From this, I learned about the *Poetry* . . . and I learned that a true gentleman keeps his son at a distance."[42]

According to this anecdote, the true gentleman does not have any private wisdom to pass on to his son; instead, he leverages the power of family attachment to encourage his son's excellence in endeavors proper to the larger community. Even were his father alive, then, the suggestion is clear that Du Fu would in any case be alone in climbing the wall tower to "study poetry." Worthy fathers had been preserving distance from their sons for over a millennium, and for as long sons had sought their fathers' approval through mastery of the literary tradition, which detached them from the private bonds of the family and immersed them in the larger inheritance of the culture as a whole.

It is this larger cultural tradition, the rest of the poem then goes on to suggest, that has the capacity to transcend time's depredations, its destruction of lineages, and its devouring of individuals. In the second couplet, for example, the tradition seems as stable as the natural world, the vast vistas of Du Fu's perch atop the wall tower taking in Mt. Tai and the sea, as well as China's most ancient political boundaries, in use from the time of the legendary sage king Yu all the way down to the present day. Amidst this stability, there has also been loss, the worn steles of the Qin and ruined palaces of the Han testifying to the collapse of empires and the limits time's passage sets against human ambition. Yet these losses have themselves been integrated into the tradition, and the text of Qin's steles and the splendor of this Han palace remain to Du Fu in famous literary works. By the end of the poem, therefore, Du Fu's "ancient thoughts" are ambivalent: both troubled by the decay of past achievements and empowered by the tradition's capacity to withstand it, incorporating its lessons into the inheritance of present poets.

In an early inkling of the virtuosic deployment of ambiguities that I will argue is characteristic of his mature verse, "ancient thoughts" (*guyi* 古意) also has another possible meaning here, indicating a common subgenre of late medieval poetry. It is unclear, that is, whether Du Fu is saying that he "always has many ancient thoughts" or that many "ancient thoughts" poems have been written on similar occasions throughout the tradition—a suspension of grammatical possibilities that pointedly blurs the distinction between the poet's mind and the minds of those poets he is imitating in the final line's troubled pacing, itself one of the oldest and most conventional closings in Chinese poetry. If Du Fu discerns in the passing of Qin and Han the prospective or recent passing of his father, then, the poem enacts the very lesson Boyu learned from Confucius: to leverage private attachments as motivation for achieving public values. In the fashion of a good Tang Classicist, Du Fu's resolve in this poem to "study poetry" endeavors to transcend the limitations of clan, family, and body to become a vessel for a cultural tradition that would span the distances between men and survive the losses to which the particulars of history are subject.

Late Medieval Tropology

Readers familiar with the dominant accounts of Chinese poetics will probably want to stop me here. The interest that Chinese critics have shown since early times in establishing historical context has often been taken as definitive of the radical differences between Chinese poetry and its counterparts in the West, and nowhere is that interest more obvious than in commentaries to the *Classic of Poetry*.[43] And it is, admittedly, true that all commentaries on that Classic do a significant amount of their exegetical work by situating individual poems in more or less precise historical circumstances.

Late medieval scholarship on the *Poetry*, however, does not argue that historical contextualization is a necessary prerequisite for poetic hermeneutics—quite the opposite, in fact. The Tang subcommentary, for instance, explains that knowledge of the *Poetry*'s historical circumstances was not necessary for the adept interpreters of the sagely reigns, such as the "numinous blind musicians" mentioned above, who could infer a poem's meaning from its sonic qualities. Instead, the historical glosses preserved in the orthodox Mao-Zheng commentary tradition (and attributed, originally, to Confucius's disciple Zixia 子夏, who learned them from the Master himself) were less a necessary supplement to the *Poetry* than a means of explaining its meaning to later readers, who lacked both the original music to which it was set and the miraculous moral intuition that had created those glosses in the first place.[44] In other words, the historical context of the *Poetry* was, according to the official Tang commentary, originally inferred from its meaning, not the reverse.

The majority of what survives to exemplify late medieval hermeneutical practice suggests that this vision of the ideal relationship between interpretation and contextualization was probably widespread. We do not have much to go on here, possibly because, as Xiaofei Tian has remarked, medieval readers of poetry seem in general to have been less obsessively concerned with getting their reading "right," and less haunted by the possibility that they were reading it "wrong," than postmedieval readers have tended to be.[45] In what we do have, however, Tang literati often appear to have considered themselves the sort of adept interpreters who did not need to rely on historical research to understand the verse they read. They frequently intuited (that is, invented) apocryphal anecdotes to contextualize poetry, and, as Christopher Nugent has pointed out in his discussion of Tang manuscript culture, they often changed its language to match what they thought it should have said.[46] Even Du Fu's poetry did not survive this practice unscathed, as we know both from the high levels of variation found in early texts and from the famous anecdote of a young Mr. Wei, who marveled at his sixteen-year-old concubine's ability to "fix" the "errors and lacunae" in his copy of Du Fu's collection, apparently without recourse to another source text.[47] These creative interpretive strategies played a role in engendering the significant *mouvance* of medieval manuscripts and left serious problems to the critics of the postmedieval period, who in their efforts to get back to "correct" interpretations have often been forced to sift large numbers of competing textual variants and anecdotal accounts.[48]

Only two large-scale historicizing commentaries on poetry survive from the late medieval period, both on the *Wenxuan*, an anthology of literature from the Han and Six Dynasties.[49] One of these, the Li Shan 李善 (d. 689) commentary, occasionally cites historical documents to support its interpretations, and later critics of the postmedieval period would often look back to it as an important precursor. Li's relatively meticulous scholarship, however, comes in for scathing criticism from the authors of the other surviving Tang commentary, the *Wuchen* 五臣 edition, which accuses him of "never having set his brush to explaining the motivating background to the compositions" included in the *Wenxuan*.[50] The charge seems overstated in light of the text that today circulates under the title of the Li Shan commentary; but whatever edition of that work the *Wuchen* editors saw, they remain nonetheless right that Li's reliance on historical research prevents him from outlining motivating contexts for the majority of the poems included in the anthology, since in most cases suitable evidence simply did not exist. The *Wuchen* editors argue, therefore, that Li Shan has not lived up to his commentarial obligation, all while unabashedly admitting that their own commentary—which provides "motivating backgrounds" for many more poems—is based on no source materials that he did not have. Indeed, it is characteristic of the *Wuchen* edition to omit any mention of sources, even where its glosses agree with Li Shan's, thus demanding that the reader trust in the authority of the commentators—who depict themselves as "refined in matters of culture, not mixing with the dust of the world" and "of lofty literary talent, living on cliffs to cultivate themselves"—rather than in independently verifiable historical evidence.[51] And given that the *Wuchen* edition seems to have enjoyed wider circulation during the Tang than did Li Shan's commentary, this assertion that historical context could be inferred rather than evidenced does not seem to have bothered contemporary readers.[52]

Since Lü Yanzuo, in his introduction to this text, works to place the *Wuchen* commentary within the tradition of *Shijing* exegesis, it is perhaps not a mere coincidence that the *Wuchen*'s hermeneutical procedures in this respect mirror those attributed to the ancient adepts who recognized the moral significance of the *Poetry*.[53] But whether or not Lü and his collaborators were explicitly modeling their commentarial practice on antiquity in this respect, their commentary follows the Mao-Zheng tradition in another way signally important for understanding the relationship between poetry and its historical ground in Tang commentaries. Following the *Poetry* model, that is, the *Wuchen* commentators intuit historical context in only enough detail to assign the *Wenxuan*'s poems to a highly limited and generalized set of possible moral and governmental situations; for the most part, the precise historical contours of those situations do not seem to have interested them.[54] The same can also be said about the many "poetry standards" (*shige* 詩格) from the eighth through the tenth centuries that assign similar moral values to contemporary poetry.[55] In this respect, Tang commentators seem to have generally agreed with Li Shan's decision—in one of the few places where his commentary does speculate into the historical ground of *Wenxuan* poems—merely to "make clear the author's greater intent, while leaving out his [more specific] hidden references."[56] As Stephen Owen has suggested, late medieval readers thus seem in general to have been interested less in an "actual particular determination of reference" and more in a limited "typology of judgment."[57]

I take this typology of poetic judgment to be an instance of a broader phenomenon I will call late medieval "tropology": the belief that the moral contours of most situations and the moral characters of most people can best be illuminated by analogy to the repeating scenarios and exemplary figures of the precedent tradition.[58] Tropology was a crucial tenet of late medieval literary culture, and it threads through most of the facets of the poetic art I have discussed thus far. It underwrites, for instance, the allusions—often long lists of them—through which late medieval writers routinely depicted the salient outlines of their own and their friends' lives. Tropology allows, moreover, for the characteristic brevity and the apparent indirectness of much late medieval poetry, permitting Du Fu to be confident, for instance, that his fellow banqueters will recognize his poem at Mr. Zuo's as praising their host's reclusive lifestyle, despite its never mentioning reclusion explicitly. And tropology explains how the editors of the Tang subcommentary to the *Poetry* and the *Wuchen* commentators on the *Wenxuan* might have thought the intuition of a poem's moral meaning could precede and justify its assignment to an ethical situation or historical moment. When the *Wuchen* commentators explain that the first of the *Wenxuan*'s "Nineteen Old Poems" (*gushi shijiu shou* 古詩十九首) is not about a woman yearning for her absent husband—as it would certainly seem to the uninitiated—but rather expresses the feelings of a virtuous male courtier "slandered by flatterers and exiled from the court," they know this not because they have historical documentation, but because it is a good poem, and they know the kinds of meanings good poems can express.[59] Having read other poems in the tradition that were written in similar situations, they possess the "other half of the tally" in their minds.

To whatever degree the *Wuchen* commentators can be taken as representative of Tang literati in general, then, their work suggests that when late medieval readers considered poetry as a moral art, they thought of it less as documenting the individual circumstances in which given poems were composed than as exemplifying normative responses to exigencies that were potentially transpersonal and transtemporal. In this sense, the basic ethical purpose of poetry was the teaching of tropology, alerting readers to the salient moral and political situations that might occur in their lifetimes and how they should react to them. If, through their assimilation of This Culture of Ours, readers knew what those situations and reactions were, then they possessed all the resources necessary for intuiting the contours of any good poem's background, and they needed to research no further. Hence, I think, the hermeneutic confidence late medieval readers and critics characteristically display.

It hardly needs to be emphasized how divergent these assumptions are from recordizing reading, which is, at least in principle, always committed to knowing as much as possible about the specific historical background of Du Fu's work, and which has therefore spawned endlessly detailed "year charts," vast commentaries on his collection, and multivolume biographies of the poet. The point to be made here, rather, is that late medieval habits of reading are often reflected in late medieval poetry in ways that make it respond only poorly to recordizing approaches. This mismatch between the two modes can be demonstrated by reference to another of Du Fu's early poems, one of the most famous in his collection.[60]

兵車行   *Ballad of the Army Wagons*

車轔轔，馬蕭蕭   Wagons rattle,
                     horses neigh,
行人弓箭各在腰   marching men, each with bow
                     and arrow at the waist.[a]

a. "Rattle" and "neigh" are onomatopoetic phrases deriving from the *Shijing*.

	耶孃妻子走相送	Moms and dads, wives and children run to see them off;
4	塵埃不見咸陽橋	in the dust you can't see the Xianyang Bridge.[b]
	牽衣頓足欄道哭	They tug at clothes, stamp their feet, block the road weeping;
	哭聲直上干雲霄	weeping's sounds touch the clouds above.
	道傍過者問行人	By the side of the road, a passerby asks the marching men,
8	行人但云點行頻	the marching men say only: They call up troops often now.
	或從十五北防河	Some from the age of fifteen go north to guard the river,
	便至四十西營田	then when they reach forty work army fields in the west.[c]
	去時里正與裹頭	When they go, the village headman wraps their headscarves;
12	歸來頭白還戍邊	those that return, white-headed, go back to the frontiers.[d]
	邊亭流血成海水	On the frontiers the blood that flows could fill an ocean's waters,
	武皇開邊意未已	but our Martial Emperor's thirst for border conquest knows no cease.
	君不聞	Haven't you heard?
	漢家山東二百州	In the lands of Han east of the mountains, two hundred prefectures,

b. The Xianyang bridge was close to Chang'an and was built by Han Wudi 漢武帝 (r. 141–87 BCE), the "Martial Emperor" of line 14.

c. "Guarding the river" refers to service in the middle reaches of the Yellow River, modern-day Inner Mongolia between Ordos and Hohhot. "The west" refers to the border with the Tibetans as well as the areas around the Tarim Basin.

d. Wrapping a headscarf was a coming-of-age ritual for boys; the point is that they are too young to be sent to the army.

16	千村萬落生荆杞	a thousand villages, ten thousand hamlets grow with thorns and briars.[e]
	縱有健婦把鋤犁	Though there be sturdy wives to grasp the plow,
	禾生隴畝無東西	grain grows over the field boundaries, one can't tell east from west.
	況復秦兵耐苦戰	And for us Qin troops, inured to hard battle,
20	被驅不異犬與雞	we're driven on, no different from chickens or dogs.[f]
	長者雖有問	Though you, sir, have asked,
	役夫敢申恨	this conscript would not dare complain.
	且如今年冬	But now in winter this year
24	未休關西卒	they haven't rested the soldiers West of the Passes;
	縣官急索租	County officials press us for taxes,
	租税從何出	but where could the taxes come from?
	信知生男惡	Truly, to have a boy child is bad;
28	反是生女好	better to have a daughter instead.
	生女猶是嫁比鄰	A daughter you can still marry to your neighbor;
	生男埋沒隨百草	a boy will be buried and be among the plants.[g]
	君不見，青海頭	Haven't you seen? By the shores of Kokonor,
32	古來白骨無人收	white bones from ancient times and none to gather them.[h]

e. "East of the mountains" refers to the heartland of Chinese civilization around Luoyang.

f. Qin was the capital region, surrounding Chang'an.

g. This section reworks an old poem by Chen Lin 陳琳 (d. 217), "The Ballad of Watering My Horse at a Pool by the Great Wall" 飲馬長城窟行: "If you have a boy child, be careful he's not conscripted; / if you have a girl, wean her on dried meats."

h. Kokonor is modern Qinghai, in the northwest. The phrase "white bones and no one to gather them" derives verbatim from the Qiyu songs 企喻歌 of the Southern Dynasties, which imagined battles on the old Han frontiers in the northwest.

新鬼煩冤舊鬼哭   The new ghosts chafe at the injustice,
　　　　　　　　　the older ghosts just weep:
天陰雨濕聲啾啾   skies darken and rain comes,
　　　　　　　　　their voices moan and moan.[i]

A number of different dates have been offered for this poem, but the general consensus is that it was written in the second half of the Tianbao period (742–56), probably sometime between 750 and 754, when the Tang engaged in a series of ill-fated campaigns on the frontiers. In his critical biography of Du Fu, the modern scholar Chen Yixin provides five pages of detailed historical background. To offer a sense of how the poem ties recordizing readers in knots, I give only a brief précis of his account.

> From the end of the Kaiyuan period [713–42] on, there had been border wars that had protected the realm's internal safety and upheld the country's unity; not all such wars can be written off. But, because Emperor Xuanzong was beginning to become benighted and entrusted government into the hands of the careerists Li Linfu 李林甫 and later Yang Guozhong 楊國忠, who wantonly engaged in military aggression in order to reap rewards for achievement on the frontiers, the Tang also launched a number of unjust wars and brought great disasters upon every race of people within the empire. Among these, the most prominent were the attacks on Shibao [a contested fort in the northwest captured in a pyrrhic victory in 749] and Nanzhao [a state in the southwest, in modern-day Yunnan, the object of a disastrous campaign from 751 to 754]. . . . These two border affairs, especially the latter, shook those both within the court and without, and the people suffered deeply. . . .
>
> In the past, this poem had been thought by many scholars to have been written on account of Xuanzong's use of troops against the Tibetans [at Shibao]. The earliest advocate of the idea that this poem was written in response to the Nanzhao campaign was the Song dynasty scholar Huang He 黃鶴 [late twelfth c.], who saw that the poem's description of grieved partings matched with the record in the history books of Xianyu Zhongtong's

---

i. According to the *Zuozhuan* 左傳, new ghosts are larger than old ghosts. The howling of ghosts was sometimes understood to cause storms, as for example in a story from the *History of the Latter Han* (*Hou Han shu* 後漢書) in which the unburied corpses of a previous massacre caused frequent rains and howling winds for several decades; the rains only stopped when the bodies were found and buried.

loss of his army at Lu'nan, whereupon [in the words of the eleventh-century *Zizhi tongjian* 資治通鑑] "Yang Guozhong sent censors to various regions to catch people and send them in chains to the army. Those traveling this way were grieved and resentful; when they were sent off by their fathers, mothers, and wives, the sound of weeping shook the wilderness."[61]

[The seventeenth-century critic] Qian Qianyi 錢謙益 [1582–1664] took this interpretation a step further, [noticing that] ". . . Du Fu does not mention Nanzhao but speaks instead of 'East of the Mountains,' 'West of the Passes,' and the northeast. . . . [This is because] at this time Yang Guozhong was rich and powerful, and Du Fu did not dare criticize him outright, so he randomly mixed in affairs in the northeast and the northwest, as if he was not speaking about Nanzhao. But Nanzhao was his deeper intent."[62]

There are several points worth noting here. The most obvious is that recordizing readers do not, in the end, have definitive proof that this poem was written about the Nanzhao campaign rather than Shibao: Qian Qianyi's explanation for why Du Fu never mentions Nanzhao is ingenious because it has to be. This question is, however, irreducibly important for recordizing reading. As Chen tells it, the Tang was involved in several wars during these years, and some of them were "justified." If Du Fu wrote this poem to complain about one of the necessary campaigns, it would be less praiseworthy than if it were written about the unnecessary campaign against Nanzhao.

No matter its fame, then, this poem remains somewhat problematic for recordizing readers. It is, however, well designed to appeal to the readerly assumptions of Du Fu's contemporaries, who would not have felt the same pressure to specify its particular historical moment. Not only is the poem signally vague about its circumstances, mentioning campaigns in several directions, but it also obviously fudges many contemporary details in order to create a picture with deep resonance in the tradition. Conscription within the lands of the empire, for example, had in fact been phased out in 737, after which Tang armies were staffed entirely with professional, volunteer soldiers eligible for significant pay and benefits, and with border peoples for whom military service was obligatory under the terms of their submission to the empire. And even before this date, military service had since 717 been relatively light: male commoners were conscripted at the age of twenty-one for a three-year term, after which they were offered financial incentives to stay but allowed to return home.[63] It is highly unlikely, there-fore, that there were white-haired old men in the 750s who had been pressed into service for their whole lives or hamlets in the heartlands de-populated by border wars. These are scenes, rather, drawn from the stock of literary tradition, and in particular from historical accounts of Han Wudi 漢武帝 (157–87 BCE), the "Martial Emperor" mentioned in line 14, whom early historians had criticized for sacrificing too much blood and treasure expanding the frontiers. By appealing to this traditional moral, Du Fu would have gratified his contemporaries' tendency to intuit a tro-pological situation from the poetry they read, rather than researching its more specific historical context.

It is true, of course, that the friends to whom Du Fu circulated this poem shortly after he wrote it would have known its occasion and would have recognized the more specific target of its criticism. And there is, in fact, some justification for suggesting that the poem might have been writ-ten between 751 and 754 since, according to the *Zizhi tongjian*, conscription was briefly authorized during this period to supply troops for the campaign against Nanzhao. Yet if Du Fu was prompted by these extraordinary con-scriptions, the poem concerns itself less with their departure from contem-porary norms than with their conformity to a moral situation that had been well described in other times. The poem's criticism of its historical mo-ment, that is, lies not in its sensitive analysis of a particular historical sit-uation, but rather in its potent rearticulation of a moral drawn from and authorized by the timeless literary tradition. It is, therefore, into this time-lessness that Du Fu is writing here. As Bai Juyi would remark in praising similar ballad-style poems of social conscience a few decades later, this is the sort of poem that could be "stored in the imperial library, so that for a hundred generations it would not disappear, and set to court music, so that emperors would hear it constantly."[64]

Lost Detail

On the late medieval model, then, poems like "Ballad of the Army Wagons" can claim perennial and immediate relevance in their articulation of tradi-tional norms. One of the consequences of recordizing reading, by contrast, is that historicizing paratexts, like that provided by Chen Yixin, become necessary to the appreciation of Du Fu's verse. Poetry's meaning, in this latter paradigm, ends up ineluctably mediated through the work of the scholars who have researched his life and times—even as many of these scholars nonetheless promise to return their readers to an intimacy with Du Fu that would, paradoxically, be impossible without their help. In a clear example of this paradox, the early commentator Lu Yin 魯訔 (1099–1175) writes that his edition of Du Fu's poetry

> organizes the collection chronologically and provides a historical preface for each poem. Thus, the political situation of the time, the cultural climate of the place where he was dwelling, the difficulty or ease of the terrain where he was, the brightness and darkness of the scenery there, and the material conditions of his lodging can all be seen. It is like accompanying Du Fu on his journeys and makes his words seem just like we are speaking with him face to face. Why should we worry [anymore] about his poems being difficult to read?

> 離而序之，次其先後，時危平，俗嫩惡，山川夷險，風物明晦，公之所寓舒局皆可概見，如陪公杖屨而遊四方，數百年間猶有面語，何患於難讀耶？[65]

In stark contradistinction to the hermeneutical visions proposed by the Tang subcommentary to the *Poetry* and the *Wuchen* commentary to the *Wenxuan*, wherein interpreters needed authoritative insight to directly intuit a given poem's meaning, Lu suggests here that the challenge of Du Fu's poetry lies merely in our temporal distance from him. The historical contextualizing information Lu provides, therefore, is supposed to allow readers to imagine Du Fu's situation so fully that they "feel that they themselves went through the tragedies he faced, of harsh conditions and evil men." For that purpose, Lu suggests, the poems on their own are incomplete, even for adept readers. They too will need Lu's research-based editing and commentary to return the collection to a state of fullness.

Authors and readers working along the general lines of the late medieval model seem to have taken a different view of the incompleteness and obscurity that inevitably accrued to poetry as it made its way through time. For them, the point of poetry was not always to be found in a clear and full evocation of a particular experience; instead, vagueness and generalizability were sometimes understood as paradigmatically poetic. As Du Fu's younger contemporary Dai Shulun 戴叔倫 (732–89) famously put it, for example, "the scenes poets evoke are like when the sun is warm on Indigo Fields and the fine jade there gives off mist: you can gaze after them, but you cannot fix them in your eyes. They are images beyond images, scenes beyond scenes—how could they be easy to discuss?"[66] Dai's was only one take on the art, and a polemical one at that; nonetheless, the sort of luminous indistinctness that his aphorism evokes was to some degree built into the very language of Tang poetry, which in some genres was "poetic" precisely to the extent that it was compressed, leaving out function words and connectives that could adequately determine the syntactic relationships between the elements of a line.[67] Such lacunae could also be poetic on the level of whole poems, as for instance in the following anecdote about the poet Zu Yong 祖詠 (ca. 699–ca. 746):

> The official examiner set the topic of "Gazing at the Lingering Snow on South Mountain." Zu Yong wrote: "South Mountain's shadowy ridge rises grandly, / massing snow at the edge of floating clouds. / Beyond the woods, the bright color of clear sky; / within the city, increasing evening chill." When these four lines were turned in to the examiner, someone rebuked him. Zu Yong replied, "That was all I had to say."
>
> 有司試終南山望餘雪詩，詠賦云：終南陰嶺秀，積雪浮雲端。林表明霽色，城中增暮寒。四句即納于有司，或詰之，詠曰意盡。[68]

"Someone" rebukes Zu Yong here because examination poems were supposed to be longer, generally six couplets rather than two; as a result, he might have felt that these four lines would fail to articulate a full response to the imagined scene. Zu's response is, as Stephen Owen has pointed out, purposefully ambiguous: it could mean either that "he ran out of ideas" or that "these four lines exhausted his meaning."[69] In its condensed ambiguity, then, the riposte reprises the poem, almost mocking the unnamed reader for being unable to "use his mind to complete the tally" by challenging him to do so again. This "someone" was not, we are meant to understand, a skilled reader, capable of seeing how fragmentation and incompletion might enable aesthetic plenitude.

In this example, we can see how late medieval readers seem to have thought of loss and lacunae as part of what made poetry a discipline worthy of hermeneutical adepts. It was, indeed, literature's ability to communicate amidst the loss of full contexts that gave it the almost religious significance it often possessed in the medieval period. To readers, it offered the ability, in the words of Gao Jian 高儉 (575–647), to "not be an immortal and yet sit face to face with antiquity, to block up one's doors and windows and yet see far into the distance."[70] And to writers, it offered hope that "even when one's hundred-year shadow is gone, one's thousand-year mind will remain."[71] Literature, in other words, allowed gifted writers and skilled readers to transcend the spatial and temporal determinants of their lives, forming against their limitations transspatial and transtemporal "friend-ships"—as Lu Chun 陸淳 (d. ca. 805) puts it in the preface to his redacted collection of the writings of Wang Ji 王績 (ca. 590–644)—"so intimate they could forget their physical bodies." As if in fulfillment of this disem-bodying ideal, Lu deleted from Wang's collection a large number of mostly social poems he did not think accurately represented the kind of person Wang really was, claiming thereby to have "completed Wang's intent (*zhi*)" by greatly reducing the amount of historical and biographical information that could be gleaned about the poet from his collection.[72] For Lu Chun, it would seem, truly knowing Wang involved liberating him from the mun-dane circumstances that circumscribed his life.

Lu Chun's assumptions here obviously contrast with the voracious historical appetite of recordizing commentary, which is not targeted at adepts but instead strives to make Du Fu's poetry accessible to all. Lu's account of poetry's ideal transcendence of mundane historical detail dove-tails nicely, however, with much of Du Fu's early verse, which often focuses on the loss that follows time's passage. In poems like the following one, for example, it is the fading of a particular moment in time that allows for the articulation of a vision that transcends it.[73]

與任城許主簿遊南池   *Visiting South Pool with*
Assistant Magistrate Xu of Rencheng

	秋水通溝洫	Autumn's waters course the field dikes;
	城隅集小船	small boats gather by the city wall.
	晚涼看洗馬	In evening cool we watch the bathing horses,
4	森木亂鳴蟬	dark trees wild with crying cicadas.
	菱熟經時雨	Water nuts have ripened through the long rains;

蒲荒八月天　　the reeds are overgrown beneath the eighth-month sky.
晨朝降白露　　Morning will bring down the white dew,
8　遙憶舊青氈　　and, far off now, I recall the old green carpet.

"The old green carpet" in the final line of this poem is a reference to a famous story. Once, thieves in the night broke into the home of the aristocrat
Wang Xianzhi 王獻之 (344–86). Encountering the intruders, Wang
merely asked them to leave him the green carpet, since it had long been in
the family; seeing him so calm, the thieves were terrified and fled.[74] On the
basis of their research into Du Fu's biography, which suggests that at the
time of writing the poet had been traveling for several months in the northeast far from home, recordizing commentators have often interpreted this
allusion as suggesting homesickness.[75] Given the themes of the rest of the
poem, however, it seems to me more likely that the "old green carpet" refers
to summer's faded verdure.[76]

To say that summer's green had been stolen would have recalled, for
a reader who knew the tradition, a text that had already been invoked by
the phrase "autumn's waters" in the opening couplet. "Autumn's Waters"
was the name of a chapter in the ancient Daoist classic *Zhuangzi* 莊子,
which used the floods of autumn to symbolize the vastness and inexora-
bility of natural transformation—and thus, ultimately, of death, which the
Zhuangzi elsewhere compared to a thief in the night.[77] The reference is apt
here in this poem of autumn and of evening, in which the wild dissolution
of nature gradually overspreads the pool. Unlike Wang Xianzhi's thieves,
this night's will pay no heed to Du Fu's wishes. Tomorrow another kind
of autumn waters, the proverbial killing dew of autumn's last month, will
fall, and the season of pleasant boat trips will be gone.

The close of night and winter is not, however, the final word of the
poem, which throughout counterbalances the intimations of coming darkness against human ingenuity in channeling them for our uses—literally, in
the field dikes, and figuratively in the men enjoying autumn's last evening
in their boats by the city wall. Indeed, the human channeling of nature's
irresistible transformations continues in the poem itself, which, like
"Zheng's Pavilion" and "Night Banquet," leverages a final imagination of
the revelers forced to disperse to suggest the fragile but also enduring
beauty of this liminal moment. In remembering the already-lost green
of summer and anticipating tomorrow's white dew, that is, Du Fu and

Assistant Magistrate Xu would have seen the apparent robustness of their present sensations thin. Yet this thinning of the present to the onrushing currents of time is not itself confined to the present moment, but is, instead, capable of being understood, imagined, and experienced transpersonally and transtemporally. Although readers of this poem who were not there at its composition might not know the precise details of the occasion, therefore—how long Du Fu had been traveling, whether or not he yearned for home—they can experience immediately the timeless structure of dissolution and preservation he found in the brevity of that darkening day.

Writing in Tradition

This vision of a poem as something "found in," "drawn out of," or "gotten from" (*de* 得) experience was common in the eighth and ninth centuries.[78] Such *trouvailles* were, by definition, not limited to the particular moment from which they derived, but rather survived it to become part of a store of such poetic coups timelessly available to readers of the poetry tradition. As I hope to have suggested, this account of poetry writing dovetails nicely with late medieval accounts of poetry reading. Because such poems were not basically constituted by the sorts of local details that would inevitably be lost with the passage of time, they could be understood immediately by authoritative readers who possessed in their minds the "other half of the tally."

Like the late medieval model in this respect, and further suggesting the broad coherence of our two paradigms of sense-making, recordizing reading likewise comes attached to a commensurate account of good writing. This point can be well demonstrated by Chen Yixin's discussion of "Visiting South Pool with Assistant Magistrate Xu of Rencheng." Chen first cites approvingly a comment on the poem by the Song dynasty critic Zhou Zizhi 周紫芝 (1082–1155).

Once in the middle of the summer by the creek, I was with a guest taking in the cool: the evening sunlight was on the mountains, cicada sounds filled the trees, and we saw two people washing their horses in the middle of Ding Creek. I said: this is what Du Fu was talking about when he wrote "In evening cool we watch bathing horses, the dark trees wild with crying cicadas." In the past when I recited this poem, I did not see its artfulness; now that I am in the place where I see what he saw, I begin to recognize how marvelous it is. When one writes poems, one really should just write what one sees: one does not have to overdo it in being novel or daring.

暑中瀕溪，與客納涼，時夕陽在山，蟬聲滿樹，觀二人洗馬丁溪中。日：此少陵所謂晚涼看洗馬，森木亂鳴蟬者也。此詩平日誦之，不見其工；唯當所見處，乃始知其為妙。作詩正要寫所見耳，不必過為奇險。[79]

Chen then glosses this comment as follows:

Not merely in creating, but also in appreciating, one needs real life experiences. The *Zhuangzi* says, "A trap is for catching fish; once one has the fish, one can forget the trap.... Words exist for containing meaning, so once one has the meaning, one can forget the words." Poetry is an art of language, and therefore it necessarily has to borrow language to express thoughts and feelings. However, what poets are good at is making people understand, and for this purpose their descriptions need not merely be clear, but moreover need to call to mind the reader's vivid life experiences. They need to make us imagine, for it to be as if we ourselves had entered into the world that they create, as sensible as reality, such that we completely forget that mere fish-trap: language.[80]

Here Chen Yixin moves fluidly between ideas of reading and ideas of writing. The basic recordizing faith that poetry mediates an experience that was once immediate to the poet has implications in both realms, instructing readers to imaginatively reconstruct poems' occasioning contexts and writers to "just write what they see." Whereas reading is an ineluctably mediated process, dependent on authority conferred either by historical learning or, as here, extensive and vivid life experiences, writing is immediate and requires no special qualifications. Both of these conclusions flow naturally from recordizing premises.

This vision was, however, impossible in the late medieval period. In order to guarantee that contemporary readers would not have to research the precise historical situations in which they were writing, writers could not merely "write what they saw." Instead—and for reasons that will be discussed in more detail over the next three chapters—late medieval intellectuals tended to be skeptical that experience was sufficient to its own interpretation or representation. It had, rather, to be filtered through the authoritative tradition: "what one sees" deciphered by and even conformed to its tropological lessons. A final, very famous example of Du Fu's early verse can be read almost as an allegory of this process.[81]

望嶽   *Gazing on the Peak*

	岱宗夫如何	What, then, is Lord Dai like?—
	齊魯青未了	Qi, there, and Lu, and still the green goes on.[a]
	造化鍾神秀	Creation concentrated spirit splendors here,
4	陰陽割昏曉	north and south slopes riving dusk and dawn.[b]
	盪胸生曾雲	Surging the breast, giving out layered clouds;
	決眥入歸鳥	homing birds entering straining eyes.
	會當臨絕頂	Someday I should look down from its highest peak,
8	一覽眾山小	in that one view, the myriad mountains small.[c]

On its most basic level, this poem is a narrative of comprehension. Having previously absorbed legends of "Lord Dai" from his reading, Du Fu arrives in the first couplet here at a vantage of the mountain, eager to see for himself what the fabled peak is really like. But though he has studied the histories detailing the fortunes of Qi and Lu, they have not prepared him for the natural vastness of Taishan, which seems to him at first an incomprehensible mass of green that swells beyond these archaic

a. The peak in question is Mt. Tai, here referred to by its archaic, honorific name Daizong. According to the *Shiji*, "The sunlit [i.e., south] side of Taishan is Lu; its shady [i.e., north] side is Qi." Qi and Lu were ancient states of Confucius's time.

b. This couplet employs what is called "borrowed parallelism," *jiedui* 借對. That is, "creation" in the third line forces us to notice that the phrase indicating the north and south slopes of Mt. Tai, *yin-yang*, can also mean "the processes of nature," a better parallel. The phrase "spirit splendors" derives from Sun Chuo's 孫綽 (314–71) "Rhapsody on Roaming to the Tiantai Mountains" 遊天台山賦, which depicts the poet traveling up a lofty mountain in his imagination.

c. This was a common literary trope, descended from Mengzi's 孟子 description of the time Confucius climbed Mt. Tai: "When Confucius climbed the eastern mountains, he saw [his home state of] Lu as small. When he climbed Mt. Tai, he saw the whole empire as small."

political boundaries. The rest of the poem, therefore, will represent an attempt to come to terms with it.

Even in this first couplet, though, readers who know the conventions of contemporary poetry can pretty well guess what such "coming to terms" will mean. Although this poem inverts the tonal pattern expected of a "regulated verse"—thus representing an early exemplar of the formal innovations for which Du Fu is rightly famed—the logical structure of that form nonetheless underlies its thematic development.[82] The first couplet, that is, announces the poem's key opposition: between the civilized tradition— suggested by the historical titles Lord Dai, Qi, and Lu—and the uncivilized vastness of the mountain. Each couplet thereafter will work over this opposition in a new way, and ultimately they will be reconciled, the tradition proving itself capable of encompassing and providing a normative interpretation to nature.

Within this overall architecture, the drama of the poem lies in its middle couplets, which threaten to lead Du Fu away from the human tradition that seems dwarfed in the first lines by the mountain's unruly hugeness. The second couplet, for instance, juxtaposes the human and the natural by means of a linguistic ambiguity in the first two characters of the fourth line, which can be read to indicate either the dark north and sunlit southern slopes of Mt. Tai, on the one hand, or, on the other, *yin* and *yang*, the two fundamental modalities of universal *qi*. On one construal, that is, the line represents a simple visual depiction of the mountain past noon-time, with one side in shadow; on the other, it represents a learned vision of the cosmos, drawing on the schematisms of traditional texts like the *Zhuangzi* 莊子, the *Yijing* 易經, and the poetry associated with "Obscure Learning" (Xuanxue 玄學)—all of which are recalled in the language of this intensely literate couplet.[83] These texts, however, were themselves positioned ambiguously within the civilized tradition. According to Tang Classicists, their metaphysical speculations threatened to lead readers into mysteries that the ancient sages had placed "beyond the square" (*fang wai* 方外) of their civilizing teachings, fearing that people might get lost in them.[84] It is no coincidence, therefore, that devotees of these mysteries often extricated themselves from the centers of the human world, pursuing contemplation in monasteries, in temples, and in reclusion on China's sacred mountains—one of the most important of which, for Daoism, was Mt. Tai itself.

Within this context, the third couplet's famously convoluted syntax can be read as suggesting Du Fu's own attraction, gazing at this famous site of Daoist pilgrimage, to such a flight into the vast mysteries of the cosmos. Here again we find an early taste of Du Fu's interest in linguistic ambiguities, as these lines' grammatical superpositions make it impossible to distinguish the poet from the mountain and the mountain from the poet. This suspension of linguistic possibilities may suggest a breakdown in the illusory distinctions between self and other against which Tang Daoists (and some of their "Obscure Learning" predecessors, not to mention contemporary Buddhists) set their teaching.[85] Or, as the great seventeenth-century critic Wang Sishi suggests, the mountain may be drawing Du Fu in, the marked difficulty of determining the poet's place in these lines implying that "his spirit is wandering" up its slopes.[86] Either way, within the tradition of poetry on Taishan traced by Paul W. Kroll, the couplet could easily have suggested to a late medieval reader an itinerary away from the core tradition of what might be called "secular" literature towards an alternative better suited to making sense of Mt. Tai's mysteries. Such an itinerary might end, for example, with Du Fu following Xie Daoyun's 謝道韞 (fl. late fourth c.) resolve in her own poem on Taishan to "dwell under its eaves [as a recluse], exhausting her heaven-given years" or Li Bai's 李白 (701–62) intention at the end of his first poem on the mountain to "cast off the secular world, oh how far away!"[87]

Yet Du Fu will not go, not yet: if he feels a call to mysteries beyond state and society, he resists it here, returning home to the human world as the sun sets on Mt. Tai. This choice is explained by the poem's final invocation of Confucius's cosmic vision from the peak. What is suggested here, I think, is nothing more than good Tang Classicist doctrine: that Confucius, the civilizing sage par excellence, was not himself without the insight sought by disciples of "Obscure Learning," Daoism, or Buddhism, all of which were thought to pry into the mysteries the sages kept secret. Even though he refused to discuss these mysteries explicitly, Confucius "embodied" (*ti* 體) them, and his civilizing teachings were designed to keep society in line with them.[88] Pledging himself, it would seem, to this Tang orthodoxy, Du Fu in the final lines reverses the resolve of Xie Daoyun and Li Bai. He will, instead, follow Confucius in his ultimate refusal to abandon human society and the cultural traditions that underwrote its flourishing, for in those cultural traditions was already all the wisdom he might gain by leaving it behind. In a precise reversal of the first couplet's confusion, he realizes here at the end of the poem that he does not need to climb the mountain after all, since he already knows from his reading what he would see from the top.

Like "Climbing the Wall Tower at Yanzhou," then, this poem is once again a self-dedication, and, like most of the poems presented in this chapter, its central drama concerns the relationship of Du Fu to the timeless tradition and of the tradition to the possibility of visions deeper, more lasting, and more significant than the mere details of individual experience can be. This account of poetry is, I have proposed, very different from the recordizing paradigm. In chapters to come, I will be suggesting that, later in his career, Du Fu does begin to worry about the relationship between poetry and particular experience, justifying thereby the recordizing project of reconstructing in great detail the historical contexts of his work. Reading his early verse through the lens provided by this project, however, has the ironic effect of concealing one of the most interesting historical narratives that can be traced in his collection: that he would only gradually come to question the late medieval models that organized his writing when he was young.

TWO

Omen and Chaos

Poems of Frustration and Foreboding (through 755)

When recordizing critics aver, as did Chen Yixin and Zhou Zizhi in the previous chapter, that a good writer will "merely write what he sees," they are not just offering a recommendation for successful poetic craft. Within the tradition of Du Fu commentary, this idea has an important moral aspect as well. Since the eleventh century, Du Fu has been seen as the Poet Historian of his era, recording what he witnessed in the years leading up to, in the course of, and in the aftermath of the An Lushan Rebellion and thereby tracing in his poetry the Tang's path to and through catastrophe. It is of crucial importance, therefore, that he should have written "what he saw": what really happened throughout those years. It is important, moreover, that he should have trained his poetic eye not just on any aspect of what was happening at the time, but on what mattered. For this, he needed to be not only a witness but a perspicacious witness, capable of appreciating the moral significance of his experience. He needed to be, to cite the other of his traditional appellations, a Poet Sage.

That he was such a perspicacious observer of contemporary events is demonstrated, for his recordizing critics, nowhere more clearly than in the verse he wrote late in the Tianbao period, in the years just preceding An Lushan's turn on the Tang capitals in 755. According to traditional Chinese historiography, these years witnessed a precipitous decline in the good government that had characterized the period of Du Fu's youth, a decline that is largely attributable to villainous presences at court, particularly the corrupt and autocratic prime minister Li Linfu 李林甫; his successor Yang Guozhong 楊國忠; and Yang's cousin Yang Yuhuan 楊玉環 (more commonly known as Yang Guifei 楊貴妃), the emperor's enthralling paramour.

According to many of his admirers, Du Fu recognized early on the misgovernance these figures had begun to breed throughout the empire, "appreciating," in the words of Chen Yixin, "the antecedents of what was to come before it happened and thus having foreknowledge that a great disaster was about to occur."[1] Recordizing readers like Chen, therefore, devote their ingenuity to unearthing the criticism that they take Du Fu to have encoded in his poetry, often in forms that are less than fully explicit.

Parts of this vision have deep roots in the Chinese tradition, going all the way back to the mythology of the *Poetry*. Other aspects, however, invert common late medieval ideas. Whereas recordizing readers see Du Fu's poetry as deriving from his accurate observation of the patent facts of his experience, for instance, late medieval intellectuals more frequently spoke of excellent verse as deriving from esoteric sources beyond the bounds of normal understanding. When late medieval poetry prefigured the fate of a dynasty, therefore, it often did so as an omen—an omen that could sometimes be obscure even to the poet himself.[2] It is this model that Du Fu's Tianbao era poetry frequently enacts, and it is in such omens that we can recognize Du Fu beginning to question the tropologies of the tradition to which he had dedicated himself in his earliest work.

A Sober "Confucian"?

Part of what is at stake in the interpretation of Du Fu's pre-Rebellion poetry is his stature as the tradition's preeminent "Confucian" poet. As Eva Shan Chou has remarked, critics from the Song dynasty onwards have split the triumvirate of great High Tang poets, Du Fu, Li Bai, and Wang Wei, among China's Three Teachings: Confucianism, Daoism, and Buddhism.[3] In truth, however, and as many scholars have shown, each of these poets engaged substantially with the other traditions as well, a religious and ideological promiscuity that was quite normal in the medieval period.[4] Through the tenth century, moreover, Du Fu tended to be depicted not as the sort of sober Confucian he has since become, but rather as a wild and unrestrained poet, after the pattern of such so-called Neo-Daoists as Xi Kang 嵇康 (223–62) or Ruan Ji.[5] For Du Fu to become the quintessential poetic representative of Confucianism, therefore, whatever had previously supported this image had to be reinterpreted as feigned, disguising his clear-headed and thoroughly Confucian political judgments beneath a veneer of unrestraint.

This common hermeneutic procedure is evident in one of the most famous interpretive coups in the history of Du Fu criticism. The poem in question is a highly formal composition whose place at the head of the regulated verse section in the oldest surviving editions of Du Fu's collection may have signaled early readers' sense of its dignity and seriousness. The verse describes Du Fu's visit to a temple dedicated to the worship of both the Daoist deity Laozi and the imperial family, which claimed him as its ancestor on the basis of a shared surname, Li 李 (Plum).[6]

冬日洛城北謁玄元皇帝廟　*On a Winter Day Paying*
My Respects at the Temple of the Mysterious
Primal Emperor, Laozi, North of Luoyang[a]

	配極玄都閟	For the Ancestral Sacrifice, the Mysterious City is shut tight;
	憑高禁禦長	resting on heights, a forbidding stockade, long.
	守柢嚴具禮	The temple's keepers are strict in maintaining ritual;
4	掌節鎮非常	in charge of the tallies, they ward off irregularities.
	碧瓦初寒外	Sapphire tiles beyond the year's first chill;
	金莖一氣旁	a golden dew-collector beside the primal *qi*.
	山河扶繡戶	Mountains and river support the figured doorframe,
8	日月近雕梁	sun and moon approach the engraved beams.
	仙李盤根大	The immortal Plum's coiling roots are great,
	猗蘭弈葉光	and the huge leaves of the Splendid Orchid glorious.[b]
	世家遺舊史	Laozi's descendants were not recorded in the histories,
12	道德付今王	but his Way and its Power are entrusted to our current king.[c]

a. Early, perhaps authorial, note: "The temple has paintings of the Five Sage Rulers [the previous emperors of the Tang] by Wu Daozi" 廟有吳道子畫五聖圖.

b. The Plum (*li*) signifies the Li family. "Splendid Orchid" was the name of a Han dynasty palace, supposedly where Han Emperor Wu was born. It may also refer to a story of Confucius finding an orchid growing in a remote valley, which he took as an image for worthy men (like Laozi) going into reclusion in periods of disorder.

c. Laozi was the supposed author of the *Classic of the Way and Its Power* (*Daodejing* 道德經).

	畫手看前輩	As for painters, when I look at recent generations,
	吳生遠擅場	it is Master Wu who far dominates the field.[d]
	森羅移地軸	His densely arrayed figures move the Earth's axis;
16	妙絕動宮牆	utter marvels stir on the temple's walls.
	五聖聯龍袞	Our Five Sage Rulers in a line of Dragon Robes;
	千官列鴈行	the thousand officials in rows like wild geese.[e]
	冕旒俱秀發	Imperial crowns stand forth together,
20	旌旆盡飛揚	while banners and pennons all fly.
	翠柏深留景	Azure cypresses deep in the lingering light;
	紅梨迥得霜	a red pear, remote, catches the frost.
	風箏吹玉柱	The jade bridges of Aeolian harps hum;
24	露井凍銀牀	the silver railing of an open well frosts.
	身退卑周室	Laozi withdrew when the Zhou House was humbled,
	經傳拱漢皇	yet his *Classic*, transmitted, made the Han emperor bow.
	谷神如不死	If "nurturing the spirit, one can avoid death,"
28	養拙更何鄉	then where now is he cultivating clumsiness?[f]

From the eleventh century to the seventeenth, this poem was something of an embarrassment to many of Du Fu's admirers, to whom the identification of Laozi as the ancestor of the Tang imperial house seemed not only so implausible as to be laughably bad political propaganda but, more important, to be symptomatic of the Tang's destructive patronage of Daoism in general.[7] In the first decades of the Qing dynasty, however, Qian Qianyi offered a new reading of the poem, by which Du Fu was not celebrating the Tang's worship of Laozi but rather criticizing it.

> In the Tianbao period, people reported that Laozi manifested his appearance and sent down a number of Daoist talismans, and Emperor Xuanzong believed them completely. This poem directly records these facts in order to

d. Wu Daozi 吳道子, a famous painter of the early eighth century.

e. The Five Sage Rulers were the five Tang emperors before Xuanzong: Gaozu, Taizong, Gaozong, Zhongzong, and Ruizong.

f. The penultimate line quotes Laozi's *Daodejing*. Laozi's "clumsiness" is ironic: as the *Daodejing* says, "great skillfulness appears to be clumsiness" to the uninitiated. Laozi had legendarily ridden an ox out of the passes to the West; his death is not recorded.

criticize the government. The first four lines say that the Daoist temple is being used as an ancestral temple: this is not canonical. The second four lines criticize the way that the splendor of the temple exceeds norms: this is not ritually correct. When Du Fu writes, "Laozi's descendants were not recorded in the histories," he is saying that, although Xuanzong had elevated the biography of Laozi to the head of the biographical section of the *Historical Records*, nonetheless, the historian had not written an account of Laozi's descendants: these are probably words of subtle criticism. Saying that "his Way and its Power are entrusted to our current king" is referring to the fact that Emperor Xuanzong himself annotated Laozi's *Classic of the Way and Its Power* and established throughout the empire Schools for Revering the Obscure, but did not necessarily know the true meaning of the Dao or its Power: these are also words of subtle criticism. The next eight lines record Wu Daozi's painting, implying that only in an age that has fallen away from the ideal can a painter get so close to the emperor. The painted crowns and flags that dazzle the eyes: is this not merely a child's game? . . . Though this poem's ultimate intent is to criticize, it is laid out with apparent beauty, and the meaning of the words is unmanifest. This is what is referred to [in the *Classic of Poetry*] as "the speaker commits no crime, but there is enough for the listener to be warned."

唐自高祖追崇老子爲祖，天寶中，見像降符，不一而足，人主崇信之極矣。此詩直記其事以諷諫也。配極四句，言玄元廟用宗廟之禮爲不經也。碧瓦四句，譏其宮殿壯麗逾制爲非禮也。世家遺舊史，謂開元中奉敕升老子、莊子爲列傳之首，序伯夷上。然太史公不列於世家，終不能改易舊史，蓋微詞也。道德付今王，謂玄宗親注道德經及置崇玄學，然未必知道德之意，亦微詞也。畫手以下八句，記吳生畫圖也，世代之寥廓如彼，畫圖之親切若此。晃旒旌斾，炫耀耳目，不亦近於兒戲乎？…此詩雖極意諷諫，而鋪張盛麗，語意渾然，所謂言之無罪，聞之足戒者也。[8]

According to Qian, the poem may seem like praise if read only for its stylistic flourishes—indeed, that was Du Fu's intention, to preserve plausible deniability in case the emperor or his court took offense, a principle derived from the properly "Confucian" *Classic of Poetry*. For an adept critic like Qian, however, the poem's message lies not in its surface beauty, but rather in the "facts it records." If we read the poem for these facts, Qian suggests, we can recognize the poem as a damning account of Xuanzong's infatuation with a heterodox and obscurantist superstition.

It is crucial to Qian's reading that the facts themselves are damning, their moral valence apparently self-evident as soon as they are articulated. A late medieval reader less certain about the significance of these "facts," however, might see the poem rather differently—perhaps taking it, as the ninth-century historian of Tang painting Zhu Jingxuan 朱景玄 did, as a good faith depiction of the temple's splendor.[9] It is true that, in almost every line, Du Fu's attention is on the artifice of the temple—its architecture, its rituals, and its murals—and on the way that artifice manifests the numinous virtue of Laozi and of the previous emperors of the Tang.[10] Though Qian's commentary obscures this focus by truncating the description of Wu Daozi's painting to a mere four couplets, it probably makes better sense to see the description of Wu's work as continuing all the way to the end of the poem, where Du Fu would be observing an image of Laozi disappearing through the mountain passes of the far west.[11] On this reading, the pointed equivocation of whether the Aeolian harps, the cypresses, and the frozen well-work are in the painting or physically in the winter scene of the temple complex would stand as praise of Wu's skill in making the realm the ancestors inhabit seem truly present.[12] And in reproducing for the reader Du Fu's uncertain experience of that obscure presence, the poem would become as it were a new painting, a new temple of verse.

If, however, the poem suggests in this way that it is art's function to manifest the obscure, it may also open itself to obscure impulses the poet cannot fully control. As Qian suggests, Du Fu does get repeatedly sidetracked here into topics that are less than entirely propitious for a laud to the house of Li. These preoccupations surface first in the fifth couplet of the poem, where the phrase "Splendid Orchid" seems to initiate a line of thought that disturbs the poet's narrative control. On the one hand, the reference seems to be to the reigning royal house and its resplendent palaces. On the other, however, it recalls a famous story about Confucius, who spent much of his life traveling from place to place vainly attempting to convince the benighted kings of his age to practice the *dao*. On one of these journeys, he came across a secluded orchid hidden in a valley and sighed that its beauty had been neglected by a blind age. "Splendid Orchids" thus came to symbolize reclusion, which could have pointed political valences when men of talent feigned "clumsiness" in order to withdraw from government service in misgoverned ages.[13] During his time on earth, Laozi himself was such a "hidden man," concealing his transcendent virtue first within a lowly archival post and then finally leaving Chinese society more decisively, out through the mountain passes to the west. This withdrawal would result in the lacuna Du Fu mentions in the ancient histories, Laozi's lowly social status preventing him from receiving a "hereditary house" biography that might have recorded the names of his descendants. And once Du Fu voices this potentially disturbing thought—which might, as Qian Qianyi suggests, cast doubt on the Li family's claim to derive from Laozi's stock—he immediately changes the subject to the magnificent painting that reaffirms Laozi's continued presence in the Tang empire.

Turning to the painting, however, does not ultimately succeed in quieting these disturbing associations. Instead, when Du Fu comes to the painting's evocation of the luxury of the Tang court, he finds his attention inexorably pulled back once again to Laozi's austere reclusion from society, symbolized (by longstanding convention) by the cypress tree in winter.[14] Here, Du Fu's biographical circumstances may be relevant. At the time of writing, most likely around the end of 749, he had spent the previous fifteen years taking the imperial exams and seeking patrons to recommend him for a government office, all without success. As in other poetry written around this same time, this continual frustration was beginning to suggest that he should give up his quest to serve the government—or at least threaten to do so in the hope of drawing succor from powerful friends. When in the last two couplets of this poem Du Fu fixates again on the question of Laozi's withdrawal from the state, then, we can sense once again the magnetic pull of these associations on his mind.

Qian Qianyi would seem to be right, therefore, in sensing that something has gone wrong in the poem's ostensible program of praising the dynasty. But if the poem may thus hint at dissatisfaction with the government, it does so in a way different from that Qian imagines. Rather than "recording facts," the poem instead manifests—unwittingly, Du Fu would have us believe—private feelings about his own personal frustrations. These personal frustrations still may speak of the government's failures, since it has failed to recognize a poet as virtuosic and a scholar as learned as Du Fu shows himself here. But such a failure is small in scale, incipient merely, and the poem is thus an obscure omen, rather than a perspicacious observation of the large-scale governmental failures that would engender the troubles to come.

Poetry's Mantic Potential

Throughout premodern Chinese history, omens commonly manifested themselves in verse.[15] The earliest instances, found in some of the oldest histories in the tradition, appear in the rhymes of children and in folk songs. In the Six Dynasties, however, we find poetic omens attributed to Buddhist monks and Daoist priests, and in the late medieval period they begin to be found in the verse of literati as well. This expansion is paralleled by changes in the ways these omens were conceptualized in contemporary texts. In the Han, poetic omens were conceptually distinct from elite literary writing, considered an "anomaly" (*yao* 妖) similar to shamanic possession by the spirits.[16] As strict distinctions between religious adepts and literati began to break down over the medieval period, however—and as elite Classicism was itself reinterpreted in such a way as to bring it into closer proximity with Buddhist and Daoist thought—it seems to have become more plausible that elite poets should be likewise able to serve as mediums, channeling the obscure forces of the cosmos into verse that could sometimes predict the fortunes of the state.

By the Tang, Classicism had come to embrace some of the orientations characteristic of other medieval Chinese intellectual traditions, such as "Obscure Learning," Buddhism, and Daoism. The early Tang scholars largely responsible for establishing the state orthodoxy divided the inherited teachings of their age between two categories, introduced summarily near the end of the previous chapter: those concerned with what was "within the square" (*fang nei* 方內) and those that speculated into what was "beyond the square" (*fang wai*). For the most part, the Classics were about what was "within the square," the daily business of ethics, ritual, and governance that was the particular province of the Ru 儒 (Confucian scholars). The ancient sages responsible for the teachings, however, had based their prescriptions for what was "within the square" on insights that were ultimately "beyond it."[17] These insights were constitutively obscure, and their pursuit was liable to lead astray all but the most gifted of interpreters. The sages' purpose in creating the Classics, therefore, was to provide lessons that would be intelligible and useful for the vast majority of us who lack the capacity to orient ourselves in the mysteries of the cosmos.

The exoteric teachings of the sages and their worthy inheritors were known, broadly, as *wen* 文, a term whose multiple valences did a great deal of work holding together late medieval thought. Meaning at its most basic something like "manifest pattern," *wen* can often be translated more grandly as "culture" or even as a shorthand for This Culture of Ours (*siwen*), the canonical tradition. *Wen* also had cosmological meanings, such as the *wen* of heaven (the celestial lights) or the *wen* of earth (rivers and mountains), both of which were understood, like the teachings of the sages, as providing manifest guides to the obscure workings of the cosmos.[18] It was also the general term, in the late medieval period, for literature. And by virtue of its place in this constellation of ideas, literature was often thought of as rendering manifest and intelligible what might otherwise be subtle and obscure.[19]

One of the clearest statements of literature's relationship to the obscure is found in Liu Xie's great treatise on *wen*, the *Wenxin diaolong* 文心雕龍. In the first chapter, "Tracing [Literature's] Source to the *Dao*" 原道, Liu provides an exalted lineage for contemporary literature, arguing that at its origin human *wen* was no different from the *wen* of the heavens or the *wen* of earth: it too was "the manifestation of the *dao*" (*dao zhi wen* 道之文). According to Liu, in other words, literature at its most normative is simply the *dao*'s self-revelation to the human mind, "sent down by the *dao* itself" through the medium of the sages, who, in turn, "used *wen* to illuminate the *dao*."[20] Authors who inherit their project, therefore, are tasked with "depicting the radiance of heaven and earth so as to enlighten the eyes of the people" and "bringing to light spiritual essences that lie concealed" (*youzan shenming* 幽贊神明) to most of us.[21]

This last phrase Liu Xie borrows from the *Yijing* 易經 (*The Classic of Change*), whose trigrams and hexagrams, not coincidentally, were understood in the late medieval period to be the ancestors of all writing and which was therefore frequently cited as defining the mission of *wen*.[22] According to the official Tang dynasty subcommentary on that Classic, the primal sage Fu Xi's 伏羲 composition of this text had played a quasi-cosmogonic role in creating the universe as it appeared to Chinese culture. Before they were represented by the trigrams and hexagrams of the *Change*, that is, the things of the world remained for most people in a state of undifferentiation: "a mysterious chaos of heaven and earth and the secret transformations of ghosts and spirits," where "people had as yet no

distinctions among them, and the myriad things were not yet differenti-
ated, not yet having their uses as clothing, food, implements, and tools."
Fu Xi, however, "had what it took to observe what was above and investi-
gate what was below, creating images for heaven and earth and thus nur-
turing the myriad things."[23] By inventing conceptual categories to organize
the infinite diversity of the world, in other words, he allowed nonsages to
perceive and to act in accordance with the latent, previously obscure order
in the cosmos.

Following this model, Tang writers often speak of literature and of
writing in general as continuing the cosmogony begun by Fu Xu's creation of
the *Yijing*. As the calligraphy theorist Zhang Huaiguan puts it, for example, in a discussion that traces the origin of characters back to the *Yijing*,

> The way of *wen* is brilliant. The sun and moon and the stars are the *wen* of
> heaven; the five sacred peaks and the four rivers are the *wen* of the earth, and
> palaces and court arrays are the *wen* of man. Characters and writing are the
> same as these: they are put to use in *wen*, and they are needed for *wen* to be
> complete. They apply names and words to nonbeing and govern and control
> the myriad beings.[24] . . . They mold and circumscribe the cosmos, separating
> and differentiating *yin* and *yang*. Through them, it becomes possible to live
> on high plains and down low by rivers; through them, the soil becomes rich
> enough to grow crops; and thus, through them, the wilds of the eight direc-
> tions are made accountable. They provide order to human affairs and make
> manifest the normative forms. Through them are lords and fathers revered,
> and through them are love and respect brought to the fulfillment of ritual.
> Old and young are differentiated, and those above and below find order.
> Thus, the great *dao* is effected by them.

文也者，其道煥焉。日月星辰，天之文也；五嶽四瀆，地之文
也；城闕朝儀，人之文也。字之與書，理亦歸一。因文爲用，相須
而成。名言諸無，宰制群有。…範圍宇宙，分別陰陽，川原高下之
可居，土壤沃瘠之可植。是以八荒籍焉，綱紀人倫，顯明正體，君
父尊嚴，而愛敬盡禮，長幼班別，而上下有序。是以大道行焉。[25]

For Zhang, writing is what makes civilization possible and the cosmos
inhabitable, for it allows us to identify general categories (such as "fine soil
for growing crops"), to share knowledge, and ultimately to organize our
social relationships into harmonious and efficient patterns. Without it, the
world would be a chaos.

Contemporary poetry was not, of course, generally tasked with category creation or information sharing. It was, however, often discussed as continuing the revelation of the universe's mysteries. Lu Cangyong 盧藏用 (ca. 660–ca. 714), for example, praises Chen Zi'ang's 陳子昂 (661–702) "Ganyu" 感遇 poems for "manifesting the subtle and explaining the hidden, almost revealing the incipiency of transformation in order to reach to the meeting place of heaven and humanity."[26] Jiaoran writes, similarly, that, "although [poetry] is not the work of the [ancient] sages, its subtlety and wondrousness is equal to the sages' achievements. The deep secrets of heaven and earth, sun and moon, and mysterious transformation, and the subtle darkness of the ghosts and spirits—if refined thought seeks in these, then the myriad images can no longer hide their wonders."[27] Writers also frequently conjoined this *Yijing* register with concepts drawn from other traditions "beyond the square," such as Buddhism and Daoism, and it was common to speak of the process of composition as an "investigation of the dark" (*mingsou* 冥搜) similar to that adepts in those traditions engaged in.[28] Whatever the vocabulary, however, the idea that good poetry should "enter the obscure" (*ru xuan* 入玄) was pervasive in the seventh through ninth centuries.[29]

"Entering the obscure" was not, moreover, merely an intellectual exercise; instead, writers were thought to be inspired by these obscurities, drawing on and channeling in their writing forces beyond common understanding. The best literature, it was often said, manifested "the aid of the spirits," was obtained through "meeting with the spirits," was created by "roaming with spirits and naturally matching tallies with them in the dark," or derived from "spirit-thought," a sort of deeper, more miraculous form of cognition to which writers sometimes had access.[30] This was a language shared by all the arts in the Tang, drawing largely from Lu Ji's 陸機 (261–303) famous "Rhapsody on *Wen*," which described literary writing as "a trial of nonbeing to demand being, a knock upon silence, seeking sound."[31] Closer to Du Fu's own time, Lü Wen 呂溫 (772–811) used many of the same figures in describing music, writing that it "comes forth from nonbeing,"[32] and Zhang Huaiguan's discussion of calligraphy, similarly, argues that true creativity occurs only when one "seeks from the void in order to establish new form, having leveled all differences and brought everything back to unity." At that point, one can access vast, unaccountable potentialities:

When one's thoughts communicate with the numinous and one's brush moves mysteriously, one's spirit matches with transformation and the transformations come forth without set pattern. . . . Obscure thought then enters into the smallest spaces, and one's uninhibited *qi* spreads through the entire cosmos. Ghosts and gods come and go as one chases the tenuous and grasps the subtle. It is a process that cannot be captured in the fish trap of words or images.

及乎意與靈通，筆與冥運，神將化合，變出無方。⋯幽思入於毫間，逸氣彌於宇内。鬼出神入，追虛捕微。則非言象筌蹄所能存亡也。[33]

Many of these same ideas are invoked by Du Fu in his early poetry. In one poem, for instance, he praises a fellow poet as "splitting primal chaos . . . and driving on the thunder," and, in another, he flatters a painter by suggesting that his materials are the universe's "primal vapor," causing the gods to complain and heaven to weep out of jealousy at his usurpation of their mysterious powers.[34]

This general vision of literature as deriving from the obscure often justified reading poetry as something like an omen. Perhaps the most common Classical citation in Tang dynasty literary discourse, for instance, was the *Yijing*'s injunction that rulers should "observe the *wen* of heaven in order to understand its transformations and observe the *wen* of man in order to complete their governance."[35] By paralleling literature (the central referent of the term "*wen* of man" in these citations) with the motions of the heavenly lights, the writers who cite this passage are suggesting that it gives insight into obscure strata of reality—serving, in the words of an early Tang history, as "the weather vane of the emotions and the pitch pipe of the spirits,"[36] by means of which the mysterious cycles of the cosmos and subtle shifts in popular mores could manifest themselves to the court. Further support for this idea would also have been found in the mythology of the *Poetry*, which was understood to have been originally collected from among the populace as a quasi-divinatory practice.[37] As the Tang subcommentary explains,

The arising of sadness and happiness is a mysterious part of what is so-of-itself; the beginnings of joy and anger are not within human control. Therefore, sparrows express their feelings in their chirping, and phoenixes dance and sing. Thus, the antecedents of poetry's logic are at one with the creation of the universe, and the use of poetry's traces changes according to its cycles.

若夫哀樂之起，冥於自然；喜怒之端，非由人事。故燕雀表啁噍之感，鸞鳳有歌舞之容。然則詩理之先，同夫開闢；詩跡所用，隨運而移。[38]

This passage explains why the commoners to whom most poems in the *Shijing* were attributed could be trusted to provide accurate intelligence about the cycles of the universe and the rise and fall of dynasties. The reason is that, insofar as their very emotions derived from mysterious processes "beyond the square," they were in their poetry effectively no different from the dancing phoenixes that were legendarily supposed to appear when the state was governed by a sage. By expressing their individual happiness or grievance, they were channeling larger and more obscure forces, revealing broad moral tendencies in the state even before they had manifested themselves in grosser signs.

Poets not infrequently appealed to something like this ideology in justifying the moral and political significance of their work. In practice, the poetry they produced along these lines probably played little role in actual governance. Yet, on the ideological level at least, the Tang governing elite seems to have set significant stock by the idea that poetry could possess a mantic significance. Poetic omens were routinely submitted to the court, including instances by close friends of Du Fu's such as the poet and official Gao Shi 高適.[39] And they were invoked to justify far-reaching governmental policies, such as Emperor Gaozu's decision, upon his successful rebellion against the Sui, to ascend the throne and found the Tang.[40]

Most important for my argument here, omens were also invoked in elite discussions of the poetic art, and traditional techniques of omen interpretation—which often involved the decoding of complicated linguistic riddles—seem sometimes to have influenced Tang poetry commentary. The clearest instance of this tendency is the *Wuchen* commentary. In his introduction to this text, Lü Yanzuo explicitly claims to read the poetry it contains as omens.

Since the time of the *Poetry*, there has been nothing greater than the *Wenxuan*. It preserves words impassioned and intense, and when we assessed the affairs [that the authors were writing about, we could tell that] they lodged their minds in the hidden and subtle, darkening the omens it produced [through them].

風雅其來，不之能尚。則有遺詞激切，揆度其事，宅心隱微，晦滅其兆。[41]

As I have suggested elsewhere, the often strikingly speculative interpretations of the *Wuchen* probably should be read as offering the sorts of interpretive coups characteristic of those mantically gifted individuals in traditional historiography who proved themselves capable of recognizing the rebuslike omens of folk songs and children's ditties.[42] Similar hermeneutical procedures are characteristic of other Tang critical works as well, particularly from the late eighth through the tenth centuries. *The Secret Meanings of the "Classic of Poetry"* (*Ernan mizhi* 二南密旨), for instance, gives a long list of poetic images and topics that can serve as "omens" (*zhao* 兆) of state situations and offers readings of individual poems in precisely this light.[43] In the *Essential Standards of the "Airs" and "Sao"* (*Fengsao yaoshi* 風騷要式), we even find the suggestion that poets may create such omens unwittingly, "criticizing the state spontaneously, without realizing it."[44]

Passions from Beyond the Square

This last quote highlights the dramatic difference between what I have been suggesting was a common late medieval vision of poetry and its relation to the state, on the one hand, and, on the other, that advocated by Qian Qianyi in his reading of "On a Winter Day Paying My Respects." For Qian, Du Fu is not channeling an omen, and he is certainly not doing so unwittingly; instead, he is reading one, observing the signs of the times and interpreting their implications. If any obscurity remains in his poetry, therefore, it is the result merely of his need to equivocate in order to preserve plausible deniability, and it is the critic's job to dissipate it, much as Qian boasted that his interpretation of this poem had "split primal chaos, hand-washing the sun and moon."[45] For a recordizing critic like Qian, the goal of reading is to get back to the clear "facts": the events, experiences, and political situations the poet saw and wrote to record. And those facts will be valuable only if the poet had the good judgment to recognize what mattered in his age and why.

When the recordizing paradigm comes to dominate the critical tradition, therefore, the moral stances open to poetry shift dramatically. What becomes valuable to critics is the perspicacity, clear-headedness, and good judgment Du Fu has, since the eleventh century, been thought to exemplify. It is no longer possible that poetry might be morally and politically important precisely in those places where things get murky, in passions that seem to go beyond their objective correlatives, and in the manifestation of subtle shifts in the cosmic or social fabric the poet himself might not fully understand. It is not possible, that is, to take Du Fu seriously when he says, in another poem from around this same time, that, "in vast confusion, my inspiration has help from the spirits."[46] But ideas along these lines were current in Du Fu's youth.

It may be significant, therefore, that he wrote many of the poems that can be most easily identified as omens of the coming chaos at sites and on topics that had associations with what lay "beyond the square," such as the Daoist temple of "On a Winter Day."[47] Another clear example of this tendency is the following poem, written on the occasion of Du Fu's visit to a Buddhist monastery in Chang'an in the company of a number of other poets.[48]

同諸公登慈恩寺塔   *A Companion Piece for "Climbing the Pagoda of Ci'en Monastery," by Various Gentlemen*[a]

高標跨蒼天	Its high crest transcends the cerulean skies,
烈風無時休	where fierce winds never rest.
自非曠士懷	Not being myself a broad-minded man,
4 登茲翻百憂	to climb here occasions a hundred fears.
方知象教力	Yet now I recognize the Teaching of Images' force,[b]
足可追冥搜	enough to pursue an investigation of the dark.
仰穿龍蛇窟	So upward we bore through the dragon's lair,
8 始出枝撐幽	emerging from the dimness of beams and struts.
七星在北戶	The Dipper is right at the northern window,

a. Early, likely authorial, note: "At the time Gao Shi and Xue Ju had already composed something" 時高適、薛據先有作.

b. The "Teaching of Images" is Buddhism.

	河漢聲西流	the River of Stars roars past heading west.
	義和鞭白日	Xihe whips along the white sun,
12	少昊行清秋	as Shaohao drives on the cool of autumn.[c]
	秦山忽破碎	Suddenly, the mountains are broken to pieces;
	涇渭不可求	the Jing and Wei Rivers cannot be found.[d]
	俯視但一氣	Looking down, I see only primal *qi*:
16	焉能辨皇州	I cannot make out the royal domain.
	廻首叫虞舜	Turning my head, I cry to Shun,
	蒼梧雲正愁	but the clouds hang gloomy over Cangwu.[e]
	惜哉瑤池飲	Alas for the banquet at Jasper Pool!
20	日晏崑崙丘	the sun grows late over the Kunlun Hills.[f]
	黄鵠去不息	The brown swan now goes off without rest;
	哀鳴何所投	crying mournfully, where will it lodge?
	君看隨陽雁	But see you the geese that follow the sun:
24	各有稻粱謀	they each have made plans for their rice.[g]

Many commentators have seen in the second half of this poem evidence of Du Fu's acumen in predicting the An Lushan Rebellion and diagnosing its causes. Pu Qilong 浦起龍 (1679–1762), for example, argues that even though the poem seems to have been written around three years before the Rebellion's outbreak,[49] "the sources of the coming disorder had already given their omens" and Du Fu had recognized them with "an acuteness that could distinguish the tip of a hair."[50] The lynchpin of Pu's reading is an allegorical interpretation of the tenth couplet's reference to the "banquet at Jasper Pool" that the Daoist Queen Mother of the West legendarily put on for the ancient King Mu of Zhou in the Kunlun mountains. Pu sees here a veiled reference to Emperor Xuanzong's infatuation with Yang

c. Xihe drives the chariot of the sun; Shaohao is the god of autumn.

d. The Jing and Wei are rivers of the capital region. Proverbially, the Jing was muddy and the Wei clear, and thus the two rivers could represent the distinction between good and bad people.

e. Shun was an ancient sage king who according to legend had died at Mt. Cangwu. The poet Qu Yuan had appealed his political frustrations to Shun's ghost in his great poem *Lisao* 離騷.

f. The banquet at Jasper pool was a fabled meeting between the ancient King Mu of Zhou 周穆王 (tenth c. BCE) and the goddess Queen Mother of the West in the Kunlun mountains.

g. The sun was a common figure for the emperor.

Guifei, who had briefly been a Daoist priestess and whose charms, according to the legend that was to grow up around the events of the time, distracted the emperor from the business of government. According to Pu, then, Du Fu has here pinpointed the cause of the disorder that would follow, but feigns acrophobia in the first lines of the poem out of concern that his companions will not understand the tone of wild desperation that overtakes it towards its end. Sighing in admiration of this device, Pu writes that "worries and troubles fill Du Fu's breast," but his "artisan mind" (*jiang-xin* 匠心) is nonetheless still in control.

The late medieval ideas discussed above, however, may suggest an alternate interpretation of the poem's increasingly wild tone. Like Luoyang's Daoist temple, this Buddhist monastery is a location, Du Fu notes, conducive to "investigation of the dark" and thus to the channeling of the confused and mysterious forces Tang intellectuals understood as productive of both poetry and omens. Reading the poem this way, Du Fu's ascent of the pagoda's towering height brings him into realms of vision beyond the superficial images of his everyday earthbound world, realms where the constellations are "right there" in the window, the rushing of the river of stars can be heard distinctly, the charioteer of the sun can be seen whipping its horses towards the horizon, and the coming of a dusk-time chill seems the sudden onset of autumn. Whatever is seen from the tower is more significant than the mere phenomenal world below, and, when finally an evening fog descends upon the landscape, Du Fu perceives it not as an innocuous natural phenomenon but rather as a terrifying reversion to the "undifferentiated, primal *qi*" from which the known, civilized world derived. Pu may be right, then, to see this fractured vision of the royal domain as prefiguring the disorder that would soon engulf the dynasty. But if the poem is an omen, its mode is the unhinged hyperbole of a poet carried away, not precise observation carefully dissembled.

Further support for this reading can be found in the poems to which this one was intended to serve as a "companion piece," particularly those of Du Fu's close friends Cen Shen 岑参 (ca. 715–70) and Gao Shi.[51] Not only do these poems' themes confirm the emphasis on the temple's connection with truths "beyond the square." More important, they suggest that Du Fu was following Cen Shen in his characteristic hyperbolic wildness[52] and taking up the theme to which Gao Shi turns at the end of his poem: his frustration at not yet having attained a significant government office. Such complaints were particularly apt to the occasion, since Ci'en Monastery was the place where the names of successful examination candidates were posted every year.[53] Du Fu had by this point repeatedly failed the official exams, and his lament in line 14 that the clouds have made it impossible to discern the clear Jing from the muddy Wei is a traditional image for the government's failure to recognize men of talent. This frustration is also expressed in the following couplet's entreaty to Shun, which echoes the archetype of all unappreciated poet-worthies, Qu Yuan 屈原, who in his great poem *Lisao* had sought reassurance from the long-deceased Shun as to the unjustness of his estrangement from his own king.[54] Like Du Fu in this poem, Qu Yuan had traveled up to heaven and looked down in dismay on the royal domain, and like Du Fu he too had compared himself to a great brown swan, going off alone into reclusion instead of fighting with other birds over scraps of food.[55] Rather than pronouncing a clear and perspicacious judgment on the empire, then, the final lines express, in a hyperbolical mode suited to "investigating the dark," Du Fu's own personal frustrations.

Frustration was an emotion that had key conceptual links to the range of concepts associated with the obscure in late medieval China. During this period, dynastic collapse was often called "primal chaos" (*caomei* 草昧), and an emperor who finally put an end to such chaos was a "sage," very much on the cosmogonic model of Fu Xi. After this act of founding, one of the emperor's central duties was to provide and maintain systems of ritual distinction, such as the imperial calendars, the official pitch pipes, standardized weights and measures, and the sumptuary codes that visibly marked differences of status on his subjects' persons.[56] Ideally, these ritual distinctions were supposed to be appropriate to the latent characteristics of their subjects, as Fu Xi's *Yijing* was "level with [the latent potentialities of] heaven and earth."[57] High officials in civil offices (*wen guan* 文官), for example, were supposed to be virtuous and brilliant, their station both corresponding to and confirming their ethical character and their talents. As a result, such high officials were frequently spoken of as "manifest" (*xian* 顯), whereas men of talent who had not yet ascended to office were "obscure" (*wei* 微)—a term that was also applied to the esoteric realities into which sages were supposed to have insight. Such men, it could be said, remained in something like a precosmogonic state, which could both suggest their propinquity and access to the realm "beyond the square" and also portend, if the state ultimately failed to recognize their virtues, the collapse of the manifest empire back into chaos.

All of these associations are latent in Du Fu's consideration, at the end of "A Companion Piece for 'Climbing the Pagoda of Ci'en Monastery,'" of giving up his search for imperial office to go, instead, into reclusion. They are even more explicit in the following poem.[58]

樂遊園歌   *Song of Leyou Park*[a]

	樂遊古園崒森爽	Ancient Leyou park towers up, dense and cool
	煙綿碧草萋萋長	with endless emerald plants growing in thick.
	公子華筵勢最高	The young lord's splendid feast finds its highest spot;[b]
4	秦川對酒平如掌	Facing our ale are Qin's rivers, flat as the palm of a hand.[c]
	長生木瓢示眞率	With a ladle of long-life wood, he displays his earnest directness,
	更調鞍馬狂歡賞	then teases us as the "horse saddler," wild with joy.[d]
	青春波浪芙蓉園	To the waves of green spring there in Lotus Park
8	白日雷霆夾城仗	comes thunder in the daylight, the entourage in the Walled Passage.[e]

a. Early, likely authorial, note: "On the thirtieth day of spring, at a banquet with Administrative Aide Yang of Helan, composed while drunk" 晦日賀蘭楊長史筵醉中作. The thirtieth day of spring was a Tang holiday.

b. The "young lord" is presumably Administrative Aide Yang, mentioned in the previous note.

c. This line echoes a famous poem by Shen Quanqi 沈佺期 (656–ca. 716), which describes the salacious pleasures of the capital.

d. The "horse saddler" seems to have been a role taken on in a drinking game: the "saddler" gave orders, and whoever disobeyed them had to drink a forfeit.

e. Lotus Park was part of a single large complex of parks in the capital along the Twisting River; the Walled Passage led from the Xingqing Palace to the Twisting River and

	閶闔晴開映蕩蕩	Clear skies, Heaven's Gates open, shining and vast,
	曲江翠幕排銀牓	by the Twisting River the azure tents are lined with silver placards.
	拂水低佪舞袖翻	Brushing the waters, turning and wheeling, dancing sleeves fly;
12	緣雲清切歌聲上	through the clouds, piercingly clear, notes of songs rise.
	卻憶年年人醉時	And I recall all the times, year upon year, I have been drunk:
	只今未醉已先悲	these days, before I get drunk, I'm already sad.
	數莖白髮那拋得	My several strands of white hair cannot be escaped;
16	百罰深杯亦不辭	a hundred forfeits of full cups, and still I don't refuse.
	聖朝亦知賤士醜	I know it's vile being lowly in this sagely reign,
	一物自荷皇天慈	when each creature receives the grace of our Heavenly Sovereign.[f]
	此身飲罷無歸處	Finished drinking, this body of mine has nowhere to go—
20	獨立蒼茫自詠詩	in a vast blur I stand alone, chanting this poem to myself.

As was the case in "On a Winter Day Paying My Respects" and "Climbing the Pagoda," the obscurity of this poem's logic and the seeming disconnect between its ostensible occasion (a joyous banquet at one of the capital's pleasure gardens) and the dark emotional tone with which it ends have encouraged influential critics to see in it an example of Du Fu's prescience.[59] Pu Qilong, for example, notes that, "at this time, the Yangs monopolized

---

was reserved for imperial outings. Leyou Park was part of the same complex but would have been some distance from the site of the imperial party, which Du Fu can see here because of Leyou Park's relative height.

f. This couplet may recall a comment of Confucius's, that, "when a state is run according to the Way, to be poor and lowly in it is a disgrace; but when it is without the Way, to be rich and noble is."

the emperor's affections and the palace was awash in lascivious pleasures, but chariots filled the passes and the tents of invading armies were scattered like clouds."[60] Chen Yixin takes the point a step further, imagining vividly the imperial extravagance Du Fu might have witnessed on the occasion. Du Fu does not much describe this extravagance, Chen explains, because the poet's character was such that "he would not wantonly publicize in his poetry that the emperor was out eating, drinking, and making merry with his favorites . . . so he equivocated with his words and made the point obscure."[61] Again, in these readings, the text of the poem is unclear, but beneath its obfuscations is a historical situation that Du Fu observed with laudable clarity.

Drunkenness, however, is both the theme and the origin of this poem—or at least so Du Fu suggests. The poem's apparently sideways logic, therefore, does not have to be explained by equivocation or avoidance of his true concerns; instead, its sudden leaps between apparently unrelated topics can be explained as a symptom of the state into which Du Fu describes himself descending, the first buzz of the party allowing him a happy appreciation of the scenery, and increasing inebriation turning a chance glimpse of the imperial outing into a spiral of depression. Given this downward trajectory, moreover, it seems at least possible that his depression results less from seeing the emperor and his favorites behaving immodestly—if they were—than from being reminded by this glimpse of the imperial party that he remains distant from the court, that this year like every year he is off drinking uselessly and that his youth—and with it his chance for ascending to high office—is passing. He "has nowhere to go" after the party breaks up because, unlike the other banqueters in his group, he has no government office, no salary, and no remaining dignity; he seems, indeed, to be the object of their jokes, drinking their forfeits until they finally tire of his company, leaving him at the end of the poem alone in the park, drunk, and sad.

Here again, recordizing criticism's vision of Du Fu as the clear-eyed Poet Sage belies his own self-depiction in the poetry of this period. As he dramatizes the production of this poem, he is driven by forces on the margins of his control, forces unleashed as the bright vision of the morning dissolves into the vast, drunken blur of the final couplet. The verse may thus be prescient of the state's coming collapse, as critics have so often suggested. But if it is, it presents itself not as a perspicacious record but rather as another omen born of frustration—and again from those realms "beyond the square" to which drunkenness was sometimes thought, in medieval China, to provide access.[62]

Portents and Patronage

If Du Fu's contemporaries could have read a portent in these poems, however, the well placed among them could also have seen them as presenting an opportunity to enact canonical ideals of government. Just as the *Poetry* was supposedly collected by the ancient courts to facilitate the formulation of policies of redress, so too are Du Fu's early poems of frustration often hard to discern from patronage pieces, written to attract the attention, sympathy, and admiration of powerful people capable of recommending a yet-unrecognized poet for office.[63] In effect, such members of the court had the ability to determine whether or not they would be omens after all.

This is another point on which the recordizing paradigm diverges from the late medieval. For recordizing critics, Du Fu saw what he saw: whether or not the empire did eventually collapse, the early stages of decline would still be worth criticizing. For late medieval readers, however, it might remain to be decided whether the poet's frustration was a symptom of dynastic decay or merely the prelude to his discovery by an enlightened court. Since poetry in the eighth century played an important role within the social ritual of appointment, the verse that a young candidate wrote and circulated could manifest his character to a powerful patron, who could then realize the talents he perceived in the poet by recommending him to an official position in which they could reach their full fruition. Poetry was thus a means by which a poet could move from a state of potentiality to one of actuality, a transition that depended on the participation of adept readers capable of both recognizing the writer and creating him as his latent talents deserved. In this sense, there might be no possibility of truth regarding the poet or the poem before its reception. At the time of writing, the poet remained within the undifferentiation that preceded the project of civilization and to which the world might return when civilization broke down.[64]

天育驃騎歌   *Song of the Fleet-Mount of the Imperial Stables*

吾聞天子之馬走千里	I've heard the horses of an emperor run a thousand leagues:[a]
今之畫圖無乃是	the one painted here is no doubt one of these.
是何意態雄且傑	What a temper on this one! vigorous, outstanding;
4 駿尾蕭梢朔風起	whishing its mettlesome tail, the north winds rise.
毛爲綠縹兩耳黃	Its coat's a pale green, its two ears are brown,
眼有紫焰雙瞳方	its eyes have purple flames, and its pupils are square.
矯矯龍性合變化	A dragon nature, tough and bold, suitable for transformation,
8 卓立天骨森開張	it stands tall, heavenly bones extending mysteriously.
伊昔太僕張景順	Some time ago, the chamberlain of the stud, Zhang Jingshun,
監牧收駒閱清峻	supervised pasture and broke the colts, observing the pure and outstanding.
遂令大奴守天育	Then he ordered the strong slaves to keep them in the imperial stables,
12 別養驥子憐神俊	caring specially for this great steed, whose divine superiority he treasured.
當時四十萬匹馬	Back then there were four hundred thousand horses,
張公歎其材盡下	but Zhang sighed at how their talents were all inferior.
故獨寫眞傳世人	So he had the portrait of this one made and transmitted to the world;
16 見之座右久更新	the longer I see it hung beside my seat, the fresher it becomes.

a. This line quotes an ancient romance, the *Story of King Mu* 穆天子傳, in which the king's horses could run a thousand leagues in a day.

年多物化空形影　　　The years grew many, the creature passed on,
　　　　　　　　　　　　leaving only this shadow,
嗚呼健步無由騁　　　with no way, alas,
　　　　　　　　　　　　to gallop out its robust pace.

如今豈無騕褭與驊騮　These days there must of course be horses
　　　　　　　　　　　　like Yaoniao and Hualiu,
20　時無王良伯樂死即休　but wanting a Wang Liang or Bole,
　　　　　　　　　　　　they simply die and are gone.[b]

Although it does not address itself to anyone in particular, this poem
is a clear plea for patronage. Du Fu suggests here that although the Kaiyuan period (713–42) was a time of sagely government, when all things were
recognized for their true worth and put to their ideal use, that flourishing
has more recently begun to fade. Nowadays fine horses—and fine men, by
implication—live ignominious lives and vanish unknown and unrecorded
back into the darkness, bereft of the opportunities to actualize their talent
that a talented observer like Zhang Jingshun might have afforded them.
Du Fu's physiognomic reading of this painted horse is intended to suggest
that he is himself such a talented observer of talent, capable of fulfilling
one of the most important responsibilities of men of high position: recognizing other men of worth for elevation into the bureaucracy. But he too
lacks office and depends on the recognition of someone else with both
talent and rank to recommend him for a post.

Read from the perspective of a potential patron, therefore, the poem
makes an almost awkwardly direct request. It does so by challenging the
reader of rank to defend his own ability to recognize talent, to demonstrate
the same insight into Du Fu's poem that Du Fu models here in his appreciation of Zhang Jingshun and his great charger.[65] In this sense, the poem
works somewhat like a chain letter: if Du Fu is right about the horse, about
the chamberlain of the stud, and ultimately about the Kaiyuan period as a
whole, then patron-readers should recognize his talent at recognizing talent
and promote him.[66] If, however, they decide to overlook him, then not only

b. Yaoniao and Hualiu were famous steeds of great antiquity; Wang Liang and Bole
were legendary men known for their ability to drive and to recognize such horses. Early
note: "It is recorded that King Mu of Zhou's horses Hualiu and Green Ears could go
30,000 *li* in a single day" 周穆王傳驊騮騄耳日馳三萬里.

will Du Fu be swallowed up into the ravening obscurity depicted in the final lines, but so too may the empire that was so recently flourishing.

Like the other patronage pieces that make up a large portion of Du Fu's early verse, the point of this poem is thus less to express the poet's sincere feelings or to document the truth of his situation than to involve others in the creation of that truth. Who Du Fu is, what his talent merits, and what he will become—all are left up to the well-placed reader. He does not protest his virtue or provide a résumé to demonstrate it; what he does, instead, is provide precedents by which potential patrons can recognize and thus create him as a familiar tropological type, the unrecognized worthy. There was a long tradition of discussing the relationship between senior officials and men of talent in terms of the recognition of exceptional horses; educated readers would have identified immediately that Du Fu was calling on a shared cultural repertoire in order to intimate their allegiance to common ideals. In this way, the poem conflates not only the possibility of meritocracy but also the continued relevance of the literati cultural project with the reader's recognition of the poet.

Much the same point can be made about this next poem as well, which offers an even more pointed challenge to Wei Ji 韋濟, the Vice-Director of the Left for the Department of State Affairs 尚書省左丞相. Du Fu addressed several poems to Wei over the years he spent in the capital, perhaps because Wei's position gave him significant influence over the Ministry of Personnel.[67]

奉贈韋左丞丈二十二韻　*Respectfully Presented to the Vice-Director of the Left, Elder Wei: twenty-two couplets*

	紈袴不餓死	Those in silk pants don't starve to death
	儒冠多誤身	but a scholar's cap often ruins a man.
	丈人試靜聽	If my elder will try listening quietly,
4	賤子請具陳	this poor fellow begs to tell you all.
	甫昔少年日	I, Fu, in the days of my youth,
	早充觀國賓	early was observed as a "guest of the realm."[a]
	讀書破萬卷	My reading had worn out ten thousand scrolls
8	下筆如有神	and my brush descended as if with a spirit.

a. This is an archaic way of saying that Du Fu sat for the second stage of the imperial examinations in the capital.

	賦料楊雄敵	In rhapsody, I expected to be Yang Xiong's peer;
	詩看子建親	in poetry, I looked on Cao Zhi as kin.[b]
	李邕求識面	Li Yong had sought to know my face;
12	王翰願卜鄰	Wang Han wanted me to settle in his neighborhood.[c]
	自謂頗挺出	I thought myself then so exceptional
	立登要路津	I would at once climb to some crucial office.
	致君堯舜上	I would make my lord greater than Yao or Shun,[d]
16	再使風俗淳	and turn the age's folkways pure again.
	此意竟蕭條	These thoughts, in the end, withered and died,
	行謌非隱淪	but I sang as I went, and did not hide away.
	騎驢三十載	I've ridden a donkey for thirty years now,
20	旅食京華春	living as a sponger in the capital spring.
	朝扣富兒門	In the mornings I knock at rich men's gates,
	暮隨肥馬塵	and at dusk I follow their plump horses' dust.
	殘盃與冷炙	Leftover goblets and cold roasts—
24	到處潛悲辛	wherever I go, I hide sadness and pain.
	主上頃見徵	A while back, His Majesty sought for men:
	欻然欲求伸	in a flash, I was going to express my talents.[e]
	青冥卻垂翅	But in the dark heavens my wings drooped,
28	蹭蹬無縱鱗	stranded on dry land, I could not ply my fins.
	甚媿丈人厚	I am deeply ashamed of your kindness to me,
	甚知丈人眞	and I deeply recognize your sincerity.
	每於百寮上	Always when you are with the hundred officers,
32	猥誦佳句新	you deign to recite my recent fine lines.
	竊效貢公喜	Secretly, I wish to emulate Lord Gong's delight,
	難甘原憲貧	for it is hard to enjoy the poverty of Yuan Xian.[f]

b. Rhyme-prose and poetry were tested on the exams. Yang Xiong 楊雄 (53 BCE–18 CE) was famous for his rhyme-prose, and Cao Zhi 曹植 (192–232) was often considered the best post-Classical poet. Both, however, encountered significant frustration in their official careers.

c. Li Yong and Wang Han were famous writers of the generation preceding Du Fu's. At this point in the Tang, literary reputation and patronage played a crucial and well-recognized role in deciding the outcome of the exams.

d. Ancient sage kings.

e. This probably refers to the special decree examination of 745, which sought unrecognized worthies who were especially gifted in any one cultural art. Du Fu apparently failed this exam, as he had failed his earlier attempt.

f. Being a close friend of Wang Ji 王吉, Gong Yu 貢禹 (first c. BCE) was overjoyed when Wang attained high office, for he knew Wang would shortly recommend him for a

	焉能心快快	How can my heart bear such misery?—
36	秖是走踆踆	all there is left me is to hurry away.
	今欲東入海	Now I am about to go east to the sea,
	即將西去秦	at once leaving Qin in the west.
	尚憐終南山	But still I love Mount Zhongnan,
40	廻首清渭濱	and turn my head to the banks of the clear Wei.[g]
	常擬報一飯	I've always planned to repay that one meal,[h]
	況懷辭大臣	and am more grieved to part from such a great official.
	白鷗波浩蕩	Yet the white gull will be in the huge waves;
44	萬里誰能馴	thousands of leagues away, who could tame it?

This is one of Du Fu's most famous early poems, largely on account of the historical information that recordizing readers have gleaned from its description of the poet's life during the years leading up to the Rebellion. In the words of his modern biographers, this poem "paints a vivid picture of the poet's straitened circumstances in Chang'an," "sketching out his image and feelings during a time at which he was dependent upon others for support."[68] Again, these metaphors suggest a sort of transcription, a writing of what was there to see had we just been there to see it. And there are indeed genuine biographical details contained in this poem, particularly the poet's experience of sitting for the special degree examination in 745, at which everyone was failed as "proof" that Li Linfu's government had left no unrecognized worthies waiting to be discovered.[69]

Whether the poem's picture of his circumstances is accurate or not, however, Du Fu has intentionally drawn its imagery from literary sources that he would have expected Wei Ji to recognize. The claim, for example, that Wang Han wanted Du Fu to "settle in his neighborhood" (or perhaps, wanted to settle in Du Fu's neighborhood) echoes the ancient statesman Yan Ying's 晏嬰 (ca. 500 BCE) injunction to site one's home according to the presence of virtuous neighbors rather than according to geomancy.[70]

---

similar post. Yuan Xian was a disciple of Confucius who kept to extreme poverty instead of toadying to the rich and powerful.

g. Both in Qin, the capital region. The clarity of the Wei was sometimes associated with good government.

h. This probably refers to the story of the commoner Ling Zhe 靈輒, who saved the life of the high official Zhao Dun 趙盾 (d. 601 BCE) three years after Zhao had saved him from starving.

Similarly, Du Fu's description of himself as having "ridden a donkey for thirty years" evokes the Eastern Han worthy Xiang Xu 向栩, who, before he gained a government position, would ride a donkey to market to beg for food,[71] as well as Tao Qian's 陶潛 (365–427) famous claim that he spent "thirty years in the snares of dust" before embarking on reclusion.[72] Even the evocative image of "leftover goblets and cold roasts" is drawn almost verbatim from Yan Zhitui's 顏之推 (late sixth c.) description of what it is like to be a musician entertaining the rich and powerful.[73] These marked quotations both demonstrate Du Fu's learning and challenge Wei Ji to enact his commitment to the values encoded within the tradition the two men shared—to align himself, that is, with the "scholar's cap" of the first couplet rather than the "silk pants" with which his descent from one of the leading clans of the empire might threaten to associate him. Although this poem provides much more of a résumé than did "Song of the Fleet-Mount," therefore, it should be understood less as a record of biographical realities than as offering Wei Ji the opportunity to define Du Fu's reality—and with it, his own.

Within this context, the poem's final image of the gull buffeted on a vast chaos represents one more intimation of the unmanifestation in which Du Fu found himself at this point of his life and to which he feared the empire might return. Yet, if it thus recalls the "vast blur" at the end of "Song of Leyou Park" and the "undifferentiated *qi*" of "Climbing the Pagoda of Ci'en Monastery," this image is more pointedly ambivalent than those poems were about the possibility Du Fu might not be promoted to office. The gull here is simultaneously pathetic and visionary, depicting the poet at once swallowed in a homeless pandemonium and yet also freed from the "taming" strictures and social roles that have been an implicit focus of the poem from its first lines' invocation of clothing-defined identities. To this point, Du Fu has expressed a willingness to take on a limited, determinate role within the bureaucracy. The striking second couplet, for example, humbles the poet by echoing the impoverished common infantryman who speaks one of Bao Zhao's 鮑照 (fifth c.) most famous ballads, asking his lord for some recompense for the long years he has spent defending the empire's frontiers.[74] At the most superficial level, Du Fu's invocation of this soldier is intended to suggest that he has served in the ranks of *wen* as faithfully as the soldier served its opposite, *wu* 武 (the military), and that, even if he has repeatedly failed the examinations, he deserves some small sinecure for having worked so long and hard. Yet the virtuosity Du Fu displays in making this argument, his ability to inhabit the voice of an illiterate soldier through highly literate allusions, also suggest his potential transcendence of the limited role he is asking Wei to assign him. If we can discern a hint of excitement in the final line's threat, it is because reclusion—as seen in the last chapter—was itself a moral stance sanctioned by the canonical tradition. Confucius, for example, had claimed that he wanted to "float on a raft on the sea" away from the disordered world of his time, and recluses for thousands of years had made their escape to China's waterlands from the hardened pathologies of failing states.[75] If Wei will not manifest his talents with a government appointment, therefore, Du Fu here suggests that he can take on another tropological role: the role of a recluse who wisely remains obscure in a state that cannot uphold the project of civilization by recognizing and promoting worthy men.

The Breaking Point

In late 755, a little over a month before the outbreak of the rebellion that would devastate the government he had worked for twenty years to break into, Du Fu was appointed to a minor post. The office was lowlier than he had hoped it would be, but it promised to relieve the poverty into which he and his growing family had fallen during the years they had been living in the capital, away from their clan's hereditary estates. In the previous year, this self-inflicted poverty had apparently grown so desperate that Du Fu's wife and children had been forced by food shortages in the capital region to relocate temporarily to Fengxian County, some hundred kilometers to the north of Chang'an. After his post was determined, therefore, Du Fu set off towards Fengxian to meet them, perhaps to bring them back to the capital with him as he started his new job. He must have begun the journey with at least some optimism that his long gamble in dissipating his family's wealth seeking government connections had finally begun to pay off. What he saw on his way, however, and what he learned on arriving at Fengxian made him question whether he had done the right thing.

To this point, I have been arguing that even Du Fu's most pessimistic and portentous early poetry fits contemporary models of what literature

should be and should do. In the very famous poem Du Fu wrote on arriving at Fengxian, however, we not only see how the late medieval ideas
that have structured his poetry in this chapter encouraged him to explore
moral stances far more inchoate than those lauded by recordizing reading.
We also begin to see how these ideas could create the conditions for the
radical break from his youthful poetics that would define his work from
this point on.[76]

自京赴奉先縣詠懷五百字   *Five Hundred Words Singing
My Feelings on Going from the Capital to Fengxian County*[a]

	杜陵有布衣	A man there is of Duling in commoner's robes,[b]
	老大意轉拙	whose thoughts have grown more clumsy with his years.
	許身一何愚	How utterly foolish, his self-appraisal!
4	竊比稷與契	secretly likening himself to Ji and Xie.[c]
	居然成濩落	In the end he's proved big and useless,[d]
	白首甘契闊	white-haired, and happy to suffer hardship.
	蓋棺事則已	When the coffin closes, then he'll stop,[e]

a. Early, probably authorial, note: "Composed at the beginning of the eleventh month
in the fourteenth year of the Tianbao Reign" 天寶十四載十一月初作.

b. Duling, Du Fu's family home, was just outside of the capital.

c. Hou Ji 后稷 and Yin Xie 殷契 were worthy ministers to the sage king Shun. They
assisted him with controlling China's primal flood, taught the common people to farm
and to abide by the five constant relationships (father-son, lord and minister, husband and
wife, old and young, friend and friend), and became the ancestors of the Zhou and Shang
dynasties, respectively. The Han dynasty writer Yang Xiong had complained of the arro-
gance of fools by saying that "they all liken themselves to Ji and Xie." Confucius, however,
had similarly "secretly likened himself" to one Old Peng.

d. This description may recall an anecdote from the *Zhuangzi*, in which Huizi could
find no use for an enormous gourd and ended up smashing it to bits. Zhuangzi laughs at
Huizi's "ineptness in using great things," saying that he could have tied the gourd to his
waist to go floating on the rivers and lakes.

e. This line derives from a discourse between Confucius and a disciple preserved in the
Hanshi waizhuan 韓詩外傳. The disciple, Zigong, complains that he has not been able
to advance past a certain point in learning from the Master and asks that Confucius let
him rest in some other, lesser activity. After Confucius tells him of the difficulty of per-
forming these other activities up to his standards, Zigong asks in despair, "Then when
does a gentleman ever rest?" Confucius answers, "The gentleman learns without cease and
only rests when the coffin is closed."

8	此志常覬豁	but with these aims, he keeps on hoping.
	窮年憂黎元	Throughout his years, he's worried for the people,
	歎息腸內熱	heaving sighs, with guts burning within.[f]
	取笑同學翁	Earning for it the laughter of old fellow students,
12	浩謌彌激烈	he sings out wildly, and with increasing fervor.
	非無江海志	He's not without the will to retire to rivers and lakes,
	蕭灑送日月	to pass his days and months aloof and serene.
	生逢堯舜君	But living under a ruler like Yao or Shun,[g]
16	不忍便永訣	he could not bear to just go off forever.
	當今廊廟具	Now the halls of state are well provisioned;
	構廈豈云缺	who could say the structure has gaps?[h]
	葵藿傾太陽	Still, like the mallow, he turns towards the sun;[i]
20	物性固莫奪	a thing's nature, of course, cannot be changed.
	顧惟螻蟻輩	Yet consider, then, the antlike sort
	但自求其穴	that only seeks a hole for itself;
	胡爲慕大鯨	why aspire to be a huge whale,
24	輒擬偃溟渤	and to sprawl across the world's great seas?[j]

f. The phrase "guts burning within" seems to derive from a story in the *Zhuangzi* in which a government official describes to Confucius the impossible political dilemma he faces. Confucius tells him that "the best thing to do is to be willing to sacrifice your life; but this is extremely difficult."

g. Yao and Shun were sage kings of antiquity.

h. This metaphor depends on the Chinese homophone *cai* 材, which means both "timber" and "talent." Du Fu is saying that the state has enough talented men, that the edifice of government does not lack any pillars or beams.

i. Emperors were traditionally compared to the sun, but this figure derives almost verbatim from Cao Zhi's declaration of loyalty to his older brother Emperor Wen of the Wei dynasty. Cao Zhi wrote, "The mallow bends its leaves, even if the sun never turns its rays upon it. Yet it will ever face the sun because of its sincerity of feeling." Since there was supposedly tension between the brothers, the allusion may bear ironic overtones.

j. The conjunction of whale and ants appears in several early texts. The earliest source of the passage may be the *Zhuangzi*, where the disciples of a Daoist master were encouraging their teacher to take a position in government. The master, however, refused to leave his reclusion, saying, "A fish that could swallow a boat, if it gets stranded on dry land, will be troubled by ants.... Therefore, birds seek to be as high as possible, and fish seek to be as deep as possible. In the same way, men who wish to preserve their lives hide themselves away."

	以茲悟生理	From this he recognizes life's truth,[k]
	獨恥事干謁	that he alone is abashed to beg for favor.
	兀兀遂至今	Foolishly persistent, he's gone on to this day—
28	忍為塵埃沒	could he bear just to disappear in the dust?
	終愧巢與由	In the end he is shamed before Chaofu and Xu You,
	未能易其節	who would not change their principles.[l]
	沉飲聊自遣	Deeply he drinks to banish such thoughts,
32	放謌頗愁絕	then lets forth a song of utmost sorrow.
	歲暮百草零	It was year's end, the plants had withered,
	疾風高岡裂	and the high hills were rent by fierce winds.
	天衢陰崢嶸	Cold darkness loomed on heaven's avenues
36	客子中夜發	as the traveler at midnight set forth.
	霜嚴衣帶斷	Severe frost snapped the sash of my coat,
	指直不得結	and with fingers numbed stiff, I could not retie it.
	凌晨過驪山	At daybreak I passed by Mount Blackstallion,
40	御榻在嵽嵲	where on the towering heights was then the royal couch.[m]
	蚩尤塞寒空	Chiyou's fog filled the cold void of the sky;[n]
	蹴蹋崖谷滑	the slopes and ravines had been trampled slick.
	瑤池氣鬱律	Vapors swelled up from Jasper Pool,
44	羽林相摩戞	where royal guardsmen rubbed and clacked.[o]
	君臣留懽娛	There lord and ministers lingered in delights
	樂動殷膠葛	while music stirred grandly over the rocky peak.
	賜浴皆長纓	Those granted baths there all bore long ribbons,

k. This moment of "realizing life's truth" may recall the recluse Xi Kang, who recognized that "the spirit depends upon the body to subsist ... one mistake can harm its life."

l. Chaofu and Xu You were ancient recluses who refused to serve even in the time of Yao. After Yao offered Xu You a position in government, Chaofu ceased his friendship with Xu You, and Xu You, distraught, went and washed out his ears. This line could also be read, "But I would not exchange principles with them."

m. The palace at Lishan, the site of natural hot springs, was where Xuanzong had taken to holding winter court. Du Fu's journey to Fengxian would have taken him past the mountain.

n. Chiyou was the inventor of warfare; in a battle against the sagely Yellow Emperor, he is said to have created a fog that lasted three days.

o. Jasper Pool was the mythological home of the goddess Queen Mother of the West and the place where she had banqueted with King Mu of Zhou. The presence of Yang Guifei may be implied here.

48	與宴非短褐	and none in short homespun joined their feasts.ᵖ
	彤庭所分帛	Yet the silks these had received at red-walled court
	本自寒女出	came originally from women cold with want,
	鞭撻其夫家	whose menfolk they'd had whipped
52	聚歛貢城闕	in greedily collecting taxes for the palace.
	聖人筐篚恩	Still, the sages' gift of baskets
	實欲邦國活	was given to preserve the state;
	臣如忽至理	and if the ministers overlooked its meaning,
56	君豈棄此物	did our lord merely throw these things away? q
	多士盈朝廷	With such officers filling the court,
	仁者宜戰慄	good men would be right to tremble.
	況聞內金盤	I've also heard the palace's golden plates
60	盡在衛霍室	are all now in the homes of imperial in-laws.ʳ
	中堂舞神仙	Within the halls, goddesses danced,
	煙霧散玉質	thick mists parted by marble flesh.
	煖客貂鼠裘	The guests were warmed by sable cloaks
64	悲管逐清瑟	while sad flutes followed clear zithers,
	勸客駝蹄羹	and urged to taste a camel's-pad stew
	霜橙壓香橘	as frosty oranges crushed fragrant tangerines.
	朱門酒肉臭	The crimson gates reeked with wine and meat;
68	路有凍死骨	on the road were bones of the frozen dead.
	榮枯咫尺異	Flourishing and withering, inches apart—
	惆悵難再述	I'm overcome by grief; it's hard to go on.
	北轅就涇渭	North I turned my yoke towards the Jing and the Wei,
72	官渡又改轍	and at the official crossing again changed track.
	羣冰從西下	Masses of ice came down from the west,
	極目高崒兀	as far as I could see, they towered up high.
	疑是崆峒來	It seemed Mount Kongtong was coming,

p. Long ribbons mark great court officers; "short homespun" refers to commoners.

q. These two couplets work over the Mao preface to one of the poems in the *Classic of Poetry*, "The Cry of the Deer" 鹿鳴: "The king feasts his ministers and worthy guests, both providing them food and drink, and giving them silks and baskets in order to express his sincere feelings. His loyal ministers are thereupon capable of giving their utmost in service."

r. "Imperial in-laws" is literally "Wei Qing 衛青 and Huo Qubing 霍去病," both Western Han generals of the second century BCE. Since both of these generals rose to prominence through their family connections with the women of the imperial court, most commentators take the line to be referring to the Yangs.

76	恐觸天柱折	and I feared it would smash Heaven's Pillar.[s]
	河梁幸未折	By luck, the bridge had not yet broken,
	枝撐聲窸窣	though its supports creaked and groaned;
	行旅相攀援	travelers clung to one another,
80	川廣不可越	the river was too wide to cross.
	老妻既異縣	My wife had gone to a county not our own;
	十口隔風雪	our ten-mouth household cut off by wind and snow.
	誰能久不顧	How could I go long without checking in on them?
84	庶往共飢渴	I'd hoped to go share their hunger and thirst.
	入門聞號咷	But, entering the gate, I heard howling:
	幼子飢已卒	my young son had already starved to death.
	吾寧捨一哀	And how could I forgo a wail of my own,
88	里巷亦嗚咽	when even the villagers were choking sobs?[t]
	所愧爲人父	What shamed me, though, was that I was his father,
	無食致夭折	and a lack of food had caused his death.
	豈知秋未登	How could I know that if the harvest was not rich
92	貧窶有倉卒	poor folk could have such calamities?
	生常免租稅	My whole life I've been exempt from taxes,
	名不隸征伐	and my name's never been on the conscription rolls.[u]
	撫跡猶酸辛	If in my experience, then, there's still bitterness,
96	平人固騷屑	of course ordinary people are desperate.
	默思失業途	I brood on those who've lost livelihoods and prospects,
	因念遠戍卒	and then think of the troops in far garrisons.
	憂端齊終南	My cares rise level with the Zhongnan Mountains;[v]
100	澒洞不可掇	an endless chaos that cannot be grasped.

Since Du Fu does not explicitly discuss the outbreak of the An Lushan Rebellion in this poem, it is generally held to have been written days before

s. Mount Kongtong was the source of the Wei River; Heaven's Pillar, the name of a mountain in the capital region. According to an old myth, Gonggong 公共 had broken one of the pillars that support the sky in a battle with the sage emperor Zhuanxu 顓頊, causing a great flood that overran all of China.

t. Confucius had emitted "a wail" when encountering a funeral, and the term had come to describe the ritually appropriate actions of grieving. It was, however, considered against ritual propriety to mourn for infants under a certain age, as Du Fu's child seems to have been.

u. Du Fu's grandfather had been a high official, and the poet had thus inherited certain economic and social privileges.

v. In the capital region. This mountain range was also a famous site of reclusion.

the news would reach him at Fengxian. The poem has therefore been touted as a paradigm work of the Poet Historian and Poet Sage, both documenting the corruption of the age and sensing with almost preternatural acuity the disaster that was about to descend upon it. The moral assurance of Du Fu's denunciation of an empire in which "crimson gates reek of wine and meat, and on the roads are bones of the frozen dead," moreover, has been praised as the voice of a "Confucian Prophet" and a "Hero of Sympathy,"[77] and the poet's turn in the final lines from his own sorrows to those of the empire has been taken as paradigmatic of his recognition, even amidst blinding grief, of the public crisis that overshadowed his personal tragedy. Yet if most recordizing readers have seen here evidence of Du Fu's consummate moral clarity, I suggest that the poem's criticism of the government and its witness to the empire's suffering is merely one moment in a more complex dialectic. Viewed in its entirety, the poem inhabits a space of moral unmanifestation that cannot be imagined within the recordizing perspective.[78]

The ethical perplexity that characterizes the poem as a whole is articulated most directly in its first thirty-two lines. Du Fu is grappling in this section with how to understand the decision he made to remain in the capital for so many years, chasing the dream of government service. Should he look back on this decision as a noble self-sacrifice, impoverishing himself and his family in the hope that he might someday be able to contribute to the greater good of the nation? Or was his persistence ultimately selfish, the result of a self-aggrandizing delusion that he alone had what it took to save his failing state? Should he have followed his inclinations to reclusion—which, in the Tang, no longer required total isolation from society but rather encompassed various comfortable occupations—so as to insulate himself and his children from the Tang's declining fortunes? Or should he simply have "begged for favor," "seeking a hole" for himself like the other "antlike" officials of the dynasty? How, in other words, should Du Fu understand his own moral being and the choices he has made, given recent events?

Several mutually contradictory visions of himself argue with one another throughout the dense tissue of allusions that makes up this first section of the poem. In the first full flowering of the interest in systematic ambiguity that characterizes many of Du Fu's most important works, every couplet here is written to accommodate multiple interpretations. Consider, for example, the second and third couplets. On one construal, Du Fu's "secretly likening himself to Ji and Xie" invokes an allusion to Yang Xiong that would tend to suggest the poet really is "foolish" and "useless," and would encourage us to read the sixth line as bitterly describing the way he has perversely enjoyed his own noble failure. On another reading, however, "secretly likening oneself" to a revered example was also something Confucius had done—and Confucius was someone who "kept at it even when he knew it was impossible," willingly suffering hardship on behalf of a state he could not save.[79] According to this more positive way of reading the section, apparently self-deprecatory terms like "foolish" and "big and useless" might bear the ironies they possess in Daoist sources, where they denote great talents that are overlooked. Then again, medieval interpreters took some of these Daoist authors to have been recluses and to have advocated reclusion in eras of disorder. These ironies, then, might equally suggest that Du Fu's choice to pursue office was genuinely foolish.

A similar tangle of self-contradictory implications could be adduced from every couplet of this first section, equally strengthening and undermining whatever interpretation we may hazard. To give just a few more examples, the figure of the whale and the ants can be construed either as excoriating officials of the time for their lack of ambition or as criticizing Du Fu himself for merely "seeking a hole" in the bureaucracy, rather than lighting out on the seas of reclusion. The poet's "shame before Chaofu and Xu You," similarly, can either straightforwardly glorify or ironically belittle the intransigence of these two legendary recluses, suggesting either that Du Fu should have followed their example or that—in an alternate grammatical construal of line 30—he could not be persuaded to adopt their principles and give over his own. Any way we read these lines they threaten to become ironic and thus to turn around on us as readers: either we have acceded to Du Fu's foolish illusions, or we have failed, like the manifestly unworthy government of his age, to recognize his virtues. The result of all these concatenating ambiguities is that we cannot confidently appraise his moral character here any more than he can himself.

It is at this point that we can see the late medieval model laying the groundwork for Du Fu's poetic evolution beyond it. In each of the poems above, his latency was forward-looking: either the poem would be an omen of troubles to come, or it would be the means by which he was recognized, brought out of obscurity, and taken into the government. *Wen* in those

poems merely threatened to break down: the poems themselves at-
tempted to keep its manifesting project alive and offered Du Fu's interlocutors chances to participate in it. In this poem, by contrast, Du Fu is
looking backwards on decisions he has previously made, decisions that
have not resulted in his following either of the tropological courses he
imagined for his life, service or reclusion. Having never had the opportunity to apply his talents to government, he cannot tell whether he really
had the stuff of a great minister or whether this aspiration was itself the
symptom of a political naïveté that would have made it more appropriate
for him to flee the collapsing polity. Having remained in a state of undifferentiated potential so long, it had become his being.[80] The *wen* of this
first section now merely manifests the obscurity in which he finds himself,
rather than envisioning ways it might be resolved. Its canonical function
has been inverted.

In an effort to redeem *wen* from the confusions of this first section,
therefore, the rest of the poem attempts to draw from its chaos—with
much the same cosmogonic resonances as "Song of Leyou Park"—a song
that will clarify his moral situation and offer possibilities for government
response. And at first, the narrative Du Fu produces does seem to lend
itself to greater moral confidence. His description of the decadent imperial
party on Mt. Blackstallion, for example, is a tissue of images drawn from
precedent texts,[81] very much in the ancient tradition of travel rhapsodies,
which paradigmatically paralleled a journey through space to a more interior
journey from confusion towards resolution, aided at every stage by the recall
of allusions to This Culture of Ours.[82] The adoption of this hopeful template
is combined, moreover, with the suggestion that the means to rectify the
situation still reside with the emperor. Although the Yang family may have
seduced Xuanzong into its luxuriance in order to peculate government valu-
ables, Du Fu reserves the possibility in the ambiguities of lines 53 to 56 that
the emperor's largesse could itself have canonical interpretations—as if he
were presenting Xuanzong with the same sort of choice he previously presented Wei Ji between a scholar's cap and silk pants. Up to a certain point,
then, this second section of the poem seems designed to restore the moral
intelligibility undermined by the first.

Upon his arrival in Fengxian, however, this intelligibility is fractured
once again. On the one hand, the poet's generosity of spirit in transcending
the death of his own son to imagine the broader sufferings of the less

privileged throughout the empire recalls the sagely ministers Hou Ji and Yin Xie, to whom he had "secretly compared himself" in the first section and who both famously worked so hard at saving the common folk from the disasters of their times that they rarely had time to look within their own doors.[83] On the other hand, however, the death of Du Fu's son was a direct result of his devotion to the project of imperial governance: he had remained in the capital all these years, spending his inheritance and subjecting his family to the deteriorating imperial economy precisely because he had "worried for the people" in much the way he is doing here. The speed with which Du Fu transitions from a "single wail" for his infant son to the troubles of the folk at large thus both speaks to his selfless concern for the state and recapitulates the moral grandiosity responsible for the child's death in the first place.[84]

As was the case in the first section of the poem, therefore, the interpretation of the ending is threatened with inescapable irony. Each detail can be read to support an account whereby Du Fu is a moral exemplar in the tradition of China's great sages—"keeping at it even when he knew it was impossible" and drawing an ethical vision out of chaos—or is, alternately, a self-aggrandizing fool who starved his own child in a doomed attempt to play this role. From this final vantage point we can recognize the ambiguous relationship between the poem's two halves, the moral chaos of the first both giving rise to the "song" that follows it and also deriving from the events that song narrates. The poem as a whole thus represents a Möbius strip of tortured attempts and failures to make sense of who Du Fu is—his culpability in the death of his son, the nobility or folly of his devotion to the state—none of which reach a clear moral conclusion. It cannot, therefore, end otherwise than did its first section: in a chaos of undifferentiation—and this time, quite explicitly, the chaos (*hong-dong* 澒洞) that prevailed before the creation of the civilized world and to which it threatened to return in moments of dynastic collapse.

From our vantage point, it is easy to read the final lines as an omen of the troubles to come. Yet this omen is one that Du Fu himself, within the poem, still cannot read. The final invocation of the Zhongnan Mountains, to the south of Chang'an, is once again ambiguous, indicating that he is looking backwards from Fengxian towards the court, but also beyond it, to a paradigmatic site of reclusion. The alternative courses that tormented him at the beginning of the poem still beckon to him now, and he cannot choose between them, cannot "grasp" what he should do next. For all its allusions to the sacred tradition and the ethical visions it contained, therefore, his *wen* has clarified nothing. Or rather, it has clarified that there is no clear moral interpretation of his experience, no rescue available through the resources of This Culture of Ours. This is the crucial recognition of this period of Du Fu's career: the moment when his poetics begins to break away from the late medieval model that had underwritten his work to this point.

THREE

Convention and Nature

The Outbreak of the Rebellion (756–57)

ays after Du Fu made his way to Fengxian to find his infant child starved to death, news of An Lushan's rebellion reached the capital. Within a month, the secondary capital of Luoyang had fallen to the rebels, and the loyalist armies had little choice but to retreat behind the natural fortifications that blocked access to the capital region around Chang'an.[1] Despite having recently been given a post, Du Fu seems—and I say "seems" because almost no poetry survives from this period to inform us—not to have returned to Chang'an to take it up. Instead, he probably remained with his family in Fengxian until the summer, at which point, sensing that the situation was turning against the imperial cause, he took them farther north away from the capital region, to Whitewater County and finally Fuzhou.

There are several ways to account for the gap in Du Fu's collection at this time.[2] It is possible that what he wrote was lost in the confusion of this tumultuous period; it is also possible that he was too preoccupied with questions of survival to spend much time writing verse. Given the poetry that he does begin to write around six months after the Rebellion's outbreak, however, his silence might also be attributable to a crisis in his art. In "Singing My Feelings on Going from the Capital to Fengxian," he had begun to question whether poetry could fulfill its traditional functions—a development that could not have come, for him, at a worse time. For other poets of the same period, verse provided an arena for assimilating the uncertainty and violence of the Rebellion to time-transcending patterns drawn from history, myth, and the natural world, patterns that explained why events had gone as they had and how the empire's predicament was likely to be resolved. Du Fu, however, could no longer rely on these patterns, and, when he does begin to write again, he writes a poetry anguished not only by the suffering of the war, but also by questions about the applicability of such traditional tropologies to contemporary experience.

In this sense, the early days of the Rebellion represent the crucible of Du Fu's poetic transformation. It is during this period that he begins to focus on the particulars of his experience in all their recalcitrance to traditional modes of sense-making, a development that begins to justify recordizing critics' vision of him as the Poet Historian. This transformation, however, is far more conflicted than it has generally seemed to such critics, for whom Du Fu's notation of the particulars of his experience has come to seem natural, an expression of the fundamental character of classical Chinese verse. For these readers, the tropological conventions of the poetic tradition are merely useful; they can be applied or subverted according to the needs of the moment. This, however, was not the vision of convention that generally prevailed in the literary discourse of Du Fu's time. Instead, traditional forms were understood as having not merely an actual but also a normative force on authors, who were tasked with assimilating the best the tradition had to offer, repeating its patterns in their own perception and action, and thus serving as a model for ages to come. To struggle with, question, and subvert the tradition's poetic conventions in the way that Du Fu does in this period, therefore, would have been in its own time a much more pointed and problematic practice.

Beyond the Breaking Point

The hypothesis that the gap in Du Fu's collection might derive from a crisis in his art draws its plausibility from the themes that animate the verse he begins to write some six months after arriving in Fengxian. Many of these poems can be understood as making poetry itself a central theme—and in particular the problem of whether the practice of writing poetry made moral sense against the violent background of the age. A number of these poems, especially those deriving from the first year of the Rebellion, give this question a resolutely negative answer, carrying forward in this respect the pessimism about poetry's potential that characterized the bitter confusions of "Singing My Feelings." It would not be until the next spring that

Du Fu would begin to explore ways of redeeming poetry's moral value, and it would not be until many years later that he would begin to find ways that would stick.

The earliest poem in Du Fu's collection that can be confidently dated to the period of the Rebellion seems to have been written in the summer of 756, when Du Fu had fled north to avoid the rebel and imperial armies then massing for a confrontation at Tong Pass. Like most of his verse that can be dated to this first year of the war, this poem displays a certain reticence in broaching the topic of the Rebellion, beginning as a relatively conventional poem praising the reclusive virtues of his host in Whitewater County, his maternal uncle Cui Xu 崔頊, and admiring the beauty of the landscape there. Yet even in this first section, Du Fu hints that he is repressing deeper concerns, fears that finally warp his vision of the natural scene and break into full explicitness in the final lines. The conceit would seem to be that he had no intention of discussing the war when he set out to write the poem but that—as was the case in several verses in the previous chapter—he gets carried away in midcourse from his ostensible theme. Here, however, the result is not a legible omen testifying to the empire's traditionally precedented entry into a cyclical phase when worthy men should hide away in reclusion. Instead, he ends the poem worrying that any attempt to assimilate current events to cycles or conventions may amount to an escapist distortion of the situation's true dangers.[3]

白水縣崔少府十九翁高齋三十韻   *Thirty Couplets on the High Studio of Old Cui, Assistant Magistrate of Whitewater County*[a]

客從南縣來	This traveler came from a county south,
浩蕩無與適	through the vastness with no place to rest.
旅食白日長	Sponging my meals, the bright days last long,
4 況當朱炎赫	even more with summer's crimson flames at full blaze.
高齋坐林杪	But in your high studio, I sit in the treetops,
信宿遊衍闃	and staying a couple of nights, I am at ease and tranquil.
清晨陪躋攀	In the cool morning, I joined you for a climb,
8 傲睨俯峭壁	and haughtily we gazed down from sheer cliffs.
崇岡相枕帶	A lofty hill supported us there:

a. Early, probably authorial, note: "Written in the fifth month of the fifteenth year of the Tianbao period (756)" 天寶十五載五月作.

曠野懷咫尺	the broad wastes fit in the space of my breast.
始知賢主人	Only then did I realize my worthy host
12 贈此遣愁寂	had gifted me this to ease sadness and care.
危堦根青冥	Perilous stairways rooted dark skies;
曾冰生漸瀝	accumulated ice formed trickling rills.
上有無心雲	Above were clouds with no will of their own;
16 下有欲落石	below were boulders about to fall.[b]
泉聲聞復息	Stream sounds were heard, then stilled again,
動靜隨所擊	running or quiet, following what it struck.
鳥呼藏其身	Birds cried out, hiding their bodies,
20 有似懼彈射	as if they feared arrows and slings.
吏隱道性情	As a hermit-clerk, you refine your being,
茲焉其窟宅	and here you make your hideaway from the world.[c]
白水見舅氏	At Whitewater I meet my uncle,
24 諸公乃仙伯	among officials, an immortal elder.
杖藜長松陰	You lean on your staff in the shade of tall pines,
作尉窮谷僻	serve as sheriff in a remote valley's depths.
爲我炊彫胡	For me you've cooked up wild rice,
28 逍遙展良覿	and then, at ease, spread a fine banquet.
坐久風頗愁	We sit long and the winds turn sad,
晚來山更碧	and as it gets late, the mountains grow green.
相對十丈蛟	Facing us, a hundred-foot flood-dragon
32 欻翻盤渦坼	flies suddenly, splitting a whirlpool.
何得空裏雷	How is it that this thunder in the sky,
殷殷尋地脈	comes rumbling along the veins of the earth?
煙氛藹嶓崒	Vapors shroud the towering peaks
36 魍魎森慘戚	as goblins gather gloomy and dreary.
崑崙崆峒顛	The summits of Kunlun and Kongdong
廻首如不隔	as I turn my heard seem not far away.[d]
前軒頹反照	Upon the front balcony falls sunset's light,
40 巉絶華岳赤	and towering over, Mount Hua turns red.

b. "Clouds with no will of their own" echoes Tao Qian's "Return!" 歸去來兮辭: "The clouds have no will in emerging from the peaks; when the birds grow tired of flying, they know to return home."

c. "Hideaway" is literally "cave dwelling," often used to describe the dwellings of immortals in cliffsides.

d. Kunlun and Kongdong are two legendarily huge mountain ranges in the far west of China. The point would seem to be that the storm has made the landscape threatening and dramatic, as those mountains were supposed to be.

	兵氣漲林巒	An air of weapons floods the forested ridges;
	川光雜鋒鏑	river glints mix in blade and arrowhead.
	知是相公軍	It is, I know, the army of the minister,
44	鐵馬雲霧積	his armored horses gathering like fog.[e]
	玉觴淡無味	Bland and savorless now is the jade goblet—
	胡羯豈強敵	how could Hu and Jie be strong foes?[f]
	長歌激屋樑	My long song beats on the roof beams,
48	淚下流衽席	and tears fall, flowing onto my seat.
	人生半哀樂	Human life is half sorrow, half joy;
	天地有順逆	in heaven and on earth, there is good and there is bad.
	慨彼萬國夫	I am moved that men from ten thousand domains
52	休明備征狄	in this glorious age will be used to fight the Di.[g]
	猛將紛填委	Fierce commanders assemble in great number,
	廟謀蓄長策	and court planners store up excellent plans.
	東郊何時開	Yet when will our eastern marches be recovered?—
56	帶甲且未釋	those bearing armor cannot yet take it off.[h]
	欲告清宴罷	Our light repast here will soon end;
	難拒幽明迫	none can resist the pressure of dark and light.[i]
	三歎酒食旁	I sigh repeatedly over my ale and food:
60	何由似平昔	how can things ever be as before?[j]

For the first thirty or so lines of the poem, Du Fu seems to be writing on the common theme of visiting a recluse. Uncle Cui's post was low, and

e. This line inverts a literary cliché drawn originally from the Han dynasty *Records of the Historian* (*Shiji*), where we read that, "when the empire first falls into difficulty, the manly and heroic all proclaim themselves kings at once, and the soldiers of all-under-heaven congregate like clouds or fog."

f. It is not clear whether this "jade goblet" refers to Du Fu's wine cup or, perhaps more likely, to the emperor's. In times of trouble, the emperor would cut down on the luxury of his diet in order to express his distress and stimulate heaven's pity. The Hu and the Jie peoples were ancient enemies of the Han.

g. The Di were an ancient, non-Chinese tribe, an enemy of the Zhou.

h. The "eastern marches" probably refers to Luoyang, the "eastern capital," recently captured by the rebels.

i. "Dark and light" is one possible interpretation of the compound *you-ming* 幽明; another is "what is of heaven and what is of humanity."

j. This line recalls a story in the *Zuozhuan* where it is said that "only when one is eating does one forget one's troubles."

so Du Fu elegantly treats him as a high-minded man who has escaped the intrigues of the court to perfect his character in communion with the beauties of the natural world. And if the poem broke off around line 30, it might be notable for its rambling length, but it would nonetheless remain within the usual range of the genre, praising the recluse's rusticity, thanking him for his hospitality, and describing the beauty of the natural scene where he lives. Readers would have no reason to wonder when exactly the poem had been written or what the political situation of the empire was at the time. The occasion would be as common as the beautiful weather Du Fu observes on his morning climb, and would demand no more investigation.

In the course of describing the natural scene, however, Du Fu begins to hint that the very conventionality of the poem may serve as an escape from something threatening. In the sixth couplet, for example, he describes the panoramic view he has from the high studio as having been "gifted to him" by Cui Xu "to ease sadness and care," and he goes on in the following lines to depict Cui's home as a "hideaway" from the troubles of the world. On the one hand, then, Cui's place of reclusion provides Du Fu with shelter from the turmoil of human history, allowing the poet to be as relaxed as the stream that merely "follows what it meets" and as placid as the "will-less clouds" that the recluse-poet Tao Qian had invoked in a famous poem as figures for the naturalness to which he aspired. On the other hand, however, the very need for safety implies threat, suggesting that Cui's reclusion might be as precarious as the boulders "about to fall" and as fearful as the birds "hiding their bodies" from hunters. The natural scene that Du Fu observes here is thus a kind of screen, both shielding the poet from his worries for the outside world and, more subtly, allowing those repressed dangers to be projected upon it.

As they prey further upon his mind, these dangers eventually transform that natural scene into a horrifying phantasmagoria. Witnessing what would seem merely a brief afternoon thundershower, Du Fu sees a cataract engorged by the rain distorted into a "hundred-foot flood-dragon," and he envisions the thickening mist about the hilltops as the gathering of demons upon the summits of the mighty mountain ranges of the west.[4] His imagination having thus grown hyperbolic, he then sees the red of the sunset bloodying Mt. Hua, near where the army of "the minister," Geshu Han 哥舒翰, was massing to defend the capital. And if this mountain range, more than a hundred kilometers to the southeast, might perhaps have been just visible on the edge of the horizon, what follows is unadulterated fantasy. What Du Fu sees in the next two couplets is, in literal terms, only the coalescence of a postpluvial fog pouring down the forested hillsides—not, as he claims, the old literary cliché of armies in a period of disorder gathering like fog. By confusing the target of this traditional metaphor for its source and by claiming to "know," moreover, that the fog is the army—as if this were a rational conclusion to draw from what he sees—the poem suggests the poet's mind may be unhinged, that the emotions he feels about the events of the time have broken through his attempts to restrain them within a conventional depiction of the timeless natural beauties of Cui Xu's hermitage.

At this point, Du Fu tries to regain control of the poem by suggesting that, in fact, the military exigencies of the time are themselves merely one moment in a larger natural cycle. Battles against the barbarian Di, Hu, and Jie peoples have occurred at intervals throughout even the most glorious of Chinese dynasties; human history alternates between joy and sorrow, order and war, just as light and dark press each other on from day to night. And since disorder is merely one phase of this cosmic cycle, Du Fu consoles himself and his uncle that this war will have an end, as all wars do; that they need not worry about it too much; indeed, that he can already see in his mind's eye the loyalist generals and ministers preparing for the capital's defense. But, in bringing up the topic of plans and troop movements, turning away from the vast scope of cosmic change and towards questions that in the present moment remain unresolved—not whether, but when, the Rebellion will end; how many will die; and whether the poet himself will survive it—this second attempt to escape into timelessness also fails to quiet the poet's cares. Historical cycles may have their moments of return, but the cycles of day and night are now pressing Du Fu towards an unknown future, and where at the beginning of the poem he complained that summer days last too long, now he wishes they might slow down. Having failed to console himself through appeal to cyclical patterns, he thus ends the poem doubting whether things will "ever be as they were before," back when poems about reclusive banquets could be merely polite, without bringing up unanswerable questions about the fate of empire.[5]

After leaving the temporary lodgings they had been afforded by Cui Xu, Du Fu took his family northwards from Whitewater to Fuzhou, which he apparently thought was far enough from both Chang'an and the northern frontier to be relatively safe. Sometime after the capital fell to An Lushan's armies in the late summer of 756, however, the poet seems to have been captured by the rebels—he is thought to have been seeking to make his way to the court-in-exile—and brought alone to occupied Chang'an.[6] It is in Chang'an that Du Fu's poetic productivity begins to pick back up again, and during the months he was held there, he wrote some of his most canonical verse. The following poem, for example, is one whose great fame has dulled the shock that must once have accompanied its distortions of contemporary convention.[7]

對雪   *Facing Snow*

戰哭多新鬼	Weeping of battles, many new ghosts;
愁吟獨老翁	chanting in sorrow, a lonely old man.[a]
亂雲低薄暮	Chaotic clouds press lower at twilight
4 急雪舞迴風	as fierce snow dances in the whirling wind.
瓢弃樽無綠	The ladle discarded, there's no green in my cup;
爐存火似紅	the brazier remains: the fire seems red.[b]
數州消息斷	From several prefectures news has been cut,
8 愁坐正書空	so sitting in sorrow, I write these words in the air.[c]

Although it is never read this way by recordizing critics—who focus on the contemporary events that lie in the background here—it is important to notice that this poem claims to be about the weather. The recent battles that begin the verse so dramatically are, as we read on, reduced to an explanation of the snowstorm, the rage of new-made ghosts being

a. According to the *Zuozhuan*, new ghosts are huge and violent.

b. The "green" is the dark color of the lees. This couplet may recall a common conceit of Six Dynasties poetry that "the troubles of the mind can make red seem green" 心之憂矣, 視丹如綠.

c. The image of "writing words in air" was a stereotyped gesture of overwhelming grief. It derives from an anecdote about the Jin dynasty general Yin Hao 殷浩 (d. 356), who lost a catastrophic battle and was dismissed from his post. He showed no appreciable signs of emotion, even to his family, but sat for days on end drawing in the air the words, "Sigh, sigh, it is strange."

traditionally thought to cause climatic anomalies. The "chaos" and "fierce-
ness" of the second couplet are, likewise, only characteristic of the clouds
and the snow, not (at least not explicitly) the human world. Even when in
the final couplet Du Fu takes up the disintegration of the empire, it is
in the context of explaining his own loneliness, why it is that he has no
companions but snow to face over his wine cup. It is, of course, impossible
to miss the fact that Du Fu is alluding here to events that other poets
would generally have discussed in genres other than the eight-line regulated verse, which was usually dedicated (as we saw in the first chapter) to
social occasions, to the articulation of more sedate emotions, and to the
observation of beautiful scenes.[8] Yet we should not miss the pretense that,
in fact, he is not breaking with this generic practice, but rather writing a
much more conventional sort of poem, centrally concerning the weather.

This claim of conventionality would likely have been both more obvious
and less plausible in the poem's own time, recognizable as part of a meditation on whether writing poetry really made sense in Du Fu's situation. The
third couplet, for instance, hints that his mind has been unhinged by present circumstances through its strange description of the still-burning bra-
zier as merely "seeming" red—an allusion to the cliché of how a troubled
mind can "disorder the eyes."[9] This suggestion is carried further by the final
line's recollection of the story of the fourth-century general Yin Hao, who
after a catastrophic defeat betrayed no outward emotion but was broken
within, endlessly scribbling obsessive nonsense in the air with his hand
when he thought he was unobserved. Although Du Fu is writing in a poetic
form conventionally suited to a banquet with friends and entertainers, he
is in fact sitting alone with no ale and only the dancing of the snow; he does
not know whether his friends are alive or dead and cannot hope that anyone
will read the words he is now writing. The allusion thus suggests that, in
these circumstances, continuing to compose poetry—and conventional,
allusive, traditional poetry in particular—may be insane.

The Claims of Convention in Du Fu's Age

In both of these poems, Du Fu depicts himself as attempting, and ultimately failing, to write in accordance with conventions no longer apt to the
historical moment. In one respect, this vision of the art's fragility would

itself have been intelligible in Du Fu's time, as several medieval critics make it clear that great poetry was not expected of ages of disorder, when writers would have little time for craftsmanship and when more immediately useful genres, such as the memorial 奏 and the call-to-arms 檄, were supposed to come to the fore.[10] It is worth remarking that in the postmedieval period, when Du Fu had risen to the pinnacle of the literary canon, this assumption gets inverted, and it becomes a cliché that ages of disorder call forth the best poetry, since it is in such strained circumstances that poets become capable of enacting the "poet historian" role that Du Fu defined for them.[11] In the late medieval period, however, poetry was often thought of as an art of peaceful times, and many theorists claimed it had reached its apogee—in moral terms at least—in the greatest eras of political stability the Chinese tradition had witnessed: the ancient Zhou dynasty, the Han dynasty, and the Tang itself.[12] This connection between political and poetic greatness was not merely coincidental, either; a homology between the regularities of a functioning empire and the regularities of good poetry underlay much medieval thought about why the art mattered as an ethical and political practice. The suggestion of poems like "Thirty Couplets on the High Studio" and "Facing Snow" that the norms of poetry had ceased to function against the backdrop of the Rebellion might, therefore, have been easily intelligible to a late medieval audience. What might not have made clear moral sense to them, I think, was Du Fu's interest in repeatedly exposing this development by continuing to write verse that explodes convention.

The idea that poetry was an art of order derived, ultimately, from late medieval hermeneutics of the *Classic of Poetry*. According to contemporary understanding, the *Poetry* had been used during the Zhou dynasty not only as a means of transmitting popular sentiment to the court, but also as a tool for the education and transformation of the people. According to what seems to have been a general consensus in medieval Classicist thought, this sort of education and transformation was necessary because people are born with widely varying dispositions (that is, "natures," *xing* 性) inclining them to a range of disparate virtues and vices, a range whose breadth was inherently inimical to the creation or maintenance of harmonious societies.[13] The rare people that sat at both ends of the dispositional spectrum—born sages and irredeemable fools—were understood to be incapable of changing: they would be either perfectly good or perfectly bad, depending upon their natural makeup. Everyone else, however, was susceptible to influence, and it was therefore the government's central task to make sure that the influences that affected its population were the right ones. This is where the *Poetry* came in. As discussed in the first chapter, the official Tang subcommentary on the Classics described poetry as deriving from an ancient institution whereby the sagely ruler commanded his subjects to listen to, to sing, and to dance out poems that he had determined embodied normative moral dispositions; the idea was that repeated embodiment of the sentiments manifested by such poems would improve the incompletely good natures of the people, thus contributing to the harmony of the state—not to mention the harmony of the natural world, the regular processes of which were thought to depend in part on correlative resonances with human society.[14] The goal of poetry, in other words, was the engendering of order in the state and in the cosmos, and for this reason it had to model order and the dispositions constitutive of order. And these dispositions, it was thought, were primarily characteristic of ordered ages.[15]

Though contemporary verse was not understood in the Tang as wholly continuous with the *Classic of Poetry*, accounts of its ethical and political significance often rested on a similar vision of most people's susceptibility to influence and lack of an innate moral compass. Li E 李諤 (fl. late sixth c.), for example, begins his famous memorial encouraging the Sui emperor to intervene in the contemporary literary scene—specifically, by punishing officials who wrote in styles he considered decadent—through appeal to the legendary governance of the ancient sage kings:

> Your minister has heard that, when the wise kings of antiquity transformed their people, they always changed the ways they heard and saw, set limits on their desires, blocked up their inclinations to perversity and dissolution, and showed them the road to purity and harmony. . . . Coming to later ages, however, the teaching and influence of the former kings gradually declined. The three patriarchs of the Wei dynasty [220–66] each valued literary phrasing more than the last, overlooking the great way of ruler and subject, and enjoying instead the minor arts of insect carving [i.e., ornate literary craftsmanship]. Those below followed those above like a shadow or an echo, and they began to compete in speeding their literary flourishes so that such writing eventually became the custom of the age. South of the Yangzi in Qi and Liang, the damage got even worse, as everyone whether noble or base, wise or foolish only worked at chanting verse. They wrote poem after poem without talking about anything more than the appearance of dew in the

moonlight and filled boxes by describing only windblown clouds. The vulgar people esteemed each other for such things, and the court used it to select men for office. . . . Thus, the more this sort of literary writing proliferated, the more disordered became governance. This is truly because they had thrown away the models of the great sages and tried to make use of what is useless. They had lost the root in chasing the branches, and, as these debased cultural currents spread throughout the land, fools took each other as teachers and models so that, the longer it went on, the worse it got.

臣聞古先哲王之化民也，必變其視聽，防其嗜欲，塞其邪放之心，示以淳和之路。⋯降及後代，風教漸落。魏之三祖，更尚文詞，忽君人之大道，好雕蟲之小藝。下之從上，有同影響，競騁文華，遂成風俗。江左齊、梁，其弊彌甚，貴賤賢愚，唯務吟詠。遂復遺理存異，尋虛逐微，競一韻之奇，爭一字之巧。連篇累牘，不出月露之形，積案盈箱，唯是風雲之狀。世俗以此相高，朝廷據茲擢士。⋯故文筆日繁，其政日亂，良由棄大聖之軌模，構無用以爲用也。損本逐末，流徧華壤，遞相師祖，久而愈扇。[16]

Li is not arguing here against the importance of literature as such, as some influential eleventh- and twelfth-century thinkers would.[17] Quite the contrary, his argument against the "frivolous" sorts of literature he sees as characteristic of the brief and tumultuous states of the Six Dynasties depends on the importance he ascribes to the more substantial, serious sorts of writing that characterized the glorious and long-lasting Zhou and Han. Recent literature, Li argues, has misled these states' malleable, imperfect populations, "changing what they saw and heard" in ways unpropitious to social harmony. What is necessary, therefore, is government intervention on the model of the *Poetry* to provide the people a proper moral standard.

Although Li E represents an extreme position in his animus against five-syllable verse (a development he attributes to the Wei period), his memorial is in other respects quite representative of the mainstream of seventh- and eighth-century literary criticism, which routinely justifies its aesthetic judgments by appealing to political history. Tang critics offered different accounts of this history to warrant either retaining or discarding the innovations of previous ages, as well as different accounts of the current dynasty's place in it to alternately glorify or denigrate contemporary literature.[18] Writing two years before An Lushan turned his armies against the capitals, for example, Yin Fan 殷璠 claimed that Emperor Xuanzong had "made all of the writers within the four seas follow the ancient ways, such that the *Poetry* of the Zhou dynasty is written again today."[19] Others disagreed, inevitably, and particularly in the wake of the Rebellion; Yuan Jie, for instance, lamented in the preface to his countercultural anthology *What Was in My Trunk [When I Fled the Rebellion]* 篋中集 that "the *Poetry* has not flourished for nearly a thousand years" because virtuous men, like the poets he selects, remain obscure and unrewarded, while the other "writers of recent ages have all imitated one another," according with the frivolous conventions of the age.[20] These positions may seem polarized, but they agree on the more fundamental premise that literature is to be judged by the political success of its era.

The most common late medieval assumption about poetry's moral significance, then, was that it was fundamentally social. As a result, when intellectuals spoke about the art as an ethical and political practice, they focused less on individual innovations than on writers' adoption of styles and concerns that could be linked up with the broader mores characteristic of a particular period of history.[21] They focused, that is, on those aspects of the poetic art that could be shared by many writers: those aspects that could become conventions. Individual virtue was always praiseworthy; the goal of literature (*wen*), however, was the iteration of that virtue, its propagation from a singularity into a whole culture (*wen*).[22] This goal provides one way of understanding the general conventionality of poetry in the period, its poets' apparent contentment to refine existing genres and themes rather than projecting the highly individuated voices that become characteristic of some later ages—partly through Du Fu's influence. Though to postmedieval critics the elaboration of these genres and themes may sometimes have seemed frivolous artifice, seventh- and eighth-century poets had good reason to see it as the work of refining a culture that had its roots in the ancient sage kings.

This complex of ideas also helps to explain why it is that nearly all surviving verse on the Rebellion by poets other than Du Fu centrally invokes generic, historical, mythic, or natural regularities to limit, transfigure, or transcend the chaos of the war. Especially at this moment, poetry was not given to simple witness: just as poets needed to impose patterning on their words in order to satisfy the metrical and euphonic specifications of traditional verse, so too did they feel compelled to find rhymes between the current events they described and the precedents of the literary tradition. In the context of the Rebellion, these conventional topoi provided writers with tools for the exercise of ordering agency, insights into the stable principles they felt must surely underlie even a world at war, and imagined realms into which they might flee the chaos of the age. For almost all the poets whose work survives other than Du Fu, poetry defused the potential unprecedentedness and transcended the disorienting singularity of their experience during the Rebellion and folded it back into intelligible patterns and tropologies.[23]

Du Fu's Rebellion-era verse would thus have stood out against the background provided by both the theory and practice of poetry in the late medieval period. In no case that survives did other poets so much as broach the possibility, as Du Fu does in "Thirty Couplets on the High Studio," that poetic attempts to transcend or transfigure the war's violence might fail. Similarly, no poet other than Du Fu suggests, as he does in "Facing Snow," that compulsive attempts to create poetic order might represent an insane response to the chaos of the time. In effect, he is playing in these poems the same game as all the other poets whose work survives from the Rebellion era: juxtaposing conventional patterns against the chaos of the age in the hope of controlling it thereby. Unlike them, however, he turns his attention to the incongruities of these juxtapositions and thus to how unsatisfying that game is in the current situation. By becoming self-conscious of his own attempts to escape the uncertainties of the present, he questions the moral foundations of the art of poetry in his time.

Convention's Untrustworthiness in Unprecedented Circumstances

In what few poems survive from the first year of the Rebellion, Du Fu consistently dwells on the hold that the conventions of the literary and cultural tradition have upon him, shaping "what he sees and hears" even when their influence is, under present circumstances, unwarranted. Such poetry continues to demonstrate, as much of the verse in the first chapter did, his dedication to the civilizing project of This Culture of Ours. But if this dedication was previously announced in hopeful tones, by now it has become tragic. The lessons of the tradition, Du Fu suggests, may not hold in present circumstances, leaving him without a clear compass for making sense of his experience and rendering his continued clutching to clichéd images and tropes a sad commentary on his unpreparedness to respond effectively to the violence of the moment. By highlighting the fallibility of the tradition, Du Fu's work of this period suggests that much more than the temporal political order has broken down in the Rebellion: in the collapse of poetic convention, he also demonstrates the collapse of his confidence that the tradition has taught him how the world both should and actually does function.

The result of these collapses is a poetry that continues to deploy convention, but that does so in ways that are shockingly novel. As in "Facing Snow," some of this novelty has disappeared with the poems' increasing fame. But even apparently simple poems—poems that are now among the first read by schoolchildren in China or students of Chinese literature abroad—would have been obviously subversive of generic expectations within Du Fu's eighth-century context. In the case of the following poem, for example, the touching simplicity that has made it so famous in fact registers how forcefully the conventions on which it draws are being twisted from their usual use.[24]

月夜   *Moonlit Night*

今夜鄜州月	Tonight the Fuzhou moon
閨中只獨看	she watches from her chamber alone.
遙憐小兒女	Afar, I long for my children there,
4 未解憶長安	too young to remember Chang'an.[a]
香霧雲鬟濕	Fragrant mist, her cloudlike hair damp;
清輝玉臂寒	cool glow, her jade arms cold.
何時倚虛幌	When by those diaphanous curtains
8 雙照淚痕乾	will we together shine our tear-tracks dry?

a. Chang'an may have several referents here. The first is the capital city itself, where Du Fu's children would presumably have lived while he was seeking an appointment. The second is Du Fu, marked by metonymy because he is currently in Chang'an. The third invokes the literal meaning of the city's name, "Long-Lasting Peace"; that is, the children may be too young to remember the prosperous period that preceded this warfare, for in their short lives they have now known poverty and war.

Poems on separated lovers unable to sleep and gazing at the moon went all the way back to the beginnings of the verse tradition, but no literati poet had ever written such a poem about his own wife. In almost all cases, poetry of this sort (often referred to as "boudoir lament," *guiyuan* 閨怨) concerned imagined, generic women, anonymous "palace ladies" yearning for their absent menfolk either in the spring, when their desires would conventionally be at their peak, or in autumn, when they would be aware of their fading youth. Such women, in other words, were poetic types; the interest of such poetry lay in the poet's handling of conventional topoi to draw out different resonances from a timeless situation. Du Fu, by contrast, is explicit here that he is talking about his own wife, the mother of his children, on some particular moonlit night of late 756 or early 757, in Fuzhou.

Even though this woman is his wife, however, she is no less imagined here than are the anonymous women in most such verses. The poem is thus strangely hybrid, importing the fictive process of "boudoir lament" into the generally nonfictional genre of first-person lyric. Within poems of this latter sort, acts of imagination are almost always marked and interpreted by elements of the verse that are presented as immediately given in experience; as such, it is striking that this poem does not contain even one couplet that describes what Du Fu is actually seeing or hearing at the moment the poem was written.[25] This unusual move would have drawn the attentions of an eighth-century reader to the motivations of the poet, whose own situation is so completely elided here. The poem's imagery would appear, to such a reader, a marked fiction, papering over the fact that Du Fu, as we learn in other poems from around the same period, does not even know whether his family survives.[26] Just as gazing at the moon, then, both proverbially assuaged but also reinforced the reality of separation,[27] so too do these conventional images expose their falseness in being deployed to console the poet, becoming as diaphanous as the curtains of the final couplet. In this sense, "Moonlit Night" simultaneously claims a continuity between Du Fu's situation and the long tradition of verse on separated lovers and also undermines that continuity to emphasize the lonely particularity of his present uncertainty.

Similar self-undermining deployments of traditional imagery can be found throughout the poetry Du Fu wrote at this time, including those poems that begin to earn him the appellation of Poet Historian through their attention to specific moments in the political and military history of the Rebellion. In the following poem, for example—written about the defeat of the loyalist armies at Qingban in the winter of 756—Du Fu suggests that the long tradition of frontier ballads from which he draws its imagery may distort his perception of the current situation.[28]

悲青坂   *Grieving over Qingban*

我軍青坂在東門	Our army was at Qingban, right at the eastern gate;
天寒飲馬太白窟	the weather cold, they watered their horses at Taibai's pools.[a]
黃頭奚兒日向西	Every day more brown-hairs and Xi lads went west to meet them,
4 數騎彎弓敢馳突	then their riders bent their bows and dared to attack.[b]
山雪河冰野蕭瑟	On the mountains, snow; on the river, ice; wind upon the moors;
青是烽煙白人骨	the dark is smoke from beacon fires; the white, human bones.
焉得附書與我軍	Whereby can I get a letter to our army?—
8 忍待明年莫倉卒	wait until next year, don't be hasty or rash.

The first couplets of this poem announce a problem. In the opening lines, for instance, the juxtaposition of the toponyms of the capital region with images drawn from the traditional ballad (*yuefu* 樂府) theme of "Watering My Horse at a Pool by the Great Wall"—which generally presented scenes on the empire's northern frontiers—highlights the poetic tradition's lack of conventional imagery for describing warfare around the capital. Then, in the second couplet, the names and directions are all wrong:

a. Mt. Taibai was about one hundred kilometers west of Chang'an. This line echoes the frontier ballad "Watering My Horse at a Pool by the Great Wall."

b. The "Brown-Haired Shiwei" 黃頭室韋 and the Xi (Tatabï or Qay) were two of the Northeastern tribes against which An Lushan's army had originally been stationed to defend the border regions; they had subsequently joined his rebel army.

the barbarians were supposed to attack from the west, not towards it, and in poetry they were usually the ancient enemies of Zhou and Han, not the present-day tribes of the northeast. Du Fu thus would seem to be acknowledging here that accurately representing the current situation will require updating traditional tropes, bringing the frontier to the heartland and the past into the present.

Even with these modifications, however, the old conventions nonetheless seem to be shaping what he "sees and hears" in ways that are not always trustworthy. As in frontier *yuefu*, for instance, the enemy are still bow-bearing nomads, even though most of An Lushan's armies were, in fact, Chinese regulars and had until recently served the Tang.[29] From his position behind enemy lines in Chang'an, moreover, all Du Fu can see of the battlefield in the distance are patches of dark and light. He identifies these patches as, on the one hand, the smoke of the fire pits traditionally set up on mountaintops to warn the heartland of coming barbarian incursions and, on the other, the piles of bleached bones that littered frontier ballads. Needless to say, neither of these identifications is remotely plausible in the present context.

As a whole, then, the poem presents a progressive meditation on the problems of applying the convention-bound art of poetry to a potentially unprecedented situation. In the final lines, Du Fu takes this meditation to its logical end, offering the army advice that would have flown in the face of traditional wisdom—winter, that is, being the season of the ancient sage kings' campaigns, and spring, the time peasants needed to be back on their land. The suggestion here—that present circumstances may not conform to inherited patterns—might have been sharply topical at the time this poem was written, given that the defeated loyalist forces at Qingban had employed outdated tactics their literatus-turned-commander, Fang Guan 房琯, had read about in ancient texts.[30] Certainly an urge to topicality, at least, is evident in Du Fu's wish that his poem might function as an urgent letter, a wish that registers how far his reflections on poetic convention were deforming the art.[31] Yet the fact that he couches this wish in terms of the conventional ballad closing "Whereby can I"— which usually indicates despair of some impossible hope—once again raises the question of whether his poetry serves any useful purpose against the background of the Rebellion. It cannot prevent the "unpredictable disasters" (another meaning of *cangcu* 倉卒, translated above as "hasty and rash") Du Fu fears await an army anachronistically adhering to classical precedents, no matter how disillusioned of convention he personally becomes.

Discovering Nature

If the maintenance and refinement of normative convention could no longer justify Du Fu's poetry, he would have to search out new sources of ethical and political significance to fill the breach. In the early days of the Rebellion, the most important such source he tried out was a cluster of concepts that can be roughly indicated by the word "nature." In medieval China, the "natural" or "self-so" (*ziran* 自然) denoted the way that things and people would be if they suffered no external compulsion—from social convention, for instance—and merely followed their own heaven-endowed "natures" (*xing* 性). This concept could, by extension, also cover the processes of the "natural world" (modern Chinese *ziranjie* 自然界), and poets in the Tang often appealed to the concept in taking up the role of the recluse, who removed himself from the corrupt cities of the empire into an insouciant intimacy with nature.

Naturalness would thus have been a logical second option for a poet witnessing the collapse of civilization, and many of Du Fu's contemporaries similarly turn their attentions to reclusion in their Rebellion-era work.[32] Naturalness was, in fact, generally not thought of as opposed to civilization in late medieval China. Although Classicists in this period generally held that most people's proper "natures" (*xing*) were imperfect, in need of normative conventions to rectify them, when society had become corrupt, those who were blessed with more elevated endowments could preserve themselves from malign influence by withdrawing from society. In this way, they could remain true to the sages' civilizing mission, even if they could not further it in their own times.[33]

As we saw in the previous chapter, Du Fu had long been interested in the possibility of adopting the recluse role, and natural scenes feature prominently in his poetry throughout 756. If I have not had much cause to dwell, however, on his reclusive fantasies in "Thirty Couplets on the High Studio," on the snowstorm of "Facing Snow," the moonlight of "Moonlit Night," or the cold mountains and moors of "Grieving over Qingban," it is because in each case these topics prove mere screens on which he can project his more fundamental concern for the troubled Tang state. But as spring returned to the broken empire in early 757, his focus would shift. Rather than writing nature as passive to interpretation, it would become a force upending his interpretations, significant in its own right.[34]

春望   *Gazing in Spring*

	國破山河在	The state shattered, its mountains and rivers remain;
	城春草木深	the city turns spring, thick with plants and trees.
	感時花濺淚	Feeling for the time: flowers spatter tears;
4	恨別鳥驚心	hating separation: birds suddenly startle.
	烽火連三月	Beacon fires span spring's three moons;
	家書抵萬金	letters from family trade for ten thousand gold.
	白頭搔更短	My white hair I've scratched even thinner,
8	渾欲不勝簪	almost to the point it will not hold a hatpin.[a]

The narrative of this famous poem hews closely to the basic medieval vision outlined above, of reclusion in the natural world as a second best refuge when society decays. At the beginning of the poem, nature and society seem radically opposed, and Du Fu's sympathies lie unambiguously with the human realm, against springtime's indifferently malevolent threat to swallow it whole, as it had done in ancient poems on ruined cities like "The Millet Is Lush" 黍離 and "The Wheat Is in Ear" 麥秀.[35] As the poem moves on, however, the antagonism between these apparent opposites begins to break down. Ambiguities in the syntax of the second couplet, for instance, allow for the suggestion that the natural world is less indifferent than it once seemed: that it is, rather, itself startled at and weeping for the Tang's collapse. In lines 5 and 6, conversely, human contrivances come to coopt the functions of nature, as nights previously lit by the natural waxing and waning of the moon are now illuminated by incessant fires of war, while natural emotion has been monetized.[36] By the poem's end, therefore, Du Fu's loyalty to the human world cannot be distinguished from his

---

a. Obsessive head scratching was a conventional sign of worry. To "throw away one's hatpin" was to give up on wearing the ceremonial headgear of government office—in other words, to become a recluse.

resolution to abandon it for reclusion in nature, since it is his very concern for the state that has prematurely aged and weakened him to the point that he has no option but to "throw away his court hatpin." Becoming a recluse, he could at least rejoin his family, and together with the birds and flowers of his hermitage he could mourn a society where men have become so vicious as to profit from war's separations.

If, however, the poem thus represents a virtuoso performance of a conventional theme, the method by which it enacts this reintegration of nature and civilization suggests an incipient reorientation of Du Fu's poetics. Whereas the poems previously discussed in this chapter all dramatized how convention and emotion might shape in advance what a poet "sees and hears," here, by contrast, Du Fu shows himself correcting his mistaken initial impressions through an effort to read his experience. In the second couplet, for example, the fact that the poet himself startles when he startles up hidden birds suggests to him a previously unsuspected sympathy, that he and they are equally afraid of the bow-bearing nomads who might be hunting them both. In the third couplet, similarly, the parallelism mandated by the regulated-verse form becomes a tool of thought, whereby he recognizes metal coins as petty parodies of the (conventionally metallic) moon, while the "connecting" or "spanning" (*lian* 連) constancy of the beacon fires travesties the natural regularities of human life that the war has fractured. Through these observations, Du Fu discovers that his social concern is not the opposite of "nature"—his or the larger world's—as he thought it might be in the first couplet. And it is this act of discovering that marks an important development in the maturation of his art, since it suggests that there may be something inherent in his experience that awaits investigation, something that This Culture of Ours has not fully described for him in advance.

This structure of discovery appears throughout much of Du Fu's verse in early 757, often turning up unexpected revelations about either his own nature or about the nature of a larger world that was, given late medieval theories of the correlative resonance between society and cosmos, startlingly unperturbed by the violence of the human one.[37] In certain poems from this period, such discoveries even come to replace the roles tradition had played in his youthful art. In the following poem, for example, it is nature, rather than tradition, that allows him to overcome the particularity of his situation, merging with others across time and space.[38]

哀江頭   *A Lament for the Riverside*

少陵野老吞聲哭	An old rustic of Shaoling weeps, choking back the sound,
春日潛行曲江曲	on a spring day pacing secretly by the Bending River's bends.[a]
江頭宮殿鎖千門	By the riverside, the palaces all have locked their thousand gates:
4　細柳新蒲爲誰綠	for whom now do the thin willows and fresh reeds turn green?
憶昔霓旌下南苑	I recall how rainbow banners once came down to this Southern Park,
苑中萬物生顏色	and everything within the park took on a bright complexion.[b]
昭陽殿裏第一人	She who was foremost then in the Palace of Shining Light,
8　同輦隨君侍君側	shared her lord's palanquin and attended at his side.[c]
輦前才人帶弓箭	And before their palanquin, palace ladies carried bows and arrows,
白馬嚼齧黃金勒	while their white horses champed at bits of yellow gold.
翻身向天仰射雲	They turned their bodies, faced the sky, shot upwards at the clouds,
12　一箭正墜雙飛翼	each arrow bringing down a pair of flying wings.
明眸皓齒今何在	Those bright eyes and gleaming teeth— where are they now?

a. The "Bending River," Qujiang 曲江, was a pleasure park in Chang'an.

b. The Bending River was part of a large complex of parks in the southeast of the city. One of these parks, Lotus Park, was also known as Southern Park.

c. "She who was foremost in the Palace of Shining Light" was the Han dynasty empress Zhao Feiyan 趙飛燕 (first c. BCE); the contemporary referent is Yang Guifei. The virtuous concubine Ban Jieyu 班婕妤, a contemporary and rival of Zhao Feiyan, had refused to ride in the same carriage with the emperor for fear of distracting him from his duties.

血污遊魂歸不得　blood stains their wandering souls:
　　　　　　　　　　they cannot be brought back.[d]

清渭東流劍閣深　The clear Wei flows eastward,
　　　　　　　　　　Sword Tower is deep;

16　去住彼此無消息　no news gets through between
　　　　　　　　　　those who went and stayed.[e]

人生有情淚沾臆　Humans are born to have feelings,
　　　　　　　　　　tears soak our breasts;

江水江花豈終極　the river water and river flowers
　　　　　　　　　　will never have an end.

黃昏胡騎塵滿城　At dusk, Hu horsemen raise
　　　　　　　　　　dust that fills the city,

20　欲往城南忘南北　and wanting to head to the southern wards,
　　　　　　　　　　I mix up south and north.[39]

Like "Gazing in Spring," this poem once again works over an apparent opposition between the human and the natural: here, between the palace women who will never return and the glories of nature that "put on their faces" (*sheng yanse* 生顏色) for no emperor, renewing themselves joyous and dispassionate year after year.[40] Again, moreover, this opposition is undermined by the progress of the poem, as Du Fu threads into it allusions that suggest, in the aggregate, that the ironic anthropomorphism of the spring plants "putting on their faces" may be matched by a tragic naturalness in the cycles of human emotion. Human feelings return, if not year after year, then at least dynasty after dynasty, displaying a timelessness and universality that transcends—and perhaps to some degree redeems— our mortal particularity as individuals.

The first of the programmatic allusions that delineate the poem's argument comes in Du Fu's self-designation as "an old rustic of Shaoling." Though it has never seemed so to critics used to referring to him as "Du

d. This probably refers most specifically to Yang Guifei, whom Xuanzong was compelled by his guard to execute on the first stage of his journey to Sichuan. It could refer to the other palace ladies mentioned above as well, as they might have been massacred by the invaders.

e. Sword Tower was a pass in Sichuan, along the route of Xuanzong's flight to Chengdu as An Lushan's armies closed in on the capital. The Wei was near Chang'an.

of Shaoling" 杜少陵 (perhaps on account of this poem), this phrase would have been marked for his contemporaries, none of whom, apparently, ever referred to themselves as being "from" Shaoling. In extant texts, Shaoling seems not to have been a neighborhood but rather a graveyard and wilderness close to the places Du Fu (like many other Tang men) usually calls home, Duling 杜陵 and Duqu 杜曲. If the poet refers to himself here— and, it should be noted, only here—as being from Shaoling, it seems likely that he hopes to recall to his readers' attention the original significance of the place, the ancient tomb mound of Han Emperor Xuan's 漢宣帝 (first c. BCE) beloved empress Xu Pingjun 許平君, who was murdered and for whom the emperor famously grieved.[41] The parallel to Xuanzong's recently murdered paramour Yang Guifei is unmistakable. By calling himself "a rustic of Shaoling," Du Fu may thus be implying that the "natural" landscape of the capital region is itself pregnant with imperial loves and losses, stretching back through history.

A second allusion is even more overt in its suggestion that recent events replay Han history. In the fourth couplet, Du Fu calls Yang Guifei "she who was foremost in the Palace of Shining Light," an appellation originally of the wicked-but-beautiful Han empress Zhao Feiyan 趙飛燕 (late first c. BCE). Unlike Zhao's more virtuous contemporary and one-time rival, Ban Jieyu 班婕妤, who had refused Han Emperor Cheng's 漢成帝 offer to ride with him in the same palanquin, Yang Guifei imitated Zhao in monopolizing the emperor's attentions.[42] Given that Emperor Cheng's misgovernment led to the accelerating disintegration of the Han empire, Du Fu thus suggests in this allusion that the denouement of Xuanzong's affair with Yang Guifei was predictable. Not only had emperors loved and lost before, but they had also loved too much before and thereby brought ruin upon their states.

The poem's last lines, finally, tie this suggestion of a timelessly repeating imperial cycle to a vision of spatial universality. As Du Fu "mixes up north and south" in the warhorse dust that shrouds the capital, heading north towards the court-in-exile rather than south towards his home at Duling, he echoes a Han dynasty gloss on a poem about a collapsing state from the ancient anthology *Songs of the Southlands* (*Chuci* 楚辭), which explains that "one whose thoughts are troubled may mix up north and south."[43] This allusion calls attention to a whole series of directional motifs throughout the poem, including this line's reference to a lyric from the southlands, the poem's consistent recall of the conventionally southern theme of imperial indulgence in sensual pleasures, and Du Fu's decision to call Lotus Park by its kenning "Southern Park."[44] The poem's most dramatic southernism, however, is the pointed ambiguity in the eighteenth line, in the phrase "river water and river flowers." The character for "river" in this line is *jiang* 江, sometimes a nonspecific word for watercourses—as in the name "Bending River," Qujiang 曲江—but more frequently the proper name of "the River," the Yangzi, which flowed past Xuanzong's exile at Chengdu towards the former seat of the romantic and doomed Southern Dynasties. In any other poem, therefore, the grandiose phrase "*jiang* water and *jiang* flowers will never have an end" would presumptively refer to the great riverine landscape of the south—certainly a more appropriate topic for such a sweeping statement than the Qujiang, a manmade pond that over the course of Chinese history was only infrequently in good repair. After this line, one might well wonder whether the poem's title, "A Lament for the Riverside," refers to the riverside where Du Fu is, or the riverside where Xuanzong now finds himself.

What all of these southernisms add up to, in a poem that also thematizes the distance between Swordgate and the Wei, is much the same point made in the suggestion that the flowers of Chang'an "put on their faces" now because they are literally the transfigurations of dead women buried there. If Du Fu "mixes up north and south," it is because there is, ultimately, no difference between them. The northern Tang emperor has lost his empire through indulgence in temporal pleasures just as the last emperors of the Chen and Sui dynasties had done in the south, and, like the southern poet of *Songs of the Southlands*, Du Fu here in the north has "troubled thoughts." The suggestion, I believe, is that there is something universal about the events of his time: that although our human passions divide us from the endlessly impassionate river water and river flowers, they are equally timeless. As a result, separations of time and space melt before the commonalities the poem discovers, and Du Fu finds an unexpected sympathy with the now deposed emperor, despite the terrible pass to which the latter's indulgences have brought the empire. Though "no news gets through between those who went and stayed," the poem has no need to tell us whether the person soaking his breast with tears is the rustic by this northern *jiang* or the onetime ruler by the southern. The two, despite their differences, share a human nature.

Human Nature in Du Fu Criticism

It is telling that Du Fu's turn to nature in "Gazing in Spring" and "A Lament for the Riverside" winds up recapitulating key late medieval principles despite beginning from a recognition, in poems like "Moonlit Night" and "Grieving over Qingban," that tradition might not prescribe an accurate form for contemporary experience. Apparently, he was not at this point ready to accept the more radical consequences that would ultimately flow from this break with the model that underwrote his early verse. In early 757, he still wanted his poetry to ally itself with the sages' civilizing project, even as he contemplated withdrawing from civilization, and he still wanted the art to raise him out of his particularity, perhaps especially as he grew increasingly isolated in Chang'an. Yet, in the end, the results of his appeals to nature do not seem to have satisfied him. He begins to see problems with the concept before the end of the year, and before 758 was over it had already ceased to play a major role in underwriting the proposed moral significance of his art.

Du Fu's abortive attempts to draw his orientation from nature and from human nature fit, however, into an important narrative of the Tang–Song transition. Claims about the normative importance of nature (*xing*) had recently become central to both Buddhist and Daoist thought, and they begin to appear in Classicist scholarship as well some four or five decades later.[45] Eventually, the idea that our shared human nature (*xing*) was the fundamental nature (*li* 理) of the cosmos would come, in the eleventh and twelfth centuries, to underwrite the Neo-Confucian (Daoxue 道學) reinterpretation of the Classics and, as Michael Fuller has discussed, a major revolution in poetic thought as well.[46] Much of recordizing criticism is also underpinned by a similar vision of shared human feelings, which renders plausible its basic faith that we can transparently understand the experiences of a poet as distant from us as Du Fu is. In this sense, Du Fu's experiments with the idea of nature in the early Rebellion period prefigure some of the larger claims that structure his criticism.

Here we face an interesting problem. On the one hand, that is, recordizing criticism clearly draws from the postmedieval intellectual currents with which it developed, and indeed recordizing critics often cite the technical terms of Neo-Confucian vocabulary to justify their interpretive practice.

The early Qing critic Chen Chunru 陳醇儒 (fl. 1661), for example, explains in the preface to his commentary on Du Fu's regulated verse:

> Talent, wisdom, learning, and force differ among ancient writers, as does the situation they met with in their lives, be it of order and disorder, success or frustration. Yet their emotional nature (*xing*) and the principle of things (*li*) has never differed. Du Fu used his access to this emotional nature and the principle of things to manifest them in poetry, and I use my access to them in reading his poetry and manifesting them in my annotations. Thus, my annotating Du Fu is the same as Du Fu annotating Du Fu, and Du Fu annotating Du Fu is the same as me annotating myself. If I were merely annotating Du Fu, that would be difficult; yet for Du Fu to annotate himself or for me to annotate myself—I have never heard that that would be difficult.

> 古人之才智學力與所遇之治亂通塞，遍不相同，而情性物理未嘗或異。以杜之性情物理而見之詩，以我之性情物理揆諸杜詩而見之注，是以我注杜者，以杜注杜也；以杜注杜者，猶之以我注我也。以我注杜則難，以杜注杜，以我注我，而以爲難者，未之前聞也。[47]

On the other hand, however, the recordizing tradition is not coextensive with Neo-Confucianism. We can find roughly this same vision of human nature throughout twentieth- and twenty-first-century Du Fu criticism as well, as, for instance, when the modern critic Xu Zong 許總 writes that "the study of literature is the study of humanity. The reason that excellent literature can be passed on for a thousand years is that it sets off resonances with the reader's emotions, and this is possible because such works are possessed of eternal human nature or 'pure human emotion' (in the words of Engels)."[48] The question, then, is how we should understand the contribution to Du Fu criticism of intellectual movements like Neo-Confucianism or Maoism: whether they predetermine and thus distort recordizing critics' readings of his work or whether these critics merely turn to Neo-Confucian or Marxist vocabularies in order to discuss dynamics inherent in the poetry itself.

As it happens, the concerns of Du Fu's poetry in the early days of the Rebellion offer a useful test case here, since in fact readers began to appreciate his unusual relationship to convention even before the Song dynasty development of Neo-Confucianism. The early-ninth-century literatus Yuan Zhen, for example, admired him for not being bound by convention, for "speaking directly about current times, without attaching his mind to following the ancients."[49] Yuan does not mean here that Du Fu never made use of ancient precedents or conventional styles; rather, the point is that he put such precedents and conventions to his own purposes without being dominated by them. All previous writers, Yuan wrote, had been limited to the style of one age, "those who loved antiquity forsaking new forms, and those who pursued [modern] ornamentation departing from [ancient] solidity." Du Fu, however,

> possessed all of the forms and force of all poets from antiquity to today and combined what others had monopolized singly. Even if Confucius [in compiling the *Poetry*] was seeking those with the most essential import, should we not still know to value sheer multiplicity? When it comes to being capable of what no one is capable of, to having no fixed preferences for or against anything, from the time of the ancient poets onwards, there has never been anyone like Du Fu.
>
> 盡得古今之體勢，而兼人人之所獨專矣。使仲尼考鍛其旨要，尚不知貴其多乎哉？苟以爲能所不能，無可無不可，則詩人以來，未有如子美者。[50]

Yuan suggests here that late medieval readers might indeed have seen Du Fu's freedom from convention as violating the homogeneity Confucius sought in purging the *Shijing* down to a core of morally exemplary verse. Yet for Yuan—who, like many of his revolutionary generation, was interested in the question of how to reorient his own relationship to the precedent tradition—this freedom is exciting rather than disturbing.[51] Du Fu, he suggests, transcends such narrow normativity, embracing instead all the literary possibilities developed throughout history.[52]

Yuan does not use a vocabulary of "nature" here. In the postmedieval period, however, when that vocabulary had already become a major intellectual force, critics would often link Yuan's vision of Du Fu's freedom from convention with claims about the naturalness of his verse. Huang Sheng 黃生 (1622–96), for instance, agreed that Du Fu's multiplicity made him the poetic counterpart of Confucius, the sage who originally "had no fixed preferences for or against anything" and who thus "gathered the great fulfillment" of human virtues by combining in his person the various strengths of previous sages.[53] If in Yuan Zhen's time, however, Confucius had been thought of as prescribing to all who were not sages a narrower normativity—This Culture of Ours—the Neo-Confucian Classicism characteristic of Huang's age now saw "This *Dao* of Ours" as commensurate with nature itself.

> Du Fu "gathered the great fulfillment" of poetry by ruminating upon the flowers and tracing the roots of [all its forms] from the *Sao* and *Elegantiae* [in antiquity] down to the Qi and Liang dynasties, and adding to this a penetrating and broadly comprehensive understanding of the Five Classics and the Three Histories. He was thus like the arrayed merchants of the five metropolises: there was no commodity he did not display. Or like a great general deploying his troops: there was nowhere he headed things did not go his way. . . . If one speaks of him in terms of his greatness, then we can say that his verse holds within it the primordial creative *qi* of the universe; if one speaks of him in terms of his subtlety, we can say that he enters into all the five normative human relationships; and if one speaks of him in terms of what is between heaven and earth, we can say that he has exhausted all there is. This is how he combines the creations of all previous eras and serves as the mold and model of This *Dao* of Ours.
>
> 杜詩所以集大成者，以其上自騷雅，下迄齊梁，無不咀其英華，探其根本，加以五經三史，博綜貫穿，如五都列肆，百貨無所不陳，如大將用兵，所向無不如意。…以言乎大則含元氣，以言乎細則入五倫，以言乎天地之間則備矣。此所以兼前代之制作，而爲斯道之範圍也與？[54]

In stark contradistinction to the visions of literary-historical decline so often invoked in late medieval discussions to ground claims about normative conventions, Huang Sheng envisions the conventions of the precedent tradition as analogous to the many commodities on sale on the market streets of a great metropolis: they do not conflict with one another as normative and debased but rather represent a richness and variety that mirrors the fecundity of the universe itself. Because they do not conflict, moreover, these conventions can serve Du Fu as a repertoire to be deployed, like troops on a battlefield, according to the demands of the situation. The vastness of Du Fu's learning thus allows him, for Huang, not only to mirror but also to do justice to the vastness of creation—to be, in a cliché Stuart Sargent has described as going back to the Song, "*Urdichter* of the *Ursprache*," the "Universal Poet" whose creativity is indistinguishable from nature's own.[55]

Beyond linking Yuan Zhen's sense of Du Fu's multiplicity with the fecundity of nature, moreover, postmedieval critics connected it with Neo-Confucian ideas about our shared human nature as well. In the preface to his great commentary on Du Fu's poetry, Wang Sishi would echo Yuan's by then well-known claims by arguing that only two poets in the post-Classical tradition truly instantiated the normative poetics of the *Shijing*—understood, that is, as "inscribing natural human emotion [in its] innumerable permutations." The first of these poets, Tao Qian, wrote before the conventions of the art had reached their full development, and, although writing came easy to him, he was thus limited in comparison to Du Fu. When it came to Du Fu, however,

> there was no book he had not read; no form he had not mastered; no famous writer from antiquity onward whose style he did not combine; and no experience, be it attainment or loss, glory or disgrace, exile or difficulty, that he did not undergo. . . . Therefore, every time he was stirred by something, there was no part of the scene that he did not enter into and no part of his true emotion he did not express; the scene and his emotion assisted each other, and there was no part of his talent that was not expressed, no aspect of the poem that did not fit with proper technique.
>
> 於書無所不讀，於律無所不究，於古來名家無所不綜，於得喪榮辱、流離險阻無所不歷。⋯ 故一有感會，於境無所不入，於情無所不出；而情境相傳，於才無所不伸，而於法又無所不合。[56]

For Wang, Du Fu lived at the consummation of poetry's formal evolution. Tao Qian was "natural" in a limited sort of way: he wrote merely what came to mind, "making poetry out of the self" (*yi wo wei shi* 以我爲詩) but without being able to do that self full justice. Du Fu, by contrast, had a complete repertoire of poetic conventions at his disposal and was able to give expression to all the possible experiences of human subjectivity. His work thus provides the most comprehensive account available of "the self"—a reality that is not ultimately individual but rather shared in much the way it was thought to be by Neo-Confucian philosophers.

If critics like Huang Sheng and Wang Sishi linked Yuan's observations to Neo-Confucian vocabularies, however, other recordizing critics appealed to other intellectual traditions. Buddhism, for example, was sometimes invoked to explain how it was that Du Fu might be simultaneously the most learned and the most natural of poets, deploying conventions appropriately to describe his experience while nonetheless managing not to be constrained by them. As Yuan Haowen 元好問 (1190–1257) writes,

> The wonder of Du Fu is like what the Buddhists talk about: being so learned as to arrive at being unlearned. When we read his poems nowadays, they seem soaked in primordial *qi*, following their objects and fully manifesting their forms. They are like the waters of the Three Great Rivers and the Five Great Lakes merging into the sea, surging and vast, without any bank; or like auspiciously glowing colored clouds, capable of a thousand, ten thousand transformations, surpassing all description. . . . Therefore, one can rightly say that no word of Du Fu's poems lacks a precedent source and also rightly say that his poetry does not come from these ancient sources.

> 子美之妙，釋氏所謂學至於無學者耳。今觀其詩，如元氣淋漓，隨物賦形；如三江五湖，合而爲海，浩浩瀚瀚，無有涯涘；如祥光慶雲，千變萬化，不可名狀。…故謂杜詩爲無一字無來處，亦可也；謂不從古人中來，亦可也。[57]

Yuan is correcting here a potential misperception that might derive from the cliché, first articulated by Huang Tingjian 黄庭堅 (1045–1105), that "no word of Du Fu's lacks a precedent source."[58] That does not mean, Yuan avers, that Du Fu's poetry is ultimately heteronomous. Rather, Du Fu's learning accomplishes a paradox best compared to a Buddhist ideal, by which the accumulation of artifice eventually allows one to break through to a state beyond it. In this state, Du Fu's verse becomes as effortlessly miraculous as the processes of the natural world.

What makes Yuan Haowen's invocation of Buddhism particularly interesting, for my purposes here, is the way it restates in a new vocabulary the insight that Huang Tingjian had articulated, originally, through Daoist metaphors. Huang took Du Fu as the central model in his advocacy of a highly allusive poetry that, he claimed, could nonetheless be more natural than less erudite sorts of composition.

When Du Fu wrote poetry or when Han Yu wrote prose, there was not a single word that did not derive from a precedent source. It's just that we later people read few books, and so we say that Han Yu and Du Fu created these phrases for themselves. But of old, those [like Du Fu and Han Yu] who were skilled at writing were truly capable of molding and smelting the myriad things, and so even when they took the stale words of old writers, their brush was like the grain of numinous cinnabar that turns iron into gold.

老杜作詩，退之作文，無一字無來處。蓋後人讀書少，故謂韓、杜自作此語耳。古之能爲文章者，眞能陶冶萬物，雖取古人之陳言入於翰墨，如靈丹一粒，點鐵成金也。[59]

Although Huang Tingjian's alchemical metaphors have occasioned much scholarly discussion, the basic point here is clear enough.[60] Like a Daoist practitioner who masters the *dao*'s "molding and smelting" of the cosmos, great writers like Du Fu can transform mere conventions into sincere statements of their own natural feelings. For Huang, indeed, Du Fu's immersion in the resources of the tradition allowed him to express his feelings fully and directly without worrying about the medium he used to express them. Having thoroughly absorbed the repertoire this tradition provided him, its elements came to him as easily as language itself, and he "never gave any thought to the writing" (*wu yi yu wen* 無意於文).[61]

Whatever their vocabulary, then, both late medieval readers and postmedieval critics have recognized that Du Fu was doing something interesting and different with poetic convention. And though recordizing critics have consistently connected this aspect of his art with a concept of "naturalness," they have drawn on a remarkably diverse range of philosophical and religious systems to do so. I would suggest, therefore, that it was not exclusively the intellectual developments of the Tang–Song transition that drove recordizing reading's initial interest in these topics—and it is certainly not these developments that drive it now. Instead, we can begin to discern here the basic pattern that will structure the discussions of Du Fu criticism throughout the rest of this book. Now that Du Fu's work has started to break away from the late medieval model, recordizing critics display a consistent insight into the problems with which he grapples, elaborated by means of the various intellectual and spiritual vocabularies available to them. These elaborations, however, tend to be recuperative, as is perhaps inevitable when it comes to a figure as canonical as Du Fu:

contemporary ideas are sought out primarily when they can explain how it might be that he had good reason to focus on the issues they describe. And recuperative reading of this sort has ambivalent implications. On the one hand, it guarantees that, even as their vocabularies change, critics will continue to concern themselves with the problems his verse manifests. On the other hand, however, it ensures they will rarely recognize how problematic these topics were for him.

Estranged from Nature and Convention

The reconciliation of nature and convention characteristic of recordizing reading results in a rather irenic account of poetry. Not only can verse no longer be the arena wherein opposed conventions battled to determine the fate of the empire—as it was, implicitly, for the late medieval period—but there is little room, furthermore, for the sorts of artistic and intellectual dilemmas with which Du Fu grappled in these early months of the Rebellion. Poetry now gives voice primarily to natural emotion, and emotion tends merely to lubricate the spontaneous, uncomplicated expression characteristic of the best verse. As Zhang Jin 張溍 (1621–78) puts it, the depth of Du Fu's emotion renders his poetry "true to the extreme of truth," with "every line coming right out of real circumstances and real affairs, as if one were seeing his heart or hearing him speak, without any artifice (*wenzi* 文字, literally "written words") intervening."[62]

When read against the particular poem Zhang is praising here, this comment showcases both recordizing reading's insight into Du Fu's rhetoric of naturalness in this period and also its insensitivity towards his self-conscious problematizing of convention. The poem in question was written in the autumn of 757, a few months after Du Fu had escaped Chang'an through the rebel battle lines to the imperial court-in-exile. On arriving there, he was rewarded for his daring by being made "Reminder of the Left" 左拾遺, the sort of office he had always hoped for, in close service to the new emperor, Suzong 肅宗. Though briefly elated, he was soon embroiled in the factional infighting of the unsettled court and returned in his poetry to the fantasies of reclusion he had previously entertained in poems like "Gazing in Spring." In the following poem, however, naturalness seems out of reach.[63]

述懷一首　　*Telling What Is in My Breast*[a]

	去年潼關破	It was last year that Tong Pass broke:
	妻子隔絕久	long I've been separated from wife and children.
	今夏草木長	But this summer, when the plants and trees grew tall,
4	脫身得西走	I escaped and was able to flee west.
	麻鞋見天子	In hemp sandals I presented myself to the Son of Heaven;
	衣袖露兩肘	my clothes showed both elbows through the sleeves.[b]
	朝廷愍生還	The court took pity on my having returned alive;
8	親故傷老醜	old friends were pained at how old and ugly I'd become.
	涕淚授拾遺	With tears I was given the post of Reminder:
	流離主恩厚	our lord's beneficence was substantial towards this refugee.
	柴門雖得去	I might have been allowed to go to my ramshackle gate,
12	未忍即開口	but I could not bring myself to open my mouth right away.
	寄書問三川	I had sent a letter inquiring of Three Rivers,
	不知家在否	not knowing whether my family survived.[c]
	比聞同罹禍	Recently I've heard all there met disaster,
16	殺戮到雞狗	butchered down to the chickens and the dogs.
	山中漏茅屋	In the mountains under a leaking thatch roof,
	誰復依戶牖	is there anyone still gazing out the doors and windows?
	摧頹蒼松根	Or at the roots of broken, graying pines,
20	地冷骨未朽	the ground so cold their bones have not yet rotted?
	幾人全性命	Even if a few are still alive and well,
	盡室豈相偶	the whole household surely will not meet again.
	嶔岑猛虎場	Mountainous and steep, that land of fierce tigers;
24	鬱結廻我首	knotted up with grief, I turn my head.
	自寄一封書	Since they last sent me a letter,
	今已十月後	it has already been ten months.
	反畏消息來	Now instead I dread that news will come—

a. Early, probably authorial, note: "This was written after I escaped from among the rebels and made it to Fengxiang" 此已下自賊中竄歸鳳翔作.

b. Wearing a gown so threadbare that both elbows showed through was a sign of Confucian commitment in the *Hanshi waizhuan*.

c. Du Fu's family was still in Three Rivers County in Fuzhou.

28	寸心亦何有	what feelings are there in this one-inch heart?[d]
	漢運初中興	The fortune of the Han now begins to rise anew,[e]
	平生老耽酒	but all my life I have been a lover of ale.
	沈思歡會處	I yearn deeply for a moment of joyous reunion,
32	恐作窮獨叟	and fear I'm an old man, at road's end alone.

As Zhang Jin implicitly recognized, this poem claims to discover the truth of Du Fu's nature, which he himself had previously misunderstood. This discovery is accomplished formally by a bookending pair of allusions to that paradigmatic poet of nature and naturalness, the recluse Tao Qian. In the third line, Du Fu quotes Tao's famous series "Reading the *Classic of Mountains and Seas*" 讀山海經詩, in which Tao describes himself happily ensconced within his rustic dwelling as the "plants and trees grow tall in mid-summer."[64] The allusion is easily missed, since Du Fu's situation is much the opposite of Tao's: he is far from home, very much in hardship, and still hoping to serve the empire. But the echo will become significant—will be discovered, as it were—in the third-to-last line of the poem, when he comes to recognize that, like Tao, he has by nature always been a "lover of ale" and that, instead of aspiring to a court post, he would rather be a recluse, in a ramshackle hut surrounded by trees grown tall, enjoying the natural bonds of family life.

Yet if the poem thus enacts the structure of learning from experience that will be Du Fu's major poetic takeaway from this period, the identification of his nature with Tao Qian's naturalness undermines Zhang Jin's claims as to the complete transparency of its artifice. Despite its apparent earnestness and simplicity, that is, the poem is highly literate and built around ironic puns. Constrained to the court-in-exile by the emperor's generosity, for example, Du Fu is "at the end of his road" (*qiong* 窮) not in the usual sense of that word—the sense recluses were "at the end of their road" when they had no path to advancement, or that Tao Qian was when

d. Traditionally, the Chinese took the seat of consciousness to be the heart. Its diminutive size, about one square Chinese "inch" (*cun* 寸), was frequently contrasted with the vastness of the feelings it could contain.

e. The Han dynasty had been restored after the Wang Mang 王莽 interregnum (9–23 CE) and lasted another two hundred years. Du Fu is suggesting that the Tang's fortunes will follow the same path.

he became so destitute he had to beg for food—but rather in the unexpected sense of having no path back to the naturalness such recluses embodied.[65] At this point in the war, he imagines, the cold pine trees surrounding his brushwood hermitage in Fuzhou will be broken and graying, sheltering not his wife and children but only their unrotted bones. Since in another life these trees could have served as conventional symbols for the fortitude of the recluse, or echoes of the famous five willows that surrounded Tao Qian's hermitage, this macabre fantasy complicates Du Fu's final recognition that he is, by nature, suited to a reclusion like Tao's.[66] After these distortions of convention, this discovery can only be ironic, a realization that his circumstances may have conspired to permanently estrange him from himself.

A short time later, Du Fu did receive a letter from his family; miraculously, they had all survived the fighting up north. Immediately, his thoughts turned again to "shouldering a hoe," as Tao Qian had famously done in his reclusion.[67] In the short time he had held his post as Reminder, Du Fu had already incurred Suzong's anger by remonstrating against the demotion of prime minister Fang Guan, who (aside from having blundered several important battles against An Lushan's army, including that at Qingban) seems to have gained a reputation for corruption and indolence. Du Fu was arrested for this offense and sentenced to punishment; before the sentence was executed, however, friends intervened to secure him a pardon and the chance to return to his post. When he was subsequently granted leave to visit his family—leave that might perhaps have doubled as a temporary dismissal—he considered giving up his governmental ambitions for good. Shortly after arriving at the hermitage he had so recently "discovered" suited his nature, however, he found nature and naturalness incapable of satisfying his restless mind.[68]

羌村 *Qiang Village*

I

	峥嵘赤雲西	Towering red clouds, and from their west
	日腳下平地	shafts of sunlight fall on level land.
	柴門鳥雀噪	A brushwood gate, sparrows clamor—
4	歸客千里至	a traveler of a thousand miles has come.
	妻孥怪我在	My wife and children are shocked I'm here;

驚定還拭淚	when their alarm settles, they wipe away tears.
世亂遭飄蕩	I was buffeted in the troubles of the age;
8　生還偶然遂	it was by chance that I was able to return alive.
鄰人滿牆頭	Neighbors crowd the tops of the walls,
感歎亦獻欷	stirred to sighs, and even weeping.
夜闌更秉燭	As night fades I once more take candle in hand,
12　相對如夢寐	and we face each other as if in a dream.

II

晚歲迫偷生	In my late years, I've been forced to steal my life,[a]
還家少歡趣	so even returning home affords little pleasure.
嬌兒不離膝	My beloved son ever hangs about my knees,
4　畏我復卻去	fearing that I might go away again.[69]
憶昔好追涼	I recall how I used to love finding cool spots here,[b]
故繞池邊樹	and therefore wander about the trees by the pond.
蕭蕭北風勁	But whistling comes the fierce north wind,
8　撫事煎百慮	and as I mull what's happened, a hundred cares simmer.
賴知禾黍收	Fortunately, I know the harvest has come in;
已覺糟牀注	I already imagine myself working my mash bin.[c]
如今足斟酌	If for now there is enough for me to drink,
12　且用慰遲暮	for the while I'll take its comfort in my twilight years.

III

群雞正亂叫	The chickens just now are squawking wildly:
客至雞鬭爭	when visitors come, they raise a ruckus.
驅雞上樹木	I drive the chickens up the trees,
4　始聞叩柴荊	and only then hear the knock at my brushwood gate.
父老四五人	Old men of the village, four or five of them,
問我久遠行	coming to visit after my long and distant travels.
手中各有攜	In their hands, each has something he brought;
8　傾榼濁復清	we tip the jars, both the thick and the clear.
苦辭酒味薄	Bitterly they tell me that the ale is weak
黍地無人耕	as there's no one to plow the millet fields.

a. The phrase rendered here as "to steal one's life" means, roughly, to eke out a disgraceful life rather than dying with honor.

b. As Yang Lun points out, Du Fu had left Qiang Village in the summer of the previous year; he was writing now in the late fall.

c. That is, Du Fu will ferment the harvested grains to make ale, as Tao Qian did in his reclusion.

	兵革既未息	And since the warfare has not yet ended,
12	兒童盡東征	all their sons are on campaign in the east.
	請為父老謌	Old men, let me make a song for you;
	艱難媿深情	I am ashamed by your deep kindness in hardship.
	歌罷仰天歎	My song finished, I look up to heaven and sigh,
16	四座淚縱橫	and tears stream freely all around.

As did Zhang Jin's comment on "Telling What Is in My Breast," critical discussions of this series both epitomize recordizing reading's insight into Du Fu's poetics in this period and showcase its smoothing of his work's internal conflicts. Fu Gengsheng 傅庚生 (1910–84), for instance, is certainly right to emphasize the unadorned directness of the poems' style and their implicit claim to thus match the common circumstances of village life they describe:

> Shen Hanguang 申涵光 [1618–77] wrote: "Du Fu's 'neighbors crowd the tops of the walls' and 'the chickens just now are squawking wildly' describe the situation of a farmer's household in the village as if I could see it before my eyes. People today who complain of not having material for poems are merely weak of talent and cowardly, for if you look at poems like these, what is there that is not material for poetry?" [It seems to me, however,] that if you write so as to be true to reality and faithfully reflect the truth, then you will naturally be able to describe feeling and scene "as if one could see it." . . . There is, in fact, nothing mysterious about this: one merely needs to write down one's real situation and true feelings, and it will be good poetry.[70]

Fu is also insightful in tying this homely, straightforward style to these poems' potential for serving as a "collective cry of grief and anguish on behalf of all the people of disordered ages, an image of people fleeing from disaster that has archetypal meaning."[71] Something like this articulation of common woes through the details of one person's experience is almost explicitly Du Fu's goal in the last couplets of the third poem. Chen Yixin therefore concurs, commenting on this series that

> the world is always the same, with certain scenes and emotions repeating themselves constantly. . . . The virtue of these poems, therefore, is just that Du Fu was able to take the common affairs and shared feelings that people

in ages of disorder all might experience and express them in common language, thus making the scene appear right in front of the reader's eyes.[72]

For Chen, further evidence for this claim lies in the frequency with which this series echoes images and scenes from Tao Qian's verse, proving, thereby, that life has certain constancies great poets can discern.

Yet insightful as these comments are, recordizing reading's emphasis on Du Fu's ideal transparency to the natural poetry of his experience also causes these critics to miss how ironic these echoes of Tao Qian prove. Read with an understanding that naturalness was itself a convention that could be subverted no less viciously than Du Fu had the other conventions of the contemporary art, these echoes suggest once again not continuities between Du Fu and Tao Qian, but rather the difficulty Du Fu has in imitating the great recluse's paradigmatic naturalness or making himself at home in reclusion. In the first poem, for instance, neither Du Fu nor his family can truly enjoy their long-awaited reunion: where his wife is "shocked" at his survival in a way that verges on reproach (*guai* 怪), he seems almost unable to see his loved ones, instead watching his neighbors over the fence and later getting up repeatedly in the night to reassure himself by candlelight that they are not, in fact, a cruel dream. In the second verse, similarly, Du Fu is so absorbed by his "simmering cares" that he cannot appreciate the cool shade by the village pond, and he is so abstracted from his family that his son fears he is about to leave again. And when he turns in the third poem to the ale Tao was famous for brewing, he finds it not only too watery to get him drunk; worse, its thinness symbolizes the collapsing empire from which he hoped it would allow him to escape.

Although the old men who bring Du Fu this ale recall the neighbor who brought a similar gift to Tao in his "Drinking Ale No. 9" 飲酒其九, therefore, this third poem represents a striking inversion of Tao's. In that poem, Tao's visitor urged him to give up his reclusion and return to life at the court, counsel that Tao rejected by reasoning that "going against one's own nature (*wei ji* 違己) is certainly a mistake."[73] For Tao, the question of what his nature was, what he truly wanted, was unproblematic, and he was happy to "enjoy a drink" with his neighbor, unperturbed by his unwanted counsel. Du Fu, however, has become deeply unsure what he wants and what his nature prescribes. Even though he is now, to all appearances, a recluse householder like Tao, he cannot keep his mind off the larger troubles of the state.

If Du Fu learned in "Gazing in Spring" that he had a deeper allegiance to nature than to the crumbling state, what he discovers over the course of these three poems is that being "natural" is not his nature after all—that naturalness, instead, is but one more convention that does not match his experience. These poems are not, therefore, evidence that all experience is inherently poetic, pace Fu Gengshen and Chen Yixin. Instead, they focus on how frustratingly unpoetic Du Fu's experience remains in this period of disorder. The convention-bound art of poetry, he has learned, cannot present his life directly or completely, any more than he could either take in at first or ultimately enjoy his long-awaited reunion with his family. Before the Rebellion, the tradition allowed him to know in advance what his experience meant and could mean. Now, by contrast, he has to learn about himself in unexpected discoveries and—as this sequential series of three poems hints—over time.

FOUR

Narrative and Experience

Poems of the Western Frontiers (late 759)

With the outbreak of the Rebellion in 755, it becomes possible to read Du Fu's poetry as a narrative, tracking both his movements and his thought from month to month. This sort of reading was not a major part of the experience of poetry in Du Fu's age, when poetry collections usually circulated without extensive historicizing commentaries, out of chronological order, and in fragments. Simple narratives were sometimes discernible within the work of particularly famous poets: readers could guess, for instance, which of Tao Qian's poems were written after he retired into his famous reclusion, which of Yu Xin's 庾信 (513–81) were written after the fall of the Liang dynasty, and roughly where most of Xie Lingyun's occasional poetry fit in the vicissitudes of his life. It had, however, never been possible to trace the development of a poet's thinking with the chronological detail that becomes characteristic of Du Fu's collection from 756 on. This point, indeed, seems not to have been lost on Du Fu himself, and in late 759 he began pointedly exploring the affordances of the new poetic form he had begun, perhaps unwittingly at first, to pioneer. In the poems to be discussed in this chapter, he considers the possibility that narrative might replace convention as the ground of poetic meaning: that his world, personality, and experience might be interpreted definitively by their unfolding in time. This project fails almost immediately. But when it does, it fails in ways that lay the groundwork for his mature verse.

In taking up this watershed moment in Du Fu's collection, I am skipping over much of his most famous work, written from the autumn of 757 until the autumn of 759. Shortly after arriving at Qiang Village, Du Fu learned that the imperial armies were on the verge of recapturing the capital, and when Emperor Suzong triumphantly returned to Chang'an in the winter of 757, he followed the procession and resumed his post as Reminder. For a brief, joyous moment after the beginning of the new year, he seems to have hoped that both empire and poetry could return to what they had been, and we find him writing court and social occasional verse scarcely distinguishable from that of the other officials who wrote with him.[1] He quickly grew discouraged again with court politics, however, and in the early autumn of 758, he was demoted to a lowly local post on the outskirts of the capital region. Over the next year, he began to write poetry that charts a deepening of the disorientation in which we left him in the last chapter. This verse, I would argue, continues to achieve its characteristic greatness not through making compelling sense of experience, but in exploring its inability to do so. But because it does not pioneer new models of moral sense-making that would shape Du Fu's mature work, I do not discuss it here.[2]

In the early autumn of 759, as the rebel army appeared poised once again to capture Luoyang, Du Fu made a momentous decision. Abandoning his post, he fled with his family to Qinzhou 秦州, a remote border commandery on the far western frontier of the empire, where he perhaps hoped they would be safe from the state's unraveling.[3] This radical and, in retrospect, rash decision marked an end to any realistic hope that he would ever serve again in the central government and thus to the aspirations that had largely defined the first forty-seven years of his life. It would, however, also mark the beginning of a renewed dedication to the art of poetry, which he began at this point to write at a clip that dwarfs the productivity of anyone the tradition had seen up to his time.[4] This productivity, in turn, seems to have enabled his experimentation with narrative.[5] In the final six months of the year, not only did he compose three unprecedentedly long narrative sequences, but he also proceeded to arrange these—via palinodic techniques built into the later sequences, which thus reflect back on the earlier—into a larger sequence of sequences: effectively, an extended narrative of his physical and spiritual progress in exile.

In linking individual poems into a narrative, these series inaugurate a new mode of poetic sense-making that provides powerful justification to some of the recordizing procedures, noted in the first chapter, that did not apply easily to his early work. Though Du Fu would largely abandon narrative sequences after 759—he writes only one more, to be discussed in the final chapter—these sets provide miniature templates for the way that recordizing critics have structured his poetic oeuvre as a whole in their chronologically organized editions and in the year charts they have composed to track his poetic productivity from month to month. In such works and in the interpretations they support and encourage, his poetry becomes a detailed and continuous dramatization of his life, almost a vast poetic series structured by a chronological logic that reaches across the boundaries of any one poem or set. In this respect, the sequences to be considered here—which were in their time a striking innovation within a tradition dominated by short, episodic forms—can be understood as first broaching some of the ideas that would become central to the recordizing account of Du Fu's significance and, gradually, to Chinese poetic reading writ large.

Narrative Discovered

Having by the time he arrived in Qinzhou effectively abandoned his ambition to serve the state, Du Fu seems to have felt the need now to conform himself to a different moral script. Reclusion was the obvious candidate, and, in the first two narrative series he wrote on the western frontiers, it is a vision of reclusion that provides the telos to his narratives. Yet he was acutely aware, as soon as he arrived in Qinzhou, that the region did not provide an obvious setting for the visionary reclusion he imagined for himself. For this reason, in the first long autobiographical series that he wrote there, he employs narrative to project the possibility that, the more he learns about the place, the more it might reveal itself an ideal spot for his hermitage after all.

"Twenty Miscellaneous Poems of Qinzhou" 秦州雜詩二十首, the title of this first series, does not much suggest that what follows will be a narrative.[6] For the first few poems, in fact, it is difficult to discern any real structure to the set, as each poem seems a self-sufficient regulated verse more concerned with the internal correspondences characteristic of the form than with any linkages between poems. At first glance, the only connection between the first and second poems in the series—which describe, respectively, Du Fu's journey west and his visit to a monastery on the outskirts of town—would seem to lie in his regret at having come to Qinzhou, which he describes in the first poem according to traditional poetic tropes of the inhospitable and barbarian western frontiers. By the third poem, however, we can begin to discern a rough sequence underlying these moments of perception and feeling.[7]

III

州圖領同谷	By the province map, it administers Tonggu;
驛道出流沙	the post-station road goes out to Flowing Sands.[a]
降虜兼千帳	Surrendered caitiffs, together a thousand tents;
4　居人有萬家	settled folk make ten thousand households.
馬驕珠汗落	From mettlesome horses pearls of sweat fall;
胡舞白題斜	on dancing barbarians, whitened foreheads tilt.[b]
年少臨洮子	The young men, the boys of Lintao,
8　西來亦自誇	even boast about coming from the west.[c]

Where the second poem ended with the poet looking back east with homesick yearning, this one finds him looking west with xenophobic concern; clearly, he does not want to be here. Although there are ten thousand settled households in the region, there remain an uncomfortable number of nomads living in tents, mobile on their horses, and dancing with ritually improper abandon, their pride in their western heritage threatening the dissolution of the imperial Qinzhou administration into the liquidity of the Flowing Sands. Yet at the same time as Du Fu continues to see here the dangerous "barbarian" nomads that did endless battle with the Han throughout several centuries of border ballads, the very fact that he is consulting a map suggests that, despite his misgivings, he is at least beginning to explore Qinzhou, possibly with an eye towards settling here. In even noting the mixed ethnicity of the region—one of the complicated facts about the Tang frontiers that rarely appears in frontier poetry—he is beginning to discover things about the place he did not expect.[8]

a. Tonggu is modern-day Cheng County 成县, about a hundred kilometers due south of Qinzhou. "Flowing Sands" is an ancient name for the Gobi Desert.

b. "Whitened foreheads" seems to refer to a passage in the *Records of the Historian*, where it was the mark of one Xiongnu tribe. "Barbarians" translates *hu* 胡, the term that originally designated the Xiongnu but had come by Tang times to serve as a nonspecific ethnonym for several groups of non-Han peoples from China's west.

c. Lintao, modern-day Lintan 臨潭, was about three hundred kilometers to the west of Qinzhou, beyond the borders of the Chinese state.

Du Fu's increasing openness to observation begins, gradually, to transform his sense of Qinzhou and, eventually, of himself. Another complicating reality of the frontier that rarely appears in frontier ballads concerned the makeup of Tang armies, which were manned in significant part by border peoples whose service was a condition of their surrender.[9] In the present moment, that meant that the "barbarian" population of Qinzhou was suffering from the effects of the Rebellion even more grievously and working harder to end it than Du Fu was himself, a point he notes explicitly in the sixth poem. Rather than seeing Qinzhou as the weird, inhuman frontier he had imagined at first, therefore, he begins to understand it as part of the Chinese cultural world and thus as a place where he could conceive of settling down.[10]

VIII

	聞道尋源使	I hear tell the envoy seeking the River's source,
	從天此路迴	came back from heaven along this route.[a]
	牽牛去幾許	From the Oxherd star, then, how far are we?
4	宛馬至今來	Fergana horses arrive here to this day.[b]
	一望幽燕隔	I gaze out towards You-Yan, cutoff:
	何時郡國開	when will those provinces be liberated?[c]
	東征健兒盡	Marched off east, our regulars are gone;
8	羌笛暮吹哀	a Tibetan flute blows sadly at dusk.[d]

The invocation in the first couplet here of the famous explorer Zhang Qian suggests that Qinzhou has been part of the Chinese world since the Han dynasty. Its location along Zhang's legendary "return" path from heaven,

a. The "envoy" is Zhang Qian 張騫 (second c. BCE), who first explored Central Asia and played a role in establishing Han dominance in the region now called Xinjiang. Since the source of the Yellow River was sometimes said to be heaven, some legends had Zhang visiting heaven on his western journey.

b. Horses from the Fergana Valley region were commonly known as "heavenly horses" 天馬, thus making them an apt parallel for the Oxherd star.

c. You and Yan were historical names for the base area of the rebels in the far northeast.

d. This flute playing might recall the "Rhapsody on Recalling Old Friends" 思舊賦 by Xiang Xiu 向秀 (227?–72). In this piece, Xiang hears the sound of a flute and is reminded of dead friends and the pleasures they shared together.

moreover, marks it as the site of one of the Han's greatest glories: the capture of the Hexi corridor that provided access to Central Asia, the Silk Road, and the "heavenly" steeds that continued to serve in Chinese armies to the present day. These Fergana horses also draw Qinzhou into the Chinese world in a less triumphant way as well. In the fifth poem of the series, Du Fu had observed that they had all but disappeared from Qinzhou's famous pasturelands, having been requisitioned to fight the rebels in the east; here he notices that Qinzhou's garrison has too marched off to its doom. All that remain now are a few lonely troops, whose flute playing—even if it is a "Tibetan" flute and thus a sign that the troops are "barbarians"—may echo the reminiscences of dead friends a flute recalled to Xiang Xiu in a famous rhapsody.[11] With the eastern part of the heartland now lost, the center of the Chinese world seems almost to have shifted westward, allowing Du Fu to see even Qinzhou's non-Chinese inhabitants as partaking of the recognizably human emotions at the core of the Chinese canon.

This revaluation of Qinzhou starts Du Fu searching for a suitable place to make a home here. He considers several possibilities, even joking that, were he able to live at the imperial post station, he would be able to feel like he was still living in the capital suburbs, with the bustle and hubbub of dignitaries passing through. Eventually, however, he comes to find the constant booming of the war drums from the Qinzhou garrison an oppressive reminder of the Tang's troubles and sets about exploring a village he has heard of in the mountains to the southeast of the county seat.[12]

XIII

	傳道東柯谷	They say that Eastbough Valley
	深藏數十家	in its depths hides a few dozen homes.
	對門藤蓋瓦	Facing their gates, wisteria covers the rooftiles;
4	映竹水穿沙	shining through bamboo, waters thread the sand.
	瘦地翻宜粟	The thin soil is surprisingly good for millet,
	陽坡可種瓜	and on the sunlit slopes one can plant melons.[a]

a. Du Fu may be thinking here of the famous melons planted by Shao Ping 召平, former marquis of Dongling, after he became a recluse following the collapse of the Qin dynasty in 206 BCE.

舩人近相報   May the boatman let me know when we get close:

8   但恐失桃花   I only fear I'll miss the peach blossoms.[b]

Comparing this poem with the third in the series reveals how much Du Fu's perspective has changed. Where at first Qinzhou seemed an outpost beyond the Chinese world, now he sees it as almost too Chinese, too bound up with the fate of the empire, and too populous with its thousand tents of barbarians and ten thousand settled families. In Eastbough Valley, therefore, he seeks to join a much smaller community of only several dozen families, an analogue, he hopes, of Tao Qian's "Peach Blossom Spring." In contrast to the third poem, where he sought out the county map to make sense of the region, here it is precisely Eastbough's hiddenness that he finds attractive, offering as it does the possibility that the place may avoid violence should the Rebellion engulf the empire as a whole. And where in the third poem Du Fu worried that the region would liquefy back into the Flowing Sands desert, here he imagines the sands of Eastbough flowing with water enough to plant melons of the sort the famous recluse Shao Ping once lived off when the empire he served collapsed.

These several echoes of the third poem in the thirteenth are not a coincidence: though unannounced by Du Fu (and, as far as I have found, unnoticed by previous critics), each poem in the series forms a parallel with its counterpart across the halfway mark, poem XI recalling poem I and poem XX recalling poem X. Through these systematic correspondences, Du Fu reflects upon what has changed during his time in Qinzhou, threading together apparently disconnected verses into a narrative that seems to have an increasingly definite drift to it. As the series moves along, in fact, even initially recalcitrant details are taken up into its advancing progress: Qinzhou's marginality to the empire in the third poem converting, for instance, from a source of worry to a sign in the thirteenth of its

b. This line refers to Tao Qian's famous story, "The Record of Peach Blossom Spring" 桃花源記. In that story, a fisherman followed the peach petals he saw floating on a stream back to a hidden valley, where a community of peaceful, hardworking folk had fled during the disorder of the Qin dynasty to make themselves an idyllic refuge from the world.

propitiousness as a site of reclusion. In this way, Du Fu's narrative procedures suggest that there might all along have been a hidden logic to his experience: that the more he learns what his life will be, the better he will understand what it has in fact been to this point, turning all his confusion and confliction into steps along the path towards their resolution. And indeed, Du Fu will end the series resolving on reclusion in Eastbough Valley, claiming to be content to spend the rest of his life there—happily, as it were, ever after.

Within narrative, however, sense is only safe at the end.[13] If later poems can change the meanings of earlier ones, then those meanings remain uncertain so long as the series remains unfinished, and any forward movement threatens to undermine the fragile narrative Du Fu has begun to discern in his experience. When in the eighteenth poem, therefore, he hears news that the Tibetans are mobilizing their armies to take advantage of Tang weakness, previously superseded worries about his non-Han neighbors in Qinzhou rise to the surface once again.[14]

XVIII

地僻秋將盡	The land is remote, autumn almost gone;
山高客未歸	mountains high, the traveler unreturned.
塞雲多斷續	Frontier clouds many, intermittent;
4　邊日少光輝	from the border sun, little light.
警急烽常報	Warning of crisis, beacon fires are constantly announced;
傳聲檄屢飛	transmitting word, calls-to-arms frequently fly.
西戎外甥國	The Western Rong are our nephew's kingdom:
8　何得迕天威	how can they defy heaven's might?[a]

If the eighth poem's focus on ethnic Tibetans in the Tang's armies helped to convince Du Fu that he could live amongst the "barbarians" of Qinzhou, this poem's return to imagery drawn from the tradition of frontier ballads—which routinely depicted war against the Tibetans—suggests

a. "Western Rong" refers here to the Tibetans, by means of an ethnonym originally applied to tribal enemies of the Zhou dynasty. The Tang had made an alliance with the Tibetans by giving their king an imperial princess in marriage; this allowed the Tang to claim that the Tibetan rulers were their "maternal nephews." "Heaven" stands for the Tang court.

that he has begun to question that conclusion. In the earlier poem, he had worried about the eastern prefectures that had been lost to the rebels; here, by contrast, he is worrying that Qinzhou and its western neighbors will be lost, as indeed it would be just three years later. Having once taken a Tang imperial princess as the bride of their king, moreover, the Tibetan royal house had accepted a familial relationship with the Tang;[15] in betraying that alliance now, they seem to Du Fu not merely strategically perfidious, but lacking in what the Chinese tradition defined as the most basic of ethical feelings, loyalty and respect within the family—a precise reversal of the humanity he had perceived in the flute playing of poem VIII. His outrage at the Tibetan attack, therefore, reminds him of loyalties he had previously sought to suppress, loyalties marked here by the transfer of "heaven"—in poem VIII, a place Zhang Qian visited by traveling west; here a metonymy for the Tang emperor and his court in Chang'an—back east from their previous western inclination. Qinzhou, that is, no longer seems to Du Fu a potential center of the world, and the progress he had made towards resolving on a life of reclusion here seems to be collapsing.

Poems XVII through XIX all articulate such hesitations, making Du Fu's final and apparently triumphant resolution in the twentieth poem to live out the remainder of his life a recluse at Eastbough Valley seem forced. And this forcedness, in turn, complicates the issue of narrative in the series as a whole. By writing his feelings towards Qinzhou as a sequence of "Miscellaneous Poems," Du Fu has implicitly disclaimed responsibility for the narrative order of the set, suggesting that it emerged spontaneously from the scattered thoughts and experiences that happened to occur to him during the time he spent there. In this supposed spontaneity, there is a claim to unmanipulated truth: the poet-protagonist is merely "discovering" a logic in his experience, a direction towards which his life has tended unawares. Yet the return near the end of the series of worries articulated in the beginning belies its overall progress, hinting that these worries tell us something deep about Du Fu that cannot be so simply superseded. In this respect, the final forcing of the ending seems a desperate attempt to recapture a narrative that has gone awry. It thus will come as no surprise when, shortly after completing these poems and declaring his intention to stay indefinitely, Du Fu decides to leave Qinzhou after all.

Narrative Redirected

If "Twenty Miscellaneous Poems of Qinzhou" ends with an attempt to force a narrative order on unruly experience, the next series Du Fu writes begins with one. This second series, a set of twelve travel poems chronicling his journey from Qinzhou south to Tonggu, opens with an announcement of its intended plot: Du Fu is heading to a paradise, where the conflicts that impeded his resolve to follow a reclusive moral script in Qinzhou will be overcome. As might be expected after the failure of the previous series, this narrative will be derailed almost immediately by realizations that undermine his stated goal. Yet Du Fu has learned something from "Twenty Miscellaneous Poems" and will not force his experience to conform to a predetermined telos. Instead, he will work to fold the very recalcitrance of his experience into a narrative of a different sort, of learning what it is about himself and his world that makes it so difficult to find the paradise he imagines in the first poem of the set.[16]

發秦州　*Leaving Qinzhou (no. 1)*[a]

我衰更懶拙	In my decline, I grow yet lazier, more dense;
生事不自謀	making a living I can't handle on my own.[b]
無食問樂土	I've no food, so I inquire about happy lands;[c]
4　無衣思南州	I've no clothes, so I long for southern climes.[d]
漢源十月交	At Hanyuan near the tenth month's turn,

a. Early, likely authorial, note: "Twelve poems recording my journey in the second year of the Qianyuan reign, going from Qin Prefecture to Tonggu County, in twelve poems" 乾元二年自秦州赴同谷縣紀行十二首.

b. "In my decline" echoes Confucius from the *Analects*: "Deep indeed is my decline! For too long I have not dreamt of the Duke of Zhou." "Lazy and dense" are conventional attributes of the recluse, who merely feigns ineptness to avoid government service.

c. The phrase "happy lands" may derive from the poem "Big Rat" 碩鼠 in the *Shijing*, wherein peasants complain of being overtaxed by their ruler: "We are going to leave you and go to a happy land." It is also a common term for Buddhist paradises, or "pure lands."

d. The phrase translated as "southern climes" may derive from a poem attributed to the exile Qu Yuan, titled "Far Travels" 遠游: "I rejoice in the fiery virtue of the southern

	天氣如涼秋	the weather is a mere autumnal chill.[e]
	草木未黃落	The plants and trees have not yellowed or shed;
8	況聞山水幽	and moreover, I hear the landscape's fine.
	栗亭名更嘉	Chestnut Pavilion's name is yet more auspicious,
	下有良田疇	and below it are good farming fields.[f]
	充腸多薯蕷	We'll fill our bellies with plentiful yams,
12	崖蜜亦易求	and cliffside honey will be easy to get.
	密竹復冬筍	Amidst its thick bamboo are winter shoots,
	清池可方舟	and its clear pools can bear linked boats.
	雖傷旅寓遠	Though pained to dwell a traveler so far from home,
16	庶遂平生遊	I hope there to complete my lifetime's roaming.
	此邦俯要衝	This territory here overlooks a strategic hub;
	實恐人事稠	truly I fear so many human affairs.
	應接非本性	Social niceties are not in my nature,
20	登臨未銷憂	and climbing for views here has not relieved my cares.[g]
	谿谷無異石	These ravines have no strange rocks,
	塞田始微收	and frontier fields have always had meager harvests.
	豈復慰老夫	What more is there here to comfort this old man?
24	惘然難久留	disappointed, it'd be hard to stay here long.
	日色隱孤戍	From the lonely outpost the sun's colors hide;
	烏啼滿城頭	the crying of crows fills the city walls.
	中宵驅車去	At midnight, I drive my wagon away,
28	飲馬寒塘流	watering my horse at the currents of cold ponds.[h]
	磊落星月高	Scattered grandly, the stars and moon on high;
	蒼茫雲霧浮	through the vast darkness float clouds and fog.

---

climes, with beautiful cassia trees flourishing in winter." The poem depicts a spirit journey to immortality.

e. By the Chinese calendar, the tenth month marked the beginning of winter. Hanyuan was a county adjacent to Du Fu's destination of Tonggu.

f. Chestnut Pavilion was a landmark near Tonggu; the name is "auspicious" because it suggests there may be (edible) chestnuts nearby.

g. This line alludes to Wang Can's 王粲 (177–217) "Rhapsody on Climbing the Tower" 登樓賦: "I climb this tower and look around in four directions, / taking this idle day to relieve my cares." This rhapsody was written during Wang Can's exile.

h. This line recalls the title of an old *yuefu* ballad, "Watering my Horse at a Pool by the Great Wall," and specifically a couplet from Chen Lin's version of that ballad: "I watered my horse at a pool by the great wall; / the water was cold, and hurt the horse's bones."

大哉乾坤内   Huge, this space twixt heaven and earth,
32   吾道長悠悠   and my way is ever far and uncertain.[i]

Qinzhou in this poem looks little like it did in Du Fu's previous fantasies
of Eastbough Valley. Yet though the ideal hermitage he hoped to find
hidden there may never have materialized, he nonetheless remains convinced—or tries to convince himself—that a paradise exists for him: that
Tonggu will be all the things Qinzhou is not, combining natural beauty,
seclusion, plenty, and warmth. As if to prove their likelihood to himself,
moreover, he imagines each of these attractions supporting all the others.
Tonggu's beauty will reside partly in its thick bamboo, bamboo that will
also provide seclusion to placid ponds upon which a recluse might drift
and food in the form of fresh shoots, which (since they are usually a spring
delicacy) will break through the winter ground there because of the southerly warmth of the region. Chestnut Pavilion, similarly, is both famed for
its beauty and promising for its name, which Du Fu takes to indicate that
there are chestnut trees around that will not, in the warm climate, have
yellowed or shed and will therefore produce nuts throughout the colder
months. There are good fields there and fine cliffs, both of which will make
for excellent vistas and abundant food. The place, that is, will satisfy the
needs of Du Fu's body and his mind, needs that seem here to be essentially
the same. In this sense, Tonggu will provide him an escape from complexity and division, finally putting an end to "his lifetime's roaming."

Endings and consummations are on Du Fu's mind here, he suggests,
because he is drawing towards the end of his life. The poem begins with
an abbreviated quotation of Confucius, who claimed that "in his decline"
he no longer dreamed of the Duke of Zhou, the sagely regent of the great
Zhou dynasty, since he knew he would no longer live up to that example.
It ends with another such quote, Confucius's late-life exclamation that his
"way (*dao* 道) is at its end": that he no longer held out hope he would be
able to bring the world to peace. Since we might expect Du Fu to invoke
these moments from Confucius's life in order to reflect on the failure of his
governmental ambitions, there is something unmistakably deflating about

---

i. "Heaven and earth" here is literally "Qian and Kun," the first two hexagrams of the
Yijing, which were understood to symbolize heaven and earth. "My way" echoes Confucius,
who exclaimed upon learning about the capture of the unicorn: "My way is at its end!"

his use of "my decline" to denote less a spiritual senescence than an inability to "make a living," and about his use of "my *dao*" to signify the literal road that lay before him.[17] Du Fu seems in this way to have banished from the poem any concern for society beyond his own physical comfort and aesthetic gratification. The problem that this journey will solve—that Du Fu is in his "decline," that he cannot keep himself or his family alive—is thus defined in a way that makes the beauty, warmth, abundance, and seclusion he imagines finding in Tonggu seem a complete answer, one that will bring his "way" to a satisfying conclusion.

If the poem is a fantasy of finding a meaningful ending, however, it also admits in its final lines that the plot Du Fu has here envisioned for himself remains at this point uncertain, capable of being proved only through the journey that lies before him. It will in fact turn out that Du Fu is not able to maintain the simplicity and singularity of purpose that characterized his initial vision of Tonggu. As he travels on, aspects of this harmony begin to come apart.[18]

鐵堂峽   *Ironhall Gorge (no. 3)*

山風吹遊子	Mountain winds blow the wanderer on;
縹緲乘險絕	tossed in the distance, we climb a sheer defile.
硤形藏堂隍	The gorge's shape conceals a palatial hall;
4　壁色立積鐵	the cliffs' colors set forth a mass of iron.
徑摩穹蒼蟠	Our path coils up, scraping the vaulted gray,
石與厚地裂	the rocks sundered from the thick earth.
修纖無垠竹	Long and graceful, bamboo without end;
8　嵌空太始雪	engraved in the void, primeval snows.
威遲哀壑底	Winding to the depths of this mournful gorge,
徒旅慘不悅	the travelers are grim, without joy.
水寒長冰橫	The water is cold, forever stretched with ice;
12　我馬骨正折	now my horse's bones are breaking.[a]
生涯抵弧矢	Between life's banks, I've confronted bows and arrows,
盜賊殊未滅	and the rebels are still far from wiped out.
飄蓬逾三年	Tossed like a tumbleweed over three years,
16　回首肝肺熱	I turn my head, liver and lungs hot.

a. This line alludes again to Chen Lin's "Watering My Horse at a Pool by the Great Wall": "The water was cold, and hurt my horse's bones."

In this poem, Du Fu starts out in much the integrality he imagined awaited him in Tonggu, if for the meantime in a less paradisiacal register. The physical and the spiritual here seem to be at one, as the poet's movements are light to the very wind, and the gorge matches the mournfulness of his traveling party. Names and things still correspond here (as the second couplet makes clear), and the landscape seems to gratify the physicalization of elevated, almost metaphysical language that had characterized the first poem's repurposing of Confucius's famous sayings. Forbidding as it is, the terrain here takes on connotations of immortality, the path winding from the natural hall built into the cliffside—a possible haunt of immortals—up to heaven, where the poet finds bamboo and snow "boundless" and "primeval"—words with mystical overtones, commonly applied to the *dao*. Bamboo and water, we recall, were paired in "Leaving Qinzhou" as well, where Du Fu imagined them in Tonggu providing him food, beauty, and seclusion.[19] To this point in his journey southwards, then, the landscape is still promising to nourish him, body, spirit, and mind.

The poem shifts direction, however, when Du Fu sees this fantasized incorporation of the landscape painfully concretized in his horse's drinking from the cold water at the base of the gorge. In this image, he at once recognizes the landscape's fundamental inhospitableness and also, in another moment that echoes the series' first poem, calls to mind Chen Lin's "Ballad of Watering My Horse at a Pool by the Great Wall." In the first poem, the echo of this ballad merely described the austerity of the western frontiers, from which he was supposedly departing for Tonggu. At this point, however, the allusion's reminder of the dangers posed to the Chinese state by marauding "barbarians" recalls his thoughts to the war still underway in the heartland. Recollecting his experiences over the past three years, Du Fu now finds his insides hot with emotion, despite the cold of the place. His mind and body come apart, and he recognizes loyalties to the state he had disclaimed in "Leaving Qinzhou."

"Ironhall Gorge" exemplifies in this way the progress of the series as a whole, which steadily undermines his fantasies even before Tonggu fails to fulfill them. Yet at the same time as his experiences along the road refuse to conform themselves to his initial plot, Du Fu also attempts to draw them into a new, emerging narrative order. He does this, once again, by ensuring that each poem in the set finds echoes in the sequence's other half—this time, two such echoes, parallel and chiastic. In this third poem of the series, for instance, Du Fu encounters "bamboo without end" and remembers the "bows and arrows" currently being used back east. It is no coincidence, then, that these images recur in the parallel ninth poem as well (the third of the series' second half), which depicts a landscape denuded of its bamboo, all of which has been made into arrow hafts to supply the armies fighting the rebels. And the tenth poem too, the chiastic pair of the third (the third to last), will also pick up on the themes of "Ironhall Gorge."[20]

積草嶺   *Massed-Plant Ridge (no. 10)*

	連峰積長陰	Linked peaks mass longstanding cold;
	白日遮隱見	the white sun alternates hidden and seen.
	颼颼林響交	Soughing, forest echoes cross;
4	慘慘石狀變	gloomy, the rock shapes change.
	山分積草嶺	The mountains split at Massed-Plant Ridge;
	路異明水縣	my road splits off from Brightwater County's.[a]
	旅泊吾道窮	As a traveler, my way is at its end;
8	衰年歲時倦	in my declining years, I weary of this season.[b]
	卜居尚百里	To divine my dwelling it's still a hundred leagues;
	休駕投諸彦	halting my harness, I'll throw in with fine men.[c]
	邑有佳主人	The town has a talented official in charge;
12	情如已會面	our feelings are as if we'd met face to face.
	來書語絕妙	In the letter that came, his words were truly fine;
	遠客驚深眷	this far traveler was startled by his deep goodwill.
	食蕨不願餘	I will eat bracken and wish for nothing more;
16	茅茨眼中見	a grass-thatched hut I see before my eyes.[d]

a. "Brightwater County" was to the southeast of Du Fu's destination of Tonggu. This road would have led back towards the heartland.

b. "My way is at its end" echoes once again Confucius's exclamation on hearing about the capture of the unicorn. "My declining years" may also echo Confucius's "in my decline," referenced in the first poem of the series.

c. "Divining a dwelling" was the ritual practice of choosing a good place to site a cottage.

d. Bracken ferns were traditionally the food of recluses. In particular, the recluses Boyi 伯夷 and Shuqi 叔齊, who refused to eat the grain of Zhou after the latter conquered the Shang, subsisted on bracken on Mt. Shouyang.

This is the first time in the series Du Fu mentions a letter inviting him to Tonggu. If he broaches the subject at this late stage, it is perhaps because after all the ardors of his lonely journey, he has become amenable to the "social niceties," and even the presence of imperial administration, he originally hoped to leave behind in Qinzhou. Finding, moreover, that this enticingly named mountain turns out to mass up only cold—a recognition that reverses the congruence of Ironhall Gorge and threatens his earlier hope that Chestnut Pavilion might promise food—he proclaims himself willing at this point to be content with harvests even more meager than those he complained about in the first poem of the set. These aspects of his initial fantasy of Tonggu have proven themselves untenable, and yet the core hope still remains: that arriving there will "complete his lifetime's roaming," providing the teleology that will finally make sense of his wandering life. Encountering in this poem a crossroads that could divert him from his stated goal, therefore, Du Fu once again inverts Confucius's lament that "my way is at its end"—this time triumphantly, if somewhat desperately as well. In the final lines, that end appears before his eyes, in the form of food and a house made of the plants that are missing on this ridgeline.

This act of envisioning recalls the end of "Ironhall Gorge," where Du Fu was also warmed amidst massed cold by thoughts of elsewhere. By this point, however, the separation of body and mind has seeped into his fantasies themselves, and the consummation he now imagines for himself no longer promises the physical comforts he once hoped for from Tonggu. In the final poem of the series, this division will reach a grotesque extreme, as Du Fu comes to recognize the importance he attaches, after all, to his estranged imperial community and the utter dispensability of the creature comforts he imagined at the journey's outset.[21]

鳳凰臺　　*Phoenix Terrace (no. 12)*[a]

| 亭亭鳳凰臺 | Rising straight up, Phoenix Terrace |
| 北對西康州 | faces West Kang Prefecture to the north.[b] |

a. Early, probably authorial, note: "The mountain is so precipitous, no one can reach its lofty peak" 山峻，人不至高頂. This mountain was past Tonggu, to the east.

b. West Kang Prefecture was an old name for Tonggu County, modern-day Cheng County, Gansu.

	西伯今寂寞	The Earl of the West is now cold and silent,
4	鳳聲亦悠悠	and the cries of the phoenix too have faded.[c]
	山峻路絕蹤	The mountain precipitous, its paths untracked;
	石林氣高浮	high through its stone forests auras float.
	安得萬丈梯	How can I get a ladder of ten thousand spans,
8	爲君上上頭	to ascend for my lord to its highest peak?
	恐有無母雛	I fear there's there a motherless chick,
	飢寒日啾啾	hungry and cold, wailing each day.
	我能剖心出	I would be able to gouge out my heart
12	飲啄慰孤愁	to feed her, consoling her lonely cares.
	心以當竹實	This heart could serve as bamboo fruit,
	炯然忘外求	its gleaming make her forget other desires.[d]
	血以當醴泉	My blood could serve as a sweetwater spring,
16	豈徒比清流	beyond compare with any clear stream.[e]
	所重王者瑞	What I value is the portent of a true king:
	敢辭微命休	dare I refuse my insignificant life's end?
	坐看綠翮長	Soon one would see her rainbow pinions grow,
20	舉意八極周	at a thought to circle the world's eight extremes.
	自天銜瑞圖	She will bear an auspicious diagram from heaven
	飛下十二樓	as she descends towards the twelve towers.[f]
	圖以奉至尊	The diagram will be presented to our Most Revered;
24	鳳以垂鴻猷	the phoenix will bestow on him the Great Plan.[g]
	再光中興業	Once more will there be the work of Restoration,
	一洗蒼生憂	washing away the cares of the common folk.[h]
	深衷正爲此	My deepest feelings are truly thus;
28	羣盜何淹留	how can the rebels linger on?

c. The "Earl of the West" was King Wen 文王 of the Zhou dynasty. In the seventh year of his reign, King Wen received the mandate of heaven, and a phoenix cried out on Mt. Qi as a portent of his virtuous rule.

d. According to the *Hanshi waizhuan*, phoenixes only eat the fruit of bamboo.

e. In the *Zhuangzi*, we read of a wonderful bird that "will only drink from sweetwater springs." According to a Tang commentary on the text, this bird was a type of phoenix.

f. A phoenix once presented such a diagram to the Yellow Emperor. The "twelve towers" thus presumably refer to those built in the capital city by the Yellow Emperor as a way to welcome the spirits, matching the twelve palaces of the immortals in the Kunlun mountains.

g. The "Most Revered" is the emperor.

h. "Restoration" originally described the restoration of the Zhou dynasty after the capital was sacked by barbarians.

The first surprise of this final poem is that it is not named "Tonggu County." Instead of describing the supposed telos of his journey, the purportedly paradisiacal hermitage site at which he has finally arrived, Du Fu instead takes up yet another mountain, past the county seat to the southeast, one he has not climbed and tells us he cannot climb.[22] Given that the poet and his family would stay in Tonggu for less than one hungry month, we can perhaps understand his decision to avoid the topic as a tacit admission of disappointment. Tonggu is not his destined end.

The failure of the fantasies that sent Du Fu to Tonggu does not prevent him, however, from imagining that that destined end still awaits him just a short distance away. Indeed, the end Du Fu envisions for himself on Phoenix Terrace Mountain both recalls and inverts his onetime fantasy of Tonggu, simultaneously fulfilling his initial hopes in unexpected ways and offering a new telos to the errant narrative of learning the series has tracked. Phoenix Terrace Mountain, that is, turns out not to be a place of plenty or of warmth, the "hungry and cold" phoenix chick he envisions crying on its summit taking over the attributes he himself sought to escape in the first poem, where he complained of lacking food and clothes. Rather than finding a place that will solve these problems for him, therefore, Du Fu imagines solving them for the phoenix, transforming his initial hopes to eat bamboo shoots and drift on limpid pools into a plan to make his body and blood the bamboo fruit and sweetwater springs that might nourish the fledgling prodigy. In this way, the poem subtly respiritualizes the first verse's physicalizing allusion to Confucius's "my way is at its end." Where, in "Leaving Qinzhou," Du Fu had applied these resonant words to his physical road ahead, here his wish that the phoenix might portend the restoration of the empire recalls the original context in which Confucius spoke them: when he heard that hunters had captured a unicorn—like the phoenix, normally the auspice of a true king—and grieved therefore that the empire would know no peace in his time.[23] These echoes of the first poem in the last thus indicate how far Du Fu has come on his journey. Where once he hoped Tonggu would be a paradise satisfying both his body and his spirit, the rigors of the road and the experiences he has had along it have taught him that no such paradise is possible: his commitments to community and the empire are too deep and the physical world too harsh. The best he can imagine now is a paradise for others, a fantasy that might satisfy his mind, if at the expense of his body.

The series thus represents a narrative of spiritual progress, of maturation from the selfish and unrealistic fantasy of "Leaving Qinzhou" to a more mature recognition of his own commitment to others.[24] At the same time, however, the schism that has intervened between body and mind over the course of his travels ends up undermining his continued hope—evident once again in this poem, which imagines a more decisive end to his "lifetime's roaming"—that the narrative of the series will ultimately reveal the sense towards which his life was tending all along. There is no physical path to the top of Phoenix Terrace Mountain, and the self-sacrificing death he imagines there is a flight of imagination only. Like the paradise of Tonggu or the grass-thatched hut he claimed to "see" on Massed-Plant Ridge, this ending is a mirage, a point Du Fu himself seems to highlight in the final lines, in which he recognizes that, no matter how sincere his feelings may be, they have no effect in the physical world.[25] Even the reasoning that encourages him to imagine finding a phoenix here—the name of the mountain—has been thoroughly discredited by his experiences at the barren Massed-Plant Ridge. Although it is possible to read the series, therefore, as a narrative of learning through experience, one that teaches him about his world and about himself, he ends up in some ways right back where he started, in a flimsy fantasy of paradise. Doubling down on the technique of forced closure noted in "Twenty Miscellaneous Poems of Qinzhou," this second series thus ends with the reassertion of a teleology Du Fu is, at this point, learning to distrust.

Narrative Undirected

Narrative having failed twice now to provide a final meaning to his life, Du Fu makes distrust of teleology the central theme of the final series he would write about his travels on the western frontiers. This distrust is built into the very structure of the set, another twelve-poem sequence whose programmatic echoes of the Qinzhou-to-Tonggu series effectively merge the two into one longer, twenty-four poem sequence, turning "Phoenix Terrace" from the end into the middle. As Du Fu travels south from Tonggu to Chengdu, he recalls at every step of the way the corresponding poem in the previous series, thereby extending the architectural interconnections that structured that set and bringing each of its poems into new affiliations that free their meaning to transform beyond the confines of its original narrative.[26] Through this formal innovation, Du Fu repudiates the hopes the past two series placed in narrative teleology, while simultaneously identifying another mode in which narrative might nonetheless be valuable as a sense-making tool. Freed now from the illusion that an ending might offer some final significance to all that's gone before, Du Fu focuses instead on narrative's ability to continually reconfigure past meanings and its promise that present experiences will unfold their significance into the future. By ensuring that the import of any given moment remains open to transformation so long as time moves forward, this new form of nonteleological narrative allows meaning to emerge beyond any end.[27]

發同谷縣　*Leaving Tonggu County (no. 1)*[a]

	賢有不黔突	Worthies have had unblackened chimneys,
	聖有不暖席	some sages, unwarmed mats.[b]
	況我飢愚人	How much more me, a hungry, foolish man:
4	焉能尚安宅	how could I value dwelling at rest?[c]
	始來茲山中	First coming here among these mountains,
	休駕喜地僻	I halted my harness, delighting in the land's remoteness.
	奈何迫物累	Yet what can I do?—I'm pressed by my encumbrances
8	一歲四行役	in one year to four forced journeys.[d]
	忡忡去絕境	Careworn, I leave this transcendent realm,
	杳杳更遠適	going far again, into the dark unknown.[e]

a. Early, probably authorial, note: "Recording my journey on the first day of the twelfth month of the second year of the Qianyuan reign from Longyou to Jiannan" 乾元二年十二月一日自隴右赴劍南紀行.

b. The "Cultivating Effort Chapter" 脩務訓 of the *Huainanzi* tells us that "Confucius had an unblackened chimney; Mozi, an unwarmed mat. Sages do not worry that mountains will be high or rivers broad but will undergo even humiliation to help the age's lord." In other sources, the respective attributes of Confucius and Mozi are reversed.

c. It is also possible that this line should be translated "could I long have rest in a dwelling?"

d. "My encumbrances" echoes the *Zhuangzi*: "He who knows the joy of heaven has no resentment of heaven, no criticism of men, no encumbrance by things, and no blame from ghosts or spirits."

e. "Transcendent realm" is a clumsy translation of the Chinese term, literally a "cut-off realm," separated from the body of the empire both spatially and qualitatively. The term

	停驂龍潭雲	I halt my team by the clouds of a dragon tarn,
12	廻首白崖石	turn my head at the rocks of White Cliff.
	臨岐別數子	At the crossroads, parting from my few friends,
	握手淚再滴	we clasped hands and tears fell again.
	交情無舊深	These friendships were not long or deep,
16	窮老多慘慼	but old and poor, there's much that makes me sad.ᶠ
	平生嬾拙意	All my life I've wanted to be lazy and dense;
	偶值棲遁跡	by chance I found here a perch to hide my tracks.ᵍ
	去住與願違	My going and staying betray my desires;ʰ
20	仰慙林間翮	I'm put to shame by the pinions in the woods.ⁱ

Du Fu's attitude towards this second journey contrasts markedly with his feelings in "Leaving Qinzhou." There, he was eager to leave where he was in pursuit of promised pleasures at his destination; here, to the contrary, he feels forced to depart but reluctant to do so. Tonggu, it turns out now he's leaving it, does fulfill many of the hopes he had of the place: it has "clear pools" and "strange rocks," and it offers a site where, "lazy and dense," he could "complete his lifetime's roaming" and cease (like a good recluse) making tracks. What the place does not resolve, apparently, is his poverty, his encumbrance by a hungry body and a famished family. These encumbrances mark the difference between him and the sages and worthies who he tries to console himself also found no rest. For whereas they went or stayed because they chose to, like the birds at the end of the poem, his travels go against his wishes, and where he's heading is not where he wants to be. If the forced ending of the previous sequence was a fantasy

---

is used famously of Tao Qian's imagined utopia in "Peach Blossom Spring": "They said to the visitor that they had fled from the disorder of the Qin dynasty, taken their wives and children and townsfolk and come to this cut-off realm, never coming forth again, from that point on separated from outsiders."

f. This couplet recalls a poem of Tao Qian's that asks: "If people understand one another, what need they be old friends?"

g. "Hiding one's tracks" was a way of speaking about reclusion.

h. "Going and staying" of one's own accord 去住自在 or without obstruction 去住 無礙 were spiritual attainments in both the Buddhist and the Daoist traditions.

i. This line may allude to another poem of Tao Qian's: "Lazy and slow, the pinions coming forth from the wood, / and before it is dusk they have returned again."

of sacrificing his body to the satisfaction of his mind, this poem is his body's revenge.

In depicting the poet forced into a tragic renunciation, "Leaving Tonggu County" sets the pattern for the first half of this set, wherein Du Fu repeatedly finds beautiful places he wishes he could remain but is compelled to leave by his responsibility for his family and his inability to make a living here on the frontiers. As this pattern plays out, however, and reluctance to leave one site gives way to appreciation of another, each departure becomes less traumatic, reconciling the poet gradually to his wandering. Consider, for example, the third poem in the series, which echoes and inverts the third of the previous set, "Ironhall Gorge."[28]

白沙渡   Whitesands Crossing (no. 3)

	畏途隨長江	The fearsome road follows the long river;
	渡口下絕岸	to the crossing we descend the sheer bank.[a]
	差池上舟楫	We climb aboard scattered boats;
4	杳窕入雲漢	dark and deep, we enter the cloudy river.[b]
	天寒荒野外	The skies are cold beyond the wilds;
	日暮中流半	the sun sets halfway in the current.
	我馬向北嘶	My horse whinnies, facing north;
8	山猿飲相喚	mountain gibbons drink, calling to one another.[c]
	水清石礧礧	Waters clear, the rocks distinct in piles;
	沙白灘漫漫	sands white, the rapids flowing slowly.[d]
	廻然洗愁辛	In a flash, wretched cares are washed away;
12	多病一踈散	my many illnesses are at once allayed.

a. The phrase translated here as "long river" usually refers to the "Long River," the Yangzi, in the south. "Sheer bank," likewise, derives from Guo Pu's 郭璞 (276–324) "Rhapsody on the Yangzi" 江賦, specifically the section describing the Three Gorges. Du Fu is, however, on the much smaller Jialing River 嘉陵江.

b. The "Cloudy River" is the Chinese name for the Milky Way.

c. The horse facing north recalls "Traveling On" from the "Nineteen Old Poems": "The north-born horse leans towards the north wind; / the bird of the south nests on a southern branch." Gibbons' calls were associated with going through the Three Gorges; hearing three calls was supposed to make one shed tears.

d. This couplet echoes another old poem, an anonymous "Yan'ge Ballad" 艷歌行: "I tell you, do not look: / if the water is clear, the rocks will be seen. / The rocks are visible, how piled up they are! / To travel far is not as good as returning home."

高壁抵嶔崟　High cliffs confront us, rough and huge,

洪濤越凌亂　as we transcend flooding waves, riotous and disordered.

臨風獨廻首　Facing the wind, I turn my head alone;

16　攬轡復三歎　then grasp the reins and repeatedly sigh.

"Ironhall Gorge," recall, was marked by a narrative of progressive separation between body and spirit: although at first the "iron hall" Du Fu found in the cliffside there seemed not only to fit the place's name but to physicalize the transcendence he was seeking on his journey, when he "turned his head" at the end of the poem, it was to return in mind to the war under way in the heartland. This poem, by contrast, describes an opposite progress. Throughout its first half, the poet's mind is elsewhere: hearing the gibbons that legendarily populate the Three Gorges down south, he sees the Jialing River as the "Long River"—the great southern Yangzi that passes through the Gorges—and embodies his wish to return home northwards in an allusion to another old poem about a horse, matching the allusion to "Watering My Horse at a Pool by the Great Wall" in "Ironhall Gorge." It is only in the second half of this verse that the mental and the physical begin to converge, as Du Fu notices that this "Whitesands Crossing" is indeed marked by beautiful "white sands," the aesthetic appreciation of which begins to allay his bodily ailments. When he turns his head in the last couplet of this poem, therefore, it is not to recall something far off, but in reluctance to leave what is here: a place where, in a physicalized metaphor, he can "transcend" the "riot" and "disorder" that characterize the world he has to go back out into. In contrast to "Ironhall Gorge," then, this poem traces a brief reintegration of body and spirit and, through it, tracks Du Fu's increasing ability to appreciate the transitory meanings of his experience without needing to project a visionary paradise for himself at the end.

Eventually, this series of transitory appreciations will coalesce in an acceptance of exile, a willingness (as Du Fu says most directly in the eighth poem of the set) not to find a perfect consummation to satisfy his desires. At the same time, however, this acceptance of exile also involves a deepening awareness of the constitutive openness of those imperfect meanings he senses in each passing experience. In its original context, for example, "Ironhall Gorge" presented Du Fu's first inkling of the threat his indelible loyalty to the failing empire posed to the fantasy that mere bodily comforts might finally satisfy him, a threat that would come to fruition finally in "Phoenix Terrace." By systematically reengaging with its imagery, however, "Whitesands Crossing" incorporates the earlier poem into a longer narrative of fissure and reconvergence. Seen from this perspective, what Du Fu learned in "Ironhall Gorge" is no longer that he would only be happy in some grotesque self-sacrifice for the greater good of the Tang. It is, instead, that our world is not hospitable to perfect consummations and that we live in it, therefore, in a constant state of precarity.[29]

劍門   *Swordgate (no. 10)*[a]

	惟天有設險	Of all the perils heaven has established,
	劍門天下壯	under heaven Swordgate is the grandest.[b]
	連山抱西南	Ranged mountains embrace the southwest;
4	石角皆北向	the rocks' sharp horns all face north.
	兩崖崇墉倚	The paired cliffs lean, towering fortifications,
	刻畫城郭狀	artfully fashioned to the shape of city walls.
	一夫怒臨關	With a single man in fury at this pass,
8	百萬未可傍	a million could not get near him.[c]
	三皇五帝前	Back under the Three Thearchs and the Five God-Kings,[30]
	雞犬各相放	everyone let their chickens and dogs run free.[d]
	後王尚柔遠	But though later kings honored "kindness to the distant,"[e]
12	職貢道已喪	their method of tribute duties was already lost.
	至今英雄人	Up to today, therefore, domineering men
	高視見霸王	gaze haughtily, presenting themselves as overlord kings.
	幷吞與割據	They'll annex neighbors and hack off territory,

a. Also named Liangshan, Swordgate Mountain was the gateway to Sichuan.

b. This line echoes the *Yijing*: "The perils of heaven cannot be scaled; the perils of the earth are mountains and rivers, hills and ridges; and kings establish perils in order to preserve their states."

c. This line echoes Zhang Zai's 張載 (d. ca. 304) "Inscription on Swordgate" 劍閣銘: "One man holding a pike could make ten thousand hesitate."

d. The "Three Thearchs and Five God-Kings" were legendary Chinese sages of great antiquity, the creators of Chinese culture and civilization.

e. "Kindness to the distant" is a policy enunciated by the sage king Shun in the *Shangshu*.

16	極力不相讓	use the utmost force and never yield.
	吾將罪眞宰	I was about to fault the True Ruler,
	意欲鏟疊嶂	wanting him to level these layered barrier-peaks.^f
	恐此復偶然	Yet perhaps this is all by chance;
20	臨風默惆悵	facing the wind, I silently despair.

As the chiastic pair of "Whitesands Crossing" and the interseries parallel of "Massed-Plant Ridge," this poem mulls once again the relationship between a place's name and its physical characteristics. Yet if the poet was previously disappointed to learn that "Massed-Plant Ridge" massed up merely cold, here he is distressed to find that Swordgate, by contrast, lives up to its name, its sharp swords of stone all pointed towards the central plain. Whereas in "Whitesands Crossing" he saw in the landscape the possibility of transcending disorder, therefore, here he sees the threat of disorder embedded within it. He thus worries that another rebellion may break out in the place to which he has fled—as indeed it would, two years later.

As was the case in its chiastic pair and interseries parallel, moreover, this poem's concern for the correspondence between toponym and reality hints at larger questions of meaning's inherence in the physical world. The first couplet here echoes the *Yijing*—the text that paradigmatically wrote meaning into the Chinese universe[31]—depicting Swordgate as a fastness established, perhaps purposefully, by heaven. At the end of the poem, however, this vision of meaning in the landscape evaporates with Du Fu's abandonment of the idea that he might task the "True Ruler" (a synonym for heaven) with leveling the pass. In these final lines, we can hear echoes of the endings of both "Whitesands Crossing" and "Massed-Plant Ridge," as well as of that other imperially significant toponym poem, "Phoenix Terrace." If "Massed-Plant Ridge," for instance, ended with the poet encouraged by the envisioned construction of a cottage in Tonggu, this poem ends with his relinquishment of an imagined destruction. Similarly, if "facing the wind" in "Whitesands Crossing" was a gesture of reluctance to leave the river, here it seems to represent resolution to continue onwards, even in depression. And if Du Fu was distraught in "Phoenix Terrace" that the

f. The "True Ruler" is an idea from the *Zhuangzi*, of a hidden being in control of transformation.

sincerity of his feelings had no effect on the empire, here he is resigned to the impotence of his imagination. Fantasies that the world might be designed with reference to human well-being—whether to content the individual, as in "Leaving Qinzhou"; to support imperial flourishing, as in "Phoenix Terrace"; or to thwart it, as here—seem to have a decreasing hold on Du Fu's mind. There is, he concludes, no hidden logic to the physical world and thus no hidden plot to individual or imperial history.[32]

成都府　*Chengdu Prefecture (no. 12)*

翳翳桑榆日	Shaded, the sun of mulberry and elm[a]
照我征衣裳	shines on my traveling clothes.[b]
我行山川異	My travels have changed the hills and streams;
4　忽在天一方	suddenly I am at one edge of the sky.
但逢新人民	All I meet are new people;
未卜見故鄉	no divining when I'll see my hometown.
大江東流去	The great river flows off east;
8　遊子去日長	the wanderer's days gone grow long.
曾城填華屋	Tiered walls packed with ornate roofs;
季冬樹木蒼	in winter's last month, the trees gray green.[c]
喧然名都會	A bustling racket in this famed metropolis;
12　吹簫間笙簧	flutes play, interspersed with reeds.[d]

a. "Mulberry and elm" is a metonymy for the evening sun, which seems to hover in the tips of their branches. It was an old proverb that, if one was unsuccessful early in life, "losing it in the eastern corner, one could get it back in mulberry and elm," that is, in one's sunset years.

b. This couplet once again echoes Tao Qian's "Return!": "The sun is shaded and about to set; / I brush against lonely pines and pace back and forth. / Why not return to reclusion?" There may also be an echo of one of Ruan Ji's "Yonghuai" 詠懷 poems: "Burning brightly, the sun falls in the west; / its lingering glow shines on my clothes." That poem ends with the couplet "The brown swan has wandered throughout the four seas; / in the midst of its road, where can it return home?"

c. "Tiered walls" refer to the elaborate mansions of Chengdu, but "Tiered Walls" 曾城 was also the name of the legendary city of the immortals in the Kunlun Mountains.

d. This line might recall the legend of Flutemaster 蕭史, who seduced Nongyu 弄玉, the daughter of Duke Mu of Qin 秦穆公. Flutemaster used his flute to call down a phoenix, on which he and Nongyu rode off together into immortality.

信美無與適	Though lovely indeed, there's no one here suits me;[e]
側身望川梁	I hunch, gazing from the river bridge.[f]
鳥雀夜各歸	At nightfall each little bird returns;
16 中原杳茫茫	the central plain is dark in the distance.[g]
初月出不高	The new moon comes out, not high;
眾星尚爭光	the many stars still vie to shine.[h]
自古有羈旅	Sojourners there've been since ancient times:
20 我何苦哀傷	why should bitter sorrows wound me?[i]

Du Fu's hard-won resistance to illusions of paradise appears throughout this poem, which both evokes and immediately passes over the immortal resonances of this bustling metropolis. Imagery of Daoist immortality has appeared throughout this series as a vocabulary for describing the stunning sites he reluctantly has had to leave along his journey;[33] it appears here as well, the description of Chengdu's "tiered walls," for instance, recalling Tiered Walls, the city of the immortals in the Kunlun Mountains, where the poet might have expected to hear transcendents playing flutes to call

e. "Though lovely indeed" is a phrase with a rich history in the poetic tradition. It originates in the *Lisao* from the *Songs of the Southlands*, spoken when the exile Qu Yuan gives up on courting the goddess Fufei. Du Fu is also thinking here of Wang Can's "Rhapsody on Climbing a Tower," which uses the same phrase in describing Wang's flight south to escape the disorder in the northlands: "Although lovely indeed, this isn't my land; / how could I stay here even a short time?"

f. The "river bridge" in question is Ten-Thousand-League Bridge 萬里橋 in Chengdu.

g. The return of the birds may recall once again Tao Qian's "On Poor Scholars": "Lazy and slow, the pinions coming forth from the wood, / and before it's dusk they have returned again." Or it might recall his "Return!": "The birds know to return when they get tired of flying."

h. This couplet echoes the *Huainanzi*: "When the sun comes out, the stars cannot be seen; this is because they cannot vie with it to shine." This allusion often has political implications; here, it may suggest the weakness of the central state. "Vie to shine" may have connotations of literary immortality as well, since the poet Qu Yuan was once said to "vie with the sun and moon in shining."

i. This line may recall the idea that strong emotions effectively drained one's life force. See, for instance, "Cultivating Longevity" 養壽, a text from the *Biographies of the Immortals* 神仙傳 purportedly authored by the long-lived Peng Zu 彭祖: "Worry, sadness, and sorrows wound men" 憂愁悲哀傷人. The line could also be translated, "Why should I be troubled by my sorrows and my pain?"

down their phoenix mounts. Yet if he was eager to imagine a phoenix in the interseries parallel of this poem, here he leaves the flutes as flutes, the tiered walls merely tiered walls. The place is "lovely indeed," as Qu Yuan had found his immortal paramour; but, like Qu Yuan, Du Fu is disappointed. It is not his land, and its people are not his—neither the friends he made in Tonggu nor a community he fully trusts to be loyal to the Tang. As the echoes and inversions of Tao Qian's poetry of reclusion make clear, Du Fu has both reached the place he will make his home and accepted that he cannot be at home here. Though he will divine a site for his dwelling in Chengdu, he would rather "divine" about returning to his hometown—something he has learned, over his plot-defying wanderings, he cannot do.

Du Fu's fantasies of finding a home for himself, a teleological end that will make sense of his life, have ended in acceptance of exile, defined both in terms of physical distance from his hometown and spiritual distance from the final consummations he sought throughout his journeys. In this respect, this last poem in Du Fu's narrative experiments represents both his disillusionment with the idea of ending and also a fitting end to the narrative of learning these series have tracked. For if Du Fu initially imagined that paradise would be a place where body and spirit might be at one, thoroughgoing exile too, surprisingly, achieves this goal. Whereas in "Leaving Tonggu" he grieved that unlike previous sages and worthies he stayed or went not by his own choice, the final couplet here makes no such distinction: there have always, simply, been sojourners. In his resultant resolution not to let sorrows harm his health, therefore, we hear an inversion of the self-conflicted, self-destructive fantasy of "Phoenix Terrace": a willingness not to end his lifetime's roaming. And insofar as "roaming" (*you* 遊) is precisely the characteristic activity of the immortals, and not harming one's life with sorrows a prescription of the immortal Peng Zu, we can also discern here an inversion of Du Fu's realization at the end of "Phoenix Terrace" that his thoughts make no difference in the real world.[34] Chengdu is not the haunt of immortals, the "happy land" he once envisioned for himself. And yet, once he accepts exile as his home, it may come a little closer to it.[35]

In recalling the imagery of moon and stars from the penultimate couplet of "Leaving Qinzhou" in the penultimate couplet here, finally, Du Fu simultaneously suggests that the series has come full circle and also acknowledges, in the rising of the new moon, that that circle remains unclosed, that time will continue forward past the end of the series. There is a hint of foreboding here: that stars should "vie to shine" with the greater lights recalls the threat of rebellion that he sensed in "Swordgate." The character of Chengdu thus remains fundamentally ambiguous, to be decided in part by what follows this poem. If there is one thing that Du Fu has learned over his travels, it is that the meaning he senses in his experience—or fails to sense there—is always provisional, open to transformation as time moves on. It is perhaps for this reason that he essentially gives up, after reaching Chengdu, on writing extended narrative sequences. Released from the idea of teleology and the banks of significance through which it channeled his verse in these series, his collection floods out into a vast, unplotted narrative, with each new poem in it capable of revising the sense of all that came before.

Narrative in the Chinese Poetry Collection

There is nothing like these series in the tradition of Chinese poetry before Du Fu. Both narratives and series exist in earlier Chinese poetry, to be sure, but both are rare, and narrative series, as Joseph R. Allen has noted, are vanishingly few. Where narrative can be found in poetic sequences, he writes, it is "a much weaker force; not until the twentieth century is it a dominant feature in the dynamics of Chinese macropoetic structures."[36] Similarly unprecedented, judging from what survives, are the complex architectonic interconnections traced here within and between these series by means of which their narratives are articulated. Also novel are the notes that Du Fu provides on the first poems of the two travel sequences, which both alert the reader to the integral character of the twelve poems that follow and provide the dates of his journeys, thus integrating the sequences into the larger narrative of his life.[37] When combined with the evidence that has been collected by Stephen Owen that Du Fu seems to have begun arranging his full collection in more or less precise chronological order at some point after the beginning of the Rebellion, these innovations may represent the beginnings of a far-reaching transformation of the Chinese poetic art.[38]

Narrative was not a major dimension of late medieval verse in general. Poetry collections, for instance, do not seem to have done much to encourage readers to string individual poems into a progressive account of a poet's experience. Though only a few partial manuscripts of poetry survive from the period, none provide information about the chronology of the poet's works or display a chronological organization.[39] We do know that two poets before Du Fu's time and one contemporary seem to have provided at least a limited chronology to their collections, with two of these three dividing their works into sections based on the sequence of their government offices.[40] As Liu Yujun 劉玉珺 has argued, however, such cases were "still in the minority and had not yet become a common phenomenon."[41] As a result, the vast majority of the poems that survive from the seventh and eighth centuries remain undatable even now that scholars are so invested in the reconstruction of poetic chronologies that they grasp at every shred of evidence to date them. At most, late medieval readers would have been provided in complete collections with a brief biographical sketch of the author, against which they might have been able to contextualize some proportion of his poetic production.[42] Given the apparent rarity of complete collections, however, and the much greater prevalence in surviving caches like the Dunhuang library cave of fragmentarily copied and entirely disorganized manuscripts, it would seem that late medieval readers did not generally look to poetry as presenting a running narrative of a poet's life or thought.

In his study of Chinese autobiography up to the Song dynasty, Kawai Kōzō 川合康三 has suggested a possible reason for the lack of narrative organization in poetry before Du Fu's time. As he tells it, Chinese literature up to this point expresses a fundamentally nonnarrative vision of the self. We can, he writes, "almost never see the self [of medieval Chinese autobiography] looking back on its own transformation in the sort of self-reflection where the self at one time sees itself having become different from the self at another time. If Western European autobiography is triggered by the discovery that within a person's human history one's past self was a different self, Chinese autobiography is rooted in the discovery that among the mass of people, one's self is different from others."[43] Accordingly, medieval Chinese autobiography was primarily interested in the delineation of the author's fundamental character, rather than its narrative transformation. And Kawai is not even talking here about poetry (that is, *shi*-poetry, as opposed to *sao*-lament or *fu*-rhapsody), which he does not think even qualifies as autobiographical in poets before Du Fu. Before Du Fu, he writes, "we can say that all poetry is taking a fixed scene as its stage and speaking the lines fitting for an appropriate role. It might be easy to say that [this poetry] is about the experience of reality, but in truth owing to convention its means of slicing and taking reality are already decided."[44]

Whether or not Kawai is right to take the case this far, when he writes that the experiences that inform late medieval poetry have generally "already been approved by precedent," he is referring to the same literary phenomenon I have referred to throughout this book as "tropology." Tropology, as he rightly suggests, has an inherent tendency to vitiate the interest of narrative as a mode of sense-making, since it foreordains what endings are possible. Consider, for example, the greatest late medieval literary autobiographies, Yu Xin's "Lament for the Southland" 哀江南賦 and Yan Zhitui's "Conceptualizing My Life" 觀我生賦, both of which conclude with summaries that assert the conformity of the experiences just narrated to lessons that could be found in the precedent tradition.[45] In this respect, these otherwise innovative autobiographies follow the model set by the preeminent genre of narrative rhapsody, the travel *fu*, which since the Han dynasty had narrated its authors' resolution of spiritual difficulties through their recall, at various places on their journeys, of canonical texts and events. This structure can also be found in some of the *shi*-poetry that provides the best precedent for Du Fu's Qinzhou-to-Chengdu sequences, that of Xie Lingyun. Xie is certainly one of the most narrative of medieval poets, and he is one of those few medieval poets, mentioned above, at least some of whose verse we know circulated in chronological order. But even if his poems routinely depict a narrative of conversion through some occasioning experience or observation, not only does the conversion depicted in each poem seem independent of every other, but most are enacted through an echo of or a recognition about some previous text.[46] In cases such as these, narrative becomes a proving ground for the analogical applicability of traditional precedents rather than an indispensable modality of meaning.

Within his late medieval literary context, therefore, Du Fu's decision to write long narrative series would have been striking. It has not, however, seemed striking to his recordizing readers. As I have already suggested, few critics over the past thousand years have had anything to say about these sequences as wholes; fewer still have discerned the plots embedded within them; and none has ever noted the complex architectures of parallel and chiastic echoes that structure them. The reason for this, I would suggest, is that there is no need to question why or how Du Fu is playing with narrative in these series when it is assumed that poetry in general has an implicit narrative character.

This assumption, characteristic of recordizing reading, once again exemplifies the paradoxical combination of insight and blindness this critical tradition displays towards the work of its favorite poet. On the one hand, that is, recordizing reading is inherently narrative in character, its interest in determining the historical occasion of each of Du Fu's poems naturally lending itself to the chronological organization of those poems into a progression of linked moments. On the other hand, because that progression is understood to be the product of historical forces rather than purposeful design, recordizing critics do not read the narrative of his work as plotted towards an end that interprets and provides significance to everything that came before. This simultaneous interest in narrative and prejudice against plot is apt to much of Du Fu's poetry—and particularly to the mode of writing he adopts after arriving in Chengdu. But the presumption that poetry will be narrative dissolves the surprise of these series, which, more than any other poems in Du Fu's collection, make narrative their central theme. Similarly, the expectation that they will be historical rather than plotted obscures their experimentation and ultimate disillusionment with plot. In essence, the recordizing tradition's alignment with the results that follow from Du Fu's thinking through narrative in these series prevents it from recognizing how he came to them.

Of course, these postmedieval assumptions about poetry and narrative are not confined to Du Fu criticism alone. Plotless historical narratives become increasingly characteristic of poetry collections written in the ninth through thirteenth centuries, as poets began to organize their work chronologically, to write and inspire chronological accounts of their poetry's composition (*nianpu*), and to become the subject of chronologically contextualizing commentary.[47] In a parallel process, moreover, critics over the last thousand years have progressively read historical and biographical narratives into the collections of Du Fu's contemporaries and predecessors, even in cases where the evidence for dating is tenuous.[48] It is impossible to say what role Du Fu's poetry might have had in spurring these developments. It might, perhaps, have been significant: some of the famous ninth- and tenth-century poets who may have popularized the practice of organizing their poetry in chronological order—poets such as Bai Juyi, Wei Zhuang 韋莊 (836?–910), and Han Wo 韓偓 (844–923)—were avowed imitators of Du Fu.[49] Du Fu is also the poet who received both the earliest and far and away the most attention from critics interested in chronology, and his poetry was the subject of at least fifty commentary editions, at least twelve different *nianpu*, and several dozen rearranged chronological editions in the Song dynasty alone.[50] Whatever the mechanisms of this cultural shift might have been, however, both poetry and criticism increasingly converged over time on a model by which the art had an inherently narrative dimension to it.

The result of this process is that Du Fu's narrative innovations have come to seem merely archetypal of the Chinese poetic tradition as a whole. In an article that exemplifies this tendency, the contemporary scholar Xie Siwei 谢思炜 writes that "autobiographicality is common among Chinese literati writers, and Du Fu is merely among them a most typical representative (*qi zhong yige zui dianxing de daibiao* 其中一个最典型的代表)."[51] It is no accident that Du Fu is here both a typical example and the most typical example. As Xie notes a sentence later, it is this common autobiographicality of Chinese poetry that "produces the obligatory practice of composing year charts (*nianpu*) and scrutinizing the historical affairs behind poetry; and the earliest Chinese year chart for a poet was written by Lü Dafang 吕大防 of the Northern Song for Du Fu." For Xie, Du Fu called for this simultaneously novel and "obligatory" treatment both "through following the established literary practice of literati authors" and through writing a new kind of "recordizing poetry" (*jishi shi* 記事詩) that fulfilled the (previously implicit) narrative tendencies of the Chinese poetic tradition before his time. Having been moved to the center of the canon, he has become unable to innovate, explore, or experiment in any but the most superficial ways.

Learning from Experience

Beyond its insight into the narrative character of Du Fu's poetry after the Rebellion—equivocal though it may be in the case of these series—recordizing reading also accurately identifies his interest in the concept of experience. As seen in the previous chapter, Du Fu had already begun experimenting in the early years of the war with the idea that he might learn progressively about himself and his world through the situations he encountered. This idea was his major takeaway from that period, and it serves as the driving force in the series discussed here, which are all narratives of learning—the latter two, significantly, from hardship.

Intuitive as the possibility of such learning might sound nowadays, this poetic structure would likely have been more marked in the late medieval period, when it was no more central to poetry than was narrative. In fact, another way of stating the point made above that tropology obviates narrative is to say that, on the late medieval model, there could only be a difference of degree, rather than of kind, between poetry occasioned by actual experience and poetry produced through tradition-informed imagination. Experience in itself was not authoritative; it could be so only if it conformed, to at least some reasonable degree, to the lessons taught by the sages and the worthy inheritors of This Culture of Ours. Though it was probably assumed in the Tang that at least a significant amount of contemporary verse derived from real experiences, it is for this reason often impossible to tell, for poems in certain genres at least, whether they describe scenes imagined on the basis of canonical learning, realities experienced firsthand, or some blend of the two.[52]

The frontier ballads (*yuefu*) that provided the template for Du Fu's initial perception of Qinzhou in "Twenty Miscellaneous Poems" provide an instructive example here. This tradition matured in the Southern Dynasties, when writers generally could have had no personal experience whatsoever of the distant northern regions the genre characteristically described; what these poets knew of the old Han frontiers they had learned primarily from Han historiography.[53] In the Tang, the old Han dynasty borderlands in the northwest were more accessible, and a number of important poets had both visited them and participated in the Tang's wars against the "barbarians" there. But in terms of their imagery, the *yuefu* written by poets who actually visited the frontiers are rarely distinguishable from those of their predecessors; indeed, the timelessness of the border wars is often the explicit theme of this body of verse.[54]

According to eighth-century critics like Yin Fan, moreover, thorough experience of the frontiers was unnecessary to the production of such poetry. All it took, he wrote, for the poet Cui Hao 崔顥 (704?–45) to "speak entirely [the affairs of] military defense far from home" was "a single peek at the border regions."[55] A famous essay by Li Hua 李華 (715?–74?) makes much the same point. In "Mourning at an Old Battlefield" 弔古戰場, Li describes a brief and utterly uneventful visit to the frontier. Though he openly admits not knowing what dynasty might have fought a battle in this place—it does not matter, since the point will be that all frontier battles are ultimately the same—he launches nonetheless into a visceral account of the suffering of the soldiers who fought here and a moving disquisition on how their example demonstrates the inherent cruelty of military expansionism.[56] For Li, actual experience is merely a prompt for the elaboration of lessons he had learned through reading.[57]

Recordizing criticism, by contrast, has always held Du Fu's personal experience to be a crucial source of both his poetry's aesthetic grandeur and its ethical significance. Writing shortly after the collapse of the Northern Song to the Jurchens, for example, Yu Ruli 喻汝礪 (d. 1143) sought to persuade his contemporaries that, because Du Fu's verse recorded his experience of a similar catastrophe, it could offer them lessons on how to deal with the exigencies of the present moment.

> The agony of bitter parting from wife and children, the torment of tax collection and military corvée, sorrow and pain, worry and hidden anguish, and the moan of having nothing to rely on: not only did all of these things press upon Du Fu, but he went through them all himself. He met with periods of flourishing order and chaotic decline, loyal worthies and flattering villains, grief and happiness, the fluctuations of rise and fall, all continuously and without any relief, and there was nothing in which his experience was incomplete.... The *Yijing* says, "Being able to completely penetrate the transformations of the world, one can then create the *wen* of all-under-heaven."[58] If Du Fu had not exhaustively experienced the great transformations of all-under-heaven, then how could he have written the greatest *wen* of all-under-heaven?
>
> 婦子老孺之騷離，賦斂征戍之棘數，哀怨疾痛、愊愊隱閔，亡聊之聲，不翅迫及其身，而親遭之。其於治亂隆廢，忠佞賢否，哀樂忻慘，起伏之變，衍迤縱肆，無乎不備。…《易》曰：「通其變，遂成天下之文。」嗟乎，非盡天下之至變，何足以成天下之至文也哉？[59]

In this quote, Yu makes a telling comparison. Because Du Fu's experience is complete in all salient dimensions and because his poetry records that experience completely, it is—as Charles Hartman puts it in an insightful discussion of Yu's inscription—a "second *Classic of Change (Yijing)*."[60] In the late medieval period, by contrast, the idea that one might produce a *Classic of Change* on the basis of experience might have been counterintuitive, since the official Tang subcommentary identifies the original as the very ground of experience itself. According to this subcommentary, before Fu Xi "looked up to conceptualize the images in the heavens and looked down to conceptualize the models of the earth," and before he encoded this conceptualization in the hexagrams of the *Yijing*, the character of the world was "blocked up and concealed" and "the nature of things was impossible to know."[61] For Yu Ruli, conversely, the representation is posterior to the learning: it merely documents what Du Fu has personally undergone. In effect, Du Fu's whole collection becomes for Yu a record of learning by experience that he and his contemporaries can reexperience for themselves to better understand their world.

Other recordizing critics suggest that because Du Fu's poetry derives from experience, readers also need to be experienced in order to read it well. From the earliest stages of the commentary tradition, it was held that "if one has not traveled ten thousand miles and read ten thousand books, one cannot read Du Fu," and over the last millennium a great many readers have claimed that their own lives prove this cliché.[62] Writing around the same time as Yu Ruli, Li Gang 李綱 (1083–1140) noted that "earlier, when I read Du Fu in times of peace, I never saw his artistry. Now, however, after I have personally experienced warfare and rebellion, whenever I chant his poems, it is as if I lived in his times, and I find his words clearly fit what is in my mind."[63] This comment sets the template for a great many appreciations of Du Fu since Li's time written at moments of crisis, from the collapse of the Southern Song to the fall of the Ming to the Second Sino-Japanese War.[64] Writing at the latter end of this series of traumas, Feng Zhi 馮至 (1905–93) reminisced that, "since the beginning of the War of Resistance, there is no one who has not directly or indirectly tasted the pain the Japanese invaders have brought the Chinese people. In these times, when I open Du Fu's poetry and begin to read, since I have myself this personal experience, I naturally can understand it one level deeper. Every word in Du Fu's poems is true . . . and, when I read these famous lines and famous poems, I feel that Du Fu was not merely the voice of the people of the Tang, but is the voice of us modern people as well."[65]

It is worth noting here that both Li Gang and Feng Zhi—and indeed Yu Ruli as well—hypostatize experience as something that can be repeated in the lives of different individuals living through different historical cataclysms. This idea that "real life truly has some basically repeating situations," in the words of Chen Yixin, is a crucial tenet of recordizing reading, ensuring that the records of an individual's experience will not be merely idiosyncratic or irrelevant to the lives of others.[66] It is important to point out, though, that however transindividual or transhistorical experience may become for recordizing readers, it should not be thought of as transcendent, in the sense of detachable from history or from the resolutely temporal details of life in this world. Instead—to anticipate the topic of the next chapter—its radical immanence is crucial to its ethical significance. Jiang Yingke 江盈科 (1553–1605), for example, contrasts Du Fu's grounding in his experience to Li Bai, the "Banished Transcendent" 謫仙, a towering and imaginative poet when he had some wine in him, but one who could not write of real hardship: "Du Fu, in comparison, was a man firm in adversity: . . . warfare, disorder, separation, hunger, cold, and sickness were all his true experiences, and the sufferings he underwent are all written in his poems."[67] Jiang immediately goes on to suggest that it is for this reason that, "when you read Du Fu's poems, you have to look at his year chart," which ties each of them to a particular historical moment. Li Gang, the editor of what he calls the first fully chronological edition of Du Fu's verse, makes the same point as well.[68]

The immanence of experience as a source of meaning is emphasized particularly clearly by Feng Zhi, the author of Du Fu's first "critical biography" (*pingzhuan* 評傳). Feng contrasts Du Fu with the philosophers who, he argues, have largely failed to solve China's problems. In attempting to abstract transcendent lessons from the world, the "cultural movements [spurred by these thinkers] had nothing to do with the people, and so, as soon as there is disorder, what the people experience is no different whatsoever from what Du Fu did."[69] By writing about his experience directly, by contrast, Du Fu provides a model for a more moral culture.

> In Du Fu, there is no transcendence, no breezy ease, only perseverant attachment (*zhizhuo* 執著): perseverant attachment to nature and perseverant attachment to human life. China has a great number of poems about nature, but who has written travel poems like Du Fu wrote from Qinzhou to Tonggu to Chengdu? . . . This was an arduous road, and these poems are not merely written out of what he saw with his eyes, but also out of what his

mind and spirit understood there, and out of his starved body walking it out step by step. . . . It is only through this spirit of perseverance that he could so powerfully write out the mountains and streams he passed through and so broadly depict the image of his age, making us feel more intimate with him, as we read his poems, than we do with any other poet of his era. Our own age is perhaps even more difficult than Du Fu's, and, for dealing with this difficulty, there is no use in flippancy or bluffing, transcendence or breezy ease. Only a spirit of perseverant attachment can conquer it. And this sort of spirit is precisely what we urgently need right now.[70]

"Perseverant attachment" was originally a Buddhist concept: the idea that we cling to the phenomena of our experience as if they were real, and despite the fact that this grasping inevitably occasions suffering. For Feng, though, the point is that experience *is* real, and irreducible to principles that can be grasped in the abstract. By writing out his suffering, Du Fu refuses to turn away from it. Though his experience may in a certain sense be timeless, therefore, his poetry provides an example of and a method for engaging productively with it in the here and now, rather than seeking to escape it into transcendent speculation.

In contrasting Du Fu's "perseverant attachment" with poets and thinkers who aimed at "transcendence" (*chaoran* 超然), Feng thus shows real insight into the three narrative series discussed in this chapter. As we saw, Du Fu set out from Qinzhou and towards Tonggu to find a paradise separated from the turmoils of this mundane earth.[71] Over the course of his journey to Chengdu, however, he became convinced by experience and reflection that no such paradise existed, that he would never escape the exile that defined his life. He would, as Feng Zhi says, have to persevere with it, finding meaning precisely in its complications, its frustrations, its refusal to offer some final, clear sense. The poetry that adopts this resolution is the subject of the next chapter.

FIVE

Vision and the Mundane

Du Fu's Years in Western Sichuan (760–65)

It is a signal tension in recordizing reading that it holds Du Fu to be special, even singular, but to be so less through exclusive, unattainable insights than through affording the dignity of classical verse to what is common, shared, and otherwise disdained. Du Fu, we are told, is great because he does what everyone could do: he "just writes what he sees," making poetry out of his real situation and true feelings. Where others seek to "transcend" such humbling, painful, or shameful experiences in wine or abstraction, he "holds to them perseveringly." As a result, we read-ers feel "more intimate with him than we do with any other poet of his era," as if his voice were our own, the voice of "all the people of disordered ages."[1] And "all the people" here has a pronounced sociological dimension as well: as Fu Gengsheng puts it, Du Fu's unusual "ability to recognize true reality [derived from] moving towards the folk," and the "realism of his verse was inextricably intertwined with its popular character."[2] He thus seems a remarkably approachable Poet Sage, as if the reason he was exceptional lay partly in his willingness not to be.

As with many of the paradoxes of recordizing reading, this one stems from a genuine insight. In Du Fu's time, poetry was often discussed as an elevated, even esoteric art, requiring poets to be learned in the high cultural tradition and, beyond this mere learning, to have access to its hidden sources in a way most people do not. Poetry, moreover, was built on exclu-sions: poetic topics were highly circumscribed to elegant, traditional ma-terials, and poets did not yet write about mundane realities in the way they would come to do from the ninth century on.[3] Instead of observing the gritty details of the common world, poets were described as transfiguring it or revealing wonders beyond our normal perception. In the years that followed his 760 arrival in Chengdu, however, Du Fu increasingly ironizes the ambitions characteristic of the late medieval art, writing verse that exposes the pretenses subtending high-cultural ideals and dwells on topics that fell beneath the attentions of elite literary forms.

Du Fu thus begins in this period to consider the possibility that he could, indeed, "just write what he saw," even in a daily life distantly removed from the elite contexts of capital poetry.[4] Yet this idea was not for him the article of faith it would come to be for recordizing readers, but rather the startling and still somewhat unassimilable implication of his ruminations in the last two periods we have considered. After questioning the capacity of traditional tropologies to make sense of his experience, that is, the poetry of his Sichuan years begins to depict their failure as revealing a previously unappreciated richness in what they overlook. This richness, moreover, turns out to inhere in the way the mundanities of his daily existence implicate the larger narrative of his life as a whole. Recordizing critics are right, therefore, to notice how often Du Fu finds meaning in the increasingly commonplace objects and affairs he concerns himself with in his exile. What they tend not to notice, however, is the surprise of this discovery, its continuing mysteriousness to Du Fu, and the roundabout ways he still felt he had to approach it. Significance was immanent in his world, just as recordizing critics suggest, but it was a significance he felt exceeded his capacity to conceptualize or represent.

Slipping the Tropological Mask

Shortly after arriving in Chengdu, Du Fu acquired a plot of land just outside the city walls and set about building a hermitage facing the Brocade River. Having accepted on his journey there that Sichuan would never be his home, he does not seem to have seriously considered himself as actualizing the traditional ideal of the recluse—a role that was paradigmatically adopted by choice rather than necessity. He had no other moral category to make sense of the life he was living, however, and the ideal still called to him even as he remained aware of his distance from it. His poetry in this period therefore employs this traditional tropology while undermining it in the same breath, as if he were simultaneously enjoying his recluse roleplay and also aware—sometimes laughing, sometimes dejected, often both at once—that it was a charade. Yet the charade itself was often what interested him. By paying attention to the ways his actual experience did not fit the recluse archetype, this poetry suggests there might be something worth taking seriously in the intricacies of a more full-bodied poetic persona and the richness of an imperfect, but real, life.

The increasing tonal complexity of Du Fu's poetry in this period is evident in some of the earliest—and most strikingly unusual—pieces he wrote after reaching Sichuan: a series of seven short quatrains presented to acquaintances in the local government he must hardly have known, requesting their help in setting up his house and grounds. Some of these requests are modest, others apparently exorbitant. Several, at least, seem to have been successful, and if they were, it is probably because this presumptuous poetasting, alternately low and soaringly poetic, allowed his interlocutors to feel they were in on the joke.[5]

憑何十一少府邕覓榿木栽　*Relying on District Defender*
He Yong to Seek Out Alder Saplings

草堂塹西無樹林	My thatched cottage, west of the trench, lacks a grove of trees;
非子誰復見幽心	if not you, who else could see this mind set on seclusion?
飽聞榿木三年大	I've heard my fill that alders get big within three years,
4　與致溪邊十畝陰	so bring me to this brookside five roods of shade.[a]

憑韋少府班覓松樹子　*Relying on District Defender Wei Ban*
to Seek Out Pine Sprouts

落落出群非櫸柳	Stately, standing apart from the herd, but not the wingnut tree;

a. "Five roods" echoes "Five Roods of Space" 十畝之間 from the *Classic of Poetry*, which is a complaint about a state that has lost all of its land, leaving each farmer with only a paltry ten *mu* (roughly equivalent to 1.25 acres or five roods). Clearly, "five roods" is not paltry in the context of this request.

青青不朽豈楊梅　　deep green that does not fade,
　　　　　　　　　　　but no mere bayberry.
欲存老蓋千年意　　I want to lodge in their old canopies
　　　　　　　　　　　thoughts of a thousand years,
4　爲覓霜根數寸栽　so seek for me some frosty stems
　　　　　　　　　　　of several inches to plant.

The run of poems from which this pair derives all presume upon Du Fu's status as a onetime official to ask local clerks for money, plantings, and elegant ceramic tableware that might render his cottage a more tropologically appropriate site for reclusion. It seems unlikely the high art of poetry had ever before been used in so transparently transactional a fashion; if it had, nothing like these poems survives in the work of any previous poet.[6] Du Fu, however, seems to have made a point of preserving them within his collection, foregrounding the fact that his attempts to affect the recluse's isolation, self-sufficiency, and naturalness in fact relied on material props too expensive for him to afford without help from the bureaucracy. Without these props, no one could see that Du Fu's thatched cottage, exposed near some drainage trench outside the city, symbolized a "mind of seclusion"; indeed, Du Fu seems himself to have found it difficult to think reclusive thoughts there without them.[7] Yet by paying attention to the government supply chains he hopes will provide him the standard accoutrements of an escape from society, these poems explode the pretenses of the trope he ostensibly seeks to enact. The result is a complex indirection, as Du Fu simultaneously depicts himself as pathetic—presenting doggerel to new-met acquaintances in hopes they might support his fragile and somewhat daft bookworm's fantasy—and also winks with his reader at this very affectation.

In suggesting that the poet is more complex than he initially presents himself, these quatrains prefigure many of the themes that will be characteristic of Du Fu's poetry throughout his Sichuan period, including in less instrumental contexts. He would similarly undermine his own pretenses at reclusion, for instance, once his house was fully supplied and when his bemused observations about the work it takes to maintain the illusion of isolation in a hermitage just outside the walls of a major city seem, therefore, directed at no one more than himself.[8]

早起　*Up Early*

春來常早起	Since spring has come, I'm always up early:
幽事頗相關	the work of seclusion really occupies me.
帖石防隤岸	I add rocks to prevent the bank from crumbling,
4　開林出遠山	thin the grove to bring out distant mountains.
一丘藏曲折	My one hill also hides twists and turns,
緩步有躋攀	and my slow strolls involve some climbing.[a]
童僕來城市	Here comes my servant boy now from the city,
8　瓶中得酒還	returning after getting ale for my jug.

Like many from his Chengdu years, this poem represents a moment of relative contentment for Du Fu after the hardships he had suffered during the Rebellion and in his journeys on the rugged frontier.[9] This serenity, however, is almost always accompanied by a self-deprecating humor hinting at the fragility of such pleasures. Manual labor had been part of the eremitic life as it appeared in poetry since the time of Tao Qian, and at first Du Fu's early rising in this poem seems merely to suggest that there is work to be done, work both necessary and beautiful. As the poem moves on, however, we learn that his is not quite the reclusion of mountains and waters that the second couplet might suggest. Instead, not only does Du Fu have a servant who could, presumably, do this work for him, but he is close enough to the city to send him there for ale. His "work of seclusion," therefore, is aimed less at sustaining a hermitage out in nature and more at improving the illusion that it is so—an illusion drinking will further. And yet it is precisely this illusion that the poem subverts.

Clearly, this is no longer the traumatic subversion of traditional tropologies that was characteristic of Du Fu's early Rebellion era poetry. Whereas those works dramatized the poet confounded by the collapse of his ethical categories, this poem and others like it show him not so much trying to make moral sense of his life as exploring its refusal to do so. In this case, the result is humorous, as if he were recognizing in himself a

a. The phrase "one hill" recalls the *Han History*'s discussion of Ban Biao: "Roaming and resting on his one hill, he wouldn't exchange his joy for the whole empire."

maturity capable of abiding imperfections. Elsewhere, however, the humor is tempered by darker implications.[10]

狂夫　*Madman*

	萬里橋西一草堂	Ten Thousand League Bridge, and to the west, 　　a single thatch cottage;
	百花潭水即滄浪	the waters of Hundred Flowers Pool 　　are my Canglang Stream.[a]
	風含翠篠娟娟靜	Wind envelops the azure bamboo, 　　quiet as it sways;
4	雨裛紅蕖冉冉香	rain soaks the red lotus, 　　more fragrant as it droops.
	厚禄故人書斷絕	Old friends with large salaries 　　have cut off their letters;
	恒飢稚子色淒涼	my children, always hungry, 　　bear forlorn complexions.
	欲塡溝壑惟踈放	That I'll soon fill some ditch just makes me 　　more careless and free:
8	自笑狂夫老更狂	I laugh at myself as a madman 　　getting madder in old age.[b]

Feigned madness in reclusion was often considered the sane approach to an age gone awry—an age, for example, in which officials with large salaries

a. Canglang Stream derives from the *Mengzi*: "Is it possible to speak with those who are not benevolent? Their perils they count safety and their defilement advantage, and thus they take joy in what destroys them. . . . There is a children's song that goes, 'When the waters of Canglang are clean, / I can wash my cap strings in them. / When the waters of Canglang are muddy, / I can wash my feet in them.' . . . [Thus,] a man brings disgrace upon himself, and only then do people disgrace him; a family destroys itself, and only afterwards do others destroy it." The song was conventionally understood to stand for the attitude of the noble man to the state: he could take office in an age of order or go into reclusion in an age of disorder, thus avoiding the disgrace and danger of serving a corrupt state.

b. "Filling a ditch" means to die in poverty without a proper burial. The phrase's locus classicus is also the *Mengzi*: "A man of high ambition does not forget that he might someday fill some ditch; a brave man does not forget that he may lose his life." In this quote, Mengzi is explaining why he has chosen not to serve the corrupt rulers of his age.

might lack the decency to remember their old friends' starving children. Yet Du Fu equivocates here as to whether his is the feigned madness of the recluse or something more serious: a lack of worldly wisdom that has harmed his family, or even the deepening result of ongoing trauma.

Each couplet of the poem is marked by these complexities. The first, for instance, intimates both the wretchedness of the poet's exile ten thousand leagues from home and the beauty and simplicity of his hermitage, scenically located here over Hundred Flowers Pool. This latter thread is picked up by the second couplet, whose minute observations suggest the recluse's affinity with nature and perhaps also Du Fu's increasing freedom from social constraint, his maintenance of inner quietude and fragrant virtue despite the storms of the age. There is, however, a bitter irony in the fact that, even as the bamboo and lotus of this couplet glow red and azure through more literal storms, the colors (*se* 色, "complexions") of his family's faces grow ever more dreary as he sits in their tumbledown cottage writing useless poetry about it. They, he suggests, may starve to death before him, leaving no one to provide him a civilized burial and thus ensuring that his final intimacy with nature will be to roll into the ditch where the lotuses bloom.[11] The laughter of the final line, therefore, which simultaneously suggests amusement at the unexpected aptness of this ending, withering disdain for himself, and helpless despair, becomes an emblem of the poem's complex moral structure.

The verse's ambivalences are also carried by its allusions, in particular its bookending references to the *Mengzi*. Both of the passages Du Fu recalls here speak of the nobility of the recluse, but in ways that have equivocal implications for his particular situation. The children's song about Canglang Stream, for instance, enjoins him not to serve a corrupt state—as he is in fact not doing—but also argues that the ruin of any family must be the fault of the family itself: by implication here, Du Fu's in his very choice to abandon his office. The allusion thus points the poet in apparently opposite directions, by which he is simultaneously the sort of man Mengzi praises and also responsible for his family's suffering. These two interpretations are not, of course, incompatible, any more than it is impossible to both grieve and laugh at the possibility of dying next to fragrant lotuses. But the unresolved suspension of these two interpretations does suggest that the realities of Du Fu's life may be more multifaceted than established moral scripts, like Mengzi's, can capture.

Poetic Apophasis

If these poems offer reflections on the nature of Du Fu's life, they also meditate on the poetic procedures by which he represents it. In revealing the pretense underwriting the ideal reclusion they initially seemed to depict, each purports to let the reader in on something behind the poet's obfuscations, fantasies, and façades, becoming a lie through which some truth is indirectly revealed. Many of Du Fu's poems from this period take on this logic of apophasis, raising topics by deflecting them and rupturing their own deceptive surfaces to intimate something more complex beneath.[12] In so doing, these poems often suggest that some rich meaning lurks in the mundanities of his daily life, but they do not claim to exhaust it.

Often, the appreciation of this structure relies upon a knowledge of Du Fu's history, and thus upon the novel form of the poetry collection he had begun to pioneer in his travel sequences. He will depict himself, for instance, enjoying the prototypical pleasures of the recluse only to hint, at the end, that he is trying to distract himself thereby from other realities, realities we may know from reading his larger collection but that are not legible in the text at hand. In the following poem, for example, the result is a joke whose lingering bitterness tempers the levity of what came before.[13]

徐步   *Strolling Slowly*

	整履步青蕪	I straighten my sandals to stroll through greening weeds;
	荒庭日欲晡	in my overgrown yard, the sun is soon to set.
	芹泥隨燕觜	Twigs and mud follow swallows' beaks;
4	花蕊上蜂鬚	flower pollen climbs on bee whiskers.
	把酒從衣濕	Taking ale, I don't mind my clothes getting wet;
	吟詩信杖扶	chanting poems, I let my cane go where it will.
	敢論才見忌	How could I claim my talents drew me spite?
8	實有醉如愚	yet truly it does happen that I get drunk as a fool.[a]

---

a. To be "like a fool" in an age of disorder was often accounted a sign of wisdom.

Huang Sheng comments: "The words 'I straighten my sandals' make me laugh out loud. Why should sandals have to be straightened? It's because they're old, worn out sandals that they trouble him to straighten them in the first place."[14] Du Fu, that is, is drunk, and drunkenly sets out to show proper decorum as he strolls through his courtyard's weeds. This light-hearted drunkenness fills the first three couplets of this poem, accounting in particular for the delicate observations of the second—visual naïveté of this sort appearing in several verses from around this period as an indication of an altered mental state simultaneously comic and profound.[15] It is no coincidence, therefore, that poetry and ale occur in parallel in the penultimate couplet, since both are implicated in this absorption of attention in the minute and the present, to the happy exclusion of everything beyond the hyperfocus of Du Fu's drunk, poetic gaze.

The repressed returns, however, in the ambiguities of the final couplet. On the one hand, recluses were supposed to feign folly as a way of avoiding conscription into the doomed governments of their times; being "drunk as a fool" could, in such cases, enact a more fundamental sobriety and good judgment. Read straight, therefore, Du Fu seems to be remarking delightedly the correspondence between his own drunkenness here and the paradigmatic drunkenness of the ideal recluse, even if he is willing to grant that, unlike other recluses throughout history, he is not hiding away from the slanders of envious rivals. On the other hand, however, if his "talents" here refer to the poetry that should have helped him earn a prestigious government office, the line takes on a mordancy that casts aspersions backwards on the drunken and trivial "poetry" of this poem itself, which in its absorption in bee pollen and swallows' mud is too foolish to draw him the sort of envy that would justify reclusion. Having wasted his talents and landed himself here in self-imposed exile, perhaps he should see himself simply as a fool, and not as feigning folly.

In taking itself as its subject in this way, this poem reflects on the functions that the poetic art had come to perform for Du Fu in Sichuan. It suggests, that is, that the activity of writing served as a sort of opiate, distracting him from the melancholy motivations that drove his obsessive composition. Precisely in offering this suggestion, however, the poem also fails to screen out the troubles he ostensibly uses it to escape, making them instead the silent center of the verse. If Du Fu thus diagnoses his poetry as a means of evading reality, this very diagnosis repurposes it into a tool for engaging with it more fully.[16]

江亭 River Pavilion

	坦腹江亭暖	I lie belly out in the river pavilion's warmth,
	長吟野望時	chanting slowly as I gaze out on the wilds.[a]
	水流心不競	The water flows—my mind does not compete;
4	雲在意俱遲	the clouds remain—my thoughts are just as slow.
	寂寂春將晚	Silent and lonesome, the spring will soon grow late;
	欣欣物自私	lush and cheerful, each thing attends itself.
	故林歸未得	Since to my old groves I cannot yet return,
8	排悶強裁詩	to hold off gloom I force myself to trim this poem.

Despite the comfortable idleness that Du Fu seems to be describing in the first six lines of this poem, the final couplet reveals that he is in fact "holding off" gloom and "forcing" himself to write. Reread from this perspective, the middle couplets reveal a tension beneath their apparent placidity. The poet notices that "each thing attends itself," that is, because the scene refuses to attend to his desires, to slow down its hints of his encroaching old age. His thoughts are slow as the clouds, similarly, not so much because he is comfortable as because he is actively trying to prevent them from running off with the water, downstream towards the east on the journey he would have to make to return to his hometown. He is gazing on the wilds and chanting poetry, that is, as a form of mental discipline, observing what is near so as to avoid thinking about what is far.

It does not work, of course: precisely by admitting this motivation, Du Fu turns the poem into a depiction of his inability to attain, via the "trimming" of this verse, the self-absorbed contentment he sees around him. This metaphor of "trimming" is a crucial clue as to why. Drawn from tailory, the metaphor applies here in two senses: first, insofar as the regulated verse form is cut to a pattern like a garment; and, second, insofar as the artistic process is one of "cutting out," of excluding parts of the fuller fabric. Yet everything Du Fu tries to cut out of this poem works its way back in. As in "Strolling Slowly," the poem's self-depiction as an escapist art renders

---

a. To lie with one's belly exposed was a paradigm of insouciance.

it, ultimately, the opposite, focusing attention on the realities of his life that register only at the margins of the verse and that we know only through reading the larger collection.

If this poem thus gestures towards the breadth of the poet's experience in history, which is too great and too painful to be captured in a short regulated verse, the apophatic technique also could be used to suggest moments of unfathomable depth. In poems like the following, for instance, Du Fu begins to hint that even the mundane phenomena of his daily world—here a springtime swelling of the Brocade River outside his gate—are rich and significant, past description.[17]

江上值水如海勢聊短述 *On the River I Encountered Waters with the Force of a Sea, and All I Wrote Was This Short Piece*

爲人性僻耽佳句	I'm a man eccentric by nature, addicted to lovely lines;
語不驚人死不休	if my words don't startle people, death would not make me rest.
老去詩篇渾漫興	Grown old now, though, my poems are just offhand whims;
4 春來花鳥莫深愁	when spring comes, you birds and flowers shouldn't worry overmuch.
新添水檻供垂釣	Recently I added a deck on the water to provide for dangling a hook,
故著浮槎替入舟	and so I'll take it as a floating raft to replace using a boat.[18]
焉得思如陶謝手	But how can I find a master poet with thoughts like Tao or Xie?[a]
8 令渠述作與同遊	I'd have them do the writing and go with them to roam.

This poem hardly touches on its occasion, which should properly have demanded a longer verse in the ancient style—or, even better, a rhapsody (*fu* 賦), the standard genre for "giving form to things" (*tiwu* 體物)—that strove to match with the force of its language the river's swollen waters.[19]

---

a. Tao Qian and Xie Lingyun—and perhaps also Xie Tiao 謝朓 (464–99)—famous poets of the Six Dynasties period.

Yet though this short regulated verse ostensibly declines to meet this challenge, some critics have seen it subtly doing so nonetheless. Chen Chunru, for example, identifies the opening couplet, in which Du Fu disclaims his lifelong obsession with startling lines, as itself among the most startling in the entire tradition. For him, therefore, the fact that a poet still capable of such a remarkable poetic statement does not even attempt a description of this vast flood speaks to the flood's vastness—even better, perhaps, than a longer piece could. The poem, we might say, becomes an analogue of the deck Du Fu suggests in the third couplet will be carried away by the onrushing waters: precisely in their inability to match up to it, both flimsy deck and flimsy poem intimate beneath them surging power.[20] This is, as Chen puts it, "writing the flood by not writing the flood."[21]

Poetic Vision in Late Medieval China

The apophatic poetics of these last several poems diverge markedly from the mainstream of late medieval thought about poetry's capacities and purposes. "All I Wrote Was This Short Piece" is particularly illuminating in this regard since it engages fairly explicitly with contemporary literary theory, some discussion of which can thus deepen our understanding of the poem both as a joke and as a statement of Du Fu's evolving poetics. In the eight lines of this regulated verse, he invokes and disclaims five ideas characteristic of contemporary literary discourse, each of which demarcated poetry's ideal distance from the mundane and highlighted the special powers attributed to successful poets by late medieval theorists. The poem, therefore, offers an opportunity to gauge how strange and startling some of his Sichuan verse would have been for his contemporaries.

The first term of literary-theoretical art that Du Fu calls on in this poem is *xing* 興 (translated atypically above as "whim"), a word with a long critical history and, for this reason, a large semantic range. Only one of its meanings is relevant here: "incipient inspiration," the excitement that accompanies and supports the dawning of good literary ideas. Though "inspiration" in this sense is not inherently incompatible with a recordizing vision of poetry, the term's use in late medieval theory often suggests that something needs to be added to raw experience before it can be used in a poem. As an eighth-century essay dubiously attributed to Wang Changling puts it, for instance, "if you have [good] images for a poem but no inspiration (*yi xing* 意興), even if you write skillfully, it will be of no use."[22]

> After a boat journey, you should go to sleep right away. When you have slept enough, the clear scenes of mountains and rivers filling your breast [from the previous day] will merge and give rise to inspirations; at this point, you should screen out all business and single-mindedly let your passions and inspirations go where they will. If you do this, whatever you write will be remarkable and untrammeled. If you find your inspiration subsiding, but your poem is not finished, wait until some later inspiration: you must not force it, and thus harm your spirit.

> 舟行之後，即須安眠。眠足之後，固多清景，江山滿懷，合而生興，須屏絕事務，專任情興。因此，若有製作，皆奇逸。看興稍歇，且如詩未成，待後有興成，却必不得強傷神。[23]

Elsewhere, this same essay mocks a poem that appears to be merely a detailed list of perceptions without an organizing concept.[24] A mere record of experience, the essay thus suggests, will not be enough. The experience, rather, needs to be integrated by a spark of inspiration that, in its unwillingness to be forced and its miraculousness when it does occur, recalls the sorts of spontaneous "meditative vision" (*jing* 境) that were pursued by medieval Buddhist adepts.[25]

> When your eye strikes upon a thing, you need your mind to strike upon it: to deeply penetrate the meditative vision (*jing*) of it, as if you had climbed the highest peak of a tall mountain and were looking down on the myriad images as if they were in the palm of your hand. When you see an image in this way, your mind sees it completely, and at this point it can be used in a poem.

> 目擊其物，便以心擊之，深穿其境。如登高山絕頂，下臨萬象，如在掌中。以此見象，心中了見，當此即用。[26]

In yet other passages, this essay suggests that writing occurs in a kind of ecstatic state in which the poet both "forgets his body" and also "places it" as one more object within the scene his mind comprehends synoptically, as if from above.[27] When Du Fu says, therefore, that he only writes on "offhand whims" (*manxing* 漫興), he is suggesting that his poetry is now the result of inspiration less single-minded, less towering, and more haphazard than the vision this essay enjoins poets to cultivate.

This claim to casualness might have been striking in the late medieval context, when the process of literary conceptualization that underwrote composition was often treated as an application of the loftiest and most mysterious capacities of the human being. Liu Xie, for example, discusses this process under the heading of "thought" (*si* 思), the second literary-critical term of art Du Fu invokes and disclaims in "All I Wrote."

> The thought in *wen* sends the spirit far. If we silently focus our attention, thought may reach back a thousand years; with an imperceptible movement of the face, our vision penetrates ten thousand leagues. As we chant poetry, the sounds of pearls and jade are breathed in and out; right there before our eyelashes furl and unfurl the forms of wind and clouds. It is thought that makes this possible: for when thought is subtle, the spirit can wander with things.
>
> 文之思也，其神遠矣。故寂然凝慮，思接千載；悄焉動容，視通萬里。吟詠之間，吐納珠玉之聲；眉睫之前，卷舒風雲之色。其思理之致乎！故思理爲妙，神與物遊。[28]

This is about as a clear a statement of the late medieval period's non-recordizing poetics as can be found in surviving materials. For Liu, literary conceptualization is not passive to experience. Instead, it is thought's freedom to roam across a thousand years and ten thousand leagues, to create clouds out of nothing and treasures from sounds, that allows us to transform even present realities into literature.

> When spirit and thought begin to move, ten thousand paths vie to sprout before them; they take square and compass to empty positions and carve and chisel what has no form. If one climbs a mountain, one's feelings will fill the mountains [or the mountains will fill one's feelings]; if one observes the sea, one's ideas will overflow the sea [or overflow with the sea]. And depending upon one's talent, one can gallop alongside the windblown clouds.
>
> 夫神思方運，萬塗競萌，規矩虛位，刻鏤無形。登山則情滿於山，觀海則意溢於海 ，我才之多少，將與風雲而並驅矣。[29]

The ambiguities of this passage, noted in the alternate translations given in brackets, follow the logic of the argument. For Liu, there can be no fundamental difference between seeing one's emotion filling the mountains and feeling the mountains filling one's emotions. Rather, the point is that both aspects of the experience are inherently formless until spirit and thought give them a unified form.[30] "Thought," therefore, operates for Liu like an army commander "determining victory without opening his tent flaps."[31] It provides the conditions that establish how experience can play out rather than merely reacting to what comes, as Du Fu suggests he now does with his "offhand whims."

For Liu Xie, therefore, "thought" is essentially creative, and in a way that may help to explain the third contemporary literary-critical commonplace gestured towards by "All I Wrote": Du Fu's reassurance to the birds and flowers that his lazy writing should no longer make them "worry overmuch." Despite what has sometimes been claimed in Western scholarship on traditional Chinese poetics—based, I believe, on the recordizing models of the later tradition, by which poets paradigmatically "transmit but do not create"—Liu's sense that literary thought is prior to experience is actually quite characteristic of late medieval literary theory, which often focuses on the quasi-cosmogonic creativity of poets.[32] The pseudo–Wang Changling, for instance, urges poets to "exert thought (*si* 思) in the space before primal *qi* has come into being," and we find pervasively in Tang aesthetic discourse the trope that artists are "creators" (*zuozhe* 作者), "participating in creation," "matching its work," or "shaking hands with the creator."[33] In some cases, poets were even thought to "compete with creation" or to "steal what is proper to it"—a trope Du Fu appeals to frequently himself, writing of artists who "plunder the caves of creation" and cause the "creator of things to complain above and heaven itself to weep."[34] In other cases, even closer to Liu Xie's claim that literary thought "carves and chisels what has no form," poets were depicted as imposing shape onto a world that would otherwise escape conceptualization. Poets thus "cage heaven and earth within form and abase all things under the brush's tip," "imprisoning the primeval void, wielding mysterious creation, deploying primal *qi* in the outstanding blade tip of their words, and pressing in upon the gapless [i.e., nonbeing, the *dao*] as they dissect it at the joints."[35] They thus follow in the tradition of the ancient sage Cang Jie 倉頡, who ensured in his invention of writing that "creation could no longer hide its mysteries, so heaven rained grain, and the spirits could no longer secret their forms, so ghosts wept by night."[36] By writing the world, that is, poets strove either to outdo it or to pin it down into a humanly significant shape. If, therefore, the birds and flowers by Du Fu's thatched pavilion no longer have to worry about him "abasing," "carving," or "revealing" them in this way, it is a sign that his literary ambitions no longer run towards such giving of fixed, humanly significant "forms to things" (*tiwu*).

It is perhaps not a coincidence, furthermore, that Du Fu should link his disinterest in "caging heaven and earth within form" to a decreased drive to produce "shocking" lines—the fourth common late medieval literary-critical trope abjured by "All I Wrote." In the Tang context, such lines would not necessarily have been shocking in the sense of unusual; rather, they might have been shocking precisely in how natural and how inevitable they seemed. Jiaoran, for instance, writes of "outstanding lines of such perfect naturalness (*tianzhen* 天眞) that they compete with creation" and that can, therefore, only be "recognized by someone who is a creator himself" and thus knows how difficult it is to come up with them.[37] For Jiaoran, this sort of naturalness may in fact require painstaking labor.

> Some say that in poetry you should not wrack your thought (*ku si*), that, if you do, it will harm the poem's naturalness. This is deeply false. Of course you need to keep your attention continuously on perilous straits and pluck the remarkable from beyond images, writing lines that stir into flight and inscribing thought of the darkest mysteries. A pearl of great rarity must surely be found under [the deadly scales of] a black dragon's chin; how much more is this the case of *wen* that communicates with the hidden and holds transformation within? It is just important that, after the piece is written, it should seem easy, as if one had gotten it without thought.

> 或曰：詩不要苦思，苦思則喪於天眞。此甚不然。固須繹慮於險中，采奇於象外，狀飛動之句，寫冥奧之思。夫希世之珠，必出驪龍之頷，況通幽含變之文哉？但貴成章以後，有其易貌，若不思而得也。[38]

Clearly, Jiaoran's interest in "naturalness" does not result in a recommendation that poets write common experiences and sentiments easily recognized by all readers—as many recordizing critics have suggested that Du Fu does. Instead, he suggests that a truly great poet will add to the repertoire of what seems natural to readers, expanding their experience of the world by drawing forth new visions from the darkness from which it derived.

Good examples of this common late medieval account of poetic creativity can also be found in the preface to Yuan Jing's 元兢 (fl. 668) *Outstanding Lines of Poets Past and Present* 古今詩人秀句, which helpfully makes clear how far this vision is from recordizing reading's interest in the experiences and feelings that any person might have. Yuan's preface focuses on examples by Xie Tiao.

> If you understand his point and the way he expresses it in *wen*, then every time you think of [his line] "A cold lamp lights my nighttime dream," it will cause your soul to be shocked from sleep in the middle of the night, and if you have seen his "The clear mirror saddens my morning locks," then always in the humid months unawares a chill will steal upon your temples.
>
> 若悟此旨而言於文，每思寒燈耿宵夢，令人中夜安寢不覺驚魂，若見清鏡悲曉髮，每暑月鬱陶不覺霜雪入鬢。[39]

For Yuan, reading these lines does not recall an experience he has had before; instead, it transforms the way he experiences the world going forward. Surely, for instance, he had previously slept beside a glowing lamp, but it never struck him as wondrous until he read Xie's poem. Great poetry, he thus suggests, should be simultaneously revelatory and, once it is articulated, inescapable. To create such works, poets cannot themselves be merely average, and they cannot simply write out the mundane experiences an average person might have. They must rather transform them.

> "A line of trees grows bright amidst the distant shadow; / the clouds turn strange colors." This couplet indeed gets something, and it can thus be called an excellent verse. Yet looking out at dusk, there is no one who does not smelt his imaginations into mist and clouds, refine his emotions into forests and peaks. . . . Therefore, a person of middling talent could perhaps occasionally get a couplet as good as this. It does not match the wondrousness of "By the setting sun the flying birds return; / sorrows come, and come without end." . . . [Here, Xie Tiao] is saying that, as he strokes his breast, his cares have nothing to light upon, and so he raises his eyes and his yearning increases. His intent can only be on the person [to whom the poem was written], but he lodges this feeling in the birds. As the sun sets, he follows

them with his gaze until he cannot see them anymore; the twilight birds return to congregate together, and so his sorrows come flying with them. How beautiful was Xie Tiao to have thought (*si*) like this!

行樹澄遠陰，雲霞成異色，誠爲得矣，抑絕唱也。夫夕望者，莫不鎔想煙霞，煉情林岫⋯中人已下，偶可得之；但未若落日飛鳥還，憂來不可極之妙者也。⋯謂捫心罕屬，而舉目增思，結意惟人，而緣情寄鳥，落日低照，即隨望斷，暮禽還集，則憂共飛來。美哉玄暉，何思之若是也。[40]

Both of the couplets discussed here derive from the same poem by Xie Tiao. Yuan is not, therefore, criticizing the first couplet—which had been praised by a critical rival—so much as identifying the second as the real locus of the poem's excellence. The latter couplet is arresting because it is something that the average person could not have seen in the same circumstances, a mental creation formed by blending scene and emotion that, in Liu Xie's words, "gallops alongside the windblown clouds." And yet when, from now on, Yuan Jing himself looks out at dusk, thinking of a distant friend, there is little doubt his experience will recall Xie Tiao's poem.

What Yuan suggests here, in effect, is that *wen* can re-create a reader's world. If, that is, a poet's "thought" can merge the raw sensory data of his perceptions and feelings into transcendent "inspirations," so too can the result of those inspirations, the poem itself, transfigure the perceptions and feelings of its readers. This is the fifth and final late medieval commonplace that Du Fu invokes in "All I Wrote," when he wishes he could go roaming on the floodwaters with a poet like Tao Yuanming, Xie Lingyun, or Xie Tiao, who might conjure for him visions he claims himself now, in his old age, unable to see. In expressing this wish, Du Fu might have been thinking of previous accounts of roaming with long-dead visionaries, such as the following by the early Tang poet Wang Bo 王勃 (650–76).

Every time I encounter a clear day between heaven and earth, I go out in my boat and chant Xie Lingyun's poem on "Going against the Current to Lonely Isle." As if in a daze, I exhaust thought of slopes and marshes, mountains and forests. [The legendary immortal isles of] Yingzhou and Fangzhang are then mysteriously before my eyes.

每遇天地晴朗，則於舟中詠大謝亂流趨孤嶼之詩。渺然盡陂澤山林之思，覺瀛洲方丈，森然在目前。[41]

Wang goes on from this comment to note that part of his enjoyment of these excursions was the poetry he composed on them, suggesting that Xie Lingyun's verse helped stimulate his own literary creativity. There is some evidence that medieval writers often used previous verse in this way, since Lu Ji describes "roaming the groves and storehouses of literature" as part of the initial process of composition, and the pseudo–Wang Changling essay recommends that poets carry with them a scroll of fine lines so that, "if they do not have any inspiration to write, they might glance at this scroll in order to unleash that inspiration."[42] By entering into the visions presented in previous poems, the suggestion is, late medieval poets could become capable of seeing their own feelings and experiences in new ways. They could then go on to write their own verse, continuing the revelation of the world's mysteries that, according to the cosmogonic mythology of This Culture of Ours discussed in chapter 2, had been initiated by Fu Xi, developed by the later sages, and sustained by worthies ever since.

It is ultimately Du Fu's place in this tradition of revelation and transfiguration that is threatened by his disavowal of these five late medieval literary-critical commonplaces. His vision has failed, and in his exile and isolation he has no one to roam with whose "thought" might transfigure his world into something beyond the mundane. Yet though this conclusion may seem bleak, the poem is also quite clearly a joke, and one whose humor lies partly in its surprising technical brilliance as a regulated verse, a form that in the middle of the eighth century was particularly associated with striking visions. Although Du Fu claims, that is, that this poem is no poem, its form pushes back, suggesting that there may be something arrestingly novel here after all, both in the unfathomable world he observes, which refuses to submit to human meaning, and in the progress of his poetic thought, which has culminated in his decision to depict it by disclaiming the ability to do so.

The Immanence of Recordizing Reading

In poems like "All I Wrote," Du Fu's increasing divergence from the late medieval model becomes the explicit topic of his verse. Poetry of this sort required a new set of ideals to make sense of it, thereby inviting the innovations of recordizing reading, which offers a very different poetics of vision. Where for late medieval theorists, poetic vision involved access to realms of insight "beyond" the mundane and beyond the reach of most people, recordizing critics often suggest that Du Fu's preeminent poetic virtue was simply getting out of his own way, allowing mundane whims of mood and scene, what could be experienced by anyone, to manifest their miraculous convergences in verse. If medieval theorists disparaged middling, uninspired poetry, therefore, these commentators have often reserved their deeper scorn for inauthenticity that would pretend to insights beyond those available to most people.[43]

Accordingly, the verse of Du Fu's Sichuan period has frequently been praised for its easy unpretentiousness, often in terms that depict this quality as a quasi-spiritual attainment. Commenting on "All I Wrote," for instance, Huang Jiashu 黄家舒 (1600–1669?) opines that "offhand whims" (*manxing*) are precisely what animate the work of a true master, who has no desire to impress others, but merely "feels inspired by whatever scene he encounters," "writing when he cannot but write and stopping when he cannot but stop."[44] Qiu Zhao'ao, similarly, suggests that "when Du Fu was young he labored for artistry, but now that he is old, he has become comfortable in the poetic realm (*shi jing* 詩境) and just casually throws this off, without suffering [the hard work of] wracked chanting (*ku yin* 苦吟)" when he "happens" (*ou* 偶) not to feel particularly inspired (*xing*).[45] And Zhao Xinghai 趙星海 (fl. 1863), likewise, writes that "having the inspiration to write long, Du Fu would write long; short, then he would write short: this is what he means when he says that, in his old age, his poetic realm (*shi jing*) became more spiritual (*shen hua* 神化)."[46] In a good example of how recordizing critics can disagree vociferously within their shared framework, Zhao actually frames his comment as a critique of Qiu's, arguing that, since no longer description of the flood could have been more striking than this short verse, Du Fu must have been "inspired" (*xing*) when he wrote it. Yet whatever their differences on this point, all these critics agree that the poem expresses a spiritual and poetic maturity that can discern and adapt to the poetry in any circumstance without forcing it into a predetermined shape.

Recordizing reading thus generally depicts poetry as deriving not from a flash of transfiguring "vision"—as it did for the pseudo–Wang Changling, who compared poetic images to the unaccountable perceptual phenomena (*jing* 境) that may appear in meditation—but rather from a poet's habitual inhabitation of a constant "spiritual realm" (*shi jing* or *jingjie* 境界).[47] Since the time of Gao Chufang 高楚芳 (1255–1308), for example, commentary on the poem "River Pavilion" has focused on Du Fu's observation in the fifth line that, "lush and cheerful, each thing attends itself," the resigned tone of which has often been interpreted as representing Du Fu's "enlightenment" or his "recognition of the *dao*"—presumably, his acceptance, after the Rebellion, that the fecundity of the natural world will not pause for human suffering.[48] Like Qiu's claim that "All I Wrote" was the product of a moment when Du Fu happened not to be inspired, this interpretation has generated some pushback, but again in ways that merely reinforce recordizing reading's disinterest in the sort of "perilous" insights so often valorized in the late medieval period. As Wang Sishi puts it, the poem's words are merely the result of "a meeting of scene and mind, and thus express the *dao* in a way that was unexpected [even to Du Fu himself]. This is probably because, in moments of ease, his innate feeling for the *dao* (*daoji* 道機) simply revealed itself naturally."[49] Pu Qilong, similarly, suggests that the "feeling for the *dao*" Du Fu shows in this poem "came from his nature and not from studying the *dao* like some Neo-Confucian."[50] Both sides of this debate, then, read the poem as displaying a wisdom that was characteristic of Du Fu at this point in his life, whether by nature or through suffering. Some critics just want to emphasize more than others that this wisdom was defined by a casual unconcern with being wise.

This latter, internally tense ideal of spiritual achievement is symptomatic of recordizing reading, which is caught between its central claim that poets should simply "write what they see" and its sense that few have ever done this so well as Du Fu. Necessary for reconciling this tension is an account of most poets as unaware that their experience is important or as incapable of getting out of their own way in describing it. As Huang Sheng puts it in his comment about "River Pavilion,"

> When people get beyond things for a moment and cease their toils, gazing at the clouds and overlooking the waters, their minds will truly experience this scene. It is merely that most have trouble speaking it out. Anyone who could speak it out would certainly be a fine poet. Yet [this poem] is merely

something thrown together of mind and eye, written out by chance (*ouran*).
Diligent effort and planning could not match it.

人從物外暫息勞生，望雲臨水，心下眞有此段光景，只是口中苦説
不出。能説得出，豈非好手？然亦心眼相湊，偶然寫成，非刻畫之
所及也。[51]

The conflicting impulses of recordizing criticism are on full display in this
comment, and for that reason it provides a useful contrast to the late medieval poetic theory discussed above. Where Yuan Jing had deprecated
even an excellent line that nonetheless could have been "gotten by a person
of middling talent," Huang here praises Du Fu precisely for writing out
what anyone might feel. And where Liu Xie had depicted poetic "thought"
planning behind its tent flaps like a skillful general, Huang suggests that
conjunctions that "happen by chance" will be more wondrous than any
that purposive planning could produce. For recordizing readers like
Huang, the world itself is rich with meaning and value. The poet's task,
therefore, is less to "exert thought in the space before primal *qi* has come
into being" than to "flow along with heaven and earth as they are transformed by the pivot of cosmic change"—as the "Retired Gentleman of
Stone Alley" 石閭居士 (identity unknown, fl. 1828?) puts it in his own
remarks on "River Pavilion."[52]

This idea of "flowing along with heaven and earth" also contrasts
markedly with the late medieval vision of poets as "creators" or as "competing with creation." Though recordizing critics do not do away entirely
with this vocabulary of creativity, they shift it in such a way as to ensure
that poets' creative work can no longer be antagonistic to that of the world
at large. Commenting on the precise observations of nature in the second
couplet of "Strolling Slowly," for instance—where "Twigs and mud follow
swallows' beaks" and "flower pollen climbs on bee whiskers"—the Retired
Gentleman of Stone Alley opines that, while other people in their bustling
overlook "the unchanging principles of things," the relaxed ease with which
Du Fu observes the swallows and bees in this poem allows him to "have
creation (*zaohua* 造化) within his breast" and to prove that "within a single
household can be found the images of heaven and earth and all the myriad
things."[53] Deng Xianzhang 鄧獻璋 (fl. 1736), similarly, comments that the
same couplet proves that great poetry is the work of the universe itself.

"This couplet's remarkable scene," he writes, "was all there before his eyes. That someone as skillful as Du Fu should have happened (*ou*) to have seen this scene [shows that] there was creation itself in his writing hand (*you huagong zai shou* 有化工在手)."[54]

This last comment is particularly revealing of the underlying shift that has occurred from late medieval to recordizing poetics. Recordizing reading, that is, seeks either to document or to participate in creation and is, in this sense, an "immanent" poetics—of much the sort Western scholarship has sometimes ascribed to the Chinese tradition as a whole.[55] This immanent poetics diverges markedly, however, from those late medieval theoretical discussions examined above, for which poetry strove either to compete with or to transform the created world by getting "beyond" it to reactivate its sources. Whether or not we would call this late medieval model "transcendent"—to recall Feng Zhi's term from the previous chapter—these two paradigms diverge on the poetic value of the everyday world Du Fu had begun to discover in his Sichuan verse. By no longer awaiting the transfiguring vision he has begun to disclaim in poems like "All I Wrote," recordizing criticism is thus faithful to some of the deeper impulses of this period's work.

Apophasis and the Immanent

There remains, however, some daylight between the poetic models of his recordizing critics and Du Fu's own experimentation in this period with ideas of immanence. His continued deployment of an apophatic rhetoric to intimate the complexities of his mundane life, in particular, suggests that this poetry sits at a transitional stage between the late medieval and recordizing models. He had begun to sense, that is, that there might be more to his life than should have been allowed by its apparent divergence from traditional scripts, but that significance continued to transcend his ability to conceptualize or represent it.

In the seventh month of 762, Du Fu's patron in Chengdu, Yan Wu 嚴武, was recalled to court, and Du Fu accompanied him on the first leg of his journey. As soon as Yan left, an insurrection broke out in the city, and Du Fu was forced to sojourn in eastern Sichuan for over a year, living off the generosity of one local official after another. On one of his journeys between such lodgings, he wrote the following two poems, which, as a set, represent a meditation on his developing poetics.[56]

早發射洪縣南途中作   *Setting Out Early from Shehong County*
Going South, Written on the Road

	將老憂貧窶	Approaching old age I worry being poor:
	筋力豈能及	my sinews' strength isn't up to it.[a]
	征途乃侵星	And now my traveling road invades on starlight,
4	得使諸病入	it might allow various illnesses in.
	鄙人寡道氣	This vulgar fellow lacks the spirit for the way,
	在困無獨立	and in difficulty I can never stand alone.[b]
	傯裝逐徒旅	Packing my bags, I follow other travelers,
8	達曙凌險澁	'til daybreak crossing rugged steeps.
	寒日出霧遲	The brumal sun is slow emerging from the fog;
	清江轉山急	the cold river rushes its turns around the hills.
	僕夫行不進	The driver struggles to make progress;
12	駑馬若維縶	my old nag is as if hobbled.
	汀洲稍疎散	But when the sandflats and isles spread out a bit,
	風景開快怏	the scenery breaks my doleful gloom.
	空慰所尚懷	In vain should it console a heart that admires such things:
16	終非曩遊集	after all, this is no pleasure jaunt like back when.
	衰顏偶一破	Yet by chance my withered face still cracks a smile;
	勝事難屢把	such splendid sights one can't often ladle up.
	茫然阮籍途	A vast blur, this road of Ruan Ji,
20	更灑楊朱泣	once more splashed with Yang Zhu's tears.[c]

a. Du Fu might be thinking here of a passage from the *Liji*: "Participation in ritual requires neither wealth from the poor nor sinews' strength from the old." The point would be that he has neither.

b. "The spirit for the way" (*daoqi* 道氣) is a double entendre here. The most common meaning of the phrase is something like the "vital breath of the *dao*," a physico-spiritual vitality that might be cultivated by religious practice. *Dao*, however, also means simply a "road," like the road upon which Du Fu is currently embarking. According to the *Daodejing*, the *dao* "stands alone and does not change."

c. This couplet contains three allusions. The first is to the story of Ruan Ji, who used to "go off driving alone on a whim, not by any major road. When he would come to the end of the carriage tracks, he would weep bitterly and return." He was weeping because in his political life he was also "at the end of his road" (*qiong* 窮): unable to advance under

通泉驛南去通泉縣十五里山水作　　*Going Fifteen Leagues*
from Tongquan Post Station South to Tongquan County,
Written in the Landscape

溪行衣自濕	Walking by the stream our clothes grew damp;
亭午氣始散	not 'til noon did the vapors start to disperse.[d]
冬溫蚊蚋在	The winter warm, mosquitoes and midges remained;
4　人遠鳧鴨亂	far from people, ducks and teals in riot.
登頓生曾陰	As we climbed and descended, layered darkness grew;
欹傾出高岸	then we emerged from the overhang of tall cliffs.
驛樓衰柳側	The station tower there, aside withered willows;
8　縣郭輕煙畔	the county walls by a bank of light mist.
一川何綺麗	How lovely, this whole river plain!—
盡目窮壯觀	I stretch my eyes to exhaust the superb view.
山色遠寂寞	The mountains' colors grow desolate in the distance,
12　江光夕滋漫	and the river's shine at sunset overflows.
傷時愧孔父	Grieving for the times, I'm ashamed before Confucius,
去國同王粲	though distant from my country, I'm like Wang Can.[e]
我生苦飄零	Yet my life too has been bitterly tossed and fallen,
16　所歷有嗟嘆	and for all I've passed through, I've got sighs.

Commenting on these two poems, critics have often been most moved by
the vulnerability Du Fu shows in admitting that he "lacks the spirit for the

---

a corrupt government. The second allusion is to the ancient philosopher Yang Zhu 楊朱,
who was said to weep whenever he came to a crossroads; according to the *Huainanzi*, he
did so because crossroads symbolized the possibility of going astray. The third allusion is
to a poem of Ruan Ji's that mentions Yang Zhu: "Yang Zhu wept at crossroads; / Mozi
grieved at the dyeing of silk. . . . / Alas for you men on the road: / how can you keep your-
selves whole?" Here "on the road" is a metaphor for being in government.

　　d. "Walking by the stream" might recall Tao Qian's "Peach Blossom Spring," in which
a fisherman "walks along a stream" 緣溪行 and finds himself in a magical utopia.

　　e. Wang Can fled south in 193 CE to escape Dong Zhuo's 董卓 violent usurpation of
the Han dynasty. While in Jiangling, he wrote his famous "Rhapsody on Climbing the
Tower," in which he complained that, "while it is truly beautiful here, it is not my home."
In that same piece, Wang alluded to Confucius: "I grieve that my hometown is cut off; /
my tears fall, and I cannot make them cease. / Of old, when Confucius was in Chen, / he
sighed about wanting to 'return home.' . . . / Human emotion is always the same in yearning for one's homeland; / how could wealth or poverty alter our minds?" Wang is referring
here to an anecdote from the *Analects* where Confucius resolved to "return home" 歸與.

way" (*daoqi* 道氣). Indeed, several commentators have gone so far as to argue that this claim shows that he does, in fact, possess precisely this spiritual excellence—the fortitude, that is, necessary to follow the *dao*. Lu Yuanchang compares Du Fu to Confucius when he and his disciples were facing starvation between Chen and Cai, arguing that

> from antiquity on, sages and worthies have often had momentary doubts about themselves when they encountered difficulty. . . . We can tell from Du Fu's saying that he "lacks the spirit for the way" that, in fact, he has it, and we know from him saying that he "cannot stand alone" that he can. By this means, he differentiates himself from those who would force themselves to put a good face on their situation.

> 古來聖賢，遭此困窮，亦有不能自信之一日。…公曰寡道氣，知其有道氣。公曰無獨立，知其能獨立。與強顏者自異。[57]

Although Du Fu in the second poem denies the resemblance to Confucius that Lu finds here—or, rather, partly because of that fact—this paradoxical comment embodies a real insight into how these poems work. Each poem depicts a shift in the poet's mood, corresponding to his shifting sense of the meaning in his experience: the first poem moving from depression to elation, and the second, from elation to depression. Yet, instead of these negations canceling out what has come before, the compound allusions with which each poem ends reintegrate the superseded mood into a more complex synthesis. Both poems thus discover in Du Fu precisely what they explicitly deny him, a "spirit for the *dao*" in his lack of the same. As a received vision of significance falls away, an alternate version of that significance is revealed beneath it.

Consider the first poem of the diptych, the argument of which does, in fact, turn upon the couplet Lu Yuanchang isolates as its most important. "Spirit for the *dao*" (*daoqi*) here is a double entendre: on the one hand, it denotes exactly that spiritual excellence intended by Lu; on the other, it refers more concretely to the physical strength requisite to undertake the road (*dao*) that lies before Du Fu on this day of hard travel. This ambivalence will echo in the final couplet of the poem, in which Du Fu invokes two allusions that similarly play upon the ambiguity of the word *dao*. The first of these allusions, to Ruan Ji's penchant for weeping where the road ends (*qiong* 窮)—a metaphor for poverty (also *qiong*) of the sort Du Fu claims for himself in the poem's first line—implies that everywhere Du Fu goes is "the end of his road," that nowhere can he find any possibility for official advancement. The second allusion, to Yang Zhu, however, complicates this first tropology, suggesting that because his life has in this sense no goal towards which he is traveling, everywhere is a crossroads marking out passed up possibilities. By continuing on towards Tongquan, specifically, he is giving up the possibility of staying on in this unexpectedly beautiful landscape to make a life for himself here as a recluse. As it turns out, therefore, precisely because Du Fu's "way" is at an end, everywhere he turns is "a way"—is (given Chinese's lack of a distinction between the definite and indefinite articles) *dao*. Unexpected significance is thus immanent, waiting to be discovered "by chance" (*ou*), at every point along his path, just as recordizing critics say it is.

This poem's reclamation of Du Fu's "spirit for the *dao*" is made possible by the juxtaposition of tropologies in its final lines, a technique he employs again in the penultimate couplet of the diptych's second verse. These compound allusions each invert an allusion in one of the alluded-to writers' works. Just as the first poem inverted Ruan Ji's invocation of Yang Zhu, that is, so too does the second twist a rhapsody by Wang Can in which Wang justifies his own homesickness by reference to Confucius's between Chen and Cai. The surface point that Du Fu is making here is simply that he should not be sighing in enjoyment of the landscape of his exile, since Confucius and Wang Can saved their sighs for their countries' troubles and their estranged homelands. In the following couplet, however, he realizes that the results of both his unjustified appreciation and their justified griefs are the same: sighs, embodied in poems like this one, which manifests his feelings as surely as Wang Can's pained rhapsody did his. Du Fu too has his share of verse sighing for the times, and he has begun to see those more morose poems as little different in character from this one, appreciating the beauties before him in this landscape. What he suggests here, in other words, is much the point recordizing readers have so often drawn from his collection: that he writes of what he sees and feels, without needing to justify his feelings through reference to the fixed moral precedents of the tradition. He may actually "feel for the moment" (*shang shi* 傷時, translated above as "grieving for the times") better than his chosen exemplars precisely by being responsive to everything its shifting vicissitudes make available.

Taken together, these poems' suggestion that everywhere Du Fu goes "is *dao*" and, therefore, that all his feelings are equally propitious for poetry, renders them as direct a statement of his evolving immanent vision as can be found in his collection. Even here, however, the emphasis is more on the surprise of discovering such richness in the falling away of traditional categories than it is on the full evocation of that richness in the poems themselves. As can be seen in another poem he wrote immediately after this pair, Du Fu seems to have doubted art's capacity to fully capture this immanent significance. Upon arriving in Tongquan County, he found on the wall of the government office building there calligraphy and a painting by Xue Ji 薛稷 (649–713), a politician, poet, and painter who had reached the highest echelons of government in the years before Xuanzong's accession to the throne. Xue had visited Tongquan County in his youth, leaving there a mural of the cranes he would famously paint on a wall of the Secretariat later in his life.[58] By this point, this mural was at least eighty years old, and, given that the government office building's collapse had now exposed to the elements the interior wall on which it had originally been painted, it would not last much longer.[59]

通泉縣署屋壁後薛少保畫鶴 *Junior Guardian Xue Ji's Crane Mural on the Back of a Wall at the Government Office Building of Tongquan County*[a]

薛公十一鶴	These eleven cranes of Lord Xue
皆寫青田眞	all portray the true ones of Greenfields.[b]
畫色久欲盡	Their painted colors, old now, are almost gone,
蒼然猶出塵	but graying, they still stand out from the dust.
低昂各有意	Curving down and stretching up, each has intent;

a. "Junior Guardian" was a title of great prestige conferred irregularly on officials of the central government, ostensibly identifying the bearer as the "guardian" of the crown prince.

b. The "Record of Yongjia Commandery" reads: "There is a washing stream that flows through the wilderness for nine miles in Greenfields. There are two cranes there that every year give birth to chicks that grow up and fly away, leaving only the father and mother to remain there permanently. They are truly lovely, perfectly white, and many say that they are fed by immortals."

	磊落如長人	imposing they stand, like giants.[c]
	佳此志氣遠	I celebrate the distance of their ambition,
8	豈唯粉墨新	not just novelty of paint and ink.
	萬里不以力	Ten thousand leagues cost no strength:
	羣遊森會神	they roam together in dark accord of spirit.
	威遲白鳳態	Winding and twisting, their white phoenix forms;
12	非是蒼鶊鄰	not these the neighbors of gray orioles.
	高堂未傾覆	But that was before the high hall collapsed,
	幸得慰嘉賓	when happily they consoled worthy guests;[d]
	曝露牆壁外	exposed to the elements outside the walls,
16	終嗟風雨頻	in the end I sigh over repeated wind and rain.
	赤霄有真骨	The red clouds hold the true bones,[e]
	恥飲洿池津	disdaining to drink from stagnant pools and fords.[f]
	冥冥任所往	Through the darkness, they go where they will;
20	脫略誰能馴	unconstrained, who could tame them?[g]

c. "Has intent" is ambiguous: it could mean that the cranes have their own intent (i.e., they are focusing on something in the painting), that their postures show intent on the part of Xue Ji, or that they "are intriguing" to the viewer. Similarly, *leiluo* 磊落 can be either "imposing" of stature or "dignified" of affect. The final two characters of the line either denote the "giants" that appear in Chinese legends or "individuals worthy of the utmost respect."

d. "Worthy guests" at a backwater like Tongquan would likely be those sent on administrative exile. Hence the consolation offered by such untrammeled beings as the cranes.

e. Du Fu uses the phrase "true bones" in other ekphrastic poetry to denote the real subject of a portrait. Elsewhere, however, the phrase is almost always used to denote the final stage in the process of attaining immortality, when the adept changes his or her mortal bones to "true bones" and leaves the mundane world behind.

f. The word "fords" here may recall a story from the *Analects* in which Confucius has his disciple "ask the ford" of two recluses. Though Confucius was literally asking where the best place might be to cross a particular river, the recluses take his question metaphorically and respond to him that he should cease trying to put the empire in order ("to cross the ford") and instead join them in reclusion.

g. The phrase translated here as "through the darkness" alludes to a passage from Yang Xiong's *Model Sayings* 法言: "Someone asked me, 'What is the gentleman like during a period of order?' I said, 'Like a phoenix.' 'What about in a period of disorder?' I said, 'Like a phoenix. . . . In an age of order it appears, and in an age of disorder it hides. It flies like a wild goose through the darkness, so how could a hunter put an arrow through it?'"

Du Fu had written a few poems on paintings in his youth before the Rebellion, including two that appear in the second chapter: "On a Winter Day Paying My Respects at the Temple of the Mysterious Primal Emperor" and "Song of the Fleet-Mount." His Sichuan years, however, represent the greatest concentration of such ekphrases in his collection, suggesting his increased interest at this time in questions of representation. These questions were particularly germane to the genre of ekphrastic poetry, which characteristically in the late medieval period praised painters by writing of their paintings' success in appearing real. This is the basic model Du Fu had adopted in his previous work along these lines, and the *trompe-l'oeil* effects that he both describes in the paintings and enacts in his poetry have long been considered an apogee of the form.[60] In his Sichuan era ekphrases, however, we begin to see a different emphasis. Where previously the paintings he described had seemed marvelously real, now their verisimilitude begins to remind him they are not. In a number of poems from this period, therefore, Du Fu ends a meditation on a painting by sighing at the absences it cannot fill: the departure of a friend, for example, or the recent death of Emperor Xuanzong.[61] In these works, Du Fu seems to be undermining others' images as relentlessly as he did, in the poems above, those recluse tropes he projected for himself.

Like most of Du Fu's ekphrastic works, this poem's basic conceit (throughout its first half, at least) is that the painting (*zhen* 眞) is real (*zhen* 眞). This conceit is substantiated through elaborate double and triple entendres that suspend within the poem's lines the shifting vision that characterized the painting's illusion. The second line of the poem, for example, encodes a whole series of different grammatical possibilities, by which the painting might consist of "portraits" (*xiezhen* 寫眞) of the legendary cranes of Greenfields (that is, Qingtian 青田 County in Zhejiang) or might alternately "depict" (*xie* 寫) the more mundane "real birds" (*zhen* 眞) of "green fields" (*qing tian* 青田)—not to mention the possibility that its cranes might be "immortals" (also *zhen* 眞), more "real" than us ephemera.[62] In the second couplet, similarly, the phrase "to stand out from the dust" (*chuchen* 出塵) can suggest that, in the most literal sense, the painted cranes are still visible through the dirt on the wall; that, by way of a common cliché, they are excellent works of art; or that, through the most usual usage of the phrase, they are emerging from the dust of the mortal world to ascend towards immortality. When Du Fu says "each has intent" (*you yi* 有意), again, it is not clear whether that intent is their own within the painting's diegetic world, Xue Ji's behind it, or the viewer's own interest (also *yi* 意) in them—whether, in other words, the poet is praising how the birds' ambitions reach far into the distance, how Xue Ji's did in painting them, or how the painting inspires the viewer's own. It is likewise difficult to decide whether the "imposing" (*leiluo* 磊落) aspect of these cranes lies in the literal size of their painted figures or in their bearing: whether they are like physical "giants" or cultural "giants" (*changren* or *zhangren*, both possible interpretations of 長人). And it is clearly true that Du Fu values the painting both for reasons that go beyond the decaying "freshness" (*xin* 新) of the paint and also beyond the "novelty" (also *xin*) of its deployment by Xue Ji. In all these cases and more, Du Fu's intensely ambiguous language blurs the distinctions between representation, reality, and the "true" reality of religious transcendence, commuting portraits into real birds into immortals, intention into performance into effect, so as to make it impossible to isolate the painting as a static artefact set in opposition to reality.

It is partly in this blurring of artifice, reality, and transcendence that the painting's "consolations," mentioned in the seventh couplet, would have lain. As Stephen Owen has noted, "worthy guests" here is a euphemism for exiles either confined to or passing through this cultural backwater.[63] Similarly "tamed" to government disposition, these worthy guests might have felt a "mysterious accord of the spirit" with these untrammeled cranes, imaginatively traveling with them ten thousand leagues without ever leaving Tongquan. The painting, moreover, might have imported new interest for them into the countryside around the office building, since the relative remoteness of the county from the empire's population centers made it all the more likely its green fields might have been occasionally visited by itinerant cranes.[64] If that was true, then Xue Ji's painting might well have transfigured these worthy guests' exile into a space of enchantment, much as Wang Bo said Xie Lingyun's poetry did for the mountains and rivers near his home. By simultaneously painting so realistically as to create the illusion of real cranes and depicting them so marvelously that they seemed immortal, the painting could be seen to enact much the same transitus between mundane reality and transcendence that was often expected of poetry in the Tang.

By the time Du Fu has gotten around to noticing the consolations the painting was supposed to offer people like him, however, he is already well into a description of its illusions' collapse through their unintended juxta-position with the real world. In an ironic inversion of the ambiguities that animated the preceding lines, he observes that these birds were never meant to be neighbors to the humble yet robust orioles that sing in the branches of nearby trees, suffering with them the wind and rain but far less resilient to their depredations. Now the painting's artefactuality is painfully obvious, its consolations apparently undermined. With a sigh, therefore, he looks up beyond the crumbling wall to the red clouds at the height of the heavens, and imagines there cranes traveling hidden through dark spaces, real birds that will not be tamed to our sordid purposes of self-deception and self-comfort. No matter how wondrous its artistry, Du Fu recognizes, this painting cannot "compete with creation" or "cage it under the brush's tip." The poem ends, therefore, as so many of Du Fu's poems in this period end: with the explosion of representation's pretense to capture the robustness of the real world.

We can observe in this ending a parable of the apophatic poetics Du Fu has developed throughout his Sichuan years. Though the *trompe l'oeil* ambiguities of the first half of the poem give way with the painting's fading to a clearer, less equivocal discourse, the final lines contain one more sur-prising equivocation: to wit, whether the "true bones" Du Fu is thinking of beyond the painting are the bones of "real" birds or of "immortals" (again, both *zhen*). As noted above, the ambiguous language of the poem's first ten lines makes it difficult to distinguish real cranes from painted cranes from immortal cranes. As the painting fades, it fails to maintain its place in this equation, and yet the suspension of the mundane and the transcendent remains intact—indeed, it might even be strengthened by the contrast they both present to the fragility of art. That something as wondrous as this painting should prove merely mortal makes the return year after year of the real cranes of green fields all the more miraculous. The collapse of artistic illusions thus reveals the surprising vitality of the real world.

Beyond Apophasis

Later on in his Sichuan years, Du Fu begins to integrate these apophatic poetics into a more direct analysis of the significance he had begun to discern in his experience. We still find in these later poems the interest in the collapse of simple tropologies and false artifices that so characterizes this period of his work in general, but the rupture of these illusions is no longer synonymous with a rupture of poetry itself. Instead of gesturing towards unrepresentable realities or breaking off at ecstatic discoveries, that is, these ruptures now become an occasion for reflection. When the mundanities of his daily existence present themselves now as pregnant with significance, they turn out to be so not in themselves, but rather insofar as they resonate, often unexpectedly, with larger narratives in his life and in history, narratives that he now begins to integrate partially into his poems. Poetry thus becomes for him in the latter days of his Sichuan sojourn less a vehicle for visions than a venue for thinking through what, exactly, his insistently but puzzlingly significant life might mean.[65]

These poetics will reach maturity in the next period of Du Fu's work, in which we find long, rambling verses on the surprising significance of chicken coops and cold noodle soup.[66] As he got further from the shock of the Rebellion and the collapse of the artistic ideologies that had guided his youthful verse, humble topics of this sort would replace the broken things and broken illusions that so often populate his Sichuan poems. In the meantime, however, an intermediate stage on this path beyond apophasis can be discerned in the following diptych, written in early 764, when Yan Wu was ordered back to Chengdu to restore order to the region. After a year and a half of homeless wandering in eastern Sichuan, Du Fu returned in the springtime to find the hermitage he had built there fallen into disrepair.[67]

水檻   *Deck on the Water*

蒼江多風飆	The gray river has many windy squalls;
雲雨晝夜飛	clouds and rain fly day and night.
茅軒駕巨浪	And my thatched porch rides huge waves—
4 焉得不低垂	so how could it help sagging low?
遊子久在外	The traveler was long abroad,
門戶無人持	and there was no one to maintain the household.[a]

a. Du Fu is saying that there was no one to maintain the buildings, but the phrase he uses generally means something more along the lines of "maintaining the family prestige."

	高岸尚爲谷	If even high cliffs become valleys,[b]
8	何傷浮柱敧	why should I grieve these floating posts lean?[c]
	扶顛有勸誡	"Raise what has fallen"—there's such a precept;[d]
	恐貽識者嗤	I fear I'll merely give those who know it cause to laugh.
	既殊大廈傾	Since this differs from a great hall's collapse,
12	可以一木支	it can be propped up by a single beam.[e]
	臨川視萬里	From the riverside, though, I can see ten thousand miles,
	何必欄檻爲	so why should I feel compelled to make a deck?
	人生感故物	In human life we're moved by familiar things;
16	慷慨有餘悲	stirred to sighing, I have grief to spare.

破船　*Broken Boat*

	平生江海心	Since my heart has ever been on rivers and lakes,
	宿昔具扁舟	in the past I prepared a small boat.[f]
	豈唯青溪上	How could it have been for this green creek alone,
4	日傍柴門遊	roaming every day by my brushwood gate?
	蒼惶避亂兵	Yet when in panic I fled disordered armies,
	緬邈懷舊丘	afar I yearned for this old home.
	鄰人亦已非	My neighbors are now no more;
8	野竹獨脩脩	there's just wild bamboo, growing tall.

b. This line alludes to "The Convergence of the Tenth Month" 十月之交 from the *Classic of Poetry*, a strident criticism of Zhou King You 周幽王 on the occasion of a solar eclipse: "Bright and loud, thunder and lightning; / it is not peaceful, it is not good. / The hundred streams roil and speed; / the mountains collapse, the crags fall. / High cliffs become valleys, / and deep valleys become peaks. / Alas for the men of our time! / how does the king not put a stop to these things?" There was also a belief in medieval China that, over a sufficiently long period of time, land and sea would change places.

c. "Floating posts" comes from Yang Xiong's "Sweet Springs Rhapsody" 甘泉賦, where the phrase describes a feature of a hyperbolically imagined palace. Du Fu seems to be taking the term in a far humbler, possibly ironic, sense.

d. This line derives from the *Analects*: "What use is the guide to a blind man if he does not support him when he totters and raise him when he's fallen?" In its original context, this was a metaphor for the work of a political advisor.

e. Wang Tong 王通 (ca. 584–617) said, to criticize someone taking office under the fragile Sui dynasty: "When a great hall is about to collapse, it cannot be propped up by a single beam."

f. The phrase "small boat" recalls the story of Fan Li, who retired from service and lived out the remainder of his days on the rivers and lakes of the southeast.

	船舷不重扣	Never again will I rap on its gunwales:
	埋沒已經秋	it's already been sunk all fall.
	仰看西飛翼	Looking up, I see west-flying wings;
12	下媿東逝流	down, I feel shame at the east-flowing stream.
	故者或可掘	The old one could perhaps be dug out,
	新者亦易求	and a new one would be easy to get.
	所悲數奔竄	But what saddens me is having fled so often,
16	白屋難久留	even in a plain cottage I couldn't stay long.

In both of these poems, Du Fu is trying to understand why these humble household accoutrements matter to him as much as they apparently do; as Stephen Owen has pointed out, they fall far beneath the threshold of what contemporary poets would have considered appropriate topics for verse.[68] Seeking an explanation, his mind turns to the tropologies of the elite tradition. The boat, he tells himself, was always meant to serve a visionary reclusion on the rivers and lakes of the far south, and the sagging porch presents an opportunity to practice the good Confucian maxim "support what totters." In both cases, however, these explanations prove unconvincing as an analysis of why he cares. Instead, he realizes that his attachment to these objects hangs on something simpler, and less publicly justifiable: that they symbolize for him the humble-but-happy life he was able to enjoy for only a short time in his thatched cottage in Chengdu.

These are, again, the apophatic poetics Du Fu has explored throughout the past few years, the richness of his mundane life appearing only in the collapse of traditional moral scripts and near the ending of both poems, which leave that mundane life hinted at but largely unrepresented. In their last lines, however, Du Fu takes the analysis a step further than he had in previous works. In these final couplets, he does not merely invoke the mundane life he so enjoyed, but also reflects on the question of why he has invested so much emotion in its pleasures. Just as the deck and boat are synecdoches of his happy hermitage in Chengdu, he realizes, so too is the thatched cottage itself a displacement of his home, the locus of all the "familiar things" and familiar people of his youth, from which the Rebellion originally forced him to "flee." Ultimately, he does not want to be at the thatched cottage—where things are not, after all, all that "familiar" (gu 故, literally "old," "long-standing")—so much as at his real "old home" back in the north. The broken deck and sunken boat, it turns out, are merely salt in the wound. And yet, as displacements of what he wants and cannot have, he finds he cares about them immensely.

Deck and boat thus come to condense within themselves the narrative of Du Fu's life in history: he sees here his youthful ambition to be a minister supporting the tottering state, his subsequent consideration of reclusion upon the swelling flood, and his humiliating flight and exile—not to mention the losses of "familiar things" and people equally suffered by others who live in "plain cottages," the common folk. The significance of these mundane items thus proves to be a network reaching out beyond the apparently circumscribed sphere of his domestic arrangements. And this network can be explored—perhaps not exhausted, but certainly explored—in verse.

A similar network of displacement and condensation can also be discerned in Du Fu's depiction, in the following famous ballad, of the fallen painter Cao Ba 曹霸, who in his glory days before the Rebellion, had previously been given the honorary title of "general" by Emperor Xuanzong.[69]

丹青引　*Song of Painting*[a]

將軍魏武之子孫	You, General, are the descendant of Wei's Warrior Emperor,[b]
於今爲庶爲清門	but now you are a commoner, if of a lofty house.[c]
英雄割據雖已矣	Although his heroic conquering is over now,[d]

a. Early note: "Presented to General Cao Ba" 贈曹將軍霸.

b. "Wei's Warrior Emperor" is the posthumous title of Cao Cao 曹操 (155–220), whose son Cao Pi 曹丕 (187–226) founded the Wei dynasty.

c. "But now is a commoner" is a citation from the *Zuozhuan*: "Surely my king knows that the descendants of the three sagely dynasties are now commoners." "A lofty house" (*qingmen* 清門) is ambiguous. The term seems generally to have meant a "pure" household, with a tradition of lofty conduct; some commentators, however, have seen Du Fu as playing here on the term's connotations of "coolness" to suggest that the household was poor (*hanmen* 寒門).

d. That is, the heroic conquering of Wei's Warrior Emperor in the wars of the Three Kingdoms period.

4 文采風流今尚存 his cultural brilliance and panache
                 survive in you still.

   學書初學衛夫人 In studying calligraphy, you first
                 studied Lady Wei;

   但恨無過王右軍 your only regret was not
                 surpassing Wang Xizhi.^e

   丹青不知老將至 When painting you did not know
                 old age's approach;

8 富貴於我如浮雲 wealth and rank to you were
                 like the drifting clouds.^f

   開元之中常引見 In the Kaiyuan reign, you were often
                 led in to audience,

   承恩數上南薰殿 several times in royal favor ascending
                 the Hall of Southern Breeze.

   凌煙功臣少顏色 The great officials of Over-the-Mists
                 were lacking in complexion;^g

12 將軍下筆開生面 where the general's brush descended,
                 living faces appeared.

   良相頭上進賢冠 On the heads of fine ministers were
                 "Promote-the-Worthy" caps;

   猛將腰間大羽箭 at the waists of fierce generals were
                 "Great Feather" arrows.^h

   褒公鄂公毛髮動 Lord Bao's and Lord E's
                 hair stirred in the breeze,

e. "Lady Wei" is Wei Shuo 衛鑠 (d. 349). Wang Xizhi 王羲之 (303–61), generally considered the greatest Chinese calligrapher, was said to have studied her style in his youth.

f. These lines are based on two passages in the *Analects*. In the first, Confucius describes himself as "the sort of person who forgets to eat in enthusiasm and in joy forgets worries, unaware that old age is coming on." In the second, Confucius says, "Eating coarse food and drinking water, and sleeping with one's arm as a pillow—happiness can also be found here. Wealth and nobility, if not obtained in the right way, are to me like drifting clouds."

g. Over-the-Mists Pavilion, within the palace compound, was where Taizong had had painted the portraits of meritorious officials of his reign. The Hall of Southern Breeze was in the Xingqing Palace.

h. "Promote-the-Worthy" caps were a type of formal court headdress indicating culture and Classical learning; "Great-Feather" arrows were famously used by Tang Emperor Taizong.

16	英姿颯爽來酣戰	their heroic forms arrived, drunk with battle.[i]
	先帝天馬玉花驄	His Late Majesty's heavenly horse, Jade-Flower Dapple,
	畫工如山皃不同	painters like mountains depicted, but none to true likeness.
	是日牽來赤墀下	That day they led it forth beneath the cinnabar stairs,
20	迥立閶闔生長風	standing tall in the gates of heaven, a steady wind came forth.[j]
	詔謂將軍拂絹素	An edict bade the general to brush the white silk;
	意匠慘淡經營中	in faint colors your artisan mind laid out the composition.[70]
	斯須九重眞龍出	In a flash from heaven's ninth tier a true dragon emerged,[k]
24	一洗萬古凡馬空	washing away at one stroke a myriad ages' common horses.
	玉花卻在御榻上	Jade-Flower then was there upon the royal dais—
	榻上庭前屹相向	upon the dais and in the courtyard, they faced each other towering.
	至尊含笑催賜金	His Majesty smiled, urging you to take the bestowed gold;
28	圉人太僕皆惆悵	the grooms and stable boys all turned melancholy.
	弟子韓幹早入室	Your disciple Han Gan long ago "entered the chamber";[l]

i. Lord Bao was Duan Zhixuan 段志玄, and Lord E was Yuchi Jingde 尉遲敬德, both among Taizong's generals.

j. Changhe 閶闔 was the legendary gate of the celestial palace and, by extension, a conventional kenning for the gates of the earthly palace.

k. "Heaven's ninth tier" is a pun, referring at once to the literal heavens above and, by convention, to the court in which Cao Ba was painting.

l. This line alludes to the *Analects*, wherein Confucius appraises one of his disciples' progress by saying "Zilu has ascended my hall, but he has not entered my chamber."

	亦能畫馬窮殊相	also good at painting horses, 　　he exhausts their unusual features.[m]
	幹唯畫肉不畫骨	Yet Han Gan paints only flesh, 　　he does not paint the bone,
32	忍使驊騮氣凋喪	and can bear to let the vigor of a Hualiu 　　wither and be lost.[n]
	將軍畫善蓋有神	The general is complete in excellence, 　　possessed of a spirit;[o]
	必逢佳士亦寫眞	meeting some fine scholar, 　　you'd always paint his portrait true.
	即今飄泊干戈際	Yet nowadays you drift at the margin 　　of spears and pikes,
36	屢兒尋常行路人	often depicting ordinary 　　passersby on the street.
	途窮反遭俗眼白	At the end of your road, it's you that meets 　　the whites of common eyes—[p]
	世上未有如公貧	in all the world there's never been 　　a person poor as you.
	但看古來盛名下	But look how from ancient times, 　　beneath the greatest names,[q]
40	終日坎壈纏其身	to the end of their days 　　hardship wrapped them up.

m. The phrase "unusual features" derives from Yan Yanzhi's 顏延之 "Rhapsody on the Russet-White Horse" 赭白馬賦: "Its strange forms arise like peaks, its unusual features shine transcendent."

n. Hualiu was a legendary steed of King Mu of Zhou.

o. "Complete excellence" derives from the *Analects*, where Confucius said that the "Shao" music was "complete in beauty and also complete in [moral] excellence." "Possessed of a spirit" suggests that there is something almost supernatural, and perhaps also compulsory, about Cao's painting.

p. The third-century poet and eccentric Ruan Ji famously displayed contempt for those he considered "common" by showing them the whites of his eyes. As discussed above, Ruan was also known for weeping whenever he came to the end of a road. The "end of the road" was a metaphor for poverty with no hope of advancement.

q. The phrase "beneath the greatest names" derives from the *History of the Latter Han*: "Beneath the greatest names, few are those whose substance lives up to them."

In keeping with Du Fu's consistent interests throughout his Sichuan period, his narrative of Cao Ba's history is, once again, a story of ruptured artistic illusions leading to a greater recognition of the artistic affordances of mundane reality. Back in his youth in the Kaiyuan era, Cao painted in very much the tropological vein in which his contemporaries were trained to write poetry. Great ministers needed "Promote-the-Worthy" caps; excellent generals, "Great Feather" arrows; special horses, "unusual features." Since the Rebellion, however, he has drifted to the southlands and is now reduced to practicing his art on less propitious subjects, common passersby who—in an inverted allusion that highlights how strange it would have been for Cao to paint them—show him the whites of their eyes as Ruan Ji once showed his to commoners. If Cao's painting once "washed away a myriad ages' common horses" and drove Xuanzong's stable boys to despair, now he is forced to depict "ordinary passersby on the street," perched, perhaps, on their common nags. His current predicament, indeed, seems almost reality's revenge for his previous "competing with creation," as if he were being forced to acknowledge its greater richness, beyond the curated images of elite culture.

Put in these terms, Cao Ba's trajectory clearly tracks Du Fu's own.[71] Du Fu too is painting a portrait in this poem, and, just as Cao depicts poor commoners on the road, there has "in all the world never been a person as poor" as him. Exiles from the elite community that was previously the audience for their arts, poet and painter thus find themselves in a surprising sort of solidarity, despite and through the breakdown of the high culture they once shared. It is perhaps not a coincidence, in this context, that the poem is bookended by depictions of failed transmission: of Cao being unable to learn the calligraphy of Lady Wei as well as had Wang Xizhi and of Cao's own disciple Han Gan failing to master his art. As one vision of tradition gives way, Du Fu finds another mode of community.[72]

This new mode of community is also a new mode of meaning. Neither the authors nor the subjects of Cao Ba's painted or Du Fu's poetic portraits actualized the ideals that This Culture of Ours strove to inculcate in society. A fallen painter as poor as Cao would probably have fallen beneath the notice of capital poetry during the boom times when he and Du Fu were young, much as common passersby would have been unpropitious material for portraits and collapsed decks incongruous applications of the lofty Confucian admonition to "support what totters." As This Culture of Ours falls apart, however, Du Fu's collapsed deck, Cao Ba's humbled paintings, and both their fractured lives become nodes in a network of significance that is less tropological than connectional and probative. In Cao's life, we catch a glimpse of Du Fu's; in Du Fu's, of the age; and, in the age, of a mysterious injustice that spans ages, guaranteeing that "beneath the greatest names, to the end of their days hardship wraps them up."

In this sense, though Du Fu continues to focus on broken things and on what is revealed when things break, this poem also represents a step beyond the apophasis that predominated earlier in his Sichuan years. At this point, he still cannot fully articulate his deepening intuition that his failed, now thoroughly mundane life might nonetheless mean more than his age's moral tropologies allowed. But by intimating that such meaning might inhere within a network of connections to the larger history of his age, this poem raises the possibility that the significance of a tropologically unprecedented existence might lie, in part, in the unexpected solidarities it can catalyze. If Cao Ba's life speaks to Du Fu because it resonates with his experience, then it is possible that his own life might equally mean something to others—perhaps, even, others beyond the narrowly constituted world of This Culture of Ours. In the next period of his work, therefore, Du Fu turns to exploring the communities in which his poetry might participate.

SIX

History and Community
Kuizhou Poems (766–68)

After leaving Chengdu in 765 and taking up residence in 766 down the Yangzi River in Kuizhou, questions of community become a defining interest of Du Fu's work. Chengdu had until recently been the nominal southern capital of the Tang empire, and he had enjoyed in the years he lived there at least a semblance of elite literary sociality. Kuizhou, by contrast, was a cultural backwater largely populated by non-Han ethnicities,[1] where he seems to have been able to make a living for himself by being one of the few educated men in the region who could supply the local satrap, Bai Maolin, with the literary grace requisite for drafting memorials to the central government and receiving elite visitors passing through the Three Gorges on journeys between Sichuan and the Jiangnan area.[2] During the two years that Du Fu spent in Kuizhou, therefore, he was acutely aware of the physical and artistic distance he had drifted from the centers of high culture in the empire. His verse often concentrated, for this reason, on the question of how he might find new communities for himself and his work, both in Kuizhou and in the tradition from which he seemed, on the surface, increasingly estranged.

This search will bring to its culmination one of the central narratives tracked throughout this book: Du Fu's progressive divergence from late medieval models of poetic significance and his increasing prefiguration of recordizing reading. As he discovers within the mundane details of his experience surprising new bases of community and connection, he becomes convinced that there may, indeed, be nothing beneath the notice of poetry, even chicken coops and cold noodle soup. These discoveries thus suggest to him, ultimately, that he can simply "record" (*ji* 記—his word) what he experiences, confident in the possibility, at least, that even if what he writes may not make full moral sense to him now, it may someday be significant to others. He thus largely abandons the late medieval vision of poetic community, which was defined by the normative enactment of This Culture of Ours. By looking, instead, to unrecognized affinities waiting to be discovered, his verse in this period finally adopts the basic metaphor of recordizing criticism.

At the same time, however, his interest in discovering new communities runs counter to the frankly nationalist impulses that have often animated recordizing critics. Because they imply that community is given rather than enacted, the recordizing ideas traced in the past several chapters—that Du Fu, the greatest of all poets, wrote from a shared human nature, of experiences all people are likely to have, and about meanings immanent in the world itself—are easily translated into claims that his Chinese readers, whether by nature or by culture, have a privileged access to fundamental truths. Frequently, these claims are advanced under threat, when the continuing relevance of his experience is cited in order to guarantee that the Chinese community will survive a current catastrophe, just as it survived the An Lushan Rebellion. Du Fu, however, was less interested in the possibility that his current community would survive than that others might be created, and that they might look very different.

Chineseness in the Late Medieval Period

If Du Fu was less invested in the idea that his future readers would be "Chinese" than those readers have been in his supposed "patriotic" (*aiguo* 愛國) loyalty to his "ancestral country" (*zuguo* 祖國), part of the reason lies in the transformation of these concepts in the transition from the late medieval to the postmedieval period. As Nicolas Tackett and Hilde De-Weerdt have recently argued, the Song dynasty witnessed a significant reorientation in the way elites imagined their community, one that, as Tackett tells it, first created China as a nation in something resembling the modern sense, "defined by a single ethnoculture and by a fixed geographic extent."[3] In the Tang, by contrast, elites identified not with a nation or an ethnicity, but rather with "civilization," and civilization was, at least in theory, capable of accepting and assimilating different peoples and of either expanding or contracting in territory. As a normative term, moreover, civilization existed in a different relationship with its others, which did not pose the same rhetorical or intellectual challenges that later rival states would pose to postmedieval Chinese empires.[4]

Late medieval intellectuals did, of course, operate with some concepts resembling ethnic and national identity.[5] Surviving evidence suggests, for instance, that many believed that there were fundamental differences between the "Chinese" (generally *hua* 華 but sometimes also *xia* 夏 or *han* 漢) and other groups—differences, moreover, that arranged themselves in a moral and biological hierarchy.[6] Yet if the Tang sometimes claimed to be the state of the *hua-xia*, these terms were also ambiguous, and could be used in ways that implicitly argued against defining the polity along ethnic lines.[7] As Charles Holcombe has noted, for example, *hua* and its common opposite, *yi* 夷 (often translated as "barbarian"), could equally be understood to import relative degrees of civilization—as when the Japanese hosts of Sillan (Korean) envoys in 723 used these terms to refer to themselves and their guests, respectively.[8] These ambiguities allowed the Tang—whose ruling house was itself, like much of the northern aristocracy, of Xianbei (Särbi) extraction—to recruit members of what might now be thought of as "non-Han" ethnic groups to settle in the heartland and to assume high posts in both the civil and military bureaucracies without thereby compromising the state's fundamental alignment with the "Chinese" tradition.[9] Partly as a result of the ambiguity of these concepts, the *hua-xia* state could be affiliated with a particular ethnic group, when it was useful to present it that way, without needing to be ethnically pure, a flexibility that partly accounts for the Tang's reputation as "China's cosmopolitan empire."[10]

When Tang intellectuals did theorize the difference between "Chinese" and "barbarians," moreover, they generally conceived of these categories not as immutable, but rather as deriving ultimately from geography. Different regions, that is, were understood as differentially shaping both the customs and the moral character of the populations they supported, thus determining their capacity to produce sages and to absorb their moral and cultural teachings.[11] This account of population difference effectively allowed that members of foreign groups could become "Chinese" (that is, "civilized") by inhabiting the traditional territory of the Chinese world and proving themselves capable of adopting its cultural and ethical norms. In some cases, this idea explicitly shaped government policy making, as for instance in 630, when it was proposed that the Türks who had surrendered to the Tang be resettled south of the Yellow River and encouraged to farm, thereby "transforming a million barbarians (*hulu* 胡虜) into *han*."[12] It was encoded into law as well in the regulation that the children of foreigners who had pledged allegiance to the Tang "would be the same as the common [Chinese] folk and would no longer be considered foreign (*fan* 蕃) households."[13] There is even some evidence to suggest that it was expected that the phenotypical markers of foreign races would disappear through generations of residence within the Central States.[14]

The possibility of assimilation through residence did not mean, however, that all that was required to be "Chinese" was submission to and inclusion in the Tang empire. Instead, the fact that "Chineseness" was equated with an ideal of culture and civilization guaranteed that certain regions and populations provided the norm against which all others would deviate by degrees. Poets in the early eighth century, for instance, clearly thought of themselves as writing primarily for an elite and relatively homogeneous community with connections to (if not always living in) the capital corridor between Chang'an and Luoyang.[15] When such poets were exiled to distant regions of the empire, therefore, they often highlighted their own "Chineseness" in contrast to the supposedly "barbaric" peoples and places amongst which they found themselves.[16] For such exiles, far from patrons and family networks, poetry served as a survival tool, allowing them to flatter and to request help from powerful patrons within the core imperial elite, and to claim to represent that elite to the Tang's colonial subjects, who were, by implication, only partly "civilized," imperfectly "Chinese."

Rather than deriving its excellence or significance from innate characteristics of the Chinese ethnonational group, therefore, poetry—specifically elite poetry—was understood to be part of the cultural repertoire that defined "Chineseness." This was, indeed, one of the crucial claims that justified the art's high-cultural status in the late medieval period, as it was seen as potentially useful in disseminating civilization to not-yet-fully civilized populations both within and beyond the empire's borders. According to legend, the verse collected in the *Classic of Poetry* had functioned in precisely this way, serving as one of the main tools by which the ancient

sagely courts incorporated their peripheries into their polities. The sage
kings, that is, had directed "local officials to use these poems to teach the
folk in their villages, and the feudal lords to use them to teach the ministers
in their capitals," thereby ensuring that everyone "from the son of heaven
to the common folk all knew these poems and were rectified" in their
behavior and their appreciation of shared norms.[17] And this ideal was not
relegated to the ancient past, either. In the preface to an imperially spon-
sored literary encyclopedia, for instance, Gao Jian wrote of *wen* not merely
as "molding and circumscribing the cosmos and bringing to light its spiritual depths," but also as "serving as teacher and model to a hundred generations, patching together and leading the world within the four seas" by
ensuring, "when used in the capital, that the many officials will be orderly,
and, when used among the villages, that the folk will be enlightened."
Through the teaching embodied in normative texts, Gao wrote, it ought
to be possible to "blend the ancient and the modern in order to make them
follow the same carriage tracks" and to allow "individuals separated by a
thousand miles nonetheless to share the same sounds."[18]

Yet if *wen* thus theoretically allowed for the extension of imperial influence throughout a territory populated by diverse cultural and ethnic
groups, the corollary was that "Chineseness" was fragile for late medieval
intellectuals, and in ways that later ethnic and nationalist identities would
not be. It was, that is, equally possible for *wen* to fully civilize the populations of the provinces and for the ritual, culture, literary refinement, and
morality that constituted *wen* to be lost even in the heartland, resulting
in its decline below the threshold of civilization.[19] This latter worry is
expressed quite clearly in Tang dynasty scholarship on the *Spring and
Autumn Annals* (*Chunqiu* 春秋), a terse history of the middle centuries of
the Zhou dynasty that, according to seventh-century exegetes like Yang
Shixun 楊士勛, had been edited by Confucius to display just how closely
the supposedly "Chinese" state was flirting with barbarity.

> Reaching the time when the Zhou house's virtue declined, human relations
> lost their order: those above weeded out no inclinations of their populaces,
> and those below merely loved and hated whatever they were inclined to. This
> made it such that in the nine provinces of the central lands only the mere
> titles and empty sacrifices survived, and, in all the eight directions, the social
> mores of the folk were indistinguishable from those of the barbarians.

Therefore, Confucius rectified the *Elegantiae* and *Lauds* [of the *Classic of Poetry*] and edited the historical records of Lu into the *Spring and Autumn Annals*.

泊乎周德既衰，彝倫失序，居上者無所懲艾，處下者信意愛憎，致令九有之存唯祭與號，八表之俗或狄或戎。故仲尼就大師而正雅頌，因魯史而修春秋。[20]

This is an unquestionably xenophobic vision of Confucius's project, which is, according to Yang, the preservation of a clear distinction between "China" and its neighbors. Yet there is nothing innate about the opposition; instead, it depends on *wen*, symbolized here by poetry and historiography. These literary institutions advanced normative values that, when practiced, ensured that the "Central States" (*zhong guo* 中國) would be "the kingdoms of ritual and righteousness."[21] For this reason, Confucius edited the text of this history to make clear that it was those values, rather than mere heredity, that defined properly "Chinese" civilization, affording Chinese titles to barbarians when they engaged in conduct worthy of praise,[22] and using barbarian titles to refer to individuals from the Central States when they transgressed moral and ritual rules.[23]

In short, then, late medieval intellectual culture would have primed Du Fu's contemporaries to conceive of "Chineseness" less as given than as a project. Their community, in other words, was defined not primarily by a shared history, but rather by the performance of textual traditions and cultural patterns that sustained the inherently friable moral links both within the empire's populations and between them and the sages at the origin of This Culture of Ours. This point is particularly clear in what survives of Tang thought about historiography. According to the official Tang subcommentary, for instance, Confucius's editing of the *Chunqiu* did not involve correcting factual information in the existing historical records, but rather merely ensured that they would conform to the "settled system for the recording of history" instituted by the sagely Duke of Zhou at the outset of the dynasty, displaying at every juncture whether the events narrated "matched with the canonical method of the Zhou" or "diverged from the standards of Zhou ritual."[24] Similar motivations were claimed as well by both official and private historiographers in the Tang, who frequently rewrote existing histories in slimmed down versions not on the basis of new archival materials, but rather to forestall divergent interpretations.[25]

Moral clarification along these lines was, moreover, the explicit purpose of Liu Zhiji's 劉知幾 (661–721) groundbreaking work of historiographical theory, *Shitong* 史通, which Liu modeled after Confucius's provision in the *Chunqiu* of standards for paring down "the overabundance of historical and archival writing" so that "readers might reach unity in their interpretations" of history.[26] The goal of such historiography, implicitly, was less to teach readers the history of their community than to sustain the possibility of real community going forward.

The prescriptive character of the "Chinese" community also ensured that whatever loyalty writers like Du Fu felt towards it would not have been the sort of "patriotism" that his critics have often ascribed to him.[27] Courtiers of the sixth and early seventh centuries not infrequently served several states in their lifetimes, a fact that forced the early Tang, which needed to make use of such men, to implicitly sanction their flexibility while nonetheless demanding adherence to its claim of righteous succession. Beyond the cultivation of the moral unanimity towards which late medieval historiography was generally aimed, therefore, the massive state-sponsored historiographical projects of the early Tang were also specifically designed to assert the fundamental Chineseness both of the states it superseded and of the young dynasty itself, which on this basis claimed the loyalty of their erstwhile subjects.[28] As Emperor Gaozu 高祖 (r. 618–26) explains in his edict commissioning these histories,

> The officials in charge of the canons [were tasked by the sage kings] with recording the ruler's words, and the scribal offices, with recording the state's affairs. By means [of the records they kept,] we can investigate successes and failures and fully understand change and continuity. Such records are also the means by which analogical models are recorded to discourage vice and encourage virtue, and through them do gentlemen with much knowledge of the past leave a mirror for the future. From Fu Xi on down, the Zhou and Qin dynasties attained this standard; the two Han dynasties passed on the lineage; the Three Kingdoms received the command; and all the way to the Jin and Song, historical records are complete. . . . [Yet when it comes to subsequent periods,] the scribal notes have not been compiled, and annals and biographies are all lacking. The years are passing and social mores have changed, and the remaining glories and lingering influence of these periods are about to be lost.

司典序言，史官記事，考論得失，究盡變通，所以裁成義類，懲惡
勸善，多識前古，貽鑑將來。伏犧以降，周秦斯及；兩漢傳緒，三
國受命。迄於晉宋，載籍備焉。⋯然而簡牘未編，紀傳咸闕。炎涼
已積，謠俗遷訛；餘烈遺風，泯焉將墜。[29]

In this edict, Gaozu performs a delicate balancing act. On the one hand,
he depicts the histories his officials will compile as manifesting, first and
foremost, the glories and the virtues of recent dynasties, dynasties his
courtiers and their ancestors are likely to have served. On the other hand,
however, he suggests that these dynasties are in danger of not being properly "Chinese," since they apparently did not follow the rules of historical
documentation established by the sages and passed down all the way to
the Jin and Song. It is up to the Tang, therefore, to write the history that
will incorporate these dynasties into what Tackett calls a "transdynastic
China," a community to which their courtiers should continue to profess
their loyalty now that it is embodied in their successor state. Yet if this
sort of ideology would have been useful in consolidating the early Tang
court, it would also have ensured that intellectuals would see their loyalty
as due to civilization as such rather than to a particular imperial instan-
tiation of it.

Nationalism in Du Fu Criticism

Many of the same tropes of identity that characterized the Tang elite perdured into the postmedieval period as well. Dynasties continued to claim
legitimate succession by writing the histories of their predecessors, for
instance, and as Peter Bol and Shao-yun Yang have shown, the idea that
"Chineseness" involved a normative culture remained central to the work
of some of the most influential postmedieval thinkers.[30] Where these
tropes appear in recordizing criticism, however, they have often shifted to
accommodate new visions of the Chinese community and its relation to
others. Because critics of this persuasion have generally perceived Du Fu
as writing his country's history during a rebellion that has retrospectively
been understood as an "ethnic conflict" (*minzu maodun* 民族矛盾), they
have frequently highlighted the way "Chinese" culture had become, for

many in postmedieval China, the property of a group whose solidarity is given rather than enacted.[31]

Du Fu criticism has served nationalist ends most obviously in moments of crisis, when "Chinese" states saw themselves under attack from groups of foreign ethnicity. An important template for such invocations of Du Fu as a symbol of patriotism was set by Wen Tianxiang 文天祥 (1236–83), a hero of loyalism during the Mongol conquest of the Southern Song. Imprisoned in the Mongol stronghold near modern-day Beijing, Wen passed his time reorganizing lines taken verbatim from Du Fu's verse into two hundred new poems that narrated the history of the Song's fall and his own experiences therein. He explained his project thus:

> As I sat in prison in You-Yan, I had nothing to do and chanted Du Fu's poems. Having become somewhat familiar with the feelings and inspirations they contained, I took his five-character lines and compiled them into quatrains. After some time at this, I had gotten two hundred such quatrains. Everything I wanted to say had already been said for me by Du Fu. Daily I thought on them without stop, and I only felt that they were my own poems and forgot that they were Du Fu's. Therefore, I know that Du Fu himself could not create poetry, but, rather, poetry is the language that inheres in human emotional nature, and we merely troubled Du Fu to speak it out for us. That I can use Du Fu's words even though he and I are separated by several hundred years—is this not because our human nature is the same?
>
> In the past people have called Du Fu's poetry a "poetic history." This is probably because he uses words chanted and sung to lodge the truth [that would elsewhere make up] historical records, and his intention of criticizing and praising contemporary figures shines brightly in them. Therefore, it is appropriate to call his poetry a history. Now, in the poems that I have compiled out of Du Fu's lines, everything from the troubles that I experienced to the epochal changes of human affairs that I witnessed are all displayed here. It is not that I intended to produce mere poetry: rather, I hope that good historians in later ages will have something to consult.

余坐幽燕獄中，無所為，誦杜詩，稍習諸所感興，因其五言，集為絕句。久之，得二百首。凡吾意所欲言者，子美先為代言之。日玩之不置，但覺為吾詩，忘其為子美詩也。乃知子美非能自為詩，詩句自是人情性中語，煩子美道耳。子美於吾，隔數百年，而其言語為吾用，非情性同哉。昔人評杜詩為詩史，蓋其以詠歌之辭，寓紀載之實，而抑揚褒貶之意燦然於其中，雖謂之史可也。予所集杜

詩，自余顛沛以來，世變人事，槩見於此矣，是非有意於爲詩者
也。後之良史，尚庶幾有考焉。[32]

Much of the argument here is implicit. The area where Wen was imprisoned, "You-Yan," was also the power base of the rebels under An Lushan,
who therefore named his court the Yan dynasty. When Wen discovers,
therefore, that Du Fu's poetry already says everything he wants to say, part
of the point is the similarity of the threat faced by both men: of barbarian
hordes invading from the northeast and overrunning the Chinese state.
There thus appears to be a certain cyclicality to history that suggests,
ultimately, that the Mongols will meet the same fate as An Lushan's
rebels, that Chinese culture will survive their depredations as it survived
An's, and that future Chinese historians will consult Wen's work just as
Wen is consulting Du Fu's. And when those future historians read Wen's
poetry, which is simultaneously Du Fu's, they will recognize that this
shared culture is in the end invulnerable to barbarian incursions because
it is built into their own "emotional nature" as well.

Wen's preface set the pattern for many poets and critics who turned
to Du Fu in times of national crisis. Hong Ye 洪業 (William Hung, 1893–
1980), to give only the most blatant example, tried to duplicate Wen's project when he was likewise imprisoned in Beijing more than 650 years later
during the Second Sino-Japanese War, and, although his Japanese jailors
denied him pen or paper—perhaps because they understood the import
of the gesture—his decision, after the war, to include this anecdote at the
head of his biography of Du Fu may have been an act of Chinese trium-
phalism.[33] Other echoes of Wen's claims have been somewhat subtler, but
we have encountered several already. If Wen implicitly identifies human
nature with Chinese culture rather than with a nature that might equally
animate its barbarian oppressors, for example, much the same argument
could also be found in Wang Sishi's claim—discussed in chapter 3—that
Du Fu fully articulated "the self" (*wo* 我).[34] Having withdrawn from public
office after the fall of the Ming to the invading Manchus, Wang is reported
to have compared Du Fu's poetry to the bracken ferns on which the ancient
worthies Boyi and Shuqi subsisted after they refused to eat the grain of
the state that conquered their own.[35] In this complex allusion, Wang suggests that his decision to focus the rest of his life on annotating Du Fu was
an attempt to enact the virtue that had come, by this point, to define the

latter's cultural image: his "loyalty to his emperor and his love of the nation" (*zhongjun aiguo* 忠君愛國).[36] Wang's claim that Du Fu wrote "the self" thus echoes Wen Tianxiang's assertion that he and his poet hero shared a single nature. And, like Wen, Wang seems to be suggesting that the shared Chineseness Du Fu's poetry epitomizes will for this reason survive whatever the northeastern invaders do, since it is built into an implicitly Neo-Confucian conception of "the self," at once universal and notably Chinese.

With the fading in modern China of the Neo-Confucian ideas about human nature and the self that once leant plausibility to the claims of Wen and Wang, critics have sought out other grounds for the group solidarity they see Du Fu's poetry articulating.[37] In the People's Republic, for instance, Xiao Difei 蕭滌非 (1907–91) cited Maoist values in arguing that Du Fu's "realist" poetry is, by its very nature, inherently patriotic.

> Du Fu saw not only the cruelty of the ruling classes, but also saw at the same time the butchery inflicted by the ethnically foreign invaders; he not only saw the people suffering every kind of disaster, saw the entire race of his ancestral country in an imminent crisis, but saw at the same time the people's drive to protect their ancestral country and enact a heroic struggle and sacrifice. This sort of huge social transformation, this sort of life-and-death battle for the survival of the nation, this bloody, vivid, and true lesson from the people not only provided Du Fu a new and great subject for his poetry— the life of the Chinese people—but also greatly elevated his recognition of reality and thus deepened his hatred of the [oppressive] ruling classes and the ethnically foreign invaders. It also increased his passionate love of his ancestral country and its people, ensuring that his poetry would have a high degree of realism and a peerlessly clear and rich popular character. It is precisely because at this time the most important conflict in society was a racial conflict that at this time the most central characteristic of Du Fu's creativity was its patriotic spirit.[38]

Xiao goes on immediately after this passage to cite discussions of dialectical materialism by both Lenin and Mao to the effect, respectively, that "our consciousness is nothing other than the reflection of the external world" and "the basic position of Marxism is that what exists outside us determines our consciousness, so that the objective reality of class conflict and ethnic conflict are responsible for establishing our thought and our feelings." The point Xiao is making in these citations is that Du Fu's loyalty to his own race and opposition to its enemies were simply the objectively correct reaction to the truth of the world in his time, just as for Wen Tian-xiang and Wang Sishi it had been the objectively correct content of human nature.

In another essay, originally published in *Renmin huabao* 人民畫報 in 1962, Xiao made the further claim that, because Du Fu's patriotism was grounded in reality, it could effectively inculcate such patriotism in readers as well.[39] This sort of argument, that Du Fu's "poetic history" can be useful for patriotic education, is found throughout modern Chinese criticism. Mo Lifeng, for instance, recommends that Chinese students read Du Fu to understand themselves:

> In the ten year period of the An Lushan Rebellion, two-thirds of the coun-try's population disappeared. Although historians can give us this concrete statistic, nonetheless it is still just a cold number. . . . But what was it really like? What was the process like? What were the details of the process? What kinds of wounds did it leave in the hearts of the people of that time? You will not find answers to these questions in the records of history. So where can you find them? In literature: in poetry: in Du Fu. . . . If we look at it this way, then Du Fu's poetry does not merely patch gaps in history, but rather plays an irreplaceable role in historical understanding.
>
> But why should we want to have this history? How does history that oc-curred two thousand or one thousand years ago concern us? The key point is that this history is our collective memory: it is engraved in the heart of the race and is at every moment influencing our lives in the present, our value systems, and our visions of what life is like. It is the great artery of the race. From this point of view, the function of Du Fu's poetry is irreplaceable, and we can with great vigor and certitude proclaim him the "Poet Historian."[40]

Since, according to Mo, the experience of the An Lushan Rebellion has shaped who Chinese readers are and will be, history is normative in a different sense than it was in the late medieval period. For late medieval intellectuals, historiographical choices were teleologically determined by the community they were supposed to create, demonstrating how norma-tive values conduce to civilization's success and deviations contribute to its decline. For Mo, by contrast, the processes of history have already created a moral community; the point of historiography is merely to appreciate better that community's inherent solidarity. The paradigmatic experience of reading Du Fu thus remains for Mo self-recognition, much as it was for Wen Tianxiang, Wang Sishi, and Xiao Difei.[41] By simply recording what happened and how it felt, Du Fu's poetry becomes a space in which generations of Chinese readers can realize their inherence in the ongoing story of the Chinese race.

Mo's comment also shows how culture's role in grounding group solidarity has changed from the late medieval period to recordizing reading, which tends to treat culture less as requiring active performance and maintenance, and more as a force in its own right. This contrast is even more pronounced in a recent article by Tan Jihe 譚繼和, which argues that "Cultural China nurtured Du Fu, and Du Fu in turn took his appreciation of and fidelity to Cultural China to produce an exceptional contribution to it."[42] Du Fu, in other words, did not have to aspire to or enact a normative culture; instead, it ineluctably shaped his consciousness, forming "the foundation of his ethnonational values" (*minzu jiazhiguan de genben* 民族价值观的根本).[43] And he, in turn, contributed to a culture that, in its capacity to attract and absorb various groups over time, has made a coherent nation out of them.

> Whether [the nation] has been at one or divided, at peace or at war, this cultural community has only become more and more cohesive, more and more close, and more and more possessed of centripetal force. This is the secret that has allowed our Chinese culture alone among the four great civilizations of the world to continue unbroken for five thousand years, and it is also the special attractiveness of Cultural China.[44]

Like the late medieval vision sketched above, Tan's account of Chinese solidarity is grounded in culture. But where This Culture of Ours was conceived of in the Tang as a set of ideals and institutions that needed to be sedulously enacted to be efficacious, Tan suggests that Chinese culture has linked people together for five thousand years because it is, in some sense, inherently attractive, perhaps inherently well adapted to what Xiao Difei called "reality" and Wen Tianxiang called "human nature." If it has thus brought various originally disparate groups together into one nation, it has done so not because sagely rulers promulgated it or worthy subjects enacted it, but rather because it worked its assimilating attraction even in periods of internal division and warfare.

As we will see below, Tan's discussion here shows significant insight into the hopes Du Fu's poetry expresses in his Kuizhou years. Yet in writing what is, in effect, a paean to the Chinese nation, even Tan displays the parochialism that is characteristic of all these recordizing critics: that they all assume their own readers will be Chinese.[45] Though Wen and Wang were writing on the brink of new dynasties, ruled and partly populated by foreigners, and though Mo and Tan looked out on an increasingly globalized world, they apparently did not look forward to Du Fu's audience or their own changing thereby. Instead, they turned to his "poetic history" to shore up their faith that the Chinese community they recognized was a given and would therefore not be disrupted by history's forward progress. Thus, although their sense that solidarity can be discovered even amidst catastrophic change tracks an important theme of Du Fu's Kuizhou verse, their conservatism diverges sharply from his interest in the possibility of finding new and different communities for himself.

Civilization's Barbarities

By the time he arrived in Kuizhou, Du Fu seems to have acquired a rather jaundiced perspective on the supposed superiority of the "Chinese" community and its culture. He did, of course, still identify with both. Even in Kuizhou, he continues to discuss the Rebellion as a war instigated by "barbarians" against the legitimate Chinese dynasty, and complaints about the alien cultural mores of the uncivilized southlands begin to appear regularly in his verse.[46] At the same time, however, he also writes several poems criticizing Chinese civilization, suggesting that it may not, ultimately, be all that different from the barbarism to which late medieval thinkers generally contrasted it.

Perhaps the most explicit such verse is the following, the second poem of a diptych that mulls the shame Du Fu feels, living out his days in obscurity far from the capital region. This shame, he reflects, is an ineliminable feature of civilization, which is underwritten by aspirations that will always exclude and devalue some individuals and groups. These aspirations are also, however, the spark that leads civilization, again and again, to conflagration and collapse.[47]

寫懷二首 Two Poems Describing My Cares, no. 2

	夜深坐南軒	In night's depths, I sat by the southern railing,
	明月照我膝	the bright moon shining on my knees.
	驚風翻河漢	A startling wind tossed the River of Stars;
4	梁棟已出日	on the roofbeams, the sun was already coming out.
	羣生各一宿	Each of the many living things had passed the night,[a]
	飛動自儔匹	the flying and the crawling naturally finding their kind.
	吾亦驅其兒	And I too hustled my sons along
8	營營爲私實	to busy themselves about our private stocks.
	天寒行旅稀	The heavens cold, travelers are few;
	歲暮日月疾	as years draw towards twilight, sun and moon speed.
	榮名忽中人	The confusion of glory and fame strikes people,[48]
12	世亂如蟻虱	and the age falls to disorder, like lice and nits.[b]
	古者三皇前	In antiquity, before the Three August Ones,
	滿腹志願畢	when the belly was full, ambition and desire ceased.[c]
	胡爲有結繩	Why did they create the knotted rope,
16	陷此膠與漆	and get us trapped here in lacquer and glue?[d]

a. "Passed the night" may recall a passage in the *Zhuangzi* in which Laozi told Confucius: "Benevolence and righteousness were merely the traveling lodge of the former kings. One can pass a night there, but one cannot dwell there for long."

b. "Lice and nits" may simply describe the messiness of an age of disorder, but it may also recall a famous passage from the *Han Feizi*: "When the empire lacks the way, sieges do not cease, and, after several years of defense, helmets and armor grow with lice and nits, and sparrows take up lodging on the tents."

c. There are various lists of the Three August Ones—legendary sage kings of great antiquity—the most common of which are Fu Xi, Shennong, and the Yellow Emperor. "When the belly was full" echoes the *Zhuangzi*: "When the wren nests within a deep forest, it does not demand more than a single branch; when the mouse drinks from a river, it does no more than fill its belly." This couplet also recalls Tao Qian's vision of the age before civilization: "Patting their bellies, they yearned for nothing."

d. According to the *Yijing*, the "knotted rope" was the precursor of writing, used to record covenants and affairs of state. "Lacquer and glue" may allude to the *Zhuangzi*: "If you use curve and plumb line, compass and square to make something right, then you carve into its natural form; if you use ropes and knots, lacquer and glue to make things firm, then you violate their natural way of being.... Thus, benevolence and righteousness

禍首燧人氏	The initiator of evil was the Great Kindler;[e]
厲階董狐筆	the stairs to disaster lay in Dong Hu's brush.[f]
君看燈燭張	Don't you see, when lamps and candles are set out,
20　轉使飛蛾密	how they make the moths fly dense around them?
放神八極外	I have roamed my spirit beyond the eight extremes,
俛仰俱蕭瑟	but in the space of a nod, it was all bleak and barren.[g]
終契如往還	In the end I understand it being "like going and returning":[h]
24　得匪合仙術	do I not thus match with the immortals' arts?[49]

The first poem of this pair ends with the claim that Du Fu has transcended the thirst for the glory that animated his youth. It is a surprise, therefore, that this second poem begins after a night he has been unable to sleep, apparently because he remains, despite the previous poem's protestations to the contrary, tormented by his failure. Recognizing its deeper hold upon his psyche, he begins to suspect that this ambition is in fact the common disease of the age, the reason it has fallen into such violence and disorder.

Civilization, Du Fu reflects, is hardly necessary if one's only goal is the maintenance of life and the satisfaction of a full belly. What it offers, instead, are more elaborate consummations, consummations that extend,

---

are just a tangle, like lacquer and glue on ropes and cords; how could you get to roam with them in the space of the Way and Power? You will merely confuse the empire!"

e. The Great Kindler was legendarily the first sage king of Chinese history, who taught men to use fire. Du Fu may be thinking here of an idea found in the Tang subcommentary to the *Liji*, that "the rituals of exalted and debased began in the time of the Kindler."

f. Dong Hu was a court historian of the Spring and Autumn period, praised by Confucius for his exemplary honesty in recording the misbehavior of those in power.

g. These lines may echo Lu Ji's "Rhapsody on *Wen*": "In [*wen*'s] origins, one recalls sight and inverts hearing, / sinks in thought and searches wide. / One's spirit speeds to the eight extremes, / and one's mind roams at heights of ten thousand yards." The phrase "in the space of a nod" recalls the *Zhuangzi*'s description of the human mind: "Be careful not to disturb the human mind. . . . It is so swift that, in the space of a nod, it can travel twice beyond the four seas."

h. In the *Liezi* we read that "death and life are like going and returning." The *Zhuangzi*, similarly, states that "the True Men of antiquity [sometimes understood in the Tang as immortals] did not know to take pleasure in life or to hate death. Coming forth occasioned no joy, going back met no resistance. Freely they came, freely they returned; that's all."

at the furthest extreme, beyond the bounds of one's lifetime to the cultural immortality offered by historiography. In this analysis, Du Fu is following the common medieval vision discussed above, whereby the time-transcending Chinese community was created and sustained by the ancient sages' serial invention of the representational and ritual technologies constitutive of *wen*. Yet when the knotted rope and the historian's brush make cultural immortality possible, they thereby, and perversely, encourage men to fight for it tooth and nail, destroying each other in the process. On this view, the sages at the very outset of Chinese culture become the initiators of its inevitable and repeating catastrophes, the primeval Great Kindler lighting the fires that would ultimately draw his descendants like moths and rage across the war-torn landscapes of Du Fu's time. The suggestion here may even be that it was the temptations built into Chinese civilization that lured the "barbarian" An Lushan to seek the imperial throne—and that Du Fu, a quintessentially Chinese literatus, is less different from him than he might wish he were.

This is iconoclastic stuff: late medieval historiography was supposed to civilize men, not engender rebellion. Yet Du Fu does not imagine that he can escape the civilization he here condemns. Instead, the poem's final bitter twist involves a recognition that it is *wen* that has allowed him to formulate this critique of *wen*, that the attitudes he articulates here not only derive from the tradition but also express the very aspirations it has ingrained in him. The final couplets thus echo any number of late medieval encomia praising *wen* for allowing men to transcend the limitations of their mortal bodies. In his edict commissioning the *History of the Jin* (*Jin shu* 晉書), to give just one example, Tang Taizong extolls historiography as making it possible for him "to roam his spirit beyond a thousand years without emerging from the palace halls and to see beyond the nine August Emperors of greatest antiquity while remaining silent behind the hanging tassels of his imperial crown."[50] To be sure, Du Fu's conclusion is diametrically opposed to Taizong's: where the latter found in the spirit journey of his reading the glories of a great tradition, Du Fu now finds only a vast barrenness. Yet this attitude too has been anticipated in the very tradition he now finds barren, and in particular, in Daoist texts like the *Zhuangzi* and the *Liezi* that were—even more ironically—sometimes understood as offering a path to another, more literal transcendence of our mortal limitations. In the compressed logic of these final couplets, then, Du Fu acknowledges that he remains unsatisfied by a full belly and that writing this poem is thus very much the vice he set out to castigate in it.

Du Fu investigates his own implication in the barbarities of civilization even more unsettlingly elsewhere in his Kuizhou era poetry. In the following poem, for example, he pantomimes the form of imperial governance—whereby the emperor's elaborate edicts would be declaimed by literati officials to an only partially comprehending local population—by directing his adolescent son Zongwu to read out an "edict" of his own to the likely non-Han servants and slaves he had at his disposal in Kuizhou (whether because he bought them, or, more likely, because he was loaned their services by his patron Bai Maolin).[51] By directing these subalterns to labor on his behalf in an elaborate and difficult piece of *wen*, Du Fu quite pointedly enacts the colonial situation in which he found himself here on the Tang's southern frontier. He does so, however, in a way so patently absurd that the poem, rather than depicting the civilizing of the poet's surroundings, ends up ironizing his attempts to do so.[52]

課伐木 *Assigning the Task of Cutting Down Trees*

課隸人伯夷、幸秀、信行等，入谷斬陰木，人日四根止，維條伊枚[53]，正直侹然。晨征暮返，委積庭內。我有藩籬，是缺是補，載伐篠簜，伊仗支持，則旅次于小安。山有虎，知禁，若恃爪牙之利，必昏黑撐突。夔人屋壁，列樹白菊，鏝爲牆，實以竹，示式遏。爲與虎近，混淪乎無良，賓客憂害馬之徒，苟活爲幸，可嘿息已。作詩付宗武誦。

I assigned the slaves Boyi, Xingxiu, Xinxing, and others the task of going into the valley to chop trees on the mountains' northern slopes.[a] Each man was to cut four trees each day and then stop, and to cut only those with branches and trunks that were straight and upright.[b] They went out in the morning and returned at dusk, building up a pile within my courtyard. I have a fence, and where there are openings, there they shall mend. They shall cut bamboo and madake and use them as

a. According to the *Rituals of Zhou*, one was supposed to cut trees from the north side of mountains in the summer and from the south side in the winter.

b. The language here echoes the *Shijing* poem "Banks of the Ru" 汝墳: "Along the banks of the Ru, / I cut down the branches and the slender trunks."

supports,[c] so that my lodging place here may become somewhat more secure. There are tigers in these mountains, but they recognize prohibitions. If they are to rely upon their sharp claws and teeth, they will certainly ambush in the dusk or dark. By the walls of their houses, therefore, the people of Kuizhou plant rows of white chrysanthemums;[54] they make their walls of plaster and reinforce them with bamboo: by this they demonstrate "fending off."[d] Since I am close here to tigers and mixed up with evil sorts, this sojourner worries about "the kind that harms horses,"[e] and I consider myself lucky merely to survive in any way I can—about this I quietly sigh. I wrote this poem and gave it to Zongwu to read out.

	長夏無所爲	In the long days of summer there is nothing to be done,
	客居課奴僕	so lodging here a sojourner, I set a task for my servants.
	清晨飯其腹	In morning's cool I fed their bellies;
4	持斧入白谷	carrying axes, they entered White Valley.
	青冥曾巓後	Behind layered ridges in the blue-dark sky,
	十里斬陰木	ten leagues away they chopped trees on the northern slopes.
	人肩四根已	Each man shouldered four and then stopped,
8	亭午下山麓	and at noon they started down to the mountains' foot.
	尚聞丁丁聲	Even now I still hear the sounds of chopping,[f]
	功課日各足	though each has fulfilled the task assigned him for the day.
	蒼皮成積委	The graying bark has formed a pile;
12	素節相照燭	in integrity, each shines on the other.
	藉汝跨小籬	I rely on you to go beyond my little fence;
	當伐苦蘆竹	as for support, I must trouble hollow bamboo.[55]

c. These two varieties of bamboo, *xiao* 篠 and *dang* 蕩, are mentioned together in the "Tribute of Yu" chapter of the *Shangshu*.

d. "Fending off" derives from the *Shijing* poem "The People Are Heavily Burdened" 民勞, which also contains the phrase "evil sorts" from the next sentence: "Let us not indulge the wily and obsequious, / in order to restrain evil sorts. / And let us fend off robbers and bandits, / who act secretly and fear the light."

e. The "kind that harms horses" derives from the *Zhuangzi*, wherein a herd boy tells the Yellow Emperor that governing the empire is just like taking care of horses: "Just get rid of those things that harm horses."

f. The phrase translated here as "chopping," *ding-ding*, comes from the *Shijing*, "Felling Trees" 伐木: "We cut trees *ding-ding*; / the birds cry out *ying-ying*."

	空荒咆熊羆	In the deserted wilderness bears and she-bears howl;
16	乳獸待人肉	nursing beasts wait for human flesh.
	不示知禁情	If you don't show them the prohibitions they recognize,
	豈唯干戈哭	you will weep not only because of the war.
	城中賢府主	In the city, the worthy governor
20	處貴如白屋	dwells in his high rank as if in a commoner's house.[g]
	蕭蕭理體淨	So severe is he, so pure in the arts of government,
	蜂蠆不敢毒	that even wasps and scorpions dare not sting.
	虎穴連里閭	Yet tigers' lairs reach right up to the villages,
24	隄防舊風俗	so defending against them is a longstanding custom here.
	泊舟滄江岸	And in mooring my boat by the gray river's bank,
	久客慎所觸	long a traveler, I worry what I might run into.
	舍西崖嶠壯	West of my dwelling the cliffs are high and huge;
28	雷雨蔚含蓄	thunder and rain have made dense cover there.
	牆宇資屢脩	My walls and roof have several times needed repair,
	衰年怯幽獨	and in my frail years, I'm afraid to be alone.
	爾曹輕執熱	You all thought little of the clinging heat,
32	爲我忍煩促	on my behalf enduring my bothersome hectoring.
	秋光近青岑	When autumn's light draws near to these green peaks,
	季月當泛菊	in fall's last month, we should float chrysanthemums.[h]
	報之以微寒	I'll repay you then in the light chill
36	共給酒一斛	by providing you all with a gallon of ale.

One can imagine how comical the scene must have been if Zongwu actually lined up these presumably illiterate slaves and struggled to read aloud to them this strange and difficult poem, with its affectation of an archaic imperial rhetoric modeled on the ancient *Classic of Documents*.[56] This humor, however, seems to be part of the point. In its very difficulty, and in the likelihood that its intended audience would understand neither its Classical resonance nor its poetic nuances, the poem thus begins to query the limitations of Chinese symbolic power out here in the distant provinces.

This question might have seemed unavoidable to Du Fu, who, as an impoverished aristocrat and a merely nominal imperial officer, was no

g. The "worthy governor" is Bai Maolin.

h. That is, on the Double Ninth Festival 重陽節, the ninth day of the ninth month, when Chinese families and friends would climb to a high place, wear ailanthus, and float chrysanthemum petals in their ale.

doubt aware that his control over these servants was less guaranteed in Kuizhou than his possession of slaves had been in his youth.[57] Here, where he had no capital and few friends, his ability to command men to work for him would have depended entirely on his claim to represent the empire and thus most tangibly on the favor of his patron in Kuizhou, Bai Maolin. It is perhaps not a coincidence, therefore, that Bai makes an appearance in this poem. Yet though Du Fu praises him as being so virtuous that, within the area under his jurisdiction, "even wasps and scorpions dare not sting," the poet seems somehow less than fully confident in the power of Bai's moral influence to protect him from "the kind that harms horses"—a resonant phrase hardly suitable for referring to literal tigers—against which he is currently reinforcing his walls and "sighing secretly" in fear. In this context, the poem's description of Bai as "dwelling in his high rank as if in a commoner's house" threatens to become ironic. The conceit's primary meaning is certainly its suggestion of Bai's humility and the graciousness of his treatment of the poet. But given that Du Fu is working on reinforcing his own "commoner's house" here, the phrase might perhaps suggest that Bai too could become food for tigers—or fodder for the kind of local uprising Du Fu had witnessed several times since the Rebellion—whatever Chinese cultural virtues he might possess.

For all the poem's apparent inanity, then, it subtly reveals the precarity of Du Fu's situation: his dependence not only on the work these slaves actually do for him, but also, more basically, on their acceptance of the imperial hierarchy the poem's declamation enacts. Yet if the poem thus begins by asserting Chinese dominance, Du Fu seeks in its second half to soften its colonial edge. As he admits after his darkly foreboding discussion of Bai Maolin, the construction he has tasked these slaves with doing for him involves not imposing civilized Chinese forms on the barbarian southlands, as we might expect given the rhetoric, but rather Du Fu's own adoption of Kuizhou's local customs. Similarly, the final lines' move to a more vulnerable and more personal register gestures towards the possibility that a less brutally hierarchical relationship might be possible between Chinese master and non-Chinese slaves. To us, the promise of a gallon of ale several months later may seem a meager reward for a day's work in the hot summer sun. For Du Fu, however, the offer has a definite symbolic meaning, inviting these nonelite servants into the elite Chinese community that customarily congregated to drink chrysanthemum-infused ale in celebration of the Double Ninth Festival.[58] In effect, Du Fu is expressing the hope that they might replace for him his long-separated family and friends, with whom he would normally share a drink on that date. If the poem began with imperial hierarchy, therefore, it ends with a gesture of fellowship.

Human as this gesture is, however—and there are others like it in the other totally unprecedented poems Du Fu wrote to slaves and servants in this period—the complications here remain troubling.[59] It is far from clear that Boyi, Xingxiu, and Xinxing would have understood the gesture, and readers who would have done so might also have recognized its enactment of a poetic trope that just barely humanized the underclass: as Wang Wei puts it, "In a distant land, friends and companions cut off, / the lonely traveler grows close with his servants."[60] The poem's grandiose imperial rhetoric, moreover, and Du Fu's direction that it should be his son who reads it out to these slaves, are not merely self-mocking jokes about the disconnect between the values the poet studied as a young man and the life he has come to live. They also represent a recognition that the only patrimony he has to bequeath his sons is the cultural learning he can no longer play fully straight, and has, moreover, almost certainly had a hard time passing on to them throughout their lifetime of flight, poverty, and domestic labor. Even as he ironizes the colonial claims of Chinese "civilization," that is, he remains dependent on them.[61] The poem is not, therefore, an unambiguous denunciation of the Chinese system of slavery or an unproblematic assertion of the humanity of the peoples on which it preyed. But it and others like it display a growing recognition of the insoluble ethical problems that followed from the inherent violence of empire.[62]

縛雞行   *Ballad of the Bound Chicken*

小奴縛雞向市賣	Our young slave bound up our chicken and headed to market to sell it;
雞被縛急相喧爭	the chicken was bound too tight and made a racket struggling.
家中厭雞食蟲蟻	Some in my house hated the chicken for eating up bugs and ants;

4	不知雞賣還遭烹	but didn't they know the chicken, if sold, would then get boiled?
	蟲雞於人何厚薄	What are bugs or chickens to us that we should treat one better or worse?
	吾叱奴人解其縛	I cursed at the slave, and had him untie its bonds.
	雞蟲得失無了時	Wins and losses between chickens and bugs will never have an end;
8	注目寒江倚山閣	I fix my eyes on the cold river, leaning against my tower in the hills.

In this simultaneously comic and disturbing little poem, Du Fu sees himself bound up in a web of casual violence. His family members, hoping to save the ants in the courtyard, unwittingly sentence their chicken to death.[63] In response, the poet—in a precise replay of his family's blindness—reasons that chickens deserve no less compassion than ants and so proceeds to mistreat his child-slave for faithfully following instructions. In self-righteously saving the chicken from unjust violence, he thus enacts it on a member of the human community he hardly recognizes as such.

Commentators have generally read this poem either as a bit of "verbal fun" or as a meditation on how to run a state (for example, by prioritizing the bureaucracy—the chicken—over the common people—the ants).[64] Its pointed resemblance to a famous parable, however, suggests that Du Fu himself recognized the irony of his reaction to the bound chicken, and is thus offering here another jaded perspective on the hierarchies of civilization.

When Zhuangzi was wandering in the Diaoling hunting park, he saw a strange bird fly up from the south. Its wings were seven feet in breadth and its eyes a full inch in diameter. It brushed against Zhuangzi's forehead and perched within a chestnut grove. Zhuangzi said, "What kind of bird is this? Its wings are huge, but it does not fly far, and its eyes are big, but it did not see me." Lifting the hem of his skirts, he strode off after it, and, taking his bow in hand, he waited for a shot. Then he saw a cicada that had just found a nice bit of shade and had forgotten itself. A praying mantis was taking advantage of cover to attack it, seeing gain and forgetting itself as well. And the strange bird was following it to profit from both, itself seeing profit and forgetting its true nature. Zhuangzi was shocked and said, "Alas! Things always encumber one another, with different kinds bringing calamity on each other." He threw down his bow and ran away, but the warden was following on his heels cursing him.

When Zhuangzi returned home, he did not go out of his courtyard for three months. When Lin Qie asked him, "Why have you recently not come out of your courtyard?" Zhuangzi replied, "I was paying attention to other forms and forgot myself, staring into muddy water and mistaking it for a clear pool. Moreover, I have heard it from the Master, 'When you go into a place, you follow its customs.' Truly, I forgot myself while wandering in Diaoling, just as the strange bird that brushed my forehead forgot its true nature while wandering in that chestnut grove. The warden therefore took me as someone worthy of execution, and that is why I have not come out of my courtyard."[65]

Like the poem, this parable describes a proliferating hierarchy of violence, with birds preying on bugs, men on birds, and men of governmental status on men of low degree. Zhuangzi's response to this vicious world is to flee it, to refuse to partake in its "customs" (*su* 俗). According to the medieval commentary on this text by Guo Xiang 郭象 (d. 312), the parable thus represents an allegory for the necessity of leaving the empire behind and taking up reclusion during an age of disorder.[66]

For Du Fu, however, this solution is not helpful: he is already in the courtyard of his "mountain pavilion" in Kuizhou precisely as a result of hiding away from a world at war. Whereas Zhuangzi thought "clear" and "muddy" waters could be distinguished, therefore, this poem's final image of the "cold river" seems pointedly ambiguous. On the one hand, the Yangzi was the path Du Fu dreamed of taking home, and it thus represented a potential escape from the humble-yet-irresolvable problems of colonial and household economy that characterized his present circumstances. On the other hand, however, the river reached in both directions from the relative safe haven of Kuizhou towards the rest of the still-embattled empire, potentially suggesting an association between the chickens and ants of his courtyard and the wars between "Chinese" and "barbarian" armies that continued to play out similarly endless enmities on a vaster stage.[67] It is far from clear, therefore, that escape is possible for Du Fu. Violent "customs" seem to bind his world—from chickens and bugs to masters and slaves, governments and rebels—into a perverse sort of community, one far broader and more problematic than the late medieval model of Chinese civilization.

Discovered Affinities

In these poems, Du Fu uses his elite Chinese art to question whether Chinese civilization is as distinct, coherent, and morally elevated as it claimed to be. This critique, however, does not encourage him to simply renounce his connections to that civilization, much less the cultural inheritance that supposedly justified its hegemony. Instead, poems like these generally work to expand and reenvision the community to which this inheritance applied, suggesting that its resources can help him discover hidden sympathies with the various "others" of his Kuizhou sojourn, including his non-Han neighbors, his servants, and even (at the furthest extreme) the fauna of his back yard. Such works do not, I think, express Du Fu's inherent affinity for all the people of his "ancestral country," nor do they enact a patrician concern to elevate and assimilate the empire's "minority peoples," as is sometimes asserted by modern critics.[68] Instead, by extending the community constituted by the Chinese tradition, he was working to reorient it and thus to solidify his own increasingly equivocal place within it.

This paradoxical dynamic can be illustrated by the following two poems. Here, Du Fu's exaggerated disdain for his "barbarian" neighbors gives way to the surprising recognition that his very distance from the center of Chinese civilization allows him to actualize in Kuizhou some of its canonical tropes.[69]

戲作俳諧體遣悶二首   *Two Poems in a Humorous Form,*
Written Playfully to Dispel Depression

I

異俗可吁怪   Different customs, so weird they make me sigh;[a]
斯人難並居   it's hard to live alongside these people.
家家養烏鬼   Each household feeds black ghosts;

---

a. This line may allude to the *Liji*: "All the places that provide dwelling for people necessarily do so according to the different qualities of heaven and earth there, whether cold or warm, dry or wet. Broad valleys and large plains have different regulations, and the people who live among them have different customs."

4	頓頓食黃魚	every meal they eat yellow fish.[b]
	舊識難爲態	Long familiarity with them makes it hard to preserve dignity;
	新知已暗疏	new acquaintances already know your details by heart.[70]
	治生且耕鑿	In the meantime for a living I'll just plow and dig a well;[c]
8	只有不關渠	all I can do is pay them no mind.

II

	西歷青羌板	In the west I crossed the plankways of the Blue Qiang;
	南留白帝城	in the south I linger by the walls of the White Emperor.[d]
	於菟侵客恨	*Wutu* encroach on this sojourner's hates;
4	粗粔作人情	*junü* are given as tokens of affection.[e]
	瓦卜傳神語	They smash tiles to transmit the spirits' words;
	畬田費火耕	slash and burn fields, toiling with fire and plowing.
	是非何處定	Yet right and wrong, where are these decided?
8	高枕笑浮生	with my head high on a pillow, I laugh at this drifting life.[f]

The joke of these poems lies in their final couplets, each of which contains an allusion that undermines the winkingly chauvinistic image of the poet built up in the previous lines. In the first poem, for example, Du Fu's

b. "Black ghosts" is one of the most notorious cruxes in Du Fu's collection. Some have suggested this is a local name for cormorants or pigs; others, that these are wrathful spirits the locals bribe to bring afflictions on their enemies. No one knows for sure.

c. This line alludes to the "Stick Toss Song" 擊壤歌 supposedly sung during the time of the sage king Yao: "When the sun comes up we rise; / when the sun goes down we rest. / We dig wells and drink, / and plow fields to eat. / What power does the emperor have over us?"

d. "Blue Qiang" is an old name for a tribe in the western regions; the White Emperor refers to Gongsun Shu 公孫述 (d. 36 CE), who set up a separatist regime in Kuizhou during the Han interregnum. A note appended to this line in early editions reads: "In recent years I went from Qin to Long, then from Tonggu County I went off to travel in Shu, and now I am lingering by Mount Wu" 頃歲自秦涉隴，從同谷縣出游蜀，留滯於巫山也.

e. *Wutu* is an old southern dialect term for tiger; *junü*, for fried honey cakes. Du Fu would have known these terms from ancient texts about the region where he found himself. It is unclear if they were still actually in use.

f. This line alludes to the *Zhuangzi*, which says of the sage that "his life is as if drifting and his death like a rest." The *Zhuangzi* also discusses the relativity of right and wrong.

complaints about his neighbors are undercut by his closing resolution simply to "plow and dig a well"—activities featured in the ancient "Stick Toss Song." According to legend, the popularity of this song manifested the good governance of the sage king Yao, whose morally transformative influence was so pervasive among his people that they could not recognize the ways it underwrote their simple, idyllic lives. This unexpected return of the quintessentially "Chinese" in a supposedly "barbarian" context suggests that the cantankerous poet presented in the poem is, in his focus on superficial sorts of ritual politeness, himself missing something important about the kind of community his uncouth neighbors have created here in Kuizhou, and the ways that community may be underwriting some of the simple pleasures of his own life here.

The second poem, similarly, carries forward this criticism of the poet's cultural prejudices, finding a precedent in the Chinese tradition itself for rising above such paltry discriminations. This precedent is, once again, the Daoist classic *Zhuangzi*, which depicts the ancient sages as having done away with narrow conceptions of "right and wrong" (*shi-fei* 是非) and thus, commensurately, as having allowed their lives to "drift" along without attempting to control them. Since Du Fu has himself drifted, in a more literal sense, on the Yangzi River down to Kuizhou, he reflects here that he might as well give up the idea that right and wrong are determined up in the capital region. In this way, he can actualize a deeply "Chinese" cultural ideal precisely in forgetting about the distinction between Chineseness and barbarity.

In both of these poems, then, the snobbish Chinese aristocrat unexpectedly finds himself in this "foreign" land living out ideals that belonged to earlier, better stages of Chinese cultural development. In poems like these, it becomes difficult to tell what represents a divergence from the Chinese tradition and what, a return to it.[71]

偶題　*Written by Chance*

| 文章千古事 | Literature is an affair of all eternity, |
| 得失寸心知 | yet its triumphs and failures are known in the mind's square inch.[a] |

a. The seat of consciousness was thought to be the heart, an organ only a square Chinese inch in size.

	作者皆殊列	Its creators are all of distinct ranks,
4	名聲豈浪垂	but fame has never been haphazardly passed down.
	騷人嗟不見	When the *Sao* poets' sighs were no longer heard,
	漢道盛於斯	the way of the Han bourgeoned in their place.[b]
	前輩飛騰入	Earlier generations got in through soaring flight;
8	餘波綺麗爲	the lingering waves did it with ornate beauty.[c]
	後賢兼舊利	Later worthies combined old strong points,
	歷代各清規	successive ages each with their own limpid norms.
	法自儒家有	Their methods I received from my scholarly family,
12	心從弱歲疲	and I tired my mind in them from youth.
	永懷江左逸	I always yearned for the ease of the River's left,
	多病鄴中奇	and was often staggered by the originality of those at Ye.[d]
	驊�皆良馬	They were Lujis all, all fine horses;
16	騏驎帶好兒	*qilin* bringing along fine sons.[e]
	車輪徒已斲	Yet, though the wheel in vain is already carved,[f]

b. The *Sao* poets are the poets of the *Songs of the Southlands* (*Chuci*), the core of which was thought to have been composed before the founding of the Han dynasty.

c. These lines seem to refer, respectively, to the vigorous poetry of the third and fourth centuries, and to the delicate verse of the fifth and sixth.

d. The "River's left" probably refers to the writers of the Eastern Jin and Southern Dynasties, the capitals of which were in the southeast. Ye was the capital of the earlier Cao-Wei dynasty.

e. This apparently simple couplet is extremely obscure and has occasioned much scholarly discussion. The reference to Lujis—Luji being the name of a legendarily fine horse—may involve an allusion to Cao Pi's "Discussion of Literature" 論文："All these seven writers ... take themselves to be Jilus [驥騄, i.e., Lujis] galloping ten thousand leagues, and so, even though they gallop at equal pace side by side, they have found it difficult to pay each other due respect." The reference to *qilin*—the Chinese unicorn—may refer to a story about the writers Xu Chi 徐摛 (474–551) and his son Xu Ling 徐陵 (507–83). When Xu Ling was only a few years old, his father once asked a famous monk to discern his destiny. The monk rubbed the crown of Xu Ling's head and told Xu Chi that the boy was a "stone *qilin* from heaven." This was a figure for great talent.

f. The "carving of the wheel" refers to the story of Wheelwright Bian 輪扁 in the *Zhuangzi*. Wheelwright Bian was carving a wheel for the Duke of Qi while the latter read a book containing the words of the ancient sages. Bian argued that such reading was useless because the essential techniques of the sages could not be transmitted in words, any more than Bian could himself transmit his wheel-carving technique to his own sons.

	堂構惜仍虧	I regret that the hall's construction is still lacking.[g]
	漫作潛夫論	In vain I wrote "Discussions of a Hidden Man,"
20	虛傳幼婦碑	for nothing circulated "young wife" steles.[h]
	緣情慰漂蕩	What "comes from feeling" merely consoled my drifting
	抱疾屢遷移	as, holding illness within, I moved several times.[i]
	經濟慙長策	Ashamed before those with good plans for the empire,
24	飛棲假一枝	I flew off to roost, borrowing this single branch.[j]
	塵沙傍蜂蠆	From dust and sand beside wasps and scorpions,
	江峽繞蛟螭	to where river and gorges have plenty wyverns and wyrms.[k]
	蕭瑟唐虞遠	Withered and fallen, from Tang and Yu far off;
28	聯翩楚漢危	continuous and unending, perils like Chu and Han.[l]
	聖朝兼盜賊	And since our sage court has to share space with rebels
	異俗更喧卑	the strange customs here grow even more harsh and base.
	鬱鬱星辰劍	Welling upwards, a sword among the stars;
32	蒼蒼雲雨池	dark and gloomy, a pool with clouds and rain.[m]

g. The figure of the hall derives from the *Shangshu*, wherein King Wu of Zhou justified his conquest of the empire by claiming to be merely "finishing the hall" his deceased father had planned out. This couplet thus suggests that Du Fu was unable to continue the projects of his predecessors.

h. "Discussions of a Hidden Man" was the name of a collection of treatises written by Wang Fu 王符 (ca. 82–167) in the Eastern Han; here the suggestion is merely that Du Fu was not prominent in the period of his life when he was seeking out a government position. "Young wife" 幼婦 is a rebus for the character "wondrous" 妙. The reference is to a piece of cryptic praise that Cai Yong 蔡邕 (133–92) wrote on the back of a stele by Handan Chun 邯鄲淳 (ca. 130–ca. 225), which, puzzled out, meant "extremely wondrous, fine words."

i. "What comes from feeling" was a common definition of poetry. "Moved several times" probably refers to Du Fu's flight to Qinzhou, from there to Chengdu, and then finally to Kuizhou.

j. This line refers to the *Zhuangzi*: "When the wren nests within a deep forest, it does not demand more than a single branch."

k. That is, Du Fu has come from the battlefields of the north to the backwater of Kuizhou.

l. Tang (Yao) and Yu (Shun) were legendary sage kings of great antiquity; they may stand here for the current emperor. "Chu and Han" refers to the intense warfare that preceded the establishment of the Han dynasty.

m. These two lines allude to stories about concealed dragons, which either serve as metaphors for Du Fu's being unrecognized down in Kuizhou or as figures for rebellions in the region. In the first story, Zhang Hua 張華 (232–300) observed a welling aura striking the stars; following it, he discovered a pair of wondrous swords, which, after his death,

	兩都開幕府	Yet though army commands have been established in both capitals,
	萬寓插軍麾	and military flags planted in ten thousand dwellings,
	南海殘銅柱	still by the southern seas remains the bronze column,
36	東風避月支	and in the east wind I can evade the Yuezhi.[n]
	音書恨烏鵲	For the "news" they bring, I hate the magpies;
	號怒怪熊羆	for their rageful howling, I blame the bears.[o]
	稼穡分詩興	But in sowing and reaping I discern inspiration for poems,
40	柴荊學土宜	and in my brushwood hut, I study what is fit for the land.[p]
	故山迷白閣	My old mountains: I have lost White Tower;
	秋水憶黃陂	autumn waters: I recall Yellow Bank.[q]
	不敢要佳句	I no longer dare demand fine lines,[r]
44	愁來賦別離	and when sorrows come, I just write of separation.[s]

turned into dragons. In the second, the great general Zhou Yu 周瑜 (175–210) argued for driving a wedge between his enemies by saying, "I fear that, when a dragon meets with rain and clouds, it is no longer a creature that can be contained in a pool."

n. The Han dynasty general Ma Yuan 馬援 (14 BCE–49 CE) set up a bronze column in the far south to mark the extent of Han sovereignty. The Yuezhi were a tribe on the western frontiers in Han times; their invocation here probably refers to the Tibetans, who had invaded western regions of the Tang empire over the past several years. The reference to the "east wind" may suggest that Du Fu intends to follow the Yangzi River farther southeast.

o. The song of the magpie was supposed to portend the arrival of a traveler; Du Fu is thus complaining that the magpies' songs are lies, since no one comes to visit him. The bears here probably allude to the "Summons of the Recluse" from the *Songs of the Southlands*: "Tigers and leopards brawl and bears and she-bears howl, the birds and beasts are frightened and lose their flocks. Come back, prince! In the mountains you cannot long remain."

p. "Studying what is fit for the land" was, according to the "Xici" commentary on the *Yijing*, the work of the primal sage Fu Xi, whose conceptualization and representation of the cosmos in that Classic represented the beginning of Chinese culture (*wen*).

q. Both White Tower Peak and Yellow Bank (also written as Imperial Bank 皇陂) were in the Chang'an area. Du Fu wrote poems on both before the Rebellion.

r. The phrase "fine lines" may recall a story from the *Shishuo xinyu*. When Fan Rongqi 范榮期 read Sun Chuo's "Rhapsody on the Tiantai Mountains," "every time he encountered a fine line, he would say, 'these are words of my kind of people'"—that is, aristocratic, cultured, Chinese people.

s. "Poems of Separation" was a poetic subgenre, anthologized under the title of "Ancient Separation" 古別離 in the *Yuefu shiji*. Guo Maoqian (1041–99), the compiler

On a surface reading, this poem narrates Du Fu's failure to inherit and uphold the literary tradition he studied in his youth. Unable to imitate its "carved wheels" or complete its "unfinished halls," he has given up on seeking fame through his verse and no longer aspires to the sort of finely crafted lines he once wrote in the landscape around the capital. Literature within the civilized tradition may be an affair of all eternity, but for him, having drifted now to the uncivilized wilderness of Kuizhou, it has become merely a means of venting his feelings. When sorrows come, he writes, no longer attempting to render his one-inch mind commensurate with the glorious tradition that has preceded him.

Yet if this poem is supposed to exemplify the new poetics it describes, having itself been "written by chance" at some point when Du Fu was feeling estranged from his youthful ambitions, it enacts this humbling of his art in an odd way. Not only is the poem a beautifully wrought and highly allusive "extended regulated verse" (*pailü* 排律), the most ornate of contemporary genres and the recent apogee of a process of cumulative metrical theorization under way since the fifth century. More important, even as Du Fu here "writes of separation" from the center of Chinese society and its literary tradition, separation was in fact one of the oldest and most perduring topics of that tradition. Even farming, the occupation Du Fu has taken up in his exile, represents a surprising return to the sources of Chinese identity, since learning "what is fit for the land" (*tuyi* 土宜) was one of the foundational accomplishments of the sage king Fu Xi, integral to his creation of the *Yijing* and, thus, to his initiation of civilization. Far from giving up on his youthful ambitions to carry on the glories of Chinese literature, then, Du Fu seems in Kuizhou to be actualizing them in ways that might not have been possible in the heartland.

In lacing a narrative ostensibly describing his fall away from elite Chinese norms with unexpected echoes of traditional precedents, Du Fu is working once again to reconfigure late medieval notions of what it might mean to inherit the tradition that defined "Chineseness" in his age. Central to this project is the redeployment of normative cultural models in nontropological ways. Having given up on the idea that such models could be unproblematically enacted in contemporary situations, he is now finding

---

of that anthology, traced the phrase "separation" back to the *Songs of the Southlands*: "No sadness is more sad than separation for life."

them relevant to his life in strange and unpredictable permutations. In this poem, for instance, the reference to Fu Xi is too specious and ironic to suggest a straightforward analogy between the poet and this legendary founder of Chinese culture. At the same time, however, the effort Du Fu is putting into learning how to farm in an unfamiliar landscape—seemingly so far removed from the elite world of Tang *wen*—does recall the primordial labors that had ultimately made possible the more complex glories of the civilized world.[72] No less than were the writers in the tradition he has failed to inherit, then, he is engaged in the work of civilization even as he is forced to do work that seems, on its surface, uncivilized. And the discovery of such resonances in unexpected places frees him up merely "to write what he feels," hopeful nonetheless that what he writes may fit into the great tradition, more broadly conceived.

Given this hope, it is no surprise that recordizing critics have often identified "Written by Chance" as Du Fu's *ars poetica*.[73] Not only does this poem suggest that he now records his emotional responses to the affairs of his life without artificially forcing them to conform to established conventions. Equally important, its discovery of his continued solidarity with the Chinese tradition, despite the apparent ruptures occasioned by the Rebellion, clearly prefigures the visions of unbreakable community favored by his recordizing commentators. Similar dynamics are, in fact, pervasive in this period of his work. In the following poems, for instance, he draws even closer to his critics' account of him as a "poet historian," noting even the most apparently mundane affairs of his daily life in a way that ties them to the fate of the empire. Yet at the same moment that these poems are the closest Du Fu comes to depicting his work as a "record" (*ji* 記) of his life, their pessimism about the Tang also shows how little he had come to invest in the "Chineseness" of his community, at least in any sense that might have been recognizable to his contemporaries.[74]

雨二首 *Rain, Two Poems*

I

青山澹無姿	The dark mountains are pale, lacking charm;
白露誰能數	white dewdrops—who can count them all?
片片水上雲	Then layer on layer, clouds over the waters,
蕭蕭沙中雨	and windy gusts, rain upon the sand.

殊俗狀巢居	Strange customs here, as if dwelling in nests;
曾臺俯風渚	from a storied terrace I look down on windblown isles.[a]
佳客適萬里	A fine traveler is going ten thousand leagues;
8 沉思情延佇	sunk in brooding, I watch him go with feeling.
挂帆遠色外	He hangs his sail beyond the farthest colors,
驚浪滿吳楚	yet frightful waves fill Wu and Chu.[b]
久陰蛟螭出	It's been dark so long the wyverns and wyrms emerge—
12 寇盜復幾許	thieves and bandits too, beyond count.

II

空山中宵陰	Empty mountains at midnight turned darker still:
微冷先枕席	a light chill first on pillow and mat.
廻風起清曙	Swirling winds rose in the cool of dawn,
4 萬象萋已碧	the myriad images lush now, emerald.
落落出岫雲	In endless profusion, clouds emerge from the peaks;
渾渾倚天石	huge and disordered, rocks lean against the sky.[c]
日假何道行	What road has the sun borrowed?
8 雨含長江白	the rain swallows the river in white.
連檣荊州舡	A series of masts, barges from Jingzhou:
有士荷矛戟	there are soldiers onboard, bearing pikes and spears.
南防草鎮慘	To the south they'll defend gloomy Grass Fort;
12 霑濕赴遠役	soaked to the bone, they head on their distant campaign.[d]
群盜下辟山	Hordes of bandits have come down Mount Pi;
摠戎備強敵	the commander fortifies against a strong foe.
水深雲光廓	Through deep waters, a vastness of clouded light,
16 鳴櫓各有適	each ringing oar has somewhere it's bound.
漁艇息悠悠	Yet here the fishermen's skiffs rest easy,
夷歌負樵客	and barbarian songs come from the wood gatherers.

a. According to the *Zhuangzi*, in antiquity, people lived in nests to protect themselves from wild animals.

b. The regions downriver to the east.

c. The image of "clouds emerging from the peaks" may recall a couplet from Tao Qian: "Clouds need no minds to emerge from the peaks; when birds tire of flying they know to return to roost." In its original context, this was a justification of reclusion.

d. Commentators identify Grass Fort as Yellow Grass Gorge, to the southwest of Kuizhou near Mt. Pi.

留滯一老翁　　Stuck lingering in this place, a lone old man:[e]
20　書時記朝夕　　I write of the times, recording dawns and dusks.[f]

These poems are part of a loose set of around fifteen written in Kuizhou under some variation of the title "Rain" ("The Rain Is Unending" 雨不絕, for instance, or "Rain Clears" 雨晴).[75] At the end of this pair, Du Fu reflects on his decision to write so many poems on such an apparently unpropitious topic. Trapped here in Kuizhou between minor rebellions upriver and down, he claims to have nothing more suitable to write about than the passage of evenings and mornings, rain and shine. Yet, in thus "writing the times" (*shu shi* 書時)—an ambiguous phrase that in the original Chinese can mean noting the time of day, the weather, the seasons, current affairs, or even the broader cultural climate of the age—Du Fu's obsessive composition recalls the responsibilities of the ancient court scribe (*shi* 史, also "historian"), charged with recording the ruler's words and activities at court "dawn and dusk." As a pseudoscribe stuck in the southlands, in fact, his situation is surprisingly reminiscent of the "Grand Scribe" (*taishi* 太史), Sima Tan, who was also once "stuck lingering" in the south, unable to document the affairs of the court. Although the last couplet of the diptych is a sigh at his estrangement from the center of civilization, therefore, it also discovers once again an unexpected connection between his experience and the canonical tradition.

Given these dynamics, it was a brilliant stroke of Wen Tianxiang's in the abovementioned verse autobiography he compiled out of Du Fu's lines to use the penultimate line of the second poem here, the allusion to Sima Tan, to describe the climax of his own story: the defeat of his armies and his capture by the Mongols.[76] Like Du Fu before him, Wen at this moment was reduced to writing a history—his recompilation of Du Fu's

e. In the time of Han Wudi, Grand Scribe Sima Tan 司馬談 (d. 110 BCE) was "stuck lingering" 留滯 in the south and was thus unable to accompany the emperor as he made his sacrificial tour of the northeast. He was so upset about not being taken along that he died of rage.

f. "Dawns and dusks" recalls "The Rain Is Not Right" 雨無正 from the *Shijing*: "Of the domains' rulers and the feudal lords, none is willing to pay court [to the king] at dawn and dusk" 邦君諸侯，莫肯朝夕.

poetry into an account of the Song's collapse—that would be of no use to his contemporaries, far from the legitimate but imperiled Chinese court. If the experience was tragic, however, the allusion was triumphant. Just as Du Fu had found in his lonely frustration a connection with Sima Tan, so too did Wen find one here with Du Fu. The records left by both previous "historians" showed him, despite his desperate circumstances, that he was not alone, that his experiences were part of a constant and recurring tradition, and that Chinese culture would thus continue forward no matter how powerful the Mongols might now seem.

Wen's reading is a powerful one, no doubt. Its polemical drive to affirm the ultimate invulnerability of the Chinese community, however, obscures Du Fu's more nuanced exploration in these poems of his simultaneous estrangement from and connection with it. For Wen, it is only the similarities between his circumstances and Du Fu's that matter, since they provide the proof that Chinese poetry is built into the recurring patterns of the world and the constant nature of the human heart. For Du Fu, however, the allusion to Sima Tan actually emphasizes the contrasts between poet and Grand Historian at least as strongly as their connections. Unlike Du Fu, Sima Tan was an actual court scribe; and where Du Fu becomes a "scribe" precisely because he is stuck here in the south, Sima Tan in similar circumstances ceased to write his records, dying instead of rage and frustration that he was unable to observe the real history being made by Han Emperor Wu in his sacrificial procession up north. The "mornings and evenings" that Du Fu is recording here—which, it might be noted, evidence local rebellions so small in scale as not to appear in surviving records[77]— are thus precisely the sort of "history" that Sima Tan preferred to die rather than to write.

Even more obviously, where Sima Tan yearned to follow the court procession up north, Du Fu ends these poems deciding not to leave Kuizhou. In both poems, he mulls the possibility of returning to regions more integral to the empire—to which the "fine traveler" was heading and for which the soldiers were preparing to fight—but reconsiders in light of the safer, more beautiful, more properly reclusive circumstances in which he finds himself here. The customs of Kuizhou may be strange, and the woodcutters may sing "barbarian" songs. But, where Wen Tianxiang would want nothing more than to escape from the Mongol stronghold and return to the Song capital, Du Fu finds that this supposedly uncivilized region offers him refuge from a state that, in its disorder, may no longer represent Chinese civilization in any sense that interests him.

Doomed States and What Survives Them

On the one hand, then, "Written by Chance" and "Rain, Two Poems" prefigure strikingly the core ideas of recordizing poetics and thus represent the culmination of one of this book's main narratives. On the other, their unexpected discoveries of contact with the tradition also diverge from the "patriotic" impulses of much recordizing criticism, suggesting less that Du Fu's Chinese identity remains despite the calamities of the age, and more that the sort of "Chineseness" that now appeals to him—if it can even be called that anymore—is far more flexible than his critics (or even his contemporaries) would have allowed. Having discarded the idea that participating in the tradition meant adopting its tropologies, he was now free to imagine other modes of belonging, even modes beyond his imagination.

Though often lionized for his steadfast loyalty to the Tang, Du Fu not only suggests throughout this period that the empire may be on the verge of its final collapse, but also considers the hopeful possibility that this collapse may allow for the consolidation of new and different communities in the future. This idea underwrites an important theme of his work in these years: the now defunct states that had once held the Kuizhou region and the cultural heroes whose works survived their destruction. In considering the monuments of these states and their heroes, he often focuses on the ways their significance had changed over time, extending offers of fellowship despite the estrangements interposed by changing polities.[78]

大曆二年九月三十日　*The Thirtieth Day of the Ninth Month of the Second Year of the Dali Reign*[a]

爲客無時了	My time as a sojourner has no final date,
悲秋向夕終	but sadness for autumn will end at eventide.
瘴餘夔子國	Miasma lingers in this country of Kui's marquis;

a. October 27, 767, the last day of autumn.

4	霜薄楚王宮	the frost is light on the palace of Chu's king.[b]
	草敵虛嵐翠	Plants rival the mountain haze's formless green;
	花禁冷葉紅	flowers prevent the cold leaves seeming red.[79]
	年年小搖落	Year after year, little shaking or falling,
8	不與故園同	not like in the gardens of my home.

This poem is based, couplet by couplet, on a lament legendarily written by the ancient poet Song Yu for Qu Yuan, anticipating the collapse of their home kingdom of Chu, which at the time contained the Kuizhou region. The lament begins:

> Sad indeed is the air of autumn! / Whistling drear, the plants and trees shake and fall, and turn to decline. / Grim and gloomy, you are on a far journey.
>
> 悲哉秋之為氣也。蕭瑟兮，草木搖落而變衰。憀慄兮，若在遠行。[80]

If one looks at Du Fu's poem with Song's in mind, the first couplet takes up autumn's "sadness," the second its "air" (*qi* 氣), the third Song's mention of "plants and trees," and the fourth his depiction of their "shaking and falling." But although Du Fu finds himself in autumn in roughly the area in which Song was supposed to have written his lament, the experiences of the two poets are surprisingly divergent. The air remains warm in Kuizhou even into the winter, and the plants shed few leaves. In fact, the scene Song describes resembles better what Du Fu imagines is happening in his hometown gardens back up north. Du Fu's sadness, then, is not the sadness of "autumn's air," which in his experience is hardly sad here in Kuizhou at all. Instead, it will continue even as autumn ends and winter begins, on the first day of the tenth month of the second year of the Dali reign.

As the weary phrase "year after year" emphasizes, Du Fu when he wrote this poem was nearing the end of his third autumn in the region of old Chu. The unplanned protraction of his sojourn here offers one explanation of the poem's strikingly "recordizing" title, suggesting that he has become acutely aware of time's simultaneously slow and too swift passage.

---

b. The Marquis of Kui was the ruler of the Kuizhou region until his state was absorbed by Chu. After this point, the Chu kings built a palace at Gaotang, near Kuizhou.

The date in the title, however, also sits uncomfortably alongside the second couplet's invocation of dead rulers and lost states, since all dates in premodern China were determined by and thus represented the ruling dynasty. Here, perhaps, we may sense the repurposing of traditional precedents we know by now to expect in Du Fu's verse from this period. For if the four cited features of Song Yu's autumn sadness fail to match Du Fu's observation, Du Fu's long exile from a collapsing state nonetheless conforms to the next, unmentioned line of Song's lament, describing Qu Yuan's exile from the capital of the soon-to-collapse state of Chu. The air of decline is thus not gone: it has merely shifted northwards, and Du Fu recognizes that, with time's march, the "Dali reign" may come to sound as sepulchral to his readers as the "palace of Chu's king" does to him. Though Song's great lament may in many respects fail to prescribe Du Fu's experience, then, it does provide a precedent for how states and the glories they sustain may vanish. And that very precedent proves that tradition can continue across even such cataclysmic divides, applying in new ways in new worlds, such that the lament of a poet exiled from a southland polity may become meaningful, a thousand years later, for a poet exiled there from a collapsing state up north.

A similar interest in doomed states and what survives them underwrites Du Fu's repeated engagements with another of the cultural luminaries of the Kuizhou region as well. Zhuge Liang 諸葛亮 (181–234) was minister and military advisor to Liu Bei 劉備 (161–223), a descendant of the Han royal house and the first ruler of Shu during the Three Kingdoms period. Kuizhou preserved two monuments to Zhuge's heroic attempts to win the empire for Shu and thus reestablish the Han dynasty: a shrine where sacrifices were offered to his spirits and the Diagram of the Eight Formations. According to the *Record of Kuizhou Commandery* 夔州都督府記 by Du Fu's younger contemporary Li Yisun 李貽孫,

> Three or four *li* farther to the west-southwest, one gets to "The Diagram of the Eight Formations" on an otherwise empty sandbar. This is what Zhuge Liang used to demonstrate his plans for mobilizing his troops. He divided his various troop formations and hid them from one another behind piled rocks. When the river swells in the springtime, it is submerged; when the waves decrease in the autumn, it is revealed. The force of creation cannot move it; thus, we see the capability of the one who created it.

又西而稍南三四里，得八陣圖，在沙州之壖。此諸葛所以示人於行
兵者也。分其列陣，隱在石磧。春而潦大則沒，秋而波減則露。造
化之力，不能推移，所以見作者之能。[81]

Du Fu too found this strange pile of rocks fascinating, but he had a different interpretation of its permanence.[82]

八陣圖   *The Diagram of the Eight Formations*

功蓋三分國	His achievements overspread kingdoms thrice divided;[a]
名成八陣圖	his fame was complete in the Diagram of the Eight Formations.[b]
江流石不轉	Though the river flows on, the stones don't roll away:
4　遺恨失吞吳	a lingering regret he failed to swallow Wu.[c]

The first couplet of this short poem contains sharp ironies, not the least of
which is the suggestion that Zhuge's fame went no further than the creation of this Diagram, which, though constructed to aid in his military
endeavors, has now come to represent their ultimate defeat. Yet if Zhuge
Liang failed to "swallow" Wu, so too has the great Yangzi River failed to
swallow the stones he piled up here on its sandbar. Stones were supposed
to "roll away," at least according to the *Shijing* poem Du Fu cites in the
penultimate line; it was the human mind, by contrast, in the firmness of
its commitments and devotions, that no force could shift. The strange
suggestion of this allusion, then, is that the stones' miraculous fixity somehow represents Zhuge Liang's frustration, the Diagram providing physical
presence to the "lingering regret" that the rising and falling waters of the

a. "His achievement overspreads" abbreviates the traditional phrase "an achievement
that overspreads all-under-heaven" 功蓋天下; this was generally the achievement of emperors. Here, however, "all-under-heaven" has been replaced with "thrice divided," a phrase
that derives from Zhuge Liang's own "Memorial on Mobilizing the Troops" 出師表,
which he wrote shortly before his disastrous final campaign.

b. The phrase "his fame was complete" might recall the *Zhuangzi*, where we read that
"those who complete accomplishments will fall, and those who complete their fame will
suffer."

c. The penultimate line alludes to "Cypress Boat" 柏舟 from the *Shijing*: "My heart is
not a stone: it cannot be rolled away."

Yangzi cannot efface from the landscape. When Du Fu faces these rocks, therefore, he seems almost to be communing with Zhuge's mind itself: hence the ambiguous grammar, which can also be construed as suggesting the "lingering regret" is Du Fu's own.

A blending of individuals along these lines is even more clearly at issue in Du Fu's other great Kuizhou era poem on Zhuge Liang, "Ballad of Ancient Cypresses" 古柏行, which pointedly conflates two different cypress groves planted near Zhuge's shrines in different locations as a way of symbolizing Du Fu's own conflation of his frustrated ambitions with those of his frustrated hero.[83] In this ballad, Du Fu imagines these monuments to Zhuge Liang's failed life allowing a paradoxical community to form among individuals who were prevented, through historical misfortune, from creating and sustaining the political communities to which they aspired. Like these ancient cypresses, then, the Diagram of the Eight Formations demonstrates the unpredictability of meaning: constructed as part of a plan for unifying the empire, it has come in its failure to catalyze a different sort of solidarity.

Much the same dynamic also characterizes Du Fu's ruminations throughout this next set of poems.[84]

詠懷古跡五首 *Five Poems Singing My Feelings on Traces of the Past*

I

支離東北風塵際 Separation in the northeast,
　　　　　　　　　　　within the windblown dust;
漂泊西南天地間 I drift and moor in the southwest,
　　　　　　　　　　　between the earth and sky.[a]
三峽樓臺淹日月 Terraces in the Three Gorges
　　　　　　　　　　　block out sun and moon;
4 五溪衣服共雲山 with the clothing of the Five Creek Tribes,
　　　　　　　　　　　I share these cloudy mountains.[b]
羯胡事主終無賴 Serving our lord, barbarians
　　　　　　　　　　　in the end untrustworthy;

a. "Windblown dust" is often a metonymy for warfare.
b. "Block out the sun and moon" could also be "linger for days and months." The "Five Creek Tribes" are an old name for the peoples of the south.

詞客哀時且未還　lamenting the times, a poet
　　　　　　　　　yet to return home.[c]

庾信生平最蕭瑟　Yu Xin's lifetime was
　　　　　　　　　dismal in the extreme,

8　暮年詩賦動江關　but in his twilight years, his poems
　　　　　　　　　moved both River and Passes.[d]

II

搖落深知宋玉悲　Shaking and falling, I know deeply
　　　　　　　　　the sadness of Song Yu;

風流儒雅亦吾師　with flair and learned grace,
　　　　　　　　　he is also my teacher.[e]

悵望千秋一灑淚　Sadly gazing, a thousand years
　　　　　　　　　at one in splashing tears;

4　蕭條異代不同時　desolate indeed, that different generations
　　　　　　　　　cannot share one age.

江山故宅空文藻　By river and mountains, his old dwelling—
　　　　　　　　　vain his literary flourishes;

雲雨荒臺豈夢思　but clouds and rain on a ruined terrace—
　　　　　　　　　could that have been a dream?[f]

c. The "barbarians" intended here are primarily An Lushan and his subordinate and successor Shi Siming 史思明, though commentators have suggested that Du Fu may also be referring to the Tang's Uighur allies and its general Pugu Huai'en 僕固懷恩.

d. Yu Xin was a sixth-century poet who lived out the remainder of his years in the north after watching his southern homeland collapse to the invasion of the "barbarian" Hou Jing 侯景 (d. 552). His "Lament for the Southland" 哀江南賦, written near the end of his life, became his most famous literary piece. "Both River and Passes" is a metonymy for "both south and north."

e. This couplet refers to the opening of Song's "Jiubian" 九辯: "Sad indeed is the air of autumn! Whistling drear, the plants and trees shake and fall, and turn to decline." Yu Xin had used the phrase "flair and learned grace" to describe Yin Zhongwen 殷仲文 and in the "Lament for the Southland" wrote of his ancestors "thatching Song Yu's dwelling"—i.e., moving to dwell in the southern lands. Du Fu may thus be saying that, like Yu Xin, he also takes Song as his teacher.

f. Guizhou 歸州 and Jingzhou 荊州, downstream from Kuizhou in modern-day Hubei, both preserved buildings that were purported to be the former dwellings of Song Yu. This couplet refers to Song's "Rhapsody on Gaotang" 高唐賦, which describes how a former king of Chu was intimate with the goddess of Shaman Mountain (near Kuizhou) in a dream. When she left him, she said that he could find her again in "the clouds of dawn

最是楚宮俱泯滅   What's worse, the Chu palace
                         has been totally destroyed;

8   舟人指點到今疑   the boatmen point it out,
                         but by now they are unsure.

III

羣山萬壑赴荊門   Through many mountains, myriad ravines
                         head off towards Jingmen;[g]

生長明妃尚有村   there's still the village there where
                         the Brilliant Consort grew up.[h]

一去紫臺連朔漠   Once she left the Purple Terrace,
                         endless dark desert;

4   獨留青冢向黃昏   all that remains is her Evergreen Grave
                         approaching brown dusk.[i]

畫圖省識春風面   In the painting, her spring-breeze face
                         he little recognized;

環珮空歸月夜魂   with girdle pendants, her moonlit-nights soul
                         uselessly returns.

千歲琵琶作胡語   For a thousand years the *pipa* has spoken
                         their barbarian tongue,

8   分明怨恨曲中論   telling clearly within the tune
                         her resentment and her grief.[j]

---

and the running rain." Commentators often suggest that Song's "Rhapsody" contained subtle political advice for the current king, intended to stave off Chu's approaching collapse.

g. Jingmen was downriver from Kuizhou in modern-day Hubei. An early note on this poem reads: "In Guizhou there is Zhaojun's village" 歸州有昭君村.

h. "The Brilliant Consort" is Wang Zhaojun 王昭君 (fl. 33 BCE), a concubine of Han Emperor Yuan 漢元帝. The emperor had so many concubines that he commissioned a painter to paint the portrait of each one so that he could conveniently choose his nighttime companions. Wang Zhaojun refused to bribe the painter, and as a result he painted her as ugly. When Emperor Yuan decided to make a present of one of his concubines to the Xiongnu Qaghan, he chose Wang Zhaojun on the basis of her portrait. When she came to take her leave, the emperor saw her beauty and regretted his mistake.

i. "Purple Terrace" refers to the Han palace in Chang'an; "dark desert" is literally "northland" desert. According to legend, Wang Zhaojun's grave was green year round despite being in the desert.

j. The *pipa*, or balloon guitar, was an instrument with a barbarian-sounding name that may well have come to China from the west; in Du Fu's time, it was often used to play

IV

蜀主窺吳幸三峽	Shu's lord came to the Three Gorges to peek at Wu,
崩年亦在永安宮	but the year he died, he was still in his palace at Yong'an.[k]
翠華想像空山裏	His halcyon banners I imagine within these empty mountains;
4 玉殿虛無野寺中	his marble palace hall hovers unreal upon this temple in the wilds.[l]
古廟杉松巢水鶴	The ancient shrine's firs and pines give nests to water cranes;
歲時伏臘走村翁	throughout the year on festival days, old villagers rush about.
武侯祠屋常鄰近	The altar room of the Martial Count is always close by,
8 君臣一體祭祀同	and as one body ruler and minister receive sacrifices together.[m]

V

諸葛大名垂宇宙	The great name of Zhuge Liang overhangs rafters and ridgepole;[n]

music associated with Central Asia. According to Shi Chong's 石崇 (249–300) "Poem on the Brilliant Consort" 王明君詞, Emperor Yuan sent a *pipa* player with Wang Zhaojun to entertain her as she traveled to the northwest. A *yuefu* (musical ballad) genre subsequently grew up around imagining the songs she would have sung on this journey; these ballads were often set to "Central Asian" musical modes.

k. "Shu's lord" was Liu Bei. During the Three Kingdoms period, he came to the Three Gorges on an ultimately unsuccessful campaign against Wu in the southeast. After his defeat, he made his way back on foot to Yufu 魚復, nearby Kuizhou, which he then renamed Yong'an (Longstanding Peace).

l. An early note on these lines reads: "The palace now is a temple; his shrine is east of the compound" 殿今為寺，廟在宮東.

m. The Martial Count is Zhuge Liang, Liu Bei's advisor and the subject of the next poem in the series.

n. "Rafters and ridgepole" (*yuzhou* 宇宙) is a common compound that often means "heaven and earth"; here it also means, more literally, "the eaves" of Zhuge Liang's shrine, where there would have been a plaque inscribed with his name in large characters.

宗臣遺像肅清高	the remnant likeness of this great official, solemn, lofty, and pure.[o]
三分割據紆籌策	A threefold division of warring regimes twisted his calculations;
4 萬古雲霄一羽毛	for ten thousand ages in the highest clouds, a single tuft of down.[p]
伯仲之間見伊呂	He looked on Yi Yin and Lü Shang as merely elder brothers;
指揮若定失蕭曹	he might have outstripped Xiao and Cao had he gained control.[q]
福移漢祚難恢復	But fortune had moved on from the Han and was impossible to regain;[r]
8 志決身殲軍務勞	his will failed, his body was destroyed, his armies toiled to no end.

Each poem in this series focuses on a southlands cultural luminary who suffered a failure of community, either losing it in their lifetimes (Yu Xin, Wang Zhaojun), having it destroyed soon after their deaths (Song Yu), or being unable to bring it into being (Liu Bei, Zhuge Liang). Yet the traces of their lives, whether in poetic, musical, or monumental form, have subsequently proven integral to the consolidation of solidarities otherwise constituted. In this sense, they not only provide Du Fu a sort of retrospective community for his own traumatic experience of social collapse—his story blending together, for instance, with Yu Xin's in the first poem of the set. Their examples also suggest, even more hopefully, that the traces of

o. The "remnant likeness" is probably a painting of Zhuge in his shrine. It is also the "image" of himself he left behind in his deeds and in his writings.

p. This line is highly obscure and has inspired numerous different interpretations. Zhuge Liang was famous for using his goose-feather fan to direct troops in battle; that may be what is intended here.

q. Yi Yin 伊尹 and Lü Shang 呂尚 were legendary ministers of the Shang and Zhou dynasties who assisted their founding rulers. Xiao He 蕭何 (d. 193 BCE) and Cao Shen 曹參 (d. 190 BCE) helped to found the Han dynasty. "Had he gained control" presumably means had he succeeded in unifying the empire under Liu Bei.

r. Because Liu Bei was a member of the Han imperial house, he claimed to be restoring the dynasty.

his life may matter someday to a broader community, one he cannot necessarily predict.

It is important to note how disparate the new communities are to which these figures have come to be significant and how little they resemble those to which they aspired in their lifetimes. The least obviously surprising, in this respect, are the transitions intimated in the first two poems, since these appear merely to follow the dynastic progress of Chinese history—the Tang inheriting the region of Song Yu's old Chu and consolidating the territories of Yu Xin's Period of Division. Yet there is a marked irony even here, given the loyalty to one particular polity that Du Fu sees as characteristic of both poets. Though Yu yearned for his southern homeland of Liang, the poetry that expressed this yearning became important to the reunified empire built on its ashes, moving readers equally north and south. And though Song wrote to save a Chu king whose palaces have been destroyed so long no trace of them remains, he now provides material for local tour guides introducing the region to officials like Du Fu from the capital in the old territory of Qin, the state responsible for wiping Chu off the map.[85]

As the series progresses, the new communities these figures catalyze become more obviously different from those they themselves imagined. Though Wang Zhaojun, for instance, grieved at being married off to a barbarian, she became a source of endless inspiration for Chinese poetry written to Central Asian music. Her legacy, in other words, involves a blending of Chinese and barbarian arts, the introduction of a "barbarian tongue" into the canonical literary tradition that thus undermines, to some degree, the hard distinction between races that might otherwise be read into her suffering at being married off to the Xiongnu.[86] In the fourth poem, similarly, Liu Bei's "Palace of Longstanding Peace" has become now a Buddhist temple (another instance of the blending of Chinese and "barbarian" cultures) that functions to consolidate a local community of mixed ethnicity and to integrate it, at an even further extreme, with nonhuman members like water cranes. These rustic and even interspecies communities are a far cry from the empire Liu Bei dedicated his life to reestablishing. But they are nonetheless communities of "longstanding peace."

These unexpected consummations do not negate the suffering of these luminaries' lifetimes, of course. Wang Zhaojun's ghost, the poet imagines, still yearns in the desert for her southern hometown; Song Yu's literary works, with their subtle moral persuasions, failed to save his king. Yet it is precisely the irreducibility of these figures' suffering that makes the series hopeful. Like Du Fu, they could not see how their lives might not be the failures they seemed. But others with other values and perspectives have understood them differently.

This hope that failed lives might someday be transformed is suggested most forcefully in the final poem, and in particular, in the ambiguity of the phrase "rafters and ridgepole" (*yuzhou* 宇宙) in its first line. Concretely, this phrase refers to the literal eaves of Zhuge Liang's shrine, where his name hung, written in "large" (*da* 大) script. Presumably this literal meaning would have been obvious in the eighth century, since, as Hoyt Cleveland Tillman has demonstrated, Zhuge Liang was not then the national hero he would become in the Song.[87] All of Du Fu's postmedieval commentators, however, take the phrase "rafters and ridgepole" in its other common sense: as a metonymy for "the heavens." On this reading, Zhuge's "great fame" (*da ming* 大名) overhangs the entire world—just as it would have had he in fact realized his ambition to restore the Han. Essentially, then, the ambiguity of this line provides a space for the transformation of Zhuge Liang from the neglected local spirit of what Du Fu describes elsewhere as a dilapidated shrine into a figure of universal approbation.[88] And since Du Fu's repeated invocation of Zhuge in his verse seems to have been influential in elevating his status in the postmedieval period, the poem could thus be said to project into the future the process observed in the preceding four, alchemizing a landmark of Zhuge's failure to reunify the empire into an unexpected fulfilment of his ambitions.

That the poem ultimately descends from this hopeful first line towards the brutal facts of the last, then, merely emphasizes once again the consistent binocularity of the series, by which the traces left by these figures' lives—their writings, their homes, the music that tells their stories, and their shrines—are simultaneously testaments to their suffering and also augurs of hope that failure may not always be final. In this sense, Du Fu's interest here in ambiguous "traces" (*ji* 跡) parallels the almost recordizing poetics of "Written by Chance," "Rain," and "The Thirtieth Day of the Ninth Month of the Second Year of the Dali Reign."[89] In those poems, he discovered that merely "writing what he felt" or "recording dawns and dusks" could connect back to the tradition in unexpected ways, even at those moments he felt most estranged from it. The humble and apparently meaningless details of his life here in Kuizhou that these poems evidenced, that is, were potentially as ambiguous as the traces of the southlands luminaries discussed in this final series. Someday, he foresaw, the still evolving narrative of his life might continue past the visions of "Chinese-ness" that defined the moral horizons of his age, retrospectively rendering its traces significant to communities as unpredictable to him as Kuizhou's rustics and river cranes would have been to Liu Bei. In the final period of his work, therefore, he turns to a more focused exploration of these ambiguities, and to the hope that he might through them be transformed.

SEVEN

Contingency and Adaptation

Last Poems (768–70)

In the early spring of 768, Du Fu and his family left Kuizhou, passing by boat through the famous Three Gorges out onto the storied waterways of Hubei and Hunan. It is unclear what ultimate destination the poet had in mind—or if he had one in mind—when he decided to uproot their lives once again for another round of hard traveling. He sometimes spoke of returning home to Luoyang or Chang'an along this route, other times of finding a new hermitage in the southlands, and still elsewhere of visionary destinations by the southern seas. Whatever plans might have lured him away from Kuizhou, however, Du Fu never made it where he was going. He died in his boat, somewhere between Changsha and Yueyang, late in 770, never having found his way home.

Aware that his time was running short, Du Fu in this period wrote a poetry whose horizons stretch beyond his death. As we saw in the last chapter, he had begun in Kuizhou to draw hope from the simple unpredictability of the future, since it promised that his apparently failed life might someday have a different and a greater meaning to others than he could recognize himself. Doubling down on this hope in his last years, his poetry comes consistently to leverage ambiguities and double entendres— even more daring than those noted in his previous verse—to depict his experience as luminous with the possibility of alternate interpretations. By recording his progress downriver in language that refuses to provide a univocal account of it once and for all, he thus suggests his openness to being transformed.

Du Fu's recordizing readers have consistently fulfilled his hopes in this regard, discovering meanings in his verse that—as already seen repeatedly—would often have surprised him. When it comes to the ideal of transformability, however, their divergence from his mature poetics is particularly ironic. At its core, recordizing reading has always maintained that the contingencies of history are not, ultimately, contingent: that they instantiate repeating situations and perduring truths, and that poetry's task is therefore merely to record them faithfully. Du Fu, by contrast, was working within a late medieval framework in which the infinite change-ability of the world was the essential problem the sages had set out to solve in their creation of This Culture of Ours. In this period of his verse, he both takes this problem for granted and inverts it, writing a poetry that would not be a source of stability, as This Culture was understood to be, but would rather change along with the world's inevitable change.

The Flux of the Medieval Chinese World

The possibility that there might not be accessible laws or regularities underlying the universe's transformations had, by the eighth century, long been central to Chinese thought. The idea derives ultimately from the antinomianism of the ancient Daoist classic *Zhuangzi*, but it gradually began to permeate Classicist scholarship in the early medieval period, particularly in the commentaries to the *Yijing* written by scholars of Obscure Learning (Xuanxue) that were eventually included in the official Tang subcommentaries.[1] By Du Fu's time, the obscurity and unpredictability of cosmic and historical transformation had not only come to serve as a crucial justification for the Classicist tradition's provision of norms capable of regulating it, but had become central to political and literary thought as well.

The *Zhuangzi* depicts a world in continual flux, whose unaccountable transformations render past precedents incapable of providing guidance in navigating present situations. One important anecdote in the text depicts a conversation between Confucius and Laozi in which Confucius complains to Laozi that, despite all his learning in the Classics, he has been unable to bring the world to order. Laozi responds,

> "The Six Classics are merely the stale traces (*chenji* 陳迹) of the former kings, not that by which they left those traces. Thus, what you are talking about are merely traces that are left by shoes, not the shoes themselves.

White fish hawks gaze at each other without moving their pupils, and trans-formation [i.e., impregnation] takes place via the wind; among insects, the male cries out upwind and the female responds downwind, and thereby transformation occurs; when it comes to creatures called *lei*, they are them-selves both male and female and so transform of themselves. Natures cannot be swapped, fates cannot be changed, time cannot be stopped, and the *dao* cannot be blocked. If you get it from the *dao*, there is nothing that is impos-sible; if you miss it, then there is nothing you can accomplish."

Confucius did not go outside for three months. After this, he again sought an audience with Laozi and said, "I've got it. Black magpies nurse, fishes lay eggs, thin-waisted wasps reproduce through transformation, and, when a younger brother comes, the older brother cries. For too long I have not played my role in transformation as a man. And since I did not play my role in transformation as a man, how could I transform men?" Laozi said, 'Yes, you've got it.'"[2]

For all its gnomic rhetoric, it is clear at least what this passage portends for the Six Classics. The Classics merely evidence the responses of the sage kings to the exigencies of particular moments in the past. Given the unpredictable transformations that characterize our world, therefore, they are unlikely to prescribe appropriate solutions to the novel demands of the present.

Less clear, however, is what exactly we are supposed to do instead of following Classical precedents, and how inimical the message here ultimately is to Classicism. These topics were matters of debate throughout the medi-eval period. The most important step towards the reconciliation of state-ments like this one in the *Zhuangzi* with Classicist ideals was made by Guo Xiang, the author of an important Xuanxue commentary on the text that strove to recenter Confucius and the sages of the Classical tradition as the text's unlikely heroes.[3] For Guo, the precedents provided by the Six Classics are indeed too rigid to apply to changing circumstances; because "the affairs of antiquity perished in antiquity, . . . and today's affairs have already trans-formed," we need instead to "transform with the times."[4] Yet even if the Classics are mere "stale traces," footprints in the dirt, they can nonetheless tell us something about the shoe that made them: in the case of the Classics, about the sages, who were capable of responding appropriately to the contin-gencies of their times, thereby bringing the world at least briefly to order.[5] In Guo's reading, therefore, what Confucius learns (or, rather, pretends to learn, since he is himself a sage) in his dialogue with Laozi is that he has to emulate not the fixed precedents of the Six Classics, but rather the sages who created them, who were adaptable to any circumstance, "riding the many transformations and treading through myriad generations."[6]

Guo Xiang is thus neither a stickler for the rules enunciated by the Classics nor a thoroughgoing antinomian. On the one hand, he takes the Classics to be too rigid to provide rules for contemporary action in the face of the endless transformations of the world; on the other, he sees the texts as nonetheless deriving from and representing the only remaining traces of sages worthy of emulation. This tension is evident in Guo's disparaging discussions of his intellectual rivals, the "Confucian scholars" (Ru 儒) who would make pedantic fidelity to the Classics a prerequisite for effective moral and political action. As he comments on a story of such "scholars" citing the *Poetry* to justify grave robbing,

> The *Poetry* and the *Ritual* are the stale traces of the former kings. "If someone uses them who is not the right person, the *dao* will not operate in vain." Thus if Confucian scholars use them to commit perfidy, of course these traces will not be worth relying on.

> 詩禮者，先王之陳迹也，茍非其人，道不虛行，故夫儒者乃有用之為姦，故迹不足恃也。[7]

This comment is interesting partly in its form. Guo's second sentence here derives verbatim from the "Xici" commentary 繫辭傳 to the *Yijing*, which was supposedly written by Confucius. Even as he disparages the Confucian Classics as "unworthy of being relied on," then, Guo is implicitly citing Confucius as an authority for his position and suggesting that he understands Confucius's true intentions better than those pettier "Confucians" who pore over his every action and injunction. Texts can still be models, but these models have to be understood correctly, and their efficacy thus depends on their being leveraged by "the right person."

Attempts like this one to lay claim to a fuller, timeless meaning behind the unreliably rigid and time-bound literal senses of a text are characteristic of Xuanxue exegesis in general and provide a justification for the many Classical commentaries that Guo and other early Xuanxue thinkers influenced.[8] According to the *Yijing* commentator Han Bo 韓伯 (317–420), for example, Confucius's "Xici" commentary teaches that "there is no constancy to transformation, and the *Yijing* therefore cannot provide fixed standards."[9] It is possible, however, for at least the most gifted among us to learn from the text how to apply the sages' constant adaptability to an inconstant world.[10]

> If one can follow [the *Yijing's*] words to gauge their import, seek their source in order to grasp the essence of their final manifestations, then the only constant fixed standard it provides is merely to adapt to transformation. One who is enlightened as to these transformations will preserve this essence; therefore the text says, "If someone uses it who is not the right person, the *dao* will not operate in vain."
>
> 能循其辭以度其義，原其初以要其終，則唯變所適，是其常典也。明其變者，存其要也，故曰苟非其人，道不虛行。[11]

As Han Bo explains it here, the *Yijing* does not provide rules but rather allows its readers to "seek the source" of the sages' words. Attaining this source, he claims, would allow one "never to be at wits' end," obviating the "hundred concerns" that otherwise bedevil anyone trying to respond appropriately to the infinite variety of the world.[12] Even though the text of the Classic represents merely the traces of sagely responses to the particular "worries and disasters of middle antiquity," therefore, adept readers will be able to understand from it "the capacity of the sages' projects to endure" through changing situations.[13] They will recognize, in other words, that contingency is not everything.

Further justification for Classical study in an inconstant world is provided by the official Tang subcommentary to Han Bo's commentary. In explaining the remark just cited, the subcommentary editors add a crucial caveat: that only a sage will be capable of grasping the source of the *Yijing's* words, since only sages are "the right person."[14] The rest of us, by contrast, should not attempt to approximate the sage's infinite adaptability, but should instead use the text to pursue a less ambitious goal.

> When the text says to "meet with an analogy [*lei*] and extend it," it means that, when one encounters some category (*lei*) of affairs, one should extend to it [that category's analogy in the *Yijing*]. . . . If one treats all the myriad affairs of the world in this way, in each case analogically extending [the

Yijing's lessons], then everything that is possible in the world will be exhaustively modeled and imaged: thus, the text says, "All the affairs possible within the world are complete in it *(neng shi bi)*."

觸類而長之者，謂觸逢事類而增長之…天下萬事，皆如此例，各以類增長，則天下所能之事，法象皆盡，故曰天下之能事畢矣也。[15]

This description of the *Yijing*'s usefulness focuses on the term *lei* 類, which simultaneously means "analogy" and "category." The claim here is that the text provides images that allow us to construct, on the basis of extended analogies, indefinitely expansible categories for things—categories that model and make tractable a world that would otherwise be too variable for nonsages to understand. The sages, that is, "created the *Yijing* . . . to analogize/categorize *(lei)* the dispositions of the myriad things and thus to make them all visible," for, had they not done so, "it would have been impossible [for most of us] to know these dispositions."[16] The *Yijing* thus functions like (and provides the primal model for) the tropologies of the literary tradition, taming the endless idiosyncrasy of individual circumstances to repeating moral situations.

Like tropologies, moreover, the categories made possible by the *Yijing* are, according to the Tang subcommentary, not only useful in helping nonsages interpret the world, but also normative, the means by which we can "aid the great void in its nurturance of all things."[17] The editors thus implicitly accept the basic critique offered by the *Zhuangzi* and by Xuanxue thinkers like Guo Xiang: that the generative matrix of the cosmos is an unknowable "void." Yet they disagree that the precedents of the Classics are therefore useless. Instead, even if these texts appear to concern "small matters" from long ago, "the analogical import of these matters is great," and, if we "grasp these analogical meanings *(yi lei* 義類) and expand them" to present circumstances, we can at least partially regularize the world and overcome the contingency that would otherwise render effective moral action impossible.[18] By following the Classics in this way, we can ensure that "the Two Norms [*yin* and *yang*, heaven and earth] will be ordered and the many things, harmonious."[19]

Politically, the major implication of this accommodation between the antinomianism of the *Zhuangzi* and the interest in precedents characteristic of Classicism was that the models of sagely governance contained in the Classics could not be implemented without alteration. Indeed, not even the ancient sage dynasties had so imitated one another. "Before the Yellow Emperor," aver the Tang subcommentaries, "people wore the skins of birds and beasts, but, later on, there were too many people and too few animals, so such skins were lacking. Therefore, the sages used silk and hemp cloths to make robes: this is an example of 'being numinous and transforming so as to make sure the people get what is appropriate to them.'"[20] The sages also recognized that change could sometimes be useful in itself, and they therefore established new calendars, weights, and measures at the outset of new dynasties, "in order to demonstrate that the ritual system has its ground in the new emperor" and is not built into the world or human society by their very nature.[21] Even in their own adaptations, however, these sages also maintained certain analogies with previous institutions, in accordance with Confucius's prediction that any dynasty that achieved success would necessarily do so by "adding to or subtracting from" a core set of constant methods. As Huang Kan puts it in his commentary to this prediction, "there is a constancy to what must change and what must be continuous."[22]

A similar need to balance change and continuity animated a great deal of late medieval literary thought as well. From the sixth through the eighth centuries, theorists debated the significance of the evident evolution of literary forms and styles that had occurred since the time of the *Shijing*, with some explicitly valorizing innovation, others seeing most of what had developed since antiquity as representing degeneration rather than progress, and the majority seeking various compromises between these extremes.[23] The most extended and perhaps the most representative discussion of the topic is found in Liu Xie's *Wenxin diaolong*. For Liu, literature has constant genres that impose normative requirements, and innovation that breaks free of these roots will not be successful. At the same time, however, "there is no limit to the techniques by which literature may transform" within the bounds demarcated by these constants, and, indeed, literature needs to change to avoid devolving into mere imitation.[24] "By transforming," he suggests, literature "can endure; by continuity, it never runs dry.... It must look to the present to establish novelty and consult antiquity to settle its models." The writer is thus tasked with "adapting to the present moment" and "riding the incipiencies of transformation," while always keeping the precedents of the literary tradition in mind.[25]

On this point, Liu is clearly indebted to a Xuanxue paradigm, and he takes the title of the chapter that discusses these issues—"Continuity and Change" 通變—from the "Xici" commentary to the *Yijing*. It is no coincidence, therefore, that his account of how it is that writers attain the capacity to adapt echoes the model Han Bo had proposed for readers of that Classic.

> If one wants to participate in the development of the literary tradition, one should enlarge its major forms. One should first widely observe and minutely inspect, gathering the head rope and grasping the tally; then one should open new roads and establish new gates, galloping far with loose reins or taking one's ease at a slower pace, relying upon one's emotions to achieve continuity [with what has come before] and depending upon one's *qi* to adapt to transformation. . . . If, however, one gnaws away at some partial understanding or brags of achievements in some single branch, this is merely galloping in a circle within a courtyard, not the free paces that can travel ten thousand leagues.

> 是以規略文統，宜宏大體。先博覽以精閱，總綱紀而攝契；然後拓衢路，置關鍵，長轡遠馭，從容按節，憑情以會通，負氣以適變。… 若乃齗齗於偏解，矜激乎一致，此庭間之迴驟，豈萬里之逸步哉！[26]

Liu Xie is invoking here the old ideal of the "comprehensive talent" (*tongcai* 通才), by which the best literary works will be the products not of specialists working to refine a particular genre or style, but rather of writers who understand what conduces to success in the literary tradition in general.[27] As Han Bo had argued with regard to the *Yijing*, one needs first to "seek the source" of the tradition's precedents, as that source will allow one to adapt to the new exigencies of the present. Having "gathered this head rope and grasped this tally," great writers will be like the founders of new dynasties, both perpetuating analogies of the precedent tradition and also breaking new ground, "opening new roads and establishing new gates," in order to "adapt to transformation." Like the founders of new dynasties, moreover, such great writers will eventually provide precedents for future generations, who will then likewise need to innovate away from their successes. Their works will thus become "stale traces" (*chenji*), fixed precedents that cannot be imitated but whose source—the deeper understanding on the basis of which they were produced—can, instead, be reactivated in adapting to new situations.

Poems That Transform

This common late medieval vision of the relationship between authors and the tradition to which they contribute represents a useful contrast to the sorts of adaptation we find in Du Fu's late work. Du Fu, I will suggest, does not attempt himself to adapt to the demands of the present moment. Instead, because he does not claim to fully comprehend the contingency of his experience, he writes poems designed to avoid becoming "stale traces" by remaining open to transformation into the future.

Contingency becomes an explicit theme in several of the earliest pieces Du Fu wrote upon leaving the Gorges. Most immediately, this theme reflects an increasing recognition of his frailty, which, if it had been on his mind for several years, was rendered all the more apparent by the difficulties he encountered on his river journey. In several of these poems, therefore, he appeals less to late medieval Classicism than to another tradition influenced by the *Zhuangzi* and its Xuanxue interpreters: the religious Daoism that sometimes promised its practitioners transcendence of the "great change" of death. In the following poem, for instance, he resolves to study Daoist techniques of immortality, if perhaps only in poetic form. The setting is 768, late spring, on his journey from Kuizhou to Jiangling 江陵 (modern-day Jingzhou).[28]

舟中 *In My Boat*

風餐江柳下　　I dine in the wind beneath river willows,
雨臥驛樓邊　　lie down in the rain beside the post station tower.[a]
結纜排魚網　　Fastened hawsers line up fishing nets;

a. This couplet alludes to a poem by Bao Zhao 鮑照 called "Written in the Voice of One Who Ascended to Heaven" 代昇天行: "I dine on the wind, entrusting myself to pines for my lodging; / I lie in the clouds, to roam through the heavens as I please." The couplet may also echo what later becomes a common set phrase for difficult journeys, "to dine in the wind and sleep in the dew" 風餐露宿, although I have not been able to find texts containing this phrase before Du Fu's time.

4	連檣並米舡	a line of masts brings together the rice boats.[b]
	今朝雲細薄	This morning the clouds were thin and light;
	昨夜月清圓	last night the moon was clear and round.
	飄泊南庭老	Drifting and mooring, I grow old in southern courts;[c]
8	祇應學水仙	I should just study to become a water immortal.[d]

The matter-of-fact simplicity of both the title and the third couplet of this poem recall the explicitly recordizing poetics of "Rain, Two Poems" in chapter 6. Again, Du Fu is noting the passing weather while held up on his journey downriver; again, the implication is both that his time has

b. This line may echo Guo Pu's "Rhapsody on the Yangzi": "When the heavens clear, and the eight winds do not soar, / boatmen then take up their oars, and travelers take hold of their rudders. / . . . Prows and sterns link together, / ten thousand leagues of lined-up masts." According to some sources, Guo Pu ultimately became a water immortal.

c. This line alludes to Yang Jiong's 楊炯 "Rhapsody on the Old Man Star" 老人星賦: "In the courts of the southern pole, / the old man star glows bright, shining and shimmering." The Old Man Star (Canopus) was thought to be an auspice of peace and longevity. Also at play in this line is the common kenning of travelers as "traveling stars," which derives from a story in Zhang Hua's 張華 *Bowu zhi* 博物志. A man living on the shores of the Yangzi River observed a raft of driftwood floating by his dwelling year after year in the eighth month. One year, he decided to get on the raft to see where it went. "For ten or more days, he still saw sun, moon, and stars, but, after this, everything became blurry and he could not sense the end of the night. After he was gone ten months or more, he suddenly came upon a place like a city, with neatly arranged dwellings. Looking afar he saw within a palace a girl weaving, and he saw a man leading his ox to drink from the bank of the river. When the oxherd saw him, he was shocked and asked, 'How did you get here?' The man told him how he had arrived and asked where he was. The oxherd answered, 'When you get to the capital of Shu [i.e., Chengdu], seek out [the diviner and Daoist] Yan Junping; he'll know.' In the end, the traveler did not get off the raft to climb the bank, and he returned [to the human world] in due time. When he got to Shu, he asked Yan Junping. Yan Junping told him, 'In that year, in that month, I saw a traveling star traverse the territory of the Oxherd Constellation.' He thus calculated that that star was the man, having at that time reached the River of Heaven."

d. Water immortals were a category of Daoist immortals, those that wandered the waters rather than dwelling in heaven or among men. A number of famous southern martyrs, including Qu Yuan and Wu Zixu 伍子胥 (d. 484 BCE), were thought to have become water immortals after their deaths. By the ninth century, moreover, the term seems to have been conventionally applied to men who spent their lives roaming the riverine regions of the south.

grown precious—the reason, perhaps, he seems to have been unable to sleep the previous night—and that he has, where he is, nothing more appropriate to write about. Yet if "Rain" expressed his frustration with a period of protracted darkness, here he is more upset by the changeability of the atmosphere and the contrast it reveals between the fluidity of the natural world and the rigidity of human responses to it, whereby even the fishermen and merchants who make their living on the water line up their fishing nets and rice boats in rectilinear patterns in response to storms that set the river willows waving in the wind.[29] In the final couplet, therefore, he envisions for himself a response that will allow him to better adapt to the unpredictable transformations of the riverscape. He will overcome his human limitations by becoming a "water immortal," one of the types of transcendents discussed in the Daoist subcommentary on the *Zhuangzi* written by Cheng Xuanying 成玄英 (fl. 636).[30]

This, at any rate, is the most obvious way of understanding the phrase "water immortal." Yet the phrase also introduces a series of ambiguities that reverberate retrospectively through the poem. Around Du Fu's time, "water immortal" was also used analogically to denote lifelong wanderers on the rivers and lakes of the southlands—wanderers who, in abandoning fixed destinations and rigid plans, might also be more flexible in adapting to the delays imposed by unpredictable storms like this one.[31] And some men who had died watery deaths, such as Qu Yuan and Wu Zixu, were also worshiped among the folk of the southlands as "water immortals," having supposedly taken on great powers after their mortal ends.[32] Depending on how we take the phrase, therefore—whether it refers to a literal Daoist immortal, a rootless wanderer, or a death on the water—the poem looks very different. Were we to take Du Fu in the final line as contemplating the Daoist arts, for example, the echoes of Bao Zhao's famous verse on immortality in the first line might suggest the indignities he hopes to transcend, allowing him to go from dining "in the wind" to "on the wind" (the same in Chinese) and from sleeping in the rain to reposing on the clouds that produce it. If, however, Du Fu resolves to be a "water immortal" of the wanderer type, then perhaps the apparent hardships of the poem's first couplet already represent the sort of this-worldly transcendence—religious ideals brought down to the mortal limitations of human life—that this kenning might imply. And, if he is suggesting that he may die out here on the water, these hardships take on another significance altogether.

Similar ambiguities can be found in the penultimate line as well. If the poem ends with Du Fu worrying about the possibility that he will die on the river, the longevous and longevity-bestowing Old Man Star he saw the night before might present a bitter contrast to himself. Unlike the dateless star, Du Fu really is growing old, far from the northern "court" where his ambitions had always been set. If, however, we take Du Fu as resolving to become an analogical "immortal," rambling through analogical "courts," the line might take on a visionary quality. In Chinese mythology, the waters on which the poet found himself were supposed to be continuous with the River of Stars, and on a clear night—as the night before had been—they would themselves have been luminous with starlight. Remembering the story of the traveler who rode a raft down the Yangzi and up into the heavens, Du Fu might be realizing that he is already the earthbound reflection of a heavenly image, and that he has thus attained the sort of intraworldly transcendence that "water immortal" wanderers enact.[33] Or, finally, if he is suggesting the possibility of studying Daoist techniques of immortality, then the parallels between himself and the star—itself legendarily an immortal in the Daoist pantheon—might suggest the propitiousness of the project.

"In My Boat" is thus polysemous through and through: it can be read coherently at least three different ways (and perhaps more). Far from providing a clear record of Du Fu's experience, it provides at best a shifting and uncertain image of his circumstances and his state of mind, which may range, depending on our choices, from dire and depressed to visionary and ecstatic. This ambiguity—or, better, transformability—is unlikely to be a mere coincidence, since it is precisely the virtue to which he aspires in the poem. Whether or not he personally will study Daoist immortality, become a destinationless wanderer, or undergo the "great transformation" of death, that is, the poem itself transcends the rigidity he criticizes in mortal men's responses to the changeability of the southlands' weather.

Similar sorts of ambiguity can be found throughout Du Fu's verse at around this time. The following poem, for instance, was written in the late winter of the same year, after he had spent a few months recuperating from illness in Gong'an county, near Jiangling. As the weather began to warm, he set out again upon the Yangzi, not knowing how far his health or the health of the empire would allow him to go.[34]

曉發公安數月憩息此縣   *Setting Out at Dawn from Gong'an*
after I Had Rested in this County for Several Months

北城擊柝復欲罷	On the north wall, they strike the watch, once more about to end;[a]
東方明星亦不遲	in the east, the Bright Star is also not slow.[b]
鄰雞野哭如昨日	Neighbors' roosters and weeping in the fields are all as yesterday,
4 物色生態能幾時	yet the beauty of the scene and my vitality— how long can these last?
舟楫眇然自此去	My boat and its oars, tiny in the vastness, leave from here
江湖遠適無前期	to rivers and lakes, traveling far, with no set stage ahead.
出門轉眄已陳跡	Turning to look as I go out the gates, it's already stale traces;[c]
8 藥餌扶吾隨所之	these herbs and tonics supporting me will go wherever I do.[d]

In this poem, Du Fu describes the passing of yet one more period of his life. The period has, apparently, not been entirely idyllic: as Jin Shengtan

a. "Striking the watch" may recall the "Xici" commentary to the *Yijing*. There we read that the sages invented the watch-rattle—"struck on doubled gates as a preparation against the approach of violent sorts"—as a stage in the increasing complexity of a civilization that had not previously known violence.

b. The "Bright Star" here is probably the Morning Star 啓明星. According to the *Shiji* and the *Han shu*, "states in which the Bright Star appears are certain to have warfare and many untoward transformations." Bright Star was also the name of an immortal.

c. Besides the *Zhuangzi* source of the phrase "stale traces" (*chenji*) cited above, it would also have recalled the "Preface to the Lanting Collection" 蘭亭集序 by Wang Xizhi: "What one has previously enjoyed becomes in the space of a nod stale traces. One cannot help but be moved by this; how much more that one's life, long or short, will eventually follow transformation, and its final set stage is extinction" 修短隨化，終期於盡.

d. "Herbs and tonics" could mean medicine for his various ailments, but could also refer to Daoist elixirs of immortality. This is the meaning of the compound, for instance, in Ge Hong's (283–343) *Baopuzi*: "Through herbs and tonics one can attain the inexhaustible."

observes, the tone of "once more" in the first line and "just like yesterday" in the third suggests that he has been up many nights in Gong'an, waiting for the watch-rattle of dawn, a military convention that no doubt reminded him of the ongoing disorder driving his neighbors to weep in the wilds.[35] Although this disorder makes him anxious to be back on rivers and lakes that preserve their beauty and vitality amidst the troubles of the human world, however, the speed he notes in the Morning Star's rise—itself a portent of warfare—testifies also to a certain trepidation at the prospect of setting out on another journey into the unknown. Frail and sick, Du Fu recognizes that his illnesses (metonymically indicated by their treatments) will follow him wherever he goes: that in leaving the neighborhood comforts of Gong'an, he may be hastening the short time that remains to him. He thus looks back as he leaves the town on another period past, a period of joys he hardly appreciated while he had them, whose end reminds him of Wang Xizhi's admonition: that "one's life, long or short, will eventually follow transformation, and its final set stage (*zhongqi* 終期) is extinction."[36] Though Du Fu says he does not know where his river journey will take him (*wu qian qi* 無前期), of course in fact he does.

As was the case with "In My Boat," however, the poem can also be read according to an alternate program of significance, unlocked by interpreting otherwise the ambiguous allusions of the final couplet. "Stale traces," as we saw above, was in the *Zhuangzi* a figure for the innovations of the ancient sages. If the allusion recalls this text rather than Wang Xizhi, then the final lines may depict Du Fu less lamenting time's passage than renouncing with some vehemence the violence of civilization. According to the "Xici," that is, both the military watch-rattle struck in the first couplet and the defensive doubled gates of the last were inventions of the sages—precedents of precisely the sort that Confucius realized he had to discard in order to "play his role in transformation." In recognizing these features of Gong'an as "stale traces," therefore, Du Fu would be forsaking the community he has found here for the ever-renewing beauty of the natural world. And this interpretation, in turn, would shift how we understand the "herbs and tonics" of the final line, whose constant companionship seemed previously to indicate the inescapability of the poet's illnesses. Given that such simples were the products of ever-renewing nature and were used by Daoist adepts in the pursuit of transcendence, the fact that he has no set stage ahead of him might indicate not the imminence of his death, but rather the possibility of entering into the endlessly flexible wandering of the immortals.

Once again, therefore, this poem does not present a clear or univocal record of a moment in Du Fu's life. Instead, it shifts before our eyes, alternately describing his depression at the closing down of possibility or his elation at its opening up. And as was the case in "In My Boat," this ambiguity does not seem to be a mere flaw in the text's construction, since the transformability it enables is a focus of the poem itself. Whether the poet will succumb to the transformations of the cosmos or attain to the adaptability of the immortals, that is, his work enacts on a textual level the changeability lamented by one of its programs of meaning and aspired to by the other. In this sense, if the poem records anything, it is the unfinished iridescence of the present moment, its capacity for meaning different things depending on what happens in the future.

In other verse from the period, this ambiguity can be focused, with virtuosic panache, into a single ambiguous character. The following poem was written a few weeks later, as Du Fu's boat arrived at Yueyang on the shores of Lake Dongting. Intending to travel down the Xiang River towards Changsha and Hengzhou, he was met by an unusual southerly blizzard that forced him to take shelter by the city, increasingly aware that any delay could be his last.[37]

泊岳陽城下   *Mooring below Yueyang*

	江國踰千里	River kingdoms for over a thousand leagues;
	山城僅百層	mountain city, merely a hundred tiers.[a]
	岸風翻夕浪	Winds from the shore churn twilight waves;
4	舟雪灑寒燈	snow on the boat spatters my cold lamp.
	留滯才雖盡	Stuck here, though my talent is used up,[b]

a. "Merely" here translates *jin* 僅, which, like the English word, is a contronym. It normally means "no more than" but can also (rarely) mean "no less than." Since "a hundred tiers" was a figure for great height, the most straightforward reading of this line should be the less common meaning, "a full hundred tiers."

b. Several famous poets were said to have "lost their talent" when they got old. The phrase "stuck here" alludes to the story of Grand Scribe Sima Tan, who was "stuck" in the southlands and died of rage and frustration at being unable to follow the emperor on a sacrificial tour.

艱危氣益增　　in hardship and peril, my temper grows.ᶜ
圖南未可料　　My journey south cannot be foretold:
8　變化有鯤鵬　　in transformation, there is Leviathan and Roc.ᵈ

As the waves rise and his light dims, Du Fu considers the possibility that he will not make it any farther. A tiny figure against a vast ground—with its thousand leagues of river kingdoms, its "full" (*jin* 僅) hundred tiers of towering rock—he is stymied by winds that would, by contrast, have supported the huge wings of the legendary Peng bird. Depleted by age and frustrated in a way that could, according to Chinese medical theory, harm his health, he worries that he will die here, stuck at the midpoint of what he hoped might be a transformative journey, incapable of following the Roc's visionary itinerary into the deeper south.[38]

Like the last two poems, however, this one can also be read according to an alternate program of significance. On the most straightforward reading of the second line, the character *jin* 僅—translated as "merely"—should mean "fully," since "a hundred tiers" is a hyperbole for vast height, greatly exaggerating the actual eminence of Yueyang Tower (which sits less than a hundred feet above the water). Read backwards from the final couplet, however, it is also possible to take *jin* in its more common sense. In this

---

c. "Temper" translates *qi* 氣, which is what one expends when one "loses one's temper" (*sheng qi* 生氣). The same word, however, can describe someone's vigor or vital force. Cao Pi famously argued in his *Dianlun* that "*qi* is the most important thing in writing literature." The cultivation of *qi* was also an important method in the Daoist attainment of immortality; to expend it wastefully in vehement emotion was thus to risk one's health.

d. "Leviathan and Roc" are Kun and Peng, a giant fish and a giant bird mentioned in the *Zhuangzi*: "In the northern deeps there is a fish whose name is Kun. Kun is so big I do not know how many thousand leagues long it is. It transforms into a bird, whose name is Peng. Peng's back is so big I do not know how many thousand leagues long it is. When it stirs up to fly, its wings are like clouds hanging from heaven. When the seas churn, it is this bird, about to move to the southern deeps. The southern deeps are the pool of heaven. . . . When the Peng is about to move to the southern deeps, it beats the water for three thousand leagues and then climbs up on the whirlwind for ninety thousand leagues, going off without rest for six months. . . . [As for why it has to fly so high,] if the accumulation of the wind is not thick enough, then it will not have the strength to support such huge wings. Therefore, the Peng will only ride the wind with ninety thousand leagues of wind below it; spreading its back against the blue sky with nothing to obstruct it, only then will it journey south."

reading, the first couplet would say that, even though the poet has traveled, as the Peng does, for over a thousand leagues on the water, the tower is *only* a hundred tiers, a paltry height in comparison to the great bird's ninety-thousand-league ascent.[39] This temporary stopover, in other words, may be just the beginning for Du Fu, since the increscent "temper" (*qi* 氣) previously understood as threatening his health could also be interpreted as the "vital energy" that was prerequisite for immortality and also the driving force behind the greatest literature—another path to the stars. In this case, the penultimate line would not express worry that the journey might not happen, but rather wonder at the possibilities that lie before him as the storm lifts his wings. After all, among the transformations of the cosmos, some are as unpredictable and as wondrous as Leviathan and Roc.

The Impossible Fixity of the Recordizing Tradition

It will be no surprise that these poems have been read rather differently by recordizing critics. "Mooring below Yueyang" presents a particularly clear example here, since its very text was altered to match a more determinate vision of what and how poetry should mean. Following an emendation first proposed by Zhao Pang 趙汸 (1319–69), many of Du Fu's most influential critics have replaced the character *jin* 僅, "merely"—the contronym whose ambivalence is the hinge on which the poem's two programs of meaning turn—with *jin* 近, resulting in a clearer descriptive sense to the second line: "I draw near this mountain city in a hundred tiers."[40] Rather than representing the ambivalence of the experience, then, the poem becomes a record of its concrete details: in the words of Qiu Zhao'ao, "The first couplet records (*ji* 記) what Yueyang is like and the second, what the scene was like when Du Fu moored his boat. The next four tell his emotion while mooring." The final lines, then, are simply emotive: "'All this means,'" Qiu avers, quoting Wang Sishi, "'is that [at this particular moment,] Du Fu was excited that his boat, in heading south, recalled the transformation of Kun and Peng, that's all.'"[41]

This example makes clear yet again the impulse of recordizing criticism to determine a poem's meaning once and for all in the moment of its composition. This impulse should, in principle, prevent poems from transforming over time, as once the contours of that moment are discovered, no new commentary should be necessary. Given the centrality of the ideal of transformativity to the sources of the Chinese tradition, however, it was impossible that it should completely disappear from Du Fu criticism—and indeed, quite the contrary, he has often been praised as the most transformative of poets, the writer whose work encompasses the most styles and whose tone and techniques change most radically from poem to poem and even within poems.[42] Yet if in this sense recordizing reading has carried forward the intellectual concerns of the late medieval period, its shifted sense of transformativity has had significant implications for Du Fu's cultural legacy. Whereas late medieval theorists like Liu Xie had leveraged the idea of transformation to guarantee that the literary tradition would remain always new, recordizing critics more often suggest that, as Du Fu adapted perfectly to the exigencies of the moment, he articulated the truth of situations that were not fundamentally contingent but were rather apt to repeat themselves throughout history. As a result, not only does the recordizing paradigm threaten its own continuance as a commentary tradition by claiming that univocal, correct interpretations of Du Fu's poems can be discovered once and for all through historical research. It has also led readers to wonder whether Du Fu's greatness threatened the tradition of poetry composition as well.

Up to the twentieth century, recordizing critics often compared Du Fu to an ideal of sagely adaptability that resembles, at least superficially, that of late medieval Classicism. As Qin Guan 秦觀 (1049–1100) puts it, for example, Du Fu's stature in poetic history mirrors Confucius's in the moral realm: just as Confucius was the "timely sage," "gathering the great fulfilment" of past worthies by deploying their various virtues only at the appropriate moment, so too did Du Fu "gather the great fulfillment" of poetry by "collecting together the strengths of other writers" and using them to "respond appropriately to whatever circumstances he encountered."[43] In the words of Zhang Jie 張戒 (*jinshi* 1124), similarly, all the poets of history who had been confined to a period or a personal style

failed to understand that everything in the world is poetry. Only Du Fu was not like this. In a mountain forest he wrote about mountain forest; in court he wrote about court; meeting skillfulness he wrote with skillfulness; meeting clumsiness he wrote with clumsiness; meeting the striking he wrote strikingly; meeting commonness he wrote commonly; sometimes letting it all go, sometimes holding back; sometimes modern and sometimes ancient. All objects, all affairs, all ideas—there was nothing, [he knew,] that was not poetry.

而不知世間一切皆詩也。惟杜子美則不然，在山林則山林，在廊廟則廊廟，遇巧則巧，遇拙則拙，遇奇則奇，遇俗則俗，或放或收，或新或舊，一切物，一切事，一切意，無非詩也。[44]

Because there was nothing in his experience that could not be perfectly recorded in verse, and because he had every possible style in his repertoire, Du Fu could simply write whatever he encountered, adapting his poetic technique in every instance to match what the moment required.

Recordizing accounts of Du Fu's adaptability, however, generally do not pay the same sort of respect to contingency that was characteristic of the Xuanxue-inflected Classicism of the late medieval period. Zhang's claim that "everything in the world is poetry" already begins to suggest that the world is constant in this respect; and if poetry is at its best when it is transparent, then the art too follows necessary laws. These claims are articulated more explicitly by the Neo-Confucian scholar Fang Qian 方潛 (1809–68) in his preface to Zhao Xinghai's commentary. For Fang, Du Fu's poetry recalls the *Yijing* as it was interpreted by Neo-Confucians: as describing a world structured always and everywhere by knowable and timeless patterns (*li* 理).[45]

Du Fu was one who lived in a time of "worries" [like the authors of the *Yijing*], and, in his being stirred by and singing about the affairs of his age, he [likewise] had "distant meanings" and "patterned language" that was "indirect but on the mark," "clear but hidden." His lodging his intentions and singing about objects is what can be called "speaking of small matters but taking from it larger analogies." And when it comes to being skilled at regulated forms but not imprisoned by them, Du Fu "mixed and combined their numbers" so that they were never exhausted and could never be fathomed. Is this not the result of his "not having a fixed standard but merely adapting to transformation?" I say, therefore, that Du Fu's poetry is poetry that connects with the *Yijing*. And yet, it is not that his poetry connects with the *Yijing*, but rather that the *Yijing* comprehends poetry....

When it comes to the many kinds of human affairs, the successive changes of worldly fortune, the transformation and arising of all things, the sequential functioning of the seasons, the extending and retracting of ghosts and spirits, the coming and going of sun and moon, and the opening and closing of heaven and earth, there is nothing that is not poetic regulation, nothing that is not poetic method, nothing that is not poetry. And all this really means is that there is nothing that is not the *Yijing*.

工部固生當憂患之時，而其感諷時事也，亦有其所謂旨遠、辭文、曲而中、肆而隱者乎？其寄意詠物也，亦有其所謂稱名小、取類大者乎？至其精於律法，而不囿於律法，參之伍之，錯之綜之，莫可窮詰，莫可端倪，則亦有其所謂不可爲典要，惟變所適者乎？竊謂杜之詩，詩而通於易者也。然而，非詩而通於易，實易之包乎詩。…以至人事之雜出，世運之遞遷，品物之化生，四時之錯行，鬼神之屈伸，日月之往來，天地之闔闢，無非律，無非法，無非詩，而實無非易。[46]

In this passage, all of the phrases enclosed in quotation marks echo Confucius's description of the *Yijing* in the "Xici" commentary. The basic point is thus clear: as Yu Ruli had implied seven hundred years earlier, Du Fu has written a new *Yijing*—albeit one that, in all the respects Fang emphasizes here, is far from new.[47] Given that the world's changes all correspond to the timeless immanent patterns of the universe, novelty cannot be a value for Fang. To the contrary, Du Fu's poetry is great because it is a repetition of the *Yi*, which, in Fang's words, "is complete when it comes to speaking of the affairs between heaven and earth."[48]

Fang's limited vision of poetic possibility may speak in part to his greater allegiance to Neo-Confucian speculation, but it recalls nonetheless comments made by other recordizing readers. We have already seen that Du Fu's critics have praised him for "exhaustively experiencing the great transformations of all-under-heaven," for fully articulating the world's "basically repeating situations," and for completely enunciating "the language that inheres in human emotional nature"—ideas that all suggest that poets might be forced in generation after generation to cover much the same ground.[49] For many writers beginning as early as the Song dynasty, these ideas seemed to threaten that "all the good language of the world had already been spoken completely by Du Fu."[50] As even the great poet Su Shi put it, also using language from the "Xici," "when poetry reached Du Fu . . . all the transformations possible for the art had already occurred; all the affairs within the world are thus complete within his work (*neng shi bi* 能事畢)."[51] Seven centuries later, Guo Songtao 郭嵩燾 (1818–91) would say much the same thing.

When the tradition arrived at Du Fu, only then was the inherent meaning of poetry able to absorb and combine all description of affairs and all categories of emotion; everything old and new, beginning and end; all of the benefits and harms, successes and failures possible in the world; all the weal and woe of the folk; all [the emotions] of parting and reuniting with friends and family; and all the glory and disgrace, sadness and happiness possible in human life. When Du Fu spoke of these things, he always reached their significance; when he mulled them over, he completely understood all their possible transformations. He thus completely exhausted [everything possible for poetry] and left nothing out.

唐杜甫氏出，指事類情，推陳始末，天下利病得失，生民之休感，親故之離合，身世之榮悴悲欣，言之必達其志，慮之必窮其變，然後詩之蘊乃旁推交通，曲盡而無遺。[52]

Though Guo is praising Du Fu's accomplishment here, the final phrase here can also be construed to suggest that Du Fu "completely consumed" everything possible for poetry and "left nothing behind" for the rest of us.[53] This is a worrisome possibility when poetry becomes ideally transparent to a world increasingly understood as structured by constant patterns.

Over the centuries, a number of critics have taken up this ambivalence in the legacy that Du Fu was understood to have left succeeding ages. According to the great Qing dynasty literary theorist Ye Xie 葉燮 (1627–1703), for instance, he had made epigones of all later poets, who were incapable of escaping his influence.

Du Fu's poetry embraces all streams and sources and comprises both the original and the transformed. He lacks nothing from before his time: the solidity and ancient elegance of the Han and Wei or the ornate beauty and dense intricateness of the Six Dynasties, the simple and distant or the alluring and lovely. Yet what came forth from Du Fu himself was not a single word or line that belonged to or imitated his predecessors. After Du Fu, however, . . . although there are dozens or even hundreds of great writers that come immediately to mind [from the Tang through the Ming], even though they all sparkle in their novelty and try to overturn precedent, nonetheless there is not one of them for whom Du Fu did not pioneer their accomplishments. This is because his skill had nowhere it did not reach, his strength had nothing it could not lift; he will forever flourish, incapable of declining. Thus, the reason that all people nowadays revere him is that they know that Du Fu, in order to be Du Fu, forged together the Han, Wei, Six Dynasties, and a hundred generations of poets that came after his time.

杜甫之詩，包源流，綜正變。自甫以前，如漢魏之渾樸古雅，六朝之藻麗穠纖，淡遠韶秀，甫詩無一不備。然出於甫，皆甫之詩，無一字句爲前人之詩也。自甫以後，⋯稱巨擘者無慮數十百人，各自炫奇翻異，而甫無一不爲之開先。此其巧無不到，力無不舉，長盛於千古，不能衰，不可衰者也。今之人固群然宗杜矣，亦知杜之爲杜，乃合漢魏六朝並後代千百年之詩人而陶鑄之者乎！[54]

Chen Tingzhuo 陳廷焯 (1853–92) is even more radical in his account of the threat Du Fu poses to later writers. For him, Du Fu is the destroyer of tradition: "Every poem of Du Fu's takes the ancients as an enemy, the hatred deep within his bones."[55]

From the *Airs* [of the *Shijing*] and the *Lisao* all the way to Li Bai, all poets inherited from one another in a single line.... But when poetry reached Du Fu it attained a sage, and when it reached Du Fu, it fundamentally transformed. Considering his abundant strength and the deep brooding of his conceptualization, none of his inheritors in the art of poetry have been able to escape his mold, and the ancient tone has never been performed again since.... From his time on, therefore, those who have studied poetry have been unable to find the *Airs* or the *Sao* and have had no choice but to take Du Fu as the limit to their endeavors.

大約自風騷以迄太白，皆一線相承。⋯詩至杜陵而聖，亦詩至杜陵而變。顧其力量充滿，意境沉鬱，嗣後爲詩者，舉不能出其範圍，而古調不復彈矣。⋯自有杜陵，後之學詩者更不能求風騷之所在，而亦不得不以杜陵爲止境。[56]

Like Guo Songtao's comment above, this too is meant as hyperbolic praise, albeit with an obvious edge. For Chen, Du Fu was too talented to accept the "fetters" that tradition placed on him; he resented and thus sought to overcome the limitations that "inheriting the single line" of poetry from antiquity up to his time would have imposed on his verse. As a result, however, he ended up placing his own fetters on later writers, for whom he came to dominate the tradition.[57]

This common image of Du Fu the devourer is far from unchallenged within postmedieval criticism. In other strands of literary commentary I have passed over in this book to focus on recordizing reading, he is also the greatest poetic teacher and model, the poet who most clearly demonstrates the range of poetic techniques available to later writers.[58] Beyond commentary, moreover, Du Fu's influence on poetic composition in China over the last millennium has been far more varied—and far less central—than Ye Xie and Chen Tingzhuo suggest.[59] Despite the cliché that poetry declined after the Tang, the massive productivity of Chinese poets throughout the last thousand years proves beyond doubt that Du Fu had not "completely exhausted" the art.

Yet even if recordizing criticism is merely one facet of Du Fu's legacy, the point to notice here is that it is explicitly inimical to the idea of either poetry or commentary as continuously transforming—and hence perduring—traditions. As a longstanding poetic paradigm, it thus presents a paradox. On the one hand, as I hope to have suggested throughout this book, its core principles have remained remarkably consistent since the Song dynasty—as, indeed, it suggests poetic principles should. On the other hand, however, it is a paradigm that, by its own lights, should have ceased to produce new scholarship as the determinate meanings of Du Fu's poems were discovered once and for all. If it has prevailed this long, therefore, it has done so not because it has convincingly solved the problems of Du Fu's verse, but rather because of the intractability of those problems themselves, which have engendered consistent disagreements about what his poems say, what realities they refer to in his life, and how his words express the virtues his readers have been sure he possessed. In this respect, recordizing criticism has been much the sort of transforming tradition that Du Fu designed his late poetry to participate in, even as it has characteristically denied that traditions should transform.

The Affordances of Difficulty

This point can be illustrated in the readings recordizing critics have given the final poem of a ten-poem set Du Fu wrote in the spring of 769 on a journey from Tanzhou to Hengzhou.[60] This series represents the culmination of Du Fu's intellectual development, containing his most mature and most explicit reflections on the question of whether his life can be considered a good one despite its apparent failures, on the problem of whether inherited moral categories provide adequate tools for understanding experience in the present, and on the dependence of moral judgment upon communities that can break down and be reconstituted in unexpected ways. It also represents perhaps the most difficult poetry in all of Du Fu: densely allusive and resolutely ambiguous, its sense depends on interconnections between poems too intricate to trace fully here. The discussion below will therefore deal with only a small portion of its complexities. In order to understand its conclusion, however, we need to start at the beginning.[61]

上水遣懷   *Unburdening My Breast While Going Upriver (no. 1)*

	我衰太平時	My decline came in an age of great peace,
	身病戎馬後	but I grew sick after the horses of war.[a]
	蹭蹬多拙爲	Losing my footing, I've often acted foolishly;
4	安得不皓首	how could I not end up white-headed?
	驅馳四海內	Driven to flight throughout the four seas,
	童稚日鮑口	my children daily eat others' gruel.
	但遇新少年	All I meet are fresh young men;
8	少逢舊親友	I rarely encounter old relatives or friends.
	低顏下色地	When I'd lower my face in these backwater places,
	故人知善誘	my comrades knew how to skillfully coax me on.[b]
	後生血氣豪	But these latter born, their blood runs proud,
12	舉動見老醜	and in my every move they see me ugly and old.
	窮迫挫囊懷	Poverty has crushed my former ambitions;
	常如中風走	I run about, always as if struck with madness.
	一紀出西蜀	Almost twelve years ago I came out to western Shu,
16	於今向南斗	and now I'm heading towards the Southern Dipper.
	孤舟亂春華	My lonely boat intrudes on spring's glory;
	暮齒依蒲柳	in twilight years I keep to cattails and willows.
	冥冥九疑葬	Dark and uncertain, that burial in the Nine Doubts:[c]

a. "My decline" echoes the *Analects*: "Confucius said, 'How severe is my decline! For a long time I have not dreamed of the Duke of Zhou.'" Medieval commentators took this as a complaint about the disorder of the age.

b. This line echoes the *Analects*, wherein we read that "the Master is good at skillfully coaxing people on" in teaching them the *dao*.

c. The Nine Doubts was a mountain range on the border of modern-day Hunan and Guangxi. It was the legendary burial place of the ancient sage king Shun.

20	聖者骨亦朽	even with a sage, the bones decay.[d]
	蹉跎陶唐人	Time has slipped past, that person of the Tao-Tang age
	鞭撻日月久	whipping on sun and moon for a long while now.[e]
	中間屈賈輩	And in between, the likes of Qu Yuan and Jia Yi
24	讒毀竟自取	in the end brought slander on themselves.[f]
	鬱沒二悲魂	Lost in the gloom, those two grieved souls,
	蕭條猶在否	withered and silent, do they still linger on here?
	崚崒清湘石	Looming up, the rocks of the clear Xiang;
28	逆行雜林藪	we travel against the current, mixing in forest and bog.
	篙工密逞巧	But the boatmen thoroughly indulge their skills,
	氣若酣盃酒	their air as if drunk on flagons of ale.
	謳謳互激遠	Their songs in turn shrill into the distance,
32	回斡明受授	at the turns clear about who gives and receives.
	善知應觸類	Fine understanding would surely "meet with the category":[g]
	各藉穎脫手	in all things, we depend on hands of unsuppressed gifts.[h]
	古來經濟才	Yet from ancient times, men with the talent for governing,
36	何事獨罕有	why are they alone so rarely found?[i]
	蒼蒼眾色晚	The vast cerulean turns the myriad colors late;
	熊掛玄蛇吼	bears hang, a dark snake roars.
	黃羆在樹顛	A brown she-bear is in a treetop,

d. This line echoes a story preserved in the *Shiji*: "When Confucius went to the state of Zhou, he sought to ask Laozi about the rituals [of the sage kings]. Laozi said, 'What you are asking about—those men's bones have already decayed, and only their words are in our ears.'"

e. Tao-Tang is the ancient sage king Yao; according to legend, he appointed Xihe to be the charioteer of the sun.

f. Qu Yuan was a worthy minister of the state of Chu who was slandered and exiled to the far south. Jia Yi, similarly, was envied for his talents and was exiled to Changsha. Both were famous writers.

g. This line echoes the "Xici" commentary: "If one meets with a category and extends to it [the *Yijing*'s examples], one can exhaust everything possible under heaven."

h. "Unsuppressed gifts" derives from the *Shiji*, where we read that a talented man is like an awl in a bag: the tip will inevitably poke through. The word "hands" here suggests easy mastery, like an "old hand" in English.

i. The word translated as "governing" is literally "organizing and fording," referring to the longstanding convention that the job of ministers was to help the state "ford the stream."

40	正為羣虎守	right now watching out for packs of tigers.[j]
	羸骸將何適	My wasted skeleton, where shall I take it?
	履險顏益厚	treading dangerous terrain, my face has grown thick.[k]
	庶與達者論	I had hoped to discuss things with men of attainment,[l]
44	吞聲混瑕垢	but I swallow sound, mingling with the flawed and defiled.[m]

解憂   *Relieving My Worries (no. 3)*

	減米散同舟	I cut back on rice, dividing it with my boatmates;
	路難思共濟	the route is hard, and I think of crossing over together.[n]
	向來雲濤盤	All the way, cloud-topping billows have whirled;
4	眾力亦不細	the strength expended by the many has not been small.[o]
	呀坑瞥眼過	Gaping pits are passed in the blink of an eye;
	飛櫓本無蔕	our flying oars are originally without set roots.[p]

j. This couplet recalls "Summoning the Recluse" from the *Songs of the Southlands,* in which the speaker tells a recluse that he will find no home out in the wilderness.

k. A "thick" face is a face that shows no shame.

l. The phrase "men of attainment" may echo the *Analects*: "Zizhang asked, 'What must a man be like to be called "a man of attainment"?' Confucius said, 'What do you mean by "a man of attainment"?' Zizhang said, 'He should be famous in the state and famous in his clan.' Confucius said, 'This is called "being famous," not "being attained." Attainment is to have an upright substance and to care about justice, to understand words and to recognize people through their appearances, and to think always about being humble to others. Such a man will be attained in the state and attained in his clan. As for a famous person, he will seem righteous on the outside but will violate righteousness in action, without, however, doubting his own righteousness.'"

m. The phrase "flawed and defiled" derives from the *Zuozhuan,* in which the Jin minister Bozong 伯宗 argues for the prudence of a shameful action by saying that "rivers and marshes take in mud, mountains and bogs store up illnesses, fine jades have flaws, and the ruler of the domain bears defilement—such is the *dao* of heaven."

n. "Crossing over together" often has a political meaning, as for example in Du Fu's "Temple of Zhuge Liang" 諸葛廟, in which we read that "lord and minister should cross over together"—that is, help each other succeed.

o. "The strength of the many" may perhaps echo the "Oath of Tang" 湯誓 from the *Shangshu*: "The king of the Xia exhausts the strength of the many and plunders his own cities. The many have become slack in his service and feel no kinship with him."

p. "Without set roots" derives from Ban Gu's "Answering a Guest's Criticism" 答賓戲. There, Ban stages a guest's critique of his own single-minded dedication to learning:

	得失瞬息間	Success or failure can happen in an instant;
8	致遠宜恐泥	in going far, one should worry about getting bogged down.�q
	百慮視安危	With a hundred concerns to see even safety as danger,
	分明曩賢計	this was clearly the calculus of past worthies.ʳ
	茲理庶可廣	This principle I hope to be able to extend;
12	拳拳期勿替	clasping it to me, I plan never to fail it.ˢ

The first poem here raises the question of whether Du Fu's life should be assessed a failure. From the outset, he compares himself with Confucius, who also might appear to have failed, having given up on saving the empire when, "in his decline," he no longer dreamed of the Duke of Zhou. Confucius's apparent failure, however, can be explained by the collapsing age in which he lived; Du Fu, by contrast, failed to achieve high office even in the Kaiyuan and early Tianbao eras, when the Tang was still at peace and well governed. He once hoped, nonetheless, that "men of attainment" would be able to look past the humiliating circumstances into which he has fallen. His old friends used to do so, at least, but now they are gone, and Du Fu can only swallow his complaints before the arrogant youngsters from whom he is forced to beg for food. Much of the series, therefore, will

"Vainly taking joy in pillowing yourself on Classics and resting on books, you hunch your body behind a barred gate, without set roots. You may send your thoughts flying beyond the bounds of the universe and drill your mind into the space of an autumn hair, submerging your spirit and remembering silently, throughout the rest of your days. But if you do not sell your vessel [i.e., take a position in government] to establish yourself or exert your function to aid the age, even if your words are like billows and waves and your writings are like spring's flowering, they will garner you no merit."

q. This line echoes the *Analects*: "Zixia said, 'Even a minor art [*dao*] will have something worth observing in it; but, if one goes far with it, I worry that one will get bogged down. For this reason, the gentleman does not take up [such minor arts].'"

r. "A hundred concerns" echoes the "Xici" commentary to the *Yijing*: "Confucius said, 'What is there to worry about under heaven? All under heaven returns to the same place, albeit via different roads; it reaches the same end despite a hundred different concerns. So what is there to worry about under heaven?'"

s. "Never to fail it" is archaic, used in both the *Shijing* and the *Shangshu* for preserving old customs. The phrase "clasping it to me" echoes the "Zhongyong" 中庸 chapter of the *Liji*: "Confucius said, 'Yan Hui is the type of man that, when he attains a virtue, he clasps it to himself and does not lose it.'"

be based on seeking analogies of his lost friends, who will understand him in ways these youngsters do not.

Analogies are, however, rendered problematic in this poem and throughout the series. As Laozi had told Confucius, the examples left by even the great sages of antiquity had decayed along with their bones; and Du Fu, in any event, finds little to value in the most obvious traditional parallels for his predicament, Qu Yuan and Jia Yi, whose ostentatious protestations of their virtue led merely to their own destruction. These problematic reflections upon tropology prompt Du Fu to question the usefulness of analogical reasoning itself. If the "Xici" commentary is right about "extending analogical categories," for instance, the boatmen tasked with ferrying him downriver should provide a good analogy for the states-men needed to accomplish the similar task of ferrying the state "across the stream"—a traditional metaphor for governance. Yet Du Fu reflects that the analogy is both apt and imperfect. On the one hand, both tasks require skillful responsiveness to unpredictable contingencies. On the other, skilled boatmen are apparently plentiful, skilled ministers tragically few.

This observation initiates a series of ruminations, continued through-out the series, on the "Xici" commentary and the analogical reasoning it prescribes. "Relieving My Worries," for instance, recalls that text once again in Du Fu's surprising claim that having "a hundred concerns" was the principle to which previous worthies held—a flat contradiction of the "Xici," which in fact explicitly discourages such scheming.[62] This invoca-tion of a traditional precedent in an unexpected sense follows the pattern of the poem in general, which does much the same thing with Ban Gu's language of "set roots" and Zixia's worry that if one "goes far" in studying a minor art, one might get "bogged down." In these allusions, Du Fu recalls canonical statements about the incommensurability of different sorts of pursuits, such as book learning, government service, and the polite enter-tainments of elite society. Yet he invokes these canonical statements to describe an endeavor, his boat journey, that can have only an analogical relationship with any of these more weighty affairs. When he aims to ex-tend the principle he has learned here to other moral domains, therefore, he is both doing what the "Xici" prescribes and also violating, in this very process, the statements he is analogizing to his experience. Insofar as this poem makes a claim that Du Fu is enacting the moral lessons of the tra-dition within the limited sphere to which his failure to achieve government office has confined him, then, it does so only paradoxically, through allusions that deny the analogy between these disparate ventures.

This strange, self-contradictory rhetoric will prove characteristic of the series as a whole. The first half of the set generally presents Du Fu claiming to actualize canonical ideals while more subtly diverging from them, whereas the second figures him apparently diverging from traditional precedents while more subtly conforming to them. By taking up the two sides of this problem—ultimately, the same problem he noted in the analogy/disanalogy between boatmen and ministers in the first poem—he mulls both the difficulties of applying traditional precedents to his experience and their continued relevance nonetheless.[63]

宿鑿石浦　　*Passing the Night by Rock Quarry Shore (no. 4)*

	早宿賓從勞	I put up early from the toils of seeking patronage;[a]
	仲春江山麗	the second month of spring, river and mountains lovely.
	飄風過無時	Yet gusting winds could pass any moment:
4	舟楫敢不繫	how would we dare not tie the boat?[b]
	回塘澹暮色	The winding dikes are pale in twilight's colors;
	日沒眾星嘒	the sun sinks, the many stars are bright.[c]
	缺月殊未生	The crescent moon has not yet come forth;
8	青燈死分翳	we cover the faint lamps at the point of their dying.
	窮途多俊異	On dead-end roads there's much that's exceptional,
	亂世少恩惠	but in a disordered age, there's little kindness.[d]

a. "The toils of seeking patronage" seems to refer to Du Fu's travails in making this journey. The phrase could also be interpreted "my entourage has toiled hard."

b. This line might recall the *Zhuangzi*, where we read: "The clever toil and the wise worry, but one who is without ability seeks for nothing. He eats his fill and roams at his ease, floating like an untied boat." According to Guo Xiang, "one who is without ability" refers to the sages.

c. This line recalls "Clouded River" 雲漢 from the *Classic of Poetry*: "I look up to heaven, and its stars are bright." In this poem, the king is complaining about disorder in the state and contrasting it to the order of the stars. The brightness of the stars here could also suggest disorder, minor lights shining while the great lights (associated with the central court) are dimmed.

d. "Dead-end roads" may recall Ruan Ji, who expressed his frustrated ambitions by weeping whenever he came to the end of a road—a physical symbol of his being unable to advance in government. "Much that's exceptional" could refer either to the beauty of the

鄙夫亦放蕩　　This base fellow has been similarly set loose;[e]

12　草草頻卒歲　　it's in travails I've mostly passed my years.[f]

斯文憂患餘　　This *wen* is what remains from worry and catastrophe,[g]

聖哲垂彖繫　　just as the sages left us their "Judgments" and "Appended Words."[h]

過津口　　*Passing Jinkou (no. 6)*

南岳自兹近　　The Southern Marchmount is close from here,

湘流東逝深　　the Xiang's flow deepens, going off to the east.[i]

和風引桂楫　　A warm breeze draws on our cassia paddles;

---

landscape on this "dead-end road" or to the character of the people who, like Ruan Ji, wind up on dead-end roads.

e. "Similarly" here presumably refers to Ruan Ji from the previous couplet, who was "wild and free," one possible meaning for the phrase translated as "set loose." The compound could also mean "sent to wander in exile."

f. "In travails" recalls "Xiang bo" 巷伯 from the *Poetry*: "Those rich people are doing fine, but this toiling person is in travails!" "Passed my years" might refer to a story in the *Kong congzi* 孔叢子 about Kong Fu 孔鮒 (3rd c. BCE), who lived in an era of disorder but spent his time studying the way of the ancient sages. When someone criticized him for not participating actively in the politics of the age, he replied: "Someone who practices war (*wu* 武) might advance and grasp his object, but for me, who studies *wen*, I can only preserve the past. Nowadays the world is in tumult, but that tumult will someday end. You might help by ending it, but I help by preserving [the past]. . . . All I can do is thus pass my years at ease [and not get involved]."

g. The phrase translated "this *wen*" most likely refers to "these poems," but the phrase also commonly means "This Culture of Ours," the sacred tradition. This is how the phrase appears in the *Analects*: "Confucius was in danger in Kuang. He said, 'King Wen is dead: does not culture (*wen*) reside in me? If heaven were to destroy this culture of ours, those who die after me will not get to participate in it. And, if heaven is not to destroy this culture of ours, then what can the people of Kuang do to me?'"

h. The phrase "worry and catastrophe" alludes to the "Xici" (that is, "Appended Words") commentary on the *Yijing*: "Was it not in middle antiquity that the *Yijing* began to flourish? Were not they who created the *Yijing* doing so out of worry for catastrophe?" According to the Tang subcommentary, this refers to the line statements (the "Judgments") of the *Yijing*, which the sages composed to forestall misunderstandings of the hexagrams in a world where the people had declined from their earlier simplicity.

i. The Southern Marchmount was Mt. Heng. The word for "going off" might recall the *Analects*: "Confucius was standing over a stream. He said, 'It goes off like this, not stopping day or night.'"

4	春日溾雲岑	spring sunlight overflows the cloudy peaks.[j]
	回首過津口	I turn my head as we pass Jinkou,
	而多楓樹林	and many are the forests of liquidambar.[k]
	白魚困密網	White fish are trapped in close-meshed nets;
8	黄鳥喧嘉音	yellow birds are raucous in lovely tones.
	物微限通塞	These creatures are small, but their fortune and adversity
	惻隱仁者心	moves a benevolent man's heart to inward pain.[l]
	瓮餘不盡酒	In my jug remains unfinished ale;
12	膝有無聲琴	on my lap there is a soundless zither.[m]
	聖賢兩寂寞	Both sages and worthies are silent and still;
	眇眇獨開襟	alone in the vast expanse, I open my lapels.[n]

j. Both the "warm breeze" and the "cloudy peaks" in this couplet echo the first stanza of Tao Qian's "Returning Birds" 歸鳥: "They beat their wings, those returning birds, / having this morning left the forest. / Afar they reached the eight extremes; / near they rested on cloudy peaks. / Where the warm breeze was not just right, / they beat their wings, seeking their intent. / They turn to their companions and cry to one another, to go rest in cool shade."

k. This line may echo one of Ruan Ji's "Yonghuai": "Deep, deep are the Yangzi's waters, and above are forests of liquidambar." Ruan Ji's couplet, in turn, derives from the "Summons of the Soul" from the *Songs of the Southlands*: "Deep, deep is the river water, and above it are liquidambar trees."

l. "Fortune and adversity" is a common compound denoting political failure and success; it appears first in the *Yijing*, where we read that one can "not go out the door and yet know whether one will meet fortune or adversity." According to the "Xici," moreover, the *Yijing* "speaks of small matters but takes from them larger analogies." The idea that a benevolent man will feel pain at the suffering of fellow creatures is a common refrain in the *Mengzi*.

m. Both the ale and the zither are reminiscent of Tao Qian. According to his biography in the *Jin History*, Tao "did not understand music but nonetheless kept a zither, though he did not bother to string it. Every time he would meet with friends to drink, he would stroke the zither and harmonize with them, saying, 'I understand only what is important about the zither; why should I bother with the sound of the strings?'" The soundless zither might also recall the legendary musician Boya 伯牙, who gave up playing music when his friend Zhong Ziqi 鍾子期 passed away, as Zhong was the only person who fully appreciated his artistry.

n. This last line might recall Wang Can's "Rhapsody on Climbing a Tower," written after he had fled disorder in the north for safe haven in the southlands: "I lean on the railing and look far, / and from the north comes a wind that opens my lapels."

"Passing the Night by Rock Quarry Shore" continues the pattern of the first half of the series, asserting continuities between Du Fu and the canonical precedents he invokes while also undermining those same analogies. Most striking in this poem is the final couplet's claim that, since he writes in response to "worries and catastrophes," his poetry (*siwen* 斯文, "this *wen*"—usually "This Culture of Ours," the sacred tradition) resembles the "Judgments" and the "Xici" commentary from the *Yijing*, which were likewise composed by King Wen and Confucius in response to "worries about catastrophe." According to the *Zhuangzi* and its Xuanxue commentators, however, the worries and the catastrophes to which the sages were responding were not, in fact, their own, but rather those of the common people. As sages, they merely responded without prejudice or concern to whatever circumstances happened to present themselves, drifting like "untied boats."[64] Du Fu, by contrast, has been traumatized by his experience, and has just demanded in the second couplet that his own boat be tied up against the contingencies of the wind.

Similar disanalogies within analogy can also be found in Du Fu's attempt, in the penultimate couplet, to compare himself to the worthies Ruan Ji and Kong Fu. Both he and Ruan Ji, for instance, can be described by the phrase *fangdang* 放蕩, but, where the recluse Ruan Ji was "wild and free" (one meaning of the phrase), Du Fu is better described as "tossed about in exile" (another). Similarly, though both he and Kong Fu have worked at *wen* in "disordered ages," he cannot, unlike Kong, "pass his years at ease" (*youyou yi zu sui* 優遊以卒歲).[65] Although he claims, therefore, to be continuing This *Wen* of Ours, Du Fu is not merely "preserving the past," as Kong Fu did. Instead, his more personal, more pained writings also represent a significant divergence from the placidity of the sages and their inheritors in the great tradition.

In the second half of the series, Du Fu seems to learn a lesson from these repeating divergences. He turns, therefore, from asserting continuities between himself and traditional precedents to meditating explicitly on the discontinuities of the world. This program begins with the observation of the inexplicably disanalogous fates of birds and fish in "Passing Jinkou," the series' sixth poem. It will continue in the next two, which reflect, first, on the disparate climates of different regions and then, ultimately, on the necessity of varying imperial governance to match such regional differences. Du Fu's conclusion, as he says in the eighth poem, is that the unpredictable variability of "heaven's vague and vast creation" ensures that "there can never be constant methods for ordering disorder" (*liluan qi hengshu* 理亂豈恒數). This sounds very close to the antinomianism of the *Zhuangzi*.

Yet even as Du Fu reflects on these explicit disanalogies, analogies nonetheless work themselves back into the poems—and with them the precedents of the canonical tradition. The language he uses in "Passing Jinkou" for the disparate fates of birds and fish, for instance, is "fortune and adversity" (*tong-sai* 通塞), an *Yijing* phrase describing alternating phases of the political cycle.[66] When he says, moreover, that these creatures move his heart "even though they are small," he is not only drawing an analogy between their fates and human affairs, but also recalling the method ascribed to the *Yijing* by the "Xici" commentary, which argues that it "speaks of small matters but takes from them larger analogies."[67] The poem also returns to the theme of lost friends, which launched Du Fu on his search for analogies in the first place. Here, he laments that he has no one with whom he might share his unfinished ale or for whom he might play his zither, past sages and worthies being too remote to take the place of his dead friends. But even as he bemoans his isolation, the very lines in which he does so clearly recall the works of previous worthies like Tao Qian, who never bothered to string his zither, and Wang Can, who was an exile far from any living friend. Though Tao and Wang are "silent" now that they are dead, and are thus unable to console Du Fu, in that silent inconsolation they are at one.

If this poem thus continues the series' focus on analogy and disanalogy, moreover, it also begins to show how they are built into its structure as well. It is not a coincidence, that is, that Du Fu returns to the theme of friendship in this sixth poem, after broaching it in the first. Like the Qinzhou-to-Tonggu and the Tonggu-to-Chengdu series examined in the fourth chapter, this sequence is structured by complex interrelations between poems in chiastic and parallel positions, which invite readers to puzzle out comparisons and contrasts between them. Beyond friendship, for instance, "Passing Jinkou" recalls a number of themes from its parallel in the first half of the set, including imagery of great southern mountains, the exile of Qu Yuan, the possibility of reclusion, animals, and the "rotting bones" of the now silent sages—themes that, had I more space to devote to them, would be well worth following out. Similar echoes characterize the last two poems of the series as well, with the ninth recalling "Passing the Night by Rock Quarry Shore" (no. 4) and the tenth once again "Unburdening My Breast While Going Upriver" (no. 1). In reading these poems, it will be worth lingering a moment over these connections.[68]

早發   Setting Out Early (no. 9)

	有求常百慮	Having demands, I feel ever a hundred concerns;
	斯文亦吾病	this *wen* is indeed my great disease.[a]
	以茲朋故多	Through it I made a great many friends,
4	窮老驅馳併	but old and poor, I've often been driven to flight.[b]
	早行篙師怠	Traveling early, the boatmen were lax,
	席掛風不正	hoisting sail with the wind not right.
	昔人戒垂堂	In the past, men warned of sitting under the eaves;
8	今則奚奔命	why should I now be rushing to command?[c]
	濤翻黑蛟躍	Breakers toss, black flood-dragons leap;
	日出黃霧映	the sun emerges, shining through brown fog.
	煩促瘴豈侵	In all the hurry, has the miasma got to me?
12	頽倚睡未醒	slumped over, I can't shake off sleep.
	僕夫問盥櫛	My servant asks me if I want to wash and comb,
	暮顏覥青鏡	but my dusky face is ashamed of the green mirror.
	隨意簪葛巾	I would, instead, casually pin on a hemp headwrap,
16	仰慚林花盛	but looking up, I'm embarrassed by the forest's flowers.[d]
	側聞夜來寇	I overhear there were robbers last night;

a. "Having demands" might recall the *Zhuangzi*: "The sages take necessity as notnecessity, and therefore they do not use military force. More common-minded people take even what is not necessity as necessity and therefore often use military force. Since they follow the path of military force, everyone comes to have demands. Thus, when one relies on military force, one's state is doomed." For "a hundred concerns," see "Relieving My Worries," above. For "this *wen*," see "Passing the Night by Rock Quarry Shore."

b. This couplet may recall the *Analects*: "A gentleman makes friends through cultured pursuits and uses these friends to support his virtue."

c. According to an old proverb, found first in the *Han shu*, "a rich young man does not sit under the eaves" where a loose roof tile might fall and injure him. The second line here is obscure, but Du Fu may be referring to seeking patrons—patrons like those discussed in "Unburdening My Breast While Going Upriver" and later on in this poem. Or perhaps he might be asking why the boatmen do not rush at his command.

d. Tao Qian famously wore a hemp headwrap, which he also used for straining ale. The hairpins might have been those that held up Du Fu's official cap.

	幸喜囊中淨	I delight at my luck, that my purse is bare.[e]
	艱危作遠客	Trouble and peril made me a far traveler,
20	干請傷直性	but seeking patronage harms my upright nature.
	薇蕨餓首陽	Gathering bracken while enduring hunger on Shouyang,
	粟馬資歷聘	or feeding my horses to provision a search for employment:[f]
	賤子欲適從	This base fellow wanted to follow them,
24	疑悞此二柄	but I worry I've mistaken these two handles.[g]

次晚洲   *Making the Stage to Late Isle (no. 10)*

	參錯雲石稠	Jumbled together, rock and cloud dense;
	坡陁風濤壯	layered in ridges, the windblown breakers huge.
	晚洲適知名	Late Isle is suited for fame;[h]
4	秀色固異狀	its splendid appearance is indeed of a different sort.
	棹經垂猿把	Our oars pass under the grasp of hanging gibbons;
	身在度鳥上	our bodies are above the crossing birds.
	擺浪散帙妨	Yet the tossing waves hinder opening my book covers,

e. Though there is no clear linguistic echo, Du Fu might be thinking here of the *Zhuangzi*'s parable of the "thief in the night": "If you hide a boat within a valley or a mountain within a marsh, you think it secure. But someone with strength comes in the night and carries it off, and you do not even know it. If you hide the small within the big, then things can get away from you. If, however, you hide the world within the world, then nothing can ever get away: this is the truth of permanent things. . . . Therefore, the sage roams where things cannot get away from him and everything is present. He takes an early death as good and old age as good, takes the beginning as good and the end as good."

f. When King Wu of Zhou conquered the decadent Shang dynasty, Boyi and Shuqi refused to eat grain grown under his jurisdiction and so went into reclusion on Mt. Shouyang, eating only bracken ferns. "A search for employment"—more literally "repeated travels in search of employment"—is a phrase often used to describe Confucius's travels throughout the states of his time in search of a ruler who appreciated him and would be willing to practice good government.

g. "Two handles" is a set phrase, originally from the *Han Feizi*, usually referring to the "handles" by which the ruler could reform his population, namely, culture and force, *wen* 文 and *wu* 武. Du Fu seems to have come up with two different handles: engagement and reclusion.

h. This line could also be read, "'Late Isle'—I have just learned its name."

8	危沙折花當	and the perilous sands prevent me snapping flowers.[i]
	羈離暫愉悅	Thus stranded abroad, such brief joys,
	羸老反惆悵	now I'm feeble and old, return to desolation.[j]
	中原未解兵	On the central plain, the warfare has not eased,
12	吾得終踈放	could I in the end be truly free?[k]

The clearest parallel between poem 4 and poem 9 is the loaded phrase "this *wen*," which appears in the last couplet of the former and the first of the latter. In "Passing the Night by Rock Quarry Shore" (no. 4), Du Fu claimed that he was continuing This Culture of Ours in his poetry, only to have that rather optimistic vision undermined by allusions pointing up significant contrasts between him and traditional exemplars. Here, by contrast, he depicts his obsession with literature as a "disease," while

i. These lines may allude to poems on the topic of friendship. The phrase "opening my book covers" appears in a poem Xie Lingyun wrote to his cousin and friend Xie Huilian 謝惠連: "I have already shared my mind with you; / happiness truly lies in this. / You climb through the ravines to seek my chamber, / and, opening my book covers, you ask what I have learned therein." "Picking flowers" probably recalls an anecdote about Lu Kai 陸凱 (198–269), who sent the following poem to his friend Fan Hua 范曄 when the latter was off in the north: "I snap a flower to give to the envoy, / who will send it along to you on the frontier. / Here in the southlands there is nothing to give you, / so for the meantime I present you this single branch of spring." "Prevent me snapping flowers" could also be translated "are fit for snapping flowers."

j. This line may recall the "Jiubian" from the *Songs of the Southlands*: "Vast and empty, stranded abroad with no living friends; / desolate, and secretly he pities himself."

k. The phrase *shufang* 踈放, translated as "truly free," is multiply ambiguous. According to Qiu Zhao'ao, it derives from the introduction to Xiang Xiu's "Rhapsody on Recalling Old Friends": "I lived close by the residences of Xi Kang and Lü An; both were men of unbridled talent. But, though Xi Kang's ambitions were distant, he was careless (*shu*); and, though Lü's mind was broad, he was wild (*fang*). Later both were executed." Taken together, the phrase comes to be a standard description of eccentrics and recluses. Taken individually, however, the words could also be translated "estranged" (*shu*) and "exiled" (*fang*), giving the sense of "banished afar." Finally, *shufang* also had a legal meaning in the Tang, denoting a reprieve from punishment: being "set free" from prison or from penalty of death. The grammar of the line is also ambiguous, as it could be read not as a question, but as an affirmative statement: "In the end, I *will* get to be truly free." "Get to" (*de* 得) could also be "forced to."

ultimately counterbalancing that pessimism with allusions that suggest unexpected conformities to traditional precedents. Even as he sighs, that is, that he has failed to grasp the tradition's "two handles"—service and reclusion: Confucius's relentless search for government office or the lofty retirement of Boti and Shuqi—he finds himself here nonetheless replicating the endless traveling of the former and the starvation of the latter.[69] And not only does this ironic convergence-in-divergence invert the divergence-in-convergence noted in the allusions of "Passing the Night" to Ruan Ji and Kong Fu; "Setting Out Early" also includes a *Zhuangzi* allusion that equally inverts the previous poem's reference to that text. There, Du Fu had demanded that his boat be tied up, thus deviating from the pattern set by the sages, who wander like "untied boats." Here, by contrast, he finds that, having no money that might tempt a "thief in the night," he seems to actualize the *Zhuangzi's* vision of the sage "roaming where things cannot escape him," where no contingency is feared because he has nothing to lose. In these parallels between the penultimate poems of the first and second halves of the series, therefore, Du Fu suggests both that he has failed in his attempts to imitate the precedents of This Culture of Ours and that, nonetheless, he often finds his failures conforming unexpectedly to strange analogies of its ideals.

Complicated parallels of this kind structure the series as a whole, producing a poetry that—it must be acknowledged—is very far from pellucid. This difficulty is, however, by design. In consistently recalling the *Yijing*, and particularly the injunction of the "Xici" commentary to "meet with categories and extend them," Du Fu seems to be revising the central epistemological paradigm of late medieval Classicism discussed above: the idea that, for most of us, the best way to understand our world is to reason analogically from examples provided by the tradition. By focusing this series on disanalogies-within-analogies and analogies-within-disanalogies, he suggests that this account of tradition's moral-epistemological significance is overly simple. Whenever he finds his experience converging with traditional precedents, he can find significant contrasts there as well; and, when he begins to wonder whether he has fully diverged from This Culture of Ours, he finds surprising connections to it. The tortured allusiveness of the series thus represents an attempt to grapple with the contingency that both prevents his life from conforming completely to traditional tropologies and also renders their precedents relevant in uncertain, often ironic, sometimes perplexing permutations.

The difficulty of this series has, moreover, ensured that its own place in the critical tradition mirrors the vision of tradition it presents. Although the final poem, for instance, is neither famous nor much discussed, commentators have suggested at least three different ways of understanding its concluding phrase, *shufang* 踈放, translated (rather lamely) above as "truly free." The earliest comment on the poem, dubiously attributed to Wang Zhu 王洙 (997–1057), reads the line as saying that Du Fu "is forced to end his life in banishment," a paradigmatic unrecognized worthy.[70] Zhao Cigong, however, takes umbrage at the idea that Du Fu would impugn the government so directly, arguing that the line is instead a statement of the depth of his commitment to the empire: given the situation up north, "how could he, in the end, feel careless and free?"[71] Tang Yuanhong 唐元竑 (1590–1647), finally, suggests that he is joking, with both good humor and subtle sadness, that "in the end, he will get to be wild and free" in reclusion, just as he always wanted.[72] If Du Fu has ruminated throughout the series, then, on the unpredictable ways that traditional precedents reflect on his experience, his own poetry has now become similarly equivocal, exemplifying a shifting range of virtues to his commentators.

Each of these readings represents a plausible interpretation of the sense of this highly ambiguous final line, and I would not be surprised, given the apparently purposeful ambiguities of his other poems in this period, if Du Fu intended each of them to be available to his readers. Other interpretations remain possible as well. In the Tang, for instance, *shufang* could also have a legal meaning: to "pardon" a criminal and release him from bondage.[73] The line can thus be understood as questioning whether Du Fu might, in the end, receive a "pardon" for his apparently failed life— precisely what he has been looking for since the first poem of the series, when he hoped to find a "man of attainment" (*dazhe* 達者) capable of seeing real virtue concealed beneath his shameful circumstances. Then as now, he was yearning for lost friends who once encouraged him when he would "lower his face in these backwater places," but—as the allusions of the fourth couplet here imply—they no longer visit him to talk about books, and he cannot send them "a single branch of spring." If anyone will "pardon" him now, it will have to be his readers.

In effect, this is the role that Wang Zhu, Zhao Cigong, and Tang Yuanhong have all taken on, each finding a different way of ensuring that the poem says something that is, in their eyes, admirable. In this example, therefore, we can see how the recordizing tradition, despite its insistence on the fixed significance of his poems, has nonetheless allowed Du Fu to transform to suit the changing moral perspectives of successive ages and diverse individuals. Although the forbidding obscurity of this set has ensured that it is not among his most famous works, it exemplifies the general difficulty of his constantly transforming, never predictable collection. This difficulty has lured critics back to Du Fu again and again, seeking to discover previously hidden analogies of their interests in China's most read poet. And it is in the transformations their discoveries engender, age after age, that he continues to receive the "pardon" he sought.

Living into Literature

To suggest that Du Fu's poetry lives in its difficulties is, of course, also to offer him a sort of "pardon." Yet this pardon is not quite the recordizing kind, whereby we would interpret his works as recording a life admirable in itself. Instead, if he transcends his apparent failures by transforming so as to speak to the shifting moral paradigms of different communities over time, then what is admirable about him is less his life per se than the way his life became poetry. Our ethical appreciation, in other words, will not appertain to the sentiments and actions of an individual in history, but rather to the way he lived into the possibilities and contingencies of tradition.

Du Fu's last works frequently depict him on this threshold between life and literature. As Stephen Owen has put it, he seems to have sensed as his time grew short that there was "something mysterious and portentous about [his southern] journey, as if he were bound in some mythic itinerary whose significance was to be revealed to him in transit."[74] He could no longer hope, however, as he had once done in Qinzhou and Tonggu, that any actual destination would deliver him the consummations he had been seeking so long. Instead, the mystery and portentousness of the journey are carried by what are essentially word games: double entendres and equivocations difficult to cash out into sense-making predicates about his life. If Du Fu's itinerary becomes "mythic," therefore, it is because literature could make it so.[75]

宿白沙驛   *Passing the Night by Whitesands Post Station*[a]

水宿仍餘照	Though I'll sleep on the water, there's still lingering sunlight;
人煙復此亭	smoke of human habitation, and then this pavilion.
驛邊沙舊白	By the post station, the sands are still their old white;
4　湖外草新青	beyond the lake, the grass is newly green.[b]
萬象皆春氣	The myriad images all have the air of spring;[c]
孤槎自客星	this solitary raft is alone a traveling star.[d]
隨波無限月	Yet following the waves, there's no end to the moonlight:
8　的的近南溟	clearly I draw near the Southern Deeps.[e]

祠南夕望   *Gazing at Dusk, South of the Shrine*

百丈牽江色	The thousand-foot tow rope drags the river's colors;[f]
孤舟汎日斜	my lonely boat floats on the sun's slant.
興來猶杖屨	When inspiration comes, I still have staff and sandals,
4　目斷更雲沙	my sight breaks off at yet more clouds and sand.
山鬼迷春竹	The Mountain Wraith is lost in spring bamboo;
湘娥倚暮花	the Xiang Maidens keep to the dusky flowers.[g]

a. An early note reads, "When first passing five *li* south of [Dongting] lake" 初過湖南五里.

b. This couplet plays on the place's toponyms: "Whitesands Post Station" and "Greengrass Lake."

c. "The myriad images" are the myriad things of the sublunary world; "images" (*xiang* 象), however, were also seen in the constellations above.

d. This line alludes to the story of the eighth-month raft from Zhang Hua's *Bowu zhi*, cited above in a note to "In My Boat."

e. The phrase translated as "clearly" here (*didi* 的的) is a double entendre: it means both "obviously" and "sparkling," referring alternately to the clarity of Du Fu's inference and the luminousness of the scene. The "Southern Deeps" derives from the *Zhuangzi*, in which it is the destination of the Roc (the Peng bird): "When the seas churn, it is this bird, about to move to the Southern Deeps. The southern deeps are the pool of heaven."

f. Du Fu was at this point traveling upstream, so his boat was being towed.

g. The Mountain Wraith and the Xiang Maidens are goddesses eulogized in the "Nine Songs" 九歌 of the *Songs of the Southlands*.

湖南清絕地　Hunan is a land of absolute pellucidity;
8　萬古一長嗟　a myriad ages, one long sigh.[h]

In "Passing the Night," the wordplay that enchants Du Fu's experience lies in the final line. He has pursued the horizon here well into the gloaming because he knows that, unlike the green grass, he will not be renewed by the coming of springtime's warmth. Yet as his time's shortness drives him on into the moonlight, and as the starry skies reflect with equal brightness in the waters below, he finds himself literally, and not at all literally, sailing on the southern deeps—both a simple description of these austral mains and the mythical "pool of heaven." The phrase translated here as "clearly" (didi 的的), moreover, can be either adverbial or adjectival, either denoting that he is "obviously" approaching the "Southern Deeps" or describing the "clear sparkling" of the waters split by his prow.[76] In this line, therefore—at once gorgeously descriptive and winkingly naïve—the clarity of the scene and the clarity of the inference are conflated, illusion and simple fact spoken in one voice. Retrospectively, it thus becomes unclear whether the poem's "images" (xiang 象) are those of the sublunar world or the constellations of the nighttime sky (also xiang). And as the scene flickers between mundane fact and supernal illusion, language and reality become indistinguishable: Whitesands has its eternal white sands, Greengrass Lake grows fresh with green grass, and the southern deeps become the Southern Deeps.

The idea that Du Fu's southward journey is a journey into literature is even more explicit in "Gazing at Dusk," written a few days later at a shrine to the two goddesses of the Xiang River—the subject, along with other regional divinities like the Mountain Wraith, of eulogies in the *Songs of the Southlands*.[77] Once again, the final couplet of the poem contains a surprising conceit that reconfigures what has preceded it. In the second couplet, Du Fu tells us he sees nothing on his walk but endless clouds and sand; read straight, the Mountain Wraith's being "lost" in the bamboo and

h. The phrase "absolute pellucidity" derives from a letter Lu Yun 陸雲 (262–303) sent his brother, Lu Ji: "In the past when I read the *Songs of the Southlands*, I did not really like them. Recently, however, I looked them over, and in truth they are like absolutely pellucid waters flowing on and on. For this reason, those who recognize this [quality], both past and present, revere them as an ancestor."

the Xiang Maidens "keeping to" the dusktime flowers both suggest, simply, that he does not see them. Yet these goddesses were tenuous presences in the *Songs of the Southlands* themselves, spurring their eulogists to sighs of passion precisely by eluding their amorous advances. When Du Fu claims in the final line to be "at one" with the authors of these ancient texts, then, his inability to distinctly perceive the goddesses here may be evidence not of their absence but rather of the elusiveness that made them so alluring in the first place. Their divinity enchants the disenchanted landscape: by not seeing them, he does.

This retrospective transfiguration of the scenes described in the middle couplets, confounding what is literally there with what is literarily there, is further strengthened by their description in the penultimate line as "absolutely pellucid." In the letter by Lu Yun to which this phrase alludes, it initially described not the southlands themselves but rather the *Songs of the Southlands*—it was, that is, a description of literary quality. Yet insofar as Du Fu is seeing the text in the landscape, the presence of the goddesses in their absence, the distinction between literary and physical beauty becomes blurred. Hunan is a land of literature, and he is being drawn in.

As Du Fu continues downriver, poetry begins not merely to be confused with life but almost to render its details irrelevant. Arriving in Tanzhou, for instance, he mulled the possibility of taking up residence at a Buddhist monastery. It is not clear, however, how much either residence or Buddhism really interested him, beyond the latter's suggestion that the world is never what it seems to the uninitiated.[78] The paradise he imagines for himself here is, rather, a paradise of verse. And that he can reach directly.[79]

岳麓山道林二寺行   *Ballad of Two Temples,*
Yuelu Mountain and Daolin

玉泉之南麓山殊   South of Jadespring,
    Yuelu Mountain is exceptional;
道林林壑爭盤紆   Daolin's forested ravines
    vie in twisting and turning.[a]

---

a. Yuelu Mountain Monastery and Daolin Monastery were both in Tanzhou. "Jade-spring" here probably refers to Jadespring Monastery in Jingzhou, which Du Fu had

	寺門高開洞庭野	One monastery's gate opens high over the wilderness of Dongting;
4	殿腳插入赤沙湖	the foot of the other's hall sticks out into Redsands Lake.[b]
	五月寒風冷佛骨	In the fifth month, cold winds chill the Buddha's bones;[c]
	六時天樂朝香爐	throughout the six divisions, celestial music pays court at the incense burners.[d]
	地靈步步雪山草	As for the numen of the place, at each step are plants from the Mountains of Snow;[e]
8	僧寶人人滄海珠	as for their saṃgha-treasure, each man is a pearl of the dark sea.[f]
	塔劫官墻壯麗敵	Their pagodas' stories and compounds' walls match in magnificence and beauty;
	香廚松道清涼俱	fragrant kitchens and piney paths equal in purity and tranquility.
	蓮花交響共命鳥	Their lotus blossoms exchange echoes from jīvajīvaka birds;[g]

---

visited on his way south. It is also possible that Du Fu is simply referring to a spring north of Yuelu Mountain Monastery.

b. Redsands Lake was to the west of Dongting Lake. Red sands might indicate the presence of cinnabar, the main ingredient of the elixir of immortality.

c. The fifth month is the height of summer. Presumably, the cold winds are on the peak of Yuelu mountain, and the incense burners of the next line are at Daolin.

d. Buddhist monasticism divided day and night into six periods. According to the *Amituo Sūtra* 阿彌陀經 (which provides a number of the details Du Fu cites throughout this poem), "In the [pure] land of that buddha [i.e., Amitābha], celestial music is constantly played. The ground is made of gold, and, throughout the six periods, heavenly mandāra flowers rain down."

e. The "Mountains of Snow" are the Himalayas; this is the translation of the Sanskrit name of that mountain range. According to the *Laṅkāvatāra Sūtra* 楞嚴經, the grasses of the Himalayas are so pure that, when yaks eat them, their dung can be used as perfume.

f. The saṃgha-treasure is one of the Three Treasures (*triratna*) of Buddhism: the Buddha, Dharma, and Saṃgha (clergy). Pearls are common metaphors for perfect excellence in Buddhist texts (and elsewhere). This couplet continues to play upon the mountainous and watery settings of the two temples, respectively.

g. Jīvajīvaka birds had two heads that each called the same name; according to the *Amituo Sūtra*, both jīvajīvaka birds and lotuses are characteristic of Amitābha's pure land.

12	金牓雙廻三足烏	their golden name plates each turn the three-footed crow.[h]
	方丈涉海費時節	Voyaging across the sea to the Immortal Isles takes a lot of time;
	玄圃尋河知有無	trace the River to the Mysterious Gardens— who knows if they're there or not?[i]
	暮年且喜經行近	In my twilight years, I delight rather in the closeness of meditative walks;
16	春日兼蒙暄暖扶	on spring days, I enjoy as well the support of sunny warmth.[j]
	飄然班白身奚適	Blown about, hair flecked with white, where is this body going?
	旁此煙霞茅可誅	beside these mists and rosy wisps, thatch can be cut.[k]
	桃源人家易制度	Here in Peach Blossom Spring, the householders enjoy lax regulations;
20	橘洲田土仍膏腴	on Tangerine Isle, the fields remain fertile and rich.[l]
	潭府邑中甚淳古	In the district city of Tan Prefecture, things have an ancient purity;
	太守庭內不喧呼	in the courtyard of the governor, there's no ruckus or clamor.
	昔遭衰世皆晦跡	In the past, those who encountered ages of decline all hid their traces;
24	今幸樂國養微軀	now I've lucked into a happy land to take care of my humble body.[m]

h. The three-footed crow is the crow in the sun; the golden name plates are so high they force the sun to turn its course.

i. The Mysterious Gardens are an abode of the immortals to the west, on the Kunlun (Himalayan) mountain range. The "Immortal Isles" is here literally "Fangzhang," one of the immortal isles in the eastern ocean. The term *fangzhang* could, however, also refer to a monk's cell.

j. "Meditative walks" is a Buddhist practice, used to prevent sleepiness. The "sunny warmth" of the springtime is likely due to the southerly location of these two temples.

k. That is, cut to roof a cottage.

l. Peach Blossom Spring was a legendary utopia, populated by folk who had fled from the imperial state. Tangerine Isle was an island in the Xiang River close to Changsha.

m. The phrase "happy land" originally derives from "Big Rat" 碩鼠 in the *Shijing*, but it is also used of Buddhist pure lands, as in the *Amituo Sūtra*.

依止老宿亦未晚	To entrust myself to the old monks here it is not too late;
富貴功名焉足圖	how could wealth, honor, deeds, or fame be worth the pursuit?
久爲野客尋幽慣	Long a traveler in the wilderness, I'm used to seeking secluded places;[80]
28 細學何顒免興孤	I've carefully studied Zhou Yong to avoid betraying my inspiration.[n]
一重一掩吾肺腑	Each fold, each layer here will be my lungs and guts;
仙鳥仙花吾友于	immortal birds and immortal flowers will be those I abide with and befriend.[o]
宋公放逐曾題壁	Lord Song, banished in exile, once wrote upon these walls,
32 物色分留與老夫	but he left part of the scene's beauty for this old man.[p]

We do not know for certain what Song Zhiwen 宋之問 (656–712) wrote on the temple wall here. Yang Lun points out, however, that the penultimate couplet of this poem echoes Song's "Lay of the High Mountain" 高山引, in which he wrote of the anguish of exile, gazing off towards the faraway northern capitals:[81]

n. Zhou Yong 周顒 was an official and a Buddhist thinker of the late fifth century who retired with his wife to a vihāra (a meditative retreat) in the mountains but accepted a high position when it was offered to him; he was subsequently mocked by Kong Zhigui 孔稚珪 (in his "Dispatch from the North Mountains" 北山移文) for engaging in a sort of false reclusion.

o. "Lungs and guts" was a phrase that often referred to intimate friends and family. "Those one befriends and abides with" are one's brothers (a phrase from the *Shangshu*). This couplet may recall a Buddhist ideal, articulated (for instance) by the Liang dynasty monk Xuanguang 玄光 in his "Discourse to Dispute Confusion" 辯惑論: "The earth and its mountains are all my old leavings, and the gray rivercourses and endless seas are my tears and blood. When one looks at it this way, who is there that is not a family member or friend?"

p. The poet Song Zhiwen had been banished to the region around the turn of the eighth century.

Each twist in the waters is a twist in my guts; / each layer of mountain a layer of grief. / The pines and catalpas [on my family's tombs] are lost in the distance; / what day will I see those I abide with and befriend?

水一曲兮腸一曲，山一重兮悲一重。松檟邈已遠，友于何日逢。[82]

For Song Zhiwen, scene and emotion joined together in alienation: all he saw was distance from his home. In invoking these lines, therefore, Du Fu is making a clear point. Where Song yearned to return to the capital and to government service, Du Fu will instead be happy here, having seen through the enticements of rank and wealth. For him, the landscape will not speak of alienation or distance but will instead be his home—or even, in a more literal interpretation of the phrase "lungs and guts," his very organs, an idea that might recall the trope of the cosmological Buddha, by which the landscapes of the world are manifestations of the enlightened being's transcendent body.[83]

Du Fu's statement that Song "left him a portion of the scenery" is an early prefiguration of the anxiety that plagued his postmedieval readers: that he had "already spoken all the good language of the world." Yet the contrast Du Fu draws between the potential home he sees in this landscape and the misery Song saw there suggests that the portion Song left him involves not so much unexplored topics as alternate perspectives on the same. In poetry, Yuelu Mountain and Daolin can be more than meets the eye, a possibility evidenced by the many descriptions here that suggest a transcendent interpretation hovering upon the mundane. The poem's references to Daolin's monks as "pearls of the ocean" and to Yuelu's vegetation as pure as the "Mountains of Snow," for instance, suggest that Du Fu may not need to travel to the dubious Immortal Isles of the eastern sea or the inaccessible Mysterious Gardens of Kunlun. Instead, he has already found in Tanzhou a "happy land" (*leguo* 樂國) full of "immortal birds and immortal flowers"—terms that can be read with either more or less transcendent significations. Where Song Zhiwen had seen here mundane misery, therefore, Du Fu imagines spending the rest of his days exploring the ways his poetry could exploit the monasteries' openness to interpretation, finding nirvana in their samsara.[84] And, in this imagination, the poem proleptically enacts the transcendence it projects, without his needing to actually make a life here—which, in the event, he would not do, being forced to leave Tanzhou after just a short time by a local rebellion.

This poem's proleptic enactment of an envisaged transcendence cannot but recall "Gazing on the Peak," in which Du Fu declared that he did not have to climb Mt. Tai to know what he would see from its summit.[85] Yet he has, in fact, come a long way from that early poetry. At this late stage in his poetic evolution, tradition no longer determines in advance what he would experience if he stayed in Tanzhou. Instead, its resources have shown him an indeterminacy of experience that may, in part, account for the remarkable flexibility and the ever-renewing optimism he displays in poems like this one, despite all the vicissitudes he has suffered. In this sense, if early poems like "Gazing on the Peak" are representative of late medieval tropology's attempt to tame contingency, the poems of his last months represent a surrender to it.[86]

白鳧行　　*Ballad of the White Duck*

君不見	Have you not seen
黃鵠高於五尺童	how the brown swan taller than a five-foot child,
化為白鳧似老翁	transforms into a white duck resembling an old man?[a]
故畦遺穗已蕩盡	The stalks of its old fields have all been shaken bare;
4　天寒歲暮波濤中	the weather's cold at year's end, and it is on the waves.
鱗介腥羶素不食	Scaly and shelled creatures reek, it never feeds on them;
終日忍飢西復東	it endures hunger all day long traveling west and then back east.
魯門鷄鶩亦蹭蹬	The frigate bird on Lu's gate was also in distress;

a. Though the above is the most obvious reading, some commentators have read the couplet differently: "Have you not seen how a child, taller than five feet like a brown swan, / transforms into an old man resembling a white duck?"

8   聞道如今猶避風   I hear that even nowadays
                                it still flees the wind.[b]

對雪   *Facing Snow*

北雪犯長沙   Northern snow invades Changsha;
胡雲冷萬家   barbarian clouds chill ten thousand homes.
隨風且閒葉   Following the wind, for a while it thins the leaves;
4   帶雨不成花   carrying rain, it does not form flowers.[c]
金錯囊徒罄   My purse is uselessly emptied of gold engravings,
銀壺酒易賒   though ale is easily advanced to those with silver jugs.[d]
無人竭浮蟻   Yet no one comes to drain the floating ants;[e]
8   有待至昏鴉   I wait, therefore, until the crows of dusk.[f]

Both of these poems consider the future of Du Fu's life and work. The deeply strange "Ballad of the White Duck," for instance, appears to be an

b. The *Guo yu* recounts that, in the seventh century BCE, a frigate bird perched on the gate of the capital of Lu. Zang Wenzhong 臧文仲, thinking it a god or prodigy, had sacrifices made to it. He was criticized for this improper religiosity by Zhan Huo 展獲, who argued that the bird must merely have been fleeing a storm on the ocean, its natural habitat. Later that same year, there was a great wind (a typhoon), and the winter was warm. Zang Wenzhong admitted that Zhan Huo must have been right.

c. The word "snow-flower" is the Chinese equivalent of the English "snowflake." "Thins" here should be understood visually: the snow comes between the viewer and the leaves but is not thick enough to white them out.

d. "Gold engravings" are "gold-engraved knife coins" 金錯刀.

e. The phrase "floating ants" refers to the frothing bubbles of the ale.

f. The *Songben* edition contains an early—perhaps authorial, perhaps spurious—note on this line: "He Xun's poem reads: 'Cold comes on the city, crossing black over the moat; the crows of dusk, their wings touching, all return'" 何遜詩云城陰度塹黑昏鴉接翅歸. No poem containing this couplet is found in He Xun's extant corpus, and the second line is suspiciously close to another of Du Fu's own poems. The phrase translated here as "wait" (*you dai* 有待) is ambiguous. It can mean to "harbor expectation" of someone's arrival, but it is also a technical term in Xuanxue and Daoist philosophy, with the meaning of "having dependence." In the *Zhuangzi*, we read that "Liezi could ride the wind, cool as you please, and could be gone for fifteen days without returning. . . . Yet although this talent allowed him to get out of walking, he still had dependence on something." Guo Xiang comments: "Without wind, he could not travel; this is having dependence. Only one for whom there is nothing he cannot ride has no dependence (*wu dai* 無代)."

allegory of the poet's translation into poetry. Though recordizing critics have predictably taken it to be offering the brown-swan-turned-white-duck as an analogical image for his aging from ambitious youth to peripatetic old man, the language in fact reads more easily in the reverse: as offering the poet as a figure for the eponymous fantastical bird.[87] By confounding the source and target of the metaphor in this way, the poem refuses to establish the concrete realities of Du Fu's life as its ultimate referent. Instead, that life also becomes an analogy for a poetic image that, the final couplet suggests, may survive beyond his death.

This suggestion, however, is carried in an allusion whose deployment both suggests again Du Fu's late interest in equivocations and also highlights the contingency to which such equivocations expose him. The original *Guo yu* story of the frigate bird revolved around competing interpretations of the bird's appearance, with Zang Wenzhong believing it a god and Zhan Huo arguing that it was, instead, just another fragile creature like us, buffeted by the vast storms of the world. In the story, Zang Wenzhong was ultimately forced to admit that Zhan Huo was right. Yet if, as Du Fu suggests here, the bird still flees the wind "even nowadays"—that is, in the text of the *Guo yu* and as a poetic trope—then Zang Wenzhong's initial imputation of divinity takes on an unexpected plausibility. The frigate bird is simultaneously fragile and immortal, an image of the way subjection to life's contingencies can become literary transcendence and literary transcendence, an endlessness of such subjection. As the white duck transforms back and forth between ambitious youth and broken old man, it becomes a symbol of Du Fu's life in poetry: hungry and homeless, but still out on the waves.

If "Ballad of the White Duck" thus takes up one way in which Du Fu's late interest in living into poetry accepts his subjection to contingency, "Facing Snow" considers the other. Though the poem seems at first merely to depict Du Fu anxious in a snowstorm to find someone who will provide him with ale, the final line's "I wait" (*you dai* 有待) can also have another, more abstract meaning. Drawing on a famous passage in the *Zhuangzi*, Xuanxue and Daoist thinkers from Guo Xiang up to Du Fu's own time used the phrase "to wait upon something" as a way of indicating heteronomy; the sage, by contrast, did not "wait upon" anything, being adaptable to any circumstance that came along.[88] If this poem, therefore, has Du Fu "waiting" from an invading barbarian snowstorm until the crows of dusk—figuratively, perhaps, from the Rebellion to his death—then it might represent a diagnosis of his life in exile, trapped in contingency, dependent on what comes.[89]

As seen throughout this chapter, however, contingency can occasion hope, and an allusion given in an early, perhaps authorial note to the final line suggests that what he has waited for throughout his life may yet come once it is ended, via his verse. Though it is difficult to be certain—for reasons I will get to in a moment—it is possible that this "Facing Snow" represents a palinode of the earlier poem by the same name, which this one seems to match in topic couplet by couplet (and which we read in the third chapter). And if indeed Du Fu is thinking here of that earlier poem, it might be no coincidence that this one concludes with an allusion to a Six Dynasties luminary. The earlier "Facing Snow" ended with a reference to the broken Jin dynasty general Yin Hao vainly "writing words in the air"—a figure for the madness of continuing to write poetry when one's only audience might be snow. In this poem, by contrast, the final allusion is to a poet, He Xun 何遜 (d. 518?), describing his own experience of being alone while watching cold weather steal upon a city towards dusk. If this note is reliable, the allusion might suggest that, for poets, writing alone is not necessarily "writing in air." Instead, Du Fu may be waiting here not merely for a contemporary to drink with, but also for readers who will have him in mind as he has He Xun and who may comfort his loneliness even after the twilight of his years.

Yet He's poem, alas, was lost by the Song dynasty—if it ever existed. Some critics have suspected, in fact, that the note is forgery, a couplet invented by some unscrupulous early commentator to "make sense" of an assuredly great poem that was otherwise—and, given this uncertainty, still remains—mysterious.[90] In both potentially discussing and powerfully demonstrating the unpredictability of its reception, "Facing Snow" thus illustrates the way Du Fu's final vision of his art surrendered his life to contingencies beyond his control. It is one of a great many poems in the dark reaches of his collection that remain poorly understood, and that continue to wait for the right reader to come along.

Conclusion

Poetry and Ethics

All of the poetic visions examined throughout this book are also ethical visions. To some degree, this connection is inevitable: what will count as good poetry will always depend in part on what it makes sense for poets to spend their time writing and readers to spend their time reading, and thus on questions of what makes for a "good life." In the premodern Chinese tradition, however, the mutual implication of poetics and ethics is foregrounded to a degree that has not always been as obvious elsewhere. Ever since Confucius legendarily included the *Poetry* among the Six Classics, those philosophers, literary theorists, and poets who took his legacy seriously have been forced to consider how the art might be important to living well, both for individuals and for the community at large.

For late medieval poets and thinkers—to recapitulate briefly here—the connection between poetry and ethics was generally anchored in the great tradition, This Culture of Ours. Most people, they assumed, would be incapable on their own of adequately conceptualizing the world or perfectly responding to its contingency, and therefore needed to rely on the models left by sages and worthies. Many of these models were embodied in texts, including literary texts, which could thus offer an arena for ethical activity. Poetry, for example, was understood to offer models of cognition, feeling, and commitment that would ineluctably shape readers' understanding of and responses to their own circumstances. One way of being a good person, therefore, involved reading good poetry and writing more of it, thereby propagating the normative models of the tradition in one's own time and transmitting them to the future.

This is the vision that largely animates the poetry of Du Fu's youth, before the Rebellion. It is not, however, the account of poetry's value that has predominantly animated his postmedieval critics in elevating him to the pinnacle of the Chinese poetic pantheon. That account—which I have labeled here "recordizing reading"—holds instead that most of us do have the resources necessary for recognizing the salient moral contours of our lives. Poetry, therefore, needs less to provide models of cognition and feeling that are transhistorically applicable and more to model the appropriate use of our capacities to understand and to feel particular situations. It is for this reason that, although Du Fu has been praised for many virtues, his perceptual acuteness and the transparency of his work are consistently at the core of critics' assessments of him: he is the Poet Sage because he is the Poet Historian. By recording what he lived through, he models for his readers a careful attention to the inherent moral truth of history.

Finally, Du Fu's own increasingly self-conscious accounts of his own poetics are also ethical visions, different from both the late medieval and the recordizing models. As responsive to his innovations as I have suggested recordizing reading often is, the epochal shift from one paradigm to the other does not track perfectly the evolution of his poetic thought throughout his lifetime. If, for instance, he did come after the Rebellion to pay closer attention to the particular ethical contours of his experience than the late medieval model generally encouraged his contemporaries to do, it was not because he was convinced that such attention would allow him to understand the moral truth of the situations he encountered. To the contrary, it was because he was bewildered by the failure of the tradition to provide adequate models of cognition or feeling for a life that was not well precedented by its exemplars. To the end of his days, therefore, he doubted not just his capacity to fully understand his experience, but also his own moral stature, having "accomplished nothing, with tears that fall like rain"—to quote the last line of his last poem, written when he was sick with the fever that would end his wandering life.[1]

Paradoxically, however, it is precisely this bewilderment—to borrow Lee H. Yearley's useful description—that forms the core of Du Fu's mature accounts of his poetry's moral meaning. These accounts revolve around his sense, articulated in the complex allusiveness of his post-Rebellion poetry, of what we might call "moral contingency."[2] Extrapolating from this poetry the rudiments of a metaethical theory, we might say that Du Fu doubts the possibility of indefinitely applicable moral categories. The conceptual tools by which we make moral judgments, he suggests, are always inherited from a past that can—and, in a world as various and changeable as ours has proven to be, often will—diverge from the exigencies of the present. As a result, not only are our values unlikely to be either universal or timeless; more important, if we pay careful attention to the details of our experience, they are unlikely to work unproblematically even here and now. In order to make satisfying moral sense of our lives, therefore, we may need more than is provided by any one moral culture at any one moment.

To the degree that it suggests that we do not have access to timeless, universal, or necessary moral truths, this rudimentary metaethical position might seem to verge on moral relativism or even moral skepticism. It is true, for instance, that the idea of moral contingency implies that values may differ across communities and over time, and it is equally true that, after the failure of This Culture of Ours, Du Fu never again considers the possibility of a community for which all ethical perplexities will have dissolved. But he is neither a relativist nor a skeptic. Instead, by observing the collapse of his own moral culture in the wake of the An Lushan Rebellion, he treats his experience as both a criterion for falsifying ethical ideas and a source for new ones—something a moral skeptic would presumably not do. And by exploring the problematic applicability of traditional concepts to the particular circumstances of his life, he offers reason to doubt whether the moral systems of any community actually serve it as well as relativism requires.[3]

I suspect, in fact, that a number of fairly robust prescriptions could be developed starting from Du Fu's decidedly nontheoretical explorations of moral contingency, and that the sequent phases of his poetic development might prove exemplary of the virtues they would enjoin.[4] At the same time, however, I doubt any elaborated moral theory could do full justice to his late poetics. Had he wanted to, he could himself have written a "philosophical" treatise, a *lun* 論 or a *zishu* 子書. If he dedicated himself instead to poetry, it may have been partly because the art fit better with his evolving moral vision, its generic affordances rendering it more apt to articulating the insufficiency of any given ethical perspective and to reaching out towards many.

Poetry as a Moral Medium

Some indication of poetry's capacity as this sort of moral medium is suggested by the structure of the thousand-year commentary tradition that has formed around Du Fu's collection. Works within this tradition predominantly endeavor to translate his verse into more straightforward, more elaborated, and more coherent propositions—much as I have done in this book. Yet the interest of those propositions always reposes implicitly on their insufficiency to the poetry itself, since were its riches to be exhausted by them, it would hardly merit commentary in the first place. In this sense, the generic expectation that poetry may require elucidation, while nonetheless remaining both more evocative and more precise than any elucidation could be, inherently predisposes the art to transcending any one articulated moral perspective.

A generic expectation of poetry's greater power as a moral medium, in comparison to more propositional forms of discourse, was a feature of Du Fu's own literary context as well, though contemporary thought turned it to different ends. According to the late medieval model, that is, it was the literary patterning of verse that made it particularly apt for conveying ethical orientations, its rhythms and intensities embodying the writer's emotions and involving the reader's body in the process of re-creating them.[5] This literary patterning, moreover, was commensurate to the patterning that poetry was supposed to promote in the body politic, *wen* as literature translating into *wen* as culture to ensure the iteration of normative values throughout society and across time. These moral imperatives were reflected in the short, occasional form of the art, which allowed its allusions to bring the weight of tradition to bear upon the present moments it characteristically discussed, thus modeling for readers the essential moral process they were subsequently expected to perform in bringing the poem's own values to bear upon their own experiences. Poetry was thus formally commensurate to the structure of morality as it was understood in the late medieval period: a system of propagating analogies that formed readers into the sort of moral adepts who would know before reading what the next good poem could say, who would "match tallies with it in their minds."

This account of the art's moral capacities underwrote Du Fu's early verse, and it was by inverting crucial features of this paradigm that he would turn his later poetry from a technology for propagating analogies into an exploration of disanalogies. Like his contemporaries, he continued to write mostly in short, highly allusive forms that allowed him to apply the resources of the past to his ongoing experience. But from the outbreak of the Rebellion onwards, his allusions are often problematic. Instead of invoking the tradition in such a way as to conform the present to it, he makes use of its resources to reflect on the obscurity, the idiosyncrasy, and the ambiguity of his experience. In this respect, his poetry rearranges the iterative chain characteristic of the late medieval model. If the ideal reader in his time was one who already embodied the values a good poem would express, Du Fu's focus on failures of precedent and interruptions in analogy ensures that his readers, no matter how steeped they might be in the cultural tradition, will not know in advance what he is trying to say. His poems become puzzles for his readers, much as the experiences they describe were puzzles to him.

Whereas the late medieval model figured poetry as a chain of normative repetitions encoding civilizational stability across time, then, Du Fu reconfigures it as a chain of bewilderment propelling a search for new ideas. Just as the collapse of his culture's moral certainties drove him to experiment with novel solutions to the puzzles of his life, that is, so too do the puzzles of his poems encourage his readers to seek out innovative interpretations to dispel their obscurities. And in both cases, the difficulty of these enigmas is crucial to their continuing interest. Not only does the problematic applicability of the tradition leave underdetermined both the moral interpretation of Du Fu's experience and the text of his poems that attempt it. When he seeks to ameliorate this underdetermination by treating individual experiences as part of a broader narrative of his life, moreover, he winds up massively overdetermining them, rendering his solutions provisional to an unknown future and his readers', likewise, dependent on convergent solutions to the rest of his verse. For these reasons, Du Fu never arrived at a final interpretation of his life's moral meaning, and his critics have always found more work to be done.

Yet although their endeavors are thus always incomplete, it is nonetheless in the ongoing attempts of such readers that we fulfill the hopes he articulates in his late works: that his problematic life should be revealed in time to have been a good one. In those rare moments when we break through bewilderment to a satisfying interpretation of a given poem, we discover the sense in what initially appeared not to make it, both to us and, in a different way, to Du Fu himself. Crucially, the over- and underdetermination of the verse ensure that the criteria by which we recognize such a discovery are rarely linguistic or historical only. Instead, just as the late medieval model required an adept reader who already knows what a good poet will say, so too can we not be fully satisfied we have understood what Du Fu is saying until it makes sense that he would have been saying it. And as our own ethical and aesthetic predilections inform our solutions to the ethical and aesthetic puzzles of his verse, a striking reorientation occurs. Suddenly, the moral divergences between individuals, eras, and ethical worlds that previously drove the obscurity of Du Fu's life and work prove, on the contrary, synergic, his disjunctive use of past precedents coming to describe the details of his present situation in a way that, from our future vantage point, seems apt and even ethically laudable. In such breakthrough moments, we thread together a tradition very different from that of the late medieval model.

Although recordizing criticism has not generally perceived itself as bringing to bear on Du Fu's work moral ideas that would have been foreign to him, it nonetheless can demonstrate the point. Not only does the millennium-spanning length of the commentary tradition testify both to the enduring obscurity of his collection and its alluring promise to someday make sense. More specifically, the assiduous historical research that animates recordizing reading attests his poetry's underdetermination; the fact that critics still generally ignore large portions of his oeuvre, after a thousand years of such research, suggests the difficulties created by its overdetermination; and the prominent role very different moral theories, from Neo-Confucianism to Maoism, have played in guiding the results of this research indicates how this combination of over- and underdetermination involves readers' ethical intuitions in its interpretation. And yet, despite these difficulties, there has hardly been a commentator who has not claimed his commentary unlocks the previously unappreciated moral significance of Du Fu's life and work. In this way, recordizing reading has been a tradition in two different senses. On the one hand, it has been remarkably consistent in its adherence to the basic idea that poetry should be a transparent record of moral truths immanent in historical experience itself. On the other, its insistence that this paradigm of poetic meaning, in fact radically new, articulates the moral significance of Du Fu's verse and the normative form of Chinese poetry since the *Shijing*—especially as both keep changing to match the evolving exigencies of different eras—reveals recordizing criticism as creatively maintaining a larger tradition whose unity, ultimately, lies in transformation.

What I have tried to suggest in this book is that it is no coincidence that this tradition, in the limited sense of the word, should also have been secretly committed to the maintenance of tradition in the larger sense as well. Instead, it has in this respect responded both to the articulated hope of Du Fu's mature work and to the poetic mechanisms he found to enact it.[6] It is, finally, this homology between the form of his verse, its moral vision, and the tradition it has created that renders his poetry more compelling than any propositional account of that vision could be—very much including my own. Indeed, if my reading of his work is onto something, it cannot, by its own lights, be complete. It is, rather, merely a means of participating in a tradition that, if we are to remain faithful to Du Fu, must always find new ways of continuing on.

A Shared Moral Project

At a certain point in this research, I thought my contribution to the tradition of Du Fu criticism might involve bringing to bear on his work the insights of recent discussions, in both literary criticism and Anglo-American philosophy, of literature's potential as a moral medium. Over the last century and particularly since the 1980s, a number of scholars have explored how homologies between literary form and content create spaces for ethical reflection that cannot be replicated in more theoretical genres, and many of their conclusions seem relevant, mutatis mutandis, to thinking about the role Du Fu's poetry has played in the moral economy of China over the last millennium.[7] Recordizing critics, in fact, have located the ethical import of his verse along each of the four main branches Joshua Landy has outlined in a recent typology of such theoretical accounts: the exemplary, the affective, the cognitive, and the formative.[8] They have, that is, taken Du Fu as exemplifying virtue in an age of disorder, as modeling the emotions that are constitutive of a rich inner life, as providing valuable information about the processes of history, and as teaching us ways of properly appreciating their significance as they play out in our own lives.

Beyond Landy's typology, the close adherence of Du Fu's poetry to the contours of his life also dovetails nicely with recent work suggesting that literature's ethical promise lies in its capacities to challenge the abstract thinking that has often dominated moral theory, to complexify the problems such theory works to solve, to ground ethical thought in the dense realities of real human lives, or to encourage us to accept the limitations incumbent upon the sort of moral beings that we are.[9] Given that most of these ideas have been developed exclusively in connection with novels from the modern West, moreover, their application to the work of a premodern Chinese poet seemed likely to be fruitful both in broadening and in specifying their claims.[10]

Yet though Du Fu may in fact have shaped his readers' moral perspectives in all these ways, the difficulty of studying this effect began to warn me away from doing so—not to mention my growing suspicion that he probably shaped different individuals and different eras differently. More important, it gradually dawned on me that the most obvious role he has played in his readers' lives did not fit along any of these lines. Rather, in building on the work of their predecessors and contributing to the cumulative edifice of historical research that supports recordizing reading, his critics have consistently attested, despite the changing details of their particular ethical and political paradigms, to the access his work has provided them to a shared moral project stretching across centuries. That Du Fu should have written in such a way as to make this possible is, I have come to think, an achievement that is ethical in character and conducive, moreover, to his readers' living better lives.

Most concretely, the participatory quality of Du Fu's poetry may render it particularly well suited to encouraging its disparate readers to see themselves as potential collaborators in a community of moral interpretation. Although, as discussed, Du Fu has often been invoked at moments of crisis to distinguish the "Chinese" from "foreign" invaders, his work nonetheless remained canonical in so-called conquest dynasties and may eventually have played some small role in shoring up their mixed communal identities. Despite his importance to Ming loyalists, for instance, the Manchu rulers of the Qing also promoted his poetry and the patriotic values it purportedly encouraged.[11] And despite simmering tensions between China and Japan, his verse has in recent years created opportunities for scholarly exchange between them, with both sides viewing it as, to greater or lesser degrees, part of their own tradition. Going forward, it is to be hoped that similar exchanges will continue between East Asia and the rest of the world.

As Du Fu recognized particularly in his Kuizhou era work, moreover, effective synchronic communities are, to a significant degree, functions of imagined diachronic solidarity. Even more than horizontal linkages, therefore, his poetry encourages his readers to imagine themselves members of a shared vertical community, across time.[12] Such transtemporal communities were always important to Du Fu, but they became even more so in his exile—a development that partially explains why, as he wrote towards a future he could not predict, his poetry became even more densely studded with allusions to the past. In his late work, these allusions no longer stake a claim to timeless wisdom, but rather suggest the commonality of the moral obscurities he thinks define our lives. As we read Du Fu, therefore, we are invited to consider the possibility that the distant past of his allusions, the middle past of his life, and the proximate past of the commentary tradition are not, ultimately, foreign to us; that instead they may contain crucial elements for our own moral futures.

In this sense, Du Fu's poetry militates against what Samuel Scheffler has called "temporal parochialism." According to Scheffler, there is a danger that, as "our sense of the connections among different human generations [becomes] increasingly impoverished," we may disregard the good reasons we have to participate in, preserve, and transmit inherited traditions, and may fail to recognize our moral dependence on the future, that "what is necessary to sustain our confidence in our values[, ultimately,] is that we should die and that others should live."[13] Scheffler identifies this temporal parochialism as a particular danger of our current moment, in which environmental and political crises threaten to leave to future generations neither the moral resources they will need to make sense of their lives nor the material resources necessary for living them well. But it is no coincidence that Du Fu too was responding to what seemed to him the imminent collapse of a great, if flawed, culture. Although the An Lushan Rebellion did not quite endanger the existence of future generations, he likewise had reason to worry that his lifetime would coincide with a decisive break between the past and the future, after which the values he learned in his youth and the tradition that informed them might be forgotten as obsolete. After all, these values and this tradition no longer worked well even for him. With the past threatening to be swallowed up into an oblivion of failed moral and political ideas and the future to become unrecognizable, human history seemed on the brink of transforming from the proving ground for the unbroken thread of This Culture of Ours to a discontinuous series in which no life could remain significant for long.

It was in response to this threat, ultimately, that Du Fu abandoned the comforting communities of late medieval poetry and late medieval ethics for a more speculative solidarity he could live only as an exile. In writing not for his contemporaries but rather for readers whose moral proclivities he could not predict, he seems to have recognized that the exigencies of enacting a particular set of settled values will always conflict with those of bridging the discontinuities between such sets. The rigor, purity, and clarity that motivate the like-minded may come to seem brittle to communities otherwise constituted, and no matter how frustrating it may be to work alongside anyone who cultivates a moral style involving irony, enigma, and plenitude, these equivocal virtues in the here-and-now can play significant roles in the long-term success of endeavors whose fruits lie in the future.[14] For this reason, although any given ethical perspective may allot some narrow space within which poetry can be moral, within the larger scope of human history, any perduring ethical accomplishment will have to be poetry, and will, as such, have to dally with incomprehension, isolation, and failure. And it is precisely as this sort of venture into the unknown that Du Fu's work is both an ethical achievement and an enduring paradox: that precisely in living a failed life according to the standards of the tradition as it was understood in his time, he ended up living well according to the transforming tradition Chinese moral poetics has actually proven to be.

Abbreviations

DFQJ   Xiao Difei 蕭滌非 et al., eds., *Du Fu quanji jiaozhu* 杜甫全集校注

LQL   Lu Qinli 逯欽立, ed., *Xian Qin Han Wei Jin Nan-Beichao shi* 先秦漢魏晉南北朝詩

QTW   *Quan Tang Wen* 全唐文, edited by Deng Hao 董浩 et al.

SB   Du Fu, *Songben Du Gongbu ji* 宋本杜工部集, edited by Wang Zhu 王洙

TPDF   Du Fu, *The Poetry of Du Fu*, translated by Stephen Owen

Notes

Note to the Reader

1. For a discussion of the rather complicated contents of the *Songben*, see Hung, "Tu Fu Again." For a more recent survey of scholarship on this still-debated edition, see Hasebe, *To Ho shibunshū*, 183–213.
2. Xiao's edition is obviously much more complete, but Owen's notes provide variants from *Wenyuan yinghua* and *Tang wen cui*, which are often inexplicably missing from Xiao's list of early variants.
3. As a rule, I avoid analyzing poems where a variant character or line radically changes the meaning of the poem; in the few instances where I find such a poem too compelling to exclude, I discuss the variant in an endnote.
4. Zhao Cigong, *Du shi jie*; Wang Sishi, *Du yi*; Qian Qianyi, *Qian zhu Du shi*; Zhu Heling, *Du Gongbu shiji jizhu*; Qiu Zhao'ao, *Du shi xiangzhu*; Pu Qilong, *Du Du xinjie*; Yang Lun, *Du shi jingquan*; Shi Hongbao, *Du Du shi shuo*; Guo Zengxin, *Du Du zhaji*; Cheng Shankai, *Du shi jianji*; Fu Gengsheng, *Du shi xi yi*; Han Chengwu and Zhang Zhimin, *Du Fu shi quan yi*; Li Shousong and Li Yiyun, *Quan Du shi xin shi*; Suzuki, *To shi*; Xiao Difei et al., *Du Fu quanji jiaozhu* (hereafter *DFQJ*); Xie Siwei, *Du Fu ji jiaozhu*; Xin Yingju, *Du shi xin buzhu*; Xu Renfu, *Du shi zhujie shangque* and *Du shi zhujie shangque xubian*; Yoshikawa, *To Ho shichū*; Zhang Zhilie, *Du shi quanji jinzhu ben*; and Zheng Wen, *Du shi jinggu*.
5. Bender, "Du Fu: Poet Historian, Poet Sage," 353–423.
6. Chen Yixin, *Du Fu pingzhuan*; *DFQJ*; and Cai Zhichao, *Du shi xinian kaolun*.

Introduction

1. Many of these dynamics have been described by previous scholars, in particular Frank Kermode in both *The Classic* and *Pleasure and Change*.
2. My sense of the Tang interpretation of This Culture of Ours is much indebted to Bol's eponymous book.
3. In this respect, I want to suggest that Du Fu experienced something like the situation described by Jonathan Lear in *Radical Hope*. Of course, the lifeworld of Tang China did not collapse entirely with the Rebellion, and most of Du Fu's contemporaries did continue to understand their lives in the old ways. Yet the seeds had been sown of the sweeping intellectual changes that were to come, and Du Fu eventually came to recognize that traditional visions of the good life had become impossible for him. In this respect, his situation might be considered intermediate between the more specific situation described by Lear in *Radical Hope* and the more general one he describes in *A Case for Irony*.

4. "Sense" and "sense-making" are not terms that have been frequently used to discuss Chinese poetics, the basic orientations of which have often been depicted as expressive and affective, sometimes in contrast to the supposedly greater focus on mimesis and its correlates—artifice, metaphysics, and allegorical truth—in Western poetics (see, for example, Miner, *Comparative Poetics*). Within this context, part of the burden of this book is to suggest that Chinese poetics has often been concerned with the cognitive and ethical questions of how we should go about making sense of our experience and our world. The terminology of "sense" and "sense-making" is borrowed, originally, from Kermode, *Sense of an Ending*. These terms have also been employed in a number of other recent studies, particularly those inspired by the hermeneutical tradition.

5. This point can be easily demonstrated from the vast quantity of reception history on Du Fu that has been published in recent years. See, for instance, Kurokawa, "Chū-Tō yori"; Jian Ending, *Qingchu Du shi*; Chen Wenhua, *Du Fu zhuan ji*; Chou Shan, "Wenxue shengyu"; Shan Chou (Chou Shan), *Reconsidering Tu Fu*; Chai Jen-nian, *Du shi Tang Song jieshou*; Sun Wei, *Qingdai Du shi*; Hartman, "Tang Poet Du Fu"; Yang Jinghua, *Songdai Du shi*; Chen Meizhu, *Qingchu Du shi*; Han Languo, *Liao Jin Yuan*; Liu Wengang, *Du Fu xue shi*; Owen, "Tang Version"; Li Gui, *Zhong Tang zhi Bei Song*; Wu Zhongsheng, *Du Fu piping*; Zou Jinxian, *Songdai Du shi*; Jue Chen, "Making China's Greatest Poet"; and Hao, *Reception*. I am indebted to this scholarship throughout this book.

6. For the aesthetics of the fragment, see Owen, *Remembrances*, 1–15.

7. See Zhang Zhonggang et al., *Du ji xulu*, 101–4. The claim is hyperbolic.

8. I will use the terms "ethical" and "moral" interchangeably throughout this book. Though I am persuaded by Bernard Williams's critique in works like his *Ethics and the Limits of Philosophy* of the narrowness of the inherited Western "system of morality," when I use either term, I hope it will be understood that I refer to the larger scope of "ethics" as Williams defines it: namely, as pertaining to the question of "how one should live."

9. I will be focusing in this book only on contrasts between the ways that Du Fu's contemporaries and his later critics discuss poetry's ethical value. Given that poetry in both medieval and postmedieval China was a social medium used among friends, between petitioners and patrons, and in political contexts, the art had a wide variety of ethical entailments that are not commonly discussed (at least not explicitly) in the literary-critical sources I will be mining. It also had a number of functions that we might reasonably term "ethical" that did not change so dramatically over time. My discussion of the relationship between Chinese poetry and ethics is thus not intended to be comprehensive.

10. On this point, see Owen, *Great Age*, 225–46 and 253–303, as well as Jiang Yin, *Dali shifeng*. There were momentous changes in the poetry of the period, but they were more geographical and social than stylistic in character. The same cannot be said, however, about other genres of intellectual activity. For discussions of the intellectual historical significance of the late eighth century, see Pulleyblank, "Neo-Confucianism and Neo-Legalism," as well as McMullen, "Historical and Literary Theory" and *State and Scholars*.

11. My discussions of the "late medieval model" of poetry's ethical significance should be understood not as simply translating a vision given entire in existing texts, but rather as an attempt to extrapolate and harmonize the most commonly discussed ideas about poetry's ethical significance from these centuries into an intellectually coherent account of the art. Not every idea proposed during this period will fit this model, not all of its aspects are equally salient in all contexts, and both individuals and groups advanced significant variants, sometimes in polemical tension with one another. (For works that emphasize such polarities, see, for instance, Wu Guangxing, *Ba shiji shifeng*, and Nagata, *Tōdai no bungaku riron*.) The ideas constitutive of this model, however, often underlie and enable such debates, and I doubt that a fundamentally different, intellectually coherent, and widely shared paradigm of poetry's moral significance can be constructed out of the materials that survive from the late medieval period. "Late medieval," it should be noted, is intended merely as a period term, denoting that there are significant continuities in poetic thought throughout these three centuries, without thereby implying that this period is somehow "belated" with respect to the medieval period as a whole.

12. I intend the admittedly ugly neologism "recordizing reading" to encompass many of the same tendencies Ji Hao has recently labeled "the mode of life reading"; for his useful history of the development of this critical mode from the Song dynasty to the advent of modernity, see his *Reception of Du Fu*. It should be stressed, as Hao does with his "mode of life reading," that recordizing reading is only one impulse within Du Fu criticism and that, despite its prevalence over the last millennium, it has been both combined with and sometimes eclipsed by other concerns (see particularly his third chapter on alternate modes of reading from the Yuan through the mid-Ming). Though I do not discuss those other concerns in any depth here, I hope nonetheless to avoid giving the impression that "recordizing reading" has been an unchanging monolith. Quite the contrary, I would consider a discussion of the ways it changes over its history a friendly amendment to my own argument here about the ways traditions inevitably change over time. I focus on aspects of recordizing reading that remain largely constant, then, to make one central point: that when the urge to treat poems as records comes on the scene, it renders many late medieval ideas about poetry impossible to sustain.

13. This transition is often discussed under the rubric of the "Tang–Song transition" first described in the 1920s by Naitō Konan 内藤湖南 (Naitō Torajirō); see especially "Gaikatsuteki Tō-Sō jidai kan" 概括的唐宋時観 in *Naitō Konan zenshū*, 8:111–19. For reviews of scholarship on this topic, see (among others) Smith and von Glahn, *Song-Yuan-Ming Transition*; Bao Bide, "Tang–Song zhuanxing"; Zhang Guangda, "Naitō Konan de Tang–Song biange shuo"; and Yinan Luo, "Study of the Changes." Though I am deeply indebted to this research, because the issues I am interested in here do not precisely track the periodization of Tang and Song, I employ period terms that do not carry the baggage associated with the Tang–Song transition, namely, "late medieval" and "postmedieval."

14. Other accounts of the transition in poetic understanding between Tang and Song have been offered, most notably in Fuller, *Drifting among Rivers and Lakes*, which remains the most sensitive account available of poetic change in Chinese history and

from which I have learned a great deal. Fuller, however, accepts a vision of Tang poetics details of which I dispute here since they have been influenced by Du Fu's retrospective dominance within the Tang canon.

15. The Han Yu "quote" that Qiu cites is almost certainly a false attribution, though Han Yu did praise Du Fu effusively elsewhere. For an excerpt from Yuan Zhen's comment, see chapter 3 below. For Han Yu's authentic comments about Du Fu, see Hua Wenxuan, *Du Fu juan,* 8–12.

16. Qiu Zhao'ao, *Du shi xiangzhu,* "Yuan xu," 1–2.

17. For other concise statements of the presumptions of recordizing reading, see (for instance) Yang Lun, *Du shi jingquan,* "Zi xu," 8; *Du shi yanzhi,* "Xu," 5; and Mo Lifeng, "Zenyang du Du Fu shi."

18. The distrust of poetry (as of "belles-lettres" in general) derives largely from Song dynasty Daoxue; on this topic, see Bol, *"This Culture,"* 300–344; Fuller, "Aesthetics and Meaning"; and Fuller, *Drifting among Rivers and Lakes.*

19. A thorough annotation of this piece can be found in Li Yunyi's commentary to *Lu Zhaolin ji jiaozhu,* 6.311–34.

20. For a discussion of Yuan Jie's life and thought, see McMullen, "Yuan Chieh."

21. For these poems, see Yuan Jie, *Xinjiao Yuan Cishan,* 3.34–36.

22. *SB* 6; *DFQJ,* 4813; *TPDF* 19.40. Line 9: *Maoshi zhushu,* 20.439b. 10: *Lunyu jishi,* 18.616. 14: For instance, *Lunyu jishi,* 3.91. 25: *Lunyu jishi,* 25.861. 32: *Laozi jiaoshi,* 13.48. 34: Yuan Jie, *Xinjiao Yuan Cishan,* 3.36. 42: See Yu Shinan 虞世南, "Bisui lun" 筆髓論, *QTW,* 138.1402b; see also Tang Taizong's 唐太宗 "Bifa lun" 筆法論, *QTW,* 7.123a. 44: *Zhouyi zhushu,* 8.171b.

23. Literally, this phrase is "the form of comparison and affective image," two of the techniques canonically attributed to the authors of the *Classic of Poetry.* As Tang Yuanhong 唐元竑 (1590–1647) points out, however, neither comparison nor affective image is employed in either of Yuan's poems; see Tang, *Du shi jun,* 4.6a. The point would seem to be merely that Yuan is imitating the *Classic of Poetry,* though more has been made of the phrase by other scholars; see, for example, Mo Lifeng, *Du Fu pingzhuan,* 312; Zhang Changdong, "Shilun Du Fu"; and Deng Fang, "Yuan Jie yuefu."

24. For this understanding of the *Poetry,* see *Maoshi zhushu,* 1.11a–20a.

25. On the concept of "understanding" in medieval China, see Shields, *One Who Knows Me,* 44–48.

26. Gao Chufang, *Ji qianjia zhupidian,* 17.1371.

27. Wang Sishi, *Du yi,* 9.313.

28. Pu Qilong, *Du Du xinjie,* 1.6.184.

29. Chen Yixin, *Du Fu pingzhuan,* 1013.

30. Mo Lifeng, *Du Fu pingzhuan,* 312–13.

31. See *Lunyu jishi,* 23.779, and *Lunyu jijie yishu,* 6.152–53. Huang Kan's 黃侃 (488–544) subcommentary to this passage in the latter is particularly revealing as to the medieval understanding of the relationship between the "worthy" and the "sage." On this topic, see Makeham, *Transmitters and Creators,* 97–127; and Ashmore, *Transport of Reading.*

32. *Zhouyi zhushu,* 8.171b. For what I take to be an exemplary medieval understanding of the significance of Yan Hui's only coming "somewhat close to incipiency," see Xie Lingyun's 謝靈運 (385–433) "Bian zong lun" 辨宗論, *Taishō,* 52.2103.224c–25a.

33. For an excellent reading of this poem that overlaps in significant ways with the one presented here, see Hsieh, "Meeting through Poetry." See also McMullen, "Du Fu's Political Perspectives."

34. For Du Fu's complaints about his social obligations in Kuizhou, see (for example) *TPDF* 21.17, "Returning at Night" 夜歸. For his poetry designated as "presentations" to dead luminaries, see 16.6–13, "Eight Sorrowful Poems" 八哀詩. For his poetry to his servants and children, see chapter 6 in this book; Patterson, "Elegies for Empire," 126–49; Jiang Xianwei, *Du Fu Kuizhou shi*, 122–43; and my "Ironic Empires."

35. As Michaela Bronstein has demonstrated, other writers in periods of trauma and transition have also become interested in the past and future of tradition. She shows that several modernist authors turned to the past in order to consider "what, exactly, was persistent about human existence—what was likely to last, rather than what would be discarded, questioned, demolished by the future" (*Out of Context*, 9). Du Fu, I will argue, was less interested in finding values that would persist, but he was similar to these authors in attempting to write for future audiences he knew would inhabit a world different from his own. For this reason, many of the larger methodological arguments Bronstein offers are relevant to my project here as well.

36. Debates about "tradition" have seethed since the Enlightenment, centering on questions of tradition's relationship to rationality, of the extent to which the modern world is (or could ever be) "detraditionalized," and of tradition's value (either as such or with regard to particular traditions). These debates are far too complex to detail here, though Shils, *Tradition*, can be recommended to interested readers as a good place to start. "Tradition" (*chuantong* 傳統) is also a fraught term in modern Chinese cultural politics in ways that inevitably influence the study of Du Fu in China today. In lieu of a thorough discussion, let me indicate simply that I am aware of the ethnonationalist connotations the concept often takes on in this context. For more on Du Fu's place in ethnonationalist discourse, see chapter 6.

37. That is, I read each of his poems in three ways: in its relation to the precedent tradition, in its interpretation by later scholars, and in the context of Du Fu's poetic development. For an argument that something like this procedure is generally necessary in the reading of premodern works, see Pollock, "Philology in Three Dimensions." For the ethical and political importance of the attempt to ground texts in their traditional contexts, see Appiah, "Thick Translation." In practice, much of the work of "thick translation" here will come in the form of excavating Du Fu's allusions. The allusiveness of his work is also discussed in E Shan Chou, "Tu Fu's Eight Laments"; Shan Chou, "Allusion and Periphrasis"; Wan Liu, "Poetics of Allusion"; Cui Yannan, "Du Fu shige"; and Nugent, "Sources of Difficulty."

38. Here it might be remarked that, on balance, Western scholars have been more interested in the epochal transformations of Chinese poetry than have Chinese scholars. In the West, indeed, there has been a cottage industry of dissertations and scholarly monographs exploring the "construction" of such-and-such great Chinese poet at the hands of later critics. This interest no doubt reflects the critical tendencies of the humanities in general over the last half-century in the Americas and Europe, but it may sometimes have more unsettling motivations as well. In his recent book *Why Literary Periods Mattered*, Ted Underwood argues that, within the Anglo-American world, ideas about the discontinuity of historical periods have long been crucial to

supporting the claims of "culture" (that is, high culture, in the Arnoldian sense) against other forms of prestige, be they hereditary or economic. Through education and wide literary sympathy, the educated middle class could effectively inherit a past that, by virtue of its purported discontinuity, can no longer be inherited in the bloodline. "The cultured individual ... [identified] with the eternity of history itself, which was grasped, not as an overarching teleology or a principle of eternal recurrence, but in the ephemeral singularities that distinguished an infinite series of different historical forms receding into the past" (143). Underwood's book might suggest a disturbing parallel between the bourgeois literature teachers he describes striving against a hereditary aristocracy, on the one hand, and, on the other, the research of newly minted Western PhDs attempting to overturn the work of Chinese scholars. My methodology here has been motivated, in part, by my awareness of the possibility that my own interest in the "transformations" of the Chinese literary tradition may have such unconscious sociological dimensions. I also want to avoid fitting a stereotype, spelled out to me by Mo Lifeng, that Westerners inherit a culture of "killing the father" (*shifu wenhua* 弑父文化).

39. This dynamic is roughly the reverse of that described by Paul de Man in *Blindness and Insight*.

40. It is a central implication of my argument that the Chinese poetic tradition has no unchanging essence that might render it alien from "our own" in the West, since at its center is a transformation. Though I will not discuss the point at length, I hope that this implication might offer a new perspective on the still-simmering debate, begun by Pauline Yu's *Reading of Imagery* and Stephen Owen's *Traditional Chinese Poetry and Poetics*, over the question of whether or not Chinese poetry begins from premises radically different from those of Western poetics. Scholars like Haun Saussy (in *The Problem of a Chinese Aesthetic* and *Great Walls of Discourse*) and Zhang Longxi ("What Is *Wen*?" and *Allegoresis*) have argued that more important similarities link the two traditions, and, in a recent article, Massimo Verdicchio ("Under Western Critical Eyes") has taken the arguments of Yu and Owen as reason to suggest that area studies as a whole are inherently inimical to the project of cross-cultural communication pursued by comparative literature (in this respect, he is taking aim at Spivak, *Death of a Discipline*, which had suggested an alliance). Paul Rouzer ("Du Fu and the Failure of Lyric"), by contrast, takes the argument in the opposite direction, showing that even Owen and Yu inevitably read Du Fu through current concerns and that we should therefore not expect to be able to (or perhaps even want to) fully appreciate a radically different literary culture. With the exception of Verdicchio, I believe, all of these scholars make useful points. The suggestion of this book, however, is that we can cut through some of their disagreements by more carefully examining the transformations of the Chinese poetic "tradition," which has not been so monolithic as to be either reliably different from or reliably similar to the Western "tradition."

41. Borges, *Everything and Nothing*, 76–78. For an earlier articulation of the same idea, see Keats, *Selected Letters*, 195. For theories of tradition that involve an agon between new writers and old, see Eliot, "Tradition and the Individual Talent," and Bloom, *Anxiety of Influence*.

ONE. Time and Authority

1. For the development of these paratextual genres, see Liu Mingjin, *Zhongguo gudai wenxue*, 390–414; Wu Hongze, "Songdai nianpu"; Zhang Bowei, *Zhongguo gudai wenxue*, 63–70; and, with specific reference to Du Fu, Xu Zong, *Du shi xue*, 25–41 and 65–74. For the development of Du Fu's *biannian* collection, see Jue Chen, "Making China's Greatest Poet," 137–88. For the origins of Du Fu commentary, see Hartman, "Tang Poet Du Fu"; Hartman, "Du Fu in the Poetry Standards"; and Yang Jinghua, *Songdai Du shi*. For broader reflections on the development of "chronological thinking" (*nenputeki shikō* 年譜的思考) in the reception of Chinese poetry in the eleventh and twelfth centuries, see Asami, *Chūgoku no shigaku*, 385–459.

2. For comprehensive listings of both surviving and lost premodern editions of Du Fu's poetry, see Zheng Qingdu et al., *Du ji shumu*; Zhou Caiquan, *Du ji shulu*; and Zhang Zhonggang et al., *Du ji xulu*.

3. They have become standard in the presentation of other poets as well, suggesting the degree to which Du Fu's reception has shaped the reading of the entire canon. I discuss this point further in chapter 4.

4. *SB* 9; *DFQJ*, 1276; *TPDF* 1.20.

5. *Wang Wei ji jiaozhu*, 4.408.

6. The first commentator to suggest this later dating seems to have been Lu Yin 魯訔 (1099–1175); see his *Caotang shi jian*, 14.333. Most editions through the mid-Qing, however, followed the interpretation of Huang He 黄鶴 (fl. 1200) given in Huang Xi and Huang He, *Bu zhu Du shi*, 17.25b–26a. The possibility of the later dating was revived (without attribution to Lu Yin) by Yang Lun 楊倫 (1747–1803); see *Du shi jingquan*, 5.218.

7. See Geng Yuanrui, "Du Fu zai Henan," 53.

8. For general treatments of print culture in China and particularly in the transition to the postmedieval world, see Inoue, *Chūgoku shuppan bunkashi* and the review by Cynthia Brokaw "Publishing, Society, and Culture in Pre-Modern China"; Brokaw and Chow, *Printing and Book Culture in Late Imperial China*; Cherniack, "Book Culture"; De Weerdt and Chia, *Knowledge and Text Production*; Chia, *Printing for Profit*; Drège, "Effets de l'imprimerie"; Poon, "Books and Printing"; and Twitchett, *Printing and Publishing*. For a discussion of the effect of printing on poetry in particular and with reference to the reception of Du Fu, see Yugen Wang, *Ten Thousand Scrolls*.

9. The concept of the *déjà lu*—the "already read," a reader's store of background texts against which any new text is interpreted—derives from Barthes, "Analyse textuelle."

10. Roughly estimating a copying rate of 1,500 graphs per hour, Du Fu's collection at its current size would have taken almost one hundred hours to copy. Using Mo Lifeng's (also rough) estimate of the size of the complete, sixty-scroll collection listed in Du Fu's biography in the *Jiu Tang shu* 舊唐書, copying it might have taken over two hundred hours. It is unlikely that the average reader would have invested enough time to make his own personal copy of a collection this large, and using a borrowed or library collection would have put limitations on the amount of historical research he could do on a given poem. For the original size of Du Fu's collection, see *Jiu Tang shu*, 190.5057, and Mo Lifeng, *Du Fu shige*, 13.

11. For Tang manuscript culture as it pertained to poetry, see Nugent, *Manifest in Words*, as well as Liu Yujun, *Siku Tangren wenji*, 21–30 and 42–53. A useful discussion of Nugent's book, with some caveats about his more radical conclusions, can be found in McMullen, "Boats Moored and Unmoored." For the role and nature of libraries, see Drège, *Bibliothèques*.

12. For the resources that Tang readers would have had for placing poetry into at least rough chronologies, see chapter 4.

13. For general discussions of reading in the medieval period, see Drège, "La lecture et l'écriture"; Jack W. Chen, "On the Act and Representation of Reading"; and Ashmore, *Transport of Reading*.

14. For the early sources of this concept, see DeWoskin, *A Song for One or Two*.

15. See *Maoshi zhushu*, 1.13b.

16. These numinous musicians also had access to the original music of the *Poetry*, which by Tang times had long been lost. See Van Zoeren, *Poetry and Personality*, especially 139–45.

17. Shi Jiaoran, *Shishi*, 1.42. For Jiaoran's poetics, see Nicholas Morrow Williams, "Taste of the Ocean."

18. See Liu Xie, *Zengding Wenxin diaolong*, 6.406 and 7.415.

19. Liu Xie, *Zengding Wenxin diaolong*, 10.592.

20. Most famously, Zhu Xi's 朱熹 (1130–1200) *Zhuzi dushu fa*.

21. *Liuchen zhu Wenxuan*, 1.1a. I have discussed this text and the implications of this claim in "Poetic Omens and Poetic History."

22. Zhang Huaiguan, "Wenzi lun" 文字論; see *QTW*, 432.4399a–b. 元 here is a standard taboo-character replacement for 玄. Zhang is writing in this text about calligraphy, but his rhetoric is representative of contemporary discourse about poetry (and painting) as well.

23. Shi Jiaoran, *Shishi*, "Shishi xu," 1.

24. On this metaphor, see Ashmore, *Transport of Reading*, 156–57.

25. Broad learning and comparative textual scholarship was, however, an ideal in Classical exegesis. See, for example, the "Shuzheng" 書證 chapter of Yan Zhitui's 顏之推 (531–91?) *Yanshi jiaxun*, 6.409–518.

26. A particularly clear example of this account of reading can be found in Zhang Yue's 張説 (667–731) grave inscription for Yin Shouzhen 尹守貞. See *QTW*, 2343b, along with my more detailed discussion of these issues in "Poet Historian, Poet Sage," 48–54.

27. *SB* 9; *DFQJ*, 68; *TPDF* 1.13. 8: For the association to Fan Li, see for instance *Taiping yulan*, 66.443b.

28. Opening and closing couplets can sometimes also be parallel, as the first couplet would be here if the variant 林風 is chosen over 風林. See *DFQJ*, 1.73.

29. Note that "darkness" and "springtime" are also opposed as instances of *yin* and *yang*, respectively. Similarly, these waters flow horizontally over the flowered paths that spread out around the banquet, whereas the stars hang down to the horizon on a vertical axis.

30. For roughly this reading of the final line, see Zhao Cigong (fl. 1163), *Du shi*, 1.20; Cai Mengbi (fl. 1200) in Lu Yin, *Caotang shi jian*, 1.19; and Pu Qilong, *Du Du xinjie*, 3.342.

31. Other evidence for this surmise can be found in the description of Mr. Zuo's "thatched hall," which suggests the recluse's rusticity and intimacy with nature, and the mention of his "few paths overgrown with flowers," which implies his isolation from the human world. Both of these images were common recluse tropes.

32. See, for example, Zhu Heling, *Du Gongbu shiji*, 1.8; Qiu Zhao'ao, *Du shi xiangzhu*, 1.22; Yang Lun, *Du shi jingquan*, 1.7; and Chen Yixin, *Du Fu pingzhuan*, 58. Even though he recognizes the allusion to Fan Li, William Hung dates the poem to the period in which Du Fu was traveling in the southeast; see *Tu Fu*, 24.

33. *Shangshu zhushu*, 3.46b. It seems to be essentially obligatory that discussions of Chinese poetry in English should, at some point, cite this statement. More attention needs to be paid, however, to the very different ways in which it was interpreted over time. The reading of the phrase I give here attempts to explain its discussion in late medieval texts, particularly the *Wujing zhengyi* 五經正義 series (the official Tang subcommentaries, preserved in the *Chongkan Songben Shisanjing zhushu*).

34. *Maoshi zhushu*, 13a–b. See also 1.11a–20b, and *Shangshu zhushu*, 3.47a. I discuss these texts at greater length in Bender, "Du Fu: Poet Historian, Poet Sage," 40–47, and a number of the points I make only summarily here are discussed more fully there.

35. See, for instance Gao Zhongwu's 高仲武 (fl. c. 779) preface to the *Zhongxing jianqi ji* 中興閒氣集, a collection of post-Rebellion poetry whose very frivolity by the moral standards of later recordizing criticism was intended to suggest that the state had been restored to flourishing. Fu Xuancong, *Tangren xuan Tangshi*, 456.

36. The term "Classicist" deserves some discussion, since it is intended to overlap with but not be identical to two terms more commonly used in describing the intellectual history of the period, namely, "Confucian" and "Ru" 儒. In this particular instance, there is little daylight between the terms: I am referring, above all, to the editors of the *Wujing zhengyi* series, who left us the most detailed record that we possess of Tang dynasty thought about the Classics, and who are undoubtedly also "Confucians" and "Ru." In other cases, however, "Classicism" is intended to be considerably broader than "Ru," which primarily denoted actual scholars of the Classics and their commentaries, and less diffuse than "Confucian," which is often used to refer to anyone evincing certain attitudes towards state service. Classicism, as I will use the term here, simply means a propensity to take the Classics seriously. Classicists could thus also be Buddhists or Daoists.

37. This important early Tang ideology is described in Bol, *"This Culture of Ours,"* 76–107. Though these were public values, there were also other contexts in which this question did not and could not arise.

38. I am thinking here, for instance, of the *fu-gu* 復古 impulse in much Tang literature. This is a huge topic, but for a brief introduction, see Owen, *Poetry of Meng Chiao and Han Yü*, 8–23.

39. SB 9; DFQJ, 8; TPDF 1.3. 1: *Lunyu jishi*, 33.1168–69. 4: *Shangshu zhushu*, 6.81a–b. 5: *Shiji*, 6.261. 6: *Wenxuan*, 11. 508–18.

40. Such is the assertion of Cai Mengbi; see Lu Yin, *Caotang shi jian*, 1.6. It is, however, unclear what documentation Cai might have had for such a claim since it does not seem to be backed up by any surviving materials.

41. The first critic to suggest that Du Fu is remembering his deceased father here seems to have been Zhang Yan 張綖 (1487–1543); see *Du Gongbu shitong*, 1.4a–b. Zhao

Cigong had earlier suggested that the syntax of the first couplet implies that this is a second visit; see *Du shi*, 1.4.

42. *Lunyu jishi*, 33.1168–69.

43. Pauline Yu in *Reading of Imagery*, for example, offers a narrative of the development of Chinese poetic thought by which historical contextualization is the most ancient form of Chinese poetic criticism.

44. See *Maoshi zhushu*, 1.13a; Van Zoeren, *Poetry and Personality*, 139–45; and my discussion of this passage in "Poet Historian, Poet Sage," 45–46. The *Zhengyi* never explicitly says whether the poems in the *Classic of Poetry* had a historicizing commentary before Confucius's time, but the implication seems to be that, in their musical form, they did not need one.

45. Xiaofei Tian, *Tao Yuanming*, 9–10.

46. There survive a great number of Tang anecdote collections containing material relating to poetry, and, if some of the anecdotes they contain might be true, a good proportion are either demonstrably false or historically questionable. For a discussion of these anecdotes, see Sanders, *Words Well Put*, and Nürnberger, *Das "Ben shi shi."* For the larger context of literati storytelling in which these anecdotes circulated, see Manling Luo, *Literati Storytelling*, and Sarah M. Allen, *Shifting Stories*. For Tang readers' frequent practice of "correcting" texts that did not make sense to them, see Nugent, *Manifest in Words*, 27–71 and 248–58, as well as Owen, "Manuscript Legacy," 303.

47. This anecdote has been discussed extensively by Tian Xiaofei and Christopher Nugent. See Xiaofei Tian, *Tao Yuanming*, 8, and Nugent, *Manifest in Words*, 14 and 229. For the anecdote, see Li Shiren, *Quan Tang Wudai xiaoshuo*, 2085.

48. The concept of *mouvance* was proposed by Paul Zumthor in his *Essai de poétique médiévale*. It originally refers to the variability of texts from medieval Europe. Bernard Cerquiglini (*Éloge de la variante*) prefers the term *variance* to separate textual variability from oral forms.

49. A small number of other commentaries survive that merely gloss individual words and provide correct pronunciations. The only surviving Tang commentary on the work of a Tang poet is the *Li Jiao zayong zhushi* 李嶠雜詠註詩 manuscript preserved at Dunhuang; for this text, see Xu Jun, *Dunhuang shiji*, 352. As Okamura Shigeru points out, however, surviving catalogs and Dunhuang fragments suggest that many other commentaries might have been written that do not survive, especially on the *Wenxuan*; see *Monzen no kenkyū*, 129. For fragments of Lu Shanjing's 陸善經 (fl. 742–58) commentary to the *Wenxuan*, see Zhou Xunchu, *Tang chao Wenxuan*.

50. *Liuchen zhu Wenxuan*, "Wuchen biao," 1.a–b.

51. *Liuchen zhu Wenxuan*, "Wuchen biao," 1.b.

52. For the relationship between the *Wuchen* and the Li Shan commentaries on the *Wenxuan*, see Knechtges, *Wen Xuan*, 52–57, and, more broadly, Chen Yanjia, *"Wenxuan" Li Shan zhu yu Wuchen zhu*.

53. *Liuchen zhu Wenxuan*, 1.1a.

54. See the more detailed discussion in my dissertation, "Du Fu: Poet Historian, Poet Sage," 56–60.

55. On this point, see my "Poetic Omens and Poetic History." For a useful discussion of the *shige* genre, see Yugen Wang, "Shige."

56. *Wenxuan*, 23.1067. This quote comes from Li's introduction to the poetry of Ruan Ji 阮籍 (210–63), which may (it is not clear) have been written by either Yan Yanzhi 顏延之 (384–465) or Shen Yue 沈約 (441–513).

57. Owen, "Poetry and Its Historical Ground," 115.

58. Although my analysis here is heavily indebted to Owen's "typology of judgment," I believe that the term "tropology" better highlights the flexible moral significance of such literary precedents in the medieval Chinese context. The tropological and the typological were two modes of biblical exegesis in the medieval West. Typological reading meant finding prefigurations of the life of Christ in the Old Testament; tropological was interpreting Old Testament stories for their moral significance. For the classic study of these modes of meaning, see Lubac, *Exégèse médiévale*.

59. *Liuchen zhu Wenxuan*, 19.1b.

60. *SB* 1; *DFQJ*, 229; *TPDF* 2.13. 1: *Maoshi zhushu*, 6.233b. 30: *LQL*, "Wei shi," 3.367. 31–32: *Chunqiu Zuozhuan*, 18.303a; *Hou Han shu*, 36.1553.

61. Chen is paraphrasing *Zizhi tongjian*, 216.6907. It is worth noting the possibility that, given the echoes between them, Du Fu's poem might have been a source for this account.

62. Chen Yixin, *Du Fu pingzhuan*, 222–26.

63. See Pulleyblank, *Background of the Rebellion*, 69–70; Lewis, *China's Cosmopolitan Empire*, 49; Graff, *Medieval Chinese Warfare*, 205–9; and Twitchett, "Hsüan-Tsung," 415–18.

64. *Bai Juyi ji*, 1.5.

65. Lu Yin, *Caotang shi jian*, "Xu," 19–20. For a similar statement from later in the tradition, see *Huang Sheng quanji*, vol. 1, "Dushi gaishuo," 20.

66. This is quoted by Sikong Tu 司空圖 (837–908) in his "Letter to Ji Pu" 與極浦書; see *QTW*, 807.8487b.

67. This point has been made in Owen, "Poetry and Its Historical Ground," 111.

68. Ji Yougong, *Tang shi jishi*, 20.503.

69. Owen, *Great Age*, 57.

70. From Gao's "Wensi boyao xu" 文思博要序; see *QTW*, 134.1357a.

71. From Liu Xie, *Zengding Wenxin diaolong*, 1.18. "Hundred-year shadow" is a metonymy for the body.

72. Lu Chun, "Shan Donggaozi ji xu" 刪東皋子集序, *QTW*, 618.6239a. For discussions of Lu's edition, see Xiaofei Tian, "Misplaced," and Warner, *Wild Deer*, 4–6.

73. *SB* 9; *DFQJ*, 25; *TPDF* 1.7.

74. See *Jin shu*, 80.2104–5.

75. See, for example, Shao Bao (1460–1527), *Ke Du Shaoling*, 20.2818; Qiu Zhao'ao, *Du shi xiangzhu*, 1.14; Pu Qilong, *Du Du xinjie*, 3.334; Yang Lun, *Du shi jingquan*, 1.4; and Chen Yixin, *Du Fu pingzhuan*, 54.

76. Following the reading of Zhao Cigong, *Du shi*, 1.17.

77. See *Zhuangzi jishi*, 3.243.

78. For the most famous discussion of poetry as *trouvaille*, see Li Shangyin's "Li He xiaozhuan" 李賀小傳, *Li Shangyin wen*, vol. 4, 2265. See also Owen, *End of the Chinese "Middle Ages,"* 107–29. Although Owen is right that this concept becomes particularly marked in the Mid-Tang, I believe it is implicit in earlier discussions of the poetic art, some of which will be quoted in chapter 5.

79. Cited in Chen Yixin, *Du Fu pingzhuan*, 54. The original passage can be found in Zhou Zizhi, *Zhupo shihua*, 1.8a–b.
80. For Chen's citation of the *Zhuangzi*, see *Zhuangzi jishi*, 9.944.
81. *SB* 1; *DFQJ*, 3; *TPDF* 1.2. 2: *Shiji*, 69.3265. 3: *Wenxuan*, 11.493. 8: *Mengzi*, 13.229.
82. Unlike standard "regulated verse," this poem rhymes on a deflected tone. It does, however, otherwise follow the rules of tonal alternation prescribed by regulated verse.
83. For the poetry of Obscure Learning, see Nicholas Morrow Williams, "Metaphysical Lyric," and Swartz, *Reading Philosophy*.
84. See *Sui shu*, 34.1003.
85. See, among many other possible examples of such statements, Cheng Xuanying's 成玄英 (fl. 636) subcommentary on the *Zhuangzi*, *Nanhua zhenjing zhushu*, 1.23–24 and 1.28–31.
86. Wang Sishi, *Du yi*, 1.2.
87. See Kroll, "Verses from on High."
88. See my "*Corrected Interpretations.*"

TWO. Omen and Chaos

1. Chen Yixin, *Du Fu pingzhuan*, 254.
2. A connection between poetry and omens has been drawn by Owen in *Traditional Chinese Poetry and Poetics*, particularly 12–53. Whereas he suggests that "Chinese poetry is the displaced vocation of the diviner," however, I will be arguing here that it was sometimes thought of in the late medieval period as the (not displaced) product of mediums.
3. See Chou, "Wenxue shengyu" and "Literary Reputations."
4. The work of Paul W. Kroll has been exemplary in this respect; see, for example, his *Dharma Bell* and his *Studies in Medieval Taoism*.
5. This vision of Du Fu is in evidence in his biography in the *Jiu Tang shu*, for example. For the early development of Du Fu's cultural image, see Jue Chen, "Making China's Greatest Poet," 75–136. "Neo-Daoism" is a misnomer for (and partly a misunderstanding of) the medieval philosophical trend discussed in the previous chapter under the heading of Obscure Learning (Xuanxue).
6. For the imperial house's deployment of their supposed descent from Laozi, see Barrett, *Taoism under the T'ang*. The following poem is *SB* 9; *DFQJ*, 173; *TPDF* 2.3. 10: Guo Xian, *Dongming ji*, 1.1a, and *Taiping yulan*, 78.2740a. 27: *Laozi jiaoshi*, 6.25. 28: *Laozi jiaoshi*, 45.183.
7. See, for example, Zhang Jie's (*jinshi* 1124) comments at *Suihantang shihua*, 2.129, and Jin Shengtan's (1608–61) at *Du shi jie*, 1.32–33.
8. This comment is worded slightly differently in the various editions of Qian's comments. This version is from his *Du Du xiaojian* 讀杜小箋, in *Muzhai chu xue ji*, cited in *DFQJ*, 181. For a slightly abbreviated version, see *Qian zhu Du shi*, 9.278.
9. See Lu Fusheng, *Zhongguo shuhua*, vol. 1, 164a.
10. As Stephen Owen notices, the verb *ye* 謁 (to visit) in the title of the poem indicates paying a respectful visit to a person, not to a place. This visit is presumably to the

dead imperial ancestors, including Laozi. For this point, and a useful discussion of this poem, see "Tang Version of Du Fu," 75.

11. Qian himself cites persuasive evidence that the painting included such a scene; see *Qian zhu Du shi*, 9.277. This departure to the west was sometimes understood as Laozi heading to India to "convert the barbarians" to Buddhism, which some Daoists understood as merely an attenuated version of Daoism.

12. On the Tang ideal of verisimilitude and illusionism in late medieval ekphrastic poetry, see Patterson, "Elegies for Empire," 149–204. For a discussion, see chapter 5 below.

13. For useful analyses of the practice and idea of reclusion, see Berkowitz, *Patterns of Disengagement*, and Ashmore, *Transport of Reading*, 56–101.

14. This convention derives, ultimately, from *Analects* 9.28; see *Lunyu jishi* 18.623.

15. For a brief survey of this material, see my "Poetic Omens and Poetic History." For more detailed studies, see Sun Rongrong, *Chenwei yu wenxue*, and Wang Xian and Xiao Jing, "Jin shiwu nian."

16. See, for instance, Wang Chong's (27–100) comments in *Lunheng*, 22.943–44 and 23.958.

17. See *Sui shu*, 34.1003. On the importance of the distinction between *fang nei* and *fang wai*, see Willard J. Peterson, "Squares and Circles." I discuss this complex of ideas more thoroughly in "Corrected Interpretations." Much of my analysis here is based on Bol, "This Culture of Ours."

18. This point is made explicitly by Shang Heng 尚衡 in "Wendao yuangui" 文道元龜, *QTW*, 394.4014a: "The origin of *wen*—was it in middle antiquity [as the "Xici" 繫辭 commentary to the *Yijing* says]? Or did it have no beginning? Heaven has five phases to distinguish its wefts; earth has five colors to distinguish its directions; and people have the five constants to distinguish their virtues. . . . If there were not the five wefts, then how could we know heaven? If there were not the five directions, then how could we know earth? If there were not the five constants, then how could people be edified? Thus, the way of *wen* goes far."

19. See, for example, Zhang Huaiguan, "Wenzi lun" 文字論, *QTW*, 432.4398b; and Li Zhou 李舟, "Dugu Changzhou ji xu" 獨孤常州集序, *QTW*, 443.4520a. For the idea that human *wen* should be understood as part of a process of "manifestation," see Owen, *Traditional Chinese Poetry and Poetics*.

20. Liu Xie, *Zengding Wenxin diaolong*, 1.1.

21. Liu Xie, *Zengding Wenxin diaolong*, 1.2. The translation of *youzan shenming* follows Owen, *Readings in Chinese Literary Thought*, 190–91, which is itself in keeping with the commentary by Han Bo 韓伯 (fourth c.) and the *Zhengyi* subcommentary; see *Zhouyi zhushu*, 9.181b.

22. See, for example, Gao Jian 高儉, "Wensi boyao xu" 文思博要序, *QTW*, 134.1357a; Shang Heng, "Wendao yuangui," *QTW*, 394.4014a; Wei Hao 魏顥, "Li Hanlin ji xu" 李翰林集序, *QTW*, 3798a; Zhang Huaiguan, "Shu duan lun" 書斷論, *QTW*, 432.4405b; Dugu Yu 獨孤郁, "Bian wen" 辯文, *QTW*, 683.6989b; and Liu Su, *Da Tang xinyu*, "Da Tang shishuo xinyu xu," 1.

23. See Zhang Huaiguan, "Shu duan lun" 書斷論, *QTW*, 432.4405b; *Zhouyi zhushu*, "Zhouyi zhengyi xu," 4b and 2a.

24. "Being" (*you* 有) and "nonbeing" (*wu* 無) are central philosophical terms in the scholarly tradition of Obscure Learning. There is, I think, no universally appropriate translation for these terms, though many have been offered. Makeham, *Transmitters*

and Creators, translates them as "having" and "not-having"; Ziporyn, *Penumbra Unbound*, as "being" and "non-being"; Ashmore, "Word and Gesture," as "extant" and "non-extant"; Puett, "Text and Commentary," as "something" and "nothingness"; Mather, "Controversy over Conformity," as "actuality" and "non-actuality"; and Wagner, *Language, Ontology, and Political Philosophy*, as "entities" and "negativity." I have translated them as "actuality" and "negativity" elsewhere—terms that I think may be more appropriate but that are also more obscure.

25. Zhang Huaiguan, "Wenzi lun" 文字論, *QTW*, 432.4398b.
26. Lu Cangyong, "You shiyi Chen Zi'ang wenji xu" 右拾遺陳子昂文集序, *QTW*, 318.2402b.
27. Shi Jiaoran, *Shishi*, "Shishi xu," 1.
28. See, for instance, *Zengding zhushi Quan Tang shi*, 714.7 and 756.32.
29. For examples of this language, see *Bai Juyi ji*, 17.1058; *Zengding zhushi Quan Tang shi*, 579.44 and 805.5; and Zhang Bowei, *Quan Tang Wudai shige*, 418.
30. See, for instance, Du Fu's own "Visiting Xiujue Temple" 遊修覺寺, *TPDF* 9.61; *Nan Qi shu*, 52.907; Shi Jiaoran, *Shishi*, "Shishi xu," 2; and Li Sizong 李嗣眞, "Shu pin xu" 書品序, *QTW*, 164.1676a.
31. See *Lu Ji ji*, 1.1–7; the translations are modified from Owen, *Readings in Chinese Literary Thought*.
32. *QTW*, 215.6308b–9a.
33. Zhang Huaiguan, "Shu duan lun," *QTW*, 312.4397b–98b.
34. See *TPDF* 3.41 and 4.7.
35. See, for example, *Chen shu*, 34.453; *Sui shu*, 76.1729; *Nan shi*, 72.1761; *Bei shi*, 83.2777; and *Bei Qi shu*, 45.601; along with more than a dozen instances in *QTW*. For a use of this same passage in a context genuinely concerned with omens, see *Jin shu*, 11.277.
36. *Nan shi*, 72.1792.
37. For the Tang understanding of this mythology, see (for instance) Cheng Boyu, *Maoshi zhishuo*, 1.2a–b; and Li Yi 李益, "Shi you liuyi fu" 詩有六義賦, *QTW*, 181.4918b–19a.
38. *Maoshi zhushu*, "Maoshi zhengyi xu," 3a.
39. See Gao Shi, "Wei Dongping Xue Taishou jin Wangshi ruishi biao" 爲東平薛太守進王氏瑞詩表, *Gao Shi ji jiaozhu*, "Shi," 305–6.
40. This incident is discussed in Bokenkamp, "Time after Time."
41. Lü Yanzuo, "Jin jizhu Wenxuan biao" 進集注文選表, *QTW*, 300.3042b.
42. See my "Poetic Omens and Poetic History."
43. See Zhang Bowei, *Quan Tang Wudai shige*, 378–81.
44. Zhang Bowei, *Quan Tang Wudai shige*, 451.
45. Qian attributes this praise to his nephew Qian Zeng 錢曾 (1629–1701). See *Qian zhu Du shi*, "Caotang shijian yuanben xu," 4.
46. See *TPDF* 3.33 and *DFQJ*, 582.
47. Other examples include poems he wrote about an imperial sacrifice to a dragon and about a period of unusual weather in the autumn of 754. See "A Companion Piece, Respectfully Offered, for Supervising Secretary Guo's 'Written on the Sacred Tarn East of the Hot Springs'" 奉同郭給事湯東靈湫作 and "Sighing at the Autumn Rain, Three Poems" 秋雨歎三首, *TPDF* 4.8 and 3.29–31.
48. *SB* 1; *DFQJ*, 295; *TPDF* 2.9. 5: This traditional kenning for Buddhism may at this point have referred to the way Buddhists used paintings and statues to provide an

analogy for the illusory nature of everyday reality; but see Greene, "'Religion of Images'?" for its original meaning. 18: *Chuci buzhu*, 1.20–25. 19: *Mu Tianzi zhuan*, 3.1a–b.

49. Pu places the poem near the end of the Tianbao period, which agrees with the conclusions of most modern commentators, who follow Wen Yiduo's argument that the poem must have been written in 752 (see "Cen Jiazhou xinian kaozheng," *Wen Yiduo quanji*, 3.101–42). Early commentators sometimes placed the poem later; Lu Yin, for example, thinks that it was written after the outbreak of the Rebellion—which might make better sense of its imagery of imperial travel.

50. Pu Qilong, *Du Du xinjie*, 1.1.9–10. Compare here modern scholar Wu Lushan 吳鷺山, who interprets this poem as illustrating that "the great disorder and crisis at the end of the Tianbao period had already been registered by Du Fu's acute political sense of smell (*zhengzhi xiujue* 政治嗅覺)"; Wu, *Du shi luncong*, 29. Wu discusses this poem under the heading "Du Fu's Realist Poetics."

51. For a comparison of the poems written on this occasion, see Mo Lifeng, *Du Fu pingzhuan*, 81–88.

52. See Owen's discussion of the equally hyperbolic "Ballad of Meipi" 渼陂行 (*TPDF* 3.12) in *Great Age*, 190–93.

53. See Wang Dingbao, *Tang zhiyan*, 1.3–4 and 3.27–28.

54. *Chuci jiaoshi*, 1.31.

55. Or so the figure was interpreted by the commentators on the *Wuchen* edition of the *Wenxuan*. The *Wuchen* commentators also understood Qu's poetic journeys through the heavens as journeys into reclusion, and they took these last images as indicating his resolve to be a "hidden one" rather than demeaning himself to get an official salary. Images of reclusion, if they are intended as such, would be appropriate to the occasion, for Du Fu often associates Buddhist monasteries, like the one at which this poem was written, with hiding away from government service. See *Liuchen zhu Wenxuan*, 33.623b.

56. For the overlaps between a religious and a political vocabulary of manifestation and hiddenness, see Nylan, "Beliefs about Social Seeing."

57. See *Zhouyi zhushu*, 7.147a.

58. *SB* 1; *DFQJ*, 214; *TPDF* 2.8. 4: *Shen Quanqi, Song Zhiwen ji*, "Shen Quanqi ji," 4.206. 18: *Lunyu jishi*, 16.540.

59. For an analysis of this poem's (lack of) logic, see Chou, *Reconsidering Tu Fu*, 165–67.

60. Pu Qilong, *Du Du xinjie*, 2.1.230.

61. Chen Yixin, *Du Fu pingzhuan*, 197.

62. For the propinquity of drunkenness to elevated spiritual states, see Nicholas Morrow Williams, "Morality of Drunkenness," as well as the essays by Tak Kam Chan and Charles Kwong in the same volume. For Du Fu's own play with this adjacency, see his "Song of Eight Drunken Immortals" 飲中八仙歌: *TPDF* 2.1 and *DFQJ*, 136.

63. For the classic studies of patronage poetry in the Tang, see Cheng Qianfan, *Tangdai jinshi xingjuan*, and Fu Xuancong, *Tangdai keju*, 247–87. In English, see Mair, "Scroll Presentation."

64. *SB* 1; *DFQJ*, 549; *TPDF* 4.1. 1: *Mu Tianzi zhuan*, 1.6b.

65. Zhang either commissioned the painting or painted it himself; the grammar allows either possibility.

66. It is worth noting here that this poem cannot provide its readers access to the painting itself—much less to the now-deceased horse behind it—through which they might independently confirm the validity of Du Fu's judgment. It may, in fact, be calling attention to this problem in the second line, in which Du Fu seems to decide that the painted horse is "no doubt" (*wunai* 無乃) one worthy of an emperor, a phrase that often in late medieval verse marks subjective (or even mistaken) judgment. The whole elaborate history that follows this decision, then, could perhaps be an extrapolation, the kind of mysterious insight I discussed in the last chapter, whereby authoritative readers proved capable of "completing the tally with their minds," recognizing wholeness where less adept readers would see only fragments.

67. *SB* 1; *DFQJ*, 276; *TPDF* 1.35. 33: *Han shu*, 72.3066. 34: *Hanshi waizhuan*, 1.11. 41: *Chunqiu Zuozhuan*, 21.365a.

68. These quotes derive from Mo Lifeng, *Du Fu pingzhuan*, 77, and Chen Yixin, *Du Fu pingzhuan*, 109, respectively.

69. For this incident, see *Zizhi tongjian*, 215.6876.

70. *Chunqiu Zuozhuan*, 42.724a.

71. *Hou Han shu*, 81.2693.

72. See *LQL*, "Jin shi," 17.991. Interestingly, both Tao's original poem and Du Fu's allusion exist in variants that read "thirteen" 十三 for "thirty" 三十, in both cases almost certainly an emendation that attempts to reconcile the more general figures with what we know about the biographies of the poets from other sources.

73. Yan Zhitui, *Yanshi jiaxun*, 7.589.

74. See *Wenxuan*, 28.1319.

75. See *Lunyu jijie yishu*, 3.56.

76. *SB* 1; *DFQJ* 264; *TPDF* 4.6. 4: *Han shu*, 87.3568 and *Lunyu jishi*, 13.431. 5: *Zhuangzi jishi*, 1.37. 7: *Hanshi waizhuan*, 8.342. 10: *Zhuangzi jishi*, 4.153. 19: *Wenxuan*, 37.1688. 21–24: *Zhuangzi jishi*, 23.773, but see also *Shiji*, 24.2495. 25: *Wenxuan*, 53.2289. 29: See *Yiwen leiju*, 36.639. 41: For other interpretations of this problematic line, see Cherniack, "Three Great Poems," 141–43. 56: *Maoshi zhushu*, 9.315a. 88: *Liji zhushu*, 7.129b.

77. For these appellations, see Schneider, *Confucian Prophet*, 87–123.

78. This is perhaps Du Fu's most famous poem nowadays, and scholarship on it is endless. For useful discussions in English, see Cherniack, "Three Great Poems," and the essays by David R. Knechtges, Lynn Struve, Wai-yee Li, and Stephen Owen in Yu et al., *Ways with Words*, 146–72. Li's essay is the most attuned to the moral ambivalence of the poem, although she reads the poem as ultimately a "narrative of resolution and control." As will become clear, I disagree with this characterization.

79. *Lunyu jishi*, 13.1029.

80. Something very much like this state has been theorized by Bernard Williams in *Moral Luck*, 20–40. Much of the essay is germane to this poem.

81. It is not, that is, the veritable record of current events that recordizing readers have often seen here: as Du Fu notes, men in the "commoners' robes" he describes himself wearing in the first lines of the poem were excluded from imperial banquets. On this point, see Chou, *Reconsidering Tu Fu*, 167–68. Susan Cherniack, similarly, has noted that Du Fu's journey should not, in fact, have taken him very close at all to Mt. Li and that he certainly could not have reached there "at daybreak" after setting out from

Chang'an in the middle of the night; "Three Great Poems," 152–53. For a recordizing critic's take on this section, see Huang Shen, *Du Fu xinying lu*, 66.

82. The comparison to travel *fu* is explored in David Knechtges's discussion of the poem in Yu et al., *Ways with Words*, 149–59.

83. See *Mengzi*, 8.199.

84. This irony is deepened by Stephen Owen's observation that Hou Ji and Yin Xie were the founders of great lineages, where Du Fu has now contributed to the death of a son. See *Great Age*, 197.

THREE. Convention and Nature

1. For the fall of the capitals, see *Zizhi tongjian*, 218.6934–39. According to this chronology, the Rebellion began on December 16, 755.

2. Various commentators have sought to fill this gap, dating several poems to the months after Du Fu arrived in Fengxian and hypothesizing on their basis that he must have returned to Chang'an before taking his family north once again. There is no good reason to believe these datings, nearly all of which depend on that variety of wishful reading to which one becomes accustomed in Du Fu commentary. Each of these poems, that is, is dated to this period because it would have been morally admirable for him to have written them at this time or morally suspect to have written them at the times to which they were assigned in earlier editions. Since none of these poems contain details that can definitively date them here, it is better to follow their placement in early collections such as *SB* and Guo Zhida, *Xinkan jiaoding jizhu*.

3. *SB* 1; *DFQJ*, 715; *TPDF* 4.16. 15: *Tao Yuanming ji*, 5.461. 44: *Shiji*, 92.2623. 60: *Chunqiu Zuozhuan*, 52.915a.

4. It is also possible that the "flood-dragon" signifies a thunderbolt.

5. The poem as a whole can be said to play with this question, since Du Fu had invoked an archaic register at its beginning as well, with the first line recalling the opening of one of the famous "Nineteen Old Poems" 古詩十九首: "A traveler came from a distant place" 客從遠方來 (see *LQL*, "Han shi," 12.333). Even in this first couplet, however, the appeal to a time-transcending "ancient" register seems to falter, the vagueness characteristic of the "old poems" disturbed by the fact that the phrase "a southern county" (*nanxian* 南縣) can also be read specifically as "South County," an old name for Fengxian. This ambiguity leaves the line suspended between generality and biographical precision, and foreshadows the tension between timeless traditional wisdom and concrete experience with which the poem ends.

6. The earliest source that claims that Du Fu was captured on his way to the court-in-exile seems to be Du Fu's biography in the *Xin Tang shu*. This detail is not in the *Jiu Tang shu*, so it is unclear whether it is a pious fiction on the part of the later historians, part of Du Fu's growing reputation for moral conduct. See *Xin Tang shu*, 201.5736.

7. *SB* 9; *DFQJ*, 748; *TPDF* 4.23. 1: *Chunqiu Zuozhuan*, 18.303a. 6: *LQL*, "Wei shi," 8.476. 8: *Shishuo xinyu*, 28.865.

8. See Bender, "Other Poetry," 38.

9. See, for instance, a poem by Wang Sengru 王僧孺: "Who knew that the mind could disorder the eyes? / Looking at crimson, it suddenly turns emerald" 誰知心眼亂，看朱忽成碧 (*LQL*, "Liang shi," 12.1766).

10. For statements to this effect, see *Zhou shu*, 41.743; *Bei shi*, 83.2778; and Gao Zhongwu 高仲武 (fl. 779), "DaTang zhongxing xianqi ji xu" 大唐中興間氣集序, *QTW*, 458.4684b.

11. For the role of the poet-historian in later ages of disorder, see Wai-yee Li, "Confronting History," and Yim, *Poet-Historian Qian Qianyi*.

12. Poetry was associated with decadent ages as well, peaceful but breeding disorder. The Southern Dynasties in particular were often depicted as having written poetry whose seductive allure played a role in the relatively swift downfall of those states. But in moralist terms, this was "bad" poetry, the nadir of the art rather than its apogee.

13. The question of the inherent morality or viciousness of human nature had been much debated in early Chinese philosophy, but it seems to have been fairly settled in the Classicism of the medieval period. For a discussion, see Makeham, *Transmitters and Creators*, 115–17 and 156–69, as well as my "*Corrected Interpretations.*"

14. For this point, see (for instance) *Zhouyi zhushu*, "Zhouyi zhengyi xu," 2a; and *Liji zhushu*, 37.669b–70a.

15. For the *Poetry*'s modeling of the dispositions characteristic of sagely ages and the claim that even the "*Changed Poems*" 變詩 express the mores promoted by the sages, see *Maoshi zhushu*, 1.15b–17b.

16. *Sui shu*, 77.2614–15.

17. See, for instance, the broadsides against poetry leveled by the Neo-Confucian philosopher Cheng Yi 程頤 (1033–1107), in Cheng Yi and Cheng Hao, *Er Cheng yishu*, 18.96a, and *Er Cheng wenji*, 10.15a–b. Here Cheng focuses his criticisms of literature on Du Fu, presumably because he was thought to be the most ethically serious of poets.

18. A great number of such accounts could be cited. For just a few produced by the so-called Four Elite Writers of the Early Tang 初唐四傑, see *QTW*, 166.1691a–b, 166.1692a–93a, 166.1693a–94b, 180.1829b–30a, 191.1930a–32b, and 198.2001a–b.

19. "Heyue yingling ji xu" 河嶽英靈集序, *QTW*, 436.4452a.

20. See Fu Xuancong, *Tangren xuan Tang shi*, 299.

21. In practice, much of Tang poetry seems unprecedented to us now. Although the wild abandon of the poetry of Cen Shen, for example, was held to reproduce some of the "wind and bone" of Wei–Jin era verse, it sounds to contemporary ears very little like this earlier poetry. Speaking in general, tropologies of all sorts are inherently creative, as the assumption of new data to old categories inevitably transforms those categories. The issue, then, is not whether late medieval poetry was path-breaking or not (it was) but how intellectuals tended to speak about it when they wanted to claim ethical significance.

22. This point is made explicitly by Xiao Yingshi 蕭穎士 (717–68) in a preface he wrote to explain one of his own poetic compositions: "Learning is about . . . imitating the canonical forms and models and adding luster to virtue and righteousness. *Wen* aims at . . . elevating those refined lessons and making manifest the truth of affairs." See *Xiao Maoting wenji*, 1.29b.

23. See my article on this topic, "Other Poetry on the An Lushan Rebellion." Li Bai is also an exception to nearly all of these claims, albeit in a way quite different from Du Fu.

24. *SB* 9; *DFQJ*, 733; *TPDF* 4.18.

25. For this point, see Ji Yun, *Yingkui lüsui kanwu*, 22.2b.

26. See *TPDF* 5.8, translated later in this chapter.

27. This point is made nicely by Wang Sishi; see *Du yi*, 2.43.

28. *SB* 1; *DFQJ*, 742; *TPDF* 4.21. 2: There are many poems under this ballad title; see for instance *LQL*, "Wei shi," 3.367.

29. David Graff estimates that only about 15 percent of the Tang's standing armies in the middle of the eighth century would have been cavalrymen; and, even if An Lushan did attract troops from various northern tribes for his rebellion, he also seems to have had popular support throughout Hebei, which had previously been considered part of the heartland of Chinese civilization and culture (*Medieval Chinese Warfare*, 208–10 and 218). Du Fu, finally, was far from unaware of the presence of "Chinese" soldiers among An's troops: he will later write in the voice of one in "Leaving the Passes, Second Series" 後出塞, *TPDF* 4.9–13; *DFQJ*, 636.

30. See *Zizhi tongjian*, 22.7004. This episode has occasioned some debate among historians; for a skeptical account, see Graff, "Fang Guan's Chariots." Du Fu would famously (and disastrously) argue on behalf of Fang Guan at court when the latter was dismissed for his inept handling of the war, so it seems unlikely that he developed a settled negative opinion of Fang for his handling of Qingban.

31. Du Fu presses these deformations to an even greater extreme in "Block Luzi" 塞蘆子 (*TPDF* 4.31; *DFQJ*, 755), written around the same time. See my discussion in "Du Fu: Poet Historian, Poet Sage," 190–95.

32. See Bender, "Other Poetry," 29–34.

33. This complex of ideas has been well discussed by Robert Ashmore in *Transport of Reading*.

34. *SB* 9; *DFQJ*, 779; *TPDF* 4.25.

35. See *Maoshi zhushu*, 6.147a, and *Shiji*, 38.1621, respectively.

36. The beacon flares may, again, be imagined here, a conventional synecdoche for war.

37. For a particularly powerful example of both these tendencies, see "Rejoicing in the Clearing Weather" 喜晴, *TPDF* 4.38; *DFQJ*, 813.

38. *SB* 1; *DFQJ*, 760; *TPDF* 4.32. 8: *Han shu*, 97.3983.

39. For a discussion of the problematic variants in this line, see Bender, "Du Fu: Poet Historian, Poet Sage," 389.

40. "Put on their faces" is an alternate translation for "took on a bright complexion" in line 6. In the few usages of the phrase that survive in Tang materials, it tends to suggest a more involuntary brightening or flushing of the face than would be suggested by "put on their faces." This second translation, however, is intended to stress the association with beautiful women.

41. See *Han shu*, 97.3966–67.

42. *Han shu*, 97.3982–84.

43. This quote derives from Wang Yi's 王逸 (ca. 89–158) commentary on the "Jiubian" 九辯. See *Chuci jijiao jishi*, 2058. As Qian Qianyi glosses the final couplet: "this is what of old people used to call 'being befuddled by emotion (情癡).'" See *Qian zhu Du shi*, 1.44.

44. Du Fu might have been thinking here of such "southern" emperors as the last emperor of the Chen dynasty, Chen Shubao 陳叔寶 (553–604), and the last emperor of the Sui dynasty, Yang Guang 楊廣 (569–618).

45. For an introduction to the idea of "nature" in Buddhism and Daoism, see Tseng, "Comparison." For a useful discussion of the introduction of these ideas into Classicism, see Barrett, *Li Ao.*

46. Fuller, *Drifting among Rivers and Lakes.*

47. Cited in *DFQJ*, 6657. Originally from Chen's *Shuchao jianzhu Du Gongbu qiyan lüshi* 書巢箋注杜工部七言律詩.

48. Xu Zong, *Du shi xue*, 263.

49. *Yuan Zhen ji*, 18.208.

50. *Yuan Zhen ji*, 16.600–601. This famous piece survives in a number of different versions, and its variants are often significant. I have followed the critical text given in Ji Qin's edition, correcting one obvious error in favor of the reading of a Song print edition he gives in his notes.

51. For the Mid-Tang reassessment of the cultural tradition, see Bol, "*This Culture of Ours*," 108–47, and Owen, *End of the Chinese "Middle Ages."*

52. The suggestion seems to be that the convention-bound poetry of the *Shijing* is a good model for most of us, but there is something beyond it: the ability to transcend convention in the way that Confucius did, a transcendence that perhaps qualified him to judge convention in the first place. Where other poets have had to subject themselves to the power of culture, that is, Du Fu is like Confucius in being "unlike any other that has come before" (*Mengzi*, 3.63) and thus being able to tame convention to his purposes rather than being shaped by it himself.

53. For the first of these quotes, see *Lunyu jijie yishu*, 9.262. For the second, see *Mengzi*, 10.232–33.

54. *Huang Sheng quanji*, vol. 2: *Du shi shuo*, "Du shi gaishuo," 21.

55. Sargent, "Can Latecomers Get There First?," 167–68.

56. Wang Sishi, *Du yi*, "Du shi jianxuan jiuxu," 1–2.

57. *Yuan Haowen quanji*, 36.24–25.

58. See *Huang Tingjian quanji*, 18.473.

59. *Huang Tingjian quanji*, 18.474–75.

60. The most in-depth treatment of Huang's poetics in English is probably Palumbo-Liu, *Poetics of Appropriation.* See also Wang, *Ten Thousand Scrolls*, and Fuller, *Drifting among Rivers and Lakes.*

61. *Huang Tingjian quanji*, 16.437.

62. Zhang Jin, *Dushutang Du shiji zhujie*, 3.479.

63. *SB* 2; *DFQJ*, 841; *TPDF* 5.8. 6: *Hanshi waizhuan*, 1.11.

64. *Tao Yuanming ji*, 4.393.

65. *Tao Yuanming ji*, 2.103.

66. See *Tao Yuanming ji*, 6.502–7.

67. See *TPDF* 5.9.

68. *SB* 2; *DFQJ*, 934; *TPDF* 5.24–26. II.5: Yang, *Du shi jingquan*, 4.158.

69. Alternately, this couplet may indicate that the boy is afraid of him and so keeps approaching and fleeing.

70. Fu Gengsheng, *Du shi sanyi*, 254.

71. Fu Gengsheng, *Du shi sanyi*, 259.
72. Chen Yixin, *Du Fu pingzhuan*, 337–39.
73. See *Tao Yuanming ji*, 3.156.

FOUR. Narrative and Experience

1. See, for instance, the famous group composition of 758, in which Du Fu composed poetry with Jia Zhi 賈至, Wang Wei 王維, and Cen Shen 岑參; these poems can be found in *DFQJ*, 994–1005.
2. I discuss the poetry of this period in "Du Fu: Poet Historian, Poet Sage," 238–75.
3. It is not entirely clear why Du Fu should have chosen Qinzhou, since hostilities with the Tibetans had already begun to eat away at Tang territory on the western frontier by this time. He seems to have had a nephew in the area and perhaps hoped to rely on him in setting up a new life.
4. With the necessary caveat that estimating poetic productivity is difficult because so much has been lost. But Du Fu has more poetry preserved from this last eleven years of his life than any previous poet other than Li Bai has for his entire career.
5. Du Fu had, before his flight to Qinzhou, written a few extended poetic series, but none structured by the complex interconnections or the narrative impetus that characterize the three long narrative sequences he wrote in the final months of this year. Given their placement in the *Songben* edition, moreover, it is possible that the two fictional narrative sequences of Du Fu's collection were also written during his time in Qinzhou. See *DFQJ*, 241–61 and 636–52. Du Fu wrote at least two nonnarrative sequences during this period as well.
6. There is not enough space here to fully translate and discuss this series or the next two. I have translated and annotated all three fully in "Three Extended Poetic Series" and discuss them in more detail in "Sense of Not Ending."
7. This series as a whole is found in *SB* 10; *DFQJ*, 1405–71; *TPDF* 7.31–50. This poem is *SB* 10; *DFQJ*, 1413; *TPDF* 7.33. 6: *Shiji*, 95.2671. There is no consensus on the meaning of the phrase "white foreheads" 白題 in this context. Some commentators think that certain western groups smeared their foreheads with white paint; others think it refers to a white hat; others think it is a white flag used in military dances.
8. For English scholarship on the tradition of frontier ballads, see Miao, "T'ang Frontier Poetry"; Marie Chan, "Frontier Poems of Ts'en Shen"; Owen, *Great Age*, 169–82; and Tian, *Beacon Fire and Shooting Star*, 323–35. The scholarship in Chinese is voluminous.
9. For the makeup of Tang armies in the eighth century, see Graff, *Medieval Chinese Warfare*, 205–26.
10. *SB* 10; *DFQJ*, 1430; *TPDF* 7.38. 8: *Wenxuan*, 16.719–22.
11. For this text, see *Wenxuan*, 16.719–22, and Knechtges, *Wen xuan*, vol. 3, 167–70. Du Fu may also be thinking here of the "Rhapsody on the Long Flute" 長笛賦 by Ma Rong 馬融 (79–166), which suggests that the flute derived originally from Tibet.
12. *SB* 10; *DFQJ*, 1446; *TPDF* 7.43. 6: *Shiji*, 53.2017. 8: *Tao Yuanming ji*, 6.479–80.
13. For this point, see Kermode, *Sense of an Ending*, and Brooks, *Reading for the Plot*.
14. *SB* 10; *DFQJ*, 1460; *TPDF* 7.48.

15. According to surviving Tang sources, the Tibetans themselves used this language in international relations. See, for instance, *Jiu Tang shu*, 196.5231.

16. This series is found in *SB* 3; *DFQJ*, 1699–1770; *TPDF* 8.27–38. 1: *Lunyu jishi*, 13.441. 3: *Maoshi zhushu*, 5.211a. 4: *Chuci buzhu*, 5.168. 20: *Wenxuan*, 11.489–92. 28: *LQL*, "Wei shi," 4.367. 32: *Chunqiu Gongyang*, 28.375a.

17. For a less ironic reading of this double entendre, see Huang Yizhen, *Du Fu zi Qin ru Shu*, 2–6. Huang's book represents an important work for anyone interested in this series or the next. See also Gao Tianyou, *Du Fu Long Shu*; Xue Shichang and Meng Yonglin, *Qinzhou shangkong*; and Wen Hulin, *Du Fu Long Shu*.

18. *SB* 3; *DFQJ*, 1711; *TPDF* 8.29. 12: *LQL*, "Wei shi," 4.367.

19. For a brilliant analysis of this imagery throughout the set, see Tian Xiaofei, "Juewu xushi" as well as "Feeding the Phoenix."

20. *SB* 3; *DFQJ*, 1750; *TPDF* 8.36. 7: *Chunqiu Gongyang*, 28.375a. 8: *Lunyu jishi*, 13.441. 16: *Shiji*, 61.2123.

21. *SB* 3; *DFQJ*, 1759; *TPDF* 8.38. 4: *Guo yu*, 1.30. 13–14: *Hanshi waizhuan*, 8.327. 15–16: *Zhuangzi jishi*, 17.605. 22: *Shiji*, 12.484.

22. For this point, see Xiaofei Tian, "Feeding the Phoenix," 106.

23. See *Chunqiu Gongyang*, 28.357a.

24. This is the basic argument of Tian Xiaofei, "Juewu xushi" and "Feeding the Phoenix."

25. Du Fu and his contemporaries would have had good Classical sanction for thinking that strong feelings (even strong feelings expressed in poetry) might have a physical effect on the world through so-called correlative resonance (*gan-ying* 感應), though it is doubtful whether they would have thought that a single private individual's feelings could exert much of an influence.

26. The parallels between these two sets were first suggested to me by Xiaofei Tian.

27. This series is found in *SB* 3; *DFQJ*, 1821–1903; *TPDF* 9.1–12. 1–2: *Huainanzi*, 19.633. 7: *Zhuangzi jishi*, 13.462. 9: *Tao Yuanming ji*, 6.479. 15–16: *Tao Yuanming ji*, 2.115. 20: *Tao Yuanming ji*, 4.364.

28. *SB* 3; *DFQJ*, 1835; *TPDF* 9.3. 2: *Wenxuan*, 12.559. 3: *Chachi* 差池 is a crux. It might mean that they climb "slowly" aboard a boat. 7: *LQL*, "Han shi," 12.329. 8: Li Dao-yuan, *Shui jing zhu*, 34.592.

29. *SB* 3; *DFQJ*, 1873; *TPDF* 9.10. 2: *Zhouyi zhushu*, 3.72b. 7–8: *Wenxuan*, 56.2411. 13: *Shangshu zhushu*, 3.43a. 19: *Zhuangzi jishi*, 2.55.

30. All early editions contain another couplet here between lines 8 and 9: "Yet pearls and jade speed to the central plain, / and the auras of Min and Emei turn gloomy" 珠玉走中原，岷峨氣悽愴. There are good reasons for thinking that this couplet is an interpolation. See my "Three Narrative Poetic Series" for an in-depth discussion.

31. For the *Yijing* as a cosmological model, see Willard J. Peterson, "Making Connections."

32. *SB* 3; *DFQJ*, 1892; *TPDF* 9.12. 1: *Tao Yuanming ji*, 5.461, and *Hou Han shu*, 17.646. 2: *Wenxuan*, 23.1074. 12: *Taiping yulan*, 178.998b. 13: *Chuci buzhu*, 1.37, and *Wenxuan*, 11.490. 16: *Tao Yuanming ji*, 4.364 and 5.461. 18: *Huainanzi*, 16.525, and *Shiji*, 84.2482. 20: *Taiping yulan*, 720.3321a.

33. Like the Buddhist themes of the previous series, and indeed a great many of the motifs of the three series discussed in this chapter, there is not the space here to fully track this program of Daoist imagery. For some further discussion, see Bender, "Three Narrative Poetic Series."

34. It is uncertain, perhaps even unlikely, that Du Fu would have been thinking of Peng Zu's advice specifically. The impulse, however, not to be wounded by emotions (one interpretation of the ambiguous phrase *ku ai shang* 苦哀傷) would have been common to much Daoist thought about cultivating longevity.

35. For Du Fu's meditations on the theme of "home" in his exile, see Jack W. Chen, "Foundings of Home."

36. Joseph R. Allen, "Macropoetic Structures," 319. See also Allen's more recent *Chinese Lyric Sequence*, especially 18–22. For narrative within Chinese poetry, see Allen, "Early Chinese Narrative Poetry"; Levy, *Chinese Narrative Poetry*; and Lin, "Time and Narration." Of these works, Allen's deals only with fictional *yuefu*, and Levy's discusses only one narrative poem before Du Fu's time. Lin deals with a number of Tang dynasty works but all after Du Fu.

37. For Du Fu's self-annotations, see Xie Siwei, *Tang Song shixue*, 98–113; as well as Xu Mai, "Du Fu shige" and "Du Fu zizhu yu shige."

38. In an unpublished lecture ("The Poet in the Scroll"), Owen proposes that, after the Rebellion, Du Fu may have begun writing his poetry on scrolls rather than on loose-leaf sheets of paper and that this choice may have resulted in the first truly chronological poetry collection in the tradition. Evidence for this possibility is largely circumstantial, but Wang Zhu's 王洙 (997–1057) collation notes do suggest that the editions he was able to collect were often in chronological order even before he set about chronologically organizing the entire collection within the two categories of "ancient-style" and "recent-style" verse. In many cases, moreover, Wang Zhu's ordering of the poems has proved more trustworthy than later scholarly reconstructions. Du Fu's early collection, however, is not in any discernible order in Wang's edition, suggesting that something likely changed after the Rebellion in the manner in which he was preserving his own verse.

39. For surviving indications of manuscript organization in the Tang, see Liu Yujun, *Siku Tangren wenji*, particularly 21–30 and 42–52. For manuscripts of poetry that survive at Dunhuang, see p. 19; see also Gao Song, *Dunhuang Tangren shiji*; Huang Yongwu, *Dunhuang de Tang shi* and *Dunhuang de Tangshi xubian*; and Xu Jun, *Dunhuang shiji*. Beyond Dunhuang, the most useful window into Tang manuscript compellation is the fragment of the Xu Hun 許渾 (*jinshi* 832) collection traced into Yue Ke's (1183–1234) *Baozhenzhai fashu zan*. For the problems of judging Tang manuscript organization from Song texts in general, see Owen, "Manuscript Legacy." For a comprehensive accounting of the survival of Tang collections into the Song, see Fan Xin, "Tangren wenji."

40. Wang Jun 王筠 (481–549) and Yan Zhenqing 顏眞卿 (708–84) are reported to have organized their collections "one office at a time" (一官一集 or 一官一體); this format would become very common in the Song. The third poet whose collection seems to have preserved some trace of chronology is Xie Lingyun; his poetry is recorded in the *Wenxuan* in precisely the order it is now understood to have been written.

41. Liu Yujun, *Siku Tangren wenji*, 52.

42. Tang prefaces to edited complete collections often mention the provision of such biographical sketches, though generally those biographies do not survive into Song and post-Song editions. For a particularly famous (and unusually long) surviving example, see Lu Cangyong's biography of Chen Zi'ang, in *Chen Zi'ang ji*, 252–56.

43. Kawai, *Chūgoku no jiden bungaku*, 25.
44. Kawai, *Chūgoku no jiden bungaku*, 208.
45. See Yu Xin, *Yu Zishan*, 94–176; and *Yan Zhitui quanji*, 307–40.
46. For Xie's allusiveness, see Owen, "Librarian in Exile," and Swartz, *Reading Philosophy, Writing Poetry*, 222–58.
47. For this process, see Wu Hongze, "Songdai nianpu," and Gong Bendong, *Song ji chuanbo*, 9–12 and 21–30. By the end of the Song, writers like Wen Tianxiang 文天祥 (1236–83) were even writing their own *nianpu*.
48. This process has been highly uneven, though at this point nearly all major poets in the tradition have received this treatment. To give the example of *nianpu*: Du Fu was the subject of his first *nianpu* in 1084; Bai Juyi likely between 1131 and 1162; Li Bai probably around 1165 (though some sources date this text to the Ming); Tao Qian around 1183; Wang Wei in the sixteenth century; Qu Yuan and Cao Zhi in the nineteenth; and Xie Lingyun, Chen Zi'ang, and Wang Can all in the first half of the twentieth. See Xie Wei, *Zhongguo lidai renwu nianpu*, and Yang Dianxun, *Zhongguo lidai nianpu*.
49. Owen ("Poet in the Scroll") has suggested that Bai Juyi began to order his collection chronologically (within categories) after reading Du Fu; the speculation is attractive but ultimately unprovable. For discussions of the chronological sections in Wei Zhuang and Han Wo, see Qi Tao's discussion in *Wei Zhuang shi ci*, vol. 2, 651–71; as well as Chen Jilong, *Han Wo shi ji*.
50. To my knowledge, Bai Juyi is the only other poet whose collection was edited (by Yang Chongxun 楊崇勳 [976–1045]) into a fully chronological edition before 1050. It is unclear how many of the editions of Du Fu's poetry put together before Wang Zhu's 1039 collation were so edited, though, as Owen notes, Wang's preface indicates that some were at least partly organized by temporal sequence (whether as the result of editorial intervention or as the remnant of Du Fu's own practice), and Su Shunqin's 蘇舜欽 1036 edition seems likely to have been. When it comes to the volume of scholarship, the only poets who compare to Du Fu in terms of the number of *nianpu* produced in the Song are Han Yu, who had ten but was mainly famous for his prose; Su Shi 蘇軾 (1037–1101), who had nine but whose life was much better known because of its recent date; and Tao Qian, who had five. For Du Fu's surviving Song dynasty *nianpu*, see Cai Zhichao, *Songdai Du Fu nianpu*.
51. Xie Siwei, "Lun zizhuan shiren Du Fu," 71.
52. This statement is, I think, patently true, but it runs against common ways of talking about Chinese poetry in the Western academy, which has often emphasized the "nonfictional" character of the art. See, for instance, Owen, *Traditional Chinese Poetry and Poetics*, 34; Miner, *Comparative Poetics*, 108; Fuller, "Weary Night"; and Mair, "Narrative Revolution," 9. I will argue against this interpretation of medieval literature in a forthcoming article. See also Ren, "Cosmogony, Fictionality, Poetic Creativity."
53. For the development of this tradition, see Tian, *Beacon Fire and Shooting Star*, 323–35.
54. The difficulty we have differentiating border poems written from experience and imagination is discussed in Timothy Wai Keung Chan, "Beyond Border and Boudoir." For perhaps the most famous example of a poem that describes the frontiers as timeless, see Wang Changling's 王昌齡 (ca. 690–756) "Going Out the Passes, two poems" 出塞二首, *Wang Changling shi zhu*, 130.

55. See Fu Xuancong, *Tangren xuan Tang shi*, 161.

56. See Li Hua, *Li Xiashu wenji*, 4.6b–8b; *Wenyuan yinghua*, 1000.4249a–b.

57. Modern critics have not always recognized this point and have indeed used frontier ballads as evidence of recordizing principles. Chen Tiemin 陳鐵民, for example, has argued that the flourishing of the genre in the years after the Tang recaptured the Han frontiers proves that "real life experience is the wellspring of literary creation." See Chen Tiemin, "Guanyu wenren chusai," 38. More recently, a few Chinese critics have begun to challenge this received view. See, for instance, Tao Chengtao, "Biansai shi shengcheng yanjiu" and "Tangdai de yinyue huanjing."

58. This passage is drawn from the "Xici" commentary to the *Yijing*; originally, it referred to the numinous power of milfoil stalks as divination tools. See *Zhouyi zhushu*, 7.154b.

59. Hu Zhongrong and Cheng Yusun, *Chengdu wen lei*, 42.25b–26a.

60. Hartman, "Tang Poet Du Fu," 71.

61. See *Zhouyi zhushu*, 8.166b.

62. The earliest source of this oft-repeated cliché seems to be Wang Zhifang 王直方, *Wang zhifang shihua* 王直方詩話, in Wu Wenzhi, *Song shihua quanbian*, vol. 2, 1152.

63. Li Gang, *Liangxi ji*, 138.4a–b.

64. Several more examples will be discussed in chapter 6.

65. The quote comes from Feng's "Du Fu he women de shidai" 杜甫和我们的时代, originally published in *Zhongyang ribao* 中央日报 on July 22, 1945, reprinted in *Feng Zhi xueshu jinghua lu*, 2.

66. Chen Yixin, *Du Fu pingzhuan*, 342.

67. See Jiang Yingke, *Xuetao shiping* 雪濤詩評, in Wu Wenzhi, *Ming shihua quanbian*, vol. 6, 5839. For the long tradition of comparing Du Fu and Li Bai, see Varsano, *Tracking the Banished Immortal*, 38–138.

68. Li claims that, before his time, all editions were only partially chronological; that is, they split Du Fu's poetry into formal sections but organized the poetry within those formal sections more or less chronologically. It is unclear whether this split was characteristic of the manuscript editions that Wang Zhu collated into his edition.

69. *Feng Zhi xueshu jinghua lu*, 3.

70. *Feng Zhi xueshu jinghua lu*, 4.

71. A Buddhist paradise, no less. For the Buddhist themes of the "Leaving Qinzhou" series, see Tian, "Feeding the Phoenix," and Bender, "Three Extended Poetic Series."

FIVE. Vision and the Mundane

1. These quotes have been discussed in earlier chapters. They derive from Zhou Zizhi, *Zhupo shihua*, 1.8a–b; *Feng Zhi xueshu jinghua lu*, 4; and Fu Gengsheng, *Du shi sanyi*, 259.

2. Fu Gengsheng, *Du shi sanyi*, 250–51.

3. Perhaps the most famous example is Mei Yaochen's 梅堯臣 (1002–60) poem about lice; see *Mei Yaochen ji*, vol. 2, 15.283. For other poems by Mei on similar topics, see Chaves, *Mei Yao-ch'en*, 178–99. A number of poems on strange topics are translated by Colin Hawes in his dissertation, "Competing with Creative Transformation." For

the idea of Chinese poetry as a "map" that is filled in progressively over the ninth century and begins, at that point, to approach "the lived world," see Owen, "Cultural Tang," in Chang and Owen, *Cambridge History*, vol. 1, 293.

4. For the "capital poetry" of the High Tang, see Owen, *Great Age*, 52–70.

5. Du Fu will, for instance, frequently talk about the pine trees he managed to plant at his hermitage. These poems are *SB* 11; *DFQJ*, 1919 and 1921; *TPDF* 9.18–19. "Alder Saplings" 4: *Maoshi zhushu*, 5.209b.

6. Stephen Owen has remarked about these poems, "We do not know if Du Fu simply preserved verses that others discarded or if he had an expanded sense of poetry in the everyday" (*TPDF*, lx). Although this is true, the humor of these poems would be much dissipated if they were, in fact, commonplace. Given the continuity between the humor here and in the poems to be considered throughout the first half of this chapter, I am inclined to think these poems would have been quite strange in his time. For Owen's tendency to read Du Fu as more a genial diarist than a driven poetic innovator, see Nicholas Morrow Williams, "Sashimi and History."

7. *Qian* 塹, translated as "trench," would normally refer to the city moat. However, historical sources indicate that Chengdu did not have a moat at this time. See *Xin Tang shu*, 222.6288.

8. *SB* 11; *DFQJ*, 2193; *TPDF* 10.6. 5: *Han shu*, 100.4205.

9. This is not always how the poem has been read. Jin Shengtan, for instance, reads the poet as "deeply pained" here by the fact that he has no real work to do (see *Du shi jie*, 2.111–12). Contrariwise, Deng Xianzhang 鄧獻璋 (fl. 1736) and Lu Yuanchang 盧元昌 (1616–after 1693) argue that Du Fu is enacting virtues here that would be useful in government. For Deng's comment, see *DFQJ*, 2197; for Lu's, see his *Du shi chan*, 12.4b.

10. *SB* 11; *DFQJ*, 1955; *TPDF* 9.28. 2: *Mengzi*, 7.118. 7: *Mengzi*, 6.94 and 10.178; the phrase is also found elsewhere in early texts.

11. Many of these points are made by McCraw in his discussion of the poem; see *Du Fu's Laments*, 24.

12. By "apophasis," I mean to gesture both to the rhetorical trope, roughly equivalent to paralipsis, and also the mode of religious discourse. For this latter usage, see for instance Sells, *Mystical Languages*.

13. *SB* 11; *DFQJ*, 2211; *TPDF* 10.10.

14. From Huang's *Du shi shuo, juan* 6; see *Huang Sheng quanji*, vol. 2, 224.

15. See, for instance, "Pouring for Myself" 獨酌 (*TPDF* 10.9; *DFQJ*, 2202).

16. *SB* 11; *DFQJ*, 2186; *TPDF* 10.5. 2: See *Shishuo xinyu*, 6.201.

17. *SB* 13; *DFQJ*, 2165; *TPDF* 10.16.

18. Note that most critics read the second line here as "Of old I prepared a floating raft to take the place of getting into a boat." I do not think this reading makes much sense in context, and we know from other poems that Du Fu did have a boat, not a raft. The headwords of both lines are thus better understood as "borrowed parallelism" 借對.

19. The paradigm for this sort of rhapsody is the description of the tidal bore in Mei Sheng's 枚乘 (d. 140 BCE) "Seven Stimuli" 七發, which can be found translated in Frankel, *Flowering Plum*, 186–211. "Giving form to things" is given as the definitive

function of the *fu* in Lu Ji's "Rhapsody on *Wen*"; see *Lu Ji ji*, 1.2, and Owen, *Readings*, 130–32.

20. My reading of this poem has been aided by Ashmore, "Recent-Style *Shi* Poetry," 184–86.

21. Cited in *DFQJ*, 2175. Originally from Chen Chunru, *Shuchao jiazhu Du Gongbu qiyan lüshi*.

22. Wang Changling (attrib.), "Lun wen yi" 論文意, in *Bunkyō hifuron*, vol. 3, "Nan," 1339.

23. *Bunkyō hifuron*, 3, "Nan," 1370.

24. *Bunkyō hifuron*, 3, "Nan," 1361.

25. For this translation of *jing* and for the use of the term in medieval Buddhist meditation, see Greene, "Visions and Visualizations" and *Chan before Chan*.

26. Wang Changling (attrib.), "Lun wen yi," *Bunkyō hifuron*, 3, "Nan," 1312.

27. *Bunkyō hifuron*, 3, "Nan," 1309–10, 1325.

28. Liu Xie, *Zengding Wenxin diaolong*, 26.369.

29. Liu Xie, *Zengding Wenxin diaolong*, 26.369. As Stephen Owen has noted, this passage is riddled with interpretive cruxes; see his *Readings in Chinese Literary Thought*, 611, for a brief discussion. For the first sentence here, I follow the interpretation of Lu Kanru and Mou Shijin, *Wenxin diaolong yizhu*, vol. 2, 87–89. Most Chinese commentators I have consulted seem untroubled by the ambiguities noted in the second sentence and do not gloss them.

30. For Liu Xie's anticipation of the postmedieval critical notion of *qing-jing jiaorong* 情景交融, see *Zengding Wenxin diaolong*, 46.567, as well as the discussion of this passage in Cecile Sun, *Pearl from the Dragon's Mouth*, 78–82.

31. Liu Xie, *Zengding Wenxin diaolong*, 26.370.

32. Mair is particularly clear on this point, writing that, "in China, the poet was not generally held to be the 'maker' of his poem but rather its 'recorder'" ("Narrative Revolution," 3). For others claiming that traditional Chinese poetics do not emphasize "creation," see, for instance, Wong, "Ch'ing," 366–67; Pauline Yu, *Reading of Imagery*, 312; and Owen, *Traditional Chinese Poetry*, 84. For arguments that there were particular periods (the early ninth century, in particular) where "creation" came into vogue, see Schafer, "Idea of Created Nature"; Kawai, "Shi wa sekai o tsukuruka?"; and Shang Wei, "Prisoner and Creator." For more general pushback against the idea that the Chinese tradition is "uncreative" (though this is not, in fact, to the point), see, for instance, Zhang Longxi, "Out of the Cultural Ghetto," 86–87; and Ren, "Cosmogony, Fictionality, Poetic Creativity."

33. See Wang Changling (attrib.), "Lun wen yi," *Bunkyō hifuron*, 3, "Nan," 1327; Li Bai, "Yu Han Jingzhou shu" 與韓荊州書, in *Li Taibai quan ji*, 26.1240; Zhang Yanyuan 張彥遠, *Lidai minghua ji* 歷代名畫記 2, in Lu Fusheng, *Zhongguo shuhua quanshu*, vol. 1, 126b; and Jia Dao 賈島 (attrib.), *Ernan mizhi* 二南密旨, in Zhang Bowei, *Quan Tang Wudai shige*, 377.

34. Shi Jiaoran, *Shishi*, "Shishi xu," 1; Wei Zhuang 韋莊, "Youxuanji xu" 又玄集序, in *Wei Zhuang ji jianzhu*, "Wei Zhuang yi wen," 456; *TPDF* 4.7, *DFQJ*, 527; and *TPDF* 6.25, *DFQJ*, 1118.

35. See *Lu Ji ji*, 1.2; and Yan Zhenqing, "Langji xiansheng Yuanzhenzi Zhang Zhihe beiming" 浪跡先生元真子張志和碑銘, *Yan Lugong wenji*, 7.16b.

36. See Zhang Yanyuan, *Lidai minghua ji* I, in Lu Fusheng, *Zhongguo shuhua quanshu*, vol. 1, 120a.

37. Shi Jiaoran, *Shishi*, "Shishi xu," 1.

38. From Jiaoran's *Shiyi* 詩議; see Zhang Bowei, *Quan Tang Wudai shige*, 208.

39. This text is preserved in the "Ji lun" 集論 section of the *Bunkyō hifuron*. See "Nan," 1540. Since it is unmarked in most editions of the collection, the attribution to Yuan Jing is less than totally certain. For a defense, see Luo Genze, *Zhongguo wenxue piping shi*, vol. 2, 27–28.

40. *Bunkyō hifuron*, vol. 3, "Nan," 1555.

41. Wang Ji, "Da chushi Feng Zihua shu" 答處士馮子華書, *Wang Wugong wenji*, 4.148.

42. Wang Changling (attrib.), "Lun wen yi," *Bunkyō hifuron*, vol. 3, "Nan," 1331.

43. Hu Shih 胡適 (1891–1962) is particularly eloquent on this point, writing that the poems of Du Fu's Sichuan period "are pure, natural joys, dashed off casually without any embellishment. . . . and lacking the affectation of recluse poetry in the High Tang." For Hu, Du Fu's capacity to write such "doggerel" (*dayou shi* 打油詩) authenticates his earnestness beyond that of "some Neo-Confucian gentleman endlessly pulling faces and droning on about his loyalty to the emperor and his love of country. . . . Precisely because Du Fu was someone who loved to laugh, therefore his sobs are all the more moving, all the more serious." See *Baihua wenxue shi*, 204–6.

44. Cited in Gu Chen, *Pijiangyuan Dushi zhujie*, "Qiyanlü juan zhi er," 32b. Huang takes this phrasing from Su Shi's description of his own writing in "Yu Xie Minshi tuiguan shu" 與謝民師推官書, *Su Shi wenji*, 19.1418.

45. Qiu Zhao'ao, *Du shi xiangzhu*, 10.810–11.

46. This comment is originally from Zhao's *Du jie chuan xin* 杜解傳新, cited in *DFQJ*, 8.2174.

47. This shift in the meaning of the term *jing* tracks developments in Chinese religious history too complex to detail here. See Greene, *Chan before Chan*, and Han, "Territory of the Sages." For a brief discussion of the development of *jingjie* as a literary concept, see Ma Xiancheng, "Fojiao 'jingjie' lilun."

48. For a broad selection of comments on "River Pavilion," see *DFQJ*, 2187–92. For the comment that started the discussion, see Gao Chufang, *Ji qianjia zhupidian buyi Du shi ji*, 7.645. For pointed criticisms of the idea that this line represents "enlightenment," see, for instance, Shao Fu, *Du lü jijie*, "Wulü juan er," 121; and Gu Chen's comment in *Pijiangyuan Dushi zhujie*, "Wuyan lü juan zhi si," 49b.

49. Wang Sishi, *Du yi*, 4.132.

50. Pu Qilong, *Du Du xinjie*, 3.2.415.

51. See "Du shi shuo," *Huang Sheng quanji*, vol. 2, 4.147.

52. Originally from Shilü jushi, *Cangyunshanfang Dulü xiangjie* 藏雲山房杜律詳解, cited in *DFQJ*, 2188.

53. Originally from *Cangyunshanfang Dulü xiangjie*, cited in *DFQJ*, 2212.

54. Originally from his *Yilan shuwu jingxuan Dushi pingzhu* 藝蘭書屋精選杜詩評注, cited in *DFQJ*, 2212.

55. Western scholarship is replete with claims that the Chinese poetic tradition, in contrast to that of the West, was always built around an "immanent" vision of meaning. See, for instance, Wong, "Ch'ing," 367; Pauline Yu, *Reading of Imagery*, 32; Jullien, *Valeur allusive*, 52; Zongqi Cai, *Configurations*, 107; Damrosch, *How to Read World*

Literature, 14; Palumbo-Liu, *Poetics of Appropriation,* 189–90; Bol, "*This Culture of Ours,*" 95; and Joseph Allen, *In the Voice of Others,* 19. Many others could be cited as well.

56. These poems are *SB* 5; *DFQJ,* 2716 and 2720; *TPDF* 11.58–59. "Setting Out," 2: *Liji zhushu,* 2.38b. 6: *Laozi jiaoshi,* 25.100. 19: *San guo zhi,* "Wei shu," 21.604. 20: *Huainanzi,* 17.583 and *LQL,* "Wei shi," 10.500. "Going Fifteen," 1: *Tao Yuanming ji jianzhu,* 6.479. 13: see, for instance, *Shiji,* 47.1942. 14: *Wenxuan,* 11.490.

57. Lu Yuanchang, *Du shi chan,* 14.18b–19a. Compare to Wang Sishi, *Du yi,* 5.158, and Shen Hanguang's 申涵光 (1620–77, *zi* Fumeng 鳧盟) marginal comment in Yang Lun, *Du shi jingquan,* 9.426.

58. See *Lidai minghua ji* 3, in Lu Fusheng, *Zhongguo shuhua quanshu,* vol. 1, 134b.

59. *SB* 5; *DFQJ,* 2733; *TPDF* 11.62. 2: *Taiping yulan,* 116.4193b. 18: *Lunyu jishi,* 36.1265. 19: Yang Xiong, *Fayan yishu,* 6.194.

60. Du Fu's ekphrastic poetry (*tihua shi* 題畫) has been extensively discussed by Patterson in "Elegies for Empire," 149–204, and by Pan in *Lyrical Resonance,* 197–230. Pan's book is the best general discussion of the ekphrastic tradition available in English, but see also Murck and Fong, *Words and Images,* especially the essay by Chaves, "Meaning beyond the Painting."

61. See *TPDF* 9.37 and 13.69; *DFQJ,* 1998 and 3207.

62. I am grateful to Robert Ashmore for pointing out some of these equivocations to me many years ago. For Daoist ideas about "reality," see Andersen, *Paradox of Being.*

63. See Owen, *Mi-Lou,* 110.

64. Though note Huang Xiufu's 黃休復 (fl. 1000) claim in his *Yizhou minghua lu* 益州名畫錄 that "before [Xue Ji painted these cranes], people from Shu had never seen them alive, and so they thought he painted them exceptionally" (Lu Fusheng, *Zhongguo shuhua quanshu,* 193a). This claim seems highly unlikely, as several species of crane are now prevalent in the region.

65. Owen has explored these poetics in his recent "Thinking through Poetry."

66. On such poems, see Bender, "Ironic Empires."

67. These poems are *SB* 5; *DFQJ,* 3155 and 3158; *TPDF* 13.42–43. "Deck," 7: *Maoshi zhushu,* 12.407a. 8: *Wenxuan,* 7.327. 9: *Lunyu jishi,* 33.1134. 11–12: Wang Tong, *Zhong shuo jiaozhu,* 3.93. "Broken," 2: *Taiping yulan,* 66.443b.

68. For Owen's reading of these poems, see *End of the Chinese "Middle Ages,"* 91–94, and *Traditional Chinese Poetry,* 116–21.

69. *SB* 4; *DFQJ,* 3200; *TPDF* 13.68. 2: *Chunqiu Zuozhuan zhushu,* 53.933b. 7: *Lunyu jishi,* 14.479. 8: *Lunyu jishi,* 13.465. 29: *Lunyu jishi,* 22.772. 30: *Wenxuan,* 14.624. 33: *Lunyu jishi,* 6.222. 37: *Shishuo xinyu,* 24.412. 39: *Hou Han shu,* 61.2032.

70. Alternately, this line might read "your artisan mind brooded gloomy as you planned the composition." The translation depends on Du Fu's familiarity with the technical terminology of painting, in particular the phrase *candan* 惨淡, which may denote a wash.

71. Many critics have pointed out parallels between poet and painter. See, for instance, Wang Sishi, *Du yi,* 6.200.

72. Stephen Owen offers an alternate interpretation of the rhetoric of lineage in this poem, by which active virtues progressively give way to the flabbiness of culture that led to the Tang's collapse. See "Thinking through Poetry," 28.

SIX. History and Community

1. According to scholars like Qi Hehui, Tan Jihe, and Jiang Xianwei, the population of Kuizhou was largely made up of what they call "Lao" 僚 (Rau) peoples. See Qi Hehui and Tan Jihe, "Du Fu Kuizhou shizhong fanying" (reprinted in Tan Jihe, *Ba Shu wenhua biansi ji*, 225–49), and Jiang Xianwei, *Du Fu Kuizhou shi*, 64. In English, see Schafer, *Vermilion Bird*; Backus, *Nan-Chao Kingdom*; Herman, "Kingdoms of Nanzhong"; and Patterson, "Du Fu's Ethnographic Imagination."

2. For Bai Maolin 柏茂林 (sometimes written 琳), see Chen Guanming and Sun Suting, *Du Fu qinjuan jiaoyou*, 121–22. For a different interpretation of Du Fu's relationship with this problematic figure, see Zhang Xiaoqing, "Du Fu yu Bai Maolin."

3. Tackett, *Origins of the Chinese Nation*, 156. See also De Weerdt, *Information, Territory, and Elite Networks*.

4. The interrelated topics of nation and ethnicity in the Tang–Song transition have been a focus of much scholarship in recent decades, not all of it in agreement about basic questions. In English, see Abramson, *Ethnic Identity*; Shao-yun Yang, *Way of the Barbarians*; Bol, "Geography and Culture"; Holcombe, "Re-Imagining China," "Immigrants and Strangers," and "Chinese Identity"; Standen, *Unbounded Loyalty*; and Zhaoguang Ge, *What Is China?* More recently see Ford, *Rome, China, and the Barbarians*, though some of the conclusions here are questionable. Chittick's *Jiankang Empire* is revelatory about the period preceding the Tang. The scholarship in Chinese is voluminous. For a useful review, see Yang, *Way of the Barbarians*, 3–20.

5. For a thoroughgoing account of the tropes of ethnicity found in surviving Tang materials, see Abramson's dissertation ("Deep Eyes and High Noses"), which in this respect is more persuasive than his book.

6. On this point, and on the significance of changing ethnonyms in the Tang–Song transition, see Shao-yun Yang, "Fan and Han," and Tackett, *Origins of the Chinese Nation*, 160–64. Tackett suggests that the more common term in the Tang, *hua*, was a toponym rather than an ethnonym: that is, it did not impute descent the way that the preferred term of later ages, *han*, would. It might be noted, with reference to the hierarchy of the races, that in the Tang the peoples of the Indian subcontinent were frequently elevated above the Chinese.

7. That is, the Tang often claimed to be the state of the *hua-xia*; for its first half, however, emperors also claimed the title of "heavenly qaghan," ruler of both China and Inner Asia. For this ideology, see Skaff, *Sui-Tang China*, 119–24, as well as Pan Yihong, *Son of Heaven*. Chen Sanping has argued that at least "the first half of the Tang might be more aptly called a Sarbo-Chinese (or Xianbeo-Chinese) regime" rather than a native Chinese one; see "Succession Struggle," 380.

8. Holcombe, "Chinese Identity," 32.

9. For the ethnicity of the Tang royal house, see Holcombe, "Xianbei."

10. For the description of the Tang as "cosmopolitan," see, for instance, Lewis, *China's Cosmopolitan Empire*.

11. See, for instance, *Zhou shu*, 49.899; and Du You, *Tongdian*, 185.4980.

12. *Jiu Tang shu*, 61.2361. For the debate in which this possibility was advanced (and ultimately rejected), see Skaff, *Sui-Tang China*, 55–58. Pages 52–72 are generally useful for a discussion of how ethnicity played out on the ground in the Tang; note in particular

the summary on page 63: "The Tang government considered foreigners desirable to attract to the empire with the expectation that the next generation would become commoners indistinguishable from Han."

13. *Da Tang liudian*, 3.15a.

14. See Zhang Zhuo, *Chaoye qianzai*, 5.124 (*Taiping guangji*, 435.3535). This anecdote has been discussed by Marc Abramson in *Ethnic Identity*, 102–3, where it is read to opposite effect, as proving that the Tang had a robust concept of hereditary ethnic difference. This, however, is simply a misreading of the anecdote, which actually shows that the recessive transmission of foreign phenotypical traits was not expected in the Tang.

15. This situation begins to change after the An Lushan Rebellion, when a number of poets fled to the southeast and set up new poetic networks in that region. Du Fu, however, seems still to have yearned for the community up north, and, as Tackett has shown in *Destruction of the Medieval Chinese Aristocracy*, the north central plain remained the home base for the Tang aristocracy until the end of the dynasty.

16. A number of the most famous poets of the early eighth century were sent into exile in the south, including Shen Quanqi 沈佺期 (656–ca. 716), Song Zhiwen 宋之問 (656–712), and Du Fu's own grandfather, Du Shenyan 杜審言 (*jinshi* 671). For their poetry from this period, see Owen, *Poetry of the Early T'ang*, 333–38, 351–62, and 376–79. For the poetry itself, see particularly *Shen Quanqi, Song Zhiwen ji jiaozhu*, 83–124 and 420–46. For the experiences of Mid-Tang intellectuals in exile in the south (albeit further east than Du Fu found himself in Kuizhou), see Ao Wang, *Spatial Imaginaries*, 195–254, though I agree with Hargett (Review, 921) that Wang may sometimes overstate how at home these exiles felt in the south.

17. This quote comes from the subcommentary in *Maoshi zhushu*, 1.12b.

18. From the preface to Gao's *Wensi boyao* 文思博要; see *Wenyuan yinghua*, 699.3606b–7b. For the imperial resonances of "unifying carriage tracks," see *Shiji*, 6.240.

19. Shao-yun Yang has argued that such declines should not be interpreted as a real loss of "Chineseness" (see *Way of the Barbarians*, 29–34). Excellent as his work is otherwise, I find his division of ritual from culture from morality from *wen* an anachronistic imposition of conceptual distinctions that we might make but that the medieval Chinese would not. See, for instance, Huang Kan's commentary on a passage in the *Analects* Huang interpreted as suggesting that a simple change in ritual dress would be equivalent to "becoming a barbarian" 爲夷狄; *Lunyu jijie yishu*, 7.199–200. For the opposite side of this point, see 5.123–4, where Huang cites Sun Chuo as arguing that what separates the barbarians from the Chinese is that the former lack "ritual and righteousness," a lack that would be remedied were a gentleman like Confucius to live among them and cause their moral transformation.

20. *Chunqiu Guliang zhushu*, "Chunqiu Guliang zhuan xu," 3a.

21. This quote comes from He Xiu's 何休 (d. ca. 175) commentary on the Gongyang tradition 公羊傳; see *Chunqiu Gongyang zhushu*, 3.38b. It is echoed as well by the Liu-Song dynasty Guliang 穀梁傳 commentator Fan Yong 范雍; see *Chunqiu Guliang zhushu*, 20.205b.

22. This interpretation of Confucius's procedure is found in Tang exegeses of all three traditions of *Chunqiu* exegesis. For examples, see *Chunqiu Guliang zhushu*, 6.59a, and *Chunqiu Gongyang zhushu*, 25.322a.

23. See, for example, *Chunqiu Guliang zhushu*, 2.23a; *Chunqiu Zuozhuan zhushu*, 7.118a–b; and *Chunqiu Gongyang zhushu*, 12.158b. Much of this material is discussed in Shao-yun Yang, *Way of the Barbarians*, alongside the *Chunqiu* scholarship of the late eighth century.

24. *Chunqiu Zuozhuan zhushu*, "Chunqiu xu," 10a.

25. For this ideal in official historiography, see Li Yanshou's 李延壽 (fl. 640) memorial to the throne on his submission of his *Northern* and *Southern* histories, in *Bei shi*, 100.3344–45. For similar statements about the private histories begun by Chen Zi'ang and Xiao Yingshi, see Lu Cangyong's "Chen Zi'ang biezhuan" 陳子昂別傳, *Wenyuan yinghua*, 793.4191a–92b; and Li Hua's "San xian lun" 三賢論, *Li Xiashu wenji*, 2.1a–5b (*Wenyuan yinghua*, 744.3886a–b). See also McMullen, *State and Scholars*, 167 and 334, nn. 27–28.

26. See Liu Zhiji, *Shitong*, 10.289–90.

27. The topic of the changing character of political loyalty from the medieval to the postmedieval period (and then subsequently within the postmedieval period) is tremendously complicated, and the literature on loyalty (and loyalty in relation to ethnicity) is large and diffuse. The best general treatment in English is Standen, *Unbounded Loyalty*, 49–63 and 149–71. See also Peterson, "P'u-ku Huai-en"; Gungwu Wang, "Feng Tao"; Jay, *Change in Dynasties*; Skaff, "Survival"; Swope, "All Men Are Not Brothers"; Wing-ming Chan, "Early-Qing Discourse"; and Yim, *Poet-Historian Qian Qianyi*; among many others. Recent work on the poet Yu Xin is also relevant here as an example of how a late medieval poet might have thought about changing dynasties. Although, as Xiaofei Tian has shown ("Yu Xin's 'Memory Palace'"), Yu was often writing specifically for a community of Liang exiles like himself, he did also write a considerable number of works expressing fealty to the Northern Zhou; see Ling, "Fame as Durable as Stone."

28. This point has been made well by Charles Holcombe ("Chinese Identity," 50–52): "By including the ethnic non-Han regimes of the fourth-century north in the *Jin shu* . . . and including both the separate lines of Northern and Southern dynasties . . . the early Tang compilation of dynastic histories reinforced a storyline that established the Tang dynasty as the legitimate heir to all of previous Chinese history." For other ways in which the Tang symbolically demonstrated its "Chineseness," see Wechsler, *Offerings*, 136–41.

29. *Tang huiyao*, 63.1090.

30. See Bol, "Geography and Culture," and Shao-yun Yang, *Way of the Barbarians*.

31. For an example of this viewpoint, see Mo Lifeng, *Du Fu shige*, 253. There can be no question that much of Du Fu's poetry, particularly in the early phases of the war, invites this vision of the Rebellion as an ethnic conflict. Du Fu frequently calls An Lushan, Shi Siming, and their sons "barbarians" and compares them to the ancient enemies of the Zhou and the Han. I discuss this issue at length in "Du Fu: Poet Historian," 220–49. Shao-yun Yang, "Reinventing the Barbarian," offers an excellent discussion of the rhetorical use of "barbarian" tropes in the Tang.

32. Wen Tianxiang, *Wen Wenshan quanji*, 16.397.

33. Hung, *Tu Fu*, vii.

34. See also Yu Ruli's comments in chapter 4.

35. This story is preserved in Quan Zuwang, *Xu Yongshang;* for the quotation, see Hao, *Reception of Du Fu,* 155. The allusion is to the "Boyi liezhuan" 伯夷列傳, *Shiji,* 61.2121–29.

36. For Ming loyalists' commentaries on Du Fu, including Wang's, see Hao, *Reception of Du Fu,* 153–205.

37. For recordizing poetics' ability to conform to various different philosophical vocabularies, see chapter 3.

38. See Xiao Difei, *Du Fu yanjiu,* 13.

39. Xiao Difei, *Du Fu yanjiu,* 283–85.

40. Mo Lifeng, *Du Fu shige,* 276–77, 281–82.

41. For a more explicit statement along these lines, see Mo Lifeng, *Du Fu shige,* 375.

42. Tan Jihe, "Du Fu yu wenhua Zhongguo," 19.

43. Tan, "Du Fu yu wenhua Zhongguo," 22.

44. Tan, "Du Fu yu wenhua Zhongguo," 21.

45. Wiliam Hung (Hong Ye) is a striking exception: he wrote his biography of Du Fu in English for a Western audience. Yet the title of this biography is telling—Du Fu is "China's Greatest Poet"—and he explains on its first page that his goal is to "enlarge the sympathetic understanding of China's people" (*Tu Fu,* vii). Du Fu thus remains the property of and the representative of the "Chinese."

46. For an analysis of Du Fu's depiction of local mores, see Zhou Jianjun, *Tangdai Jing Chu,* 184–212; and, in English, Patterson, "Du Fu's Ethnographic Imagination."

47. SB 7; DFQJ, 5292; TPDF 20.104. 5: *Zhuangzi jishi,* 14.517. 12: *Han Feizi,* 7.156. 14: *Zhuangzi jishi,* 1.24; and Tao Qian, *Tao Yuanming ji jianzhu,* 3.219. 15: *Chunqiu Zhouyi zhushu,* 8.168b. 16: *Zhuangzi jishi,* 8.321. 17: *Liji zhushu,* 1.10a. 18: *Chunqiu Zuozhuan zhushu,* 21.365b. 21: *Wenxuan,* 17.763. 22: *Zhuangzi jishi,* 11.371. 23: *Zhuangzi jishi,* 6.229.

48. This line is a notorious crux. Triangulating from variants in early editions, I suspect that 忽 may be a corruption of 惑, which is how I have translated the line. 感 is also an attractive early variant; I would then translate, "Glory and fame stir people inwardly."

49. This couplet has often been read according to a variant (金/合) that would change the meaning to "are these not the Buddha's arts?" Though I do my best throughout this book to avoid poems that have variants that change the sense of the poems, it is not clear what this would mean in context, and I strongly suspect the received reading is correct.

50. *Jin shu,* "Xiu Jin shu zhao," 3305.

51. Du Fu's domestic arrangements are difficult to discern. He certainly had the use of at least one Lao 獠 (Rau) slave, whom the poet identifies as such in "To Be Shown to the Lao Slave Aduan" 示獠奴阿段 (*TPDF* 15.6; *DFQJ,* 3546); another slave girl he calls Aji 阿稽 was probably also Lao, given medieval notices on the naming conventions among these southern peoples (see *Wei shu,* 101.2248). The other servants he mentions are of less certain ethnicity and less certain legal status. It is not clear, moreover, whether he owned or employed these servants himself, since he probably did not have the money to buy or support them at this point (though he almost certainly had owned slaves earlier in his life). It is possible that he had access to them

and to other categories of "debased" 賤 laborers through his connections to Kuizhou's regional government, which, like other southern commands, was in charge of a large number. On the complicated legal categories under which "debased" laborers were attached to the government or to private individuals in the Tang, see Li Jiping, *Tangdai nubi zhidu*; also useful are Hori, *Chūgoku kodai no mibunsei*, and Chu Gansheng, *Nubi shi*. In English, the institution of non-Han slavery in the Tang is discussed briefly in Schafer, *Golden Peaches*, 40–47, and in Abramson, *Ethnic Identity*, 133–38. For Du Fu's poems to his Lao slaves, see Patterson, "Du Fu's Ethnographic Imagination."

52. *SB* 6; *DFQJ*, 4556; *TPDF* 19.7. Preface: *Zhou li zhushu*, 16.248a; *Maoshi zhushu*, 1.43b; *Shangshu zhushu*, 6.82b; *Maoshi zhushu*, 17.630b; *Zhuangzi jishi*, 24.833. 9: *Maoshi zhushu*, 9.327a.

53. 校 here is clearly an error for 枚.

54. These "white chrysanthemums," *baiju* 白菊, have occasioned a great deal of scholarly consternation, and a number of variant characters have been suggested. The invocation of the Double Ninth festival at the end of the poem, however, may perhaps suggest that chrysanthemums are indeed intended here.

55. This section of the poem is highly obscure, resulting in a number of variant readings in early texts. I suspect Du Fu may be referring simultaneously to his slaves and the wood that they have brought him.

56. One cannot know whether he would have read out the preface, which is the most difficult part of the text; the verse, however, is no light reading itself.

57. Du Fu had been given a position in the Ministry of Works 工部 during his later years in Chengdu, but he never went to take up the post, and perhaps was never supposed to do so.

58. For the poetic theme of the Double Ninth Festival, see Davis, "Double Ninth."

59. For a discussion of several of these poems, see Patterson, "Elegies," 126–49.

60. Wang Wei, "Staying Over in Zhengzhou" 宿鄭州, *Wang Wei ji jiaozhu*, 1.39. The general sentiment appears in several places in Tang verse.

61. I discuss this paradox more thoroughly in "Ironic Empires."

62. *SB* 7; *DFQJ*, 4350; *TPDF* 18.18. I have benefitted from an unpublished paper by Mai Huijun.

63. Chen Yixin argues that "family members" is code for Du Fu's wife, who had taken to Buddhism in this time; see *Du Fu pingzhuan*, 965. The Buddhist injunction not to harm any sentient being could very well be at issue in this poem.

64. See Chou, *Reconsidering Tu Fu*, 179; and, for an earlier example of how the poem was read as a bit of absurdity, see Li Yindu's 李因篤 (1631–92) comment in *DFQJ*, 4353. For the political reading, see, for instance, the comments of Xie Jingchu 謝景初 (1020–84) preserved in Cai Zhengsun, *Shilin guangji*, 2.31a, and of Lu Yuanchang, *Du shi chan*, 25.16b.

65. *Zhuangzi jishi*, 7.695–98. Much of this text could be translated differently. I have generally followed Guo Xiang's rendering here, as Du Fu is likely to have known the text with Guo's commentary.

66. See *Nanhua zhenjing zhushu*, 7.399. Guo is less than fully explicit here, though his point can be inferred from his statement about needing to adapt to the "easiness" or "danger" of an age. For a more direct statement, see Cheng Xuanying's subcommentary at the end of the passage.

67. The "coldness" of the water may be relevant here, as fall and winter were the traditional seasons of warfare with the barbarians.

68. See, for instance, Jin Qihua, *Du Fu shi*, 133–37; and Jiang Xianwei, *Du Fu Kuizhou shi*, 98–120.

69. SB 16; *DFQJ*, 5171; *TPDF* 20.85–86. I.1: *Liji zhushu*, 13.435a. I.7: *Taiping yulan*, 189.1044a. II.3: *Chunqiu Zuozhuan zhushu*, 21.370b. II.4: *Chuci buzhu*, 9.208. II.8: *Zhuangzi jishi*, 15.539.

70. The phrase translated "know your details by heart" (*anshu* 暗疏) is uncertain. This is its usual sense in medieval texts. Most commentators take it character-by-character to mean something like "cold and distant," though it never appears in this meaning elsewhere, so far as I can find.

71. SB 15; *DFQJ*, 4194; *TPDF* 18.1. 15: Cao Cao et al., *San Cao ji*, "Wei Wendi ji," 178. 16: *Chen shu*, 26.325. 17: *Zhuangzi jishi*, 13.490–91. 18: *Shangshu zhushu*, 13.193b. 20: *Shishuo xinyu*, 11.318. 21: *Wenxuan*, 17.766. 24: *Zhuangzi jishi*, 1.24. 31: *Jin shu*, 36.1075–76. 32: *San guo zhi*, 54.1264. 38: *Chuci buzhu*, 12.234. 40: *Zhouyi zhushu*, 8.166b. 43: *Shishuo xinyu*, 4.144. 44: *Chuci buzhu*, 2.72.

72. Stephen Owen has discussed Du Fu's interest in rethinking the nature of empire in his "Thinking through Poetry."

73. See, for instance, Wang Sishi, *Du yi*, 8.262; Weng Fanggang, *Du shi fuji*, 15.16a–b; and Liang Yunchang, *Du yuan shuo Du*, 14.13b (940). In English-language scholarship, A. R. Davis also takes this poem as the central poetical statement of Du Fu's collection; see *Tu Fu*, 99–102. The most insightful reading of the poem I have come across is by Wang Hao 汪浩, *Shurentang du Du shi* 熟人堂讀杜詩, cited in *DFQJ*, 4204.

74. SB 6; *DFQJ*, 3702; *TPDF* 15.49–50. I.6: *Zhuangzi jishi*, 19.994. II.5: *Tao Yuanming ji jianzhu*, 5.461. II.19: *Shiji*, 130.3295.

75. It is impossible to tell how many of these poems Du Fu might have written about any one spell of rainy weather, since our earliest editions separate them by genre. I say "around fifteen" because some of these poems do not appear in one or another early edition and are thus attributed to Du Fu with less than complete certainty.

76. See "The Tongfu defeat" 同府之敗, in Wen Tianxiang, *Wen Wenshan quanji*, 16.415.

77. Shannan East Circuit 山南東道 was under the command at this time of Liang Chaoyi 梁崇義, who was nominally loyal to the Tang but not truly under its control. The upriver rebellion is so uncertain no one even knows for sure what Grass Fort is.

78. SB 16; *DFQJ*, 5205; *TPDF* 20.76.

79. Alternately, this line might be translated "flowers survive the cold leaves turning red."

80. *Chuci buzhu*, 8.182.

81. *QTW*, 544.5515a–b. The Diagram of Eight Formations was a traditional pictorial genre for illustrating military strategy; the great military strategist Sunzi 孫子, for example, was supposed to have composed one. Later mythology devised other purported purposes for Zhuge's Diagram, turning it into a maze from which his enemies could not escape. I cannot find evidence that such ideas were current in the Tang.

82. SB 16; *DFQJ*, 3572; *TPDF* 15.13. 1: *San guo zhi*, "Shu shu," 35.919. 2: *Zhuangzi jishi*, 20.680. 3: *Maoshi zhushu*, 2.74b.

83. See *TPDF* 15.70; *DFQJ*, 3575.

84. SB 15; *DFQJ*, 3841; *TPDF* 17.34–38. II.1: *Chuci buzhu*, 8.182. II.2: Yu Xin, *Yu Zishan ji zhu*, 1.46 and 2.104. II.6: *Wenxuan*, 19.875–76. III.8: *Wenxuan*, 27.1291. I have benefitted from an unpublished paper by Mai Huijun.

85. This interpretation assumes that critics are right to think that the fifth line of the poem, "vain his literary flourishes," refers to his being unable to effectively persuade the king of Chu to adopt a less ruinous course. For an example of a critic advancing this position, see Jiang Shaomeng's 蔣紹孟 (n.d.) comment cited in Yang Lun, *Du shi jingquan*, 13.651.

86. Much of the music that was popular in the Tang came from Central Asia, including much of the music that underlay the *yuefu* tradition. We have little access to this music nowadays, but for a useful study, see Tao Chengtao, "Biansai shi."

87. Tillman, "Reassessing Du Fu's Line."

88. See *TPDF* 15.12; *DFQJ*, 3569. Shrines are, however, often dilapidated in Tang poetry; the frequency of the trope raises doubts about its particular accuracy here.

89. "Traces" is a technical term of medieval philosophy that will be discussed in the next chapter. It refers to the way that records of a given figure's actions can fail to accurately manifest the true motivations that gave rise to those actions. This technical usage is highly relevant to these poems. Where most medieval Xuanxue thinkers valorize "what made the traces" over the "traces" themselves, Du Fu is placing his hope in the latter.

SEVEN. Contingency and Adaptation

1. The history narrated briefly here is extraordinarily complex, and it has been the subject of a great deal of scholarship. For an English introduction to the history of *Yijing* scholarship, see Richard J. Smith, *Fathoming the Cosmos*. For the text's transformation from a key to the cosmos's regularities to a statement of its unfathomability, see Meyer, "Correct Meaning," 75–146. For the Tang subcommentary, see Meyer as well as my "*Corrected Interpretations.*"

2. *Zhuangzi jishi*, 5.532–33.

3. For a study of Guo's commentary in English, see Ziporyn, *Penumbra Unbound*.

4. *Nanhua zhenjing zhushu*, 5.281.

5. For Guo's interpretation of the metaphor of shoes and traces, see *Nanhua zhenjing zhushu*, 5.304.

6. *Nanhua zhenjing zhushu*, 3.170. Confucius's pretending is not mentioned in this passage, but it is a cornerstone of Guo's commentary that Confucius was a sage, and Laozi was not.

7. *Nanhua zhenjing zhushu*, 9.527.

8. On the meaning-structure of Xuanxue exegesis, see Ashmore, "Word and Gesture."

9. *Zhouyi zhushu*, 8.172b. For Han's interpretation of the phrase "fixed standards" (*dianyao* 典要), see 8.174b.

10. It seems to have been the faith of Xuanxue in general (pace Makeham in *Transmitters and Creators*) that talented individuals could learn, through studying the obscure, to approximate the wisdom of the sages. This was a point made explicitly by Sun Chuo in his Xuanxue commentary on the *Analects*: "The *Yijing* fully penetrates the principles of the myriad things between heaven and earth, . . . and thus it is possible for one to exhaust learning and fully understand these mechanisms. One does not have to be born a sage to do so." See *Lunyu jijie yishu*, 1.15.

11. *Zhouyi zhushu*, 8.174a.

12. *Zhouyi zhushu*, 8.169a.

13. *Zhouyi zhushu*, 8.173a and 8.167b.

14. See *Zhouyi zhushu*, 8.174a–b.

15. *Zhouyi zhushu*, 7.154a.

16. *Zhouyi zhushu*, 8.166b.

17. *Zhouyi zhushu*, 7.154a.

18. *Zhouyi zhushu*, 8.172b.

19. *Zhouyi zhushu*, "Zhouyi zhengyi xu," 2a.

20. *Zhouyi zhushu*, 8.167b.

21. *Liji zhushu*, 34.618a.

22. Huang Kan, *Lunyu jijie yishu*, 1.24–26. For the *Zhengyi*'s statement to a similar effect, see *Liji zhushu*, 34.617b: "When sages assume the throne, there is that they change [from past dynasties] and that they do not." This principle was invoked in court debates as well. See, for instance, Cui Mian's 崔沔 (637–739) "Jia biandou zeng fu jiyi" 加籩豆增服紀議, *Wenyuan yinghua*, 764.4015b, which also usefully makes the point that only sages can create anew, whereas worthies merely transmit what they have created.

23. Some of these issues have been discussed in English-language scholarship with regard to the literary culture of the Liang dynasty; see for instance Tian, *Beacon Fire*; Nicholas Morrow Williams, "Literary Controversy"; and Ping Wang, *Age of Courtly Writing*. They have been touched on in the Tang by McMullen in "Historical and Literary Theory." For an interpretation of the whole of the premodern Chinese literary tradition along these lines, see Liu Wenzhong, *Zhengbian—Tongbian—Xinbian*.

24. Liu Xie, *Zengding Wenxin diaolong*, 6.397.

25. Liu Xie, *Zengding Wenxin diaolong*, 6.398.

26. Liu Xie, *Zengding Wenxin diaolong*, 6.398.

27. See Owen, *Readings in Chinese Literary Thought*, 215. This ideal is elaborated by Cao Pi 曹丕 (187–226) in his *Dianlun* 典論; see Cao Cao et al., *San Cao ji*, "Wei Wendi ji," 1.177–79.

28. *SB* 17; *DFQJ*, 5528; *TPDF* 21.65. 1–2: *Wenxuan*, 28.1330. 4: *Wenxuan*, 12.569. 7: *QTW*, 190.1922; and *Bowu zhi*, 10.111.

29. For a reading along these lines, see Zhang Jin, *Dushutang Du shiji zhujie*, 18.1735.

30. See, for instance, *Nanhua zhenjing zhushu*, 6.328.

31. According to Yuan Jiao 袁郊 (late ninth c.), this kenning was applied during his lifetime to Du Fu's contemporary Tao Xian 陶峴; see Yuan Jiao, *Ganze yao*, 3. It is not clear how common this kenning might have been for similar wanderers.

32. See Wang Jia, *Shiyi ji*, 10.235; and *Yue jue shu*, 4.326.

33. This suggestion is even more explicit in other poems written around the same time; see, for instance, *TPDF* 21.43; *DFQJ*, 5455.

34. *SB* 18; *DFQJ*, 5649; *TPDF* 22.22. 1: *Zhouyi zhushu*, 8.168a. 2: *Han shu*, 26.1291. 7: *Zhuangzi jishi*, 14.533; and *Jin shu*, 80.2099. 8: Ge Hong, *Baopuzi*, 6.124.

35. Jin Shengtan, *Du shi jie*, 4.246.

36. Wang Xizhi, *Jin Wang Youjun ji*, 2.93a–94a (335–37).

37. *SB* 18; *DFQJ*, 5667; *TPDF* 22.28. 5: *Shiji*, 130.3295, and, for instance, *Song shu*, 51.1480. 6: Cao Cao et al., *San Cao ji*, "Wei Wendi ji," 178. 7–8: *Zhuangzi jishi*, 1.2–6.

38. For an interpretation of the poem along these lines, see Owen, "Self's Perfect Mirror."

39. Owen offers and dismisses this interpretation in *TPDF*, vol. 6, 392.

40. See Zhao's *Du lü Zhao zhu*, "juan shang," 72. The emendation has been accepted by important critics, including Wang Sishi, Qiu Zhao'ao, and Yang Lun. Those critics that reject the emendation often do so with explicitly recordizing explanations; see, for instance, Zhou Zhuan's 周篆 (1642–1706) comment in his *Du gongbu shiji jijie* 杜工部詩集解, cited in *DFQJ*, 5669. Note that the emendation is patently implausible. Even if the two characters are phonetically close (they were not homonyms in Middle Chinese), no scribe would have heard *jin* 近 and written *jin* 僅, the *lectio difficilior*. Owen's preference for *jin* 近 on the basis of parallelism is also not convincing, since *jin* 僅 is equally parallel.

41. Qiu Zhao'ao, *Du shi xiangzhu*, 22.1945. Surviving editions of Wang's comment read slightly differently; see Wang Sishi, *Du yi*, 10.363.

42. See, for particularly good examples of this common trope, Zhang Yuan, *Du shi huicui*, "Zi xu," 1b–2a, and Ye Xie, *Shi yuan*, "Neipian xia," 44. Owen has discussed Du Fu's "shifting style" in *Great Age*, 183–224.

43. Qin Guan, *Huaihai ji*, 22.4a–b.

44. Zhang Jie, *Suihantang shihua*, 1.103–4.

45. Fang explicitly attributes his understanding of the *Yijing* to the teachings of Cheng Yi and Zhu Xi. For a basic introduction to Neo-Confucian exegesis of the *Yi*, see Richard J. Smith, *Fathoming the Cosmos*, 127–39. For Cheng Yi's *Yijing* scholarship, see "Ch'eng I and the Pattern of Heaven-and-Earth," in Kidder J. Smith et al., *Sung Dynasty Uses*, 136–68; Hon, *Yijing and Chinese Politics*, 110–40; and Cheng Yi's *Yi River Commentary on the "Book of Changes,"* trans. Harrington. For Zhu Xi's, see *Sung Dynasty Uses*, 169–205, as well as Zhu Xi's *Original Meaning of the Yijing*, trans. Adler.

46. Originally from a preface to Zhao's *Du jie chuan xin*; reproduced in *DFQJ*, "Fulu er," 6684–85.

47. For Yu Ruli, see chapter 4.

48. This is a quotation from the *Yijing* itself; see *Zhouyi zhushu*, 7.149b. It is worth noting the difference between the *Zhengyi* (Tang) reading of this passage and Cheng Yi's reading. Where the *Zhengyi* says that "the *dao* of change and continuity fills heaven and earth," Cheng Yi argues that the *Yijing* is complete because "the underlying principles of the myriad things are always and everywhere the same" 萬物之理无有不同. See Cheng Yi, *Yichuan xiansheng Zhouyi jingzhuan*, 9.11b.

49. These ideas are discussed in chapters 3, 4, and 6. Hu Zhongrong and Cheng Yusun, *Chengdu wen lei*, 42.26a; Chen Yixin, *Du Fu pingzhuan*, 342; Wen Tianxiang, *Wen Wenshan quanji*, 16.397.

50. This statement is attributed to Li Nangong 李南公 (*jinshi* before 1069) in Chen Fu's 陳輔 (*jinshi* 1057) *shihua*, preserved in Zeng Zao, *Lei shuo*, 57.13b.

51. *Su Shi wenji*, 70.2210–11.

52. *Guo Songtao shi wen ji*, "Wenji" 4.41.

53. This idea actually went all the way back to the late Tang. In a preface for a poem on crabapple blossoms, Xue Neng 薛能 (*jinshi* 846) thanked heaven that Du Fu had never written on the topic and that therefore he still had an opportunity to do so. This preface inaugurated a poetic cliché that persisted into the Song. See Chen Si, *Haitang pu*, "juan shang," 8a–b.

54. Ye Xie, *Shi yuan*, "Neipian shang," 11–12.

55. Chen Tingzhuo, *Baiyuzhai cihua*, 9.217.

56. Chen Tingzhuo, *Baiyuzhai cihua*, 9.216–17.

57. As Chen explains, writers after Du Fu could only see the sources of their tradition through the distorting lens he provided; for this reason, his transformation of the tradition "could not be fathomed." This argument prefigures my own, though I would apply it to critics rather than poets.

58. For a discussion of this strand of criticism, see, for instance, Xu Guoneng, "Lidai Du Fu shixue." In English, see Hao, *Reception*, 94–122.

59. Du Fu's influence on particular poets is difficult to study. For a fascinating recent article on modern poets' engagement with his work, though, see David Wang, "Six Modernist Poets."

60. This series is *SB* 8; *DFQJ*, 5708, 5715, 5718, 5760, 5755, 5774, 5777, 5780, 5784, and 5788; *TPDF* 22.39–48. Note that *DFQJ* splits the set up and assigns its various members (on flimsy evidence) to different parts of Du Fu's southern journey, though they appear together in the earliest surviving editions of his collection. As far as I know, no commentator has ever noticed that these ten poems are a set.

61. *SB* 8; *DFQJ*, 5708 and 5718; *TPDF* 22.39 and 22.41. "Unburdening," 1: *Lunyu jishi*, 13.441. 10: *Lunyu jishi*, 17.594. 20: *Shiji*, 63.2140. 33: *Zhouyi zhushu*, 7.153b. 34: *Shiji*, 16.2366. 35: *Shangshu zhushu*, 10.140a. 39–40: *Chuci buzhu*, 12.234. 43: *Lunyu jishi*, 25.867. 44: *Zuozhuan zhushu*, 24.407b. "Relieving," 2: *DFQJ*, 4708. 4: *Shangshu zhushu*, 8.108b. 6: *Wenxuan*, 45.2016. 8: *Lunyu jishi*, 38.1307. 9: *Zhouyi zhushu*, 8.169a. 12: *Liji zhushu*, 31.881a.

62. *Zhouyi zhushu*, 8.169a. See also the other surviving medieval comment on this passage: Guan Lang, *Guanshi yizhuan*, 6.19b. The idea that the sages might have "a thousand concerns" is, however, found in the *Yanzi chunqiu*, 6.411. And Lu Zhaolin 盧照鄰 inverts the "Xici" quotation in one of his essays, suggesting that the sages did in fact have "a hundred concerns"; see his "Wu bei wen" 五悲文, *QTW*, 166.1697b.

63. *SB* 8; *DFQJ*, 5760 and 5774; *TPDF* 22.42 and 22.44. "Passing the Night," 4: *Zhuangzi jishi*, 32.1040. 6: *Maoshi zhushu*, 1.63b. 12: *Maoshi zhushu*, 12.429b, and *Kong congzi*, 6.8a–b. 13: *Lunyu jishi*, 17.579, and *Zhouyi zhushu*, 8.173a. "Passing Jinkou," 2: *Lunyu jishi*, 18.610. 3–4: *Tao Yuanming ji jianzhu*, 1.53. 6: *Wenxuan*, 23.1075, and *Chuci buzhu*, 9.215. 9: *Zhouyi zhushu*, 6.132b. 10: see for instance *Mengzi*, 3.54. 12: *Jin shu*, 94.2463. 14: *Wenxuan*, 11.490.

64. For Guo Xiang's interpretation of this parable, which makes the point that it is the sages who drift like untied boats, see *Nanhua zhenjing zhushu*, 32.592.

65. See *Kong congzi*, 6.8a–b. It is worth noting that this story itself seems to be an allusion to a story of Confucius's own retirement to "leisure" 優哉游哉 in *Shiji*, 47.1918 (among other sources); Du Fu could have been thinking of either story or of both.

66. *Zhouyi zhushu*, 6.132b.

67. *Zhouyi zhushu*, 8.172b.

68. *SB* 8; *DFQJ*, 5780 and 5784; *TPDF* 22.47 and 22.48. "Setting Out," 1: *Zhuangzi jishi*, 32.1046. 3: *Lunyu jishi*, 25.878. 7: *Han shu*, 49.2270. 18: *Zhuangzi jishi*, 6.243. "Making," 7: *Wenxuan*, 25.1199. 8: *Taiping yulan*, 970.4432a. 9–10: *Chuci buzhu*, 8.183. 12: *Wenxuan*, 16.720.

69. This point might perhaps be strengthened by the variant character in the penultimate line, which in *Wenyuan yinghua* reads: "I seem to have understood (*wu* 悟) these

two handles" instead of "I seem to have mistaken (*wu* 悞) these two handles." In a few surviving texts from Dunhuang, "understood" 悟 is written with the character "mistaken" 悞, suggesting either that the two homophonous characters (both pronounced *nguH* in Middle Chinese) were capable of interchangeable use in Tang scribal practice or that they were sometimes confused. Though it is not possible to say for certain whether Du Fu meant to use a character that could be interpreted either way, we can at least observe that such a choice would fit with his penchant, in this period, for exploiting linguistic ambiguities as well as with the program of this series in particular. For texts from Dunhuang where these characters are interchanged, see for instance Pan Chonggui, *Dunhuang bianwen ji*, 2.279–83, 2.283, and 8.1266.

70. See Guo Zhida, *Xinkan jiaoding*, 16.15b. Note that, although this colloquial sense of *de* 得 is not listed in the *Hanyu da cidian* until the Qing, it appears in popular literature in the Tang. See Jiang Lansheng and Cao Guangshun, *Tang Wudai yuyan cidian*, 89.

71. Zhao Cigong, *Du shi jie*, "Yi zhi juan zhi si," 1387.

72. Tang Yuanhong, *Du shi jun*, 4.27b.

73. See, for instance, *QTW*, 92.958b, 107.1097a, and 847.8896a.

74. Owen, "Self's Perfect Mirror," 98.

75. The first poem is *SB* 18; *DFQJ*, 5696; *TPDF* 22.36. The second is *SB* 18; *DFQJ*, 5703; *TPDF* 22.38. "Passing," 8: *Zhuangzi jishi*, 1.2. "Gazing," 7: Yan Kejun, *Quan shanggu*, "Quan Jin wen," 102.2042b.

76. Pu Qilong argues both meanings are in play; see *Du Du xinjie*, 3.6.586.

77. See *Chuci buzhu*, 2.54–119.

78. Earlier in his life, Du Fu at various points displays a greater interest in Buddhism per se. For a discussion of Du Fu's attitudes towards the religion, see Liu Kebing, *Du Fu yu fojiao*; in English, see Rouzer, "Refuges and Refugees."

79. *SB* 8; *DFQJ*, 5732; *TPDF* 22.62. 6: See *Taishō* 1762.368a23–24. 7: See *Taishō* 1799.916a14–15. 24: *Maoshi zhushu*, 5.212a. 28: *Wenxuan*, 43.1957–61. 29–30: *Shangshu zhushu*, 18.273b and *Taishō* 2102.49b14.

80. The text of this couplet is problematic; my translation follows the generally accepted emendation of Zhou Yong for He Yong. Most commentators also accept the variant "Xie Ke" 謝客 for "traveler in the wilderness" 野客, understanding the phrase as referring to Xie Lingyun by his child name, "Guest" 客.

81. Yang Lun, *Du shi jingquan*, 19.968.

82. See *Shen Quanqi, Song Zhiwen ji jiaozhu*, "Song Zhiwen ji jiaozhu," 3.557. Tao Min speculates that this poem was written during Song's banishment to Qinzhou 欽州 in the far south; it is not impossible that he would have passed through Tanzhou on the way there.

83. The cosmological Buddha was a common trope of Chinese Buddhist art in the Six Dynasties and early Tang, whereby a map of the cosmos would be displayed on a statue of the Buddha's body. The underlying Buddhological idea is that the basic nature of all things is Buddha nature, so all things are ultimately the Buddha. On this topic, see for instance Howard, *Imagery of the Cosmological Buddha*.

84. This sort of transformation of the landscape is common in Buddhist literature. The most famous example is in the *Vimalakīrti Nirdeśa* 維摩詰所説經, *Taishō* 475.538c20, in which the Buddha reveals that our world is in fact a pure land by touching the earth with his foot.

85. See chapter 1.
86. The first poem is *SB* 8; *DFQ J*, 5934; *TPDF* 23.19. The second is *SB* 18; *DFQ J*, 5919; *TPDF* 23.14. "Ballad," 7: *Guo yu*, 4.164.
87. See, for an early example, the comment attributed to Shi 師 in Wang Zhu (attrib.), *Fenmen jizhu Du gongbu shi*, 23.11a.
88. For a discussion of the concepts of "having dependency" and "not having dependency" as they feature in medieval Daoism, see Kroll, "Poetry Debate."
89. At least some association between crows and death is suggested in a ninth-century story from the *Chu Hedong ji* 出河東記, in which the "Crow Caw Realm" 鴉鳴國 is said to be where ghosts go when they die. See *Taiping guangji*, 384.3066–67. It is unclear whether Du Fu would have known this story or others like it.
90. See, for instance, Zhu Heling, *Du Gongbu shiji jizhu*, 20.814. Shi Hongbao disputes Zhu's reasoning but does not disagree with his conclusion (*Du Du shi shuo*, 23.226).

Conclusion

1. *TPDF* 23.49; *DFQ J*, 6093.
2. See Yearley, "Ethics of Bewilderment." The idea of "moral contingency," in particular, is suggested on pp. 448–49, though Yearley does not use these words. More generally, the literature on contingency in ethics is vast. Recent work has considered the contingency that operated in the evolution of our moral attitudes; the dependence of our moral obligations on our circumstances; and the operation of so-called moral luck, those factors outside of our control that may play a role in rendering our decisions good or bad. Cultural differences in moral thought have also been extensively discussed and theorized, largely from a metaethical perspective, and the results of such metaethical deliberation have sometimes influenced more positive moral theorizing, for instance by relativists and by many recent "postmodern" thinkers (see Bauman, *Intimations*). In a few cases, the contingency of our moral perspectives has been explicitly theorized as a possible source of positive values; one famous example, albeit idiosyncratic, is Rorty, *Contingency, Irony, and Solidarity*. This is perhaps the closest contemporary position I know of to Du Fu's, though I have also been influenced in my thinking about Du Fu by the account of moral historicity in Taylor, *Sources of the Self*.
3. Without going down the rabbit hole of skeptical and relativist moral theorization, it should, I think, be enough to say that the rough position hinted at in Du Fu's poetry is far more limited than skeptics' and relativists' tend to be. He does not commit, that is, to the impossibility of real moral knowledge, to the unreality of moral truths, or to the unboundedness of moral variation over time. Instead, he merely disclaims for himself any access to transhistorical constancies, assuming that even should such objective moral truths exist, we come to know them primarily through a community-mediated and thus historically contingent past. If moral values are real, therefore, and if we happen to know them, that is a matter of luck—luck that Du Fu was fairly convinced, by the end of his life, he did not have.
4. To give an example from the fifth chapter, his interest in topics excluded from high-cultural discourse might be seen to display an appropriate respect for the possibility

that inherited categories may not capture everything of value. Or, to take another from the sixth, his willingness to imagine solidarities across ethnic and cultural divides might reflect a recognition that moral communities are not grounded in unchanging verities and are thus liable to shift. Both of these virtues could reasonably be recommended to anyone whose values turn out to be merely contingent.

5. For the bodily effects of poetry, see *Maoshi zhushu*, 1.13a–b. I discuss this text extensively in "Poet Historian, Poet Sage," 43–47.

6. This is not to suggest that the moral vision preceded or finally decided his poetic development. Quite the opposite: the form was a gift, an affordance of the late medieval model as it broke down to a poet who had been, in his youth, devoted to it even more completely than most of his contemporaries. And this form may well have guided the development of his thought.

7. The idea that certain ethical perspectives are best articulated in literary genres was influentially theorized by Nussbaum in *Love's Knowledge*. Since her groundbreaking early work, it has been taken up by a number of theorists, representing a wide variety of moral perspectives. For a survey of such positions, the so-called Literary Turn in analytic philosophy, see Hämäläinen, *Literature and Moral Theory*. Meretoja, *Ethics of Storytelling*, 1–37, is a useful complement, considering continental philosophy as well.

8. See Landy, *How to Do Things*, 3–19.

9. Work along these lines is too multifarious to cite in full, but see, for instance, Adamson, "Against Tidiness"; Diamond, "Difficulty of Reality" and "Anything but Argument?"; Murdoch, "Nostalgia"; Phillips, "Allegiance and Change"; and Martha Nussbaum's broader projects in *Love's Knowledge*, *Poetic Justice*, and *Cultivating Humanity*.

10. A few critics have considered the ethical affordances of poetry as well, though each notes that the novel has been more at the center of recent thought. See, for instance, Altieri, "What Differences Can Contemporary Poetry Make in Our Moral Thinking?" and "Lyrical Ethics"; Eskin, *Ethics and Dialogue*; and David-Antoine Williams, *Defending Poetry*.

11. See Hao, *Reception*, 206–33.

12. I hope to echo here Gadamer's concept of the "festive," discussed in *Relevance of the Beautiful*, 3–65. The community Du Fu's work should sustain, however, is less timeless than Gadamer imagines art being. Much of my approach throughout this book has been informed by *Truth and Method*.

13. Scheffler, *Why Worry?*, 3; *Equality and Tradition*, 287–311; and *Death and the Afterlife*, 108. Note that Scheffler is interested primarily in more "conservative" (small *c*) traditions that "hand down . . . values from generation to generation." See *Equality and Tradition*, 304–5.

14. For the ethical potentials of irony, enigma, and plenitude, see (among other works) Nehamas's account of Socrates in *Art of Living*.

Works Cited

Abramson, Marc Samuel. "Deep Eyes and High Noses: Constructing Ethnicity in Tang China." PhD diss., Princeton University, 2001.

———. *Ethnic Identity in Tang China*. Philadelphia: University of Pennsylvania Press, 2008.

Adamson, Jane. "Against Tidiness." In *Renegotiating Ethics in Literature, Philosophy, and Theory*, edited by Jane Adamson, Richard Freadman, and David Parker, 84–110. Cambridge, U.K.: Cambridge University Press, 1998.

Allen, Joseph R. *The Chinese Lyric Sequence: Poems Paintings, Anthologies*. Amherst: Cambria Press, 2020.

———. "Early Chinese Narrative Poetry: The Definition of a Tradition." PhD diss., University of Washington, 1982.

———. *In the Voice of Others: Chinese Music Bureau Poetry*. Ann Arbor: Center for Chinese Studies, University of Michigan, 1992.

———. "Macropoetic Structures: The Chinese Solution." *Comparative Literature* 45, no. 4 (1993): 305–29.

Allen, Sarah M. *Shifting Stories: History, Gossip, and Lore in Narratives from Tang Dynasty China*. Cambridge, Mass.: Harvard University Asia Center, 2014.

Altieri, Charles. "Lyrical Ethics and Literary Experience." *Style* 32, no. 2 (1998): 272–97.

———. "What Differences Can Contemporary Poetry Make in Our Moral Thinking?" In *Renegotiating Ethics in Literature, Philosophy, and Theory*, edited by Jane Adamson, Richard Freadman, and David Parker, 113–33. Cambridge, U.K.: Cambridge University Press, 1998.

Andersen, Poul. *The Paradox of Being: Truth, Identity, and Images in Daoism*. Cambridge, Mass.: Harvard University Asia Center, 2019.

Appiah, Kwame Anthony. "Thick Translation." *Callaloo* 16, no. 4 (1993): 808–19.

Asami Yōji 浅見洋二. *Chūgoku no shigaku ninshiki: Chūsei kara kinsei e no tenkan* 中国の詩学認識：中世から近世への転換. Tokyo: Sōbunsha, 2008.

Ashmore, Robert. "Recent-Style *Shi* Poetry: Heptasyllabic Regulated Verse." In *How to Read Chinese Poetry: A Guided Anthology*, edited by Zong-qi Cai, 181–97. New York: Columbia University Press, 2008.

———. *The Transport of Reading: Text and Understanding in the World of Tao Qian*. Cambridge, Mass.: Harvard University Asia Center, 2010.

———. "Word and Gesture: On Xuan-School Hermeneutics of the Analects." *Philosophy East and West* 54, no. 4 (October 2004): 458–88.

Backus, Charles. *The Nan-Chao Kingdom and T'ang China's Southwestern Frontier.* New York: Cambridge University Press, 1981.

Bai Juyi 白居易. *Bai Juyi ji jianjiao* 白居易集箋校. Edited by Zhu Jincheng 朱金城. Shanghai: Shanghai guji chubanshe, 1988.

Bao Bide 包弼德 (Peter K. Bol). "Tang–Song zhuanxing de fansi: yi sixiangshi de bianhua wei zhu" 唐宋轉型的反思：以思想史的變化爲主. *Zhongguo xueshu* 3, no. 1 (2000): 63–87.

Barrett, Timothy Hugh. *Li Ao: Buddhist, Taoist, or Neo-Confucian?* London Oriental Series 39. Oxford: Oxford University Press, 1992.

———. *Taoism under the T'ang: Religion and Empire during the Golden Age of Chinese History.* London: Wellsweep, 1996.

Barthes, Roland. "Analyse textuelle d'un conte d'Edgar Poe." In *Semiotique narrative et textuelle*, edited by Claude Chabrol. Paris: Librairie Larousse, 1973.

Bauman, Zygmunt. *Intimations of Postmodernity.* London: Routledge, 2003.

Bei Qi shu 北齊書. By Li Baiyao et al. Beijing: Zhonghua shuju, 1972.

Bei shi 北史. By Li Yanshou 李延壽. Beijing: Zhonghua shuju, 1974.

Bender, Lucas Rambo. "The Corrected Interpretations of the Five Classics (*Wujing Zhengyi*) and the Tang Legacy of Obscure Learning (*Xuanxue*)." *T'oung Pao* 104, no. 1 (2019): 76–127.

———. "Du Fu: Poet Historian, Poet Sage." PhD diss., Harvard University, 2016.

———. "Ironic Empires." In *Reading Du Fu: Nine Views*, edited by Xiaofei Tian, 56–74. Hong Kong: Hong Kong University Press, 2020.

———. "Other Poetry on the An Lushan Rebellion: Notes on Time and Transcendence in Tang Verse." *Harvard Journal of Asiatic Studies*, nos. 1–2 (2019): 1–48.

———. "Poetic Omens and Poetic History." Unpublished essay.

———. "The Sense of Not Ending." Unpublished essay.

———. "Three Narrative Poetic Series from Du Fu's Exile on the Western Frontiers." *Journal of Oriental Studies* 51.1 (2021).

Berkowitz, Alan J. *Patterns of Disengagement: The Practice and Portrayal of Reclusion in Early Medieval China.* Stanford: Stanford University Press, 2000.

Bloom, Harold. *The Anxiety of Influence: A Theory of Poetry.* Oxford: Oxford University Press, 1973.

Bokenkamp, Stephen R. "Time after Time: Taoist Apocalyptic History and the Founding of the T'ang Dynasty." *Asia Major* 7, no. 1 (1994): 59–88.

Bol, Peter K. "Geography and Culture: The Middle-Period Discourse on the Zhong Guo—the Central Country." In *Kongjian yu wenhua changyu: kongjian zhi yixiang, shijian yu shehui de shengchan* 空間與文化場域：空間之意象、實踐與社會的生產, edited by Ying-kui Huang 黃應貴, 61–106. Taipei: Hanxue yanjiu zhongxin, 2009.

———. *"This Culture of Ours": Intellectual Transitions in T'ang and Sung China.* Stanford: Stanford University Press, 1992.

Borges, Jorge Luis. *Everything and Nothing.* New York: New Directions Publishing, 1999.

Brokaw, Cynthia J. "Publishing, Society, and Culture in Pre-Modern China: The Evolution of Print Culture." *International Journal of Asian Studies* 2, no. 1 (January 2005): 135–65.

Brokaw, Cynthia Joanne, and Kai-wing Chow. *Printing and Book Culture in Late Imperial China.* Berkeley: University of California Press, 2005.

Bronstein, Michaela. *Out of Context: The Uses of Modernist Fiction.* Oxford: Oxford University Press, 2018.

Brooks, Peter. *Reading for the Plot: Design and Intention in Narrative.* Oxford: Clarendon Press, 1984.

Bunkyō hifuron huijiao huikao 文鏡秘府論彙校彙考. Compiled by Henjō-Kongō (Kukai) 遍照金剛 (空海). Edited by Lu Shengjiang 盧盛江. Beijing: Zhonghua shuju, 2006.

Cai Zhengsun 蔡正孫. *Shilin guangji* 詩林廣記. In *Yingyin wenyuange siku quanshu.*

Cai Zhichao 蔡志超. *Du shi xinian kaolun* 杜詩繫年考論. Taipei: Wanjuanlou tushu gufen youxian gongsi, 2012.

———. *Songdai Du Fu nianpu wu zhong jiaozhu* 宋代杜甫年譜五種校注. Taipei: Wanjuanlou tushu gufen youxian gongsi, 2014.

Cai, Zongqi. *Configurations of Comparative Poetics: Three Perspectives on Western and Chinese Literary Criticism.* Honolulu: University of Hawai'i Press, 2002.

Cao Cao 曹操, Cao Pi 曹丕, and Cao Zhi 曹植. *San Cao ji* 三曹集. Changsha: Yuelu shushe, 1992.

Cerquiglini, Bernard. *Éloge de la variante: histoire critique de la philologie.* Paris: Seuil, 1989.

Chai Jen-nien 蔡振念. *Du shi Tang Song jieshou shi* 杜詩唐宋接受史. Taipei: Wunan tushu chuban gufen youxian gongsi, 2001.

Chan, Marie. "The Frontier Poems of Ts'en Shen." *Journal of the American Oriental Society* 98, no. 4 (1978): 420–38.

Chan, Timothy Wai Keung. "Beyond Border and Boudoir: The Frontier in the Poetry of the Four Elites of Early Tang." In *Reading Medieval Chinese Poetry: Text, Context, and Culture*, edited by Paul W. Kroll, 130–68. Leiden: Brill, 2015.

Chan, Wing-ming. "The Early-Qing Discourse on Loyalty." *East Asian History* 19 (2000): 27–52.

Chang, Kang-i Sun, and Stephen Owen, eds. *The Cambridge History of Chinese Literature.* Cambridge, U.K.: Cambridge University Press, 2010.

Chaves, Jonathan. "'Meaning beyond the Painting': The Chinese Painter as Poet." In *Words and Images: Chinese Poetry, Calligraphy, and Painting*, edited by Alfreda Murck and Wen Fong, 431–57. Princeton: Princeton University Press, 1991.

———. *Mei Yao-ch'en and the Development of Early Sung Poetry*. New York: Columbia University Press, 1976.

Chen Chunru 陳醇儒. *Shuchao jiazhu Du Gongbu qiyan lüshi* 書巢箋注杜工部七言律詩. Woodblock print. Jinling: Lianghengtang, Kangxi 61 (1722).

Chen Guanming 陳冠明 and Sun Suting 孫愫婷. *Du Fu qinjuan jiaoyou xingnian kao* 杜甫親眷交遊行年考. Shanghai: Shanghai guji chubanshe, 2006.

Chen, Jack W. "Foundings of Home: On Du Fu and Poetic Success." In *Reading Du Fu: Nine Views*, edited by Xiaofei Tian, 15–26. Hong Kong: Hong Kong University Press, 2020.

———. "On the Act and Representation of Reading in Medieval China." *Journal of the American Oriental Society* 129, no. 1 (2009): 57–71.

Chen Jilong 陈继龙. *Han Wo shi ji kao lüe* 韩偓事迹考略. Shanghai: Shanghai guji chubanshe, 2004.

Chen, Jue. "Making China's Greatest Poet: The Construction of Du Fu in the Poetic Culture of the Song Dynasty (960–1279)." PhD diss., Princeton University, 2016.

Chen Meizhu 陳美朱. *Qingchu Du shi shiyi chanshi yanjiu* 清初杜詩詩意闡釋研究. Tainan: Hanjia chubanshe, 2007.

Chen, Sanping. "Succession Struggle and the Ethnic Identity of the Tang Imperial House." *Journal of the Royal Asiatic Society* 6, no. 3 (1996): 379–405.

Chen shu 陳書. By Yao Silian 姚思廉 et al. Beijing: Zhonghua shuju, 1972.

Chen Si 陳思. *Haitang pu* 海棠譜. In *Yingyin wenyuange siku quanshu*.

Chen Tiemin 陈铁民. "Guanyu wenren chusai yu shengTang biansai shi de fanrong" 关于文人出塞与盛唐边塞诗的繁荣. *Wenxue yichan*, no. 3 (2002): 23–38.

Chen Tingzhuo 陳廷焯. *Baiyuzhai cihua* 白雨齋詞話. Shanghai: Shanghai guji chubanshe, 2009.

Chen Wenhua 陳文華, ed. *Du Fu zhuan ji Tang Song ziliao kaobian* 杜甫傳記唐宋資料考辨. Taipei: Wenshishe, 1987.

Chen Yanjia 陈延嘉. "*Wenxuan*" Li Shan zhu yu Wuchen zhu bijiao yanjiu 《文选》李善注与五臣注比较研究. Changchun: Jilin wenshi chubanshe, 2009.

Chen Yixin 陈贻焮. *Du Fu pingzhuan* 杜甫评传. Beijing: Beijing daxue chubanshe, 2003.

Chen Zi'ang 陳子昂. *Chen Zi'ang ji* 陳子昂集. Edited by Xu Peng 許鵬. Beijing: Zhonghua shuju, 1960.

Cheng Boyu 成伯璵. *Maoshi zhishuo* 毛詩指説. In *Yingyin wenyuange siku quanshu.*

Cheng Qianfan 程千帆. *Tangdai jinshi xingjuan yu wenxue* 唐代進士行卷与文學. Shanghai: Shanghai guji chubanshe, 1980.

Cheng Shankai 成善楷. *Du shi jianji* 杜诗笺记. Chengdu: Ba Shu shudian, 1989.

Cheng Yi 程頤. *The Yi River Commentary on the "Book of Changes."* Translated by L. Michael Harrington. New Haven: Yale University Press, 2019.

———. *Yichuan xiansheng Zhouyi jingzhuan* 程先生周易經傳. Yuan print edition, held in Zhejiang tushuguan.

Cheng Yi 程頤 and Cheng Hao 程顥. *Er Cheng wenji* 二程文集. Edited by Hu Anguo 胡安國 and Tan Shanxin 譚善心. In *Yingyin wenyuange siku quanshu.*

———. *Er Cheng yishu* 二程遺書. Edited by Zhu Xi 朱熹. In *Yingyin wenyuange siku quanshu.*

Cherniack, Susan. "Book Culture and Textual Transmission in Sung China." *Harvard Journal of Asiatic Studies* 54, no. 1 (1994): 5–125.

———. "Three Great Poems by Du Fu: 'Five Hundred Words: A Song of My Thoughts on Traveling from the Capital to Fengxian,' 'Journey North,' and 'One Hundred Rhymes: A Song of My Thoughts on an Autumn Day in Kuifu, Respectfully Sent to Director Zheng and Adviser to the Heir Apparent Li.'" PhD diss., Yale University, 1989.

Chia, Lucille. *Printing for Profit: The Commercial Publishers of Jianyang, Fujian (11th–17th Centuries)*. Cambridge, Mass.: Harvard University Asia Center, 2002.

Chittick, Andrew. *The Jiankang Empire in Chinese and World History*. Oxford: Oxford University Press, 2020.

Chongkan Songben Shisanjing zhushu fu jiaokan ji 重刊宋本十三經注疏附校勘記. Edited by Ruan Yuan 阮元. Taipei: Yiwen yinshu guan, 1981.

Chou, [Eva] Shan. "Allusion and Periphrasis as Modes of Poetry in Tu Fu's 'Eight Laments.'" *Harvard Journal of Asiatic Studies* 45, no. 1 (1985): 77–128.

———. "Literary Reputations in Context." *T'ang Studies* 10–11 (1992): 41–66.

———. *Reconsidering Tu Fu: Literary Greatness and Cultural Context*. Cambridge, U.K.: Cambridge University Press, 1995.

———. "Tu Fu's Eight Laments: Allusion and Imagery as Modes of Poetry." PhD diss., Harvard University, 1984.

———. "Wenxue shengyu de hanyi" 文學聲譽的涵義. *Jiuzhou xue kan* 3, no. 2 (1989): 53–65.

Chu Gansheng 褚贛生. *Nubi shi* 奴婢史. Shanghai: Shanghai wenyi chubanshe, 1994.

Chuci buzhu 楚辭補注. With annotations by Wang Yi 王逸 and Hong Xingzu 洪興祖. Beijing: Zhonghua shuju, 1983.

Chuci jijiao jishi 楚辭集校集釋. Edited by Cui Fuzhang 崔富章 and Li Daming 李大明. *Chuci xue wenku* 楚辭學文庫. Wuhan: Hubei jiaoyu chubanshe, 2003.

Chunqiu Gongyang zhuan zhushu 春秋公羊傳注疏. With annotations by He Xiu 何休 and Xu Yan 徐彥. In *Chongkan Songben Shisanjing zhushu fu jiaokan ji*.

Chunqiu Guliang zhuan zhushu 春秋穀梁注疏. With annotations by Fan Ning 范寧 and Yang Shixun 楊士勛. In *Chongkan Songben Shisanjing zhushu fu jiaokan ji*.

Chunqiu Zuozhuan zhushu 春秋左傳注疏. With annotations by Du Yu 杜預, Kong Yingda 孔穎達, et al. In *Chongkan Songben Shisanjing zhushu fu jiaokan ji*.

Cui Yannan 崔燕南. "Du Fu shige yongdian chutan" 杜甫诗歌用典初探. PhD diss., Shandong daxue, 2008.

Da Tang liudian 大唐六典. By Tang Xuanzong 唐玄宗 and Li Linfu 李林甫. Beijing: Zhonghua shuju, 1984.

Damrosch, David. *How to Read World Literature*. Chichester, U.K.: Wiley-Blackwell, 2009.

Davis, A. R. "The Double Ninth Festival in Chinese Poetry: A Study of Variations upon a Theme." In *Wen-Lin: Studies in the Chinese Humanities*, edited by Tse-tsung Chow, 45–64. Madison: University of Wisconsin Press, 1968.

———. *Tu Fu*. New York: Twayne Publishers, 1971.

de Man, Paul. *Blindness and Insight: Essays in the Rhetoric of Contemporary Criticism*. Oxford: Oxford University Press, 1971.

De Weerdt, Hilde Godelieve Dominique. *Information, Territory, and Elite Networks: The Crisis and Maintenance of Empire in Song China*. Cambridge, Mass.: Harvard University Asia Center, 2015.

De Weerdt, Hilde Godelieve Dominique, and Lucille Chia, eds. *Knowledge and Text Production in an Age of Print: China, 900–1400*. Leiden: Brill, 2011.

Deng Fang 邓芳. "Yuan Jie yuefu de 'bixing tizhi' ji qi dui xin yuefu de yiyi: cong 'Chongling xing' ji xiangguan zheng lunwen tanqi" 元结乐府的"比兴体制"及其对新乐府的意义——从《舂陵行》及相关政论文谈起. *Yuefu xue*, no. 1 (2010): 221–237.

DeWoskin, Kenneth J. *A Song for One or Two: Music and the Concept of Art in Early China*. Ann Arbor: Center for Chinese Studies, University of Michigan, 1982.

Diamond, Cora. "Anything but Argument?" *Philosophical Investigations* 5, no. 1 (January 1982): 23–41.

————. "The Difficulty of Reality and the Difficulty of Philosophy." *Partial Answers: Journal of Literature and the History of Ideas* 1, no. 2 (2003): 1–26.

Drège, Jean Pierre. *Les bibliothèques en Chine au temps des manuscrits: jusqu'au Xe siècle*. Paris: École française d'Extrême-Orient, 1991.

————. "Des effets de l'imprimerie en Chine sous la dynastie des Song." *Journal asiatique* 282, no. 2 (1994): 409–42.

————. "La lecture et l'écriture en Chine et la xylographie." *Études chinoises* 10, nos. 1–2 (1991): 77–112.

Du Fu. *The Poetry of Du Fu*. Translated by Stephen Owen. Boston: De Gruyter, 2016.

————. *Songben Du Gongbu ji* 宋本杜工部集. Edited by Wang Zhu 王洙. Xu guyi congshu facsimile edition. Shanghai: Shangwu yinshu guan, 1957.

Du shi yanzhi 杜詩言志. Anon. Huaiyin: Jiangsu renmin chubanshe, 1983.

Du You 杜佑. *Tongdian* 通典. Beijing: Zhonghua shuju, 1988.

Eliot, T. S. "Tradition and the Individual Talent." In *Selected Prose of T. S. Eliot*, edited by Frank Kermode, 37–45. New York: Harcourt Brace Jovanovich, 1975.

Eskin, Michael. *Ethics and Dialogue: In the Works of Levinas, Bakhtin, Mandel'shtam, and Celan*. Oxford: Oxford University Press, 2000.

Fan Xin 樊昕. "Tangren wenji Songdai shengcun zhuangkuang yanjiu" 唐人文集宋代生存状况研究. PhD diss., Yangzhou daxue, 2014.

Feng Zhi 冯至. *Feng Zhi xueshu jinghua lu* 冯至学朮精华录. Beijing: Beijing shifan xueyuan chubanshe, 1988.

Ford, Randolph B. *Rome, China, and the Barbarians: Ethnographic Traditions and the Transformation of Empires*. Cambridge, U.K.: Cambridge University Press, 2020.

Frankel, Hans H. *The Flowering Plum and the Palace Lady: Interpretations of Chinese Poetry*. New Haven: Yale University Press, 1976.

Fu Gengsheng 傅庚生. *Du shi sanyi* 杜詩散译. Xi'an: Shaanxi renmin chubanshe, 1979.

————. *Du shi xi yi* 杜詩析疑. Xi'an: Shaanxi renmin chubanshe, 1979.

Fu Xuancong 傅璇琮. *Tangdai keju yu wenxue* 唐代科举与文学. Xi'an: Shanxi renmin chubanshe, 1986.

————, ed. *Tangren xuan Tang shi xinbian* 唐人選唐詩新編. Xi'an: Shanxi renmin jiaoyu chubanshe, 1996.

Fuller, Michael A. "Aesthetics and Meaning in Experience: A Theoretical Perspective on Zhu Xi's Revision of Song Dynasty Views of Poetry." *Harvard Journal of Asiatic Studies* 65, no. 2 (2005): 311–55.

———. *Drifting among Rivers and Lakes: Southern Song Dynasty Poetry and the Problem of Literary History.* Cambridge, Mass.: Harvard University Asia Center, 2013.

———. "'Weary Night:' The Role of Ritual and Corporeal Selfhood in Grounding the Classical Chinese Poetic Tradition" "倦夜"——对中国古典传统中肉身诗学的反思. *Zhongguo xueshu* 38 (2017): 119–37.

Gadamer, Hans-Georg. *The Relevance of the Beautiful and Other Essays.* Cambridge, U.K.: Cambridge University Press, 1986.

———. *Truth and Method.* Translated by Joel Weinsheimer and Donald G. Marshall. New York: Crossroad, 1989.

Gao Chufang 高楚芳, ed. *Ji qianjia zhupidian buyi Du shi ji* 集千家註批點補遺杜詩集. With annotations by Liu Chenweng 劉辰翁. Du shi congkan. Taipei: Datong shuju, 1974.

Gao Shi 高適. *Gao Shi ji jiaozhu* 高適集校注. Edited by Qinshan Sun 孫欽善. Shanghai: Shanghai guji chubanshe, 1984.

Gao Song 高嵩. *Dunhuang Tangren shiji canjuan kaoshi* 敦煌唐人詩集殘卷考釋. Yinchuan: Ningxia renmin chubanshe, 1982.

Gao Tianyou 高天佑. *Du Fu Long Shu jixingshi zhuxi* 杜甫陇蜀纪行诗注析. Lanzhou: Gansu minzu chubanshe, 2002.

Ge Hong 葛洪. *Baopuzi neipian jiaoshi* 抱朴子內篇校釋. Edited by Wang Ming 王明. Beijing: Zhonghua shuju, 1985.

Ge, Zhaoguang. *What Is China? Territory, Ethnicity, Culture, and History.* Translated by Michael Hill. Cambridge, Mass.: The Belknap Press, 2018.

Geng Yuanrui 耿元瑞. "Du Fu zai Henan" 杜甫在河南. *Zhengzhou daxue xuebao* 1986, no. 4: 45–54.

Gong Bendong 巩本栋. *Song ji chuanbo kaolun* 宋集传播考论. Beijing: Zhonghua shuju, 2009.

Graff, David A. "Fang Guan's Chariots: Scholarship, War, and Character Assassination in the Middle Tang." *Asia Major* 22, no. 1 (2009): 105–30.

———. *Medieval Chinese Warfare, 300–900.* London: Routledge, 2002.

Greene, Eric M. *Chan before Chan.* Honolulu: University of Hawai'i Press, 2021.

———. "The 'Religion of Images'? Buddhist Image Worship in the Early Medieval Chinese Imagination." *Journal of American Oriental Society* 138, no. 3 (2018): 455–84.

———. "Visions and Visualizations: In Fifth-Century Chinese Buddhism and Nineteenth-Century Experimental Psychology." *History of Religions* 55, no. 3 (2016): 289–328.

Gu Chen 顧宸. *Pijiangyuan Dushi zhujie* 辟疆園杜詩註解. Woodblock print. Wuxi: Pijiangyuan, Kangxi 2 [1663].

Guan Lang 關朗. *Guanshi yizhuan* 關氏易傳. With annotations by Zhao Rui 趙蕤. Edited by Fan Qin 范欽. In *Fanshi ershiyi zhong qishu* 范氏二十一種奇書. *Hanji quanwen ziliaoku* 漢籍全文資料庫 digital edition of a Ming woodblock print. Zhongyang yanjiuyuan zixun kexue yanjiusuo 中央研究院資訊科學研究所, ed. Taipei: Zhongyang yanjiuyuan jisuan zhongxin, 2000.

Guo Maoqian 郭茂倩, ed. *Yuefu shiji* 樂府詩集. Beijing: Zhonghua shuju, 1998.

Guo Songtao 郭嵩燾. *Guo Songtao shi wenji* 郭嵩燾诗文集. Changsha: Yuelu shushe, 1984.

Guo Xian 郭憲. *Dongming ji* 洞冥記. In *Yingyin wenyuange siku quanshu*.

Guo yu 國語. Attributed to Zuo Qiuming 左丘明. With annotations by Wei Zhao 韋昭. Shanghai: Shanghai guji chubanshe, 1978.

Guo Zengxin 郭曾炘. *Du Du zhaji* 讀杜劄記. Shanghai: Shanghai guji chubanshe, 1984.

Guo Zhida 郭知達. *Xinkan jiaoding jizhu Du shi* 新刊校定集注杜詩. Beijing: Zhonghua shuju, 1982.

Hämäläinen, Nora. *Literature and Moral Theory*. New York: Bloomsbury, 2015.

Han Chengwu 韩成武 and Zhang Zhimin 张志民. *Du Fu shi quan yi* 杜甫诗全译. Shijiazhuang: Hebei renmin chubanshe, 1997.

Han, Christina Hee-Yeon. "Territory of the Sages: Neo-Confucian Discourse of Wuyi Nine Bends Jingjie." PhD diss., University of Toronto, 2011.

Han Feizi jijie 韓非子集解. By Han Fei 韓非. Edited by Wang Xianshen 王先慎. Beijing: Zhonghua shuju, 1998.

Han Languo 赫蘭國. *Liao Jin Yuan Du shi xue* 遼金元杜詩學. Zhengzhou: Henan renmin chubanshe, 2012.

Han shi waizhuan jinzhu jinyi 韓詩外傳今註今譯. Edited by Lai Yanyuan 賴炎元. Taipei: Taiwan shangwu yinshu guan, 1972.

Han shu 漢書. By Ban Gu 班固. Beijing: Zhonghua shuju, 1962.

Hanyu da cidian 漢語大詞典. Edited by Luo Zhufeng 羅竹風 et al. 12 vols. Shanghai: Hanyu da cidian chubanshe, 1990–93.

Hao, Ji. *The Reception of Du Fu (712–770) and His Poetry in Imperial China*. Leiden: Brill, 2017.

Hargett, James M. Review of *Spatial Imaginaries in Mid-Tang China: Geography, Cartography, and Literature* by Ao Wang. *The Journal of Asian Studies* 78, no. 4 (November 2019): 920–21.

Hartman, Charles. "Du Fu in the Poetry Standards (*Shige*) and the Origins of the Earliest Du Fu Commentary." *T'ang Studies* 28 (December 2010): 61–76.

———. "The Tang Poet Du Fu and the Song Dynasty Literati." *Chinese Literature: Essays, Articles, Reviews (CLEAR)*, no. 30 (2008): 43–74.

Hasebe Tsuyoshi 長谷部剛. *To Ho shibunshū no keisei ni kansuru bunkenga-kuteki kenkyū* 杜甫詩文集の形成に関する文献学的研究. Suita: Kansai daigaku shuppanbu, 2019.

Hawes, Colin S. C. "Competing with Creative Transformation: The Poetry of Ouyang Xiu (1007–1072)." PhD diss., University of British Columbia, 1996.

Herman, John. "The Kingdoms of Nanzhong: China's Southwest Border Region Prior to the Eighth Century." *T'oung Pao* 95, nos. 4/5 (2009): 241–86.

Holcombe, Charles. "Chinese Identity during the Age of Division, Sui, and Tang." *Journal of Chinese History* 4, no. 1 (January 2020): 31–53.

———. "Immigrants and Strangers: From Cosmopolitanism to Confucian Universalism in Tang China." *T'ang Studies* 20–21 (2003): 71–112.

———. "Re-Imagining China: The Chinese Identity Crisis at the Start of the Southern Dynasties Period." *Journal of the American Oriental Society* 115, no. 1 (1995): 1–14.

———. "The Xianbei in Chinese History." *Early Medieval China* 2013, no. 19 (December 1, 2013): 1–38.

Hon, Tze-Ki. *The Yijing and Chinese Politics: Classical Commentary and Literati Activism in the Northern Song Period, 960–1127.* Albany: State University of New York Press, 2005.

Hori Toshizaku 堀敏一. *Chūgoku kodai no mibunsei: ryō to sen* 中国古代の身分制：良と賤. Tokyo: Kyūko shoin, 1987.

Hou Han shu 後漢書. By Fan Ye 范曄. Beijing: Zhonghua shuju, 1965.

Howard, Angela Falco. *The Imagery of the Cosmological Buddha.* Leiden: Brill, 1986.

Hsieh, Daniel. "Meeting through Poetry: Du Fu's 杜甫 (712–770) 'Written in Accord with Prefect Yuan's "Ballad of Chongling."'" *T'ang Studies* 32, no. 1 (2014): 1–20.

Hu Shih 胡適. *Baihua wenxue shi* 白話文學史. Shanghai: Shanghai guji chubanshe, 1999.

Hu Zhongrong 扈仲榮 and Cheng Yusun 程遇孫, eds. *Chengdu wen lei* 成都文類. In *Yingyin wenyuange siku quanshu.*

Hua Wenxuan 華文軒, ed. *Du Fu juan: shangbian* 杜甫卷上編. Gudian wenxue yanjiu ziliao huibian 古典文學研究資料彙編. Beijing: Zhonghua shuju, 1964.

Huainanzi 淮南子. Edited by Liu Wendian 劉文典. Beijing: Zhonghua shuju, 1989.

Huang Shen 黃珅. *Du Fu xinying lu* 杜甫心影錄. Nanjing: Jiangsu guji chubanshe, 1991.

Huang Sheng 黃生. *Huang Sheng quanji* 黃生全集. 4 vols. Anhui: Anhui daxue chubanshe, 2009.

Huang Tingjian 黃庭堅. *Huang Tingjian quanji* 黃庭堅全集. Edited by Liu Lin 劉琳 et al. Chengdu: Sichuan daxue chubanshe, 2001.

Huang Xi 黃希 and Huang He 黃鶴, eds. *Bu zhu Du shi* 補注杜詩. In *Yingyin wenyuange siku quanshu.*

Huang Yizhen 黃奕珍. *Du Fu zi Qin ru Shu shige xiping* 杜甫自秦入蜀詩歌析評. Taipei: Liren shuju, 2005.

Huang Yongwu 黃永武. *Dunhuang de Tang shi* 敦煌的唐詩. Taipei: Hongfan shudian, 1987.

———. *Dunhuang de Tang shi xubian* 敦煌的唐詩續編. Taipei: Wenshizhe chubanshe, 1989.

Hung, William. *Tu Fu: China's Greatest Poet.* Cambridge, Mass.: Harvard University Press, 1952.

———. "Tu Fu Again." *Tsing Hua Journal of Chinese Studies* 10, no. 2 (1974): 1–60.

Inoue Susumu 井上進. *Chūgoku shuppan bunkashi: shomotsu sekai to chi no fūkei* 中国出版文化史 :書物世界と知の風景. Nagoya: Nagoya daigaku shuppankai, 2002.

Jay, Jennifer W. *A Change in Dynasties: Loyalty in Thirteenth-Century China.* Bellingham: Western Washington University, 1991.

Ji Yougong 計有功. *Tang shi jishi jiaojian* 唐詩紀事校箋. Edited by Wang Zhongyong 王仲鏞. Chengdu: Ba Shu shudian, 1989.

Ji Yun 紀昀. *Yingkui lüsui kanwu* 瀛奎律髓刊誤. Congshu jicheng xubian. Shanghai: Shanghai shudian, 1994.

Jian Ending 簡恩定. *Qingchu Du shi xue yanjiu* 清初杜詩學研究. Taipei: Wenshizhe chubanshe, 1986.

Jiang Lansheng 江藍生 and Cao Guangshun 曹广顺, eds. *Tang Wudai yuyan cidian* 唐五代语言词典. Shanghai: Shanghai jiaoyu chubanshe, 1997.

Jiang Xianwei 蔣先伟. *Du Fu Kuizhou shi lungao* 杜甫夔州詩论稿. Chengdu: Ba Shu shushe, 2002.

Jiang Yin 蔣寅. *Dali shifeng* 大歷诗風. Shanghai: Shanghai guji chubanshe, 1992.

Jin Qihua 金启华. *Du Fu shi luncong* 杜甫诗论丛. Shanghai: Shanghai guji chubanshe, 1985.

Jin Shengtan 金聖歎. *Du shi jie* 杜詩解. Edited by Zhong Laiyin 鐘來因. Shanghai: Shanghai guji chubanshe, 1984.

Jin shu 晉書. By Fang Xuanling 房玄齡 et al. Beijing: Zhonghua shuju, 1974.

Jiu Tang shu 舊唐書. By Liu Xu 劉昫 等 et al. Beijing: Zhonghua shuju, 1975.

Jullien, François. *La valeur allusive des catégories originales de l'interprétation poétique dans la tradition chinoise: contribution à une réflexion sur l'altérité interculturelle.* Paris: École française d'Extrême-Orient, 1985.

Kawai Kōzō 川合康三. *Chūgoku no jiden bungaku* 中国の自伝文学. Tokyo: Sōbunsha, 1996.

———. "Shi wa sekai o tsukuru ka? Chū Tō ni okeru shi to zōbutsu" 詩は世界を創るか : 中唐における詩と造物. *Chūgoku bungaku hō* 44 (1992): 92–119.

Keats, John. *Selected Letters of John Keats*. Cambridge, Mass.: Harvard University Press, 2002.

Kermode, Frank. *The Classic: Literary Images of Permanence and Change*. Cambridge, Mass.: Harvard University Press, 1983.

———. *Pleasure and Change: The Aesthetics of Canon*. Edited by Robert Alter. Oxford: Oxford University Press, 2004.

———. *The Sense of an Ending: Studies in the Theory of Fiction*. Oxford: Oxford University Press, 2000.

Knechtges, David, trans. *Wen xuan or Selections of Refined Literature*. 3 vols. Princeton: Princeton University Press, 1982.

Kong congzi 孔叢子. Attributed to Kong Fu 孔鮒. Sibu congkan. Shanghai: Shangwu yinshu guan, 1922.

Kroll, Paul W. *Dharma Bell and Dhāraṇī Pillar: Li Po's Buddhist Inscriptions*. Kyoto: Scuola italiana di studi sull'Asia orientale, 2001.

———. "A Poetry Debate of the Perfected of Highest Clarity." *Journal of the American Oriental Society* 132, no. 4 (2012): 577–86.

———. *Studies in Medieval Taoism and the Poetry of Li Po*. Farnham, UK: Ashgate, 2009.

———. "Verses from on High: The Ascent of T'ai Shan." *T'oung Pao* 69, no. 4 (1983): 223–60.

Kurokawa Yōichi 黒川洋一. "Chū Tō yori Hoku Sōmatsu ni itaru To Ho no hakken ni suite" 中唐より北宋末に至る杜甫の発見について. *Shitennōji joshi daigaku kiyō* 3 (1970): 81–112.

Landy, Joshua. *How to Do Things with Fictions*. Oxford: Oxford University Press, 2012.

Laozi jiaoshi 老子校釋. Edited by Zhu Qianzhi 朱謙之. Beijing: Zhonghua shuju, 1984.

Lear, Jonathan. *A Case for Irony*. Cambridge, Mass.: Harvard University Press, 2011.

———. *Radical Hope: Ethics in the Face of Cultural Devastation*. Cambridge, Mass.: Harvard University Press, 2006.

Levy, Dore Jesse. *Chinese Narrative Poetry: The Late Han through T'ang Dynasties*. Durham, NC: Duke University Press, 1988.

Lewis, Mark Edward. *China's Cosmopolitan Empire: The Tang Dynasty*. Cambridge, Mass: The Belknap Press, 2009.

Li Bai 李白. *Li Taibai quan ji* 李太白全集. Edited by Wang Qi 王琦. Beijing: Zhonghua shuju, 1977.

Li Daoyuan 酈道元. *Shui jing zhu jiaoshi* 水經注校釋. Edited by Chen Qiaoyi 陳橋驛. Hangzhou: Hangzhou daxue chubanshe, 1999.

Li Gang 李綱. *Liangxi ji* 梁谿集. In *Yingyin wenyuange siku quanshu*.

Li Gui 李贵. *Zhong Tang zhi Bei Song de dianfan xuanze yu shige yinge* 中唐至北宋的典范选择与诗歌因革. Shanghai: Fudan daxue chubanshe, 2012.

Li Hua 李華. *Li Xiashu wenji* 李遐叔文集. In *Yingyin wenyuange siku quanshu*.

Li Jiping 李季平. *Tangdai nubi zhidu* 唐代奴婢制度. Shanghai: Shanghai guji chubanshe, 1986.

Li Shangyin 李商隱. *Li Shangyin wen biannian jiaozhu* 李商隱文編年校注. Edited by Liu Xuekai 劉學鍇 and Yu Shucheng 余恕誠. Beijing: Zhonghua shuju, 2002.

Li Shiren 李时人, ed. *Quan Tang Wudai xiaoshuo* 全唐五代小说. 5 vols. Shaanxi: Shaanxi renmin chubanshe, 1998.

Li Shousong 李寿松, and Li Yiyun 李翼云. *Quan Du shi xin shi* 全杜诗新释. Beijing: Zhongguo shudian, 2002.

Li, Wai-yee. "Confronting History and Its Alternatives in Early Qing Poetry." In *Trauma and Transcendence in Early Qing Literature*, edited by Wilt L. Idema, Wai-yee Li, and Ellen Widmer, 73–98. Cambridge, Mass.: Harvard University Asia Center, 2006.

Liang Yunchang 梁運昌. *Du yuan shuo Du* 杜園說杜. Beijing: Shumu wenxian chubanshe, 1995.

Liezi jishi 列子集釋. Edited by Yang Bojun 楊伯峻. Beijing: Zhonghua shuju, 1979.

Liji zhushu 禮記注疏. With annotations by Zheng Xuan 鄭玄 and Kong Yingda 孔穎達. In *Chongkan Songben Shisanjing zhushu fu jiaokan ji*.

Lin, Tsung-Cheng. "Time and Narration: A Study of Sequential Structure in Chinese Narrative Verse." PhD diss., University of British Columbia, 2006.

Ling, Chao. "Fame as Durable as Stone: Yu Xin's (513–581) Inscriptional Literature in the Chinese Cultural Memory." PhD diss., Yale University, 2019.

Liu Kebing 鲁克兵. *Du Fu yu fojiao guanxi yanjiu* 杜甫与佛教关系研究. Hefei: Anhui daxue chubanshe, 2014.

Liu Mingjin 刘明今. *Zhongguo gudai wenxue lilun tixi: Fangfa lun* 中国古代文学理论体系:方法论. Shanghai: Fudan daxue chubanshe, 2000.

Liu Su 劉肅. *Da Tang xinyu* 大唐新語. Edited by Xu Denan 許德楠 and Li Dingxia 李鼎霞. Beijing: Zhonghua shuju, 1984.

Liu, Wan. "Poetics of Allusion: Tu Fu, Li Shang-Yin, Ezra Pound, and T. S. Eliot." PhD diss., Princeton University, 1992.

Liu Wengang 劉文剛. *Du Fu xue shi* 杜甫學史. Chengdu: Ba Shu shushe, 2012.

Liu Wenzhong 刘文忠. *Zhengbian—Tongbian—Xinbian* 正变 • 通变 • 新变. Nanchang: Baihuazhou wenyi chubanshe, 2005.

Liu Xie 劉勰. *Zengding Wenxin diaolong jiaozhu* 增訂文心雕龍校注. Edited by Huang Shulin 黄叔琳 and Li Xiang 李詳. Beijing: Zhonghua shuju, 2000.

Liu Yujun 劉玉珺. *Siku Tangren wenji yanjiu* 四庫唐人文集研究. Chengdu: Ba Shu shushe, 2010.

Liu Zhiji 劉知幾. *Shitong tongshi* 史通通釋. With annotations by Pu Qilong 浦起龍. Shanghai: Shanghai guji chubanshe, 1978.

Liuchen zhu Wenxuan 六臣注文選. Compiled by Xiao Tong 蕭統. With annotations by Li Shan 李善 et al. Beijing: Zhonghua shuju, 1987.

Lu Fusheng 盧輔聖, ed. *Zhongguo shuhua quanshu* 中國書畫全書. 14 vols. Shanghai: Shanghai shuhua chubanshe, 1993.

Lu Ji 陸機. *Lu Ji ji* 陸機集. Beijing: Zhonghua shuju, 1982.

Lu Kanru 陆侃如 and Mou Shijin 牟世金, eds. *Wenxin diaolong yizhu* 文心雕龙译注. Jinan: Qi-Lu shushe, 1981.

Lu Qinli 逯欽立, ed. *Xian Qin Han Wei Jin Nan Beichao shi* 先秦漢魏晉南北朝詩. Beijing: Zhonghua shuju, 1983.

Lu Yin 魯訔, ed. *Caotang shi jian* 草堂詩箋. With annotations by Cai Mengbi 蔡夢弼. Taipei: Guangwen shuju, 1964.

Lu Yuanchang 盧元昌. *Du shi chan* 杜詩闡. Siku quanshu cunmu congshu. Jinan: Qi-Lu shushe, 1997.

Lu Zhaolin 盧照鄰. *Lu Zhaolin ji jiaozhu* 盧照鄰集校注. Edited by Li Yunyi 李雲逸. Beijing: Zhonghua shuju, 1998.

Lubac, Henri de. *Exégèse médiévale : les quatre sens de l'Écriture*. Paris: Aubier, 1959.

Lunyu jijie yishu 論語集解義疏. With annotations by He Yan 何晏 and Huang Kan 黄侃. Congshu jicheng. Shanghai: Shangwu yinshu guan, 1936.

Lunyu jishi 論語集釋. Edited by Cheng Shude 程樹德 et al. Beijing: Zhonghua shuju, 1990.

Luo Genze 羅根澤. *Zhongguo wenxue piping shi* 中國文学批評史. Shanghai: Gudian wenxue chubanshe, 1957.

Luo, Manling. *Literati Storytelling in Late Medieval China*. Seattle: University of Washington Press, 2015.

Luo, Yinan. "A Study of the Changes in the Tang–Song Transition Model." *Journal of Song-Yuan Studies* 35 (2005): 99–127.

Ma Xiancheng 马现诚. "Fojiao 'jingjie' lilun yu gudai wenlun yijing shuo de xingcheng" 佛教"境界"理论与古代文论意境说的形成. *Xueshu luntan*, no. 4 (2000): 83–87.

Mair, Victor H. "The Narrative Revolution in Chinese Literature: Ontological Presuppositions." *Chinese Literature: Essays, Articles, Reviews (CLEAR)* 5, nos. 1/2 (1983): 1–27.

———. "Scroll Presentation in The T'ang Dynasty." *Harvard Journal of Asiatic Studies* 38, no. 1 (1978): 35–60.

Makeham, John. *Transmitters and Creators: Chinese Commentators and Commentaries on the Analects.* Cambridge, Mass.: Harvard University Asia Center, 2003.

Maoshi zhushu 毛詩注疏. With annotations by Kong Yingda 孔穎達 et al. In *Chongkan Songben Shisanjing zhushu fu jiaokan ji.*

Mather, Richard B. "The Controversy over Conformity and Naturalness during the Six Dynasties." *History of Religions* 9, nos. 2/3 (1969): 160–80.

McCraw, David R. *Du Fu's Laments from the South.* Honolulu: University of Hawai'i Press, 1992.

McMullen, David L. "Boats Moored and Unmoored: Reflections on the Dunhuang Manuscripts of Gao Shi's Verse." *Harvard Journal of Asiatic Studies* 73, no. 1 (2013): 83–145.

———. "Du Fu's Political Perspectives: His Outlook on Governorships and His Response to Yuan Jie's Daozhou Verses." *T'ang Studies* 37, no. 1 (January 1, 2019): 81–110.

———. "Historical and Literary Theory in the Mid-Eighth Century." In *Perspectives on the T'ang,* edited by A. F. Wright and D. Twitchett, 307–42. New Haven: Yale University Press, 1973.

———. *State and Scholars in T'ang China.* Cambridge, U.K.: Cambridge University Press, 1988.

———. "Yuan Chieh and the Early Ku-Wen Movement." DPhil diss., University of Cambridge, 1968.

Mei Yaochen 梅堯臣. *Mei Yaochen ji biannian jiaozhu* 梅堯臣集編年校注. Edited by Zhu Dongrun 朱東潤. Shanghai: Shanghai guji chubanshe, 1980.

Mengzi yizhu 孟子譯注. Edited by Yang Bojun 楊伯峻. Beijing: Zhonghua shuju, 1988.

Meretoja, Hanna. *The Ethics of Storytelling: Narrative Hermeneutics, History, and the Possible.* Oxford: Oxford University Press, 2018.

Meyer, Andrew Seth. "The Correct Meaning of the Five Classics and the Intellectual Foundations of the Tang." PhD diss., Harvard University, 1999.

Miao, Ronald. "T'ang Frontier Poetry: An Exercise in Archetypal Criticism." *Ch'ing-Hua Hsüeh-Pao* 10, no. 2 (1974): 114–41.

Miner, Earl. *Comparative Poetics: An Intercultural Essay on Theories of Literature.* Princeton: Princeton University Press, 1990.

Mo Lifeng 莫砺锋. *Du Fu pingzhuan* 杜甫评传. Nanjing: Nanjing daxue chubanshe, 1993.

———. *Du Fu shige jiangyan lu* 杜甫诗歌讲演录. Guilin: Guangxi shifan daxue chubanshe, 2006.

———. "Zenyang du Du Fu shi" 怎样读杜甫诗. *Gudian wenxue zhishi* 5 (2000): 3–10.

Mu Tianzi zhuan 穆天子傳. With annotations by Guo Pu 郭璞. Sibu congkan. Shanghai: Shanghai shangwu yinshu guan, 1936.

Murck, Alfreda, and Wen Fong. *Words and Images: Chinese Poetry, Calligraphy, and Painting*. Princeton: Princeton University Press, 1991.

Murdoch, Iris. "Nostalgia for the Particular." *Proceedings of the Aristotelian Society* 52 (1951): 243–60.

Nagata Tomoyuki 永田知之. *Tōdai no bungaku riron: "fukko" to "sōshin"* 唐代の文学理論 : 「復古」と「創新」. Kyoto: Kyōto daigaku gakujutsu shuppankai, 2015.

Naitō Torajirō 内藤虎次郎. *Naitō Konan zenshū* 内藤湖南全集. 14 vols. Tokyo: Chikuma shobō, 1969–76.

Nan Qi shu 南齊書. By Xiao Zixian 萧子顯 et al. Beijing: Zhonghua shuju, 1972.

Nan shi 南史. By Li Yanshou 李延壽. Beijing: Zhonghua shuju, 1975.

Nanhua zhenjing zhushu 南華眞經注疏. With annotations by Guo Xiang 郭象 and Cheng Xuanying 成玄英. Beijing: Zhonghua shuju, 1998.

Nehamas, Alexander. *The Art of Living: Socratic Reflections from Plato to Foucault*. Berkeley: University of California Press, 1998.

Nugent, Christopher M. B. *Manifest in Words, Written on Paper: Producing and Circulating Poetry in Tang Dynasty China*. Cambridge, Mass.: Harvard University Asia Center, 2010.

———. "Sources of Difficulty: Reading and Understanding Du Fu." In *Reading Du Fu: Nine Views*, edited by Xiaofei Tian, 111–29. Hong Kong: Hong Kong University Press, 2020.

Nürnberger, Marc. *Das "Ben shi shi" des Meng Qi*. Wiesbaden: Harrassowitz Verlag, 2010.

Nussbaum, Martha Craven. *Cultivating Humanity: A Classical Defense of Reform in Liberal Education*. Cambridge, Mass.: Harvard University Press, 1997.

———. *Love's Knowledge: Essays on Philosophy and Literature*. Oxford: Oxford University Press, 1990.

———. *Poetic Justice: The Literary Imagination and Public Life*. Boston: Beacon Press, 1995.

Nylan, Michael. "Beliefs about Social Seeing: Hiddenness (Wei 微) and Visibility in Classical-Era China." In *The Rhetoric of Hiddenness in Traditional Chinese Culture*, edited by Paula M. Varsano, 53–78. Albany: State University of New York Press, 2016.

Okamura Shigeru 岡村繁. *Monzen no kenkyū* 文選の研究. Tokyo: Iwanami shoten, 1999.

Owen, Stephen. *The End of the Chinese "Middle Ages": Essays in Mid-Tang Literary Culture.* Stanford: Stanford University Press, 1996.

———. *The Great Age of Chinese Poetry: The High Tang.* New Haven: Yale University Press, 1981.

———. "The Librarian in Exile: Xie Lingyun's Bookish Landscapes." *Early Medieval China* 10–11, no. 1 (2004): 203–26.

———. "The Manuscript Legacy of the Tang: The Case of Literature." *Harvard Journal of Asiatic Studies* 67, no. 2 (2007): 295–326.

———. *Mi-Lou: Poetry and the Labyrinth of Desire.* Cambridge, Mass.: Harvard University Press, 1989.

———. "The Poet in the Scroll: Du Fu's Collected Poems in Manuscript." Unpublished manuscript.

———. "Poetry and Its Historical Ground." *Chinese Literature: Essays, Articles, Reviews (CLEAR)* 12 (1990): 107–18.

———. *The Poetry of Meng Chiao and Han Yu.* New Haven: Yale University Press, 1975.

———. *The Poetry of the Early T'ang.* New Haven: Yale University Press, 1977.

———. *Readings in Chinese Literary Thought.* Cambridge, Mass.: Harvard University Press, 1992.

———. *Remembrances: The Experience of the Past in Classical Chinese Literature.* Cambridge, Mass.: Harvard University Press, 1986.

———. "The Self's Perfect Mirror: Poetry as Autobiography." In *The Vitality of the Lyric Voice: Shih Poetry from the Late Han to the T'ang,* edited by Shuen-fu Lin and Stephen Owen, 71–102. Princeton: Princeton University Press, 1986.

———. "A Tang Version of Du Fu: The *Tangshi leixuan* 唐詩類選." *T'ang Studies* 25 (2007): 57–90.

———. "Thinking through Poetry: Du Fu's 'Getting Rid of the Blues' (*Jie men*)." In *Reading Du Fu: Nine Views,* edited by Xiaofei Tian, 27–40. Hong Kong: Hong Kong University Press, 2020.

———. *Traditional Chinese Poetry and Poetics: Omen of the World.* Madison: University of Wisconsin Press, 1985.

Palumbo-Liu, David. *The Poetics of Appropriation: The Literary Theory and Practice of Huang Tingjian.* Stanford: Stanford University Press, 1993.

Pan Chonggui 潘重規, ed. *Dunhuang bianwen ji xinshu* 敦煌變文集新書. Taipei: Wenjin chubanshe, 1994.

Pan, Daan. *The Lyrical Resonance between Chinese Poets and Painters: The Tradition and Poetics of Tihuashi.* Amherst, N.Y.: Cambria Press, 2010.

Pan Yihong. *Son of Heaven and Heavenly Qaghan: Sui-Tang China and its Neighbors*. Bellingham: Western Washington University, 1997.

Patterson, Gregory M. "Du Fu's Ethnographic Imagination: Local Culture and Its Contexts in the Kuizhou Poems." *Chinese Literature: Essays, Articles, Reviews (CLEAR)* 37 (2015): 29–65.

———. "Elegies for Empire: The Poetics of Memory in the Late Work of Du Fu (712–770)." PhD diss., Columbia University, 2003.

Peterson, Charles A. "P'u-ku Huai-en 僕固懷恩 and the T'ang Court: The Limits of Loyalty." *Monumenta Serica* 29, no. 1 (1970): 423–55.

Peterson, Willard J. "Making Connections: 'Commentary on the Attached Verbalizations of the *Book of Change*.'" *Harvard Journal of Asiatic Studies* 42, no. 1 (1982): 67–116.

———. "Squares and Circles: Mapping the History of Chinese Thought." *Journal of the History of Ideas* 49, no. 1 (1988): 47–60.

Phillips, D. Z. "Allegiance and Change in Morality: A Study in Contrasts." In *Interventions in Ethics*, edited by D. Z. Phillips, 24–41. London: Palgrave Macmillan UK, 1992.

Pollock, Sheldon. "Philology in Three Dimensions." *Postmedieval: A Journal of Medieval Cultural Studies* 5, no. 4 (2014): 398–413.

Poon, Ming-sun. "Books and Printing in Sung China (960–1279)." PhD diss., University of Chicago, 1979.

Pu Qilong 浦起龍. *Du Du xinjie* 讀杜心解. Beijing: Zhonghua shuju, 1961.

Puett, Michael. "Text and Commentary: The Early Tradition." In *The Oxford Handbook of Classical Chinese Literature*, edited by Wiebke Denecke, Wai-yee Li, and Xiaofei Tian, 112–22. Oxford: Oxford University Press, 2017.

Pulleyblank, Edwin G. *The Background of the Rebellion of An Lu-Shan*. London: Oxford University Press, 1955.

———. "Neo-Confucianism and Neo-Legalism in T'ang Intellectual Life, 755–805." In *The Confucian Persuasion*, by Arthur F. Wright, 77–114. Stanford: Stanford University Press, 1960.

Qi Hehui 祁和晖, and Tan Jihe 譚繼和. "Du Fu Kuizhou shizhong fanying de minzu wenti" 杜甫夔州诗中反映的民族问题. *Caotang*, no. 2 (1984): 26–37.

Qian Qianyi 錢謙益. *Muzhai chu xue ji* 牧齋初學集. Woodblock print. Qu Shisi 瞿式耜, Chongzhen 16 (1643).

———. *Qian zhu Du shi* 錢注杜詩. Shanghai: Shanghai guji chubanshe, 1979.

Qin Guan 秦觀. *Huaihai ji* 淮海集. In *Yingyin wenyuange siku quanshu*.

Qiu Zhao'ao 仇兆鰲. *Du shi xiangzhu* 杜詩詳注. Beijing: Zhonghua shuju, 1979.

Quan Tang wen 全唐文. Edited by Deng Hao 董浩 et al. Beijing: Zhonghua shuju, 1987.

Quan Zuwang 全祖望. *Xu Yongshang qijiu shiji* 續甬上耆舊詩集. Siming: Siming wenxian she, 1918.

Ren, Yong. "Cosmogony, Fictionality, Poetic Creativity: Western and Traditional Chinese Cultural Perspectives." *Comparative Literature* 50, no. 2 (1998): 98–119.

Rorty, Richard. *Contingency, Irony, and Solidarity.* Cambridge, U.K.: Cambridge University Press, 1989.

Rouzer, Paul. "Du Fu and the Failure of Lyric." *Chinese Literature: Essays, Articles, Reviews (CLEAR)* 33 (December 2011): 27–53.

———. "Refuges and Refugees: How Du Fu Writes Buddhism." In *Reading Du Fu: Nine Views,* edited by Xiaofei Tian, 75–92. Hong Kong: Hong Kong University Press, 2020.

Sanders, Graham Martin. *Words Well Put: Visions of Poetic Competence in the Chinese Tradition.* Cambridge, Mass.: Harvard University Asia Center, 2006.

San guo zhi 三國志. By Chen Shou 陳壽. With annotations by Pei Songzhi 裴松之. Beijing: Zhonghua shuju, 1982.

Sargent, Stuart H. "Can Latecomers Get There First? Sung Poets and T'ang Poetry." *Chinese Literature: Essays, Articles, Reviews (CLEAR)* 4, no. 2 (July 1982): 165–98.

Saussy, Haun. *Great Walls of Discourse and Other Adventures in Cultural China.* Cambridge, Mass.: Harvard University Asia Center, 2001.

———. *The Problem of a Chinese Aesthetic.* Stanford: Stanford University Press, 1993.

Schafer, Edward H. *The Golden Peaches of Samarkand: A Study of T'ang Exotics.* Berkeley: University of California Press, 1963.

———. "The Idea of Created Nature in T'ang Literature." *Philosophy East and West* 15, no. 2 (1965): 153–60.

———. *The Vermilion Bird: T'ang Images of the South.* Berkeley: University of California Press, 1967.

Scheffler, Samuel. *Death and the Afterlife.* Oxford: Oxford University Press, 2014.

———. *Equality and Tradition: Questions of Value in Moral and Political Theory.* Oxford: Oxford University Press, 2010.

———. *Why Worry about Future Generations?* Oxford: Oxford University Press, 2018.

Schneider, David K. *Confucian Prophet: Political Thought in Du Fu's Poetry (752–757)*. Amherst, New York: Cambria Press, 2012.

Sells, Michael Anthony. *Mystical Languages of Unsaying*. Chicago: University of Chicago Press, 1994.

Shangshu zhushu 尚書注疏. With annotations by Kong Anguo 孔安國, Kong Yingda 孔穎達, et al. In *Chongkan Songben Shisanjing zhushu fu jiaokan ji*.

Shao Bao 邵寶. *Ke Du Shaoling xiansheng shi fenlei jizhu* 刻杜少陵先生詩分類集註. Du shi congkan. Taipei: Datong shuju, 1974.

Shao Fu 邵傅. *Du lü jijie* 杜律集解. Du shi congkan. Taipei: Datong shuju, 1974.

Shen Quanqi 沈佺期 and Song Zhiwen 宋之問. *Shen Quanqi, Song Zhiwen ji jiaozhu* 沈佺期宋之問集校注. Edited by Tao Min 陶敏 and Yi Shuqiong 易淑瓊. Beijing: Zhonghua shuju, 2001.

Shi Hongbao 施鴻保. *Du Du shi shuo* 讀杜詩説. Shanghai: Shanghai guji chubanshe, 1983.

Shi Jiaoran 釋皎然. *Shishi jiaozhu* 詩式校注. Edited by Li Zhuangying 李壯鷹. Beijing: Renmin chubanshe, 2003.

Shi Sengyou 釋僧祐, comp. *Hongming ji jiaojian* 弘明集校箋. With annotations by Li Xiaorong 李小榮. Shanghai: Shanghai guji chubanshe, 2013.

Shields, Anna M. *One Who Knows Me: Friendship and Literary Culture in Mid-Tang China*. Cambridge, Mass.: Harvard University Asia Center, 2015.

Shiji 史記. By Sima Qian 司馬遷. Beijing: Zhonghua shuju, 1972.

Shils, Edward. *Tradition*. Chicago: University of Chicago Press, 1981.

Shishuo xinyu jiaojian 世説新語校箋. By Liu Yiqing 劉義慶. Edited by Xu Zhen'e 徐震堮. Beijing: Zhonghua shuju, 1984.

Skaff, Jonathan Karam. *Sui-Tang China and Its Turko-Mongol Neighbors: Culture, Power and Connections, 580–800*. Oxford: Oxford University Press, 2012.

————. "Survival in the Frontier Zone: Comparative Perspectives on Identity and Political Allegiance in China's Inner Asian Borderlands during the Sui-Tang Dynastic Transition (617–630)." *Journal of World History* 15, no. 2 (2004): 117–53.

Smith, Kidder, Jr., Peter K. Bol, Joseph A. Adler, and Don J. Wyatt. *Sung Dynasty Uses of the I Ching*. Princeton: Princeton University Press, 1990.

Smith, Paul Jakov, and Richard von Glahn, eds. *The Song–Yuan–Ming Transition in Chinese History*. Cambridge, Mass.: Harvard University Press, 2003.

Smith, Richard J. *Fathoming the Cosmos and Ordering the World: The Yijing (I Ching, or Classic of Changes) and Its Evolution in China*. Charlottesville: University of Virginia Press, 2008.

Song shu 宋書. By Shen Yue 沈約. Beijing: Zhonghua shuju, 1974.

Spivak, Gayatri Chakravorty. *Death of a Discipline*. New York: Columbia University Press, 2003.

Standen, Naomi. *Unbounded Loyalty: Frontier Crossings in Liao China.* Honolulu: University of Hawai'i Press, 2007.

Su Shi 蘇軾. *Su Shi wenji* 蘇軾文集. Beijing: Zhonghua shuju, 1986.

Sui shu 隋書. By Wei Zheng 魏徵 et al. Beijing: Zhonghua shuju, 1973.

Sun, Cecile Chu-chin. *Pearl from the Dragon's Mouth: Evocation of Feeling and Scene in Chinese Poetry.* Ann Arbor: Center for Chinese Studies, University of Michigan, 1995.

Sun Rongrong 孙蓉蓉. *Chenwei yu wenxue yanjiu* 谶纬与文学研究. Beijing: Zhonghua shuju, 2018.

Sun Wei 孙微. *Qingdai Du shi xue shi* 清代杜诗学史. Jinan: Qi-Lu chubanshe, 2004.

Suzuki Torao 鈴木虎雄. *To shi* 杜詩. Tokyo: Iwanami shoten, 1966.

Swartz, Wendy. *Reading Philosophy, Writing Poetry: Intertextual Modes of Making Meaning in Early Medieval China.* Cambridge, Mass.: Harvard University Asia Center, 2018.

Swope, Kenneth. "All Men Are Not Brothers: Ethnic Identity and Dynastic Loyalty in the Ningxia Mutiny of 1592." *Late Imperial China* 24, no. 1 (August 21, 2003): 79–129.

Tackett, Nicolas. *The Destruction of the Medieval Chinese Aristocracy.* Cambridge, Mass.: Harvard University Asia Center, 2014.

———. *The Origins of the Chinese Nation: Song China and the Forging of an East Asian World Order.* Cambridge, U.K.: Cambridge University Press, 2017.

Taiping guangji 太平廣記. Edited by Li Fang 李昉 et al. Beijing: Zhonghua shuju, 1961.

Taiping yulan 太平御覽. Edited by Li Fang 李昉 et al. Beijing: Zhonghua shuju, 1995.

Taishō shinshū daizōkyō 大正新修大藏經. Edited by Takakusu Junjirō 高楠順次朗 and Watanabe Kaigyoku 渡邊海旭. Tokyo: Taishō issaikyō kankōkai, 1924–32.

Tan Jihe 谭继和. *Ba Shu wenhua biansi ji* 巴蜀文化辨思集. Chengdu: Sichuan renmin chubanshe, 2004.

———. "Du Fu yu wenhua Zhongguo" 杜甫与文化中国. *Du Fu yanjiu xuekan* 114, no. 4 (2012): 19–26.

Tang huiyao 唐會要. Edited by Wang Pu 王溥. Beijing: Zhonghua shuju, 1990.

Tang wen cui 唐文粹. Edited by Yao Xuan 姚鉉. Photoreprint of 1139 edition. Beijing: Beijing tushuguan chubanshe, 2006.

Tang Yuanhong 唐元竑. *Du shi jun* 杜詩攟. In *Yingyin wenyuange siku quanshu.*

Tao Chengtao 陶成涛. "Biansai shi shengcheng yanjiu" 边塞诗生成研究. PhD diss., Nanjing daxue, 2014.

————. "Tangdai de yinyue huanjing yu yuefu biansai shi de fanrong: jianlun Tangdai biansai shi 'qinli biansai' zhiwai de 'xiangxiang biansai'" 唐代的音乐环境与乐府边塞诗的繁荣——兼论唐代边塞诗"亲历边塞"之外的"想象边塞." *Du Fu yanjiu xuekan*, no. 3 (2018): 81–89.

Tao Qian 陶潜. *Tao Yuanming ji jianzhu* 陶淵明集箋注. Edited by Yuan Xing-pei 袁行霈. Beijing shi: Zhonghua shuju, 2003.

Taylor, Charles. *Sources of the Self: The Making of the Modern Identity*. Cambridge, Mass.: Harvard University Press, 1989.

Tian, Xiaofei 田晓菲. *Beacon Fire and Shooting Star: The Literary Culture of the Liang (502–557)*. Cambridge, Mass.: Harvard University Asia Center, 2007.

————. "Feeding the Phoenix: Du Fu's Qinzhou-Tonggu Series." In *Reading Du Fu: Nine Views*, edited by Xiaofei Tian, 93–108. Hong Kong: Hong Kong University Press, 2020.

————. "Juewu xushi: Du Fu jixingshi de fojiao jiedu" 觉悟叙事: 杜甫纪行诗的佛教解读. *Shanghai shifan daxue xuebao* 47, no. 1 (2018): 106–13.

————. "Misplaced: Three Qing Manuscripts of a Medieval Poet." *Asia Major* 20 (2007): 1–23.

————. *Tao Yuanming and Manuscript Culture: The Record of a Dusty Table*. Seattle: University of Washington Press, 2005.

————. "Yu Xin's 'Memory Palace': Writing Trauma and Violence in Early Medieval Chinese Aulic Poetry." In *Memory in Medieval China: Text, Ritual, and Community*, edited by Wendy Swartz and Robert F. Company, 124–57. Leiden: Brill, 2018.

Tillman, Hoyt Cleveland. "Reassessing Du Fu's Line on Zhuge Liang." *Monumenta Serica* 50, no. 1 (January 2002): 295–313.

Tseng, Chih-mien Adrian. "A Comparison of the Concepts of Buddha-Nature and Dao-Nature of Medieval China." PhD diss., McMaster University, 2014.

Twitchett, Denis. "Hsüan-Tsung (reign 712–56)." In *The Cambridge History of China*, vol. 3: *Sui and T'ang China*, edited by Denis Twitchett and John K. Fairbank, 333–463. Cambridge, U.K.: Cambridge University Press, 1978.

————. *Printing and Publishing in Medieval China*. New York: Frederic C. Beil, 1983.

Underwood, Ted. *Why Literary Periods Mattered: Historical Contrast and the Prestige of English Studies*. Stanford: Stanford University Press, 2013.

Van Zoeren, Stephen. *Poetry and Personality: Reading, Exegesis, and Hermeneutics in Traditional China*. Stanford: Stanford University Press, 1991.

Varsano, Paula. *Tracking the Banished Immortal: The Poetry of Li Bo and Its Critical Reception*. Honolulu: University of Hawai'i Press, 2003.

Verdicchio, Massimo. "Under Western Critical Eyes: Du Fu." *Comparative Literature Studies* 54, no. 1 (2017): 211–28.

Wagner, Rudolf G. *Language, Ontology, and Political Philosophy in China: Wang Bi's Scholarly Exploration of the Dark (Xuanxue)*. Albany: State University of New York Press, 2003.

Wang, Ao. *Spatial Imaginaries in Mid-Tang China: Geography, Cartography, and Literature*. Cambria Sinophone World Series. Amherst, N.Y.: Cambria Press, 2018.

Wang Changling 王昌齡. *Wang Changling shi zhu* 王昌齡詩注. Edited by Li Yunyi 李雲逸. Shanghai: Shanghai guji chubanshe, 1984.

Wang Chong 王充. *Lunheng jiaoshi* 論衡校釋. Edited by Huang Hui 黃暉. Beijing: Zhonghua shuju, 1990.

Wang, David Der-wei. "Six Modernist Poets in Search of Du Fu." In *Reading Du Fu: Nine Views*, edited by Xiaofei Tian, 143–64. Hong Kong: Hong Kong University Press, 2020.

Wang Dingbao 王定保. *Tang zhiyan* 唐摭言. Beijing: Zhonghua shuju, 1960.

Wang, Gungwu. "Feng Tao: An Essay on Confucian Loyalty." In *Confucian Personalities*, edited by Arthur Wright and Denis Twitchett, 123–45. Stanford: Stanford University Press, 1962.

Wang Ji 王績. *Wang Wugong wenji: Wu juan ben hui jiao* 王無功文集：五卷本會校. Edited by Han Lizhou 韓理洲. Shanghai: Shanghai guji chubanshe, 1987.

Wang Jia 王嘉. *Shiyi ji* 拾遺記. Beijing: Zhonghua shuju, 1981.

Wang, Ping. *The Age of Courtly Writing: Wen Xuan Compiler Xiao Tong (501–531) and His Circle*. Leiden: Brill, 2012.

Wang Sishi 王嗣奭. *Du yi* 杜臆. Shanghai: Shanghai guji chubanshe, 1983.

Wang Tong 王通. *Zhong shuo jiaozhu* 中説校注. Edited by Zhang Pei 張沛. Beijing: Zhonghua shuju, 2013.

Wang Wei 王維. *Wang Wei ji jiaozhu* 王維集校注. Edited by Chen Tiemin 陳鐵民. 4 vols. Beijing: Zhonghua shuju, 1997.

Wang Xian 王嫻 and Xiao Jing 肖婧. "Jin shiwu nian shichen yanjiu zongshu" 近十五年诗谶研究综述. *Lanzhou jiaoyu xueyuan xuebao* 26, no. 1 (n.d.): 48–53.

Wang Xizhi 王羲之. *Jin Wang Youjun ji* 王右軍集. Taipei: Taiwan xuesheng shuju, 1971.

Wang, Yugen. "*Shige*: The Popular Poetics of Regulated Verse." *T'ang Studies* 22 (2004): 81–125.

———. *Ten Thousand Scrolls: Reading and Writing in the Poetics of Huang Tingjian and the Late Northern Song*. Cambridge, Mass.: Harvard University Asia Center, 2011.

Wang Zhu 王洙, attrib. *Fenmen jizhu Du gongbu shi* 分門集注杜工部詩. Sibu congkan. Taipei: Datong shuju, 1974.

Warner, Ding Xiang. *A Wild Deer amid Soaring Phoenixes: The Opposition Poetics of Wang Ji*. Honolulu: University of Hawai'i Press, 2003.

Wechsler, Howard J. *Offerings of Jade and Silk: Ritual and Symbol in the Legitimation of the T'ang Dynasty*. New Haven: Yale University Press, 1985.

Wei, Shang. "Prisoner and Creator: The Self-Image of the Poet in Han Yu and Meng Jiao." *Chinese Literature: Essays, Articles, Reviews (CLEAR)* 16 (1994): 19–40.

Wei shu 魏書. By Wei Shou 魏收. Beijing: Zhonghua shuju, 1974.

Wei Zhuang 韋莊. *Wei Zhuang ji jianzhu* 韋莊集箋注. Edited by Nie Anfu 聶安福. Shanghai: Shanghai guji chubanshe, 2002.

———. *Wei Zhuang shi ci jian zhu* 韦庄诗词笺注. Edited by Qi Tao 齐涛. 2 vols. Jinan: Shandong jiaoyu chubanshe, 2002.

Wen Hulin 温虎林. *Du Fu Long Shu dao shige yanjiu* 杜甫陇蜀道诗歌研究. Beijing: Zhongguo shehui kexue chubanshe, 2015.

Wen Tianxiang 文天祥. *Wen Wenshan quanji* 文文山全集. Shanghai: Guoxue zhengli she, 1936.

Wen Yiduo 聞一多. *Wen Yiduo quanji* 聞一多全集. Shanghai: Kaiming shudian, 1948.

Weng Fanggang 翁方綱. *Du shi fuji* 杜詩附記.. Xia Qinbang 夏勤邦 hand-copied edition, 1909.

Wenxuan 文選. Compiled by Xiao Tong 蕭統. With annotations by Li Shan 李善. Shanghai: Shanghai guji chubanshe, 1996.

Wenyuan yinghua 文苑英華. Edited by Li Fang 李昉 et al. Beijing: Zhonghua shuju, 1966.

Williams, Bernard. *Ethics and the Limits of Philosophy*. Cambridge, Mass.: Harvard University Press, 1985.

———. *Moral Luck: Philosophical Papers 1973–1980*. Cambridge, U.K.: Cambridge University Press, 1981.

Williams, David-Antoine. *Defending Poetry: Art and Ethics in Joseph Brodsky, Seamus Heaney, and Geoffrey Hill*. Oxford: Oxford University Press, 2010.

Williams, Nicholas Morrow. "Literary Controversy at the Liang Court Revisited." *Early Medieval China* 2015, no. 21 (2015): 63–92.

———. "The Metaphysical Lyric of the Six Dynasties." *T'oung Pao* 98, nos. 1–3 (2012): 65–112.

———. "The Morality of Drunkenness in Chinese Literature of the Third Century CE." In *Scribes of Gastronomy: Representations of Food and Drink in Imperial Chinese Literature*, edited by Isaac Yue and Siufu Tang, 27–43. Hong Kong: Hong Kong University Press, 2013.

———. "Sashimi and History: On a New Translation of Du Fu." *China Review International* 21, nos. 3/4 (2014): 201–44.

———. "The Taste of the Ocean: Jiaoran's Theory of Poetry." *Tang Studies* 31 (2013): 1–37.

Wong, Siu-kit. "*Ch'ing* in Chinese Literary Criticism." PhD diss., Oxford University, 1969.

Wu Guangxing 吴光兴. *Ba shiji shifeng: tansuo Tang shishi shang "Shen-Song de shiji" (705–805)* 八世纪诗风——探索唐诗史上"沈宋的世纪"(705–805). Beijing: Shehui kexue wenxian chubanshe, 2013.

Wu Hongze 吴洪泽. "Songdai nianpu kaolun" 宋代年谱考论. PhD diss., Sichuan daxue, 2006.

Wu Lushan 吴鹭山. *Du shi luncong* 杜诗论丛. Hangzhou: Zhejiang wenyi chubanshe, 1983.

Wu Wenzhi 吴文治, ed. *Ming shihua quanbian* 明詩話全編. Nanjing: Jiangsu guji chubanshe, 1997.

———, ed. *Song shihua quanbian* 宋詩話全編. 10 vols. Nanjing: Jiangsu guji chubanshe, 1998.

Wu Zhongsheng 吴中胜. *Du Fu piping shi yanjiu* 杜甫批评史研究. Beijing: Zhongguo shehui kexue chubanshe, 2012.

Xiao Difei 萧涤非. *Du Fu yanjiu* 杜甫研究. Jinan: Qi-Lu chubanshe, 1980.

Xiao Difei 萧涤非 et al., eds. *Du Fu quanji jiaozhu* 杜甫全集校注. 12 vols. Beijing: Renmin wenxue chubanshe, 2014.

Xiao Yingshi 蕭穎士. *Xiao Maoting wenji* 蕭茂挺文集. In *Yingyin wenyuange siku quanshu*.

Xie Siwei 谢思炜. *Du Fu ji jiaozhu* 杜甫集校注. Shanghai: Shanghai guji chubanshe, 2015.

———. "Lun zizhuan shiren Du Fu: jian lun Zhongguo xi xifang de zizhuanshi chuantong" 论自传诗人杜甫—兼论中国和西方的自传诗传统. *Wenxue yichan*, no. 3 (1990): 68–76.

———. *Tang Song shixue lunji* 唐宋诗学论集. Beijing: Shangwu yinshu guan, 2003.

Xie Wei 谢巍. *Zhongguo lidai renwu nianpu kao lu* 中国历代人物年谱考录. Beijing: Zhonghua shuju, 1992.

Xin Tang shu 新唐書. Edited by Ouyang Xiu 歐陽修, Song Qi 宋祁, et al. Beijing: Zhonghua shuju, 1995.

Xin Yingju 信应举. *Du shi xin buzhu* 杜诗新补注. Zhengzhou: Zhongzhou guji chubanshe, 2002.

Xu Guoneng 徐國能. "Lidai Du Fu shixue shifalun yanjiu" 歷代杜詩學詩法研究. PhD diss., Taiwan shifan daxue, 2001.

Xu Jun 徐俊. *Dunhuang shiji canjuan jikao* 敦煌詩集殘卷輯考. Beijing: Zhonghua shuju, 2000.

Xu Mai 徐邁. "Du Fu shige zizhu luelun" 杜甫詩歌自注略論. *Du Fu yanjiu xuekan*, no. 3 (2010): 32–38.

———. "Du Fu zizhu yu shige jingyu de kaituo" 杜詩自注與詩歌境域的開拓. *Anhui daxue xuebao*, no. 6 (2010): 34–38.

Xu Renfu 徐仁甫. *Du shi zhujie shangque* 杜詩注解商. Beijing: Zhonghua shuju, 1979.

———. *Du shi zhujie shangque xubian* 杜诗注解商榷续编. Chengdu: Sichuan renmin chubanshe, 1986.

Xu Zong 許總. *Du shi xue fawei* 杜詩學發微. Nanjing: Nanjing chubanshe, 1989.

Xue Shichang 薛世昌 and Meng Yonglin 孟永林. *Qinzhou shangkong de feng-huang: Du Fu Longyou shi xulun* 秦州上空的凤凰：杜甫陇右诗叙论. Beijing: Zhongguo shehui kexue chubanshe, 2013.

Yan Kejun 嚴可均, ed. *Quan shanggu sandai Qin Han Sanguo Liuchao wen* 全上古三代秦漢三國六朝文. Beijing: Zhonghua shuju, 1965.

Yan Zhenqing 顏眞卿. *Yan Lugong wenji* 顏魯公文集. Woodblock print. Sanchangwuzhai congshu. Zhijing xuezhai, Daoguang 27 [1847].

Yan Zhitui 顏之推. *Yan Zhitui quanji yizhu* 颜之推全集译注. With annotations by Zhang Aitang 张霭堂. Jinan: Qi-Lu shushe, 2004.

———. *Yanshi jiaxun jijie* 顏氏家訓集解. Edited by Wang Liqi 王利器. Beijing: Zhonghua shuju, 2002.

Yang Dianxun 杨殿珣, ed. *Zhongguo lidai nianpu zonglu* 中国历代年谱总录. Beijing: Shumu wenxian chubanshe, 1996.

Yang Jinghua 楊經華. *Songdai Du shi chanshi xue yanjiu* 宋代杜詩闡釋學研究. Beijing: Zhongguo shehui kexue chubanshe, 2011.

Yang Lun 楊倫. *Du shi jingquan* 杜詩鏡銓. 2 vols. Shanghai: Shanghai guji chubanshe, 1980.

Yang, Shao-yun. "Fan and Han: The Origins and Uses of a Conceptual Dichotomy in Mid-Imperial China, ca. 500–1200." In *Political Strategies of Identity Building in Non-Han Empires in China*, edited by Julia Schneider, Francesca Fiaschetti, and Julia Schneider, 9–35. Wiesbaden: Harrassowitz Verlag, 2014.

———. "Reinventing the Barbarian: Rhetorical and Philosophical Uses of the *Yi-Di* in Mid-Imperial China, 600–1300." PhD diss., University of California, Berkeley, 2014.

———. *The Way of the Barbarians: Redrawing Ethnic Boundaries in Tang and Song China*. Seattle: University of Washington Press, 2019.

Yang Xiong 楊雄. *Fayan yishu* 法言義疏. Edited by Wang Rongbao 汪榮寶 and Chen Zhongfu 陳仲夫. Beijing: Zhonghua shuju, 1987.

Yanzi chunqiu jishi 晏子春秋集釋. Edited by Wu Zeyu 吳則虞. Beijing: Zhonghua shuju, 1962.

Ye Xie 叶燮. *Shi yuan, shi mei, shi fa tanyou: "Yuan shi" pingshi* 诗源, 诗美, 诗法探幽：《原诗》评释. With annotations by Lü Zhimin 吕智敏. Beijing: Shumu wenxian chubanshe, 1990.

Yearley, Lee H. "Ethics of Bewilderment." *Journal of Religious Ethics* 38, no. 3 (2010): 436–60.

Yim, Lawrence C. H. *The Poet-Historian Qian Qianyi.* London: Routledge, 2009.

Yingyin wenyuange siku quanshu 景印文淵閣四庫全書. Compiled by Ji Yun 紀昀 et al. Taipei: Taiwan shangwu yinshu guan, 1983–86.

Yiwen leiju 藝文類聚. Compiled by Ouyang Xun 歐陽詢. Edited by Wang Shaoying 汪紹楹. Shanghai: Shanghai guji chubanshe, 1999.

Yoshikawa Kōjirō 吉川幸次郎. *To Ho shichū* 杜甫詩注. 5 vols. Tokyo: Chikuma shobō, 1977–83.

Yu, Pauline. *The Reading of Imagery in the Chinese Poetic Tradition.* Princeton: Princeton University Press, 1987.

Yu, Pauline, Peter Bol, Stephen Owen, and Willard Peterson, eds. *Ways with Words: Writing about Reading Texts from Early China.* Berkeley: University of California Press, 2000.

Yu Xin 庾信. *Yu Zishan ji zhu* 庾子山集注. Edited by Ni Fan 庾信 and Xu Yimin 許逸民. Beijing: Zhonghua shuju, 1980.

Yuan Haowen 元好問. *Yuan Haowen quanji* 元好問全集. Edited by Yao Dianzhong 姚奠中 and Li Zhengmin 李正民. Taipei: Shanxi renmin chubanshe, 1990.

Yuan Jiao 袁郊. *Ganze yao: fu lu* 甘澤謠：附錄. Congshu jicheng chubian. Changsha: Shangwu yinshu guan, 1939.

Yuan Jie 元結. *Xinjiao Yuan Cishan ji* 新校元次山集. Edited by Yang Jialuo 楊家駱. Zhongguo xueshu mingzhu. Taipei: Shijie shuju, 1964.

Yuan Zhen 元稹. *Yuan Zhen ji* 元稹集. Edited by Ji Qin 冀勤. Beijing: Zhonghua shuju, 1982.

Yue jue shu jiaoshi 越絕書校釋. Edited by Li Bujia 李步嘉. Wuchang: Wuhan daxue chubanshe, 1992.

Yue Ke 岳珂. *Baozhenzhai fashu zan* 寶眞齋法書贊. Taipei: Shijie shuju, 1962.

Zeng Zao 曾慥. *Lei shuo* 類説. In *Yingyin wenyuange siku quanshu.*

Zengding zhushi Quan Tang shi 增订注释全唐诗. Edited by Chen Yixin 陈贻焮 et al. 5 vols. Beijing: Wenhua yishu chubanshe, 2001.

Zhang Bowei 張伯偉, ed. *Quan Tang Wudai shige huikao* 全唐五代詩格彙考. Nanjing: Jiangsu guji chubanshe, 2002.

———. *Zhongguo gudai wenxue piping fangfa yanjiu* 中国古代文学批评方法研究. Beijing: Zhonghua shuju, 2002.

Zhang Changdong 蔣长栋. "Shilun Du Fu de 'bixing tizhi'" 试论杜甫的"比兴体制." *Qiusuo*, no. 1 (1997): 96–100.

Zhang Guangda 张广达. "Naitō Konan de Tang–Song biange shuo ji qi yingxiang" 内藤湖南的唐宋变革说及其影响. *Tang yanjiu* 11 (2005): 5–71.

Zhang Hua 張華. *Bowu zhi jiaozheng* 博物志校證. Edited by Fan Ning 范寧. Beijing: Zhonghua shuju, 1980.

Zhang Jie 張戒. *Suihantang shihua jiaojian* 歲寒堂詩話校箋. Edited by Chen Yingluan 陳應鸞. Chengdu: Ba Shu shushe, 2000.

Zhang Jin 張溍. *Dushutang Du shiji zhujie* 讀書堂杜詩集註解. Du shi congkan. Taipei: Datong shuju, 1974.

Zhang, Longxi. *Allegoresis: Reading Canonical Literature East and West*. Ithaca, N.Y.: Cornell University Press, 2005.

———. "Out of the Cultural Ghetto: Theory, Politics, and the Study of Chinese Literature." *Modern China* 19, no. 1 (1993): 71–101.

———. "What Is *Wen* and Why Is It Made So Terribly Strange?" *College Literature* 23, no. 1 (1996): 15–35.

Zhang Xiaoqing 张晓庆. "Du Fu yu Bai Maolin jiaoyou kaolun: jian shizheng 'Lanjing cheng Bai zhongcheng' deng shiti zhi" 杜甫与柏茂琳交游考论—兼释证《览镜呈柏中丞》等诗题旨. *Hunan daxue xuebao* 11, no. 5 (2010): 102–5.

Zhang Yan 張綖. *Du Gongbu shitong* 杜工部詩通. Du shi congkan. Taipei: Datong shuju, 1974.

Zhang Yuan 張遠. *Du shi huicui* 杜詩會粹. Siku quanshu cunmu congshu. Jinan: Qi-Lu shushe, 1997.

Zhang Zhilie 张志烈, ed. *Du shi quanji jinzhu ben* 杜诗全集今注本. Chengdu: Tiandi chubanshe, 1999.

Zhang Zhonggang 张忠纲, Zhao Ruicai 赵睿才, Qi Wei 綦维, and Sun Wei 孙微, eds. *Du ji xulu* 杜集叙录. Jinan: Qi-Lu shushe, 2008.

Zhang Zhuo 張鷟. *Chaoye qianzai jijiao* 朝野僉載輯校. Edited by Hao Runhua 郝润華 and Mo Qiong 莫琼. Jinan: Shandong renmin chubanshe, 2018.

Zhao Cigong 趙次公. *Du shi Zhao Cigong xianhou jie jijiao* 杜詩趙次公先後解輯校. Edited by Lin Jizhong 林繼中. Shanghai: Shanghai guji chubanshe, 1994.

Zhao Pang 趙汸. *Du lü Zhao zhu* 杜律趙註. Du shi congkan. Taipei: Datong shuju, 1974.

Zheng Qingdu 郑庆笃, Jiao Yuyin 焦裕银, Zhang Zhonggang 张忠纲, and Feng Jianguo 冯建国, eds. *Du ji shumu tiyao* 杜集书目提要. Jinan: Qi-Lu shushe, 1986.

Zheng Wen 鄭文. *Du shi jinggu* 杜詩繫詁. Chengdu: Ba Shu shudian, 1992.

Zhou Caiquan 周采泉. *Du ji shulu* 杜集書錄. Shanghai: Shanghai guji chubanshe, 1986.

Zhou Jianjun 周建軍. *Tangdai Jing Chu bentu shige yu liuyu shige yanjiu* 唐代荆楚本土詩歌與流寓詩歌研究. Beijing: Zhongguo shehui kexue chubanshe, 2006.

Zhou li zhushu 周禮注疏. With annotations by Zheng Xuan 鄭玄 and Jia Gongyan 賈公彥. In *Chongkan Songben Shisanjing zhushu fu jiaokan ji*.

Zhou shu 周書. Edited by Linghu Defen 令狐德棻 et al. Beijing: Zhonghua shuju, 1971.

Zhou Xunchu 周勛初, ed. *Tang chao Wenxuan jizhu huicun* 唐鈔文選集註彙存. Shanghai: Shanghai guji chubanshe, 2000.

Zhou Zizhi 周紫芝. *Zhupo shihua* 竹坡詩話. In *Yingyin wenyuange siku quanshu*.

Zhouyi zhushu 周易注疏. With annotations by Wang Bi 王弼, Kong Yingda 孔穎達, et al. In *Chongkan Songben Shisanjing zhushu fu jiaokan ji*.

Zhu Heling 朱鶴齡. *Du Gongbu shiji jizhu* 杜工部詩集輯注. Edited by Han Chengwu 韓成武 et al. Baoding: Hebei daxue chubanshe, 2009.

Zhu Xi 朱熹. *The Original Meaning of the Yijing: Commentary on the Scripture of Change*. Translated by Joseph A. Adler. New York: Columbia University Press, 2019.

———. *Zhuzi dushu fa* 朱子讀書法. Edited by Zhang Hong 張洪 and Qi Xi 齊熙. In *Yingyin wenyuange siku quanshu*.

Zhuangzi jishi 莊子集釋. Edited by Guo Qingfan 郭慶藩 and Wang Xiaoyu 王孝魚. Beijing: Zhonghua shuju, 1985.

Ziporyn, Brook Anthony. *The Penumbra Unbound: The Neo-Taoist Philosophy of Guo Xiang*. Albany: State University of New York Press, 2003.

Zizhi tongjian 資治通鑑. By Sima Guang 司馬光. Beijing: Zhonghua shuju, 1956.

Zou Jinxian 邹进先. *Songdai Du shi xue shulun* 宋代杜诗学述论. Beijing: Zhongguo shehui kexue chubanshe, 2016.

Zumthor, Paul. *Essai de poétique médiévale*. Paris: Éditions du Seuil, 1972.

Index

Harvard-Yenching Institute Monograph Series

(Most Recent Titles)